The Object of

Java™

SECOND EDITION

Introduction to
Programming Using
Software Engineering
Principles

The Object of

java™

SECOND EDITION

Introduction to
Programming Using
Software Engineering
Principles

David D. Riley

PEARSON

Addison
Wesley

Boston San Francisco New York
London Toronto Sydney Tokyo Singapore Madrid

Publisher	Greg Tobin
Senior Acquisitions Editor	Michael Hirsch
Editorial Assistant	Lindsey Triebel
Managing Editor	Patty Mahtani
Cover Design	Joyce Cosentino Wells
Cover Image	© 2005 Steve Allen / Brand X Pictures
Media Producer	Bethany Tidd
Senior Marketing Manager	Michelle Brown
Marketing Assistant	Dana Lopreato
Senior Manufacturing Buyer	Caroline Fell
Text Design, Production Coordination, Composition, and Illustrations	Gillian Hall, The Aardvark Group

Access the latest information about Addison-Wesley titles from our World Wide Web site: http://www.aw.com/cs

Many of the designations used by manufacturers and sellers to distinguish their products are claimed as trademarks. Where those designations appear in this book, and Addison-Wesley was aware of a trademark claim, the designations have been printed in initial caps or all caps.

Library of Congress Cataloging-in-Publication Data

Riley, David D., 1951–
    The object of Java : introduction to programming using software engineering principles /
    David D. Riley.-- 2nd ed.
        p. cm.
    ISBN-13: 978-0-321-33158-3
        1. Java (Computer program language) 2. Computer software--Development.
        3. Object-oriented programming (Computer science) I. Title.
    QA76.73.J38R54 2005
    005.13'3--dc22   2005019950

ISBN 0-321-33158-3

2 3 4 5 6 7 8 9 10—CRW—09 08 07 06

This book is dedicated to my wife, Sandra, and children,
Kasandra and Derek. These three remarkable individuals
provided endless assistance, encouragement, and inspiration.

Contents

3 Introduction to Design and Implementation   75

4 Methods   117

5 Primitive Data   165

6 Supplier Classes   199

7 Logic and Selection   259

11 Containers   473

12 Introduction to Arrays   515

13 File Input and Output   561

14 Recursion   605

15 Applications and Applets   633

Preface

The Object of Java–the title directly parallels the objectives of this book. Java was designed as a vehicle for modern software development. Similarly, this text was designed as a vehicle for instruction in modern software development. Both are powered by the object-oriented paradigm and properly driven with sound software engineering practices. The goal of this book is to convey programming skills, object-oriented skills, software engineering skills, and Java skills–and through these skills to provide a firm foundation for future study in computer science.

The target audience is students in Introduction to Programming courses. IEEE/ACM Curriculum 2001 refers to these courses as CS101 or CS111. It is not necessary that readers have written computer programs before, but their having a reasonable level of analytic sophistication is important. A background of three years of high school mathematics is all that is required to understand the notations in the book.

New in This Edition

Use of AWT and Swing

The first edition of *The Object of Java* relied upon an author-supplied library of graphic-related classes. As of Java 5, this material is surprisingly easy to present using standard Java libraries. With this change, students no longer need to devote time to learning nonstandard software. The fundamental approach of the first edition of this book has been preserved; there is still a heavy reliance upon using external classes and the same gentle introduction to applications involving GUIs remains—now using *AWT* and *Swing* classes.

Complete Use of Java 5

This second edition fully incorporates the features of Java 5 that deserve presentation in an introductory programming course.

Generics: One significant enhancement to Java 5 is the incorporation of generic data types. Now bag and list containers can be properly defined as Bag<ItemType> and SimpleList<ItemType>, rather than BagOfObject and SimpleListOfObject. This enhances the applicability of data containers and significantly improves type safety.

Autoboxing: Java 5 support for autoboxing and autounboxing is integrated into the presentation. Wrapper classes are still included, but far less time is devoted to this topic as a result of these important new language features.

enum: Enumerated data types that are a staple in many programming languages are now supported in Java. This new language feature is integrated into the discussion of writing your own classes. The built-in ordinal and name methods are also covered and enumerated types appear in several code examples.

***for* loop:** The *for* loop has been enhanced by a special version for iterating over collections. This form of the loop is presented as a more elegant way to express simple container processing. The discussion of this version of the for statement is presented for both lists and arrays. The limitations of this special version of the for statement are also examined.

assert statement: Providing for testable assertions in the form of the assert statement is a significant language enhancement. The assert statement is explored, along with its usefulness for debugging, in Chapter 7 on logic and selection.

Scanner: The new java.util.Scanner class provides an improved, type-safe way to translate primitive literals in textual form into primitive values. This class is utilized to show how to translate from String, JTextField, and files. Using Scanner makes it more convenient to handle GUI input of primitive type.

Objects Centric—Even More

The focal point of this book has always been object-orientation. To make that even clearer, Chapter 1 begins with initial examples demonstrating the use of multiple classes. Instead of the traditional "hello world," this revision explores a more object-oriented program to simulate a robot vehicle. Chapters 2 and 3 have also been altered to clarify how software engineering applies in the proper object-oriented (O-O) context.

Improved Orthogonality

Every attempt has been made to make the example classes in the text consistent with Java standards. Documentation has been changed to make it display better with javadoc tools. The bag and list classes are now inherited from standard Java interfaces, using the same `hasNext`, `next`, `add`, and `remove` methods. Preconditions and postconditions have been rewritten to use UML's Object Constraint Language notation.

More Complete Programs

Programming is learned from examples. One of the hallmarks of the first edition of this book was the inclusion of more than 70 complete programs. In this edition, the number of complete programs is increased to more than 80. A few of these new inclusions are of case study length.

Object Orientation and Java

In the words of James Gosling and Henry McGilton, "To function within increasingly complex network-based environments, programming systems must adopt object-oriented concepts." Such emphasis on object orientation requires more than an "objects first" curriculum; it requires an objects-centric approach. Software classes, methods, inheritance, and event-driven code should be as much in the current programming repertoire as variables, loops, and arrays. The goal of the objects-centric approach goes well beyond a presentation of object terminology. The objects-centric approach seeks to educate software developers who are able to reason with object orientation.

Part of the beauty of the objects-centric approach is that it subsumes the older imperative and functional paradigms. In order to use object-oriented programming (OOP), programmers must still write assignment instructions, pass parameters, return values from functions (nonvoid methods), and become proficient with all of the basic control structures. This means that when students are transitioning from OOP to other programming paradigms, they encounter few of the obstacles that are often experienced when transitioning in the opposite direction.

The ideas and approach of this book are based upon many years of experience using the O-O approach in Introduction to Programming classes. Recently, instructors have used the Java programming language. Java works well in introductory courses because it incorporates a reasonable implementation of the object model, and it is ubiquitous in both academic and professional circles. Java has the added benefit of a C-like notation. This is helpful for students who may use C, C++, or C# in the future. As Gosling and McGilton put it, "The Java programming language is designed to be object-oriented from the ground up."

Software Engineering Emphasis

Like good writing, good programming requires skill and discipline. The guidelines and techniques of software engineering are critical for developing such skill and discipline. A software engineering emphasis is evident throughout this book. The following features are specifically included to convey proper software engineering.

Software Engineering Hints

You will find Software Engineering Hints sprinkled throughout the chapters. These offer a collection of software-developer "best practices." A Software Engineering Hint might suggest how to format a language construct for good programming style or it might explain how experienced programmers approach a common design problem.

Programming by Contract

The importance of specifications is amplified by OOP. Method preconditions and postconditions, as well as class invariants, are especially critical for conveying code behavior. Such assertions are used consistently to document examples and to define example classes. Programming by contract is introduced in Chapter 2 and used regularly thereafter. Additional discussions about logical expressions, loop invariants, and special assertion notations are included. Class specifications in this form are supplied in HTML format.

Patterns

The software engineering principle of design patterns reminds us that our software development skills are often based on our memory for commonly used structures. This book extends the notion to include patterns for frequently encountered code expressions, instructions, algorithms, and design patterns that serve as programming templates. These patterns are highlighted so that the reader may become familiar with a commonly required solution and learn how and when it is applicable.

Software Testing

Testing is a part of any good software engineering model. Special sections are included to ensure that the reader will develop basic debugging skills, as well as knowledge of simple path testing and black box testing.

The Java Inspector

Software engineering studies confirm that the most useful of all testing comes in the form of informal desk checks, code reviews, and walkthroughs. Such practices require fundamental knowledge of what to "check," "review," or how to "walk through." Every chapter provides this information in the form of The Java Inspector. These end-of-chapter sections not only provide a useful review of salient points from the chapter, but also they present practical "how to" ideas.

UML

Pictures play a key role in object-orient design and programming. Numerous object diagrams are interspersed throughout to illustrate the runtime nature of computation. Class diagrams are frequently included to depict the visible interface of a class and to picture relationships among various classes. In addition, activity diagrams are included to show control flow.

To remain true to the software engineering theme, this book restricts diagramming notations to those from the Unified Modeling Language (UML). Using UML diagrams exposes students to the same notations that have become standard in the software development industry. The subset of UML used in this book is summarized in Appendix E.

Order of Topics

Teaching OOP in CS1 courses has taught us several lessons. Arguably, the most important discovery has been how sensitive this material is to proper ordering. Instructional time is the scarcest of resources in today's programming courses; there is no time to waste. After experimenting with various alternatives, we have found that the order of topics in this text works well for our students.

You may notice that the table of contents of this book is unique. The objects-centric approach demands that key object-oriented material be presented as early as possible so that it can be properly applied throughout the text.

Chapter 1 begins with a brief overview of objects and classes—a "preview of coming attractions." An example object-oriented program is used to illustrate some basic notations, the software development tools (editors, compilers, and virtual machines), and to provide a glimpse of the overall process of software development. This chapter is expected to require no more than one class period of coverage.

Objects-Centric

Chapter 2 begins with the basic object-oriented construct: the method call. After demonstrating how to perform methods upon objects, the chapter continues to examine simple sequences of these instructions. It also explores declaring, instantiating, and assigning objects. Including the swap algorithm as a code pattern helps to illustrate object bindings. The chapter includes all of the Java facilities needed to write initial programs.

Early O-O Strategies

Chapter 3 is a unique blend of basic software design skills and some additional language facilities. In this chapter, the reader is shown a prototyping strategy for attacking programming problems in an OOP context. Under the assumption that every beginning student is expected to write several programs, this strategy helps to answer the "Where do I begin?" questions. Chapter 3 also discusses other fundamental software development skills, such as selecting good identifier names and using output instructions (`System.out.println`) to assist in debugging.

Methods

The method call, which is the primary instruction of OOP, is introduced   in Chapters 1 and 2 and explored more fully in Chapter 4. This presentation also examines how to create methods, including such issues as parameter passage, local variables, and nonvoid methods.

Primitive Types

Only after the reader has gained experience with objects, classes, and methods in four chapters, does the presentation turn to primitive data types in Chapter 5. We have found that delaying a discussion of primitive types, such as numeric expressions, eliminates many early distractions. This approach allows the reader to become relatively comfortable with manipulating reference data before confronting the issue that Java treats numbers in a nonobject-oriented way. The later presentation of primitive types also tends to expose primitive variables as anomalies (although sensible anomalies), in an object-oriented environment. It takes no more time to present primitive expressions at this later time, and it definitely improves the students' comfort level with reference data/objects.

Writing Supplier Classes

There appears to be a significant cognitive difference between writing client code that utilizes other classes and writing the supplier-side code of those external classes. Chapter 6 is included to assist readers in making the leap. This chapter not only confronts design decisions of which class is the best site for a particular method, but also explores the importance of proper information hiding and encapsulation.

Control Structures

Why not present selection and loops before Chapters 7? The answer is that delaying the discussion of these control structures allows object-oriented topics to be explored earlier, and therefore used throughout more of the remainder of the course. When presented later, the utility of if instructions and while loops is fairly obvious, and students eagerly assimilate such useful material. In the object-oriented model, control structures are no longer the centerpiece of programming skills. Nonetheless, selection and repetition are still important programming tools, and we have found this placement to provide students with sufficient exposure to master these constructs.

Delaying the presentation of selection and repetition is possible, in part, because of event-driven code. A quick glance at the programming assignments and examples in this book should provide convincing evidence that interesting and challenging programming is quite possible without selection instructions or loops.

Using extensive event-driven programming has other benefits. Event-driven code is a natural companion of OOP. We are all accustomed to the behavior of buttons, menus, and scrollbars that rely upon event-driven control. Indeed, the program-control model tends to be awkward for anyone who has grown up with graphical user interfaces.

Inheritance

The core of the object-oriented tools and techniques is covered in three phases:

1. utilizing objects, classes, and methods (Chapters 1–4)
2. writing supplier-side code (Chapter 6)
3. using inheritance (Chapters 8–9)

It would be wonderful to introduce inheritance earlier, but we have had the best success with presenting inheritance beginning at roughly the middle of the course. This timing still permits sufficient opportunity to use inheritance in many course projects.

Containers—Including Arrays

Chapter 11 is included to separate the issues of container classes from the specific concepts of arrays (Chapter 12). The inherently sequential nature of a list makes it a bit easier to use than a direct access container, such as an array. More importantly, a list is a better example of the object-oriented approach for implementing a container (data structure). Since Java integrates array notation into the language, an array gives the initial appearance of being unlike other objects. Chapter 11 also takes the opportunity to include useful discussions of genericity, the Object class, wrapper classes, and a sorting algorithm that is naturally suited to lists—insertion sort.

Order Dependencies

Although the order of presentation in this text works well at our institution, many factors can dictate the need for variations. Therefore, every reasonable effort was made to minimize dependencies of topics. Figure P.1 diagrams significant chapter dependencies. An arrow in this diagram is drawn from A to B to indicate that Chapter B relies substantially upon the material presented in Chapter A.

This book is an attempt to be as inclusive of topics as is reasonable. In an ideal world, it would be nice to cover all 15 chapters in one course. This is a considerable undertaking, and we suspect that most courses will sacrifice coverage of part or all of some of the later chapters.

Appendix A is also included for those faculty who prefer to begin with an introduction to computer hardware. This material can be used as an introductory chapter, or as outside reading material. The choice to place this material in an appendix was made because it lies outside the object model focus.

Figure P.1   Chapter dependencies

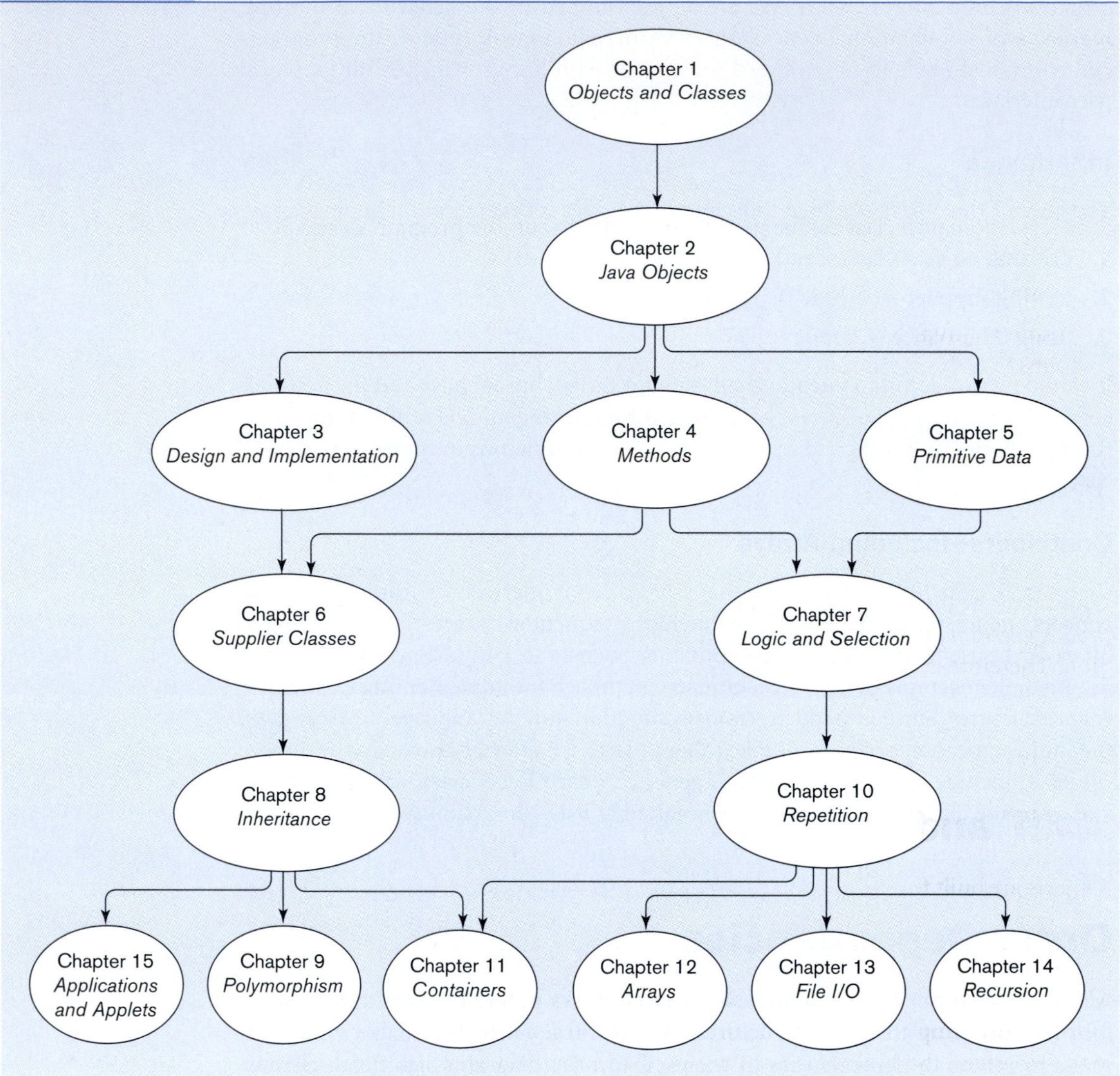

Chapter 1
Objects and Classes

Chapter 2
Java Objects

Chapter 3
Design and Implementation

Chapter 4
Methods

Chapter 5
Primitive Data

Chapter 6
Supplier Classes

Chapter 7
Logic and Selection

Chapter 8
Inheritance

Chapter 10
Repetition

Chapter 15
Applications and Applets

Chapter 9
Polymorphism

Chapter 11
Containers

Chapter 12
Arrays

Chapter 13
File I/O

Chapter 14
Recursion

Applications or Applets—Your Choice

The programs in this book are all written in such a way that they can be executed either as Java applications or as Java applets. Each program incorporates a class called `Driver` that defines a controller object for the program.

The *run.java* class, illustrated below, is included to use the program as an application.

```
public class run {
    public static void main(String args[]) {
        Driver driver = new Driver();
    }
}
```

The *AppletRun.java* class can be used if you prefer to run the program as an applet.

```
import javax.swing.JApplet;
public class AppletRun extends JApplet {
    public void AppletRun() {
        Driver driver = new Driver();
    }
}
```

The details of the distinction between applications and applets, along with *run.java* and *AppletRun.java*, are considered Java-isms that detract from the early presentation. Therefore, a complete discussion of these issues is delayed until Chapter 15.

AWT and *Swing* Libraries

Objects are built from classes, and classes come from libraries. Therefore, an objects-centric approach would be incomplete without the inclusion of software libraries. This book uses standard libraries from J2SE 5.0: *AWT* and *Swing*.

Using these libraries makes it possible to develop Java programs that display animations, utilize simple list data structures, or access real calendar and clock information. However, the bulk of classes are used to provide a graphical user interface (GUI) for student-written Java code.

Why Use Graphical Libraries?

In our experience, there seems to be no collection of classes that motivates beginning programmers better than GUI libraries. This motivation is sufficiently strong that we have found that the *AWT* and *Swing* libraries require very little of our precious lecture time. After we have demonstrated the basics in one or two initial lectures, our students are quite capable of teaching themselves about Java classes by reading their specifications.

Graphical classes also have the pedagogical advantage of visibility. The GUI objects provide a fertile field for examples of objects and object relationships that are easily visualized.

The final reason for using GUI classes is that the alternative seems to be the same tired interactive terminal stream type I/O that CS1 courses have used for 30 years. A generation that was raised with compact disks and electronic games will find terminal I/O artificial and unappealing.

Opening Black Boxes

Bertrand Meyer has defined the concept of "successive opening of black boxes" as a pedagogical approach that begins with the use of predefined components (i.e., the black boxes) that little by little reveals the tools and techniques that were used to compose the black boxes. As an example black box, this text avoids the distraction of static methods early in the presentation by using the aforementioned run.java static class to instantiate an initial Driver object. The reader is initially asked to ignore the run.java class until later in the text when static methods are explained and the code for the run.java class is shown as an illustration.

When a black box is employed and the reader is expected to assume something "on faith," a special Closed Black Box section, accompanied by the appropriate icon, appears in the text. Correspondingly, Opening the Black Box sections indicate locations in the book where these black box concepts are revealed.

Supplements

The following supplementary materials are available to all readers at http://www.aw.com/cssupport:

- the source code for the example programs used in the book (more than 80 programs)
- class diagrams and specifications in HTML form for key classes/features examined in the book

In addition, the following supplements are available to qualified instructors. Visit our Instructor Resource Center (http://www.aw.com/irc) or send email to computing@aw.com for information on how to access them:

- a complete set of answers to all exercises
- source code for sample solutions to programming exercises
- PowerPoint lectures that parallel the chapter presentations

Acknowledgments

I am indebted to Barbara Barkauskas, Keith Burand, and Kasilingam Periyasamy for their trust, helpful comments, and friendship. These fine colleagues had sufficient faith in this project (or perhaps it was disappointment with other textbooks) that they were willing to teach for a full year from a manuscript of the first edition of this book. Barb deserves a special commendation because she also consented to act as a reviewer. She provided the unique perspective of one who teaches the material precisely this way.

I am also grateful for the remarkable collection of talented reviewers from widely varying programs that the folks at Addison-Wesley contracted for both this and the previous edition. Good reviewers probe, question, suggest, and criticize, and these knowledgeable computer scientists did all of that.

Thomas W. Bennet, Mississippi College
Glenn Blank, Lehigh University
Randy Bower, Jacksonville University
Jonathan Bredin, Colorado College
Robert Burton, Brigham Young University
Charles Costarella, Antelope Valley College
W. Sam Chung, Pacific Lutheran University
Eck Doerry, Northern Arizona University
Adrian German, Indiana University
Daniel P. Gill, Purdue University
Aaron J. Gordon, Metropolitan State College of Denver
Le Gruenwald, University of Oklahoma
H. Paul Haiduk, West Texas A & M University
Mark S. Hutchenreuther, California Polytechnic State University
Cerian Jones, University of Alberta
Michael A. Long, California State University, Chico
Blayne E. Mayfield, Oklahoma State University
Bina Ramamurthy, State University of New York at Buffalo
John M. Samaras, Valdosta State University
Carolyn J. C. Schauble, Colorado State University
Marc L. Smith, Colby College
John A. Trono, Saint Michael's College
Phil Ventura, State University of New York at Buffalo

Dave Riley

Preface for the Student

Why have you decided to take this course? Are you committed to a career as a computer scientist? Are you seeking to sharpen your analytic problem-solving skills? Are you testing the waters to see if computer programming might be in your future?

Whatever your reason, it is important to realize that the lifeblood of computer science is software development. This is why a large part of the computer science curriculum is devoted to the study of how to develop software. This book is an introduction to computer science in the form of an introduction to software development.

Learning to develop software is a participatory sport. You don't learn to write poetry by merely reading it, and you won't learn to create software by just reading this text or listening to your instructor. You need to do it. You will find several programming assignments suggested at the end of each chapter. Plan to write at least one program per chapter using these or other assignments.

Problem-solving lies at the heart of software development. Your problem-solving skills will grow as you develop software. Sometimes it will be frustrating and sometimes it will be energizing. Computer scientists find excitement in tackling problems. The more difficult the path that leads to the solution, the greater the feeling of accomplishment when the program is written.

Software Engineering Hints

The world's understanding of software development has matured through the years to the point that we now refer to the best practices as "software engineering." Software engineering principles and processes can be complicated, especially in an introduction to software development. However, software engineering is really just a collection of procedures that we know to be effective, and it is always wise to learn from the experience of others.

Like any craftsman, the software engineer must learn how best to use the tools of the craft. Sprinkled throughout this text you will find highlighted Software Engineering Hints. These hints offer "how to" suggestions. Often they discuss how software engineers choose from alternative approaches or solutions. It is a good idea to read each Software Engineering Hint as you read the associated section.

A secondary reason for including the Software Engineer Hints is to help you gain some appreciation for future software engineering issues you may encounter. Software development, like other problem solving, tends to follow a three-step sequence:

1. Analyze the problem.
2. Design a solution.
3. Implement the solution.

Unfortunately, Steps 1 and 2 are difficult, if not impossible, to appreciate fully prior to a thorough understanding of Step 3. Therefore, software development is generally taught in the opposite order. In other words, we begin by studying how to implement a solution. The Software Engineering Hints provide a glimpse at the problem analysis and design steps as a means to see important connections in software development.

The Java Inspector

One practice that has proven invaluable in software engineering is the inspection. The names "design review," "code inspection," "structured walk-through," and "desk check" refer to different kinds of inspections. An inspection is really just what its name implies: an informal analysis, or perusal of some aspect of the software. Just as a painter must step back from a painting to discover imperfections, so too must a software engineer step back from the software to find problems and potential improvements. The Java Inspector sections are included to provide guidance on how to inspect software. Just like Software Engineering Hints, it is best to examine The Java Inspector both before and after you have had the opportunity to utilize the chapter's material.

Successively Opening Black Boxes

Imagine that you are asked to learn to speak a new language and that you are told you must speak only in complete sentences. This analogy is remarkably close to what it is like to begin to develop software (computer programs) using any modern programming language. The difficulty is that you will be expected to create complete programs almost from the very start. However, it is impossible to learn all of the rules for punctuation and grammar of any useful language without taking your time.

Terminology

The computing industry has spawned a rather rich vocabulary of its own. Just a few years ago, if you mentioned "the Web," most people would assume you were talking about spiders. Today, we tell friends to "email me" as frequently as we ask them to "give me a call."

Software development also has its own terminology. Some of these terms may be familiar to you, but most are probably new. Throughout the book, the most important vocabulary is identified and these terms appear boldfaced when they first occur. You will also find a summary of key terms at the end of each chapter.

A Final Comment

If you are reading this book as an assigned text for a course, then I am honored that your instructor has chosen this book. However, I did not write this text for instructors; I wrote it for you, the student. With the assistance of the good folks at Addison-Wesley, some fine colleagues in my department, and some excellent reviewers, I've tried to make the organization logical, the presentation clear, and the writing readable. The first semester that I used an early draft of this material I did so in parallel with another well-known textbook, and my students told me that they greatly preferred my manuscript. (Of course, I was the one who assigned their grades at the end of the semester, not the author of the other textbook. ;-) So you are the true judge of the quality of this book. If you find that it helps you to begin your journey into computer science, then my efforts will be successful.

Dave Riley

Objects and Classes

An object in possession seldom retains the same charm that it had in pursuit.

—Pliny the Younger

Objectives

- To provide a basic definition of an object as an entity with state and behavior
- To present the fundamental similarities and differences between objects and their classes
- To provide an initial example of how objects and classes can be used to construct a simple program
- To introduce the notation of class diagrams
- To explain the edit-compile-run process and its realization for the Java programming language
- To introduce the terminology of the waterfall software development model and use it to illustrate the role of various key processes in software development

*T*he world is a collection of **objects**. When you (an object) got up this morning you might have retrieved a box of cereal (another object) from the cupboard (still another object) and poured cereal into a bowl (a fourth object). Then you turned to the refrigerator (an object) to remove a gallon of milk (an object) to cover your cereal. Just as objects play a central role in "real life," they can also play a central role in computer programming.

1.1 ■ Objects Everywhere

Examining objects with a bit more care leads to the conclusion that every object has two facets:

- its state
- its behavior

The **state** of an object is made up of the object's particular characteristics. The amount of milk within the carton, the location of the milk carton, and whether or not the carton is open, are characteristics that contribute to the state of the milk carton. Of course, an object's state changes as time passes. When a milk carton is opened, its state changes; and the state changes again as the milk is poured out. The changeable nature of state means that state is related to time.

A refrigerator also exhibits state. For example, the temperature inside the refrigerator is a significant part of its state. When the refrigerator's door is closed, the state of the refrigerator includes the fact that the light within is off. As the door is opened and the light turns on, the state of the refrigerator has changed.

Behavior refers to tasks that can be performed by or upon an object. Typically, behavior takes the form of operations. For example, the act of pouring milk from a carton is an operation that is part of the normal behavior for a milk carton. Other common operations for a milk carton include opening the carton and placing it in the refrigerator. Operations such as standing on the carton or using it to paint a picture are not considered typical behavior for a milk carton.

Objects are routinely categorized into groups, also known as **classes**. The milk carton in your hand is a particular object; it belongs to a class called "milk container." Similarly, the refrigerator in your home belongs to the class of all refrigerators.

Classes define the state and behavior that is shared by all of the class members. An operation, like pouring milk, is part of the milk container class because it is common to all milk container objects.

1.2 ■ Objects in Software

A **program** is a collection of instructions that, when performed, cause a particular task to be performed on a computer. Individuals who write programs are, therefore, called **programmers**. The terms **software** and **code** refer to a collection of one or more programs, so we refer to programmers as **software developers**.

Today, the strategy most often employed by knowledgeable software developers is called **object-oriented programming (OOP)**. A programmer using an object-oriented (O-O) strategy begins by selecting objects that can collectively solve a given problem.

To illustrate the role of objects in programs, consider a computer program to simulate a simple robot vehicle. (NASA undoubtedly used many such programs in the design of the Mars Rovers.)

Writing software begins with the **program requirements**—a statement of the specific purpose of the software. Below is an informal set of software requirements for our robot simulator.

Robot Simulator: Program Requirements

The program displays two windows. One window contains a simulated two-dimensional road course and the robot. The course includes orange cones to mark barriers. The second window contains two user control buttons—one labeled "Turn" and the other labeled "Step."

Initially, the robot image is in the upper left corner of the road course window and headed toward the right. Several barrier cones are placed in this road course window (see Figure 1.1).

The user controls the program execution by clicking on the control buttons. Clicking the Turn button causes the robot cart to change its direction of travel by a rotation of 90 degrees in the clockwise direction. The travel direction is indicated by the robot's image. Clicking the Step button causes the robot to move slowly forward by a distance equal to half of the robot's length. Robots are not allowed to move off the window or through barriers, so clicking the Step button has no effect in such situations.

The program requirements document suggests the use of several objects. One way to discover objects in requirements is to search for nouns. Key nouns in the robot simulator requirements include: the robot, a road course window, a control window, barriers (cones), the Turn button, and the Step button.

Once a programmer identifies the objects in the program, the next step is to find or create a class corresponding to each object. Classes are essential because they serve as the sources of code for an object-oriented program. In fact, it is correct to say that an object-oriented program consists of a collection of classes.

software *Hint*
engineering
Object-oriented design begins by selecting the objects. A good O-O designer looks for nouns in the program requirements because they often indicate the key objects needed for a solution.

Figure 1.1   Two windows for the robot simulator

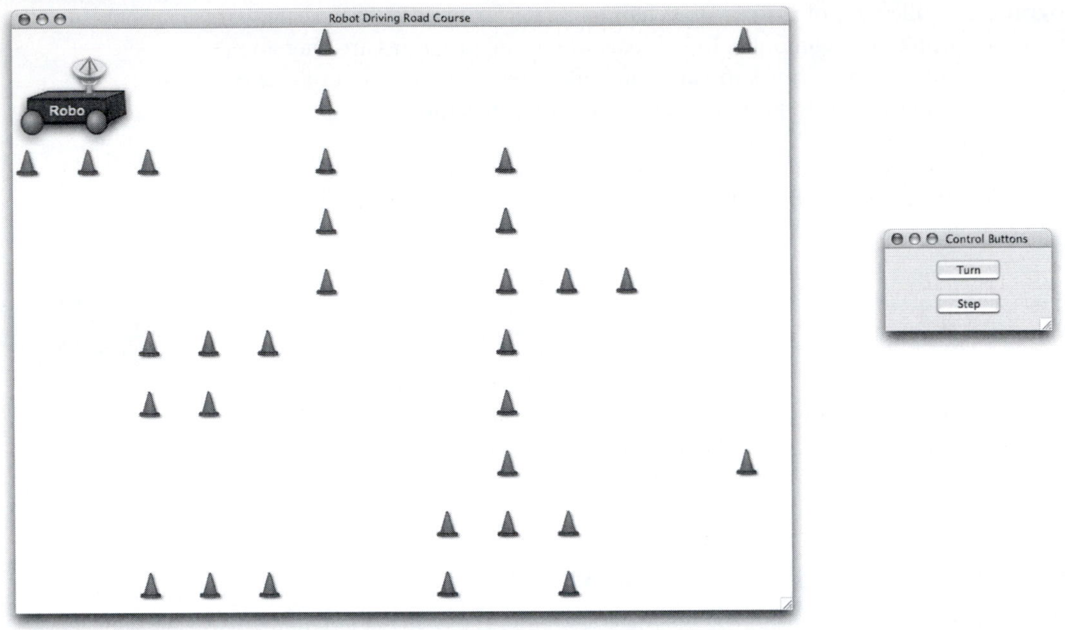

software *Hint*
engineering
Programmers
should always try
to reuse existing
software, rather
than waste time
creating some-
thing that already
exists.

Ideally, a programmer **reuses** an existing class, as opposed to writing the code for a new class. Software reuse by a programmer makes sense in the same way that an architect designs new structures from commonly available lumber with standard dimensions or an engineer designs new automobile engines using spark plugs that are available at most hardware stores.

For the robot simulator program, it is safe to assume that there are standard classes for building user interface buttons and software windows. However, there are several classes for this program that are likely to be unique to this kind of robot simulator. The following classes form a good beginning of the program:

- `Barrier`
- `ControlWindow`
- `RoadCourse`
- `Robot`

The `Barrier` class contains the instructions for maintaining the state of each road barrier cone. The state of a `Barrier` object includes position and size information as well as the window in which the cone image is displayed. The behavior of a `Barrier` object consists of operations to create such objects, locate them within some window and draw the orange cone image.

Sometimes objects are composed from other objects. Such is the case with `RoadCourse` objects. A `RoadCourse` consists of a window, one or more `Robot` objects, and numerous `Barrier` objects. A `RoadCourse` must be able to display the proper images and to maintain the location of each.

The `ControlWindow` object is also composed of other objects—a window and two buttons. The act of clicking each button must interact with the behavior of the robot.

The `Robot` class plays a pivotal role in the robot simulator program. A `Robot` object must interact with the other objects. A `Robot` moves about a `RoadCourse` window, responds to button clicks from the `ControlWindow`, and must not run over `Barrier` objects.

The four classes (`Barrier`, `ControlWindow`, `RoadCourse`, and `Robot`) are not sufficient to provide a complete program. We still need some way to start program execution and create the necessary objects. In this book, we adopt the convention of using an additional class, called `Driver`, as a starting point. The `Driver` typically creates and coordinates the execution of other objects that are involved in the program's execution. Figure 1.2 reveals the code for a proper `Driver` class to be used in the robot simulator program. Future programs will have different `Driver` classes depending upon their requirements.

> **software engineering** *Hint*
>
> The name Driver was chosen for the initial object because it is this object that initiates, *drives,* and coordinates the program's execution.

Closed **Black Box**

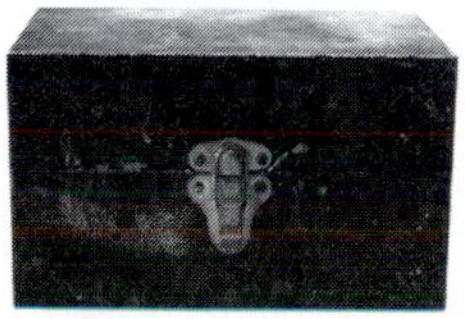

Programming languages are like all foreign languages—the initial exposure to a written sample is somewhat mysterious. The `Driver` code in Figure 1.2 is included to illustrate a few key points about the software and its connection to the programming process. However, don't worry too much about the particulars now. It is best to think of the notational details of this example as a black box to be opened (explained) in future chapters.

Figure 1.2

`Driver` class for the Robot Simulator program

```java
/**
 * Driver class for the Robot Simulator program
 */

public class Driver {
    private RoadCourse course;
    private Robot robo;
    private ControlWindow buttonWin;

    public Driver() {
        course = new RoadCourse();
        robo = new Robot( course );
        course.placeRobotOnRoad( robo );
        buttonWin = new ControlWindow( robo );
    }
}
```

object declarations

instructions

The execution of an object-oriented program begins with an initial object. This initial object plays a special role because it serves as the starting point for the entire program and often coordinates much of the program's activity. In this book, a `Driver` class provides the code for the initial object.

The state of an object depends upon its components (other objects). This particular `Driver` object includes three component objects, declared in the two lines that begin with the word `private`.

1. The `course` object is declared to belong to the `RoadCourse` class.
2. The `robo` object is declared to belong to the `Robot` class.
3. The `buttonWin` object is declared to belong to the `ControlWindow` class.

An object's behavior is determined by **instructions** (also called **statements**) When a program executes, the program's instructions are performed. There are four instructions for the `Driver` coded in Figure 1.2. These instructions are found in the four lines following the `public Driver() {` line.

■ The first instruction will cause a new `RoadCourse` object, named `course`, to be constructed.

■ The second instruction will cause a new `Robot` object, named `robo`, to be constructed. The name `course` is included in this instruction to permit the `robo` object to interact with the `course` object.

■ The third instruction will place the `robo` object upon the `course` to be constructed.

■ The fourth instruction will create a `ControlWindow` object called `buttonWin`, sharing the `robo` object so that when the user clicks `buttonWin` objects, the result is applied to `robo`.

The other four classes in the program also contain declarations and instructions. For example, the `ControlWindow` class must declare and create two button objects. Similarly, the `RoadCourse` class creates objects for the `course` window and its barriers.

The robot simulator example illustrates the tools that a software developer must use to write a program. A program is built from classes that the programmer writes or reuses. Classes are composed from statements, and these statements are used in such a way that they manipulate objects to perform desired tasks.

The work of a programmer is something like that of a songwriter. A songwriter composes songs and a programmer writes classes. A song is composed from notes and words, and a class is composed from declarations and instructions. A performer takes the notes and lyrics of a song and performs the music. A computer takes the declarations and instructions of a program and executes the program. Sometimes the results of a program execution are images drawn on a computer screen, sometimes they are complex calculations, and sometimes they retrieve and update important information.

1.3 ■ Anatomy of a Software Class

Since all of the code in object-oriented programs resides within classes, the skilled programmer needs to be familiar with writing and using classes. Indeed, most of this book is devoted to learning how best to compose classes. This section introduces the basics.

A **software class** consists of two groups of members:

■ attributes

■ methods

An **attribute**, often represented by an **instance variable**, is an entity that names a single characteristic of an object's state. A **method** is an operation that can be performed upon an object. It is useful to picture the attributes and methods as a **class diagram** with the following general form.

software *Hint*
engineering

Pictures are often helpful when designing software. One particularly useful picture is the class diagram.
A class diagram shows the key features of a class, including

■ class name
■ class attributes
■ class methods

The best time to draw class diagrams is *before* writing the code, because it often reveals helpful programming issues.

The class diagram is a rectangle with three compartments separated by two horizontal lines. The top compartment contains the name of the class, the middle compartment lists the attributes of the class, and the bottom compartment shows the class methods.

This class diagram notation is part of the **Unified Modeling Language** (**UML**). UML is the most widely used set of notations in today's software engineering industry.

The class diagram for Driver class of Example 1 is shown in Figure 1.3. The class diagram for Driver specifies that this class contains three attributes: course, robo, and buttonWin. Notice that each attribute is preceded by the name of the class to which it belongs.

Figure 1.3

Class diagram for Driver class of the Robot Simulator

The methods of the class are listed in the bottom compartment of the class diagram. The only method in the Driver class has the same name as the class (Driver). It may seem strange for a method to have the same name as its class, but this is common in some programming languages.

The robot simulator program also makes use of other classes. Class diagrams for three of these classes are shown in Figure 1.4. This figure illustrates a couple of additional notations that are typical of class diagrams.

Neither the RoadCourse, Robot, nor JButton (its full name is javax.swing. JButton) class diagram includes any attributes; the attribute region of each class diagram in Figure 1.4 is left blank. When attributes are omitted in this way, it means that either the class has no attributes or (more often) the attributes of the class aren't relevant to the discussion at hand.

The list of methods shown within a class diagram can also be incomplete. The "..." notation in the RoadCourse, Robot, and JButton diagrams indicates that there are more methods in these classes than are shown. The additional methods are not shown because they are not needed for this program.

You may also notice that the, placeRobotOnRoad, rotateClockwise, moveByOneStep, and repaint methods are preceded by the word void. The inclusion of void is commonly used in Java to denote a method that is designed for updating.

UML class diagrams frequently include headings to categorize the class methods. These headings are bracketed within « » symbols. In Figure 1.4, the RoadCourse,

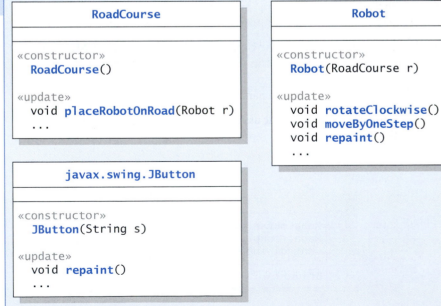

Figure 1.4

Class diagrams for RoadCourse, Robot, and JButton

`JButton`, and `Robot` methods are categorized as *constructor* methods, while the others are *update* methods. The distinction between constructor and update categories will be explained in Chapter 2.

1.4 ■ The Difference between Objects and Classes

An object is very closely associated with the class to which it belongs. The attributes of an object are defined by its class. An object's behavior is restricted by the methods that are included in its class. The instructions that are executed by an object are the instructions that are written in the class. However, there are significant differences between objects and classes.

A class

- is a template that defines attributes and methods.
- is written by a programmer as a part of a program.
- does not exist when programs execute, except in the form of one or more member objects.
- is static in the sense that its code cannot be altered during program execution.
- is named by a class name.

An object

- must belong to some class.
- exists during the time that a program executes.
- must be explicitly declared *and* constructed by the executing program.
- has attributes that can change in value and methods that can execute during program execution. (The class to which the object belongs defines these attributes and methods.)
- is often referenced using a variable name.

Classes can be compared to automobile assembly lines. The purpose of an automobile assembly line is to produce cars, just as the purpose of a class is to produce objects. A single assembly line is designed to produce a single basic type of car. Similarly, the objects from the same class all share common characteristics.

Each object must **belong** to one particular class. The `robo` object from Figure 1.2 belongs to the `Robot` class. This means that the program is permitted to perform `Robot` methods (operations) upon `robo`. This also means that performing `Driver` methods or `RoadCourse` methods upon `robo` is *not* permitted; these methods are designed for a different kind (class) of objects. Sometimes two different classes have methods with the same name; this is the case for the `repaint` method—`repaint` is permissible on *both* `JButton` and `Robot` objects.

Every object belongs to a single class, but it is possible for a class to have numerous member objects. The `Driver` class could be revised to create not one, but two `Robot` objects. Each of these objects would have its unique attribute values, just as two cars from the same assembly line might be painted different colors. However, both robot objects are the product of the same assembly line called `Robot`, and this class membership defines the methods that can be performed upon them.

1.5 ■ Edit, Compile, and Run

The discussion of classes and objects raises a fundamental distinction between actions that occur during program execution and actions that occur prior to program execution. In order to explore these issues, it is useful to examine the process that is used to bring a program into production.

Computers are **hardware**; that is, they are made of electrical circuits, perhaps with a few mechanical devices. A key part of the hardware is a unit called the **main memory**. The main memory stores each object, including all of its attributes.

The **processor** is another key device within every modern computer. The processor is responsible for executing the program. Unfortunately, processors are restricted to executing only primitive types of instructions, known as **machine instructions**. Machine instructions are extremely difficult for humans to read and write, because they are designed for the convenience of the computer hardware—not the programmers. Therefore, modern software development relies upon **high-level programming languages**. The term high-level implies that the languages are closer to a notation that is comfortable for programmers.

The use of a high-level language dictates the need for a three-step process to bring a program from the programmer's mind into production. Figure 1.5 illustrates this process. Step 1 occurs when the programmer types the program into the computer. A programmer uses a software tool, called an **editor**, to perform this task. Each software class is typed into the editor, and the editor is used to save each class in a separate **file** (generally on the computer's disk storage). Such files are often called **source code** because they are the original (source) program components as created by the programmer.

In order to type the source code, a programmer must first choose a particular **programming language**. Each programming language has its own unique notations and conventions, just as each natural language has its distinctive conventions.

In this text, all programs are written in a programming language called **Java**. Java is the result of a research project directed by James Gosling and funded by Sun Microsystems. In May 1995, Sun formally announced the new language. Java shares many of its notations with the earlier C and C++ programming languages, as well as the more recent C# language. Java incorporates several different language features, including specific features to support object-oriented programming and World Wide Web applications.

Figure 1.5   The edit-compile-run process

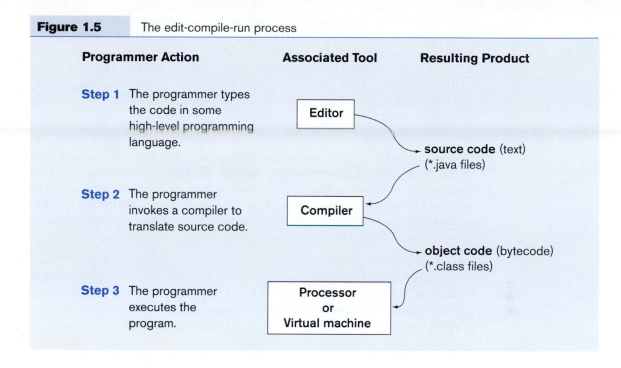

When programming in Java, the programmer usually stores each class in a separate file and the name of each file should be the same as the class with ".*java*" appended. For example, the `Driver` class would be stored in a file named *Driver.java*. It is most convenient to gather all of the files for the classes of a single program within the same folder. For the robot simulator program, the following files would be collected within the same program folder: *Barrier.java*, *ControlWindow.java*, *Driver.java*, *RoadCourse.java*, and *Robot.java*.

Note that Java is a **case-sensitive language**, which means that capitalization patterns must be identical if they are to refer to the same thing. Case sensitivity dictates that "driver," "DRIVER," and "DriVeR" are different names. Some file systems are also case sensitive.

Once the classes have been stored in source files, the second step is to **compile** the source code. A **compiler** is a program that translates source code into an executable form. Assuming the compiler detects no errors in the source code, it stores the translated form of each class in its own file. Each of these translated **object code** files is named the same as the original class with ".*class*" appended. In other words, the Java compiler reads the *Driver.java* file and stores the translated form of this class in a second file called *Driver.class*. (The source file remains unaltered by the compilation process.) One common procedure for compiling code is to place the source code files into a single folder, making certain that the folder is the working folder (current directory), and then enter the following command.

```
javac *.java
```

software *Hint*
engineering

Compilers are extremely unforgiving. In English, a missing comma or semicolon is often unimportant, but not so for a compiler. The wise programmer reviews source code for typographical errors and avoids using conventions that encourage such errors.

In the event that the programmer mistypes the program, the compiler will detect an error. These errors are called **compile-time errors** or **syntax errors**; they are errors in the allowable **syntax** or form of the code. When a syntax error is detected, it is reported by the compiler and no object code is produced. Such an error is a signal to the programmer to return to the editor, rewrite the source code, and compile again. It may take several repetitions of edits and compiles before the programmer corrects the code.

When all syntax errors are fixed and the classes compiled, the third step is to **execute** (or **run**) the program. Many compilers produce object code that is in machine code format, so the computer's processor can execute such object code directly. Most Java compilers do not translate into machine code; instead, their object code is stored in a format known as **bytecode**. Like machine code, bytecode is in a form that is of little value to humans, but unlike machine code, bytecode cannot be directly executed by a processor.

One solution to the problem of how to execute bytecode is to use a **Java Virtual Machine** (or **Java VM**) to execute the code. The Java VM is another program that knows how to execute the ".*class*" files. A Java VM can be invoked by typing "`java`" followed by a blank and the name of the class where execution is to begin. In the case of robot simulator, the folder contains a class called "run.class" that is an appropriate starting class for this code. (The `run` class is used by most examples in this text in order to create an object of type `Driver`, thereby invoking the `Driver` constructor method.) A typical command to execute the program is:

```
java run
```

Java supports two kinds of programs: applications and applets. Chapter 15 examines the notations and behaviors of each. The robot simulator program has been described as an **application**. The differences between applets and applications is sufficiently minor that any of the programs in this book can be transformed into either with the addition of a couple of simple files.

Program execution begins by loading the program's instructions into the memory of the computer, then executing those instructions one by one. As the program executes, objects are constructed, modified, and inspected as directed by the program's instructions. These objects occupy memory space. If the programmer uses the right instructions in the proper order, then the program's execution produces the intended result.

When the robot simulator application is executed, the two windows shown in Figure 1.1 appear as the result. The windows may look slightly different on computers with different operating systems. However, the windows will always include the robot, barriers, and buttons shown.

The Java bytecode that is created by a compiler on one computer can generally be executed on any Java VM running on any computer. The ability to easily transport executable code from one computer to another is called **portability**; it is the primary reason for using a compiler that produces bytecode rather than machine code. Machine code is not portable because each family of computer processors has its own machine code.

Just as there are compile-time errors, there are also **logic errors**. A logic error occurs when a program doesn't perform the intended task. Sometimes logic errors are so grievous that they can be detected by the Java VM, in which case an error is reported to the programmer. These reported errors are known as **runtime errors**. However, many times the program with a logi-

software *Hint*
engineering

Beginning programmers sometimes make the mistake of believing that a program is correct if the compiler fails to find syntax errors. The wise programmer knows that logic errors can occur independently and are frequently more difficult than syntax errors to find and correct.

caerror appears to run normally but simply produces incorrect results. For example, the program designed to display *a* robot within a robot course window may not include the robot image, may display a different image, or there may be no window at all.

Programming errors, whether they are compile-time errors or logic errors, are also called **faults**. More informally, faults are called **bugs**. The process of identifying faults is referred to as **testing**, and the act of testing together with correcting faults is known as **debugging**.

Some programmers prefer to use an **Integerated Development Environment** (IDE), rather than command line interfaces and commands such as **javac** and **java**. An IDE provides a single application for editing, compiling, and executing programs. Most IDE actions are possible by clicking a button or selecting an item from a menu. This

software *Hint*
engineering

Programs are neither correct nor incorrect by themselves. It makes sense to talk about program correctness only with respect to the specified purpose of the program. Programmers must scrutinize and rescrutinize the specifications (requirements) documents throughout the process of writing and testing their code.

book, and its example programs, are designed to be independent of any IDE, but the use of an IDE is always encouraged. Well-known Java IDEs include BlueJ, Eclipse, Code Warrior, and JBuilder, Appendix F contains a few more details about how to compile and run programs using Microsoft Windows without an IDE.

1.6 ■ Introduction to Software Engineering

In the 1970s it became apparent that much of the world's software was being created by haphazard methods. Unlike other engineering disciplines with strict rules for how to approach a new design and how to measure the quality of a product, computer programming was a kind of "grab bag" of programming strategies often learned through on-the-job experiences. The term **software crisis** was frequently used to describe a software industry in which programming projects rarely met schedules and the resulting software typically contained many faults. The phrase "computer error," which usually means "software error," became a common excuse for many everyday problems.

The result of this bit of history was a new emphasis on **software engineering** as a disciplined approach to software development. Today's software developers practice their craft on sizable programs consisting of thousands, or even millions, of instructions. Teams of cooperating software developers, devoting hundreds of collective years of time, are required for this so-called **programming in the large**. This book explores the fundamental tools of the software development trade. The examples and exercises are necessarily smaller than large-scale programming, but it is essential to keep in mind that the ultimate goal is to develop the habits and skills needed for programming in the large.

Large programming projects usually follow a pattern known as a **software lifecycle**. There are numerous models of software lifecycles. One of the earliest models, called the **waterfall model**, is illustrated in Figure 1.6. While there are many different lifecycles employed by today's software engineer, the waterfall model is sufficient for this discussion, because it provides the basic engineering activities needed to develop programs.

software *Hint*
engineering

Introductory computer science texts tend to concentrate on issues relating to the implementation phase of the software lifecycle. However, history shows that implementation is easier (and faster) when more effort is invested in analysis and design.

The waterfall model describes the process of creating a program as a five-step procedure. The process begins with the **analysis phase** in which the software developer must analyze the problem to be solved. The purpose of analysis is to discover what the customer wants and to formulate a detailed set of software requirements.

The **design phase** of software development is when the basic structure of the program is chosen. Object-oriented design includes tasks such as identifying the objects needed in the program and outlining the classes and their relationships. Documents such as class diagrams are produced during the design phase.

The actual code for each class is created during the **implementation phase**. The difference between the design phase and the implementation phase is analogous to the difference between the job of an architect and a contractor. Design work produces the architectural blueprint whereas implementation turns the blueprint into bricks and mortar. Any software implementation must be expressed using the notation of some programming language, but designs are often language independent.

The waterfall model suggests that the implementation phase is followed by a **testing phase** in which the code is tested for correctness with respect to its requirements. Software rarely ends its lifecycle with testing. Most significant programs live through

Figure 1.6

The waterfall model of software development

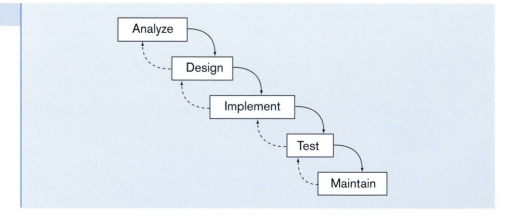

many revisions (also called versions or releases). Each revision purports to improve the software by correcting earlier deficiencies and/or adding new and improved features. The process of modifying the code to produce later revisions is known as the **maintenance phase**.

Few, if any, software development projects follow the exact five-step sequence of the waterfall model. For most projects, testing is an ongoing process, not just a single step between implementation and maintenance. It is also commonplace to discover a deficiency during the implementation that requires revisiting the basic design or the requirements documents. Despite the imperfections in the waterfall model, all programmers can benefit by understanding the five phases of the model because they represent five fundamental activities of software engineering.

1.7 ■ A Sample of Object-Oriented Software Development

To glimpse the way that a large object-oriented programming project might proceed and its relationship to the phases of the waterfall model, consider the task of automating a grocery store. The software development project begins by analyzing the entire grocery operation to discover the requirements of the software. During the analysis phase, senior software developers meet with the storeowners to understand their needs and wishes for the software. The developers also study the store's equipment, including the computer upon which the software will execute and customer checkout devices and systems for recording new inventory arrivals. Store policies and personnel responsibilities are also investigated during this project phase.

Once the storeowners and the senior programmers agree on a set of system requirements, software design begins. The initial stages of software design, sometimes called **high-level design**, are likely to rely heavily upon information gathered during the analysis phase. As the design phase begins, objects are identified and classes emerge. Suppose the grocery store has 14 checkout lanes, each equipped with bar code scanners, credit card readers, and manually operated cash drawers. Additionally, the store receives weekly printed price lists from suppliers. Objects found in analyzing such a system include:

- a bar-coded can of beans
- the cash drawer in register 3
- the order form to be submitted to a supplier
- the cash stored in the store's safe
- a single sale by credit card

The objects must be grouped into classes, such as `BarCodedProduct`, that include objects like corn chips and bars of soap. Similarly, a `CashDrawer` class has member objects that include the cash drawers in use at checkout lanes, as well as cash drawers that are being counted by the store bookkeeper.

The design process proceeds to identify the attributes and methods of each class. For example, the attributes of `BarCodedProduct` include items like the product's name, the supplier, the cost, the selling price, the current inventory, and the bar code number. The operations that are performed upon bar-coded objects, such as *change the price* and *sell one item* become methods of the class. Figure 1.7 contains a sample class diagram that might result from designing the `BarCodedProduct` class.

It is common for the process to discover unexpected objects during the design phase. For example, consideration of the `BarCodedProduct` class and its `quantityOnHand` attribute might lead to the need for an out-of-stock-alert object. There are likely to be hundreds of classes needed for the grocery store system.

An architect creates house plans by performing a kind of high-level design to draw graphical blueprints. But an architect must also supply more detailed descriptions of things such as wall thickness, materials, and insulation requirements. Similarly, software designers must perform both high-level design and **detail design**. Writing a class diagram is usually viewed as high-level design, but supplying precise specifications for the behavior of each of the class's methods is considered detail design. An example of a detail design decision is whether or not to design the `sellOneItem` method so that it triggers immediate product orders when inventory is low.

After the desired behavior for a method is completed within the detailed design, the method can be implemented. During the implementation process, a software developer writes the actual Java instructions (the code) that execute when the method is invoked. The developer, and others, are likely to examine and test the code under various conditions to ensure that it performs the intended task.

Figure 1.7

Class diagram for BarCodedProduct

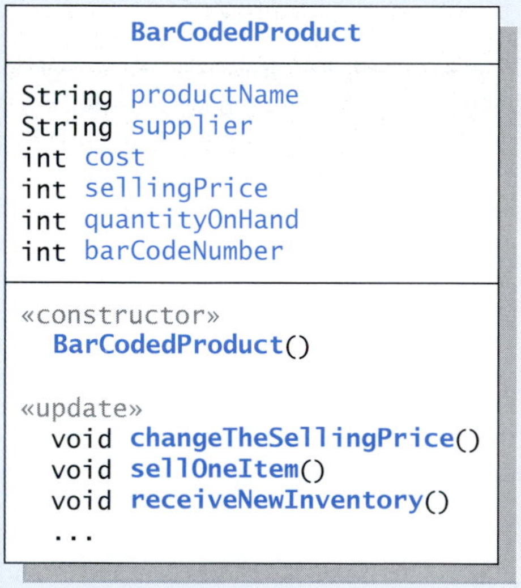

The execution of the complete program consists of a collection of objects that perform methods upon one another. When an item is scanned for sale by the checkout scanner object, a method must be called to update the quantity on hand from the product object and another method might add the item's cost to the customer's bill object. It is the combined execution of numerous methods upon many objects that belong to various classes that characterizes a typical running object-oriented program.

Inspector

Software engineering teaches that the most productive way to improve code quality is to perform frequent and thorough desk checks. A **desk check** consists of scrutinizing the code manually. Compilers can discover syntax errors and executing a program can uncover certain logical errors. However, many of these errors can be avoided if the programmer simply spends a little time examining the code.

Below is a collection of hints on what to check when examining code that involves the concepts of this chapter.

■ Compilers are uncompromising. Spell and punctuate precisely. The Java syntax rules presented throughout the book are a guide.

■ Java is case sensitive. Check for proper use of capitalization.

■ Check every class to be certain that it is stored in a file named with the class name and the "*.java*" suffix.

■ Organize your programs into folders. Java often relies upon related classes to be organized within the same folder.

■ Before a program can be executed, it must be compiled properly. Always check for the presence of syntax errors prior to executing your program.

Terminology

analysis phase (of software development)

application (in Java)

attribute

behavior

belong (as an object "belongs" to a class)

bug

bytecode

case-sensitive language

class (in software)

class diagram

code

compile / compiler

compile-time error

debug

design phase (of software development)

desk check

detail design

editor

edit-compile-run process

execute

fault

file

hardware (of a computer)

high-level design

high-level programming language

implementation phase (of software development)

instance variable

instruction

integrated development environment
   (IDE)

Java (programming language)

Java Virtual Machine (Java VM)

logic error

machine instruction

main memory (computer memory)

maintenance phase

member (of a class)

method

object

object code

object-oriented programming (OOP)

portability

processor

program

program correctness

program requirements

programmer

programming in the large

programming language

reuse (of software)

run

runtime error

software

software class

software crisis

software developer

software engineering

software lifecycle

source code

state

syntax

syntax error

testing

testing phase (of software
   development)

Unified Modeling Language (UML)

waterfall model (of software
   development)

Exercises

1. Consider an object called cruise ship. Which of the following would you classify as contributing to the state of the cruise ship, and which is better associated with its behavior?

   a. the ship's color

   b. the act of slowing the ship down to five knots per hour

   c. the length of the ship's deck

   d. turning the ship back toward its home port

2. For each of the following objects, select a class to which it and other objects belong.

   a. your mother

   b. Sun Microsystems

   c. your favorite item of clothing

d. the writing utensil you use most often

e. your favorite pet

3. Identify as many objects as you can within each of the following requirements statements.

a. Write a program to draw a clown with a red nose and green hair.

b. Write a program to simulate a farm tractor pulling a plow through a field.

c. Write a program to show three dogs leaping through three hoops.

4. For each class diagram below, identify the name of the class, the name of each attribute, the class to which it belongs, and the name of each method.

a.

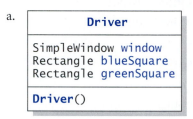

b.

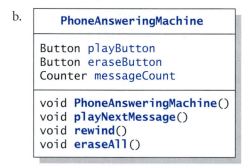

5. Each statement below lists an activity that might take place within the development of a particular piece of software. As best fits, label each activity as

analysis phase
design phase
implementation phase
testing phase
maintenance phase

a. Sending an early version of the software to a group of prospective buyers to get their reaction

b. Formulating a collection of classes from the program requirements

c. Writing the code for a particular method

   d. Correcting syntax errors

   e. Discussing a typical scenario for how the software should function

   f. Announcing Version 1.2 of the program

Programming Exercises

1. Compile and run the robot simulator program. This may require assistance to learn how to use the Java compiler and runtime environment on your system. Don't forget to include the `run` class.

2. Use your editor to remove the third instruction from the robot simulator `Driver` class (Figure 1.2). (The third instruction consists of the following line.)

   ```
   course.placeRobotOnRoad( robo );
   ```

   When you compile and run this new version of the program, you should see a window with no robot.

3. Use your editor to remove a semicolon anywhere from the `Driver` class of the robot simulator program (Figure 1.2). Recompile the program to see how the Java compiler reports compile time errors.

Introduction to Java Objects

2

Objectives

- To introduce the basic Java language concepts necessary to write an initial program in the form of a class called `Driver`
- To present the concept of syntax diagrams as a notation to be used in defining Java syntax throughout this text
- To describe the syntax and semantics of a sequence of statements
- To describe the syntax and semantics of a parameterless method call instruction
- To describe the syntax of an assignment instruction used to construct new objects
- To describe the syntax and usage of instance variable declarations
- To examine the need for class specifications and present a means for expressing them in the form of class invariants, as well as method preconditions and postconditions
- To describe the syntax of Java comments and suggest how best to use comments to express software specifications

- To present the concept of simple divide and conquer strategies for developing software
- To describe the syntax of Java identifiers and discuss the importance of careful identifier selection
- To introduce parameter passage as a means of passing an argument to a method

How does a programmer "speak" Java? Much of this book is devoted to explaining the Java programming language and how to express your programs in Java. This chapter focuses on the basics of how to write a single-class Java program.

2.1 ■ Syntax Diagrams

Every programming language has two defining characteristics:

- syntax
- semantics

Syntax refers to form and semantics refers to meaning. Spelling and punctuation within a program are syntax issues, whereas the program's behavior at runtime depends upon its semantics.

To maintain the necessary precision for illustrating syntax, this text uses a notation known as **syntax diagrams**. Language designers often use syntax diagrams to define the syntax of their programming language and programmers frequently consult syntax diagrams to determine how to express their solutions in a manner that is acceptable to the compiler.

A complete definition of a programming language consists of many separate syntax diagrams. Each syntax diagram is a picture containing text and arrows that define a single portion of the language's notation. As an initial example, we use Figures 2.1, 2.2, and 2.3 that define a particular set of English sentences. Each of these figures contains a separate syntax diagram.

Every syntax diagram has a name that identifies the portion of syntax that it represents. Figure 2.1 names its syntax diagram *FourSentences*. Correct syntax is defined by any path that proceeds all the way from the arrow entering the diagram on the left through the arrow leaving the diagram on the right. Any such path through defines a syntactically valid sequence of symbols based upon the order that symbols are

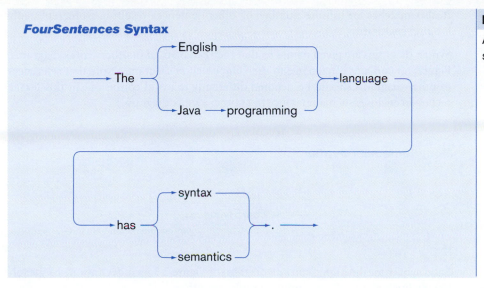

Figure 2.1

An example
syntax diagram

encountered along the path. The *FourSentences* diagram defines four possible paths
and, therefore, four sequences of symbols. These four alternatives are:

- The English language has syntax.
- The English language has semantics.
- The Java programming language has syntax.
- The Java programming language has semantics.

Any one of these alternatives is valid syntax for *FourSentences*. Furthermore, there
are no other syntactically valid *FourSentences* alternatives.

Sometimes syntax diagrams contain arrows that loop backward. Figure 2.2 illustrates this type of syntax diagram.

The *WhyProgram* syntax diagram from Figure 2.2 matches each of the following
sentences:

- Programming is subtle.
- Programming is very subtle.
- Programming is very, very subtle.
- Programming is very, very, very subtle.

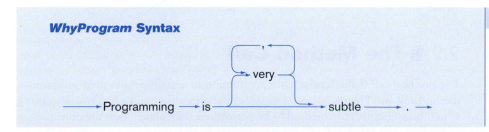

Figure 2.2

A second syntax
diagram

It also matches an infinite number of other sentences resulting from repeatedly looping backward.

Syntax diagrams are given names so that they can be used in other syntax diagrams. Figure 2.3 contains a reference to the *FourSentences* diagram. (Note that references to other diagrams should be denoted differently to avoid confusion. In this text, a rectangle encloses such a reference to another syntax diagram.)

Figure 2.3

A third syntax
diagram

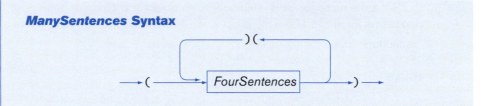

ManySentences **Syntax**

Valid syntax for the *ManySentences* diagram of Figure 2.3 includes any one of the following lines, along with an infinite number of others.

- (The English language has syntax.)
- (The English language has semantics.)
- (The Java programming language has syntax.)
- (The Java programming language has semantics.)
- (The English language has syntax.) (The English language has syntax.)
- (The English language has syntax.) (The English language has semantics.)
- (The English language has syntax.) (The Java programming language has syntax.)

Most programming languages contain a certain amount of flexibility that is ignored by syntax diagrams. The issue of **separators** is one particular topic ignored by syntax diagrams. The sentences described as valid for the preceding syntax diagrams contain blanks between consecutive words, despite the fact that the syntax diagrams do not contain blanks. Blanks are used as **separators** between consecutive symbols of English sentences. Java allows various kinds of white space (one or more blanks, tabs, or ends of lines) to serve as separators. Unless otherwise stated, white space is permitted, but not required, wherever an arrow is placed in a syntax diagram.

Sometimes a version of a syntax diagram is labeled abridged in an early presentation because it is incomplete. Appendix B includes a more complete definition of Java syntax.

2.2 ■ The Method Call

The **method call** is the fundamental instruction in any object-oriented program. A method call (see Figure 2.4) involves two things: an object and a method. Executing a method call causes the method to be performed (executed) upon the object.

Figure 2.4   ***ParameterlessMethodCall*** description (abridged version of *MethodCall*)

Syntax

Notes

- *ObjectRef* is the name (or valid reference) to an object and *MethodName* is the name of a nonconstructor method from the class to which the *ObjectRef* object belongs.
- No separators are permitted before or after the period.

Semantics

Executing *ParameterlessMethodCall* causes the method to be performed upon the object.

To see how method calls are used, suppose that the task is to draw lines on a computer window. Further assume the use of a preexisting `DrawingGizmo` class. The following class diagram describes `DrawingGizmo` to have at least six nonconstructor methods named `moveForward`, `turnClockwise`, `turnCounterclockwise`, `dontDraw`, `draw`, and `delay2Sec`.

```
DrawingGizmo
────────────────────────

«constructor»
   DrawingGizmo()

«update»
   void moveForward()
   void turnClockwise()
   void turnCounterclockwise()
   void dontDraw()
   void draw()
   void delay2Sec()
   ...
```

If `pencil` is the name of an object belonging to the `DrawingGizmo` class, then according to the rules of *ParameterlessMethodCall*, each of the following are valid Java instructions.

```
pencil.moveForward();
pencil.turnClockwise();
pencil.turnCounterclockwise();
pencil.dontDraw();
pencil.draw();
pencil.delay2Sec();
```

The following illustrate some *invalid* attempts at method call instructions. (The reason that each is invalid is explained on the right.)

`pencil.moveForward;`	*(missing parentheses)*
`pencil.moveforward();`	*(misnamed method—moveforward should be moveForward)*
`chalk.moveForward();`	*(incorrect object name—chalk)*
`pencilmoveForward();`	*(missing period)*
`pencil .moveForward();`	*(blanks not permitted prior to the period)*
`pencil.DrawingGizmo();`	*(constructor methods cannot be called with this syntax)*

The last invalid instruction points out that Java divides methods into two categories: those that are **constructors** and those that are not. Constructor methods are easily identified because they always have the same name as their class. As we will see later, constructor methods are called using a different syntax.

When a method call is executed, that method is applied to the indicated object. Therefore, executing the instruction

```
pencil.moveForward();
```

causes the `pencil` object to move forward. If there is a second `DrawingGizmo` object, named `pen`, then the following Java instruction is appropriate to move the `pen` object.

```
pen.moveForward();
```

In object-oriented terminology, executing a method is often referred to as sending a **message**. So the execution of the previous instruction can be explained as a `moveForward` message being sent to the `pen` object. Thinking about objects this way is helpful in understanding that a program is nothing more than a collection of objects that are sending and responding to messages.

2.3 ■ Instruction Sequences

Executing a single instruction performs one task, such as moving a `DrawingGizmo` object forward a short distance or causing it to turn. However, a more complete task generally requires many instructions. To allow for such tasks, Java supports a *StatementSequence*, as described in Figure 2.5. (Note that Java instructions are also referred to as "statements.")

When a **sequence of statements** executes, each of the statements is executed in turn. That is, the first statement executes, and when it completes, the second statement executes; when the second statement completes, the third statement executes, and so forth. As an example, executing the following sequence of Java statements/instructions causes the `pencil` object to begin drawing, move forward twice, turn clockwise, and then move forward three more times—precisely in that order.

```
pencil.draw();
pencil.moveForward();
pencil.moveForward();
pencil.turnClockwise();
pencil.moveForward();
pencil.moveForward();
pencil.moveForward();
```

Figure 2.5   *StatementSequence* description

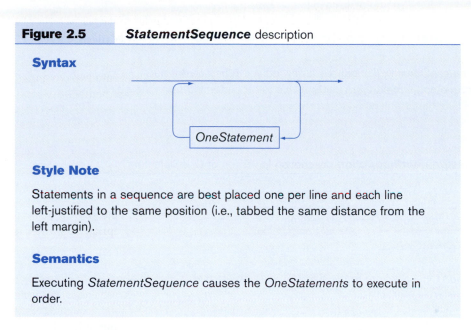

Syntax

Style Note

Statements in a sequence are best placed one per line and each line left-justified to the same position (i.e., tabbed the same distance from the left margin).

Semantics

Executing *StatementSequence* causes the *OneStatements* to execute in order.

2.4 ■ Constructing and Assigning Objects

Before an executing program can call a method (send a message), first it must **construct** the object that is to receive that message. Figure 2.6 defines the syntax used to create objects.

According to this description of `ParameterlessConstruction`, the notation for constructing an object consists of the keyword `new` followed by a constructor method call. For example, evaluating the following expression constructs a `DrawingGizmo` object.

```
new DrawingGizmo()
```

Such a construction is called an **instantiation**, because it creates an *instance* (an object) of type `DrawingGizmo`. An **assignment instruction** (see Figure 2.7) is frequently used in conjunction with an object instantiation in order to make a complete instruction, as well as give the object a name.

Figure 2.6   *ParameterlessConstruction* description (a version of *Expression*)

Syntax

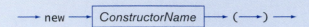

Note

ConstructorName is the name of a constructor method.

Semantics

Evaluating *ParameterlessConstruction* causes a new object to be constructed
and the constructor method named *ConstructorName* to be performed upon the object.

Figure 2.7   *AssignmentInstruction* description (a version of *OneStatement*)

Syntax

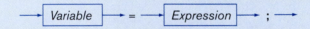

Note

The type of *Expression* must conform to the declared type of *Variable*.

Semantics

Executing *AssignmentInstruction* causes *Expression* to be evaluated.
Variable is assigned the result of the *Expression* evaluation.

Executing an assignment instruction assigns (or binds) a variable name to the result
of an expression evaluation. If the expression in the assignment instruction is an
object instantiation, then the result of executing an assignment instruction is to construct a new object and to bind the **variable** to that object. The following instruction
is an example:

```
pencil = new DrawingGizmo();
```

Following the execution of the above instruction, a new `DrawingGizmo` object has
been constructed. The name `pencil` is bound to this new object so the variable
refers to the object.

Assume that a program has two `DrawingGizmo` variables: `pen` and `pencil`. Prior to
executing any instructions, these variables are considered to be unbound. In Java an
unbound variable is said to be `null`. This means that the state of `pen` and `pencil`
prior to any bindings can be pictured as follows. The downward lines in this picture
don't connect to anything because the variables are unbound.

Programmers must be cautious about variables that are null. Attempting to execute a method call on using a name that is null results in a runtime error something like the following:

```
Exception Occurred:
java.lang.NullPointerException
...
```

This error is avoided by binding a variable to an object prior to applying methods to the variable. For example, executing the following statements causes two separate DrawingGizmo objects to be created, each bound to one of the variables. This binding is pictured in the form of object diagrams to the right of the instructions. The shaded rectangles represent objects, showing both the name of the object (before the colon) and the class to which the object belongs (after the colon).

```
pen = new DrawingGizmo();
pencil = new DrawingGizmo();
```

```
      pen                    pencil
       ◆                      ◆
  ┌──────────────────┐  ┌─────────────────────┐
  │ pen : DrawingGizmo│  │ pencil : DrawingGizmo│
  └──────────────────┘  └─────────────────────┘
```

Assignment instructions can also be used to assign one variable to another. (Any variable name by itself is considered a valid *Expression*.) When one variable is assigned to another, the result is for the left variable to take on the same value/binding as the one on the right. The second instruction in the example below illustrates this concept.

```
pen = new DrawingGizmo();
pencil = pen;
```

```
        pen      pencil
         ◆        ◆
     ┌────────────────────┐
     │ : DrawingGizmo      │
     └────────────────────┘
```

As can be seen in the picture above, pencil becomes bound to the same object as pen. In other words, the single object has two variable names. In a sense, the two variables are **aliases** for each other. (Since there are two names for the same object, the object name is omitted within the object rectangle.) Failure to recognize aliases can lead to programmer confusion. For example, normally a method performed upon pencil would have no effect upon the pen object. However, if the two variables are aliases, then any change to one is effectively a change to both.

Sometimes assigning one variable to another produces objects, known as **orphans**. An orphan is an object that is no longer bound to anything. The example below shows how the object previously bound to `pencil` becomes orphaned when the third assignment instruction executes.

```
pen = new DrawingGizmo();
pencil = new DrawingGizmo();
pencil = pen;
```

```
         pen       pencil
          ◆          ◆
          └──────────┤
     ┌─────────────┐ ┌─────────────┐
     │: DrawingGizmo│ │: DrawingGizmo│
     └─────────────┘ └─────────────┘
```

Creating such orphans is not necessarily a bad thing, as long as this was the programmer's intent. However, it is important to remember that an orphaned object becomes inaccessible to program instructions. Java virtual machines automatically recover any computer memory space that might otherwise have been lost to orphan objects.

It is also possible to create orphans by instantiating another object. Each of the two instructions below constructs a new object and binds that object to `pencil`. Since a variable can be bound to one object at a time only, the object bound by the first instruction becomes an orphan when the second instruction executes.

```
pencil = new DrawingGizmo();
pencil = new DrawingGizmo();
```

```
                     pencil
                       ◆
                       │ ╲
     ┌─────────────┐   ┌──────────────────────┐
     │: DrawingGizmo│   │pencil : DrawingGizmo │
     └─────────────┘   └──────────────────────┘
```

Assigning `null` to a variable is yet another way to create an orphan. The first instruction below instantiates a `DrawingGizmo` object, and the second causes the object to become orphaned by assigning to `pencil` the value `null`.

```
pencil = new DrawingGizmo();
pencil = null;
```

```
              pencil
               ◆
               │ (null)
                    ┌─────────────┐
                    │: DrawingGizmo│
                    └─────────────┘
```

Programmers should take care not to create unnecessary objects, or orphan necessary objects.

2.5 ■ Coding Patterns and Swapping

Some programming ideas occur with enough frequency to be called **patterns**. A pattern is a general programming template that is used in many programs. Coding patterns are programming expressions or instruction sequences that are useful for solving many problems.

One such coding pattern is known as a **swap**. The swap pattern is applicable in any situation where the objects assigned to two variables must be interchanged. Such an interchange provides insight into the behavior of assignment instructions.

Suppose that a program is using the variables `leftPen` and `rightPen` for two `DrawingGizmo` objects. Further assume that the `leftPen` object has visually moved to the right side of the `rightPen` object, which causes the programmer to wish to swap the assignments of the two variables. A typical mistake made by novice programmers is to attempt to perform the interchange with the following code:

```
leftPen = rightPen;
rightPen = leftPen;
```

A logic error can be discovered by tracing the execution of these instructions. Prior to the execution of this code, it is presumed that each variable is bound to some object as shown in the object diagram below.

Executing the first instruction (`leftPen = rightPen;`) results in the following:

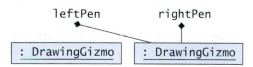

Executing the second instruction changes nothing, because both variables are already bound to the right object.

The key shortcoming of the previous attempted swap is that the first instruction causes one of the objects to be orphaned. This shortcoming can be resolved by using a third `DrawingGizmo` variable—call it `tempGizmo`. The resulting swap code is shown below.

```
tempGizmo = leftPen;
leftPen = rightPen;
rightPen = tempGizmo;
```

Suppose that prior to this code the three variables are bound as follows:

Below is the state following the execution of the first instruction:

```
tempGizmo = leftPen;
```

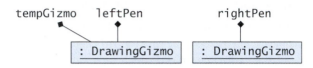

Next is the state following the execution of the second instruction:

```
leftPen = rightPen;
```

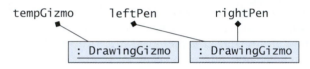

> software **engineering** *Hint*
>
> Just as basketball players recognize certain typical defenses, programmers learn to recognize software patterns. Knowing commonly used patterns like swapping is essential in software engineering.

Below is the state following the execution of the third instruction:

```
rightPen = tempGizmo;
```

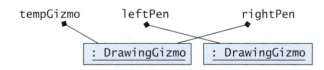

This three-instruction sequence can be extended to a coding pattern by considering any two variables—call them *varA* and *varB*. Figure 2.8 contains this pattern.

Figure 2.8

Swap pattern for interchanging *varA* and *varB*

aThirdVar = varA;

varA = varB;

varB = aThirdVar;

2.6 ■ Putting It Together in a Java Class

Every Java variable must be declared before it can be used. Figures 2.9 and 2.10 describe a common way to accomplish a declaration. Variables declared as described in these figures are known as **instance variables**.

Syntax

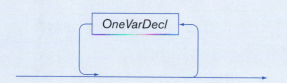

Figure 2.9

InstanceVarDecls
description

Style Notes

- Each variable declaration should be on a single line and left-justified one tab setting (three or four spaces).
- Variable names should be meaningful.
- Variable names should be nouns or noun phrases.

Syntax

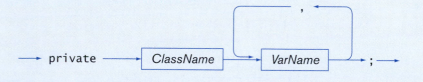

Figure 2.10

PrivateVarDecl
description
(a version of
OneVarDecl)

Note

Each *ClassName* and *VarName* must be named by an *Identifier*.

Usage

Each *VarName* is declared to have a type of *ClassName*, and the scope of this declaration is the class in which it is included.

Below are two example declarations that appropriately declare the instance variables discussed earlier: pencil and pen.

```
private DrawingGizmo pencil;
private DrawingGizmo pen;
```

Since both variables are declared with the same class, the two lines can be combined into the following equivalent one-line declaration:

```
private DrawingGizmo pencil, pen;
```

The declarations of instance variables and the code that manipulates the objects bound to those variables is typically placed within the same class. Figure 2.11 describes a *DriverClass* for the purpose of writing a class that combines variable dec-

Figure 2.11

DriverClass
description
(abridged ver-
sion of *Class*)

Syntax

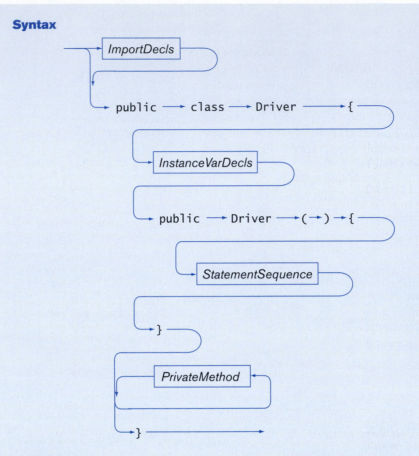

Semantics

When a `Driver` object is instantiated, the *StatementSequence* code is executed.

Notes

■ *PrivateMethod* is described in Chapter 4.

■ *ImportDecls* is described in Chapter 3.

Style Notes (for enhancing code readability)

■ The line beginning `public class` and ending with { should be on a single line and left justified. The final } symbol should also be left aligned.

■ All *InstanceVarDecls*, should be indented by one tab (three or four spaces) from the left.

■ The line beginning `public Driver()` should be indented by one tab, as well as the matching (second from the last) } symbol. *StatementSequence* lines should be indented two or more tabs.

larations and executable instructions. *DriverClass* contains many of the aspects of the complete Java class syntax, and will be expanded in future chapters.

software *Hint*
engineering

The `Driver` Java class described in Figure 2.11 is designed to allow flexibility in writing initial programs with minimal programming language distractions. To produce a working program, the programmer only needs to supply the desired code in place of `StatementSequence` and any necessary variable declarations in place of `InstanceVarDecls`.

> The overall layout of a class has a dramatic impact on its readability. The best conventions for class layout are to use tab style indentation with tab distances of either three or four spaces. The `public class` line and final `}` symbol should be left justified. Variable and method declarations within the class need a minimum indentation of one tab.

Figures 2.12 and 2.13 provide a complete `Driver` class containing the Java code explained thus far and an image of the window that results from the execution of that code. This particular program declares a single variable named `pencil`. This program begins execution by constructing a new `DrawingGizmo` object, binding the `pencil` name to the object. The remainder of the `Driver` method applies various `DrawingGizmo` methods to `pencil`.

There is one file constraint that must be observed when compiling and running the code in Figure 2.12. The `DrawingGizmo` class must be available to `Driver`. The easiest way to accomplish this is to include a *DrawingGizmo.class* file in the same folder as the *Driver.java* file.

Closed
Black Box

> The syntax of Java, like any new language, may raise questions for the first-time reader. Why is the word `public` placed at the front of the class line and also at the beginning of the `Driver` constructor method? What is the meaning of the `private` prefix in front of the `pencil` declaration? Why all of the parentheses and braces?
>
> For now, these things must be taken on faith. The meaning of `private` and `public` declarations, as well as Java punctuation, are topics that will be explored later; it is premature to worry about these details at this stage.

Figure 2.12 illustrates a second coding pattern. This pattern is the most fundamental of all object-oriented coding patterns because it describes the preliminary steps that are necessary in order to call a method. Figure 2.14 contains this so-called declare-instantiate-bind pattern.

The three-step pattern from Figure 2.13 is perhaps the most fundamental of all coding patterns in object-oriented programming. This pattern outlines the three requirements that need to be observed in order to call a method upon a variable without error.

The first step of the declare-instantiate-bind pattern is to declare the variable. Java, like most modern programming languages, does not permit a variable to be used

Figure 2.12

Example
Driver class
to manipulate
pencil

```java
public class Driver {
    private DrawingGizmo pencil;

    public Driver() {
        pencil = new DrawingGizmo();
        pencil.draw();
        pencil.moveForward();
        pencil.moveForward();
        pencil.moveForward();
        pencil.turnClockwise();
        pencil.turnClockwise();
        pencil.turnClockwise();
        pencil.moveForward();
        pencil.turnClockwise();
        pencil.turnClockwise();
        pencil.moveForward();
        pencil.turnClockwise();
        pencil.turnClockwise();
        pencil.moveForward();
        pencil.turnClockwise();
        pencil.turnClockwise();
        pencil.moveForward();
    }
}
```

Figure 2.13

Image produced
by executing the
program in
Figure 2.12

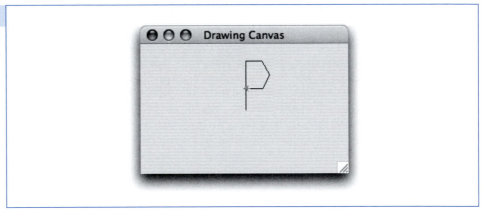

without declaration. The program in Figure 2.12 carries out this first step with the
following instance variable declaration.

```java
private DrawingGizmo pencil;
```

After this declaration, both the name of the variable, pencil, and its class association, DrawingGizmo, are known.

Figure 2.14

Declare-
instantiate-bind
coding pattern

Three steps are essential prior to calling a method upon any variable.

Step 1: *Declare* the variable, specifying the class to which it belongs.

Step 2: *Instantiate* an object with a class conforming to the variable.

Step 3: *Bind* the variable (declared in Step 1) to the object instantiated in Step 2.

After these three steps, methods can be called freely upon the variable.

As described in Section 2.4, a newly declared variable, such as `pencil`, is initialized to `null`; and calling a method upon a `null` variable results in a runtime error. Therefore, the variable must be assigned an object prior to calling a method. Steps 2 and 3 explain that this requires both *instantiating* and *binding* the object—in that order. Often instantiating and binding occurs in the same instruction, as in the following example from the Figure 2.12 program.

```
pencil = new DrawingGizmo();
```

Once an object is instantiated (`new DrawingGizmo()`) and bound (=) to `pencil`, then, and only then, the code is free to call methods upon that variable.

2.7 ■ Programming by Contract

An accomplished software engineer would find prior descriptions of the `DrawingGizmo` class to be excessively vague. Where and how is the `DrawingGismo` tool's movement displayed? How far does the tool move in a single `moveForward` call? What is the initial position of a newly constructed `DrawingGizmo`? These and other similar questions cannot go unanswered if the programmer is expected to compose programs that correctly satisfy their requirements.

The imprecise nature of code, like that in Figure 2.12, stems from a vague understanding of the behavior of `DrawingGizmo`. The `DrawingGizmo` class diagram (shown in Section 2.2) and the names of the `DrawingGizmo` methods provide clues regarding the behavior of `DrawingGizmo` objects, but they lack precision and completeness.

One widely accepted solution to the problem of ill-defined class behavior is to provide **class specifications**. A class specification for `DrawingGizmo` contains sufficient explanation about the state and behavior of `DrawingGizmo` objects so that a programmer can confidently use such objects.

The notation used for expressing class specifications in this text consists of two elements:

- a **class invariant**
- **precondition/postcondition** specifications for each method

software *Hint*
engineering

A complete class specification must include the information from the class diagram plus:

- a class invariant
- a specification for the behavior of each method

Method behavior specifications consist of:

- an optional precondition
- a postcondition

A class invariant defines a collection of facts that are true about class objects. The name invariant comes from the understanding that these facts must be true throughout the object's execution lifetime. A suitable invariant for the `DrawingGizmo` class is given in Figure 2.15. From this invariant, it is discovered that a `DrawingGizmo` object appears as an arrow within a *Drawing Canvas* window. The invariant also specifies that each DrawingGizmo object is either in a *drawing* mode or a *moving* mode.

The class invariant doesn't tell the whole story because it fails to explain anything about the behavior of the various class methods. To be complete, a class specification must also include specifications for each method. Such a method specification includes two parts:

1. preliminary conditions that are required for the method to execute properly (known as the method's precondition)

2. changes that result from executing the method (known as the method's postcondition)

Together, the precondition and postcondition form a **software contract**. This contract states the following:

The Precondition/Postcondition Contract

If   the calling code ensures the precondition is true at the time it calls the method,

then   the postcondition is guaranteed to be true at the time the method completes execution.

This Precondition/Postcondition Contract places a burden on the code that calls any method. This so-called calling code is responsible for ensuring that the state of execution satisfies the precondition portion of the contract. The role of the precondi-

Figure 2.15

DrawingGizmo class invariant

Invariant

A `DrawingGizmo` object:

- appears as an arrow within the *Drawing Canvas* window (the window is 260 pixels wide and 160 pixels high)

and

- is either in drawing mode or in moving mode.

tion is to identify requirements for using the method. Violating a precondition should be considered a logic error.

As long as the precondition is true when the method is called, the contract states that the method is obligated to ensure the postcondition is true when the method finishes. In other words, the postcondition is the portion of the specification that defines the actions that are performed when the method executes.

Figure 2.16 provides specifications for the five methods from the DrawingGizmo class. This notation denotes preconditions as **pre** and postconditions as **post**. *All of*

software *Hint*
engineering

The use of preconditions, postconditions, and invariants to guide the programming process is widely known as *design by contract*.

Constructor Methods

```
public DrawingGizmo()
```
   post: A new DrawingGizmo object is created and placed in the center of the *Drawing Canvas* window. (Note that if two tools occupy the same location, only one will be visible.)
   and This object is set to drawing mode (and therefore colored green).
   and The arrow for this object is pointing up.

Update Methods

```
public void draw()
```
   post: This object is set to drawing mode (and therefore colored green).

```
public void dontDraw()
```
   post: This object is set to moving mode (and therefore colored red).

```
public void turnClockwise()
```
   post: This object is rotated by 30 degrees clockwise from its previous direction.

```
public void turnCounterclockwise()
```
   post: This object is rotated by 30 degrees counterclockwise from its previous direction.

```
public void moveForward()
```
   pre: At least 20 pixels separate this object from the *Drawing Canvas* edge in its path.
   post: This object is moved in the arrow's direction 20 pixels from its previous location.
   and If this object is in drawing mode, a line segment is drawn across the 20 pixel path just traversed.

```
public void delay2Sec()
```
   post: The DrawingGizmo delays all activity for two seconds, then resumes.

Figure 2.16

DrawingGizmo method specifications

the terms of the assertions must be true to satisfy the specification. To emphasize this, the terms are separated by **and**. For example, the specifications make it clear that immediately after executing a `DrawingGizmo` constructor, the associated object will be positioned in the center of the window *and* it is in drawing mode (i.e., it is colored green) *and* its arrow is pointed up.

The precondition for `moveForward` specifies that the programmer using a `DrawingGizmo` must take care not to let it get too close to the edge of the window before calling `moveForward`. Notice that the Precondition/Postcondition Contract explains the situation when the precondition is true, but makes no promises for the outcome when the precondition is false. Therefore, if `moveForward` is called when the `DrawingGizmo` is 20 or fewer pixels (roughly 100 pixels equal one inch) from the window edge ahead of it, then the behavior of the `moveForward` method is unpredictable. (Obviously, programmers must avoid such situations where preconditions are not true.)

Sometimes there are no constraints on calling a method. In these situations, it is common to omit the precondition. This means that it is possible to execute the `DrawingGizmo` constructor method at any time, regardless of any particular state of execution. Similarly, there is no precondition for calling the `draw`, `dontDraw`, `delay2Sec`, `turnClockwise`, or `turnCounterclockwise` methods.

Even without the presence of a precondition, there is one precondition that is understood for every method except constructors. As explained previously, a runtime error will occur whenever a method is called upon a variable name that is `null`. Therefore, with or without a precondition, all nonconstructor methods have an implicit precondition that the object to receive the message must be non-null. Constructor methods are an exception to this rule because their purpose is to create a new object.

Writing class specifications takes practice. Effective specifications communicate accurately and succinctly. The items in postconditions should not explain unnecessary detail, but they must include enough information for the programmer to understand behavior precisely. The `DrawingGizmo` specifications are given in English, which is informal. Such informality tends to improve readability, but can result in ambiguities. Later in this text, slightly more formal notations are introduced for expressing specifications.

Armed with the `DrawingGizmo` specifications from Figure 2.16, we can now analyze the behavior of the Figure 2.12 `Driver` method. The first instruction from this method is repeated below:

```
pencil = new DrawingGizmo();
```

This causes the `DrawingGizmo` constructor method to construct a new object and assign the object to the `pencil` variable. The postcondition for the `DrawingGizmo` method specifies that the new tool is centered in the *Drawing Canvas* window as a green arrow pointing up.

software *Hint*
engineering

Every nonconstructor method has an implicit precondition, which is:

The object upon which this method is applied is not null.

software *Hint*
engineering

To be truly useful, a class specification must have four characteristics. It must be:

■ *precise*
■ *concise*
■ sufficiently *complete*
■ *accurate* with respect to intended class behavior

The next four instructions in this program are as follows:

```
pencil.draw();
pencil.moveForward();
pencil.moveForward();
pencil.moveForward();
```

When the first of these three instructions executes, the `pencil` object is set to the drawing mode and the arrow is turned green. This instruction is unnecessary for a newly constructed `DrawingGizmo` object, but is not harmful. Executing the next three methods moves the arrow forward (upward) by 60 pixels, drawing a line across this path. Notice that the preconditions of both of these method calls are met, since `pencil` is near the center of the window and the window is 160 pixels high. (The window height is given in the class invariant.)

The next four instructions are as follows:

```
pencil.turnClockwise();
pencil.turnClockwise();
pencil.turnClockwise();
pencil.moveForward();
```

The postcondition for the `turnClockwise` method states that the object should be turned 30 degrees clockwise. This means that executing the first three lines above causes `pencil` to rotate by a total of 90 degrees (i.e., point to the right); then the last instruction draws another 20 pixel line segment.

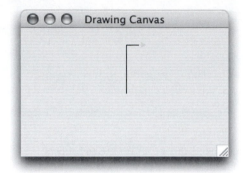

The remaining nine instructions are shown below.

```
pencil.turnClockwise();
pencil.turnClockwise();
pencil.moveForward();
pencil.turnClockwise();
pencil.turnClockwise();
pencil.moveForward();
pencil.turnClockwise();
pencil.turnClockwise();
pencil.moveForward();
```

Executing these instructions causes the `pencil` to perform the same task three consecutive times—rotate 60 degrees and then draw a 20 pixel line. The resulting window shows the result of this program.

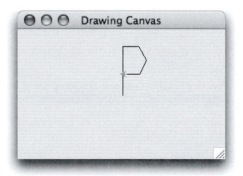

When the complete program is executed, you are unable to view the intermediate stages of execution. Instead, all that is visible is this final form of the window. Section 2.9 explores this characteristic of execution, along with the `delay2sec` method.

2.8 ■ **Comments**

Class specifications can be made available in a number of different formats. The specifications used within this book are included in HTML (Web page) format to make them most accessible when programming. It is also important to embed class specifications within the source code. This makes the specifications readily accessible to future maintenance programmers, as well as handy for the initial implementation.

The device used by programmers to place specifications within a program is called a **comment**. Figure 2.17 describes the Java comment. Comments allow text to be placed at almost any location within a program without altering the program's runtime behavior.

Syntactically, there are two possible types of comments:

1. single line comments

2. multiline comments

software *Hint*
engineering

Although they play no role in program execution, comments are critically important within a program. It is a good idea to include comments in the following places:

■ at the beginning of every class to indicate the author, date, and other identifiers

■ throughout the class to provide specifications (especially in the form of class invariants, preconditions, and postconditions

■ any place where the code might otherwise be confusing

Syntax

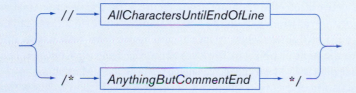

Figure 2.17

Comment
description

Notes

■ A comment is permitted anywhere that a separator, such as a blank, is allowed.

■ *AllCharactersUntilEndOfLine* denotes any sequence of characters as terminated by the first end of line encountered.

■ *AnythingButCommentEnd* denotes any sequence of characters and/or ends of lines as terminated by the first occurrence of */.

■ By convention, comments that immediately precede a class or a method begin with an extra asterisk (/**).

Semantics

Comments do nothing at runtime.

The single line comment begins with "//" and continues through the end of the same text line. A multiline comment can spread across several lines of text. Multiline comments begin with "/*" and extend until the first subsequent instance of "*/". This means that a two-line comment such as:

```
/** @author David D. Riley
 *  @version May 9, 2005
 */
```

software *Hint*
engineering

software engineering Hint

Java programmers follow certain conventions in how to write and where to place comments. It helps other programmers to read your comments if you follow these conventions.

can also be written as two consecutive single line comments.

```
// @author David D. Riley
// @version May 9, 2005
```

Major comments should begin with /** and following lines should be prefixed with an asterisk (*). The expected locations for major comments are before each class and before specifications.

Figure 2.18 shows an improved version of the `Driver` class from Figure 2.12. This improved code is the same except for the inclusion of initial comments to identify the author and date and appropriate specifications.

2.9 ■ Observing Execution

When you execute the program from Figure 2.18 you see the final form of the *Drawing Canvas* window with the letter P completely formed; you can't observe the `DrawingGizmo` object while it moves and turns. The reason you are unable to observe the `pencil` object as it moves about the *Drawing Canvas* is because of the way that the Java VM executes. We will cover how the VM executes your program in the discussion of events in Chapter 4; for now it is sufficient to know that the VM is responsible for both executing your program and updating the computer display as a result of your program's execution. The VM grants a higher priority to executing the program, so in the case of this `DrawingGizmo` example, the VM doesn't actually update the *Drawing Canvas* until the program has finished executing.

software engineering Hint

Learning to use a Java debugger (included with most IDEs) is time well spent. Every software developer spends considerable time tracking down runtime errors in their program code. A debugger can significantly reduce debugging time.

Programmers often prefer to "slow the program down a bit" so that they can observe the program's behavior. This is especially true when the program does not behave as expected. Perhaps the best way to accomplish this is to use a **debugger**. If you use an IDE, then your IDE probably includes a debugger that allows you to control your program's execution by pausing it at specified locations. Debuggers generally include facilities for inspecting the state of variables when you pause execution.

`DrawingGizmo` includes one additional method, `delay2Sec`, to assist with debugging with or without a debugger. Executing `delay2Sec` causes the Java VM to pause

Figure 2.18

Improved version
of an earlier
Driver class

```java
/** @author David D. Riley
 *  @version May 9, 2005
 *
 *  This class draws a block letter "P" that is
 *  60 pixels high and about 30 pixels wide upon
 *  a window named Drawing Canvas.
 */
public class Driver {
    private DrawingGizmo pencil;

    public Driver() {
        pencil = new DrawingGizmo();
        pencil.draw();
        pencil.moveForward();
        pencil.moveForward();
        pencil.moveForward();
        pencil.turnClockwise();
        pencil.turnClockwise();
        pencil.turnClockwise();
        pencil.moveForward();
        pencil.turnClockwise();
        pencil.turnClockwise();
        pencil.moveForward();
        pencil.turnClockwise();
        pencil.turnClockwise();
        pencil.moveForward();
        pencil.turnClockwise();
        pencil.turnClockwise();
        pencil.moveForward();
    }
}
```

execution for two seconds and update the *Drawing Canvas* window. For example, consider the program revision shown in Figure 2.19.

When this last version of Driver executes, it will pause three times—each time for two seconds and each time displaying an intermediate version of the letter P. Figure 2.20 shows the three intermediate views of *Drawing Canvas*.

Figure 2.19

A Driver class
including calls
to delay2Sec

```java
/** @author David D. Riley
 *  @version May 9, 2005
 *
 *  This class draws a block letter "P" that is
 *  60 pixels high and about 30 pixels wide upon
 *  a window named Drawing Canvas.
 */
public class Driver {
    private DrawingGizmo pencil;

    public Driver() {
        pencil = new DrawingGizmo();
        pencil.draw();
        pencil.moveForward();
        pencil.moveForward();
        pencil.delay2Sec();
        pencil.moveForward();
        pencil.turnClockwise();
        pencil.turnClockwise();
        pencil.turnClockwise();
        pencil.moveForward();
        pencil.delay2Sec();
        pencil.turnClockwise();
        pencil.turnClockwise();
        pencil.moveForward();
        pencil.delay2Sec();
        pencil.turnClockwise();
        pencil.turnClockwise();
        pencil.moveForward();
        pencil.turnClockwise();
        pencil.turnClockwise();
        pencil.moveForward();
    }
}
```

2.10 ■ Refining Algorithms— Divide and Conquer

Carpenters assemble furniture from raw materials such as lumber, glue, and paint.
Similarly, software developers assemble programs from classes and their component
declarations and instructions. The software assembly phase is often called **implementation** or **coding**.

Figure 2.20   Three intermediate *Drawing Canvas* images

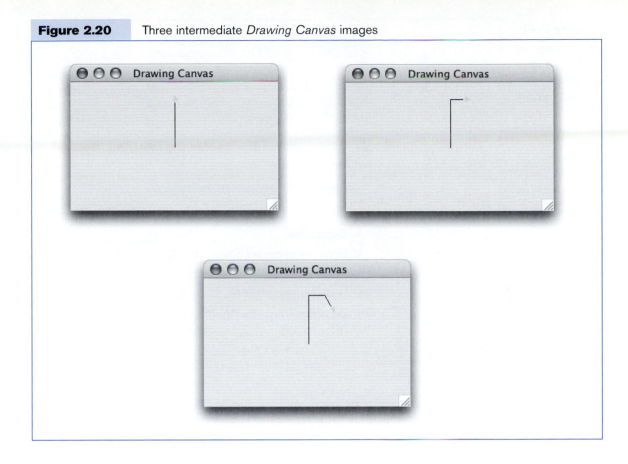

Implementation is not possible without a strategy. A carpenter relies upon a strategy to assemble all of the parts properly. Similarly, good programming requires development strategies to compose each program.

Perhaps the most useful of all design strategies is called **divide and conquer**. As its name implies, a divide and conquer strategy consists of two parts:

1. *Divide* a larger component into its constituent subcomponents.
2. *Conquer* each of the subcomponents.

Dividing and conquering is fundamental to object-oriented software development. O-O design first divides a problem into its constituent objects, and then conquers the objects by identifying or creating a software class for each object. Next, O-O design proceeds to divide each class into its attributes and methods, and then *conquers* each attribute and method by supplying its code. Both of these uses of divide and conquer are revisited throughout the book.

As an example of a divide and conquer approach, consider writing a method that uses `DrawingGizmo` to create an underlined X, as shown in Figure 2.21.

Figure 2.21

A five-step algorithm to draw an underlined X

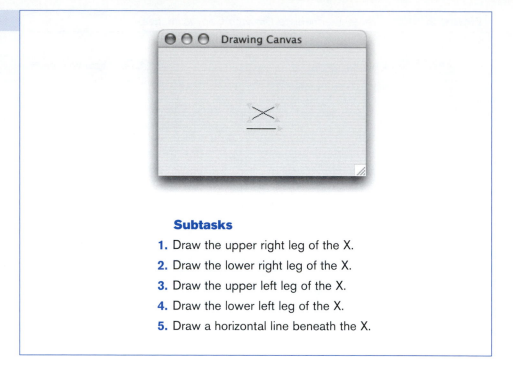

Subtasks

1. Draw the upper right leg of the X.

2. Draw the lower right leg of the X.

3. Draw the upper left leg of the X.

4. Draw the lower left leg of the X.

5. Draw a horizontal line beneath the X.

This particular program is sufficiently complicated that it is advisable to apply divide and conquer. Figure 2.21 illustrates a five-stage procedure to create the underlined X. This shows that a single task can be partitioned into separate subtasks.

The five-stage procedure from Figure 2.21 uses a design technique typically employed by good software developers. The subtasks are expressed in English, instead of Java or any other programming language. Programmers frequently use such informal notations during a design process. The five subtasks do not constitute a syntactically valid Java program, but they form an **algorithm** that can eventually be transformed into a Java program.

software *Hint*
engineering

In the early stages of software design it is often better to use informal notations, such as English sentences, to express algorithms. This facilitates progress by avoiding programming language details.

The term *algorithm* refers to any collection of instructions (or subtasks) that define a procedure for performing some task. Humans frequently think algorithmically. There are algorithms for creating your favorite chocolate cake. There are algorithms for driving from your home to the nearest department store. Your morning routine is also an example of an algorithm. None of these algorithms is likely to be coded Java, but all of them consist of a specific sequence of subtasks that, when performed in order, produce a desired result. Java software also consists of algorithms. In a Java program, the algorithms often take the form of a method, such as those written in prior `Driver` constructors.

The particular five-part algorithm in Figure 2.21 is not the only solution for drawing this particular checked box. A slightly different algorithm would draw the underline before the X, and yet a third algorithm would draw the X as one subtask instead of separating it into four subtasks. As with most programming problems, there are many possible algorithms.

The Figure 2.21 algorithm demonstrates the divide phase of a *divide-and-conquer* strategy. The task has been divided into an algorithm with five subtasks. In order to complete the program, the programmer must conquer each subtask. The technique of dividing a single stage/subtask into its own algorithm is commonly called **refinement**, and the repeated application of divide-and-conquer to refine one task into subtasks, then subtasks into sub-subtasks, and so on, is known as **stepwise refinement**.

Subtask 1 from Figure 2.21 is conveniently refined from

Draw the upper right leg of the X.

into the following four Java statements:

```
xUpperRightPen = new DrawingGizmo();
xUpperRightPen.turnClockwise();
xUpperRightPen.turnClockwise();
xUpperRightPen.moveForward();
```

Note that this code uses the name xUpperRightPen for a DrawingGizmo object that draws the upper right leg of the X. (Section 2.11 presents additional suggestions for how to choose names.) Refining the second subtask from the algorithm proceeds similarly. One option for this refinement results from the observation that fewer statements are needed to create a new DrawingGizmo object than to reposition the xUpperRightPen object for drawing the next leg of the X. Therefore, the **Subtask 2**

Draw the lower right leg of the X.

is refined into:

```
xLowerRightPen = new DrawingGizmo();
xLowerRightPen.turnClockwise();
xLowerRightPen.turnClockwise();
xLowerRightPen.turnClockwise();
xLowerRightPen.turnClockwise();
xLowerRightPen.moveForward();
```

Refinement of **Subtask 3** and **Subtask 4** is simplified by the observation that the left legs of the X are mirror images of the right legs. This means that the left legs can be drawn using counterclockwise rotations in place of the clockwise rotations used to draw the right legs. The resulting refinements are as follows:

software *Hint*
engineering

When the desired task for any method becomes complicated (more than six or seven instructions), programmers are well advised to use a design strategy such as refinement.

Draw the upper left leg of the X.

refines into:

```
xUpperLeftPen = new DrawingGizmo();
xUpperLeftPen.turnCounterclockwise();
xUpperLeftPen.turnCounterclockwise();
xUpperLeftPen.moveForward();
```

and

Draw the lower left leg of the X.

refines into:

```
xLowerLeftPen = new DrawingGizmo();
xLowerLeftPen.turnCounterclockwise();
xLowerLeftPen.turnCounterclockwise();
xLowerLeftPen.turnCounterclockwise();
xLowerLeftPen.turnCounterclockwise();
xLowerLeftPen.moveForward();
```

Refinement of **Subtask 5** is clearly more involved than the previous four subtasks. When a subtask is sufficiently complex it is preferable to refine it into noncode subtasks. For example,

Draw a horizontal line beneath the X.

can be refined into the following:

5.1 *Create a* `DrawingGizmo` *and move it left of the X.*

5.2 *Turn 90 degrees counterclockwise and move down below the X.*

5.3 *Turn 90 degrees counterclockwise and draw a horizontal line below the X.*

To complete, the code in each of the remaining three sub-subtasks must be refined into code.

Subtask 5.1

Create a `DrawingGizmo` *and move it left of the X.*

can be refined as follows:

```
underlinePen = new DrawingGizmo();
underlinePen.dontDraw();
underlinePen.turnCounterClockwise();
underlinePen.turnCounterClockwise();
underlinePen.turnCounterClockwise();
underlinePen.moveForward();
```

Subtask 5.2

Turn 90 degrees counterclockwise and move down below the X.

can be refined as follows:

```
underlinePen.turnCounterClockwise();
underlinePen.turnCounterClockwise();
underlinePen.turnCounterClockwise();
underlinePen.moveForward();
```

Finally, **Subtask 5.3**

Turn 90 degrees counterclockwise and draw a horizontal line below the X.

can be refined into the following six Java statements:

```
underlinePen.turnCounterClockwise();
underlinePen.turnCounterClockwise();
underlinePen.turnCounterClockwise();
underlinePen.draw();
underlinePen.moveForward();
underlinePen.moveForward();
```

The complete refinement is summarized in Figure 2.22. The non-Java parts of the algorithm are shaded in blue with their refinement to their right. The original algorithm is shown in the left column.

The process of refining algorithms in the manner demonstrated by this example is called **top-down design**. Top-down design proceeds from a so-called high level algorithm (Subtasks 1 though 5) and successively refines the highest level task until the final subtasks can be expressed in a programming language.

Following this top-down design, the original algorithm has been transformed into the sequence of Java instructions. These instructions are gathered with the appropriate instance variable declaration and class syntax in Figure 2.23. Blank lines are included in this program to separate the code into the portions corresponding to the five parts of the original algorithm.

Figure 2.22

Refinement of
the underlined
X algorithm

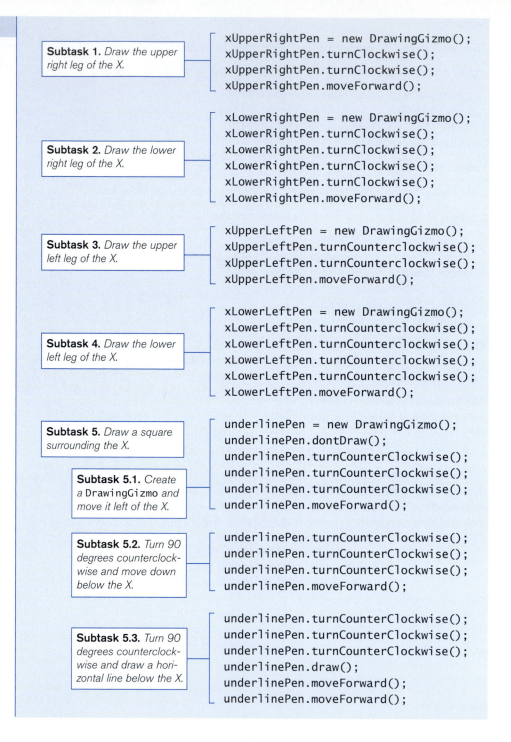

Subtask 1. *Draw the upper right leg of the X.*

```
xUpperRightPen = new DrawingGizmo();
xUpperRightPen.turnClockwise();
xUpperRightPen.turnClockwise();
xUpperRightPen.moveForward();
```

Subtask 2. *Draw the lower right leg of the X.*

```
xLowerRightPen = new DrawingGizmo();
xLowerRightPen.turnClockwise();
xLowerRightPen.turnClockwise();
xLowerRightPen.turnClockwise();
xLowerRightPen.turnClockwise();
xLowerRightPen.moveForward();
```

Subtask 3. *Draw the upper left leg of the X.*

```
xUpperLeftPen = new DrawingGizmo();
xUpperLeftPen.turnCounterclockwise();
xUpperLeftPen.turnCounterclockwise();
xUpperLeftPen.moveForward();
```

Subtask 4. *Draw the lower left leg of the X.*

```
xLowerLeftPen = new DrawingGizmo();
xLowerLeftPen.turnCounterclockwise();
xLowerLeftPen.turnCounterclockwise();
xLowerLeftPen.turnCounterclockwise();
xLowerLeftPen.turnCounterclockwise();
xLowerLeftPen.moveForward();
```

Subtask 5. *Draw a square surrounding the X.*

Subtask 5.1. *Create a* DrawingGizmo *and move it left of the X.*

```
underlinePen = new DrawingGizmo();
underlinePen.dontDraw();
underlinePen.turnCounterClockwise();
underlinePen.turnCounterClockwise();
underlinePen.turnCounterClockwise();
underlinePen.moveForward();
```

Subtask 5.2. *Turn 90 degrees counterclockwise and move down below the X.*

```
underlinePen.turnCounterClockwise();
underlinePen.turnCounterClockwise();
underlinePen.turnCounterClockwise();
underlinePen.moveForward();
```

Subtask 5.3. *Turn 90 degrees counterclockwise and draw a horizontal line below the X.*

```
underlinePen.turnCounterClockwise();
underlinePen.turnCounterClockwise();
underlinePen.turnCounterClockwise();
underlinePen.draw();
underlinePen.moveForward();
underlinePen.moveForward();
```

Figure 2.23

Driver class to draw an under-lined X

```
public class Driver {
    private DrawingGizmo xUpperLeftPen, xUpperRightPen;
    private DrawingGizmo xLowerLeftPen, xLowerRightPen;
    private DrawingGizmo underlinePen;

    /** post: This class draws an X within a horizontal
     *        line beneath. */
    public Driver() {
        xUpperRightPen = new DrawingGizmo();
        xUpperRightPen.turnClockwise();
        xUpperRightPen.turnClockwise();
        xUpperRightPen.moveForward();

        xLowerRightPen = new DrawingGizmo();
        xLowerRightPen.turnClockwise();
        xLowerRightPen.turnClockwise();
        xLowerRightPen.turnClockwise();
        xLowerRightPen.turnClockwise();
        xLowerRightPen.moveForward();

        xUpperLeftPen = new DrawingGizmo();
        xUpperLeftPen.turnCounterclockwise();
        xUpperLeftPen.turnCounterclockwise();
        xUpperLeftPen.moveForward();

        xLowerLeftPen = new DrawingGizmo();
        xLowerLeftPen.turnCounterclockwise();
        xLowerLeftPen.turnCounterclockwise();
        xLowerLeftPen.turnCounterclockwise();
        xLowerLeftPen.turnCounterclockwise();
        xLowerLeftPen.moveForward();

        underlinePen = new DrawingGizmo();
        underlinePen.dontDraw();
        underlinePen.turnCounterclockwise();
        underlinePen.turnCounterclockwise();
        underlinePen.turnCounterclockwise();
        underlinePen.moveForward();
        underlinePen.turnCounterclockwise();
        underlinePen.turnCounterclockwise();
        underlinePen.turnCounterclockwise();
        underlinePen.moveForward();
        underlinePen.turnCounterclockwise();
        underlinePen.turnCounterclockwise();
        underlinePen.turnCounterclockwise();
        underlinePen.draw();
        underlinePen.moveForward();
        underlinePen.moveForward();
    }
}
```

2.11 ■ **Selecting Identifiers**

During the process of program design, the programmer must frequently choose names for various program entities. For example, the designer of the previous program (see Figure 2.23) chose to name five drawing objects xUpperRightPen, xLowerRightPen, xUpperLeftPen, xLowerLeftPen, and underlinePen.

Names for program entities are called **identifiers**. In addition to naming instance variables with identifiers, such as underlinePen, programs also name classes with identifiers, such as Driver and DrawingGizmo, and methods, such as moveForward, turnClockwise, turnCounterclockwise, draw, and dontDraw. Figure 2.24 explains the Java rules for identifiers.

Certain identifiers, like class have special meaning in Java. These identifiers are called **reserved words**. Figure 2.25 enumerates all Java reserved words. Programs are not permitted to use reserved words to name other program entities.

To make Java programs easier to read, software developers follow two important conventions:

1. Identifiers should be descriptive of the entities they name.

2. If the identifier contains multiple English words, then each word (except possibly the first) should begin with a capital letter.

Figure 2.24

Identifier description

Syntax

An *Identifier* begins with either an alphabetic letter (a through z or A through Z) or an underscore (_) and is followed by zero or more consecutive alphabetic letters, digits (0 through 9) and/or underscores. Dollar signs ($) are also permitted within identifiers but are generally reserved for system use.

Notes

■ Java is case sensitive, so two identifiers with the same sequence of letters but different capitalization are considered different identifiers.

■ Some identifiers are reserved words (see Figure 2.25) and may not be used for other purposes.

■ A separator *must* be used immediately after the identifier when the symbol just after the identifier is an alphabetic character, an underscore, or a digit.

Style Note

When selecting an identifier, the programmer should generally capitalize the first letter of any English word embedded within.

Figure 2.25   Java reserved words

abstract	finally	public
boolean	float	return
break	for	short
byte	generic	static
case	goto	super
cast	if	switch
catch	implements	synchronized
char	import	this
class	instanceof	throw
const	int	throws
continue	interface	transient
default	long	true
do	native	try
double	new	void
else	null	volatile
extends	package	while
false	private	
final	protected	

A descriptive name, such as DrawingGizmo, assists any programmer who reads the code. Similarly, capitalizing individual words in an identifier makes it easier to read the name. For example, the identifiers turnClockwise and moveForward are easier to read than turnclockwise and moveforward.

Another convention generally followed in Java programs, is to capitalize the first letter of an identifier that names a class name and use a lowercase letter to begin other identifiers. This first-letter convention allows the class identifiers to be distinguished at a glance.

It is also best to select an identifier based upon its usage. Identifiers that are nouns or noun clauses are preferable for variables, classes, and non-void methods. (Non-void methods are discussed later.) Void methods, like the ones shown thus far, are better named with identifiers that are action verbs or verb phrases.

software *Hint*
engineering

The readability of code can be dramatically affected by an intelligent choice of identifiers. The following conventions should be observed when selecting an identifier.

■ Every identifier must be descriptive of the entity it names.

■ Every English word embedded within an identifier should begin with an uppercase letter.

■ Class name identifiers should begin with an uppercase letter and other identifiers should not.

■ Identifiers naming classes, variables, and non-void methods should be nouns or noun phrases.

■ Identifiers naming void methods should be action verbs or verb phrases.

2.12 ■ A Second Example of Refinement

As a second example of top-down design, consider the task of making a cheese pizza. In particular, the pizza should be made according to the following recipe.

Using a premixed ball of crust dough, flatten the dough to the desired thickness. Next, pour two cups of pizza sauce onto the dough. Spread the sauce evenly across the dough. Spread three cups of mozzarella cheese on top. Cook the pizza for 15 minutes at 400 degrees Fahrenheit.

Cooking recipes are algorithms because they explain a procedure for preparing some kind of food. The cheese pizza recipe is no exception. This recipe can be recast as a five-stage algorithm as shown in Figure 2.26.

As explained earlier, the first step in any object-oriented design is to identify the objects. In the case of the pizza recipe, the objects seem to be

- dough (crust)
- sauce
- cheese
- oven

Often a software developer can find existing software classes from which to construct the necessary objects. It is important to discover such classes early, because they impact the way the design needs to proceed toward implementation. In this case, assume that the five classes diagrammed in Figure 2.27 have been discovered for use in implementing the cheese pizza recipe.

The plus sign (+) shown in Figure 2.27 is a notation commonly used within class diagrams. A plus sign prefix on a method of a class diagram indicates that this method is available for use outside of the class. (Alternatives to the plus sign will be explained in subsequent chapters.)

A second important difference between Figure 2.27 and earlier presentations of methods is the inclusion of **parameters**. Parameters are indicated in a class diagram by the name of a type (class) inside the parentheses following a method. Figure 2.27 shows that the following methods have parameters: `placeInOven`, `pourInto` (from both the `Sauce` and `Cheese` classes), and `pourOnto`.

Figure 2.26

Top-level algorithm for making a cheese pizza

Subtask

1. Using a premixed ball of crust dough, flatten the dough to the desired thickness.
2. Pour two cups of pizza sauce onto the crust.
3. Spread the sauce evenly across the crust.
4. Spread three cups of mozzarella cheese on top.
5. Set pizza oven to 400 degrees Fahrenheit and cook pizza for 15 minutes.

Figure 2.27   Class diagrams for pizza-related classes

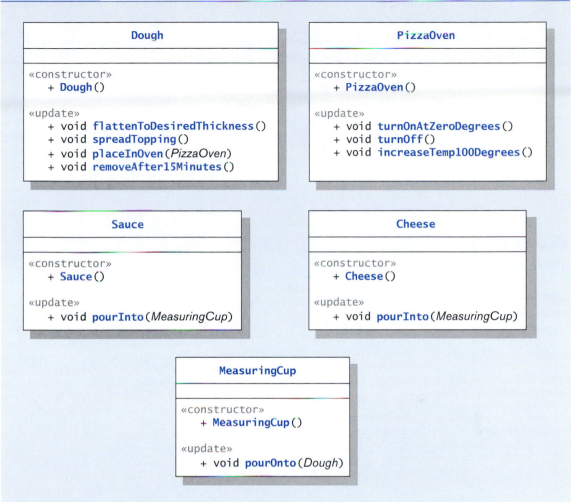

The use of parameters often stems from the need to involve multiple objects in a single method. For example, the act of pouring pizza sauce into a measuring cup involves two objects—the sauce and the cup. Using a parameter permits one object to be **passed** to a method performed upon a second object. As a second example, the following instruction is used to cause a Dough object, called crust, to be placed into the PizzaOven named oven.

```
crust.placeInOven(oven);
```

The five classes from Figure 2.27 introduce a new object into the algorithm that was not obvious by reading the original pizza recipe. In particular, it will be necessary to use measuring cups to transfer sauce and cheese to the dough. This additional class will impact the subsequent refinement of the algorithm.

The next stage of the top-down design is to refine each of the subtasks from the top-level design. Figure 2.28 shows an algorithm that results from refining each of the five individual subtasks.

The second-level refinement from Figure 2.28 names several objects. The objects are listed below, along with the class to which each belongs.

- crust—of type Dough
- sauceCup—of type MeasuringCup
- mySauce—of type Sauce
- cheeseCup—of type MeasuringCup
- oven—of type PizzaOven

Figure 2.28

The second-level algorithm for making a cheese pizza

```
// 1.  Using a premixed ball of crust dough, flatten the dough
//     to the desired thickness.
     crust = new Dough();
     crust.flattenToDesiredThickness();

// 2.  Pour two cups of pizza sauce onto the crust.
     sauceCup = new MeasuringCup();
     mySauce = new Sauce();
     mySauce.pourInto(sauceCup);
     sauceCup.pourOnto(crust);
     mySauce.pourInto(sauceCup);
     sauceCup.pourOnto(crust);

// 3.  Spread the sauce evenly across the crust.
     crust.spreadTopping();

// 4.  Spread three cups of mozzarella cheese on top.
     cheeseCup = new MeasuringCup();
  // 4.2. Use cheeseCup to spread three cups of mozzarella on
  // the pizza.

// 5.  Set pizza oven to 400 degrees Fahrenheit and cook
//     pizza for 15 minutes.
     oven = new PizzaOven();
     oven.turnOnAtZeroDegrees();
  // 5.3. Set the temperature to 400 degrees.
     crust.placeInOven(oven);
     crust.removeAfter15Minutes();
     oven.turnOff();
```

The designer has been careful to select proper Java identifiers for these object names. In writing the program for this algorithm, the programmer must provide declarations for these five instance variables.

When the six instructions from Stage 2 execute, sauceCup and mySauce are instantiated. The mySauce.pourInto(sauceCup); instruction causes the measuring cup to be filled with sauce, then the sauceCup.pourOnto(crust); empties the cup onto the pizza crust. These two instructions are repeated to pour a second cup of sauce on the crust. The decision to use a separate MeasuringCup variable, called cheeseCup, in Stage 4 was made in order to use a clean cup for the cheese. (The sauceCup might be messy.)

It is evident that another level of refinement is needed, because there are two instructions (Stage 4.2 and Stage 5.3) in the Figure 2.28 algorithm that are not yet expressed in Java. The complete program in Figure 2.29 results from refining these two comments and including the necessary instance variable declarations.

2.13 ■ Calling Methods with Parameters

The concept of parameters is demonstrated in the cheese pizza example from the previous section. The DrawingGizmo class also demonstrates the use of parameters by way of the moveBy, delayBy, and turnBy methods (not previously presented). Figure 2.30 contains a more complete class diagram for DrawingGizmo that reveals these two additional methods.

Like instance variables, every parameter has both a name and a type. As shown in the DrawingGizmo class diagram, moveBy, turnBy, and delayBy each have a single parameter of type int. A type of int denotes that these parameters are of integer type. Sometimes, as is the case in Figure 2.30, the class specification does not include names for parameters. However, parameter names are always included in class specifications. Figure 2.31 contains the specifications for moveBy, turnBy, and delayBy.

Parameter names are useful for expressing a method's preconditions and postconditions. For example, consider the turnBy postcondition.

post: This object is rotated by a degrees clockwise from its previous direction.

This postcondition asserts that the DrawingGizmo object has been rotated by a degrees clockwise from the direction of the object immediately prior to the method call. Consider the following Java statement:

```
pencil = new DrawingGizmo();
pencil.turnBy(90);
```

Following the execution of these two statements, the pencil object will be directed to the right (90 degrees clockwise from the upward direction). Whenever a method containing parameters is called, the method call must specify an **argument** for each parameter. The value 90 is an argument in the preceding call to turnBy.

Figure 2.29

Program to
make a cheese
pizza

```java
public class Driver {
    private Dough crust;
    private MeasuringCup sauceCup, cheeseCup;
    private Cheese mozzarella;
    private PizzaOven oven;
    private Sauce mySauce;

    /** post:  A cheese pizza is ready to eat. */
    public Driver() {
        crust = new Dough();
        crust.flattenToDesiredThickness();
        sauceCup = new MeasuringCup();
        mySauce = new Sauce();
        mySauce.pourInto(sauceCup);
        sauceCup.pourOnto(crust);
        mySauce.pourInto(sauceCup);
        sauceCup.pourOnto(crust);
        crust.spreadTopping();
        cheeseCup = new MeasuringCup;
        mozzarella = new Cheese();
        mozzarella.pourInto(cheeseCup);
        cheeseCup.pourOnto(crust);
        mozzarella.pourInto(cheeseCup);
        cheeseCup.pourOnto(crust);
        mozzarella.pourInto(cheeseCup);
        cheeseCup.pourOnto(crust);
        oven = new PizzaOven();
        oven.turnOnAtZeroDegrees();
        oven.increaseTempBy100Degrees();
        oven.increaseTempBy100Degrees();
        oven.increaseTempBy100Degrees();
        oven.increaseTempBy100Degrees();
        crust.placeInOven(oven);
        crust.removeAfter15Minutes();
        oven.turnOff();
    }
}
```

```
DrawingGizmo
-------------------------------
-------------------------------
«constructor»
  DrawingGizmo()

«update»
  void moveForward()
  void turnClockwise()
  void turnCounterclockwise()
  void moveBy(int)
  void turnBy(int)
  void dontDraw()
  void draw()
  void delay2Sec()
  void delayBy(int)
  ...
```

Figure 2.30

DrawingGizmo class diagram (including moveBy and turnBy)

`public void turnBy(int a)`

post: This object is rotated by a degrees clockwise from its previous direction.

`public void moveBy(int d)`

pre: At least d pixels separate this object from the *Drawing Canvas* edge in its path.

post: This object is moved in the arrow's direction d pixels from its previous location.
and If this object is in drawing mode, a line segment is drawn across the d pixel path just traversed.

`public void delayBy(int t)`

post: The `DrawingGizmo` delays all activity for t milliseconds, then resumes.

Figure 2.31

Specifications for moveBy and turnBy (from DrawingGizmo)

The description of *MethodCallWithParameters* in Figure 2.32 explains that each argument must also conform to the class of its corresponding parameter. For now, conformance should be interpreted to mean that both must have the same type or class. The previous call to `turnBy` is valid because 90 is a valid integer. However, a syntax error results from a statement such as

```
pencil.turnBy(90.3);
```

because `90.3` is a real number, not an integer.

Parameter passage permits methods to have broader application. The `turnBy` method can be used as a replacement for both `turnClockwise` and `turnCounterClockwise`. For example, instead of the following Java statement:

```
pencil.turnClockwise();
```

the Java statement below is an alternative that accomplishes the same task.

```
pencil.turnBy(30);
```

Figure 2.32   *MethodCallWithParameters* description (abridged version of *MethodCall*)

Syntax

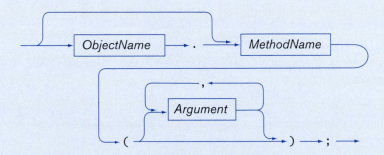

Notes

■ *ObjectName* is the name of an object, and *MethodName* is the name of a nonconstructor method from the class to which the *ObjectName* object belongs.

■ No separators are permitted before or after the period.

■ The number and class type of each *Argument* must conform to the class of the corresponding parameter.

Semantics

1. Executing *MethodCallWithParameters* causes each argument to be assigned to its corresponding parameter, followed by an execution of the method body.

2. If *ObjectName* is omitted, the call is assumed to be to a local method.

Similarly, the Java statement

```
pencil.turnCounterclockwise();
```

is equivalent to

```
pencil.turnBy(-30);
```

Sometimes using a parameter reduces the number of necessary instructions. The following three instructions:

```
pencil.turnClockwise();
pencil.turnClockwise();
pencil.turnClockwise();
```

can be replaced more succinctly with the following single statement:

```
pencil.turnBy(90);
```

In addition, the `turnBy` method can perform many directions that are impossible using only `turnClockwise` and `turnCounterclockwise`. Using `turnBy`, a `DrawingGizmo` can be directed in any one of 360 different directions. Without turnBy, only twelve directions are possible.

Inspector

Below is a collection of hints on what to check when examining code that involves the concepts of this chapter.

- To a programmer, syntax diagrams are like dictionaries. Just as you look up words in a dictionary when writing prose, it is equally important to refer to syntax diagrams when writing programs. Appendix B contains a syntax diagram collection for Java.

- Checking a program's style can easily improve readability and may also uncover well-hidden problems. A key style issue raised in this chapter is proper indentation. See Figure 2.11 for proper class indentation. All statements in the same sequence should be indented by the same amount.

- Objects must be instantiated before calling a method upon them. Check to ensure constructor method calls precede the use of variables to avoid runtime errors.

- Every assignment instruction should be checked to see if it will create an orphan object at runtime.

- Any variable used within a section of code must be declared in some way. Checking for variable declarations is a good idea.

- When performing a desk check, keep class diagrams and class specifications handy. If the program being checked uses another class, then it is helpful to consult the specifications of the class's behavior.

- If a precondition is violated, then the program's behavior is unpredictable. Therefore, it is wise to review each method call to ensure that the precondition will be satisfied.

- Classes that make use of other classes require extra attention. The Java compiler and Java VM can locate outside classes as long as they are in the same folder as the class using them. This is why any class that uses `DrawingGizmo` must have the *DrawingGizmo.class* file in its folder.

- It is easy to forget either the "/*" (at the beginning) or the "*/" (at the end) of a multiline comment. Checking to see that these symbols occur in matched pairs avoids potentially confusing compile-time errors. Also, remember that one multiline comment cannot be nested inside another.

- Retain higher (earlier) levels of a top-down design. These earlier steps can be compared to the resulting code to check for omissions.

- Checking identifiers can greatly improve readability. Are instance variables named with nouns? Are methods named with verbs? Is the first letter of each class name uppercase and the first letter of each variable and method lowercase? Most importantly, are the names meaningful?

> ■ For every method call, check to see that the number and type of the arguments in the call are the same as the number and type of the parameters expected by the method.

Terminology

algorithm	orphan
alias (via variable names)	parameter
argument (in parameter passage)	pass
assignment instruction	pattern
bind (a variable name to an object)	postcondition
class invariant	precondition
class specifications	refinement
comment (within a program)	reserved word
constructor (method)	semantics
debugger	send (a message)
design by contract	separator (in Java syntax)
divide and conquer	sequence of statements
higher-level algorithm	software contract
identifier	stepwise refinement
instance variable	swap
instantiation	syntax
message (as used to call a method)	syntax diagram
method call	top-down design
new (the Java reserved word)	variable
null	

Exercises

1. Suppose that you are writing a class that has declared three objects named redWagon, blueWagon, and greenWagon. All of these variables belong to a class called Wagon, and the Wagon class contains two methods, as shown in the following class diagram:

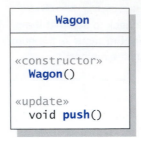

Each part below is an attempted instruction that is either a method call (see Figure 2.4) or an assignment instruction (see Figures 2.6 and 2.7). Identify whether or not each instruction has correct Java syntax.

a. `redWagon.push();`

b. `redWagon.push;`

c. `greenWagon.Wagon();`

d. `blueWagon.pull();`

e. `redWagon = new push();`

f. `redWagon = new Push();`

g. `blueWagon = new Wagon();`

h. `redWagon = new blueWagon;`

i. `redWagon = new redWagon.push();`

2. Figures 2.9 and 2.10 show how to declare instance variables.

a. Show the complete declaration of the instance variable `redWagon` from Exercise 1.

b. Give a single declaration that declares *all* three `Wagon` variables: `redWagon`, `blueWagon`, and `greenWagon`. (See Exercise 1 for a description of these variables.)

3. Trace the execution of each of the following statement sequences by drawing an object diagram after each instruction. Identify every orphan that is created, and every alias that occurs by this execution.

a.
```
greenWagon = new Wagon();
blueWagon = new Wagon();
redWagon = new Wagon();
greenWagon = blueWagon;
redWagon = blueWagon;
```

b.
```
greenWagon = new Wagon();
blueWagon = greenWagon;
redWagon = blueWagon;
```

```
c. greenWagon = new Wagon();
   blueWagon = null;
   greenWagon = blueWagon;
   redWagon = greenWagon;

d. greenWagon = new Wagon();
   blueWagon = greenWagon;
   greenWagon = new Wagon();
   redWagon = greenWagon;
   greenWagon = new Wagon();
   blueWagon = greenWagon;
   greenWagon = new Wagon();
   redWagon = greenWagon;
   greenWagon = new Wagon();
```

4. Write a segment of Java code that swaps the object bound to blueWagon with the object bound to redWagon. (You may use greenWagon any way you wish.)

5. Even if the push method has no precondition, there is still an implicit precondition for the following instruction. What is it?

   ```
   greenWagon.push();
   ```

6. Each part below makes a statement regarding one or more of the following assertions.

   ■ class invariant

   ■ method precondition

   ■ method postcondition

   Select all of the previous assertions that function as described.

   a. If the method is to function properly, this condition must be true at the time the method is called.

   b. If the method is functioning properly, this condition must be true at the time the method completes.

   c. Ensuring this condition is the responsibility of the programmer writing the code for the method.

   d. Ensuring this condition is the responsibility of the programmer writing the code that calls the method.

7. Show the lines that are drawn in the *Drawing Canvas* window as a result of executing each of the following Java Driver constructors.

a. ```
public class Driver {
    private DrawingGizmo pencil;
    public Driver() {
        pencil = new DrawingGizmo();
        pencil.draw();
        pencil.moveForward();
        pencil.dontDraw();
        pencil.moveForward();
    }
}
```

b. ```
public class Driver {
    private DrawingGizmo pencil;
    public Driver() {
        pencil = new DrawingGizmo();
        pencil.moveForward();
        pencil.moveForward();
        pencil.dontDraw();
        pencil.turnClockwise();
        pencil.moveForward();
        pencil.draw();
        pencil.draw();
        pencil.turnClockwise();
        pencil.turnClockwise();
        pencil.turnClockwise();
        pencil.moveForward();
        pencil.turnClockwise();
        pencil.moveForward();
    }
}
```

c. ```
public class Driver {
    private DrawingGizmo pencil, pen;
    public Driver() {
        pencil = new DrawingGizmo();
        pen = new DrawingGizmo();
        pen.dontDraw();
        pen.turnClockwise();
        pen.moveForward();
        pen.turnClockwise();
        pen.draw();
        pencil.moveForward();
        pen.moveForward();
    }
}
```
```

8. Using the complete definition of DrawingGizmo, show the lines that are drawn in the *Drawing Canvas* window and the final position of the DrawingGizmo object that results from executing each of the following Java Driver constructors.

a.
```java
public class Driver {
    private DrawingGizmo pencil;
    public Driver() {
        pencil = new DrawingGizmo();
        pencil.turnBy(150);
        pencil.moveBy(40);
        pencil.turnBy(120);
        pencil.moveBy(40);
        pencil.turnBy(120);
        pencil.moveBy(40);
    }
}
```

b.
```java
public class Driver {
    private DrawingGizmo pencil;
    public Driver() {
        pencil = new DrawingGizmo();
        pencil.dontDraw();
        pencil.moveForward();
        pencil.turnBy(90);
        pencil.draw();
        pencil.moveForward();
        pencil.dontDraw();
        pencil.moveBy(10);
        pencil.draw();
        pencil.moveForward();

        pencil.turnBy(90);
        pencil.moveForward();
        pencil.dontDraw();
        pencil.moveBy(10);
        pencil.draw();
        pencil.moveForward();

        pencil.turnBy(90);
        pencil.moveForward();
        pencil.dontDraw();
        pencil.moveBy(10);
        pencil.draw();
        pencil.moveForward();
```

```
                    pencil.turnBy(90);
                    pencil.moveForward();
                    pencil.dontDraw();
                    pencil.moveBy(10);
                    pencil.draw();
                    pencil.moveForward();

                    pencil.dontDraw();
                    pencil.turnBy(135);
                    pencil.moveBy(35);
                    pencil.turnBy(-135);
        }
    }
```

9. Imagine that `pencil` is an instance variable of type `DrawingGizmo` that is located near the left edge of its window and directed to the right. Refine each of the following algorithms into a short piece of Java code using `pencil`. These algorithms are simple enough that this refinement can occur in a single step.

    a. Rotate `pencil` 90 degrees in the counterclockwise direction.

    b. `pencil` draws two 20-unit horizontal line segments separated by 20 units.

    c. `pencil` draws three stair steps heading downward from its initial position.

10. Imagine that `pencil` is an instance variable of type `DrawingGizmo` that is located near the left edge of its window and directed to the right. Perform top-down design on each of the following algorithms, converting them into a piece of Java code using `pencil`. Do not attempt to translate each of these directly into code. Instead, you should refine each algorithm gradually into subalgorithms.

    a. Use `pencil` to draw the number 950 on the window.

    b. Use `pencil` to draw the word STEP in block letters on the window.

    c. Use `pencil` to draw a house that contains two windows and a door.

Programming Exercises

1. Compile and run the program called *Driver* (Figure 2.12).

2. Write a program that uses a `DrawingGizmo` object to create a square that has sides 40 pixels long.

3. Write a program to display the "HI" message shown on the next page. The letters should be 40 pixels tall.

4. Write a program that draws two side-by-side rectangles that are 40 pixels high and 20 pixels wide. Use two different DrawingGizmo objects to draw them in parallel. In other words, one object should draw the left rectangle and one should draw the right, and immediately after each action of the left DrawingGizmo object, the right object should take the corresponding action. Include a delay of a half second at the end of drawing each side. (The final image is shown below.)

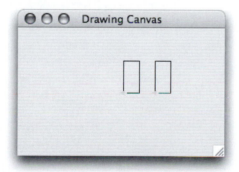

5. Write a program that draws a regular pentagon and a five-pointed star. The pentagon must be regular with sides that are 40 pixels long. The vertices of the pentagon must be the same as the points of the star. Note that you will need to use the methods described in Section 2.13. (The final image is shown below.)

Introduction to Design and Implementation

3

I would propose to call this limit the 'span of absolute judgment,' and I maintain that for unidimensional judgments this span is usually somewhere in the neighborhood of seven.

—George A. Miller

Objectives

- To introduce the need for using class library code
- To examine how the Java compiler locates library code
- To present prototyping as a strategy for developing software
- To introduce the Color and Label classes from the *java.awt* library
- To introduce the JFrame class from the *javax.swing* library
- To examine three additional classes for drawing simple graphics: Line, Rectangle, and Oval
- To describe the Java import declaration and its role for accessing external software class
- To introduce the use of commenting out code and output instructions, such as System.out.println, for use in debugging

75

By now it should be obvious that writing a Java program typically involves the use of many different classes. This chapter introduces a few preexisting classes and how to integrate them into designing programs. A prototyping approach is also examined as an effective technique for programmatic design.

3.1 ■ Introduction to Standard Classes

Object-oriented programming relies upon the ability to "borrow" existing software in the sense that programs frequently include objects whose software classes have been written by other programmers. There are three common sources of software:

1. software classes you write
2. software classes included in the standard Java library distribution
3. nonstandard software classes written by another programmer to which you have access

Chapter 2 presented a technique for writing your own `Driver` class. Many of the example programs make use of a class called `DrawingGizmo` in several of its programming examples. The `DrawingGizmo` class was written by another programmer—the author of this book. Your program can include `DrawingGizmo` objects as long as you include the *DrawingGizmo.class* file within the same file folder as your *Driver.java* file.

software **engineering** *Hint*

There are numerous Java standard classes not presented in this book and the classes that are presented can only be explained in part. You are encouraged to explore the standard classes more fully.

`DrawingGizmo` might be useful for a few introductory programming assignments, but there are other much more important classes. The best known are the so-called "standard classes." Standard classes get their name from the fact that they are distributed with every proper implementation of Java. Standard classes are standardized by a process that allows the Java community to review and comment on new proposals. Just like the English language has changed over time, the standard classes can change in different versions of the language.

Most of the standard classes include many more methods than can be explored in this book. However, several standard class features are presented and used in examples throughout this and future chapters.

The Java standard classes are grouped into libraries. Each class library includes classes that share a common purpose. At this time, there are three master groups of standard libraries: *java*, *javax*, and *org*. The classes used in this book come from the *java* and the *javax* groups. The *java* group includes the original standard libraries, while the "*x*" suffix in *javax* refers to the fact that these libraries were originally considered extensions. The *org* libraries are essentially the product of various standards organizations.

The standard libraries Java includes for the purpose of supporting **graphical user interfaces** (**GUI**), which is pronounced "goo-ee," are *AWT* and *Swing*. GUI libraries allow the user to interact with a computer through objects such as windows and buttons. The *AWT* library is the older of the two and is part of the *java* library group. The *Swing* library relies largely upon *AWT* classes, and *Swing* classes are located within the *javax* library group.

One of the commonly used standard classes used by both *AWT* and *Swing* is `java.awt.Color`. (Actually, the name of the class is `Color`, but since it is part of the *java.awt* library, its full name is `java.awt.Color`.) Objects belonging to the `java.awt.Color` class are graphical colors that can be used to determine the appearance of various visual objects. For example, two common methods used among the standard graphical classes, and also used by the `DrawingGizmo` class, are:

```
public void setBackground(java.awt.Color c)
```
    post: The background color of this object is *c*.

```
public void setForeground(java.awt.Color c)
```
    post: The foreground color of this object is *c*.

In the case of a `DrawingGizmo`, a call to `setBackground` resets the color of the drawing canvas and a call to `setForeground` assigns a new color to the drawing object. That object continues to draw with the assigned color as long as it is in drawing mode and `setForeground` is not called again. Figure 3.1 illustrates a program to draw a triangle in which the right side is colored gray, and the left side and base are colored white all within a black window. The drawing that results from executing this program is shown in Figure 3.2.

The colored triangle program demonstrates how the `Color` class can be used to define both a parameter type and color values. The `setForeground` method has a single parameter of type `Color`. The color gray is passed as an argument to this method using the following syntax:

```
pencil.setForeground(java.awt.Color.gray);
```

Similarly, setting the drawing color to white is accomplished by the following statement.

```
pencil.setForeground(java.awt.Color.white);
```

There are thirteen possible colors that are defined within the `Color` class and therefore can be used as arguments when calling `setBackground` or `setForeground`. These color values are shown in Figure 3.3.

Figure 3.1

Program to draw a colored triangle and its *Drawing Canvas*

```java
public class Driver {
    private DrawingGizmo pencil;

    public Driver() {
        pencil = new DrawingGizmo();
        pencil.setBackground(java.awt.Color.black);
        pencil.dontDraw();
        pencil.moveBy(50);
        pencil.draw();
        pencil.turnBy(150);
        pencil.setForeground(java.awt.Color.gray);
        pencil.moveBy(80);
        pencil.turnBy(120);
        pencil.setForeground(java.awt.Color.white);
        pencil.moveBy(80);
        pencil.turnBy(120);
        pencil.moveBy(80);
    }
}
```

Figure 3.2

Image produced by executing the program in Figure 3.1

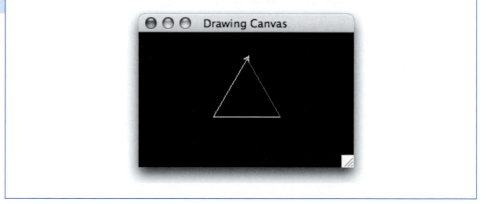

Figure 3.3

Color constant values

```
java.awt.Color.black          java.awt.Color.magenta
java.awt.Color.blue           java.awt.Color.orange
java.awt.Color.cyan           java.awt.Color.pink
java.awt.Color.darkGray       java.awt.Color.red
java.awt.Color.gray           java.awt.Color.white
java.awt.Color.green          java.awt.Color.yellow
java.awt.Color.lightGray
```

3.2 ■ Import Declarations

Although it may seem lengthy, the expression `java.awt.Color.black` is necessary for the Java compiler to locate the `black` object. You might think of this expression like your postal address. The mail service does not know where to deliver a letter unless you include the name of the recipient, the street address, the town, state, and country. Similarly, the Java compiler cannot find members of a class (like the color red) unless you specify the name of the standard library group (`java`), followed by the library (package) within that library group (`awt`), followed by the class from within the library (`Color`), and finally the object's name (`black`). Periods separate the parts of the expression. Notice that Java syntax prohibits such expressions from being reordered, i.e., they must proceed left to right from general to specific. Figure 3.4 details this expression.

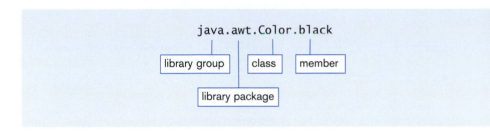

Figure 3.4

A fully qualified expression for a standard class member

Fortunately, the Java language designers also included the concept of an **import declaration**. There are two uses for import declarations:

1. they assist the compiler in locating packages of software that are located outside of the current file folder

2. they permit some abbreviation in expressions that refer to class members.

An `import` declaration is a line placed before the `public class` line. Each import declaration specifies one or more files/folders that the compiler should search to locate external classes. Figure 3.5 provides more detail.

When one class makes use of members from a second class, then the Java compiler first searches for the external class file within the current folder (i.e., the folder of the class that is being compiled). If the compiler is unable to find the external class within this folder, then import statements are used by the compiler to locate the appropriate class.

Java programming environments generally use the **path** and **classpath** system variables to determine the addresses of major library folders.[1] The *fileSpecs* folder (named in Figure 3.5) specification must specify a file pathname that is relative to *path* or *classpath*.

software *Hint*
engineering

Import declarations are widely used to simplify expressions that refer to members of standard classes. When more than one class is to be imported from the same library then the * notation is useful in your import declaration.

---

1. The classpath system variable is usually predefined to identify the standard Java library folders. When a new library is added, the classpath system variable must be updated to include the library.

Figure 3.5

ImportDecls
description

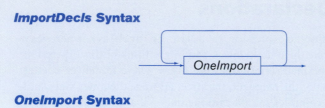

ImportDecls **Syntax**

OneImport **Syntax**

Note

fileSpecs denotes the pathname of a file from among the preset user, system, and boot libraries. The notation uses a period as a separator between consecutive folder/file names.

Usage

The class in which the *ImportDecls* is included can access the imported classes.

Any class that abbreviates `Color` object names, such as `Color.green`, must include an import declaration such as the following.

```
import java.awt.Color;
```

An alternative `import` that allows access to all classes in the `awt` folder uses an asterisk (`*`) in place of `Color` as shown below.

```
import java.awt.*;
```

Black Box

Java is designed to be extensible in the sense that programmers can add their own libraries. This permits software development groups to tailor the Java environment to their own programming needs. Chapter 14 examines how to create and use user libraries.

Figure 3.6 illustrates the use of an `import` declaration This program is identical to the program from Figure 3.1, except for the inclusion of the import declaration and the corresponding abbreviated notation for specifying colors.

When a class is imported, the notation used to refer to members of that class can be abbreviated in the same way as if the class were located within the same file folder. In other words, you can omit names of library groups and packages outside of import declarations. In the case of color values the "`java.awt.`" prefix can be omitted when naming the `red` and `blue` objects. Therefore, an expression such as

```
import java.awt.Color;
public class Driver {
    private DrawingGizmo pencil;

    public Driver() {
        pencil = new DrawingGizmo();
        pencil.dontDraw();
        pencil.moveBy(50);
        pencil.draw();
        pencil.turnBy(150);
        pencil.setForeground(Color.red);
        pencil.moveBy(80);
        pencil.turnBy(120);
        pencil.setForeground(Color.blue);
        pencil.moveBy(80);
        pencil.turnBy(120);
        pencil.moveBy(80);
    }
}
```

Figure 3.6

Program to draw a colored triangle using an import declaration

`java.awt.Color.red` can be shortened to `Color.red`. The same abbreviations are permitted if the import declaration in Figure 3.6 is changed to

```
import java.awt.*;
```

3.3 ■ javax.swing.JFrame

The *AWT* library's `Color` class is only a small part of the standard GUI libraries. This section explores another class that is useful for creating visible images. GUIs rely upon graphical drawings that appear on the **computer display** (**screen**). The **window** is the primary object that GUIs use to support these drawings. Each window is a rectangular region of the screen that is devoted to displaying graphical elements created by the associated program. The region called *Drawing Canvas* used by `DrawingGizmo` objects is a window. Some types of windows permit the user to provide control, such as dragging the window to a different location, resizing the window, and closing the window. The primary *Swing* class for creating such windows is called **JFrame**. (There is an analogous class within the *AWT* library named `Frame`.) A class diagram including many `JFrame` methods is shown in Figure 3.7.

This class diagram introduces a new notation that is common for class diagrams. A minus sign (-) has been inserted in front of all class attributes. A minus sign prefix signifies that a feature is *not* available for use outside the class. In other words, the five `JFrame` attributes cannot be used by other programs. The reason that these five

Figure 3.7

JFrame class
diagram

```
                    java.swing.JFrame
  ───────────────────────────────────────────────
    – int x
    – int y
    – int width
    – int height
    – Color backColor
  ───────────────────────────────────────────────
    «constructor»
      + JFrame(String)
      ...

    «update»
      + void add(java.awt.Component, int)
      + void remove(java.awt.Component)
      + void repaint()
      + void setBackground(java.awt.Color)
      + void setBounds(int, int, int, int)
      + void setLayout(java.awt.LayoutManager)
      + void setVisible(boolean)
      ...
```

attributes are included in the class diagram is that they are helpful for describing the class behavior. Methods also share this notation. Prefixing with a plus sign (+) signifies that the attribute or method is available for public use, and prefixing with a minus sign (−) means that the attribute or method is private to the class and not available elsewhere.

The class specification in Figure 3.8 includes more detailed information about JFrame.

Figure 3.8

javax.swing.
JFrame class
specification
(*continues*)

Invariant

A JFrame object...

■ is a rectangular window.

■ is placed on a computer screen with its upper left corner *x* pixels from the left and *y* pixels from the top. (The upper left corner of the screen is (0, 0).)

■ has usable dimension of *width* pixels from side to side and *height* pixels from top to bottom; this region has a background color of *backColor*.

A JFrame with a gray *backColor* on a white screen is shown on the next page.

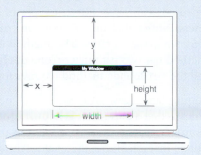

Figure 3.8

`javax.swing.`
`JFrame` class
specification
(*continued*)

Constructor Methods

public **JFrame**(String *s*)

> **post:** A new JFrame (window) object is created
> **and** *s* is displayed as a label in the bar at the top of the JFrame
> (Note that this method needs to be followed by calls to setBounds
> and setVisible in order to make the object appear.)

Update Methods

public void **add**(java.awt.Component *pic*, int *j*)

> **pre:** *j* == 0 for best results

> **post:** The *pic* graphical object will be drawn upon this JFrame.

public void **remove**(java.awt.Component *pic*)

> **post:** The *pic* graphical object will be removed from this JFrame.

> **note:** Nothing occurs if *pic* was not added to this JFrame at the time of
> the call.

public void **repaint**()

> **post:** Causes the Java virtual machine to update the display of this object
> as soon as possible.

public void **setBackground**(java.awt.Color *c*)

> **post:** *backColor* == *c*

public void **setBounds**(int *initX*, int *initY*, int *w*, int *h*)

> **post:** *x* == *initX* **and** *y* == *initY*
> **and** *width* == *w* **and** *height* == *h*

public void **setLayout**(java.awt.LayoutManager *m*)

> **pre:** *m* == null (for use in this book)

> **post:** Objects added to the frame will be arranged via *m*

public void **setVisible**(boolean *b*)

> **post:** *b* == *true* **implies** this JFrame is made visible and brought to the
> foreground (in front of other windows).

Chapter 2 introduced the concept of parameters and arguments. The JFrame class demonstrates that methods can have different types of parameters and different numbers of parameters. Notice that the JFrame constructor method has a single parameter of type String, the setVisible method has a parameter of type boolean, the add method has two parameters (one of type java.awt.Component and of type int), and the setBounds method requires four int parameters.

software **engineering** *Hint*
Programmers must always take care to get the order of method arguments, and their types, to match the parameters.

Like most programming languages, Java uses a technique known as **positional parameters**, which means that a parameter is known by its order (position) among all other parameters for the particular method. For example, it is always the first parameter of setBounds that establishes the *x* value (the distance separating the left edge of the computer display and the JFrame) while the third setBounds parameter always determines the width of a JFrame.

The variety of different types of parameters from these JFrame methods may seem a bit overwhelming. However, there are only a few possibilities to consider for now. Figure 3.9 summarizes the kinds of arguments you will want to use in early assignments. Later chapters will explain all of these data types in more detail.

The standard Java GUI libraries use a common two-dimensional coordinate scheme. In such a scheme, x represents the horizontal coordinate of any screen position and y represents the vertical coordinate. The class invariant for JFrame indicates that the upper left corner of a JFrame has *x* and *y* values that measure the distance to the upper left corner of the computer screen. (When x = 0 and y = 0, the JFrame is located in the screen's upper left corner—this might be partially obscured if your operating system includes a menu bar across the top of the screen.) The value of x increases from left to right and the value of y increases from top to bottom.

Figure 3.9

Some arguments for boolean, int, Color, Component, LayoutManager, and String types

Parameter Type	Useful Arguments
boolean	either true or false Example: true
int	any integer constant Examples: 17 -3256
java.awt.Color	color value constants (see Figure 3.3) Examples: Color.black Color.lightGray
java.awt.Component	any valid Label, Rectangle, Oval or Line object (See Sections 3.4 and 3.5 for a discussion of these classes.)
java.awt.LayoutManager	null
String	any consecutive sequence of printable characters enclosed within double quotation marks Example: "objects are fun!")

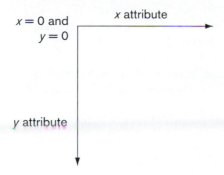

It is also typical in Java to measure screen distances in terms of **pixels** (an abbreviation for picture elements). Computer displays range from about 1024 to 1600 pixels horizontally and 768 to 1200 pixels vertically. The x and y values for a JFrame object measure its distance (in pixels) from the left and top edge, respectively, of the computer display. The class specification of JFrame also illustrates the Java standard of using *width* and *height* attributes to represent size (in pixels) of the displayable region of a JFrame.

The class specifications in this text often make use of special Java notations. Two consecutive equal signs (i.e., "==") is one such notation that appears frequently (see Figure 3.8). Java uses two consecutive equal signs as the notation for "equals," whereas a single equal sign denotes assignment. Therefore, the specification for the setBounds method states that following this method's execution, the JFrame is located initX pixels from the left edge of the screen ($x ==$ initX) and initY pixels down from the top of the screen ($y ==$ initY).

Creating a JFrame object should be viewed as a four-statement coding pattern:

1. Instantiate a JFrame object (calling the JFrame constructor).
2. Establish the dimensions and position of the JFrame (calling setBounds).
3. Assign a layout manager to the JFrame (calling setLayout).
4. Force the JFrame to be displayed (calling setVisible).

Note that while Step 1 must occur first, the remaining three steps may occur in any order. A program that demonstrates this pattern is given in Figure 3.10. The import declarations in this program are used to import *both* the Color class and the JFrame class.

This program instantiates two JFrame objects, one called window and the other called blackWindow. When the window object is displayed, it is titled "First Window" by virtue of the string argument to the JFrame constructor. This window is 300 pixels wide, 200 pixels high with its upper left corner 50 pixels from the top and left of the computer screen. The blackWindow object, is titled "Black Background" and its dimensions cause it to overlap the window object.

Figure 3.11 displays the two windows as they appear when the program executes. The reason that blackWindow is on top of window is that the setVisible method is last called on blackWindow. The reason that the two windows have a different

Figure 3.10

Program to
construct two
JFrames

```java
import java.awt.Color;
import javax.swing.JFrame;
public class Driver {
        private JFrame window, blackWindow;

    public Driver() {
        window = new JFrame("First Window");
        window.setBounds(50, 50, 300, 200);
        window.setLayout(null);
        window.setVisible(true);

        blackWindow = new JFrame("Black Background");
        blackWindow.setBounds(150, 150, 250, 125);
        blackWindow.setLayout(null);
        blackWindow.setBackground(Color.black);
        blackWindow.setVisible(true);
    }
}
```

Figure 3.11

Image produced
by executing the
program in
Figure 3.10

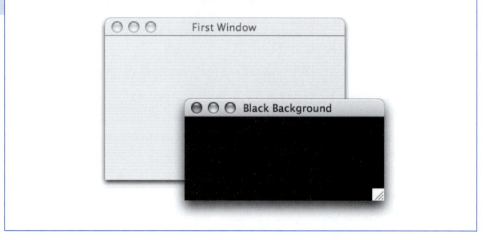

color is that `setBackground` is called to assign a black background color to `blackWindow`; window uses the default background color because `setBackground` is not called upon the `window` object.

The need for `setLayout` results from the way that `JFrame` objects manage their content. Every `JFrame` utilizes a special object, known as a layout manager, to arrange graphics that are displayed within the window. Using `null` as an argument to `setLayout`, disables all automatic layout manager control for the `JFrame`. Some programmers refer to this as a **null layout manager**.

3.4 ■ java.awt.Label

The purpose of a GUI window is to display other GUI objects. Therefore, the *Swing* classes treat JFrame as though it were a container—its content being the GUI objects it displays. Two JFrame methods are provided to include (add) new things to the content or to eliminate (remove) GUI items.

There are dozens of classes for creating objects that can be added or removed from a JFrame—one such class, called Label, is used for displaying text messages. Label is a standard class within the *AWT* library; its class diagram and class specification are given in Figures 3.12 and 3.13.

Label objects are useful for displaying messages within windows. Displaying a Label requires a four-step pattern:

1. Create a Label object, specifying the text for the message (calling Label).
2. Assign the Label a position and dimensions (calling setBounds).
3. Add the Label to a container such as a JFrame (calling add on the container).
4. Inform the Java virtual machine that the Label display should be updated (calling repaint).

The Java drawing mechanisms require that you always create a graphical object, assign it a location, and add it to some visible container, such as a JFrame. It does not matter whether setBounds is called before or after calling add, and calling

software
engineering *Hint*

When in doubt, err on the side of caution. For example, it is best to call repaint *every* time that a displayed object is changed. Sometimes the Java VM will not update the screen without a call to repaint, and other times it will.

Figure 3.12

java.awt.Label
class diagram

java.awt.Label
– int *x*   – int *y*   – string *text*   – Color *foreColor*   – Color *backColor*
«constructor»   + **Label**(*String*)   ...   «update»   + void **setBackground**(*java.awt.Color*)   + void **setForeground**(*java.awt.Color*)   + void **setBounds**(*int, int, int, int*)   + void **repaint**()   ...

Figure 3.13

`java.awt.Label`
class specifica-
tion

Invariant

A `Label` object...

- is a string of text.
- should be added to a container object with its upper left corner *x* pixels from the left and *y* pixels from the top. (The upper left corner of the container is (0, 0).)
- when it is contained within a proper GUI container the value of text is displayed in color *foreColor* in a rectangular region; this region has a background color of *backColor*.

Below is a `Label` with *text* == "message," a white *backColor* and a black *foreColor*.

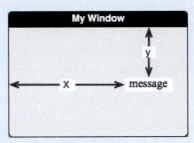

Constructor Methods

`public Label(String s)`

    post: A new `Label` object is created
             and *text* == *s*
             and *foreColor* == `Color.black`
             and *backColor* is transparent
             (Note that `Label`s do not appear until added.)

Update Methods

`public void setBackground(java.awt.Color c)`

    post: *backColor* == *c*

`public void setForeground(java.awt.Color c)`

    post: *foreColor* == *c*

`public void setBounds(int initX, int initY, int w, int h)`

    post: *x* == *initX* **and** *y* == *initY*
             and *width* == *w* **and** *height* == *h*

`public void repaint()`

    post: Causes the Java virtual machine to update the display of this object as soon as possible.

repaint is optional, depending upon the circumstances. However, it is best to be safe and call repaint, to encourage the Java VM to update the Label portion of the computer screen. Figure 3.14 shows a program that uses four Label objects. Figure 3.15 shows the corresponding JFrame that is created and displayed by the program.

```java
import java.awt.*;
import javax.swing.JFrame;
public class Driver {
    private JFrame window;
    private Label cityEngland, cityFrance, cityJapan, cityUSA;

    public Driver() {
        window = new JFrame("Cities of the World");
        window.setBounds(50, 50, 400, 300);
        window.setLayout(null);
        window.setBackground(Color.white);
        window.setVisible(true);

        cityEngland = new Label("London");
        cityEngland.setBounds(100, 200, 120, 20);
        cityEngland.setForeground(Color.green);
        window.add(cityEngland,0);
        cityEngland.repaint();

        cityFrance = new Label ("Paris");
        cityFrance.setBounds(250, 30, 100, 20);
        cityFrance.setForeground(Color.blue);
        window.add(cityFrance,0);
        cityFrance.repaint();

        cityJapan = new Label ("Tokyo");
        cityJapan.setBounds(30, 75, 100, 20);
        cityJapan.setForeground(Color.red);
        window.add(cityJapan,0);
        cityJapan.repaint();

        cityUSA = new Label ("New York City");
        cityUSA.setBounds(225, 250, 150, 20);
        cityUSA.setForeground(Color.white);
        cityUSA.setBackground(Color.blue);
        window.add(cityUSA,0);
        cityUSA.repaint();
        window.repaint();
    }
}
```

Figure 3.14

Program to display labels

Figure 3.15

Image produced
by executing the
program in
Figure 3.14

The program in Figure 3.14 begins by creating a JFrame object, called window. The program goes on to create four Label objects (cityEngland, cityFrance, cityJapan, and cityUSA). Each Label names a different city in the corresponding country and each is set to a different foreground color by calls to setForeground. The cityUSA object also is assigned a background color; this is why the "New York City" string appears to be surrounded by a filled rectangle. When no background color is assigned the background of a Label remains transparent.

The add method deserves more explanation. You *must* call the add method in order to cause a Label to appear on the computer screen. If the following instruction is deleted from the Figure 3.14 program, then the word "Paris" would not appear in the JFrame.

```
window.add(cityFrance,0);
```

In addition to placing an object within a container, a call to add also has the effect of removing that same object from any prior placement. In other words, GUI objects can only be displayed within one container at any time. Attempting to add the same Label to two windows fails to do so. Instead, the second add effectively undoes the first. In addition, adding a Label to the same JFrame a second time has no effect. For example, the following code

```
window.add(cityUSA,0);
window.add(cityUSA,0);
window.add(cityUSA,0);
```

yields the same result as the single statement:

```
window.add(cityUSA,0);
```

It is possible for two Label objects to overlap. When this occurs the Label that was added last will partially obscure the Label that was added earlier In fact, this is the purpose of the second parameter; when the second parameter is zero (0), this signifies to place the new item "on top of" all prior added objects. Therefore, the following code

```
cityEngland = new Label("London");
cityEngland.setBounds(100, 200, 120, 20);
cityEngland.setForeground(Color.blue);
cityEngland.repaint();
cityUSA = new Label ("New York City");
cityUSA.setBounds(110, 205, 150, 20);
cityUSA.setForeground(Color.white);
cityUSA.setBackground(Color.gray);
cityUSA.repaint();
window.add(cityEngland,0);
window.add(cityUSA,0);
```

causes cityUSA to overlap cityEngland as shown below:

L**New York City**

However, if the last three lines are reordered as follows

```
window.add(cityUSA,0);
window.add(cityEngland,0);
```

the overlap looks like this:

London**New York City**

The remove method undoes the work of an add. Therefore, executing the following statement causes the cityUSA to be removed from any prior placement (i.e., the Label becomes invisible).

```
window.remove(cityUSA);
```

If there was no prior placement, then executing the statement above does nothing.

3.5 ■ Nonstandard Classes (Rectangle, Oval, and Line)

As previously mentioned, programmers are not limited to using only classes from the standard libraries. It is also possible to use classes that are supplied by another programmer. This section proposes new classes—Rectangle, Oval, and Line. These classes are not included in the *AWT* or *Swing* libraries. Instead, these classes were written by the author to be used in conjunction with the standard library classes.

Black Box

The standard libraries include many useful classes, such as Color, JFrame, and Label. However, not everything is provided so directly. The *AWT* library does not include any classes that can be directly instantiated as simple graphical objects like rectangles, ovals, or lines. Even though these classes are not included, *Swing* provides the functionality required for programmers to create their own such classes. The Rectangle, Oval, and Line classes used in this chapter are built this way. The code for these classes is revealed and explained in Chapter 8.

As their names suggest, Rectangle, Oval, and Line are designed to display graphical images (geometric solids) of the indicted shape. Objects belonging to any of these classes are similar to java.awt.Label objects in the way they rely on the use of the add and repaint methods. For example, the code in Figure 3.16 creates a blue rectangle with a black oval immediately to its right. Figure 3.17 shows the window that results from executing this program. Notice that the images associated with blueRectangle and blackOval appear as filled solids.

The code from Figure 3.16 illustrates several issues. This program does not include any import declarations for Rectangle and Oval classes; this is acceptable as long

Figure 3.16

Program to display a rectangle and oval

```
import java.awt.Color;
import javax.swing.JFrame;
public class Driver {
    private JFrame window;
    private Rectangle blueRectangle;
    private Oval blackOval;

    public Driver() {
        window = new JFrame("the window");
        window.setBounds(50, 50, 300, 200);
        window.setLayout(null);
        window.setBackground(Color.white);
        window.setVisible(true);
        blueRectangle = new Rectangle(100, 100, 50, 30);
        blueRectangle.setBackground(Color.blue);
        window.add(blueRectangle, 0);
        blueRectangle.repaint();
        blackOval = new Oval(150, 100, 50, 30);
        window.add(blackOval, 0);
        blackOval.repaint();
    }
}
```

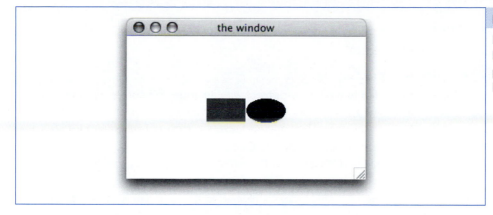

Figure 3.17

Image produced by executing the program in Figure 3.16

as the *Rectangle.class* and *Oval.class* files are located in the same folder as *Driver.java*. The statements that instantiate `Rectangle` and `Oval` objects make it clear that the corresponding constructors have four parameters. The parameters of the `Rectangle` and `Oval` constructors specify, respectively, the *x* and *y* location, the width and the height of each object. Once again, the `setBackground` method is used to establish the color of each object. (Black is the default color.) Figures 3.18 and 3.19 detail these and other behaviors via a class diagram and specifications for the `Rectangle` class.

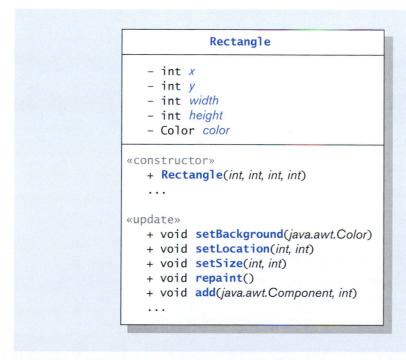

Figure 3.18

`Rectangle` class diagram

Figure 3.19

Rectangle
class
specification
(*continues*)

Invariant

A Rectangle object...

- is drawn as a rectangular solid.

- should be added to a container object with its upper left corner *x* pixels from the left and *y* pixels from the top. (The upper left corner of the container is (0, 0).)

- when it is contained within a proper GUI container the rectangle appears in color *color* and the dimensions of the rectangle are given by *width* and *height*.

- if necessary, the rectangle image is clipped to the boundaries of its container.

Below is a black `Rectangle` added to My Window.

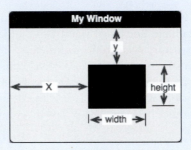

Constructor Methods

`public Rectangle(int initX, int initY, int w, int h)`

> **post:** A new Rectangle object is created
> **and** color == `Color.black`
> **and** x == *initX* **and** y == *initY*
> **and** width == *w* **and** height == *h*
> (Note that `Rectangles` do not appear until added.)

`...`

Update Methods

`public void setBackground(java.awt.Color c)`

> **post:** *color == c*

`public void setLocation(int intX, int initY)`

> **post:** *x == initX* **and** *y == initY*

`public void setSize(int w, int h)`

> **post:** *width == w* **and** *height == h*

Figure 3.19

Rectangle class
specification
(*continued*)

```
public void repaint()
```
   post: Causes the Java virtual machine to update the display of this object as
           soon as possible.

```
public void add(java.awt.Component pic, int j)
```
   pre: *j* == 0 for best results.

   post: The *pic* graphical object will be drawn upon this Rectangle.

The Oval class is the same as Rectangle, except for the name of the constructor
(Oval) and the image that is displayed (a solid oval, rather than a solid rectangle).
The *x, y, width,* and *height* values apply to the Oval at the location of its maximum
dimensions.

The Java GUI classes generally adopt a known as **relative coordinates.** Each graphical container (such as java.swing.JFrame has a boundary defined by its *x, y,
width,* and *height* values. When a graphical object is added to a component, the
added object is placed at a location *relative* to the container. That is, the component's
upper left corner (rather than the upper left corner of the screen) is treated as *x* ==
0 and *y* == 0 for purposes of positioning the added object.

The Java GUI classes also use a technique known as **clipping.** When a graphical
object is added to a container, any portion of the added object that lies outside the
boundaries of the container is said to be *clipped*—which means that the external
region is not visible. For example, consider the following segment of code.

```
blackOval = new Oval(-25, 100, 50, 30);
window.add(blackOval, 0);
```

The blackOval object has an x value of –25, which means that half of the object lies
to the left (outside the boundaries) of the window in which it is contained. Such a
placement results in the left half of the oval being clipped as shown below.

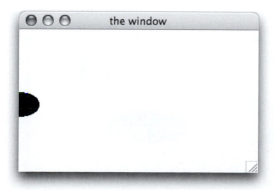

It is also possible to add Rectangle and Oval objects to other Rectangle and Oval objects. When adding to an Oval, note that its boundary is rectangular, not curved. Figure 3.20 contains a more extensive example that demonstrates this.

Closed

Black Box

The add method has another unusual characteristic in that it results in a hidden binding. It happens that every object is bound to the object to which it is added. Consider the execution of the following.

```
someRectangle = new Rectangle(30, 30, 30, 30);
window.add(someRectangle, 0);
someRectangle = null;
```

When this instruction sequence completes execution, someRectangle is bound to a 30 by 30 Rectangle by virtue of the first instruction. After the object is added, someRectangle is assigned null. The 30 by 30 rectangle does *not* disappear, however. The add method has bound this rectangle to window, so the graphical object will continue to be visible even when it has no variable name binding.

Figure 3.20

Example of image clipping and overlay

```
blackOval = new Oval(100, 100, 100, 40);
window.add(blackOval, 0);
bigSquare = new Rectangle(50, 20, 100, 100);
bigSquare.setBackground(Color.lightGray);
blackOval.add(bigSquare, 0);

smallSquare = new Rectangle(200, 30, 40, 40);
smallSquare.setBackground(Color.gray);
window.add(smallSquare, 0);
whiteOval = new Oval(210, 50, 20, 15);
whiteOval.setBackground(Color.white);
window.add(whiteOval, 0);
window.repaint();
```

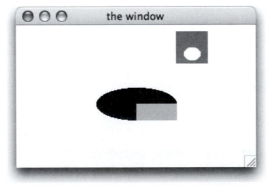

The Line class differs from Rectangle and Oval in two significant ways:

1. The Line constructor specifies line endpoints, not *x, y, length,* and *width.*

2. It does not make any sense to add to a Line.

The class diagram and specifications from Figures 3.21 and 3.22 contain the details.

A Line object appears as a line segment. The Line constructor uses its four parameters to specify the endpoints of the line segment. (This is different from Rectangle and Oval parameters.) The first two parameters specify, respectively, the *x* and *y* coordinates of one endpoint, while the last two parameters give the *x* and *y* coordinates for the line's other endpoint.

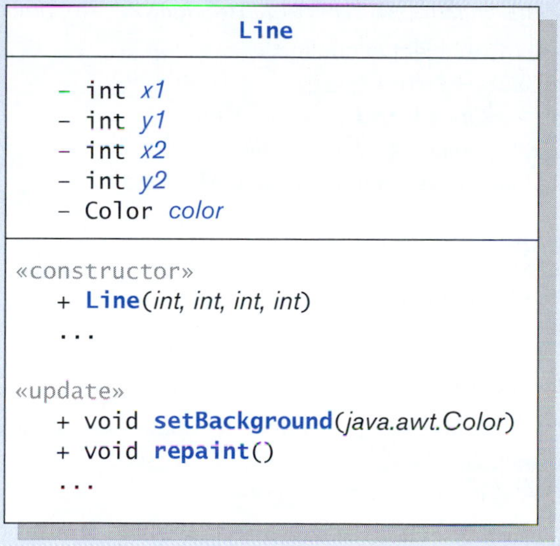

Figure 3.21

Line class diagram

Figure 3.22

Line class specification (*continues*)

Invariant

A Line object...

- is drawn as a line segment.
- should be added to a container object with one end located *x1* pixels from the left and *y1* pixels from the top and the opposite end located *x2* pixels from the left and *y2* pixels from the top. (The upper left corner of the container is (0, 0).)
- when it is contained within a proper GUI container the line segment appears in color *color*.
- if necessary, the line image is clipped to the boundaries of its container.

Figure 3.22

Line class
specification
(*continued*)

Below is a black Line added to My Window.

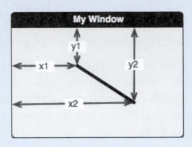

Constructor Methods

public **Line**(int *initX1*, int *initY1*, int *initX2*, int *initY2*)

> **post:** A new Line object is created
> **and** *color* == Color.black
> **and** *x1* == *initX1* **and** *y1* == *initY1*
> **and** *x2* == *initX2* **and** *y2* == *initY2*
> (Note that Lines do not appear until added.)

Update Methods

public void **setBackground**(java.awt.Color *c*)

> **post:** *color* == *c*

public void **repaint**()

> **post:** Causes the Java virtual machine to update the display of this object as
> soon as possible.

3.6 ■ Prototyping

Section 2.10 examined stepwise refinement (top-down) as a design strategy for writing software. In this section we introduce a different strategy, called **prototyping**. The process of prototyping consists of developing a sequence of programs, known as **prototypes**. The early prototypes provide partial functionality only, but are sufficient to exhibit key aspects of the desired program behavior. Each succeeding prototype adds functionality.

Software that produces graphical images is often well suited to prototyping. A customer purchasing this program may not know, or care to specify, details of color or placement. Prototypes can be used to assist the customer in making these software requirements decisions. For example, consider the problem of drawing a caricature of a caterpillar. An initial prototype of code and the associated picture are shown in Figures 3.23 and 3.24.

Figure 3.23

A first prototype
for the caterpillar
program

```java
import java.awt.Color;
import javax.swing.JFrame;
public class Driver {
    private JFrame theWindow;
    private Oval head, frontSegment, midSegment, rearSegment;

    public Driver() {
        theWindow = new JFrame("The Pede");
        theWindow.setBounds(30, 30, 500, 250);
        theWindow.setLayout(null);
        theWindow.setVisible(true);
        head = new Oval(110, 70, 84, 84);
        theWindow.add(head, 0);
        frontSegment = new Oval(180, 100, 50, 50);
        theWindow.add(frontSegment, 0);
        midSegment = new Oval(230, 100, 50, 50);
        theWindow.add(midSegment, 0);
        rearSegment = new Oval(280, 100, 50, 50);
        theWindow.add(rearSegment, 0);
        theWindow.repaint();
    }
}
```

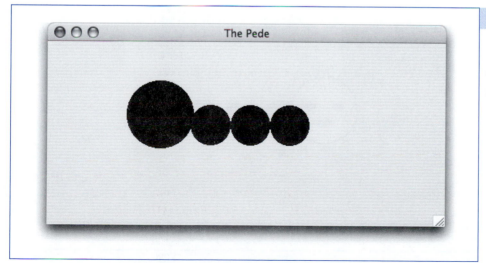

Figure 3.24

Image produced
by executing the
caterpillar
program in
Figure 3.23

This prototype makes use of a JFrame object, named theWindow, and four Oval objects. Following the instantiation of theWindow, each of the four Ovals is instantiated and added to theWindow. The final instruction ensures the display of all objects.

The customer can execute this first prototype and observe the drawing produced. This allows the customer to make key decisions. It is also important to note that the programmer has not invested much time in the prototype, so the cost of changing the requirements are minimal. Suppose that the customer decides that this three-segment body and enlarged head are good, but legs and a face are needed. A second prototype might take the form shown in Figure 3.25. The newly inserted statements are boldfaced in Figure 3.26.

The second prototype overlays the head with a white face containing two eyes and a mouth. All are drawn as Oval objects. The second prototype also includes just one leg, hoping to get the customer's reaction. The additional legs are easier to include once the desired leg form has been determined. For the final program, assume that the customer wants the following changes:

- The mouth should be turned up in a smile.
- The head must appear in front (not behind) the front body segment.
- Each leg needs a "foot" pointing forward.

Figure 3.27 contains the desired drawing.

The two most difficult tasks in reaching this final program are

- The mouth should be turned up in a smile.
- The head must appear in front (not behind) the front body segment.

Figure 3.25

Image produced by executing a second prototype for the caterpillar program

```
import java.awt.Color;
import javax.swing.JFrame;
public class Driver {
    private JFrame theWindow;
    private Oval head, frontSegment, midSegment, rearSegment;
    private Oval face, leftEye, rightEye, mouth;
    private Rectangle frontLeg;

    public Driver() {
        theWindow = new JFrame("The Pede");
        theWindow.setBounds(30, 30, 500, 250);
        theWindow.setLayout(null);
        theWindow.setVisible(true);
        head = new Oval(110, 70, 84, 84);
        theWindow.add(head, 0);
        face = new Oval(2, 2, 80, 80);
        face.setBackground(Color.white);
        head.add(face, 0);
        leftEye = new Oval(15, 30, 15, 10);
        leftEye. setBackground (Color.blue);
        face.add(leftEye, 0);
        rightEye = new Oval(50, 30, 15, 10);
        rightEye. setBackground (Color.blue);
        face.add(rightEye, 0);
        mouth = new Oval(25, 50, 30, 10);
        face.add(mouth, 0);
        mouth. setBackground (Color.red);
        frontSegment = new Oval(180, 100, 50, 50);
        theWindow.add(frontSegment, 0);
        frontLeg = new Rectangle(200, 150, 10, 20);
        theWindow.add(frontLeg, 0);
        midSegment = new Oval(230, 100, 50, 50);
        theWindow.add(midSegment, 0);
        rearSegment = new Oval(280, 100, 50, 50);
        theWindow.add(rearSegment, 0);
        theWindow.repaint();
    }
}
```

Figure 3.26

A second prototype for the caterpillar program

Turning the mouth into a smile is accomplished by creating an extra Oval. The initial Oval is a red mouth. A smile results from placing a white Oval on top of the red one. The following instruction sequence draws such a mouth:

Figure 3.27

The final
caterpillar
drawing

```
mouth = new Oval(25, 50, 30, 10);
mouth.setBackground(Color.red);
face.add(mouth, 0);
mouthCover = new Oval(0, 0, 30, 5);
mouthCover.setBackground(Color.white);
mouth.add(mouthCover, 0);
```

The easiest way to make the head cover the first body segment is to move the statement that adds `head` to `theWindow` so that it occurs sometime *after* the statement that adds `frontSegment`. The following order accomplishes the necessary task:

```
theWindow.add(frontSegment, 0);
theWindow.add(head, 0);
```

software *Hint*
engineering

Prototyping is an
efficient strategy
for a developer
to craft a working
program.

The caterpillar example illustrates that prototyping is useful for discovering requirements, but there are many other reasons for using prototyping. One reason is that prototyping assists with debugging. Since each prototype alters only a portion of the code, the most likely location to begin searching for the cause of an error is one of these alterations.

3.7 ■ Debugging: Commenting Out Code and Using System.out.println

Design by prototyping highlights the closely interconnected nature of the design, implementation, and testing activities. By definition, a prototyping strategy requires repeated design of implementation prototypes, each of which should be tested prior to proceeding to the next prototype.

Even the most careful programmers make errors. If those errors are syntactic, such as a misspelled variable identifier or a misplaced comma, then the compiler reports the error, and the programmer can make the necessary correction.

As mentioned in Chapter 1, logic errors do not generally involve bad syntax. Instead, a logic error is an incorrect algorithm that results from faulty thinking. Logic errors can be more difficult for a programmer to locate and correct because

- They are not manifest until runtime.
- They may or may not result in a reported error.
- They may not cause trouble for every program execution.

For example, suppose that the caterpillar program (discussed in the previous section) was rewritten so that leftEye is placed upon rearSegment, rather than face. This is not a syntax error because it is valid Java code to add one Oval (leftEye) to another Oval (rearSegment). Therefore, the Java compiler will not report any errors for this new program.

Logic errors, like the misplaced leftEye, are sometimes discovered when the program executes. There are two possible runtime manifestations of this particular error:

1. If the add method is called prior to constructing either leftEye or rearSegment, then a null pointer exception occurs.

2. If the add method is called after both leftEye and rearSegment are constructed, then the left eye image is drawn in the wrong location.

Debugging can be difficult because logic errors can take so many different forms. In addition, it is often difficult to associate the visible behavior of a logic error with its cause.

The first step in debugging logic errors is to **trace** the program to identify its cause. In a program trace, the programmer pretends to be the Java VM and executes the program. Each instruction is considered in the order that it would be executed by the VM, and as each is considered, the programmer records the result. (This record is typically a picture of the state of each program object.) Throughout this book there are examples of program traces, sometimes using pictures of the resulting graphical output (like the examples in this chapter), and sometimes using object diagrams (like Section 2.4).

Occasionally a logic error is so ornery that manual tracing does not help. In such cases, it is wise to seek additional information about the details of program behavior. If you use an IDE, you probably have access to a debugger. Debuggers are useful tools for discovering logic errors.

To illustrate logic errors and debugging issues consider the erroneous early prototype of the caterpillar program shown in Figure 3.28.

When this prototype executes, only one of the caterpillar's body segments is visible. The Resulting JFrame image is shown in Figure 3.29. Obviously, this prototype contains logic errors that result in an image without the middle and rear caterpillar body segments.

Figure 3.28

An erroneous prototype for the caterpillar program

```java
// This prototype contains two logic errors.
import java.awt.*;
import javax.swing.JFrame;

public class Driver {
    private JFrame theWindow;
    private Oval head, frontSegment, midSegment, rearSegment;

    public Driver() {
        theWindow = new JFrame("The Pede");
        theWindow.setBounds(10, 10, 500, 250);
        theWindow.setLayout(null);
        theWindow.setVisible(true);
        head = new Oval(110, 70, 80, 80);
        theWindow.add(head, 0);
        head.repaint();
        frontSegment = new Oval(180, 100, 50, 50);
        theWindow.add(frontSegment, 0);
        frontSegment.repaint();
        midSegment = new Oval(230, 100, 0, 50);
        theWindow.add(midSegment, 0);
        midSegment.repaint();
        rearSegment = new Oval(180, 100, 50, 50);
        theWindow.add(rearSegment, 0);
        rearSegment.repaint();
    }
}
```

Figure 3.29

theWindow displayed by Figure 3.28 prototype

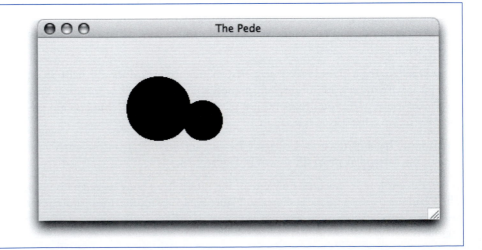

Apart from the use of an IDE debugger there are two other techniques that programmers can employ to modify code so that it might reveal its own logic errors.

1. **commenting out code**

2. injecting **System.out.println** instructions

The technique of commenting out code, as its name suggests, consists of modifying code by transforming one or more sections of the code into comments. In Java, a section of code can be turned into a comment by prefixing the section with /* and suffixing with */. The modified program is then recompiled and executed and its execution behavior is compared to other executions. Hopefully, the differences (or similarities) in program execution reveal the logic error.

The technique of commenting out code is particularly effective in narrowing down the location of a problem. For example, consider the erroneous prototype from Figure 3.28. A programmer might begin debugging by commenting out all of the code that is supposed to draw the middle and rear segments. The code below shows how to do this by turning the last six lines of the Driver constructor into a comment.

```
theWindow = new JFrame("The Pede");
theWindow.setBounds(10, 10, 500, 250);
theWindow.setLayout(null);
theWindow.setVisible(true);
head = new Oval(110, 70, 80, 80);
theWindow.add(head, 0);
head.repaint();
frontSegment = new Oval(180, 100, 50, 50);
theWindow.add(frontSegment, 0);
frontSegment.repaint();
/*
  midSegment = new Oval(230, 100, 0, 50);
  theWindow.add(midSegment, 0);
  midSegment.repaint();
  rearSegment = new Oval(180, 100, 50, 50);
  theWindow.add(rearSegment, 0);
  rearSegment.repaint();
*/
```

When the resulting program is compiled and executed, it behaves exactly like the Figure 3.29 prototype. This confirms that the head portion and first body segment are being drawn as expected by the Figure 3.28 code. This experiment also narrows down the source of the logic error to somewhere within the last six lines of code.

software *Hint*
engineering

Java does not support nested comments. In other words, you cannot include one /* ... */ comment within another because the first */ terminates the last /*.

When commenting out code, you need to take care to avoid commenting out a section of code that includes a comment using the /* .... */ notation.

As a second experiment, the body of `Driver` could be modified a second time as follows:

```
theWindow = new JFrame("The Pede");
theWindow.setBounds(10, 10, 500, 250);
theWindow.setLayout(null);
theWindow.setVisible(true);
head = new Oval(110, 70, 80, 80);
theWindow.add(head, 0);
head.repaint();
frontSegment = new Oval(180, 100, 50, 50);
theWindow.add(frontSegment, 0);
frontSegment.repaint();
midSegment = new Oval(230, 100, 0, 50);
theWindow.add(midSegment, 0);
midSegment.repaint();
/*
  rearSegment = new Oval(180, 100, 50, 50);
  theWindow.add(rearSegment, 0);
  rearSegment.repaint();
*/
```

This version of the prototype restores the three statements that are supposed to draw the middle segment of the caterpillar. However, when this code is compiled and executed there is no change from the preceding two executions. Clearly, the three statements that were restored to execution are not working, but what task do these three statements accomplish? This question might be answered with a third experiment that comments out the statements that draw the caterpillar's head and front segment, such as the following `Driver` code:

```
theWindow = new JFrame("The Pede");
theWindow.setBounds(10, 10, 500, 250);
theWindow.setLayout(null);
theWindow.setVisible(true);

/*
  head = new Oval(110, 70, 80, 80);
  theWindow.add(head, 0);
  head.repaint();
  frontSegment = new Oval(180, 100, 50, 50);
  theWindow.add(frontSegment, 0);
  frontSegment.repaint();
*/
midSegment = new Oval(230, 100, 0, 50);
theWindow.add(midSegment, 0);
midSegment.repaint();
```

```
/*
rearSegment = new Oval(180, 100, 50, 50);
theWindow.add(rearSegment, 0);
rearSegment.repaint();
*/
```

Executing this code results in a JFrame that displays nothing. This means that neither the head nor first body segment are obscuring the middle segment. This result should clue the programmer to focus on the three statements that create, add, and repaint the middle segment. Of course, the logic error is the third argument to the Oval constructor—a width of zero.

The second technique frequently employed by programmers that uses the program to assist with its own debugging, is to use a statement known as System.out.println. All Java objects support this method as a way to output objects' runtime state. System.out.println is a method call with a single parameter, and when it is called, the state of its argument is output to the **standard output stream**. When executing a program from a command line such as *Command Prompt* for Windows, *Terminal* for OS X, or a command shell for Unix, the standard output stream is the same window where commands are typed.

Three typical calls to System.out.println are shown below.

```
System.out.println(frontSegment);
System.out.println(midSegment);
System.out.println(rearSegment);
```

Suppose these three instructions are appended as the last instruction in the Driver class from Figure 3.28. When this modified prototype is executed, an example like the one shown in Figure 3.30 is displayed.

The three lines in Figure 3.30 that begin with "Oval" show the output that results, respectively, from the three System.out.println instructions. The first four numbers on each line give the *x, y, width,* and *height* for the oval at the time the instruction was executed. In this case, these instructions reveal that frontSegment and rearSegment have the same *x* values and the same *y* values, which is the reason that the rear segment is not properly located.

software *Hint*
engineering

Inserting System.out.println calls at key locations is helpful for observing runtime behavior and for debugging. Some programmers build these instructions into their program and prefix them with "//" to turn off the output when it is not needed. This technique of leaving these instructions as comments makes it easier to reactivate them for future debugging.

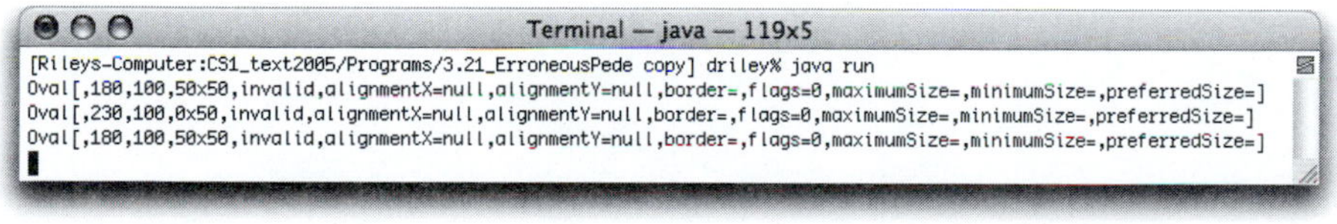

Figure 3.30

Terminal window

When `System.out.println` calls are "sprinkled" among program instructions, it is possible to observe changes in state that occur during program execution. This kind of output provides valuable trace information for debugging. These instructions should be removed or turned into comments for the production program.

Closed
Black Box

There are a couple of things that may seem odd about `System.out.println`. Its name is long and unusual. Furthermore, it is strange to have a method that accepts arguments of virtually any type. The reasons behind these features are explained in Chapters 9 and 15.

Inspector *Java*

Below is a collection of hints on what to check when examining code that involves the concepts of this chapter.

■ There are only two ways for your class to have access to other classes: These other classes are located within the same file folder as yours, or an `import` declaration is included at the top of your class.

■ If Color constants are used, then check for either

```
import java.awt.Color;
```

or

```
import java.awt.*;
```

■ When using the add command for container classes, remember that the placement is relative to the upper left corner of the background object, and not necessarily relative to the window or the computer display.

■ A frequent problem when using graphics is that some graphical object does not appear at runtime. Below is a checklist of probable reasons. They should be checked in the order they are listed.

1. The program terminated with a runtime error prior to adding the object.

2. The object was never added.

3. The object was added, but not repainted. (Calling repaint is not always needed, but it is not harmful.)

4. The object is located outside the boundaries of its underlying background.

5. The object is covered up by another object.

6. The Java VM is having difficulty updating the window. (This is a remote possibility, but it happens with certain operating systems, complicated graphics, and/or graphics that overlap boundaries.) Sometimes resizing a Java window will cause it to redraw properly.

Terminology

java (library of standard classes)

javax (library of standard classes)

`java.awt`

`javax.swing`

AWT

Color

clipping

commenting out code

computer display (screen)

JFrame (`javax.swing.Frame`)

graphical user interface	relative coordinates
GUI	standard output stream
implementation	`System.out.println`
import declaration	*Swing*
`Label` (`java.awt.Label`)	trace
null layout manager	user
pixel	window
prototype	

Exercises

1. Top-down design and prototyping provide techniques for progressing gradually toward a final program. However, they do so in different ways. Identify each of the following statements as either a top-down concept or a prototyping concept.

   a. Writing a research paper beginning with an outline is similar to this design technique.

   b. This technique can be described as somewhat like "trial and error."

   c. This technique is better suited to an ongoing involvement from the customer(s).

   d. The very first version of the code might be the last using this technique.

2. A class diagram (shown below) and class specifications (on the next page) for a class called `AlarmClock`. Using this class show how to perform a prototype design of a program to set two alarm clocks. One alarm should be set for 5 o'clock and the other for 4:32.

AlarmClock
– int *hour* – int *minute*
«constructor»   + **AlarmClock**()

«update»
  + void **advanceOneHour**()
  + void **advanceOneMinute**()
  + void **advanceTenMinutes**()

Invariant

An AlarmClock object...

- keeps track of a single alarm time in terms of *hour* and *minute*
- cannot distinguish between A.M. and P.M. times
- has attribute values restricted to the following ranges:
  $1 \leq hour \leq 12$ **and** $0 \leq minute \leq 59$

Constructor Method

public **AlarmClock**()

> **post:** A new AlarmClock object is created with attributes as follows:
> *hour* == 1 **and** *minute* == 0

Update Methods

public void **advanceOneHour**()

> **pre:** *hour* < 12

> **post:** The value of *hour* is one unit greater than before this method was called.

public void **advanceOneMinute**()

> **pre:** *minute* < 59

> **post:** The value of *minute* is one unit greater than before this method was called.

public void **advanceTenMinute**()

> **pre:** *minute* < 50

> **post:** The value of *minute* is 10 units greater than before this method was called.

3. ```
private JFrame window;
private Rectangle rectA, rectB;
private Oval oval, circle;
```

Using the instance variable declarations above, sketch the images or output that result from executing each of the following segments of code.

a. ```
window = new JFrame();
window.setBounds(10, 10, 200, 100);
window.setVisible(true);
window.setLayout(null);
rectA = new Rectangle(50, 20, 100, 30);
rectA.setBackground(Color.black);
window.add(rectA, 0);
```

```
   rectB = new Rectangle(50, 60, 5, 30);
   rectB.setBackground(Color.gray);
   window.add(rectB, 0);
   window.repaint();

b. window = new JFrame();
   window.setBounds(10, 10, 200, 100);
   window.setVisible(true);
   window.setLayout(null);
   rectA = new Rectangle(20, 10, 100, 30);
   rectA.setBackground(Color.black);
   window.add(rectA, 0);
   rectB = new Rectangle(50, 60, 5, 10);
   rectB.setBackground(Color.white);
   window.add(rectB, 0);
   window.repaint();

c. window = new JFrame();
   window.setBounds(10, 10, 200, 100);
   window.setVisible(true);
   window.setLayout(null);
   rectA = new Rectangle(50, 20, 200, 30);
   rectA.setBackground(Color.green);
   window.add(rectA, 0);
   rectB = new Rectangle(50, 60, 10, 100);
   rectB.setBackground(Color.blue);
   rectA.add(rectB, 0);
   circle = new Oval(0, 0, 20, 20);
   circle.setBackground(Color.red);
   rectB.add(circle, 0);
   oval = new Oval(160, 50, 100, 40);
   oval.setBackground(Color.yellow);
   window.add(oval, 0);
   window.repaint();

d. window = new JFrame();
   window.setBounds(10, 10, 200, 100);
   window.setVisible(true);
   window.setLayout(null);
   oval = new Oval(10, 10, 50, 50);
   window.add(oval, 0);
   oval = new Oval(20, 20, 50, 50);
   window.add(oval, 0);
   oval = new Oval(30, 30, 50, 50);
   window.add(oval, 0);
   window.repaint();
```

e.
```
window = new JFrame();
window.setBounds(10, 10, 200, 100);
window.setVisible(true);
window.setLayout(null);
oval = new Oval(10, 10, 50, 50);
rectangle = new Rectangle(20, 20, 70, 70);
rectangle.setBackground(Color.red);
rectangle.add(oval, 0);
window.add(oval, 0);
window.repaint();
```

f.
```
window = new JFrame();
window.setBounds(10, 10, 200, 100);
window.setVisible(true);
window.setLayout(null);
oval = new Oval(10, 10, 50, 50);
window.repaint();
```

g.
```
window = new JFrame();
window.setBounds(10, 10, 200, 100);
window.setVisible(true);
window.setLayout(null);
oval = new Oval(10, 10, 50, 50);
window.add(oval, 0);
window.add(oval, 0);
window.repaint();
```

h.
```
window = new JFrame();
window.setBounds(10, 10, 200, 100);
window.setVisible(true);
window.setLayout(null);
oval = new Oval(10, 10, 50, 50);
window.add(oval, 0);
oval.setSize(100, 25);
oval.setLocation(50, 20);
window.repaint();
```

i.
```
window = new JFrame();
window.setBounds(10, 10, 200, 100);
window.setVisible(true);
window.setLayout(null);
oval = new Oval(10, 10, 50, 50);
window.add(oval, 0);
System.out.println(window);
System.out.println(oval);
```

Programming Exercises

1. Write a program that produces a window with the following image. The face is yellow on a black background. The mouth is red. The eyes are black.

2. Write a program that produces a window with the following image. The pattern is blue on a white background.

3. Write a program that produces a window with the following image. The snake eye has a blue pointed iris and a small black slit for a pupil. The background of the window is gray.

Methods

*Though this be madness,
yet there is method in 't.*

—William Shakespeare

Objectives

- To examine the need to partition large algorithms into subprograms
- To explore the syntax and semantics of private methods
- To examine the concept of parameter passage
- To introduce non-void methods
- To present local variables in support of objects needed only within one method
- To introduce event handling and a `ThreeButtons` class for simple button handling
- To introduce result and previous value notations for expressing postconditions

Methods are the code repositories of an object-oriented program. Prior chapters have shown how programmers use external classes and call preexisting methods. This chapter explores how methods are written and called within the same class.

4.1 ■ The Need for a Subprogram

software *Hint*
engineering
Programmers
decompose their
code into subpro-
grams because
shorter segments
of code are easi-
er to implement,
debug, and read.
A good rule of
thumb is to divide
code into pieces
that fit on one
computer screen
or less.

Novels are written in chapters. Manuals are divided into sections. A television miniseries is shown in episodes. Whether by chapter, section, or episode, humans seem to prefer to have their information partitioned into segments. Therefore, it is not surprising that good computer programs are subdivided into smaller portions.

Historically, computer programs have been constructed from **subprograms**. Each subprogram performs some portion of the complete task of the program. More important, each subprogram can be designed, implemented, and tested as a separate entity. The use of subprograms is, therefore, an effective way to partition a lengthy algorithm into smaller modules.

A method is a subprogram. When code becomes long or repetitive, it is often helpful to be able to decompose the task into separate methods. Such decomposition has the effect of modularizing code into smaller pieces that are easier to write and read. As an example, consider writing a program to make a backup copy of an audio compact disk. Figure 4.1 explains background information on compact disks.

For this program, it is necessary to assume that the computer running the program will have two CD drives, at least one of which is capable of burning CDs. Figure 4.2 contains an algorithm designed to copy one audio CD that contains eight tracks (songs) onto another.

software *Hint*
engineering
If the same task
is repeated sev-
eral times, it is a
likely candidate
to become a sub-
program. One
such example is
found in Steps 3
through 9 of
Figure 4.2.

Even though there are nine steps in the algorithm for copying the 8-track CD, there appear to be just three different tasks. The first step of the algorithm is unique, and represents one task. The second step copies the first track of the source CD onto the destination CD. The last seven steps are all identical, so they represent the same task being performed seven times. These three different tasks are potential candidates for individual subprograms (methods).

Figure 4.3 contains a partial program for this algorithm. The Figure 4.3 program is missing the subprograms indicated by the nine numbered comments within the code.

The `Driver` class in Figure 4.3 includes the declarations for two instance variables: `sourceCD` and `destinationCD`. The designer of this program decided to refine the first step of the algorithm into two Java instructions that instantiate `sourceCD` and

Figure 4.1

Information about compact disks

Compact disks, also known as CDs, are flat plates of plastic that can store various types of data. An audio CD is a CD that stores data representing sound (usually music). A CD player spins the CD under a beam of light and a sensor detects the associated reflections. Sensing the reflected light beam is called reading the disk's data.

The audio data on the disk is stored in groups, known as **tracks**. One track generally corresponds to a separate song. The tracks are arranged in concentric circles from the inside of the CD outward, as shown in the picture below.

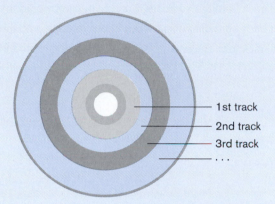

There are three kinds of devices (drives) capable of reading CDs; they are called CD-ROM, CD-R, and CD-RW. Two of these devices (CD-R and CD-RW drives) can also write new data onto the proper types of compact disks. The process of writing to a CD is called burning.

destinationCD. Such instructions rely upon a fictional class called CDdrive,[1] described by the following class diagram.

```
┌─────────────────────────────────────┐
│             CDdrive                 │
├─────────────────────────────────────┤
│                                     │
├─────────────────────────────────────┤
│  «constructor»                      │
│     + CDdrive()                     │
│                                     │
│  «update»                           │
│     + void setToFirstTrack()        │
│     + void advanceToNextTrack()     │
│     + void readTrackIntoBuffer()    │
│     + void burnTrackFromBuffer()    │
└─────────────────────────────────────┘
```

---

1. CDdrive is a class invented for this example and not a part of the software supplied with this text.

Figure 4.2

Algorithm for copying an 8-track CD

Step

1. Initialize both the source CD drive and the destination CD drive.
2. Read the first track from the source CD and burn a copy onto the destination CD.
3. Read the next track from the source CD and burn a copy onto the destination CD.
4. Read the next track from the source CD and burn a copy onto the destination CD.
5. Read the next track from the source CD and burn a copy onto the destination CD.
6. Read the next track from the source CD and burn a copy onto the destination CD.
7. Read the next track from the source CD and burn a copy onto the destination CD.
8. Read the next track from the source CD and burn a copy onto the destination CD.
9. Read the next track from the source CD and burn a copy onto the destination CD.

Figure 4.3

Partial Driver to copy an 8-track CD

```java
public class Driver {
    private CDdrive sourceCD;
    private CDdrive destinationCD;

    /** post: destinationCD has the a copy of the 1st eight
     *         tracks from sourceCD
     */
    public Driver() {
        sourceCD = new CDdrive();
        destinationCD = new CDdrive();
        // 2) Copy first track from sourceCD to destinationCD
        // 3) Copy the next track from sourceCD to destinationCD
        // 4) Copy the next track from sourceCD to destinationCD
        // 5) Copy the next track from sourceCD to destinationCD
        // 6) Copy the next track from sourceCD to destinationCD
        // 7) Copy the next track from sourceCD to destinationCD
        // 8) Copy the next track from sourceCD to destinationCD
        // 9) Copy the next track from sourceCD to destinationCD
    }
}
```

The CDdrive class contains a method to instantiate an object (CDdrive), a method to position the read/burn mechanism at the first track (setToFirstTrack), and a method to advance the read/burn mechanism from one track to the next (advanceToNextTrack).

The readTrackIntoBuffer method is designed to read data from the current track, and the burnTrackFromBuffer is designed to burn data to the current track. Both readTrackIntoBuffer and burnTrackFromBuffer make use of a reserved segment of computer memory called a **buffer**. Executing `readTrackIntoBuffer` causes this buffer to receive a copy of the current track from the CD drive. Executing `burnTrackFromBuffer` causes whatever track was last placed into the buffer to be burned onto the current track of the CD.

4.2 ■ Private Parameterless Methods

Java subprograms take the form of methods. Figure 4.4 describes the kind of method that can be used to accomplish the necessary subprogram tasks needed for the CD copying program. This particular version of method is called **private**, because it is called only within its class.

From Figure 4.4 it is evident that private methods have a syntax that is similar to the `Driver` constructor method. The differences are

- the `private` prefix
- a `void` qualifier before the class name
- a method name other than `Driver`

| **Figure 4.4** | ***PrivateVoidParameterlessMethod*** description (abridged version of *PrivateMethod*) |

Syntax

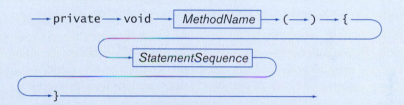

Semantics

When this method is called, the *StatementSequence* code is executed.

Note

MethodName is an identifier. Each parameterless method within the same class must have a unique name.

Style Notes

- The line beginning with `private` and ending with "{" should be on a single line and one tab setting inside the containing class. The final "}" symbol should also be aligned directly under `private`.
- All *StatementSequence* instructions should be indented at least one tab inside private.
- *MethodName* should be an action verb or a verb phrase.
- Precondition and postcondition clauses are a good inclusion in each method.

Closed

Black Box

In Java, the `private` and `public` prefixes are important, but they may seem confusing to a novice programmer. The following rules are sufficient for now.

1. The `Driver` class is `public`.

2. The `Driver` constructor method is `public`.

3. `leftAction`, `midAction`, and `rightAction` (see Section 4.8) are `public`.

4. Everything else is `private`. This includes all nonconstructor methods and all instance variables within the `Driver` class.

Chapter 6 will clarify the meaning of these declarations, and explain in more detail how to select between `public` and `private`.

software *Hint*

engineering

The selection of the name of a method deserves care. The name should reflect the task that the method performs. It helps to use action verbs or verb phrases for void methods.

Below is an example private method that can be used in the CD copy program as the subprogram to advance both drives by one track, then copy the new track from `sourceCD` to `destinationCD`.

```
private void copyNextTrack() {
    sourceCD.advanceToNextTrack();
    destinationCD.advanceToNextTrack();
    sourceCD.readTrackIntoBuffer();
    destinationCD.burnTrackFromBuffer();
}
```

The code between the initial "{" and last "}" symbols of a method is often called the method **body**. Every method body consists of a sequence of statements (instructions). The body of `copyNextTrack` contains four instructions.

A private method executes in response to a **method call** (or **method invocation**), instruction. When a method is called, its body executes. Following the method body execution, the method is said to **return** to the location of the call. Figure 4.5 shows the syntax for calling a private parameterless method.

All methods that are members of the same class are accessible throughout that class. As Figure 4.5 indicates, the syntax for calling a method within the same class is different from calling external methods; there is no object prefix required within the same class. For example, the `Driver` class simply includes the following instruction in order to call the `copyNextTrack` method:

```
copyNextTrack();
```

The execution of the call instruction above behaves as if the body of the `copyNextTrack` method were substituted in its place.

This runtime behavior of a method call can be pictured in the form of an **activity diagram** (another Unified Modeling Language diagram form). Activity diagrams show the sequence of activities or actions that occur at runtime. Figure 4.6 contains an excerpt of code that calls `copyNextTrack`, along with an activity diagram to illus-

Figure 4.5	***PrivateVoidParameterlessMethodCall*** description (abridged version of *MethodCall* and a possible *OneStatement*)

Syntax

Notes

- *MethodName* is the name of a nonconstructor method from the same class as this call.
- No separators are permitted before or after the period.

Semantics

Executing *PrivateVoidParameterlessMethodCall* causes the method to be executed.

Figure 4.6	Activity diagram for calling copyNextTrack

Code Excerpt (from the Driver class)

```
. . .
// Instruction before the call
copyNextTrack();
// Instruction after the call
. . .
```

Activity Diagram

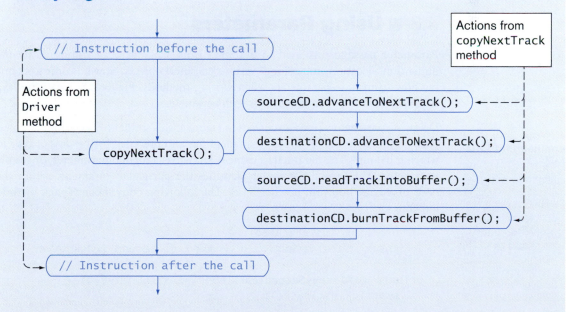

trate how this code executes. The action boxes (rectangles with rounded sides) on the left represent the execution of instructions from the `Driver` method, and the actions on the right represent the body of `copyNextTrack`. This figure demonstrates that executing the call instruction causes the body of the method to execute followed by a return to the code following the call.

The complete program for copying an 8-track CD is shown in Figure 4.7. This class contains three methods—the `Driver` constructor and two `private` methods. When `Driver` executes, it instantiates both `CDdrive` variables, then calls the `copyFirstTrack` method. Following the return from this first call, the `Driver` method proceeds to call the `copyNextTrack` method seven times in succession, thereby copying the remaining seven tracks.

Figure 4.7 also illustrates the use of specifications (in comment form) for private methods. Each of the three methods includes an appropriate set of *precondition* (pre) and *postcondition* (post) clauses. The use of these specifications demonstrates how each method can be thought of as a self-contained algorithm (a subprogram) that is part of the complete solution.

It should be noted that the 8-track CD copy problem can be solved by other programs that do *not* contain `private` methods. The most obvious such program results from replacing each call of a `private` method with the body of that method. The resulting `Driver` method is over 30 instructions long, which is probably acceptable. However, the `private` methods, as shown in Figure 4.7, do a better job of clearly delineating and explaining the subalgorithms; they are easier to read, and easier to modify. For larger programs, the advantage of using `private` methods becomes even more obvious.

4.3 ■ Using Parameters

Parameter passage was used in examples from Chapter 3 to communicate the dimensions, location, and color of various graphical objects. Now it is time to examine how to include parameters when writing methods. Figure 4.8 shows the Java requirements for `private` methods with parameters.

software *Hint*
engineering

Methods are subprograms within classes, so their formatting style parallels that of a class. Their bodies should be indented from the surrounding curly braces.

Declaring parameters (see *ParamDecls* in Figure 4.8) is similar to declaring variables. Each parameter must be named by an identifier and preceded by the class or type to which it belongs. The parameter's name is known as a **formal parameter**, or simply **parameter**. The formal parameter identifies the particular parameter within the body of the method (but nowhere else). The following `copySecondTrack` method illustrates.

```
/** pre:   s instantiated and d instantiated
 * post:  first track of d == copy of second track of s
 */
private void copySecondTrack(CDdrive s, CDdrive d) {
   s.setToFirstTrack();
```

```
public class Driver {
    private CDdrive sourceCD;
    private CDdrive destinationCD;

    /** post:  destinationCD has a copy of the 1st eight tracks
     *         from sourceCD
     */
    public Driver() {
        sourceCD = new CDdrive();
        destinationCD = new CDdrive();
        copyFirstTrack();
        copyNextTrack();
        copyNextTrack();
        copyNextTrack();
        copyNextTrack();
        copyNextTrack();
        copyNextTrack();
        copyNextTrack();
    }

    /** pre:   sourceCD instantiated and destinationCD instantiated
     * post:   sourceCD positioned at first track
     *         and destinationCD positioned at first track
     *         and 1st track of destinationCD == 1st track of
     *             sourceCD
     */
    private void copyFirstTrack() {
        sourceCD.setToFirstTrack();
        destinationCD.setToFirstTrack();
        sourceCD.readTrackIntoBuffer();
        destinationCD.burnTrackFromBuffer();
    }

    /** pre:   sourceCD instantiated and destinationCD instantiated
     * post:   sourceCD positioned at next track (from time of
     *         call) and destinationCD positioned at next track
     *         and current track of destinationCD == current
     *         track of sourceCD
     */
    private void copyNextTrack() {
        sourceCD.advanceToNextTrack();
        destinationCD.advanceToNextTrack();
        sourceCD.readTrackIntoBuffer();
        destinationCD.burnTrackFromBuffer();
    }
}
```

Figure 4.7

Program to copy an 8-track CD

Figure 4.8   *PrivateMethod* and *ParamDecls* description

PrivateMethod Syntax

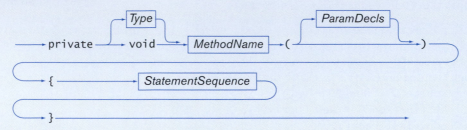

ParamDecls Syntax

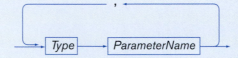

Semantics

When this method is called, each *ParameterName* is assigned its corresponding argument. Then the *StatementSequence* code is executed.

Notes

- *MethodName* is an identifier. Each method within the same class must either have a unique name or a different number and/or types of parameters.

- *ParameterName* is an identifier that identifies the formal parameter.

- *Type* can be any accessible class name or Java primitive type.

- The use of *Type*, rather than `void`, in a private method is described in Section 4.5.

Style Notes

- The line beginning with `private` should be one tab setting inside the containing class. The final "}" symbol should also be aligned directly under `private`.

- The initial "{" should be on the end of the first line of the method, or directly underneath `private` (in the event that there is no room on the first line).

- All *StatementSequence* instructions should be indented at least one tab inside `private`.

- If void is used, then *MethodName* should be a verb or a verb phrase. Otherwise, it should be a noun or noun phrase.

- Precondition and postcondition clauses are good inclusions in each method.

```
      s.advanceToNextTrack();
      s.readTrackIntoBuffer();
      d.setToFirstTrack();
      d.writeTrackFromBuffer();
   }
```

The copySecondTrack method has two formal parameters: s and d. Both parameters belong to the CDdrive class. When this method executes, s and d are assigned their corresponding arguments. Consider the execution of the following method call:

```
   copySecondTrack(sourceCD, destinationCD);
```

At the time this method is called, the parameter passage behavior is equivalent to executing these two instructions.

```
   s = sourceCD;
   d = destinationCD;
```

The resulting execution of the copySecondTrack body burns a copy of the second track from s, which is an alias for sourceCD, onto the first track of d, an alias for destinationCD. If a different call, like the following, is used, then the association of formal parameter to argument is different:

```
   copySecondTrack(sourceCD, blankCD);
```

During the execution of this new call instruction, s is assigned sourceCD as before, but d is assigned blankCD. This has the effect of copying from sourceCD onto blankCD.

Formal parameters are eliminated (but not necessarily the corresponding arguments) following each method execution. Therefore, parameters cannot be used outside their method, and calling the same method multiple times results in new argument assignments every time with no lingering formal parameter values from previous calls.

As a second example of parameter passage, consider the following colorAndAdd method. This method uses the Rectangle and Color classes described in Chapter 3.

```
/** pre:    theWindow has been instantiated
  *         and r has been instantiated
  *         and c is a valid Color
  * post:   r is set to color c
  *         and r is added to theWindow
  */
private void colorAndAdd(Rectangle r, Color c) {
   r.setBackground(c);
   theWindow.add(r, 0);
   r.repaint();
}
```

The `colorAndAdd` method has two formal parameters with different types. The first parameter is a `Rectangle` named `r` and the second parameter is a `Color` (`java.awt.Color`) named `c`. Figure 4.9 shows the execution of the following method call with three object diagrams. This figure contains an activity diagram followed by three snapshots of the state of computation. These snapshots take place just before, during, and just after the execution of the method that is initiated by the following call:

```
colorAndAdd(rectangle, Color.green);
```

Prior to executing `colorAndAdd` there are three relevant objects: a `Rectangle` object named `rectangle`, a `JFrame` object named `theWindow`, and a `Color.green` object. When `colorAndAdd` is called, the two arguments from the call instruction are assigned to the corresponding formal parameters as if the following instructions were executed:

```
r = rectangle;
c = Color.green;
```

Figure 4.9 illustrates the resulting situation by showing that the first parameter (`r`) is bound to the `rectangle` object and the second parameter (`c`) is bound to the `Color.green` object. The resulting execution of the method's second instruction

```
r.setBackground(c);
```

> **software engineering** *Hint*
>
> The code example pictured in Figure 4.9 includes a variable called rectangle. It is a common practice to use variable names that are similar to the name of the class to which they belong. The convention of using a lowercase letter at the beginning of a variable and an uppercase letter at the beginning of a class avoids conflicts, even when the same name is used for a variable and its class.

causes `rectangle` to be colored green because both `r` and `rectangle` are bound to the same object. The formal parameters are destroyed when the method returns, so they have been removed from the final snapshot in Figure 4.9.

Figure 4.10 contains a program that uses the `colorAndFill` method to draw a window containing three blue squares, as shown in Figure 4.11. This program includes three call instructions like the one just explained.

Parameter passage adds pliability to a method because the same method can be applied to different arguments. The `colorAndAdd` method is applied to three different `Rectangle` objects in the three squares program.

4.4 ■ Local Variables

Methods are truly subprograms in the sense that each method has its own environment. Each method has its own

- name
- executable body of instructions
- formal parameters

Figure 4.9   Objects before, during, and after calling `colorAndAdd`

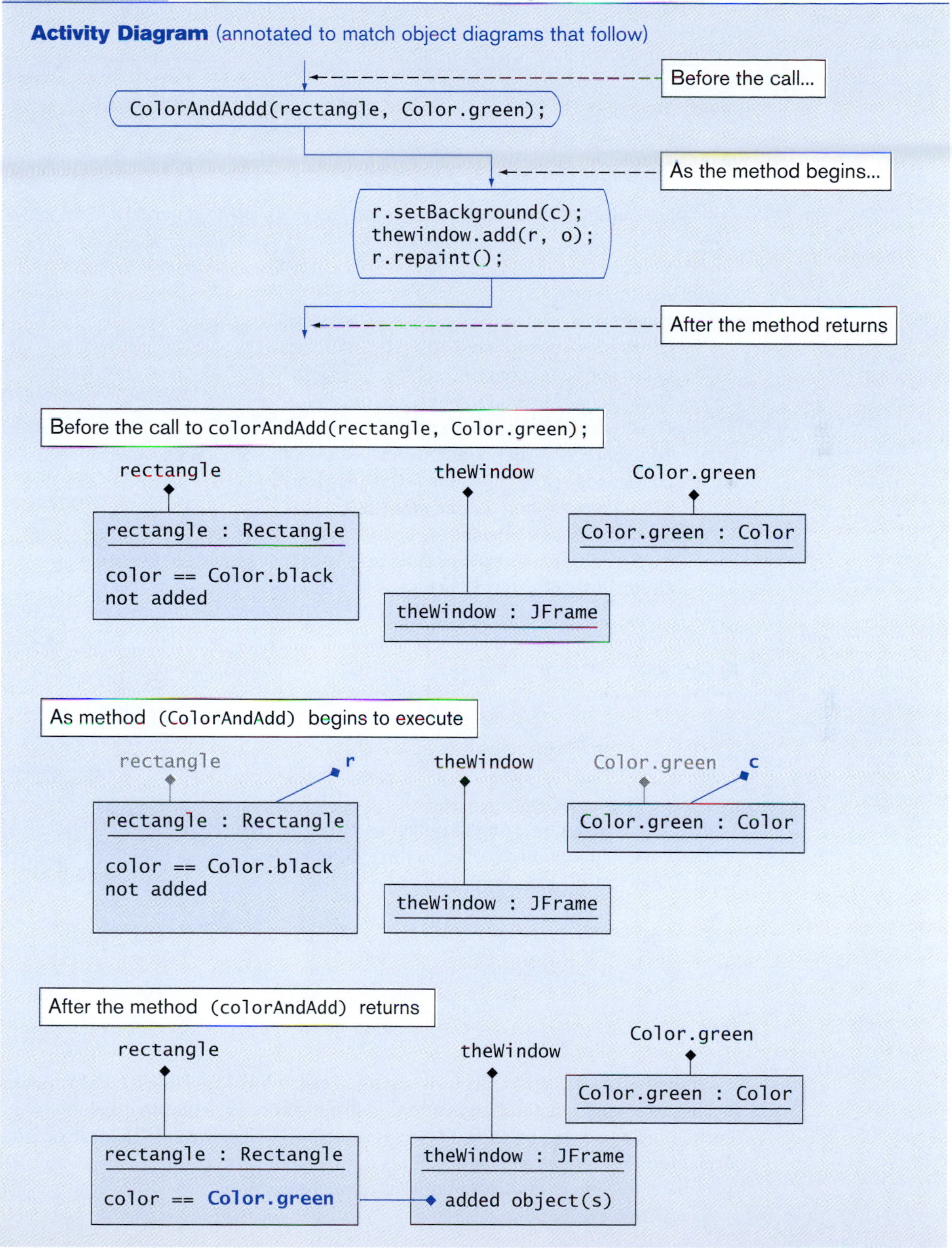

Activity Diagram (annotated to match object diagrams that follow)

```
ColorAndAddd(rectangle, Color.green);  ⊣------------------  Before the call...

                          r.setBackground(c);  ⊣-----------  As the method begins...
                          thewindow.add(r, o);
                          r.repaint();

                                              ⊣------------  After the method returns
```

Before the call to `colorAndAdd(rectangle, Color.green);`

```
        rectangle              theWindow              Color.green

   rectangle : Rectangle                         Color.green : Color

   color == Color.black
   not added
                            theWindow : JFrame
```

As method (`ColorAndAdd`) begins to execute

```
        rectangle        r     theWindow         Color.green    c

   rectangle : Rectangle                     Color.green : Color

   color == Color.black
   not added
                          theWindow : JFrame
```

After the method (`colorAndAdd`) returns

```
        rectangle              theWindow              Color.green

                                              Color.green : Color

   rectangle : Rectangle    theWindow : JFrame

   color == Color.green   ◆ added object(s)
```

Figure 4.10

Three squares
program

```java
/** Three Squares Program
 *      Author: David Riley
 *      Date: January 2005
 */
import java.awt.*;
import javax.swing.JFrame;
public class Driver {
    private JFrame theWindow;
    private Rectangle leftSquare, midSquare, rightSquare;

    /** post:  a window with three blue filled squares is drawn */
    public Driver() {
        theWindow = new JFrame("The Window");
        theWindow.setBounds(10, 10, 450, 250);
        theWindow.setLayout(null);
        theWindow.setBackground(Color.white);
        theWindow.setVisible(true);
        leftSquare = new Rectangle(100, 100, 50, 50);
        colorAndAdd(leftSquare, Color.blue);
        midSquare = new Rectangle(200, 100, 50, 50);
        colorAndAdd(midSquare, Color.blue);
        rightSquare = new Rectangle(300, 100, 50, 50);
        colorAndAdd(rightSquare, Color.blue);
    }

    /** pre:    theWindow has been instantiated
     *          and r has been instantiated
     *          and c is a valid Color
     *   post:  r is set to color c
     *          and r is added to theWindow
     */
    private void colorAndAdd(Rectangle r, Color c) {
        r.setBackground(c);
        theWindow.add(r, 0);
        r.repaint();
    }
}
```

Each method can also have its own variables, called **local variables**. Local variables belong to a single method's execution, unlike instance variables that belong to the entire object and can be shared by several methods. The syntax of a local variable declaration (described in Figure 4.12) is similar to the syntax for declaring a formal parameter, together with the optional assignment portion.

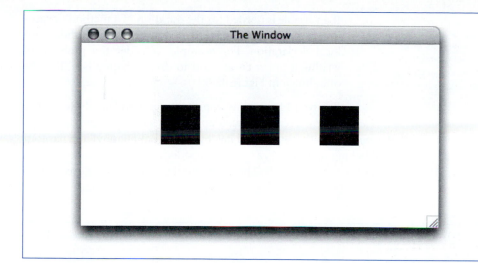

Figure 4.11

Image produced by executing the program in Figure 4.10

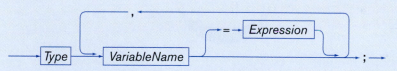

Figure 4.12

LocalVariableDecl description

Syntax

Semantics

- Executing *LocalVariableDecl* causes each *VariableName* to begin its lifetime. (The lifetime ends when the method returns.)
- If the optional = *Expression* syntax is used, then *Expression* is evaluated and the result is assigned to *VariableName*. If = *Expression* is not included, then *VariableName* is assigned a default value (null for objects).
- The lifetime of *VariableName* ends with the completion of execution of its method.

Notes

- The type of *Expression* must conform to *Type*.
- *Type* can be any accessible class name or primitive type.

Style Notes

- Local variable declarations are best placed immediately after "{".
- Local variable naming conventions should follow the same style as instance variable naming.

software
engineering *Hint*

Local variables are best suited to situations in which the need for an object is restricted to the execution of a method. Local variables are the preferred alternative to instance variables, whenever both would work.

If a variable is needed for the duration of a method's execution only, then that variable is an obvious candidate for local declaration. For example, consider the problem of writing a `private` method to draw a happy face, like the one shown in Figure 4.13.

Figure 4.14 contains a `private` method to draw such a happy face. This `makeHappyFace` method requires a single parameter that is an `Oval` with a width and height of 100. `makeHappyFace` has four local variables, all belonging to the `Oval` class. These local variables are declared in the first statement of the method body. Thereafter, local variables can be used within

Figure 4.13

A happy face image

Figure 4.14

makeHappyFace method

```
/** pre:   f has been constructed with a radius of 100
 *  post:  f is colored yellow
 *         and two black eyes are added to f
 *         and a black smile is added to f
 */
private void makeHappyFace(Oval f) {
    Oval leftEye, rightEye, mouth, mouthCover;
    f.setBackground(Color.yellow);
    mouth = new Oval(20, 20, 60, 60);
    f.add(mouth, 0);
    mouthCover = new Oval(-10, -30, 80, 80);
    mouthCover.setBackground(Color.yellow);
    mouth.add(mouthCover, 0);
    leftEye = new Oval(20, 30, 15, 15);
    f.add(leftEye, 0);
    rightEye = new Oval(65, 30, 15, 15);
    f.add(rightEye, 0);
}
```

the method's body in the same way as instance variables. The lifetime of the four local variables comes to an end when makeHappyFace completes its execution. Fortunately, the images that are produced by the variables remain, because they have been added. (Recall that the add command binds the graphical object to the container object to which it is added.)

software *Hint*
engineering

Methods are an effective means for shortening the overall program when repetitive tasks are involved. For example, the program in Figure 4.15 draws four happy faces by calling makeHappyFace four times, as opposed to having four similar copies of the code.

Private methods are particularly helpful for applying the same operation to different objects by passing each object as an argument in a separate method call. Figure 4.15 illustrates with a method to create a window with four happy faces. Each of the four calls to the makeHappyFace method passes a different Oval object.

One difference between local variables and instance variables is that each method call creates a *new set* of the method's local variables. These local variables are available to the method throughout the remainder of its execution, and the variable names cease to exist once the method returns. As a result, the execution of the Driver method, shown in Figure 4.16, is four separate happy faces with four separate left eyes, four separate right eyes, and four separate mouths.

```java
/** post: a window with four happy faces is drawn */
public Driver() {
    theWindow = new JFrame("The Window");
    theWindow.setBounds(10, 10, 250, 250);
    theWindow.setLayout(null);
    theWindow.setBackground(Color.white);
    theWindow.setVisible(true);
    topLeftFace = new Oval(30, 10, 100, 100);
    makeHappyFace(topLeftFace);
    theWindow.add(topLeftFace, 0);
    topLeftFace.repaint();
    topRightFace = new Oval(140, 10, 100, 100);
    makeHappyFace(topRightFace);
    theWindow.add(topRightFace, 0);
    topRightFace.repaint();
    botLeftFace = new Oval(30, 120, 100, 100);
    makeHappyFace(botLeftFace);
    theWindow.add(botLeftFace, 0);
    botLeftFace.repaint();
    botRightFace = new Oval(140, 120, 100, 100);
    makeHappyFace(botRightFace);
    theWindow.add(botRightFace, 0);
    botRightFace.repaint();
}
```

Figure 4.15

Driver to make four happy faces

Figure 4.16

Image produced by executing the program in Figure 4.15

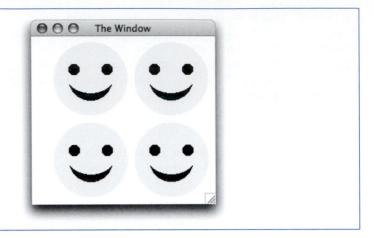

4.5 ■ Non-Void Methods

Java supports three categories of method: void, non-void, and constructor. Often void methods are labeled as *update* or *mutator* because when a void method is applied to an object the intent is to change (mutate) the object in some way. Constructor methods are different in the sense that they create the object. As we shall see in this section, non-void methods play a third role.

Earlier in the book, calling a method was described as sending a message. One object (sometimes referred to as the "caller object") sends a message to another object (the "called object"). The called object executes its method body and then returns to the caller. For void methods, the purpose of the caller is usually to update or mutate the target of the called object. Parameter passage provides a mechanism for the caller to share objects (arguments). For example, in order for the makeHappyFace method to place a mouth upon a face object, it sends the following add message to the f (face) object.

```
f.add(mouth, 0);
```

Java's style of parameter passage is a one-way form of communication in the sense that the caller's actual arguments are assigned to the called object's formal parameters, but the called object cannot alter the binding of any argument. This restriction means that the execution of the above add method cannot alter the mouth object by virtue of this parameter. The advantage to the caller is that the argument object is protected from rebinding.

Figure 4.17 illustrates the outcome of an attempt to rebind a parameter. When testReturn is called, it is passed an argument (oneOval) that is null. The execution of the testReturn method constructs a new object and binds the formal parameter a to the newly constructed object. However, this new binding has no effect upon oneOval, which is still null. Executing this program results in a run-

```
/* This program is a vain attempt to return
 * a new object via parameter passage.
 */
import java.awt.*;
public class Driver {
    private JFrame window;
    private Oval oneOval;

    public Driver() {
        JFrame window = new JFrame("the window");
        window.setBounds(10, 10, 500, 400);
        window.setLayout(null);
        window.setVisible(true);
        testReturn(oneOval);
        window.add(oneOval, 0);          // This line fails.
    }

    private void testReturn(Oval a) {
        a = new Oval(10, 10, 20, 20);    //This line is useless.
    }
}
```

Figure 4.17

Erroneous attempt to return an object via a parameter

time error, because oneOval is still null when the add instruction executes in the Driver constructor.

Java's style of parameter passage prohibits passing rebound information back to the caller. However, the language includes a different mechanism that permits methods to return data. Such a method is called a **non-void** method. The name non-void method stems from a syntax that replaces the "void" with the method's return type (i.e., the name of the type/class for the object to be returned). A non-void method returns a single object for each call.

Below is an example non-void method. The placement of the Oval identifier just after private signifies that redDot is a non-void method to return an object of type Oval. Executing redDot causes a new Oval object, called dot, to be instantiated. The method causes dot to be colored red.

> software engineering *Hint*
>
> Identifiers that represent nouns or noun phrases are best for naming non-void methods.

```
private Oval redDot() {
    Oval dot;
    dot = new Oval(0, 0, 20, 20);
    dot.setBackground(Color.red);
    return dot;
}
```

Figure 4.18 **Non-voidReturnInstruction** description (a possible *OneStatement*)

Syntax

$$\longrightarrow \text{return} \longrightarrow \boxed{\textit{Expression}} \longrightarrow ; \longrightarrow$$

Notes

■ The type of *Expression* must conform to the declared type of the surrounding method.

■ Non-void methods require a `return` instruction.

Semantics

Executing *Non-voidReturnInstruction* causes *Expression* to be evaluated and its value returned to the place of the call.

Style Note

It is best to locate a `return` instruction at the bottom of the method body.

The `redDot` method on the previous page also illustrates the use of a new instruction, namely the **return instruction**. A `return` instruction is required for every non-void method, and the preferred location for a `return` is the last instruction of the method. Figure 4.18 describes this instruction.

Executing a `return` instruction results in two actions:

1. *Expression* is evaluated.

2. The method's execution is terminated and the value of *Expression* is returned to the point of the call.

> **software engineering *Hint***
>
> Non-void methods are best designed to modify nothing, except the object returned. If a method must alter any objects, it is advisable to use a void method and to alter the objects passed as arguments.

Non-void methods are sometimes called **functions**. Just like a mathematical function, a non-void method yields a value. Also like a function, non-void methods are invoked as expressions. In other words, a non-void method is called a bit differently than void methods. The call to a non-void method is properly located anywhere in the code where an *Expression* of the method's type is permitted. One good location for such a call is at the right side of an assignment instruction. For example, consider the following instruction:

```
theOval = redDot();
```

When this instruction executes, the `redDot` method is called. The value of the expression in the subsequent `return` instruction (i.e., a newly instantiated `circle` object) is returned and assigned to `theOval`.

As a second example of a non-void method, suppose we wish to write a program that displays messages that look like bordered signs. These bordered signs should contain a short string message surrounded by a light gray border that appears to have mitered corners. Figure 4.19 illustrates producing a window that contains two such bordered signs, as shown in Figure 4.20.

Figure 4.19

Bordered signs program

```java
import java.awt.*;
import javax.swing.JFrame;
public class Driver {
    private JFrame window;
    private Rectangle topSign, bottomSign;

    /** post:  a window with two bordered signs is drawn */
    public Driver() {
        window = new JFrame("The Window");
        window.setBounds(10, 10, 250, 180);
        window.setLayout(null);
        window.setBackground(Color.white);
        window.setVisible(true);
        topSign = borderedSign(Color.green, "Home, Sweet Home");
        topSign.setLocation(50, 20);
        window.add(topSign, 0);
        bottomSign = borderedSign(Color.red, "Computers Rule!");
        bottomSign.setLocation(50, 90);
        window.add(bottomSign, 0);
        window.repaint();
    }

    /** post:  result == a rectangle 150 pixels wide
     *            and 50 pixels high
     *         and result has a border colored gray with mitered
     *            corners
     *         and the message s is displayed on result
     *         and the color of the center of result is c
     */
    private Rectangle borderedSign(Color c, String s) {
        Rectangle result;
        Line upperLeft, upperRight, lowerLeft, lowerRight;
        Label message;
        result = new Rectangle(0, 0, 150, 50);
        result.setBackground(Color.lightGray);
        upperLeft = new Line(0, 0, 9, 9);
        result.add(upperLeft, 0);
        upperRight = new Line(149, 0, 140, 9);
        result.add(upperRight, 0);
        lowerLeft = new Line(0, 49, 9, 40);
        result.add(lowerLeft, 0);
        lowerRight = new Line(149, 49, 140, 40);
        result.add(lowerRight, 0);
        message = new Label(s);
        message.setBounds(10, 10, 130, 30);
        message.setBackground(c);
        result.add(message, 0);
        return result;
    }
}
```

Figure 4.20

Image produced by executing the program in Figure 4.19

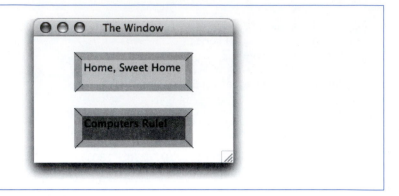

The Driver class for the bordered windows program includes a non-void method called borderedSign. This borderedSign method returns a Rectangle object that has a Label and four Line objects (to give the appearance of mitered corners) added to the Rectangle. The Driver constructor calls borderedSign twice in order to produce two different signs, using the following six statements:

```
topSign = borderedSign(Color.green, "Home, Sweet Home");
topSign.setLocation(50, 20);
window.add(topSign, 0);
bottomSign = borderedSign(Color.red, "Computers Rule!");
bottomSign.setLocation(50, 90);
window.add(bottomSign, 0);
```

Each sign is assigned to a separate variable (topSign and bottomSign). Each sign is positioned using setLocation and added to the window JFrame.

Local variables are used within the borderedSign method for the Label and Line objects, so that once the Rectangle is returned there are no variables to provide access. In other words, there are no variables for altering the colors or positions of any of the Line or Label objects from outside the borderedSign method.

4.6 ■ Standard Non-Void Methods

Now that we have seen how to call non-void methods, it is possible to discuss additional methods available from classes that were not described earlier because they are non-void. Figure 4.21 contains a more complete version of the Rectangle class that points out some of these previously unmentioned methods.

Five new methods are revealed in Figure 4.21: getX, getY, getWidth, getHeight, and getBackground. Each method returns the corresponding property from the Rectangle object. For example, the following instruction assigns the color of a

```
Rectangle
----------------------------------------
- int x
- int y
- int width
- int height
- Color color
----------------------------------------
«constructor»
    + Rectangle(int, int, int, int)

«update»
    + void setBackground(java.awt.Color)
    + void setLocation(int, int)
    + void setSize(int, int)
    + void repaint()
    + void add(java.awt.Component, int)
    ...

«query»
    + int getX()
    + int getY()
    + int getWidth()
    + int getHeight()
    + java.awt.Color getBackground()
    ...
```

Figure 4.21

Class diagrams for `Rectangle` including query methods

`Rectangle` object bound to the `myRectangle` variable to a `java.awt.Color` variable named `theColor`.

```
theColor = myRectangle.getBackground();
```

Notice that the notation for calling non-void methods from external classes requires that the method is prefixed with the name of the object. This is no different from calling a void method.

Figure 4.21 labels the non-void methods as **query** methods because they are used to query or inspect some particular attribute. Some programmers also refer to non-void methods as **inspector** methods. The convention of beginning a query method with the word *get* is frequently used in the standard Java libraries.

These methods make it possible to write a method, call it `rectangleClone`, that can make a duplicate of any Rectangle. Such a method follows.

software engineering Hint

It is best to use a noun or noun phrase to name a non-void method. An alternative naming convention used in the standard libraries is to begin the name with *get*.

```
/** post:   result is newly instantiated
 *          and result.getX() == r.getX()
 *          and result.getY() == r.getY()
 *          and result.getWidth() == r.getWidth()
 *          and result.getHeight() == r.getHeight()
 *          and result.getBackground() == r.getBackground()
 */
private Rectangle rectangleClone(Rectangle r) {
   Rectangle result;
   result = new Rectangle(r.getX(), r.getY(),
                          r.getWidth(), r.getHeight());
   result.setBackground(r.getBackground());
   return result;
}
```

The rectangleClone method has a single parameter, r, of type Rectangle and the method returns a second Rectangle that has the same position, dimensions, and color as r. The code of the method uses method calls, such as r.getX() as arguments to other methods. This is allowed because calls to non-void methods may occur anywhere that an expression is permitted.

Now that non-void methods have been presented, it is also time to take a closer look at the JFrame class. Technically, when objects are added to a JFrame, they are not really added to the JFrame object itself; instead, they are added to the JFrame's **content pane**. You can think of the content pane as a rectangle that is automatically included with every JFrame in order to provide a canvas upon which other objects can be added.

The JFrame class includes a non-void method, called getContentPane, to permit access to its content pane. As shown in Figure 4.22, getContentPane returns an object of type Container (from the *AWT* library). This means that applying methods such as add, remove, setBackground, and setLayout to a JFrame actually causes them to be applied to the JFrame's content pane. For example, consider the following instruction that adds a Rectangle called myRect to a JFrame called window:

```
window.add(myRect, 0);
```

The identical result is accomplished using the following code:

```
java.awt.Container contentPane = window.getContentPane();
contentPane.add(myRect, 0);
```

Taking advantage of the fact that non-void methods represent objects, the following instruction is yet a third way to express this behavior:

```
window.getContentPane().add(myRect, 0);
```

In fact, prior to Version 1.5.0 of Java it was not possible to add directly to a JFrame. Instead, one of the later two alternatives were necessary. In Version 1.5.0, the Java language designers modified JFrame so that add, remove, and setLayout could be

Figure 4.22   Class diagrams for `javax.swing.JFrame` and `java.awt.Container`

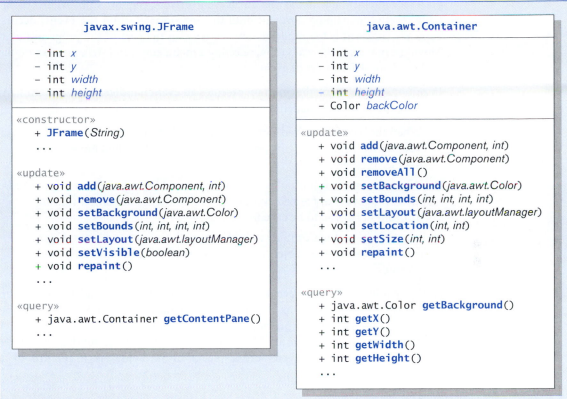

called upon a `JFrame`, not just its content pane. However, it is still important to know about the content pane, because it is best to call methods like `getHeight` and `removeAll` on the content pane. If, for example, you call `removeAll` upon a `JFrame`, then the content pane is removed, and the objects from subsequent adds are not visible.

4.7 ■ Introduction to Event Handling

All of the programs examined thus far can be described as **program-driven** code. As the name implies, program-driven code executes under the control of the program. The execution of each instruction is triggered by the completion of the program's previous instruction.

Program-driven code is not well suited to modern computer interfaces that involve user interaction. When a user strikes a key or moves the mouse, it is expected that these actions will have an immediate impact upon the program. However, program-driven code is incapable of the necessary immediate response.

A different style of program execution, known as **event-driven** code, is more appropriate for interacting with the user. In an event-driven program, some code is essentially reactive, remaining dormant until the appropriate action (an **event**) occurs. Typically, an event is the result of some activity on the part of the program's user. Moving a mouse, clicking a button, selecting a menu entry, and striking a key on the keyboard are all examples of events.

In response to an event, the program executes an **event handler**. In Java, event handlers are methods with predefined names. Events occur in situations such as:

- When the mouse is moved from a location outside a rectangle to inside, then a `mouseEntered` event occurs upon the rectangle and a `mouseEntered` event handler is called.

- When the mouse is positioned over a button and the mouse button is pressed, then an `actionPerformed` event occurs upon the button object causing `actionPerformed` to be called.

- When the user drags certain kinds of sliders, then a `changeEvent` event occurs upon the slider object and the associated `stateChanged` method executes.

Notice that in each case the event is associated with some object and a method with a prescribed name. This book includes a special class, called `ThreeButtonFrame` that uses event handling to provide more user control over program execution. A `ThreeButtonFrame` object is just like `javax.swing.JFrame` except that it has three buttons horizontally arrayed across the bottom. Below is a picture of a `ThreeButtonFrame` object.

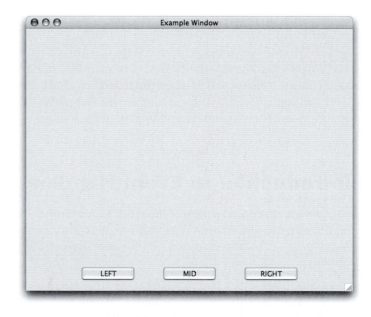

In order to make use of such an object three things are necessary:

1. The folder containing the *Driver.java* file also includes the *ThreeButtons.java* file. (*ThreeButtons.java* is a prewritten class, included with the CD accompanying this text; the code in this class is explained in later chapters.)

2. The `Driver` class syntax must follow the special syntax shown in Figure 4.23.

3. The program must declare and instantiate a `ThreeButtonFrame` object within the `Driver` class.

A `ThreeButtonFrame` object supports three different kinds of events, one event for clicking each of its three buttons. When the LEFT button is clicked, a `leftAction` event occurs; when the MID button is clicked, a `midAction` event occurs; and when the RIGHT button is clicked, a `rightAction` event occurs. To make event handling more convenient, every one of these events is handled by a method with a name corresponding to the associated event. These three methods (event handlers) must be located within a `Driver` class, using the syntax of Figure 4.24.

There are three new requirements for a `Driver` class that wishes to use a `ThreeButtonFrame` object.

1. The public class line of `Driver` must include the following syntax following the class name:

   `extends ThreeButtons`

   (This requires that the *ThreeButtons.java* file is present within the same folder as *Driver.java*.)

2. `Driver` must declare and instantiate a `ThreeButtonFrame` object. This object has a default size of 600 by 500, and includes the left, mid, and right buttons.

3. The `Driver` class must include three void parameterless methods named `leftAction`, `midAction`, and `rightAction`, and each must be specified as `public` rather than `private`. These methods will serve as event handlers for the respective `ThreeButtonFrame` buttons.

Closed
Black Box

Event handling via `ThreeButtonFrame` can look like magic at first. As you run the program, every click to one of the three window buttons "magically" calls the corresponding event-handler method. Of course, this is not really magic; instead, this event handling requires careful coordination by the Java VM and the software provided by the *ThreeButtons.java* file.

Chapters 8 and 15 explain details that make it possible for `ThreeButtonFrame` to provide for event handling in this way. Later chapters also demonstrate other ways to handle Java events.

Figure 4.23   *DriverForThreeButtons* syntax diagram (abridged version of *Class*)

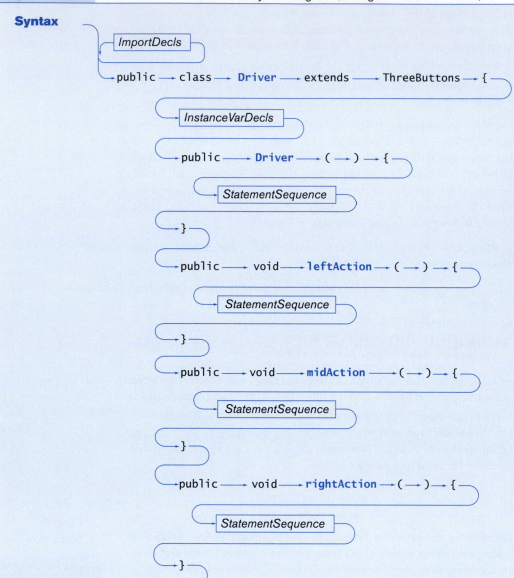

Note

The leftAction, midAction, and rightAction methods can serve as event handlers for ThreeButtonFrame objects.

Figure 4.24 contains the class diagram for this kind of Driver class. The three event handler methods are illustrated in this diagram. Figure 4.25 contains a sample Driver class.

It is typical for event-driven programs to begin with a segment of program-driven code to initialize the objects needed to accomplish event handling. In the Figure 4.25 program, the Driver method serves to perform this needed initialization. When Driver completes, a ThreeButtonFrame has been created and a Rectangle object (bound to square) has been added to the window. Note that ThreeButtonFrame objects are the same as JFrame objects, except that they contain three buttons and have a default size of 600 by 500.

Following the execution of the Driver method, the program execution becomes truly event driven. The program becomes inactive until the user chooses to click on one of the three buttons. If the user clicks on the LEFT button, then an event occurs, and the leftAction method executes as the event handler. Similarly, a user click to the MID button generates an automatic call to midAction, and a click on the RIGHT button invokes rightAction. Following the execution of any event handler, the program returns to an inactive state, awaiting the next event.

For the particular program in Figure 4.25, each event handler recolors the square object. A leftAction event colors square green, a midAction event colors square red, and a rightAction event colors square blue.

The period of program inactivity between consecutive events is actually quite important to the Java VM. This apparent "down time" from program execution is used by the Java VM to do things such as update the computer display. The instruction

    square.repaint();

included within each event handler informs the Java VM that the square object needs to be redrawn. Calls to repaint do not ensure immediate screen updates, but they should be included in order to assist the Java VM to update the display properly when it has the opportunity.

software engineering *Hint*

The Java VM is designed to make use of program inactivity between events to do housekeeping chores, like graphical update.

To make this work properly, a programmer should follow two rules:

1. Write event handlers that execute quickly. (This maximizes the free execution time allotted to the VM.)

2. Call repaint for any graphical object that changes in appearance.

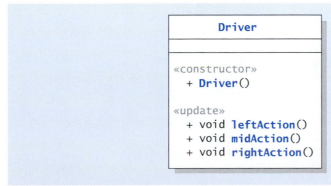

Figure 4.24

Class diagram for Driver used with *ThreeButtonFrame*

Figure 4.25

Program to
recolor a square

```java
import java.awt.*;
public class Driver extends ThreeButtons {
    private ThreeButtonFrame window;
    private Rectangle square;
    /** post:   a window with a 100 by 100 filled black square
     *                is drawn
     *          and button actions control recoloring of the
     *                square
     */
    public Driver() {
        window = new ThreeButtonFrame("Square Recoloring
            Window");
        window.setLayout(null);
        square = new Rectangle(250, 150, 100, 100);
        window.add(square, 0);
        square.repaint();
    }

    /** pre:    square is constructed
     * post:    square is colored green and square is repainted
     */
    public void leftAction() {
        square.setBackground(Color.green);
        square.repaint();
    }

    /** pre:    square is constructed
     * post:    square is colored red and square is repainted
     */
    public void midAction() {
        square.setBackground(Color.red);
        square.repaint();
    }

    /** pre:    square is constructed
     * post:    square is colored blue and square is repainted
     */
    public void rightAction() {
        square.setBackground(Color.blue);
        square.repaint();
    }
}
```

4.8 ■ Postcondition Notation

A method's postcondition must always reflect the task performed when the method
executes. Each postcondition is expressed in the form of an assertion regarding the
state of computation at the time that the method returns. Sometimes this state
involves instance variables from the class and sometimes it involves parameters that
were passed to the method. For example, the following method is passed a
Rectangle; and the method colors its parameter blue, assigns it new dimensions,
and places it upon an instance variable, called window. The postcondition reflects all
of these changes using the names window and r to refer to the objects that are
altered.

```
/** pre:    r is instantiated
 *  post:   r.getBackground() == Color.blue
 *          and r.getWidth() == 100 and r.getHeight() == 50
 *          and r has been added to window
 */
public void positionColorAndPlace(Rectangle r) {
    r.setBackground(Color.blue);
    r.setSize(100, 50);
    window.add(r, 0);
}
```

It *is* proper for a postcondition to refer to

- formal parameters from its class
- instance variables from its class

However, it is *not* proper for a postcondition to refer to

- arguments passed to the method
- local variables of the method
- local variables of other methods
- inaccessible instance variables of other classes

Parameters are known by their formal parameter names within a method. Therefore,
they should also be known by their formal parameter names within the precondition and postcondition. The arguments that are passed to these parameters are
determined by the calling code and should not appear anywhere in the precondition
or postcondition.

When a method returns, all of its local variables are eliminated and are no longer
available at the time the postcondition applies. Similarly, local variables from other
procedures and inaccessible instance variables are not available for use within a
method, so they also should not be used within the method's postcondition (or precondition).

Non-void methods have another object that must play a role in their postcondition, namely the object returned by the method. This book uses the convention of calling this object `result`. For example, a method that returns an `int` value that is double its parameter can be expressed with the following postcondition.

```
/** post:  result == k * 2 */
public int parameterDoubled(int k) {
    return k * 2;
}
```

Since `result` is a name for the object returned, it is proper to use `result.` as a prefix to attributes of the return object. For example, consider the following method:

```
/** post:   result.getX() == 100 and result.getY() == 20
 *          and result.getWidth() == 5
 *          and result.getHeight() == 5
 *          and result.getBackground() == Color.black
 */
public Rectangle newBlackSquare() { ... }
```

software engineering *Hint*

The name *result* should be avoided as a variable name. One acceptable exception is for a non-void method that instantiates the object it returns. In such cases, the name *result* may be used for a local variable bound to the return object.

The notation `result.getX()` refers to the x coordinate of the `result` object. So the above postcondition describes that the `Rectangle` returned by the method has an upper left corner at (100, 20), is a square with five pixels on each side, and is colored black.

When a method must instantiate a new object to be returned, some programmers find it convenient to name the object as a local variable called `result`. This is the one time when a local variable makes sense in a postcondition. Following is a `newBlackSquare` method that illustrates using `result` for a local variable.

```
/** post:   result.getX() == 100 and result.getY() == 20
 *          and result.getWidth() == 5
 *          and result.getHeight() == 5
 *          and result.getBackground() == Color.black
 */
public Rectangle newBlackSquare() {
    Rectangle result;
    result = new Rectangle(100, 20, 5, 5);
    result.setBackground(Color.black);
    return result;
}
```

Sometimes postconditions must refer to previous values of a parameter of an instance variable. For example, imagine a program to maintain the credit card balance and a method called `chargeIt` to post a new charge to the account. The primary impact of posting a new charge is to add this new charge to the account, thereby increasing the amount due. One way to denote a postcondition for such alterations is illustrated as follows:

```
/** post: amountDue == amountDue@pre + newCharge */
public void chargeIt(int newCharge) { ... }
```

The postcondition for `chargeIt` uses **@pre** as an expression suffix. This use of **@pre** is called a **previous value notation** because the suffixed expression denotes the value from the time the method *begins* to execute (i.e., the time at which the precondition was true). Any postcondition expression without an @pre suffix is referring to the expression's state at the *end* of the method's execution. Therefore, `chargeIt`'s postcondition describes that the resultant amount due consists of the amount due prior to executing the method plus the value of the `newCharge` parameter.

4.9 ■ java.awt.Container– A Design Example

This section explores the design of a particular program to draw and manipulate coffee cups. Several concepts of this chapter are revisited along the way. The particular software requirements for this program are explained in Figure 4.26.

From these requirements, three objects are evident:

1. a window of type `ThreeButtonFrame`
2. a red coffee cup
3. a blue coffee cup

Furthermore, the use of `ThreeButtonFrame` dictates syntax for `Driver` that follows the form shown in Figure 4.23.

One of the key parts of the design for this program is the code to draw a coffee cup with the shape shown in the picture above. Because this task is nontrivial, it is reasonable to design a separate method to construct a cup object. It is also wise to use a non-void method to return the cup as a single graphical unit.

The coffee cup picture seems to be a composition of four ovals: a black oval for the top of the cup, a colored oval for the handle, a white oval for the "hole" in the center of the handle, and a portion of a filled colored oval for the cup body. There are two difficulties in drawing this image:

- grouping the four ovals into a single graphical unit
- clipping off the top and bottom of the oval that forms the body of the cup

Both of these difficulties can be solved with the same *java.awt* class, called **Container**. This class was introduced earlier (see Figure 4.22) as the class for `JFrame` content panes. Figure 4.27 provides specifications for `java.awt.Container`.

Figure 4.26

Requirements for the coffee cup program

Initial State

The program displays a `ThreeButtonFrame` object containing two coffee cups. Both cups are roughly 40 pixels wide and 20 pixels high. One coffee cup is centered near the top of the window and is colored red. The second coffee cup is centered just above the MID button and is colored blue.

LEFT   Every time the LEFT button is clicked, the red coffee cup moves downward by five pixels and the blue coffee cup moves upward by five pixels.

MID   Every time the MID button is clicked, the two coffee cups are relocated to their positions from the initial state.

RIGHT Every time the RIGHT button is clicked, the red coffee cup moves to its left by 10 pixels and the blue coffee cup moves to its right by 10 pixels.

Figure 4.27

`java.awt.` `Container` class specifications (*continues*)

Invariant

A `java.awt.Container` object...

- is a transparent rectangular region.
- should be added to a container object with its upper left corner *x* pixels from the left and *y* pixels from the top. (The upper left corner of the container is (0, 0).)

Below is a `Container` added to the content pane of a `JFrame`. The `Container` is shown in black, although it would be transparent on an actual computer display.

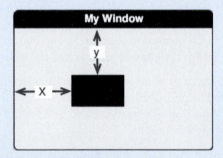

Constructor Methods

`public` **`Container`**`()`

    post: A new `Container` object is created
           and *backColor* is transparent.

          (Note that `Container`s also do not appear until added.)

. . .

Update Methods

public void **add**(java.awt.Component *c*, int *j*)

  pre: *j* == 0

  post: *c* is placed on top of this Container located c.getX() pixels from the left and c.getY() pixels from the top of this Container.

public void **remove**(java.awt.Component *c*)

  post: The *c* graphical object will be removed from this Container.

  note: Nothing occurs if *c* was not added to this Container at the time of the call.

public void **setBackground**(java.awt.Color *c*)

  post: *backColor* == *c*

public void **setBounds**(int *initX*, int *initY*, int *w*, int *h*)

  post: *x* == *initX* **and** *y* == *initY* **and** *width* == *w* **and** *height* == *h*

public void **setLayout**(java.awt.LayoutManager *m*)

  post: *m* is established as the layout manager for this Container.

  note: For this book an argument of null is suggested. This method does not need to be called except for the content pane of a JFrame.

public void **setLocation**(int *initX*, int *initY*)

  post: *x* == *initX* **and** *y* == *initY*

public void **setSize**(int *w*, int *h*)

  post: *width* == *w* **and** *height* == *h*

public void **repaint**()

  post: Causes the Java virtual machine to update the display of this Container, and its content, as soon as possible.

. . .

Query Methods

public java.awt.Color **getBackground**( )

  post: *result* == *backColor*

public int **getX**( )

  post: *result* == *x*

public int **getY**( )

  post: *result* == *y*

public int **getWidth**( )

  post: *result* == *width*

public int **getHeight**( )

  post: *result* == *height*

. . .

Figure 4.27
java.awt.
Container class
specifications
(*continued*)

The java.awt.Container objects are intended for use as backgrounds upon which to place other *AWT* or *Swing* objects. A Container shares most of its properties and all of its methods (excepting constructors) with the Rectangle and Oval classes discussed in Chapter 3. In fact, it is correct to say that Rectangle and Oval are specialized types of Container; all three classes share the same update and query methods. The only significant difference between Rectangle, Oval, and Container is their appearance: a rectangle, an oval, or a transparent region.

Another characteristic shared by all three classes is the way they clip added images. Executing the code segment below demonstrates how to use a Container for clipping and Oval in the shape of a coffee cup body.

```
cupBackground = new Container();
cupBackground.setBounds(0, 5, 30, 15);
cup = new Oval(0, -18, 30, 35);
cupBackground.add(cup, 0);
```

The result of executing this code is pictured in Figure 4.28. Only the colored portion of the cup object is actually visible, since the gray portions lie outside of a Container named cupBackground.

Container objects are a good way to group other graphical *AWT* and *Swing* objects into a single graphical object. The complete coffee cup image consists of the Container shown in Figure 4.28 along with an Oval cup handle with an Oval hole in the handle and an Oval for the top of the cup. If all four of these parts of the coffee cup are placed upon the same underlying Container, they behave as a group.

A complete Driver class for this program is shown in Figure 4.29. The work of constructing a coffee cup is performed by a method called newCup. This method instantiates and returns a Container object upon which all of the parts of the coffee cup have been placed. The parameter of the newCup method determines the color of the cup, so that the same method can be used to create different colored cups. In this program, newCup is called once to create the red cup and once to create the blue cup.

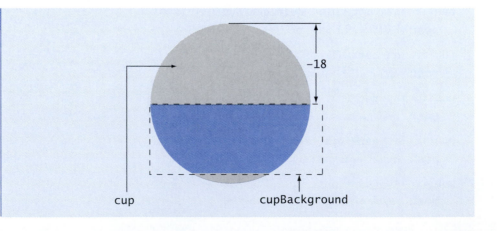

Figure 4.28

A cup Oval placed upon cupBackground (a Container)

```java
import java.awt.*;
public class Driver extends ThreeButtons {
    private ThreeButtonFrame window;
    private Container redCup, blueCup;
    /** post:  a window is created
     *         and redCup is repositioned at the top center of
     *            window
     *         and blueCup is repositioned at the bottom center
     *            of window
     */
    public Driver() {
        window = new ThreeButtonFrame("Move the Cups");
        window.setVisible(true);
        window.setLayout(null);
        window.setBackground(Color.white);
        redCup = newCup(Color.red);
        window.add(redCup, 0);
        blueCup = newCup(Color.blue);
        window.add(blueCup, 0);
        midAction();
    }


    /** post:  result is a new Container with a coffee cup
     *         colored c on top
     *         and result.getWidth() == 40 and
     *            result.getHeight() == 20
     */
    private Container newCup(Color c) {
        Container background, cupBackground;
        Oval cup, handle, handleCenter, top;
        background = new Container();
        background.setBounds(0, 0, 40, 20);
        handle = new Oval(28, 1, 8, 13);
        handle.setBackground(c);
        handleCenter = new Oval(2, 2, 4, 9);
        handleCenter.setBackground(Color.white);
        handle.add(handleCenter, 0);
        background.add(handle, 0);
        cupBackground = new Container();
        cupBackground.setBounds(0, 5, 30, 15);
        cup = new Oval(0, -18, 30, 35);
        cup.setBackground(c);
        cupBackground.add(cup, 0);
        background.add(cupBackground, 0);
        top = new Oval(0, 1, 30, 6);
        background.add(top, 0);
        return background;
    }
```

Figure 4.29

A program to draw two coffee cups (*continues*)

Figure 4.29

A program to draw two coffee cups (*continued*)

```
/** pre:    redCup instantiated and blueCup instantiated
 * post:    redCup.getY() == redCup.getY()@pre + 5
 *          and blueCup.getY() == blueCup.getY()@pre - 5
 */
public void leftAction() {
    int newX, newY;
    newX = redCup.getX();
    newY = redCup.getY() + 5;
    redCup.setLocation(newX, newY);
    redCup.repaint();
    newX = blueCup.getX();
    newY = blueCup.getY() - 5;
    blueCup.setLocation(newX, newY);
    blueCup.repaint();
}

/** pre:    redCup instantiated and blueCup instantiated
 * post:    redCup is repositioned at the top center of window
 *          and blueCup is repositioned at the bottom center
 *              of window
 */
public void midAction() {
    redCup.setLocation(280, 30);
    redCup.repaint();
    blueCup.setLocation(280, 400);
    blueCup.repaint();
}

/** pre:    redCup instantiated and blueCup instantiated
 * post:    redCup.getX() == redCup.getX()@pre - 10
 *          and blueCup.getX() == blueCup.getX()@pre + 10
 */
public void rightAction() {
    int newX, newY;
    newX = redCup.getX() - 10;
    newY = redCup.getY();
    redCup.setLocation(newX, newY);
    redCup.repaint();
    newX = blueCup.getX() + 10;
    newY = blueCup.getY();
    blueCup.setLocation(newX, newY);
    blueCup.repaint();
}
}
```

There are six local variables declared in newCup. The background variable represents the Container upon which the coffee cup is constructed. Additional local variables are used for the individual parts of the cup. These variables are properly declared to be local to newCup because they are not used elsewhere in the program.

One of the advantages of placing objects upon an underlying Container is that they can be moved around as a unit. A red coffee cup is added to a ThreeButtonFrame via the following two statements:

```
redCup = newCup(Color.red);
windowPane.add(redCup, 0);
```

The same cup is then moved (as a whole unit) to the top center of the window by using the following statement:

```
redCup.setLocation(280, 30);
```

Moving the cups, as required for clicks of the LEFT and RIGHT buttons, is accomplished using the setLocation method in a more complex manner. For example, LEFT button click is supposed to move the cups vertically (redCup moves downward and blueCup moves upward, each by five pixels). The solution to this code is to use the query (non-void) methods called getX() and getY(). These methods return the current location of the object. The following statements cause redCup to remain unchanged in its horizontal (X) position and move appropriately in the vertical (Y) direction:

```
int newX, newY;
newX = redCup.getX();
newY = redCup.getY() + 5;
redCup.setLocation(newX, newY);
```

Local variables called newX and newY are assigned the new position, and then a call to setLocation repositions the cup. Likewise, the statements below

```
newX = blueCup.getX() + 10;
newY = blueCup.getY();
blueCup.setLocation(newX, newY);
```

software *Hint*
engineering

The newX and newY local variables are not really necessary in the coffee cup program because the expressions for the new cup locations can be passed directly via the parameter list. At first, it may seem easier to write the code *with* the local variables. However, you should try to use more complex expressions for arguments. The brevity of the final (single-statement) version is generally considered more readable.

cause the blue cup to move to its right by 10 pixels, as required by rightAction.

Since arguments can be expressions, it is also possible to call non-void methods within the argument list. For example, the three-statement code segment to move blueCup can be abbreviated into the following single statement:

```
blueCup.setLocation(blueCup.getX()+10, blueCup.getY());
```

Notice that the statement eliminates the need for the newX and newY local variables.

Inspector

Below is a collection of hints on what to check when examining code that involves the concepts of this chapter.

- Methods that are too long become difficult to read. Check for methods that are longer than one computer screen. Find a way to break up long methods into logical pieces.

- The `public` and `private` prefixes should be checked so that most things are `private`. For now, the exceptions are the `Driver` class, the `Driver` constructor method, and the `leftAction`, `midAction`, and `rightAction` event handlers.

- Remember to include the `void` type when declaring methods that are not functions. A quick scan can detect missing the missing `void`. Do not forget that constructor methods, like `Driver`, must *not* include void.

- Always check method call instructions to be certain that their argument lists match the parameter list in number, type, and order.

- Non-void methods should be called by an expression within an instruction, unlike void methods where the call is a complete instruction.

- Remember to include a return instruction in the body of all non-void methods.

- When using `ThreeButtonFrame` objects, ask three questions:

  1. Is extends `ThreeButtons` included as a suffix on the `public class` line of `Driver`?

  2. Are the `leftAction`, `midAction`, and `rightAction` parameterless void methods included in `Driver`?

  3. Does the `Driver` code construct a `ThreeButtonFrame` object?

- When using graphical images, each event handler method should be reviewed to ensure that `repaint` is called for any displayed object whose appearance has changed.

Terminology

@pre (postcondition clause notation)	event-driven code
activity diagram	event handler
body (of a method)	formal parameter
buffer	function
Container (java.awt.Container)	local variable
event	method call

method invocation

non-void method

parameter

parameter passage

previous value (postcondition clause notation)

private (method)

program-driven code

public (method)

query method

result (postcondition clause notation)

return instruction

subprogram

ThreeButtonFrame

ThreeButtons class

Exercises

1. Which of the following should be declared using `public` and which should be declared using `private`?

   a. the `Driver` class

   b. the `Driver` constructor method

   c. the `leftAction` method

   d. any instance variable of the `Driver` class

   e. private methods of the `Driver` class that aren't event handlers

2. Below are three parameterless methods that are included within your `Driver` class.

```
private void makeRedDot() {
    circle.setBackground(Color.red);
}
```

```
private void drawGraySquare() {
    Rectangle graySquare;
    graySquare = new Rectangle(20, 20, 50, 50);
    graySquare.setBackground(Color.gray);
    window.add(graySquare, 0);
}
```

```
private void makeSpottedContainer() {
    Oval spot;
    spottedContainer = new Container();
    spottedContainer.setBounds(0, 0, 100, 100);
    spot = new Oval(30, 30, 20, 20);
    spot.setBackground(Color.red);
    spottedContainer.add(spot, 0);
}
```

a. Each of these methods makes use of an instance variable that *must* be declared in `Driver`. Name each instance variable.

b. Draw a picture of the `window` that results from executing the following code. (Assume that `window` is declared to be an instance variable of type `JFrame`.)

```java
public Driver() {
    window = new JFrame("Window");
    window.setBounds(10, 10, 500, 500);
    window.setLayout(null);
    window.setVisible(true);
    drawGraySquare();
    makeSpottedContainer();
    window.add(spottedContainer, 0);
    window.repaint();
}
```

c. Draw a picture of the window that results from executing the following code. (Assume that `window` is a `JFrame` instance variable and that `circle` is an `Oval` instance variable.)

```java
public Driver() {
    window = new JFrame("Window");
    window.setBounds(10, 10, 500, 500);
    window.setLayout(null);
    window.setVisible(true);
    makeSpottedContainer();
    drawGraySquare();
    window.add(spottedContainer, 0);
    circle = new Oval(20, 20, 50, 50);
    window.add(circle, 0);
    makeRedDot();
    window.repaint();
}
```

d. What happens at runtime when the program from part (c) is modified to remove the two instructions involving `circle`?

3. Use the following private method to complete parts (a) and (b).

```java
private void makeGreenBorderedDot(int x, int y, JFrame w) {
    Oval dot, border;
    dot = new Oval(x, y, 100, 100);
    dot.setBackground(Color.green);
    w.add(dot, 0);
    border = new Oval(0, 0, 100, 100);
    dot.add(border, 0);
}
```

a. Assuming that window is a JFrame instance variable, explain why the Java compiler detects a syntax error in each of the following instructions.

```
makeGreenBorderedDot();
makeGreenBorderedDot(20, 20);
makeGreenBorderedDot(20, window, 20);
```

b. Show the results of executing the following code. (Assume that window is a JFrame instance variable.)

```
public Driver() {
    window = new JFrame("Window");
    window.setBounds(10, 10, 300, 300);
    window.setVisible(true);
    window.setLayout(null);
    makeGreenBorderedDot(20, 20, window);
    makeGreenBorderedDot(150, 0, window);
    makeGreenBorderedDot(80, 80, window);
    window.repaint();
}
```

4. Use the following private method to complete parts (a) through (c). (Note that s*2 denotes s multiplied by 2 and s*3 means s multiplied by 3.)

```
private Container makeChex(int s) {
    Rectangle leftSquare, rightSquare, topSquare,
        bottomSquare;
    Container result;
    leftSquare = new Rectangle(0, s, s, s);
    rightSquare = new Rectangle(s*2, s, s, s);
    topSquare = new Rectangle(s, 0, s, s);
    bottomSquare = new Rectangle(s, s*2, s, s);
    result = new Container();
    result.setBounds(0, 0, s*3, s*3);
    result.add(leftSquare, 0);
    result.add(rightSquare, 0);
    result.add(topSquare, 0);
    result.add(bottomSquare, 0);
    return result;

}
```

a. Assuming that the only two instance variables are window (belonging to JFrame) and container (belonging to Container), explain why the Java compiler detects a syntax error in each of the following instructions:

```
window.makeChex(100);
container.makeChex(100);
container = makeChex(100, container);
container = makeChex(s);
```

b. Assuming that the only two instance variables are window (belonging to JFrame) and container (belonging to Container), explain why the following instruction is wrong. (Incidentally, the Java compiler will *not* detect this as an error.)

```
makeChex(100);
```

c. Show the results of executing the following code. (Assume that window is a JFrame instance variable and smallContainer and largeContainer are Container instance variables.)

```java
public Driver() {
    window = new JFrame("Window");
    window.setBounds(10, 10, 270, 270);
    window.setLayout(null);
    window.setVisible(true);
    largeContainer = makeChex(90);
    window.add(largeContent, 0);
    smallContainer = makeChex(30);
    window.add(smallContent, 0);
    window.repaint();
}
```

5. Explain each of the following postconditions in a few English sentences:

a.
```
/** post:   result == a + b */
private int mysteryMethod1(int a, int b) { ... }
```

b.
```
/** pre:    spot1 and spot2 are both instantiated
 *  post:   spot1 == spot2@pre
 *          and spot2 == spot1@pre
 */
public void mysteryMethod2(Oval spot1, Oval spot2) { ... }
```

c.
```
/** pre:    spot1 and spot2 are both instantiated
 *  post:   spot1.getWidth() == spot1.getWidth()@pre - 1
 *          and spot2.getBackground() == Color.green
 */
public void mysteryMethod3(Oval spot1, Oval spot2) { ... }
```

6. On the next page is a Driver class that is supposed to create a circle on a ThreeButtonFrame and allow the user to halve the size of the circle by clicking the left button and double the size of the circle by clicking the right button. (Note that the two setSize method calls correctly accomplish these respective tasks.) This code contains several errors. Fix them.

```
import java.awt.*;
public class Driver extends ThreeButtons{
    private ThreeButtonFrame window;
    private Oval circle;
    /** post:   a window with a 100 by 100 black circle is
     *          drawn
     */
    public Driver() {
        window = new ThreeButtonFrame("Circle Resizer");
        window.setLayout(null);
        window.setVisible(true);
        window.add(circle, 0);
        window.repaint();
    }
    /** pre:    circle is instantiated
     * post:  circle is double the size of prior circle
     */
    public void leftAction() {
        int newWidth, newHeight;
        newWidth = circle.getWidth * 2;
        newHeight = circle.getHeight() * 2;
        circle.setSize(newWidth, newHeight);
        circle.repaint();
    }

    /** pre:    circle is instantiated
     * post:  circle is half the size of prior circle
     */
    public void rightEventHandler() {
        circle.setSize(getWidth()/2, getHeight()/2);
        circle.repaint();
    }
}
```

Programming Exercises

1. A 7-segment display is sometimes used in devices such as calculators to display decimal digits (0–9). The concept of a 7-segment display is to use seven bars arranged as shown in the window below. By lighting some of the seven bars, and not others, any digit can be displayed legibly. (The window on the next page displays the digit 8 by lighting all seven bars.)

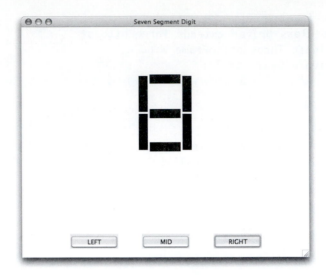

Write a program that uses this concept together with `ThreeButtonFrame` so that initially the program displays the digit 8 with black bars, as shown above. Thereafter, the buttons behave as follows:

LEFT   Causes the digit to become a 2 with all bars colored red.

MID   Causes the digit to become a 7 with all bars colored orange.

RIGHT Causes the entire digit to move to the right by two pixels.

Include the use of the following private methods in your program:

`removeAllBars();`   to remove all seven bars from their placement.

`colorBars(Color);`   to recolor all seven bars to the color of the method's argument.

2. Write a method that returns a symbol that looks like a U.S. Interstate sign, similar to the one shown in the upper left corner of the window below. (This sign has a blue bottom and a red border across the top.) This method needs two parameters to pass the coordinates of the upper left corner of the road sign. Call your method appropriately to fill the window with the eight signs as arranged below.

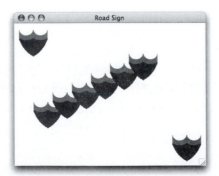

3. Write a program to utilize a ThreeButtonFrame and use other private methods efficiently. Initially your program should draw four log cabin quilt blocks centered in the middle of the window. A log cabin block consists of nine rectangles arranged and sized as shown below. Each of your blocks should consist of eight Rectangle objects with a blank center. You may color all of the blocks as you choose with three restrictions: all blocks must be filled; no two blocks that touch on their sides may have the same color; and the leftmost block is red for one block, black for another block, dark gray for one block, and light gray for the remaining block. When all blocks are added initially, only one block is visible, because they are all placed on top of each other. The button clicks should behave as follows:

LEFT   Each of the four quilt blocks must move two pixels closer to their respective corners. Note that if the center of each quilt block is empty, the blocks underneath should show through as they move.

MID   This button does nothing.

RIGHT This button should cause each quilt block to move in the opposite direction as the LEFT button.

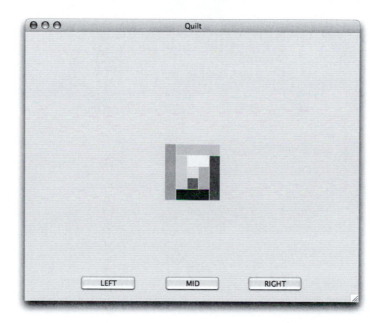

Primitive Data

5

FORTRAN (Formula Translator) is an algebraic, formula-type procedural language developed primarily to meet typical scientific processing.

—Information Technology for Management, Glossary

Objectives

- To explore the similarities among and differences between primitive types and reference types
- To examine integer data types, including `int`, `short`, `byte`, and `long`
- To examine real data types, including `double` and `float`
- To examine the order in which numeric expressions are evaluated at execution time
- To explore mixed-type numeric expressions and the use of casting
- To introduce the `Math` library class and some of its more useful methods and constants
- To demonstrate how to create numeric constants and non-void primitive methods in Java
- To examine a few common numeric expression/instruction patterns
- To examine the `char` data type

N umbers have always played a key role in computer programming. In the earliest programming languages, the instructions themselves, were numbers. Today, computers frequently manipulate numeric data, whether that data represents scientific formulas, accounting ledger information, or engineering calculations.

5.1 ■ Primitive Types

Object-oriented programming makes use of data in many forms. All instance variables and local variables presented thus far in this text have been **reference types**. The name "reference" derives from the fact that a variable of this type *refers* (is bound) to its object. Each reference object derives its type from a class.

There are eight Java data types that are too simple to require the overhead of a reference. These "simpler" data types are called **primitive types**. Primitive types have three characteristics that distinguish them from reference types.

1. Primitive types are *atomic* in the sense that they contain no attributes (instance variables).

2. Primitive types are *built into* the Java language, requiring no external class.

3. A primitive variable represents a *value*, rather than an object binding.

The complete list of primitive types is given in Figure 5.1. As the names in this figure imply, the majority of the primitive types are devoted to storing numbers.

Primitive types are similar to classes, since programs can use them to specify the types of instance variables, local variables, parameters, and methods. However, primitive type data have key differences, mostly related to efficiencies that can result from the simpler, built-in types. These differences will become clearer as the types are examined.

Figure 5.1 The primitive data types		
	boolean	float
	byte	int
	char	long
	double	short

To illustrate the difference between reference and primitive types further, consider the following set of local variable declarations. The first statement declares two reference (Oval) variables, and the second declares two primitive (int) variables. Below the two statements is an object diagram that depicts the result of executing these declarations.

```
Oval theOval, assignedOval;
int theInt, assignedOval;
```

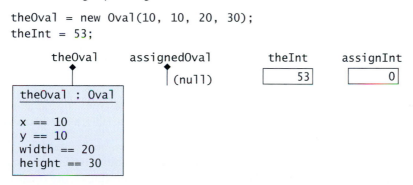

The reference variables are pictured as bindings (null at this time), while the primitive variables are shown as boxes. The initial value of a reference variable is null, and the initial value of an int variable is 0.[1] Note that the boxes used above are one of two optional object diagram notations for primitive variables. The alternative is to give the name of the variable, followed by "==", followed by its value. For example, theInt == 0.

Now consider what happens when the following two statements are executed. Once again, the resulting object diagram is shown after the code.

```
theOval = new Oval(10, 10, 20, 30);
theInt = 53;
```

Executing the assignment to a reference variable assigns a binding to that variable. Executing the first assignment above causes theOval to be bound to a newly instantiated Oval object. By contrast, the assignment to a primitive variable assigns a value, not a binding. The above assignment to theInt illustrates this. This object diagram also illustrates the alternate notation for primitive variables. Apparently, inside the Oval object there are four int variables (x, y, width, and height). A byproduct of instantiating an Oval object is the assignment of these four variables to values from the corresponding constructor arguments.

Suppose that the program continues to execute the following two instructions. Each of these statements assigns one variable to another of the same type.

---

1. While you should be aware that variables are automatically initialized, remember that reliance upon these initial values is a bad software engineering practice.

```
assignedOval = theOval;
assignedInt = theInt;
```

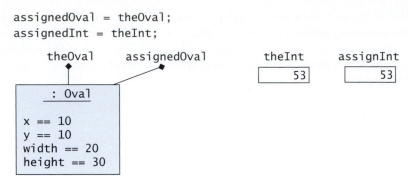

When one reference variable is assigned to another, the binding is copied. By contrast, assigning one primitive variable to another copies the value. So while a subsequent method call to theOval will also modify assignedOval, primitive variables remain independent.

5.2 ■ Primitive Integer Data Types

The **int** data type is arguably the most commonly used Java data type for integer data. (This data type was encountered previously as a parameter type for such methods as setLocation and setSize.) A variable of type int can store any non-negative or negative integer with nine or fewer decimal digits. Figure 5.2 contains a summary of int.

Figure 5.2 describes the key characteristics of the int data type. The name of the type, int, can be used to declare the type of an instance variable, a local variable, a parameter, or the return type of a method.

A **constant**, also called a **literal**, is a single value of the primitive type that is acceptable Java notation. For example, Java permits all of the following as int constants.

```
73
+64710
0
-3
```

The Java syntax for constants is generally similar, but not identical, to common mathematical notations. In the case of int constants, blanks and/or commas are *not* permitted within a constant, even though such notations are frequently used for everyday communication among people.

Illegal constant attempts:

```
1,000,025  //commas not permitted within constant
6 521      //white space not permitted within constant
```

Figure 5.2 contains a partial listing of int operators. Each operation is described in terms of its syntax and mapping. A **prefix operator** is an operator that syntactically

Name of the Type: `int`

Usage: An `int` is an integer within the range from −2,147,483,648 through 2,147,483,647.

Constants: Any consecutive sequence of nine or fewer decimal digits (0–9) optionally preceded by a "+" or "−" symbol.

Prefix Operator (`int` → `int`)

[++ and -- cannot be applied to constants or constant expressions.]

Syntax	Semantics
-	negation
++	auto-increment
--	auto-decrement

Infix Arithmetic Operators (`int` × `int` → `int`)

Syntax	Semantics
+	addition
-	subtraction
*	multiplication
/	division (quotient)
%	remainder after integer division (modulo)

Infix Relational Operators (`int` × `int` → `boolean`)

Syntax	Semantics
==	equal to
!=	not equal to
<	less than
<=	less than or equal to
>	greater than
>=	greater than or equal to

Postfix Operator (`int` → `int`)

[++ and -- cannot be applied to constants or constant expressions.]

Syntax	Semantics
++	auto-increment
--	auto-decrement

Figure 5.2

Summary of the `int` data type (operators abridged)

precedes the expression to which it applies. For example, any integer expression may be preceded by a dash (−) to cause the expression to be negated.

The proper syntax for an **infix operator** is to place it *between* its operands. For example, adding the integer twenty-five to three is denoted as follows in Java.

```
25 + 3
```

Postfix operators must be placed *after* the expression to which they apply. Java has two common postfix operators (auto-increment and auto-decrement). These operators can be applied to variables to increase (auto-increment) the variable's value by one or decrease (auto-decrement) the variable's value by one.

Figure 5.3 summarizes the syntax of expressions of `int` type. This syntax diagram includes operators and constants that were previously described in Figure 5.2.

Many of the Java int expressions borrow their notation from common arithmetic expressions. Below are two examples.

```
17 + 3 / 2
(25 + 14) * (80021 - 3422)
```

The asterisk (`*`) symbol denotes multiplication, and the slash (`/`) denotes integer division. An integer division results from dividing two integer expressions, and the result of an integer division is an integer quotient. Therefore, the expression

```
17 / 3  evaluates to  5
```

and the expression

```
-5 / 4  evaluates to  -1
```

Figure 5.3 **IntExpression** syntax (abridged version of *Expression*)

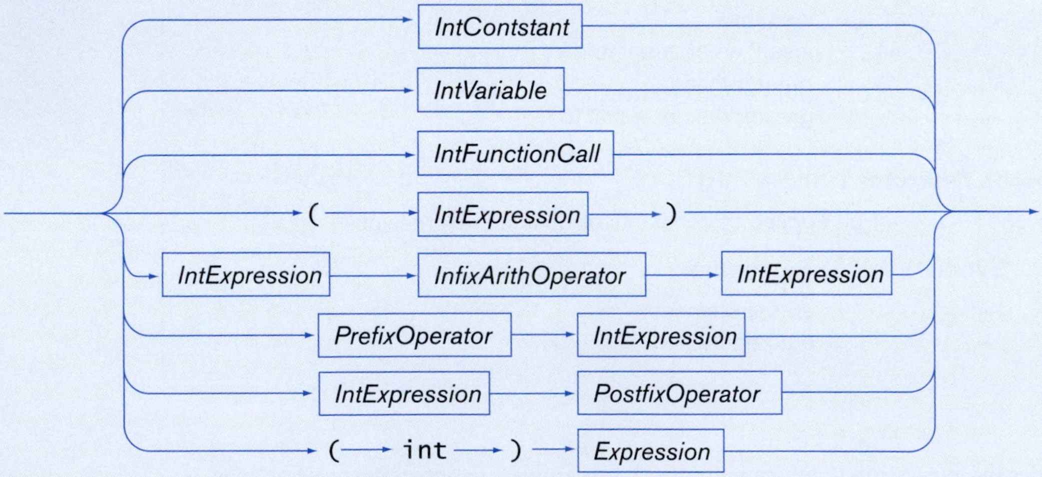

When the % operation is applied to two positive integers, the result is the remainder of an integer division. Therefore, the expression

17 % 3   evaluates to 2

Negative operands do not change the magnitude of the result of evaluating a % expression, and the result of the expression will have the same sign as the first operand. The examples below illustrate.

-17 % 3   evaluates to -2
17 % -3   evaluates to 2
-17 % -3   evaluates to -2

Assignment instructions can be used to assign values to int variables. Three example assignment instructions are listed below. (The identifiers must be declared as int variables.)

```
slicesOfBread = 24 * 10;        assigns 240 to slicesOfBread
jarsOfJelly = 100 + 1000;       assigns 1100 to jarsOfJelly
quartsOfMilk = 2000 - 2016;     assigns -16 to quartsOfMilk
```

If an int variable is used within an expression, then the variable's value is substituted for the variable when the expression evaluates. Consider the following instruction sequence.

```
dereksAge = 19;
kasandrasAge = dereksAge + 2;
```

When the second instruction executes, the value of dereksAge (19) is added to 2 in order to assign kasandrasAge the value 21.

Frequently, instructions are used to alter the existing value of an int variable. For example, executing the following instruction doubles the value of a variable.

```
cupsOfYogurt = cupsOfYogurt * 2;
```

Similarly, the following instruction decreases the value of jarsOfPeanutButter by 1.

```
jarsOfPeanutButter = jarsOfPeanutButter - 1;
```

The postfix auto-decrement operator provides an alternative Java notation for decrementing by one. Below is an example Java instruction that has the same behavior as the one above.

```
jarsOfPeanutButter--;
```

The ++ symbol also provides a more abbreviated notation for incrementing by 1. For example, executing the instruction

```
sandrasAge = sandrasAge + 1;
```

has the same result as executing

```
sandrasAge++; .
```

Java uses explicit rules to govern the order in which `int` operations are performed. These rules dictate the value of each `int` expression. For example, the `int` expression

    7 + 9 / 2

evaluates to 11, because 9/2 is evaluated prior to the "+" operation. The order in which operations are performed depends upon the **precedence** of the associated operators. Operators with higher precedence are performed before operators with lower precedence. In the preceding expression the "/" operator has higher precedence than "+".

Expression evaluation also depends upon the order in which equal precedence operators. For example, the expression

    6 * 2 / 3

evaluates to 4 (the correct answer) if "*" is performed first, and evaluates to 0 (incorrect) if "/" is performed first. With just a few exceptions, Java operators of equal precedence are performed left to right. Figure 5.4 contains a table of the important `int` operators, their precedence, and the order in which they are performed. Appendix C contains a more complete listing.

Java also supports parenthesized expressions. When parentheses are used, the expressions within are evaluated prior to their adjacent operators. Parentheses take priority over precedence. For example, the following expression evaluates the average (mean) of its two `int` variables because the addition is performed before the division.

    (dereksAge + kasandrasAge) / 2

There are three other Java data types for integers. They are named **byte**, **short**, and **long**. The differences between the four integer types is the amount of computer storage required for each, and correspondingly, the range of integer values that can be assigned to each. Figure 5.5 summarizes these differences. For example, a variable of type `byte` requires a quarter of the memory space needed to store a variable of

Figure 5.4

Precedence of selected int operators

Precedence	Operator	Operation	Order within
highest	--	postfix autodecrement	left to right
	++	postfix autoincrement	
	--	prefix autodecrement	right to left
	++	prefix autoincrement	
	-	unary minus	
	/	division	left to right
	*	multiplication	
	%	remainder	
	+	addition	left to right
lowest	-	subtraction	

Figure 5.5	Summary of Java integer data types		
Type	**Storage Size**	**Minimum Value**	**Maximum Value**
byte	8 bits	−128	127
short	16 bits	−32,768	32,767
int	32 bits	−2,147,483,648	2,147,483,647
long	64 bits	−9,223,372,036,854,775,808	9,223,372,036,854,775,807

type `int`. However, a `byte` variable is restricted to storing values within the range from −128 through 127. The same operators are supported by all four integer data types.

5.3 ■ Differences between Primitives and References

Primitive type data often exhibits behavior that appears to be different from the behavior of reference data. In fact, data of either type can be thought of as objects, but there are differences between primitive objects and nonprimitives (reference objects).

Examining how each type of data is stored inside a computer provides insight into the differences. Every variable of primitive type is associated with its own cell of computer memory. From the previous discussion of integer data types, it should be clear that the size of the memory cell depends upon the particular type. An `int` variable occupies a memory cell that is 32 bits long, while a `long` variable requires a 64-bit cell. This association between variable and memory cell does *not* require a `new` operation. In fact, the `new` operation is not permitted on primitive data. Consider the following local variable declaration.

```
int carCount;
```

This declaration causes `carCount` to begin its lifetime, and the variable is immediately associated with a 32-bit memory cell, as pictured by the rectangle below.

carCount ` [              0]`

Notice that the rectangle (memory cell) in the picture above appears to have a value of zero (0). The value in the memory cell contains what the programmer thinks to be the "value of the variable." Memory cells always store some value, and Java supports initialization of variables in certain cases. However, it is generally advisable for the program to assign its own initial values. The following instruction illustrates such an assignment.

```
carCount = 35;
```

software
engineering *Hint*

Java automatical-
ly initializes many
variables. The
wise programmer
avoids automatic
initialization by
always assigning
a value to a vari-
able before using
the variable's
value.

The outcome of executing this instruction is pictured below.

carCount | 35 |

Notice that an assignment to a primitive variable changes the variable's value, not its binding, as it would for a reference variable. In fact, the association of a variable name to a particular memory cell will not change throughout the lifetime of the instance variable. Furthermore, no two variables share the same memory cell.

When a primitive variable is used within an expression, the variable evaluates to its cell content (variable value). Therefore, executing the third instruction in the following instruction sequence causes vehicleCount to be assigned the value 100 (the sum of the values of carCount and truckCount).

```
carCount = 35;
truckCount = 65;
vehicleCount = carCount + truckCount;
```

Parameter passage of primitive data is also impacted by this memory cell association. Java uses a style of parameter passage that is formally known as **parameter passage by value**. Parameter passage by value treats each formal parameter like a local variable that receives a copy of the *value* of its corresponding argument at the time a method is called. For example, consider the following private method.

```
/** pre:    fRect is instantiated and sRect is instantiated
 *  post:   fRect is moved d pixels to the right
 *          and sRect is moved d/2 pixels to the right
 */
private void slideRects(int d, Rectangle fRect, Rectangle sRect)
{
    fRect.setLocation(fRect.getX()+d, fRect.getY());
    d = d / 2;
    sRect.setLocation(sRect.getX()+d, sRect.getY());
}
```

Suppose that the above method is called as follows.

```
slideRects(velocity, blueRectangle, greenRectangle);
```

When this call executes, the formal parameter d receives a copy of the value of velocity. The first statement within the method moves fRect (blueRectangle) to the right by d (velocity) pixels. Execution of the second statement in the method reduces d by one half, so the third statement will move sRect (greenRectangle) to its right by one half of velocity. It is important to notice that there is no further interaction between argument and parameter; velocity will not change value by executing slideRects, even though d changes value.

In reality, there is no difference between primitive data parameter passage and reference parameter passage in Java. In both cases, parameter passage behaves as though an assignment instruction is executed at call time for every parameter. The assignment assigns the argument to the parameter. For reference data, the assignment copies a binding; for primitive data, the assignment copies a value.

Every reference variable is also associated with its own cell of memory. The cell of the reference variable stores the **address** of the object that is bound to the variable. When a reference variable is first declared, its cell stores `null`, which is the address of nothing. When one reference variable is assigned to another, the value (address) is copied, so both variables are bound to the same object. In passage of a reference expression, a copy of the argument's value (an object address) is assigned to the formal parameter. This is why the method cannot alter the binding of an argument.

5.4 ■ Real Numbers (float and double Types)

Integer data are incapable of storing numbers that require nonwhole parts. Mathematicians use a class of numbers, known as **real numbers** to include values that lie between consecutive integer values. The number 3.2 is an example of a real number that is not an integer. Java includes two primitive data types for storing real number values. These types are known as `double` and `float`. Figure 5.6 describes the `double` data type.

The operations that Java supports on real expressions are essentially the same as those for integer expressions. Figure 5.6 points out that all of the `int` operators can also be applied to `double` operands. Of course, `double` operations produce real number results, so the division operator (/) performs real number division when applied to `double` expressions.

The syntax of a `double` constant is also distinct from Java integer constants. A syntax diagram for this syntax is given in Figure 5.7. The *Eformat* suffix permits using a scientific notation. For example, `3.92E+5` denotes $3.92 * 10^5$ or 392,000.

The `float` type in Java is nearly the same as `double`. The only differences stem from a variation in memory size.

■ `float` values occupy 32 bits while `double` values occupy 64 bits.

■ `float` constants use the `double` syntax with an "f" character appended.

The fixed size of `float` and `double` storage imposes two limitations upon representing real numbers—limited accuracy and a restricted range of values. Figure 5.8 summarizes these restrictions.

Java cannot always store the exact value of a real number. This limitation is a byproduct of the fixed length of the memory cells used to store `double` (64 bits) and `float` (32 bits) values. Even the mathematician cannot express all real numbers exactly in a limited number of digits. For example, the value 1/3 must be approximated to 0.3333 when using only four **significant digits** of accuracy. (Significant digits include all digits excluding any leading or trailing zeros.)

Figure 5.6

Summary of the `double` data type (operators abridged)

Name of the Type: `double`

Usage: A `double` is a real number with fifteen significant digits of accuracy.

Constants: Any consecutive sequence of zero or more decimal digits (0–9) followed by a decimal point, followed by any consecutive sequence of zero or more decimal digits. (There must be a minimum of one digit either before or after the decimal point.) The entire constant may be prefixed by a "+" or "–" symbol, and an E-format suffix is optional.

Prefix Operator (`double` → `double`)

[++ and -- cannot be applied to constants or constant expressions.]

Syntax	Semantics
-	negation
++	auto-increment
--	auto-decrement

Infix Arithmetic Operators (`double` × `double` → `double`)

Syntax	Semantics
+	addition
-	subtraction
*	multiplication
/	division
%	remainder after removing maximum integral multiple of the divisor

Infix Relational Operators (`double` × `double` → `boolean`)

Syntax	Semantics
==	equal to
!=	not equal to
<	less than
<=	less than or equal to
>	greater than
>=	greater than or equal to

Postfix Operator (`double` → `double`)

[++ and -- cannot be applied to constants or constant expressions.]

Syntax	Semantics
++	auto-increment
--	auto-decrement

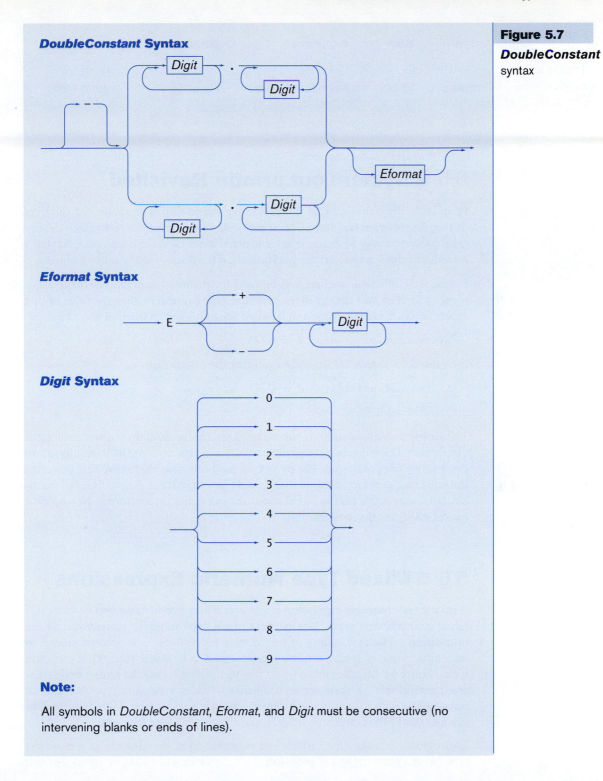

DoubleConstant Syntax

Eformat Syntax

Digit Syntax

Figure 5.7

DoubleConstant
syntax

Note:

All symbols in *DoubleConstant*, *Eformat*, and *Digit* must be consecutive (no intervening blanks or ends of lines).

Figure 5.8	Type	Size	Accuracy	Minimum	Maximum
Limitations of double and float	double	64 bits	15 significant digits	about 10^{-308}	about 10^{308}
	float	32 bits	7 significant digits	about 10^{-38}	about 10^{38}

5.5 ■ System.out.println Revisited

Frequently, programmers find it useful to be able to display the values of variables during the program execution. This is particularly important for testing and debugging code, as a way to examine intermediate states of various objects. Chapter 3 introduced the System.out.println method for displaying the state of objects.

Fortunately, this same method can be used for primitive expressions. If the argument to System.out.println is a primitive type expression, then the value of that expression is displayed. For example, when the following instruction executes

```
System.out.println(25 + 3 * 2);
```

the value 31 is displayed. Similarly, executing the instruction

```
System.out.println(98.2 - 0.4);
```

displays the value 97.8.

The println method outputs the value of its argument and then terminates the output line. Therefore, two consecutive calls to System.out.println results in two consecutive lines of output. The **print** method offers an alternative that performs the same task as println except that it does not terminate an output line. For example, two consecutive calls to System.out.print cause their values to be displayed consecutively on the *same* line.

5.6 ■ Mixed Type Numeric Expressions

A **mixed type numeric expression** is any expression that involves two or more different numeric data types. Java permits mixed type numeric expressions. At the foundation of Java's handling of mixed type expressions, is a concept known as **widening**. Some of Java's primitive types are said to be **wider** than other primitive types. Figure 5.9 describes this relation among the data types. The arrows in this diagram extend from a narrower to immediately wider type. Any type that can be reached by a path following one or more arrows is a wider type. Therefore, double is wider than float, and both double and float are wider than int.

Conceptually, a wider type variable can represent all of the values from a narrower type (with a potential loss of precision when converting to float or long). For this

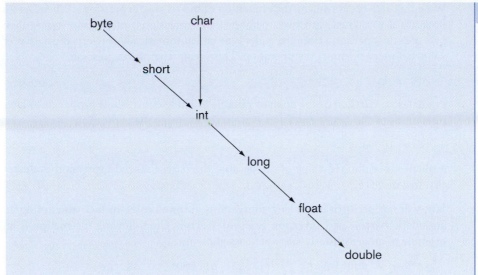

reason, Java considers a conversion from narrower to wider to be a **safe conversion**. Such safe conversions are often performed automatically. Java considers any primitive type to conform to any wider primitive type. This permits an `int` expression to be assigned to a `double` variable or a `long` argument to be passed to a parameter of type `float`. In fact, all of the following assignment instructions result in the appropriate widening type conversion. (The type of each variable is indicated by its name.)

```
doubleVar = floatVar;
doubleVar = longVar;
doubleVar = intVar;
doubleVar = shortVar;
doubleVar = byteVar;
doubleVar = charVar;
floatVar = longVar;
floatVar = intVar;
floatVar = shortVar;
floatVar = byteVar;
floatVar = charVar;
longVar = intVar;
longVar = shortVar;
longVar = byteVar;
longVar = charVar;
intVar = shortVar;
intVar = byteVar;
intVar = charVar;
shortVar = byteVar;
```

Widening also occurs during the evaluation of mixed type expressions. Whenever an operator is evaluated with two operands (subexpressions) of different types, then Java uses the operation from the wider type and automatically converts the narrower value before performing the operation. This means that the expression

```
7.0 / 2
```

evaluates as 7.0/2.0 or the double value 3.5. These conversions propagate to later operations of the same expression as well. For example the expression

```
(8 + 10.3) / 3
```

evaluates to a double value of 6.1 because the parenthesized expression evaluates first to a double.

Java will *not* perform narrowing conversions automatically. In fact, attempting an automatic narrowing conversion is a syntax error. The following instruction is an example of an erroneously attempted assignment.

```
intVar = doubleVar; // illegal attempt to narrow
```

Similarly, passing a wider argument to a narrower parameter is not permitted.

Narrowing is not performed automatically because it is considered unsafe. It is unsafe to convert a long value to a short because the long value may be outside the range of possible short values. Likewise, it is unsafe to convert from double to int because an int cannot store the fractional part of the double value.

Java provides a mechanism, known as a **cast**, so programmers may force unsafe conversions to occur in selected instances. The cast syntax and semantics are described in Figure 5.10.

The evaluation of a cast is called **casting**. Java permits casting any primitive expression to a narrower type. Casting from a double to a float may result in a loss of accuracy, but otherwise the value is maintained.

Figure 5.10

CastExpression description (abridged version of *Expression*)

Syntax

$$\longrightarrow (\longrightarrow \boxed{Type} \longrightarrow) \longrightarrow \boxed{Expression} \longrightarrow$$

Notes

- *Type* is an identifier that names a data type (primitive type or class name).
- Some casts are not allowed because the types are incompatible.

Semantics

When a *CastExpression* executes, the *Expression* is evaluated then converted to the data type specified by *Type*.

When a real type is cast to an integer type, **truncation** occurs. Truncation means that any fractional portion of the value is lost (*not* rounded). So the expression

```
(int) 24.8
```

evaluates to an `int` value of 24. Similarly, the expression

```
(long) -91.6
```

evaluates to a `long` value of –91.

A cast has higher precedence than any operator, except the prefix operators. Therefore, the following instruction produces a compile time error.

```
intVar = (int) 25.2 + 16.9;  // this contains a syntax error
```

This instruction should be written either as

```
intVar = (int)(25.2 + 16.9);
```

or

```
intVar = (int)25.2 + (int)16.9;
```

depending upon the intended result.

5.7 ■ Primitive Methods (Including Math)

There are many uses for methods that return a primitive type value. In this section, we discuss three example applications of such methods.

- methods to return attributes of graphical objects
- methods to perform common mathematical operations
- methods created by the programmer to return primitive values

Many *AWT* and *Swing* classes are defined in terms of four attributes: *x*, *y*, *width*, and *height*. Figure 5.11 reviews these attributes by showing an `Oval` object added to the content pane of a `JFrame` object.

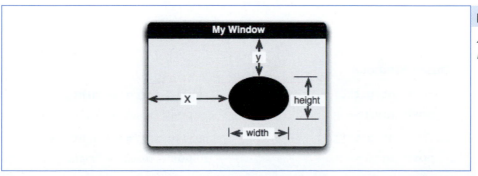

Figure 5.11

x, *y*, *width*, and *height* attributes

Sometimes it is useful for a program to be able to inspect these values at runtime. Methods that return an attribute are often referred to as **query methods**. In Chapter 4, we saw several such query methods named "get___". Figure 5.12 repeats the specifications for four commonly used methods.

software **Hint**
engineering

Names of the form "get___" are used frequently within the Java libraries to name query methods. This is an acceptable naming convention, even though it violates the preferred style of using nouns to name functions.

A sample use of a query occurs when moving a `Label` relative to its previous position. The following method call is designed to move a `Label`, called `lab`, down by half of its height.

```
lab.setLocation(lab.getX(), lab.getY()+lab.getHeight()/2);
```

Not all methods returning primitive values are query methods. The standard Java library includes a class, called **Math,** which supplies a number of methods that perform commonly used mathematical functions. These are the kinds of functions often found on many calculators. Figure 5.13 describes some of the `Math` methods. Using the `Math` class requires no `import` declaration, but a "`Math.`" prefix is needed.

`Math` methods may be called from anywhere that an expression of the same type is permitted. For example, assuming that `side1` and `side2` are double variables that store the lengths of the shorter sides of a right triangle, the following instruction assigns the proper value to `hypotenuse` (another `double` variable).

```
hypotenuse = Math.sqrt(side1 * side1 + side2 * side2);
```

Since arguments are expressions, sometimes an argument contains another nonvoid method call argument. For example, the preceding instruction can be written equivalently as follows.

```
hypotenuse = Math.sqrt(Math.pow(side1,2) + Math.pow(side2,2));
```

Executing this instruction requires that `Math.pow` be called twice. The value of the two arguments can then be passed to the `Math.sqrt` method.

`Math` contains many of the common mathematical functions, such as square root (**sqrt**); absolute value (**abs**–three versions for three different types of numbers); exponentiation (**pow**); logarithmic functions (**log** and **exp**); and trigonometric functions (**sin**, **cos**, and **tan**).

In addition to the predefined primitive methods, programmers can also define their own methods for returning primitive values. The following method illustrates.

Figure 5.12

Query methods included in most graphical classes

Query Methods

```
public int getX()              public int getWidth()
    post:  result == x             post:  result == width

public int getY()              public int getHeight()
    post:  result == y             post:  result == height
```

```
private double average(double d1, double d2) {
    return (d1 + d2) / 2.0;
}
```

This `average` method accepts two double parameters and returns the average (arithmetic mean) of its parameter values. The `average` method demonstrates once again, that the `new` operation is not used to create primitive type data.

```
/* post: result == the absolute value of d */
double Math.abs(double d)

/* post: result == the absolute value of f */
float Math.abs(float f)

/* post: result == the absolute value of j */
int Math.abs(int j)

/* post: result == b raised to the power e */
double Math.pow(double b, double e)

/* post: result == f rounded to the nearest integer */
int Math.round(float f)

/* post: result == d rounded to the nearest integer */
long Math.round(double d)

/* post: result == the square root of d */
double Math.sqrt(double d)

/* post: result == the cosine of d (radian measure) */
double Math.cos(double d)

/* post: result == the sine of d (radian measure) */
double Math.sin(double d)

/* post: result == the tangent of d (radian measure) */
double Math.tan(double d)

/* post: result == the natural logarithm of d */
double Math.log(double d)

/* post: result == the constant e raised to the power d */
double Math.exp(double d)

/* post: result == a random value such that 0.0<result<1.0 */
double Math.random()
```

Figure 5.13

Selected methods from the Math class

5.8 ■ Constants (final)

Mathematicians and scientists often use the concept of a **constant** to describe a value that is unchanging. The acceleration due to earth's gravity is a constant and so are the Golden Ratio and Euler's constant. Java supports the concept of a constant as well.

The `Math` class includes two constants for the well-known mathematical constants, Π and E. Like other Java language parts, constants are named by identifiers. Figure 5.14 contains more detail.

The reserved word **final** provides a means of creating constants in Java. From Figure 5.14 it is evident that both `Math.E` and `Math.PI` are constants, and they are both of type `double`.

Constants are used almost interchangeably with variables in Java. For example, the following instruction will calculate and assign the area of a circle with a radius stored in the variable `circleRadius`.

```
circleArea = circleRadius * circleRadius * Math.PI;
```

The significant difference between a `final` variable and other variables is that a `final` variable can only be assigned a value once. (For instance variables, such an assignment *must* occur before the end of the constructor method.) Any attempt to alter the value of a `final` variable results in an error.

software
engineering *Hint*

A constant is a variable whose value does not change during execution. It is preferable to declare such data as **final** (constant) because the compiler prohibits accidentally changing the constant's value.

Programmers can declare their own constants. Figure 5.15 shows the appropriate syntax for such declarations. The *FinalPrivateVarDecl* syntax is used to specify constants whose scope is the entire class, and *FinalLocalVariableDecl* is a notation used to declare constants that are local to a method. A *FinalPrivateVarDecl* can be placed anywhere an instance variable declaration is permitted, and a *FinalLocalVariableDecl* can be located anywhere that a local variable can be declared.

Figure 5.15 points out that any constant can, and should, be assigned a value as part of its declaration. Below is a sample declaration that can be placed within a class to create a constant named `pintsPerGallon`.

```
private final int pintsPerGallon = 8;
```

Figure 5.14

Constants from the Math class

```
/** E is the natural base for logarithms
 *     (roughly 2.7182818284590452354) */
final double Math.E

/** PI is a circle's circumference / diameter
 *     (roughly 3.14159265358979323846) */
final double Math.PI
```

Figure 5.15   *FinalPrivateVarDecl* (a possible *OneVarDecl*) and
LocalVariableDecl (a possible *OneStatement*)

FinalPrivateVarDecl **Syntax**

FinalLocalVariableDecl **Syntax**

Semantics

A constant has the same scope and may be used in the same places as a variable with one exception—constants can only be assigned once; and for instance variables, the assignment must occur before the end of the constructor method.

Notes

- The type of *Expression* must conform to *Type*.
- *Type* can be any accessible class name or primitive type.

5.9 ■ Numeric Expression Patterns

Some numeric expressions occur with sufficient frequency that they deserve to be considered common patterns. Good software developers are familiar with these expression patterns and know how to apply them. The first pattern is designed to retain accuracy that might otherwise be lost by integer division. Such accuracy can be retained by forcing a real division, rather than integer division. The pattern to accomplish this is shown in Figure 5.16.

```
(double) integerExpression / integerExpression ;
```

Figure 5.16

Expression pattern for double division with int expressions

A related pattern is required when a real expression (say of type `double`) must be assigned to an integer variable. A cast is often used in such a case. Applying the cast to the entire expression generally requires a set of parentheses around the expression. Figure 5.17 shows this pattern.

There are many occasions when the value of a real expression must be *rounded* to the nearest integer, rather than truncated. The `Math` class includes methods to round `float` expressions to `int` and `double` expressions to `long`. Figure 5.18 demonstrates how to use these methods to round expressions, along with a pattern for rounding without using `Math` methods.

Another common pattern that occurs frequently in programs is an instruction that increases the value of an integer variable by one. There are two ways to accomplish this instruction in Java; both are shown in Figure 5.19.

The Figure 5.19 pattern is essentially a counting pattern, because if it is performed repeatedly the effect is to cause the variable to count upward as in 2, 3, 4, 5, . . . In some cases, programs need to count within a restricted range. For example, a variable could be used to count from 0 to 4, repeatedly, as in the sequence 0, 1, 2, 3, 4, 0, 1, 2, 3, 4, . . . This kind of counting is accomplished by the assignment instruction pattern shown in Figure 5.20.

A final numeric expression pattern occurs when the program needs an integer that is randomly generated over a contiguous range. For example, a program simulating the roll of a die may need to model one roll as an integer from 1 through 6. The fol-

Figure 5.17

Assignment pattern for assigning `double` to `int`

```
intVar = (int) (doubleExpression);
```

Figure 5.18

Two expression patterns for rounding

```
intVar = (int) Math.round ( doubleExpression );
```

or

```
intVar = (int) ( doubleExpression + 0.5 );
```

Figure 5.19

Two expression patterns for incrementing a variable by one

```
integerVar = integerVar + 1;
```

or

```
integerVar ++;
```

$$integerVar = (integerVar + 1) \% (n + 1);$$

lowing Java instruction assigns to the `int` variable, `oneDie`, one of the integers from one through 6 with equal probability for each.

```
oneDie = (int)(Math.random() * 6.0) + 1.0 ;
```

This instruction relies on the `Math` method, called `random`, and the fact that `random` returns random `double` values between (but not equal to) 0.0 and 1.0. This single instruction can be extended into a pattern expression for generating any range of integers, as shown in Figure 5.21.

$$(int) \ (Math.random() \ * \ (high - low + 1)) + low$$

5.10 ■ char Data Type

Many computer applications process textual data. A word processor assists users in preparing documents of textual data. A compiler translates the text of a source program into object code. An e-mail program assists with reading and composing electronic messages (typically in textual form).

Not surprisingly, Java includes built-in facilities to support text processing. The simplest data type associated with textual data is the primitive `char` type. Figure 5.22 summarizes `char`.

A value of `char` data can be either a single **printable character** or a single nonprintable character. The printable characters include

- uppercase and lowercase alphabetic letters (A–Z and a–z)
- decimal digits (0–9)
- punctuation marks (period, comma, etc.)
- and special characters (#, $, *, etc.)

Figure 5.22

Summary of the char data type

Name of the Type: char

Size: two bytes

Usage: a single (unicode) character

Constants: Any printable character enclosed within single quotes (no intervening blanks permitted). Escape sequences can also be used to specify constants.

Postfix Operator: (char → char)
[cannot be applied to constants or constant expressions]

Syntax	Semantics
++	auto-increment
--	auto-decrement

Widening: char automatically widens to int, long, float, or double

The printable characters can be used as char constants, as long as they are enclosed within single quotation marks. For example, the following are all valid literals of type char.

```
'A'
'4'
'?'
```

Some special char constants cannot be written using the above notation. For these characters, Java supports an **escape sequence** notation. An escape sequence consists of a backslash character (\) followed by a second character. The two-symbol escape sequence is enclosed within single quotation marks to form a char constant. Figure 5.23 includes commonly used escape sequences for char constants.

Figure 5.23

Escape sequence char constants

Character	Escape code constant
single quotation mark (')	'\''
double quotation mark (")	'\"'
backslash character (\)	'\\'
backspace	'\b'
tab	'\t'
linefeed (new line)	'\n'
form feed	'\f'
carriage return	'\r'

Some escape sequences are designed to denote nonprintable characters. Nonprintables include, for instance, tabs and linefeed characters. Other char constants requiring the use of escape sequences include the single quotation mark, the double quotation mark, and the backslash.

Since computer storage encodes everything in numeric form, char constants also have a numeric value. Java uses the **unicode** encoding scheme to encode char values. There are more than 65,000 characters included in unicode. The first 128 characters are known as the **ASCII characters**. Figure 5.24 shows the encoding for the ASCII portion of the unicode alphabet.

Figure 5.24   The first 128 unicode characters

Dec	Hex	char	Dec	Hex	char	Dec	Hex	char	Dec	Hex	char
0	0000	\<NUL\>	35	0023	#	70	0046	F	105	0069	i
1	0001	\<SOH\>	36	0024	$	71	0047	G	106	006A	j
2	0002	\<STX\>	37	0025	%	72	0048	H	107	006B	k
3	0003	\<ETX\>	38	0026	&	73	0049	I	108	006C	l
4	0004	\<EOT\>	39	0027	'	74	004A	J	109	006D	m
5	0005	\<ENQ\>	40	0028	(	75	004B	K	110	006E	n
6	0006	\<ACK\>	41	0029	)	76	004C	L	111	006F	o
7	0007	\<BEL\>	42	002A	*	77	004D	M	112	0070	p
8	0008	\<BS\>	43	002B	+	78	004E	N	113	0071	q
9	0009	\<HT\>	44	002C	'	79	004F	O	114	0072	r
10	000A	\<LF\>	45	002D	–	80	0050	P	115	0073	s
11	000B	\<VT\>	46	002E	.	81	0051	Q	116	0074	t
12	000C	\<FF\>	47	002F	/	82	0052	R	117	0075	u
13	000D	\<CR\>	48	0030	0	83	0053	S	118	0076	v
14	000E	\<SO\>	49	0031	1	84	0054	T	119	0077	w
15	000F	\<SI\>	50	0032	2	85	0055	U	120	0078	x
16	0010	\<DLE\>	51	0033	3	86	0056	V	121	0079	y
17	0011	\<DC1\>	52	0034	4	87	0057	W	122	007A	z
18	0012	\<DC2\>	53	0035	5	88	0058	X	123	007B	{
19	0013	\<DC3\>	54	0036	6	89	0059	Y	124	007C	|
20	0014	\<DC4\>	55	0037	7	90	005A	Z	125	007D	}
21	0015	\<NAK\>	56	0038	8	91	005B	[	126	007E	~
22	0016	\<SYN\>	57	0039	9	92	005C	\	127	007F	\<DEL\>
23	0017	\<ETB\>	58	003A	:	93	005D	]	...	...	
24	0018	\<CAN\>	59	003B	;	94	005E	^			
25	0019	\<EM\>	60	003C	<	95	005F	_			
26	001A	\<SUB\>	61	003D	=	96	0060	z	\<...\>		
27	001B	\<ESC\>	62	003E	>	97	0061	a	denotes a nonprint-		
28	001C	\<FS\>	63	003F	?	98	0062	b	able character		
29	001D	\<GS\>	64	0040	@	99	0063	c			
30	001E	\<RS\>	65	0041	A	100	0064	d			
31	001F	\<US\>	66	0042	B	101	0065	e	⎵		
32	0020	⎵	67	0043	C	102	0066	f	denotes a		
33	0021	!	68	0044	D	103	0067	g	space/blank		
34	0022	"	69	0045	E	104	0068	h			

Figure 5.24 also illustrates that each char value has a numeric equivalent. The numeric value of a character is the value resulting from widening a char to an int. The columns labeled "Dec" show the decimal numeric equivalent for the corresponding char values. For example, the character 'Y' has a numeric value of 89 and '{' has a value of 123. Notice that the numeric value of decimal digits is different from what might be expected. The character '2' has a numeric value of 50 and '9' has a numeric value of 57. Any char expression is converted to its numeric equivalent by a cast to int.

Java recognizes one additional form of escape sequence for any char constant. This notation consists of a backslash (\) followed by a lower case "u" followed by the hexadecimal equivalent of the character. Figure 5.24 indicates the hexadecimal equivalent for the ASCII characters in the columns labeled "Hex." Using this escape code notation, the character '+' can be expressed as '\u002B' and 'q' is expressed as '\u0071'.

Sometimes it is useful to increment a char variable from one character to the next. Such a pattern can be used to advance the value of a char variable from one alphabetic letter to its successor or from one decimal digit character to the next. Figure 5.25 shows two patterns for accomplishing such char incrementation.

The first pattern is the simpler one, but the second pattern illustrates how char expressions can be widened automatically, as well as how to cast an int expression to a char.

Figure 5.25

Two patterns incrementing char variables

$$charVar\ ++$$

or

$$charVar = (char)\ (charVar + 1);$$

5.11 ■ Design Example– Dynamic Histogram

This section examines a particular program that makes use of primitive numeric data in several ways. The software requirements for this program are to display a window with three buttons and a histogram that reflects the number of times that each button has been clicked. More specifically, there is a blue filled rectangle immediately above each button. The height of each of these rectangles must be relative to the percentage of clicks of its neighboring button.

Figure 5.26 shows a snapshot of a portion of the program's execution when the buttons left to right have been clicked, respectively, 3, 2, and 5 times. For this snapshot, the height of the left bar is 30 percent of the maximum possible height. The middle bar is 20 percent of its maximum possible height, and the right bar is 50 percent of its maximum possible height.

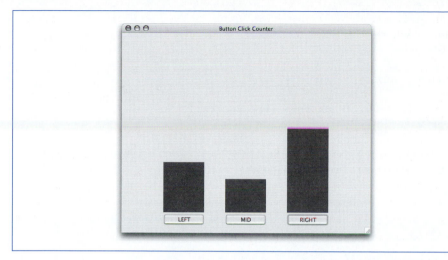

Figure 5.26

Histogram after
3, 2, and 5 clicks

A Driver class for this histogram program is shown in Figure 5.27. This program uses ThreeButtonFrame and the corresponding leftAction, midAction, and rightAction event handler methods.

The three blue histogram bars are represented by three variables: leftBar, midBar, and rightBar. Three int variables store the number of times the three buttons are clicked. These variables are leftClickCount, midClickCount, and rightClickCount. An int constant, named maxBarHeight, stores the maximum possible height of a blue bar as 400 pixels.

When a button click event calls the appropriate event handler, such as leftAction, the corresponding click counting variable is incremented by an instruction like the following.

```
leftClickCount++;
```

The redrawHistogram method is called after each click count variable update. In turn, redrawHistogram calls redrawOneBar once for each of the three bars. The second argument to the redrawOneBar method is the appropriate click count variable (an int).

The redrawOneBar method contains several examples of primitive expressions. Perhaps the most interesting is the following instruction, which is designed to calculate the height of a histogram bar.

```
newHeight = (int)((double)c / totalClicks * maxBarHeight);
```

This instruction uses two of the patterns that were presented in Section 5.9 (see Figures 5.16 and 5.17). The (double) cast is essential in the above instruction. If this cast is removed and more than one button is clicked, then the division always evaluates to zero and so does the bar height. By casting to double, the bar height evaluates accurately, rather than truncating fractional values. The outer cast to int is required in order to narrow the expression's value to an int type, as required by the int variable, newHeight.

Figure 5.27

Driver for
button click
histogram

```java
import java.awt.*;
/** Moving Histogram Program
 *  Author: David Riley
 *  Date: January, 2005
 */
public class Driver extends ThreeButtons{
    private ThreeButtonFrame histoWin;
    private Rectangle leftBar, midBar, rightBar;
    private int leftClickCount, midClickCount, rightClickCount;
    private final int maxBarHeight = 400;

    /** post:  A window is displayed that contains a histogram of
     *         the number of times that each window button is clicked
     *         as a percentage of the total number of such clicks.
     */
    public Driver() {
        histoWin = new ThreeButtonFrame("Button Click
            Histogram");
        histoWin.setLayout(null);
        leftClickCount = 0;
        midClickCount = 0;
        rightClickCount = 0;
        leftBar = newBar(100);
        histoWin.add(leftBar, 0);
        midBar = newBar(250);
        histoWin.add(midBar, 0);
        rightBar = newBar(400);
        histoWin.add(rightBar, 0);
        histoWin.repaint();
    }

    /** pre:   leftBar, midBar and rightBar are constructed
     *  post:  leftClickCount == leftClickCount@pre + 1
     *         and all bars of the histogram are properly updated
     */
    public void leftAction() {
        leftClickCount++;
        redrawHistogram();
    }

    /** pre:   leftBar, midBar and rightBar are constructed
     *  post:  midClickCount == midClickCount@pre + 1
     *         and all bars of the histogram are properly updated
     */
    public void midAction() {
        midClickCount++;
        redrawHistogram();
    }
```

```
/** pre:   leftBar, midBar and rightBar are constructed
 * post:   rightClickCount == rightClickCount@pre + 1
 *         and all bars of the histogram are properly updated
 */
public void rightAction() {
    rightClickCount++;
    redrawHistogram();
}


/** post:   result is a filled blue rectangle
 *          and result.getWidth() == 100
 *          and result.getX() == j
 */
private Rectangle newBar(int j) {
    Rectangle tmp = new Rectangle(j, 0, 100, 0);
    tmp.setBackground(Color.blue);
    return tmp;
}


/** pre:   leftBar, midBar, and rightBar are constructed
 * post:   all bars of the histogram are properly updated
 */
private void redrawHistogram() {
    redrawOneBar(leftBar, leftClickCount);
    redrawOneBar(midBar, midClickCount);
    redrawOneBar(rightBar, rightClickCount);
}


/** pre:   r is constructed
 * post:   the y and height attributes of r are adjusted to a
 *         new height of maxBarHeight *
 *         (c/(leftClickCount+midClickCount+rightClickCount))
 */
private void redrawOneBar(Rectangle r, int c) {
    int totalClicks, newHeight;
    totalClicks = leftClickCount + midClickCount
        + rightClickCount;
    newHeight = (int)((double)c / totalClicks
        * maxBarHeight);
    r.setLocation(r.getX(), 430-newHeight);
    r.setSize(r.getWidth(), newHeight);
    r.repaint();
}
}
```

Inspector

Below is a collection of hints on what to check when examining code that involves the concepts of this chapter.

- Reference data must be instantiated before it is used, but primitive data does not permit instantiation. When you check to be certain that reference variables are nonnull, check also to be certain that there is no illegal attempt to use a new operation on primitive data.

- The most common errors in numeric expressions stem from a misunderstanding of operator precedence. It is wise to check each numeric expression to be certain that operations will be evaluated in the correct order. When in doubt, use parentheses.

- Watch out for division on integer operands. Because the fractional part is lost, an integer division often produces unwanted results. The patterns from Figures 5.16 and 5.17 are useful in avoiding such problems.

- Remember that a cast to an integer *truncates*; it does not round. The *Math* class provides methods for rounding.

- Constants (`final` variables) can only be assigned once, and this is best done within their declaration statement.

Terminology

abs (Math function)	log (Math function)
address (of a memory cell)	long data type
byte data type	Math (library class)
cast	mixed type numeric expression
char data type	parameter passage by value
cos (Math function)	PI (Math constant)
double data type	postfix operator
E (Math constant)	pow (Math function)
exp (Math function)	prefix operator
E-format	random (Math function)
final	real number
float data type	reference type
infix operator	round (Math function)
int data type	safe type conversion

short data type

tan (Math function)

significant digit

truncation

sin (Math function)

widening

sqrt (Math function)

wider (type)

System.out.println

Exercises

1. What is the *type* (int, double, float, etc.) of each of the following Java expressions?

a. 19 / 3

b. (int)71.7 - 2 * 3

c. (7 + 2.3) * 3

d. (7 % 3) + (int)18.6

e. 2 + (int)1.9 - 2.3f

f. ((long)7 / 2) * 1.1

2. What is the *value* of each expression in Exercise 1?

3. What value is assigned to the int variables j and n as a result of executing each of the following instructions. (Assume that j has an initial value of 3 and n has an initial value of 16.)

a. j++;

b. n = n * 2;

4. What is output by each of the following instructions?

a. System.out.println(7 - (3 * 2.1));

b. System.out.println(7 - 3 * 2.1);

c. System.out.println(13 % (2+1));

d. System.out.println((int) 4.8);

e. System.out.println((double)1 / 8 + 2);

5. For each of the following pairs of types, identify which is the wider type. (Note that it is possible for neither type to be wider than the other.)

a. int or double

b. int or short

   c. `int or float`

   d. `long or short`

   e. `byte or short`

6. What is the type and the value of each of the following expressions?

   a. `Math.abs(-3.4) + Math.abs(3.4)`

   b. `Math.abs(7 - 10 * 2)`

   c. `(int)(Math.PI * 2)`

   d. `Math.round(17 / 3.0f)`

   e. `Math.sqrt(Math.abs(-3) + 22)`

   f. `Math.pow(3, Math.pow(Math.sqrt(4.0), 2))`

   g. `Math.cos(Math.PI)`

7. Each of the following is an incorrect attempt to write a method that returns the average (arithmetic mean) of three `int` numbers as accurately as possible, using a `double` return type. Some of these attempts contain syntax error, and others contain logic errors. Identify specifically what is wrong with each attempt.

   a.
```
private double average3(int n1, int n2, int n3) {
    return (double)n1 + (double)n2 + (double)n3 / 3.0;
}
```

   b.
```
private double average3(int n1, int n2, int n3) {
    double result;
    result = new ((n1 + n2 + n3) / 3.0);
    return result;
}
```

   c.
```
private double average3(int n1, int n2, int n3) {
    double result;
    result = (double)(n1 + n2 + n3) / 3.0);
    return result;
}
```

   d.
```
private double average3(int n1, int n2, int n3) {
    return (double(n1) + double(n2) + double(n3)) / 3;
}
```

8. Consider the following method.

```
public int m2(int z) {
    return z * 2;
}
```

What is output by each of the following instructions?

a. `System.out.println(m2(25));`

b. `System.out.println(m2(7) + m2(m2(3)));`

c. `System.out.println(m2(m2(m2(5)+1) + m2(1)));`

9. What is the range (i.e., smallest possible number and largest possible number) that can be assigned to the double variable, d, as a result of executing each instruction below.

a. `d = Math.random() * 5;`

b. `d = 2 + (int)(Math.random() * 7);`

c. `d = 2 + (int)Math.random() * 7;`

d. `d = d % 25;`

10. Precisely what is output by executing each of the following instructions?

a. `System.out.println('A');`

b. `System.out.println('A' + 3);`

c. `System.out.println((char)98);`

d. `System.out.println((char)51);`

e. `System.out.println('\\');`

f. `System.out.println('\u0071');`

g. `System.out.println((char)('A' + 1));`

11. Write a Java method for each of the following.

a. This method is a correct version of the `average3` method from Exercise 7.

b. This method returns a double value and has a single parameter of type `int`. When called, the method returns the area of a circle whose radius is equal to the parameter.

c. This method returns the length of a line segment given (as four parameters) the coordinates of the endpoints of the line segment. The parameters and return value should all be of type `double`.

Programming Exercises

1. Write a program to simulate a sunrise. Your program must begin with a black window and a "sun" that has a diameter of 100 pixels, but is not yet visible. Using a `ThreeButtonFrame`, the MID button should cause the sun to rise and the other buttons behave as described on the next page.

LEFT   This button is for zooming in on the sun. Clicking this button causes the sun to be enlarged by 20 percent. It is important to recenter the sun to the same center point whenever it enlarges.

MID   This causes the sun to raise by 2 percent of its current diameter.

RIGHT   This button is for zooming out from the sun. Clicking this button causes the sun to be reduced in size by 30 percent. It is important to re-center the sun to the same center point whenever it reduces its size.

2. Write a program using `ThreeButtonFrame`. Initially, this program must display a green lollipop in the middle of the window. This initial lollipop consists of a green filled circle that is 100 pixels in diameter upon a "stick" constructed from a `Rectangle` that is 100 pixels long and 5 pixels wide. The bottom edge of the green circle should just touch the stick, and the stick must be centered horizontally with the green disk. The three buttons of the window have the following behavior.

LEFT   The stick of the lollipop is resized to a length that is randomly selected from 50 through 150, and the green disk is automatically repositioned to stick precisely atop the new stick length.

MID   The disk portion of the lollipop is resized to have a diameter that is randomly selected from 70 through 120. The upper left corner of the disk does not change as a result of this resizing, but the stick must be repositioned to be horizontally centered and just touch the bottom of the disk.

RIGHT   The entire lollipop moves to its right. The first time that the RIGHT button is clicked the lollipop moves 1 pixel to its right; the next time it moves 2 pixels to its right; the next time it moves 3; etc.

3. Use a `ThreeButtonFrame` to draw line segments using the `Line` class. The initial line segment is black and connects points $(0, 0)$ to the opposite corner of the window. Thereafter, the buttons behave as described below.

LEFT   Clicking this button draws a new red line segment with one endpoint that is selected randomly from the region *below* the diagonal of the original (black) line segment. The second endpoint for your new line segment must be the midpoint of the most recently drawn line segment, regardless of color.

MID   This button redraws the original black line segment.

RIGHT   Clicking this button draws a new green line segment with one endpoint that is selected randomly from the region *above* the diagonal of the original (black) line segment. The second endpoint for your new line segment must be the midpoint of the most recently drawn line segment, regardless of color.

Supplier Classes

For Nature did that want supply.

—John Dryden

Objectives

- To introduce the client-supplier relation, the associated concept of composition, and examine the role of supplier classes and client classes in a complete program
- To show an additional class diagram notation for composition
- To explore the differences between `public` and `private` declarations
- To revisit the Java notation for qualified expressions
- To introduce scope and lifetime rules for variables and methods
- To explore various issues of class design including selecting the best location for a feature and properly hiding information to create thin interfaces
- To examine the notions of read-only and write-only access to data and to demonstrate a technique for implementing both kinds of restricted access
- To introduce the concept of reusing an identifier and examine Java rules for such reuse, including method overloading
- To introduce the `String` data type for implementing a character string

- To introduce the Scanner as a means for converting String data to primitive data
- To examine the concept of enumerated data types
- To introduce the JTextField class from the *Swing* library

*T*he **client-supplier relation** is common in the retail industry. Every grocery store is the client of suppliers who deliver daily stock for the grocer's shelves. Meanwhile, that same grocer is a supplier for customers (clients) who shop at the store daily. The electronic world is also no stranger to clients and suppliers. Internet Web servers act as suppliers to client computers that download Web pages, and e-mail servers supply electronic mail messages to their clients.

6.1 ■ Clients and Suppliers in Software

The concept of **clients** and **suppliers** also plays a central role in object-oriented software development. In software development, the clients and suppliers are classes. A client class is one that borrows the facilities of another class (known as the supplier class). Sometimes the client calls a method or accesses an attribute from the supplier. Sometimes the client class uses the supplier class for one of the following:

- a variable type
- a parameter type
- the return type of one or more nonvoid methods

Figure 6.1 illustrates with a simple Driver class that constructs a window and adds a red Oval to that window. The location and size of the Oval is selected randomly.

The Driver class in this example is a client of three classes: JFrame, Oval, and Math; this means that these three classes are all suppliers to Driver. The JFrame and Oval classes are suppliers because Driver includes instance variables belonging to these classes. Math is a supplier because Driver uses one of its methods, namely random.

Since they serve as types for one or more variables, JFrame and Oval have a special relationship with Driver, known as **composition**. The term "composition" means that a client class is *composed* of instance variables and thereby of the classes that supply types for these instance variables. Another name used for composition is **aggregation**; a client class is an aggregate of its instance variables. Composition/aggregation is such an important relationship that class diagrams are often annotated with connecting lines to point out this relationship. The usual notation, as shown below, is to draw a line segment connecting the composition to its supplier with a diamond on the composite (client) end of the line.

This aggregation/composition notation can be used to diagram the program from Figure 6.1. Figure 6.2 contains such a diagram for the three classes.

Previous chapters have explored how to write client code. In this chapter, the focus changes to an examination of how to add supplier code.

```java
import javax.swing.JFrame;
import java.awt.Color;
/** Random Oval Program
 *  Author: David Riley
 */
public class Driver {
    private JFrame window;
    private Oval redOval;

    /** post:  A window is displayed
     *         and a randomly sized red oval is displayed.
     */
    public Driver() {
        window = new JFrame("Random Red Oval");
        window.setBounds(10, 10, 600, 500);
        window.setVisible(true);
        window.setLayout(null);
        redOval = new Oval((int)(Math.random()*600),
            (int)(Math.random()*500),
            (int)(Math.random()*600),
            (int)(Math.random()*500));
        redOval.setBackground(Color.red);
        window.add(redOval, 0);
        window.repaint();
    }
}
```

Figure 6.1

Program to draw a random oval

Figure 6.2

Class diagram
showing
composition

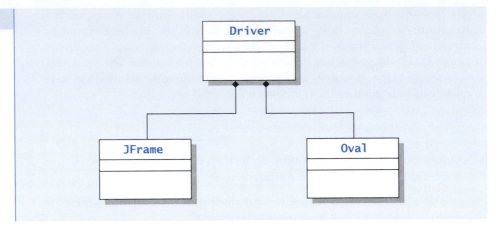

6.2 ■ **Another Client**

Suppliers of manufactured goods must seek to provide the services most desired by their clients. Similarly, supplier classes should be designed to provide the best possible services to client classes. The "services" that a class supplies take the form of methods and instance variables. The Container class supplies update methods such as setBackground and setLocation, as well as query methods like getX and getHeight. The Math class supplies constants such as PI and functions like Math.sqrt and Math.random. The instance variables, constants, and methods of a class are said to be **encapsulated** members of that class.

Java uses the **private** and **public** prefixes to control member encapsulation. A feature that is declared to be public is available anywhere. Features that are declared to be private are the "private domain" of the class. Private features are encapsulated within the class, and not available elsewhere. This use of public and private apply to instance variables, methods, and classes alike.

Consider the banking community. The primary data type for banking software is probably not an int or a double, but some form of *money*. It seems that a supplier

Opening
the Black Box

The Driver classes encountered thus far have used fussy rules regarding the use of public and private. The Driver class, along with the Driver constructor method, are public because they must be used elsewhere in order to create an initial Driver object. Likewise, the leftAction, midAction, and rightAction methods are public because they are called from event handling objects that are external to Driver.

Other Driver methods and instance variables are declared to be private. This is done to keep such features localized within the class, since they are not needed outside. These choices of how to use public and private are important software engineering decisions that will be explained later.

class that provides ways to store and manipulate money would be useful for programmers developing banking software. Figure 6.3 contains the class diagram specifications for such a supplier class, called MoneyUSA. Figure 6.4 contains the class specifications for MoneyUSA.

A variable of type MoneyUSA will represent a single amount of money. A single program may declare as many MoneyUSA variables as needed.

The members of MoneyUSA include

- a constructor (MoneyUSA) that has five parameters for different amounts of dollars and coins
- a valueInCents method to return the numeric value (in cents) of the money
- a valueInDollars method to return the dollar value of the money (as a double)

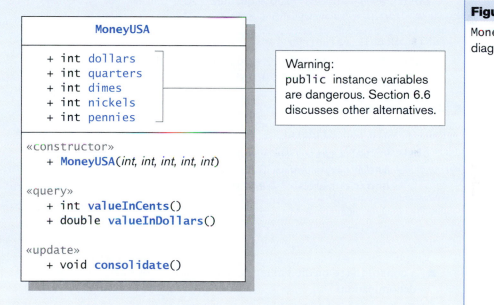

Figure 6.3

MoneyUSA class diagram

The MoneyUSA class declares several public instance variables. As the warnings in Figures 6.3, 6.7, and 6.8 suggest, public instance variables are generally a poor choice. In this particular situation, public instance variables are tolerable, and they are included because they help to illustrate important concepts.

In Section 6.6, an Opening the Black Box feature explains how to write the MoneyUSA class without the use of public instance variables.

Closed
Black Box

Figure 6.4

MoneyUSA class
specifications

Invariant

A MoneyUSA object maintains a monetary amount as an integer count of dollars, quarters, dimes, nickels, and pennies so that dollars >= 0 and quarters >= 0 and dimes >= 0 and nickels >= 0 and pennies >= 0.

Constructor Method

public **MoneyUSA** (int *dol*, int *q*, int *di*, int *n*, int *p*)

   pre: *dol* >=0 **and** *q* >= 0 **and** *di* >= 0 **and** *n* >= 0 **and** *p* >= 0

   post: dollars == *dol* **and** quarters == *q* **and** dimes == *di*
           and nickels == *n* **and** pennies == *p*

Query Methods

public int **valueInCents**()

   post: *result* == dollars * 100 + quarters * 25 + dimes * 10
                + nickels * 5 + pennies

public double **valueInDollars**()

   post: *result* == (dollars * 100 + quarters * 25 + dimes * 10
                + nickels * 5 + pennies) / 100.0

Update Method

public void **consolidate**()

   post: valueInCents() == valueInCents()**@pre**
        and 0 <= quarters <= 3 **and** 0 <= dimes <= 2
        and 0 <= nickels <= 1 **and** 0 <= pennies <= 4

■ a `consolidate` method to replace large numbers of small coins with larger denominations

■ five instance variables to keep track of the exact number of each coin/dollar bills in the money

Every feature of the MoneyUSA class is declared to be `public`. Class diagrams use a plus sign (+) to highlight the fact that an instance variable or a method is `public`, while a minus sign (-) indicates a private feature.

Notice that the methods called `valueInCents` and `valueInDollars` are labeled «query». This means that they are nonvoid methods that return some attribute or characteristic of the object. A client program can *query* a MoneyUSA object to retrieve its monetary value either in cents (by calling `valueInCents`) or in dollars (by calling `valueInDollars`).

Figure 6.5 contains an example of a Driver class that is a client of MoneyUSA. The Driver class contains a constructor method and a private method, called printMoney.

The Driver constructor method declares a local variable called cash that belongs to the MoneyUSA class. This variable is assigned a value by the following instruction.

```
cash = new MoneyUSA(1, 5, 1, 4, 2);
```

Executing the above instruction calls the MoneyUSA constructor, thereby initializing the monetary amount to consist of one (1) dollar, five (5) quarters, one (1) dime, four (4) nickels, and two (2) pennies and binds this new Money object to the cash variable. The next instruction calls the private printMoney method, passing cash as an argument. When printMoney returns, the following instruction is executed:

```
cash.consolidate();
```

This instruction calls the consolidate method. According to the MoneyUSA specifications, consolidate revises coin counts into the largest possible denominations

Figure 6.5

Client class for MoneyUSA

```java
/** Money Test Program
 * Author: David Riley
 */
public class Driver {
    public Driver() {
        MoneyUSA cash;
        cash = new MoneyUSA(1, 5, 1, 4, 2);
        printMoney(cash);
        cash.consolidate();
        printMoney(cash);
        cash.pennies = cash.pennies * 2;
        printMoney(cash);
    }

    private void printMoney(MoneyUSA m) {
        System.out.println(m.valueInCents());
        System.out.println(m.valueInDollars());
        System.out.println(m.dollars);
        System.out.println(m.quarters);
        System.out.println(m.dimes);
        System.out.println(m.nickels);
        System.out.println(m.pennies);
    }
}
```

without changing the total value of the money. In other words, a call to `consoli-date` should change every five pennies into a nickel, every two nickels into a dime, every two dimes and a nickel into a quarter, and every four quarters into a dollar. For example, if the total value of cash is $2.57, then a call to `consolidate` will ensure that this money is stored as two (2) dollars, two (2) quarters, no (0) dimes, one (1) nickel, and two (2) pennies.

The `Driver` constructor includes the following instruction:

```
cash.pennies = cash.pennies * 2;
```

This is an assignment instruction that accesses a public instance variable. The notation

```
cash.pennies
```

denotes the `pennies` variable that is a part of the `cash` object. Therefore, this assignment instruction can be explained as doubling the number of pennies in the `cash` object. Figure 6.6 generalizes the notation used to reference this variable.

Figure 6.6   *ObjectReference* description

Syntax

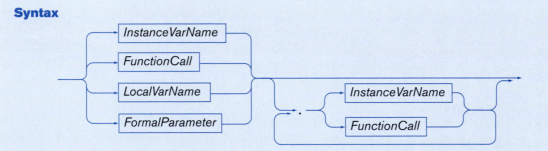

Syntax

- *InstanceVarName* is the name of an instance variable that is accessible in this context (scope).
- *FunctionCall* is the name and argument list for a nonvoid method that is accessible in this context (scope).
- *LocalVarName* is the name of a local variable (valid only if used within a method that includes a declaration for this variable).
- *FormalParameter* is the name of a formal parameter (valid only if used within a method that declares such a parameter).

Notes

- *ObjectReference* can be used anywhere that an object of the same type is permitted.
- *ObjectReference* may be used to the right of an assignment operator only if it ends with a variable or parameter name.

This description of *ObjectReference* from Figure 6.6 defines the alternative ways to identify an object in Java. An object can be referred to using

- a variable name
- a nonvoid method call (that returns the object)
- a local variable name
- the name of a formal parameter

Of course, variable names, method calls, and formal parameters are valid only if used within the proper context. This context refers to the scope of each name. Java scope rules are examined in Section 6.4.

The *ObjectReference* description also shows that any of these four items can be used as a qualifier to be followed by a period and a different instance variable name or method call. Figure 6.5 makes use of this notation to refer to the number of quarters in a parameter (m) of type `MoneyUSA`

```
m.quarters
```

and to call `MoneyUSA` methods using expressions like the one below:

```
m.valueInDollars()
```

Expressions like those described by Figure 6.6 are often called **qualified expressions** because of the qualifiers on the left of the period. The `valueInDollars` must be *qualified* by m in order to identify the object to which the method is applied.

6.3 ■ **Suppliers**

When implementing a supplier class, the best place to start is the class diagram and class specifications. A class diagram shows the public features of the class, including such things as instance variable types and method names with parameter lists. The class specification goes even further by providing the software contracts (preconditions, postconditions, and class invariants) that define the desired behavior of the class.

Figure 6.7 contains code for the `MoneyUSA` supplier class. This class consists of the same five instance variables and four methods as seen in the class diagram and specification. Even the assertions from the class specification are retained in this class to assist in code readability

The syntax used by a supplier class is no different from other classes. Like all classes, `MoneyUSA` must include a constructor method that has the same name as the class. Executing the `MoneyUSA` constructor method causes the values of its parameters to be assigned to the corresponding instance variables. Notice that while the `Driver` class needs to use notation such as

```
cash.dimes
```

software
engineering *Hint*

Writing a supplier class should start with the class diagram and class specification. These two documents dictate the features of the class and specify their behavior.

Figure 6.7

MoneyUSA class

```java
/** Class Invariant
 *    A MoneyUSA object maintains a monetary amount as an integer
 *    count of dollars, quarters, dimes, nickels, and pennies and
 *    dollars>=0 and quarters>=0 and dimes>=0 and nickels>=0 and
 *    pennies>=0  */
public class MoneyUSA {
    public int dollars;
    public int quarters;
    public int dimes;
    public int nickels;
    public int pennies;
```

> Warning:
> public instance variables
> are dangerous. Section 6.6
> discusses other alternatives.

```java
    /** pre:   dol>=0 and q>=0 and di>=0 and n>=0 and p>=0
     * post:   dollars == dol and quarters == q and dimes == di
     *         and nickels == n and pennies == p  */
    public MoneyUSA(int dol, int q, int di, int n, int p) {
        dollars = dol;
        quarters = q;
        dimes = di;
        nickels = n;
        pennies = p;
    }

    /** post:   result == dollars*
     *          100+quarters*25+dimes*10+nickels*5+pennies  */
    public int valueInCents() {
        return dollars*100+quarters*25+dimes*10+nickels*5+pennies;
    }

    /** post:   result == (dollars*
     *          100+quarters*25+dimes*10+nickels*5+pennies)/100  */
    public double valueInDollars() {
        return valueInCents() / 100.0;
    }

    /** post:   valueInCents() == valueInCents()@pre
     *          and 0<=pennies<=4 and 0<=nickels<=1
     *          and 0<=dimes<=2 and 0<=quarters<=3  */
    public void consolidate() {
        int remainingCents = valueInCents();
        dollars = remainingCents / 100;
        remainingCents = remainingCents % 100;
        quarters = remainingCents / 25;
        remainingCents = remainingCents % 25;
        dimes = remainingCents / 10;
        remainingCents = remainingCents % 10;
        nickels = remainingCents / 5;
        pennies = remainingCents % 5;
    }
}
```

to reference an instance variable from another class, inside the MoneyUSA class the variable

    dimes

is accessed using only its name.

The consolidate method is a good example of how class specifications are transformed into the necessary code. The method's postcondition asserts that executing consolidate does not alter the total monetary value of its object, but it may need to adjust the counts of individual denominations so they fall within ranges (such as $0 <= $ pennies $<= 4$). The algorithm to accomplish this is similar to the procedure a cashier uses to make change.

The first step in consolidate is to declare a local variable as follows.

    int remainingCents = valueInCents();

This line not only declares a new remainingCents variable, but it also initializes its value to the total number of cents in the MoneyUSA object. The next instruction is

    dollars = remainingCents / 100;

Executing this instruction assigns to dollars the maximum number of whole dollars that exist within remainingCents. The next instruction

    remainingCents = remainingCents % 100;

subtracts the value of these dollars from remainingCents. At this point in the execution, the value of remainingCents must be less than 100. The next two instructions are designed to assign to quarters the maximum number of quarters in remainingCents and subtract their value from remainingCents. Similar instructions remove as many dimes and nickels as possible. Finally, pennies is assigned the value of remainingCents that is left over after the value of all larger denominations are subtracted.

Most classes are not just a supplier or a client, but serve as both a client of some classes and a supplier to others. Figure 6.8 illustrates such a class, called PersonalBudget. The PersonalBudget class is a client of MoneyUSA by virtue of three instance variables: cashOnHand, outstandingBalance, and savings. These three variables maintain the three related aspects of a person's finances. The body of the PersonalBudget constructor method consists of three calls to the MoneyUSA constructor to initialize the three instance variables to zero.

The totalAssets method illustrates how PersonalBudget accesses the different MoneyUSA variables. Executing the instruction

```
assets = new MoneyUSA(cashOnHand.dollars + savings.dollars,
    cashOnHand.quarters + savings.quarters,
    cashOnHand.dimes + savings.dimes,
    cashOnHand.nickels + savings.nickels,
    cashOnHand.pennies + savings.pennies);
```

Figure 6.8

PersonalBudget
class

```java
public class PersonalBudget {
    public MoneyUSA cashOnHand;
    public MoneyUSA outstandingExpenses;
    public MoneyUSA savings;
    public PersonalBudget() {
        cashOnHand = new MoneyUSA(0, 0, 0, 0, 0);
        outstandingExpenses = new MoneyUSA(0, 0, 0, 0, 0);
        savings = new MoneyUSA(0, 0, 0, 0, 0);
    }

    /** pre:   0<=dol and 0<=q and 0<=di and 0<=n and 0<=p
     * post:  savings is savings@pre + dol*100+q*25+di*10+n*5+p
     *            cents consolidated into the largest possible
     *        denominations.
     */
    public void addToSavings
            (int dol, int q, int di, int n, int p) {
        savings.dollars = savings.dollars + dol;
        savings.quarters = savings.quarters + q;
        savings.dimes = savings.dimes + di;
        savings.nickels = savings.nickels + n;
        savings.pennies = savings.pennies + p;
        savings.consolidate();
    }

    /** pre:   cashonHand is constructed and savings is
     *         constructed
     * post:  result = the value of cashOnHand plus savings
     *        consolidated into the largest possible
     *        denominations
     */
    public MoneyUSA totalAssets() {
        MoneyUSA assets;
        assets =
            new MoneyUSA(cashOnHand.dollars + savings.dollars,
            cashOnHand.quarters + savings.quarters,
            cashOnHand.dimes + savings.dimes,
            cashOnHand.nickels + savings.nickels,
            cashOnHand.pennies + savings.pennies);
        assets.consolidate();
        return assets;
    }

    // additional methods can be included here

}
```

> Warning:
> public instance
> variables are dangerous.
> Section 6.6 discusses
> other alternatives.

constructs a new MoneyUSA object and assigns it to the local assets variable. Notice that the number of dollars in assets becomes the total of the number of dollars in the cashOnHand and savings objects.

To illustrate how PersonalBudget can be a supplier as well as a client, consider the following Driver class:

```
public class Driver {
    private PersonalBudget myBudget;
    // additional variables and methods can be included here
}
```

This latest Driver class is a client of PersonalBudget because it declares an instance variable, called myBudget, which belongs the PersonalBudget class.

The composition relationships among the three classes (Driver, PersonalBudget, and MoneyUSA) is pictured in Figure 6.9. The number "3" on the line connecting PersonalBudget to MoneyUSA denotes the fact that PersonalBudget contains three instance variables of type MoneyUSA.

Class diagrams, like Figure 6.9, illustrate several useful relationships. However, class diagrams cannot capture the behavior of objects at runtime. A common method to draw runtime relationships is with object diagrams. Figure 6.10 is a sample object diagram for the three classes.

An object diagram includes a separate rectangle for each reference object. The variable name of an object and its class appear underlined on the first line of the rectangle. The class to which the object belongs is preceded by a colon. Lines are drawn

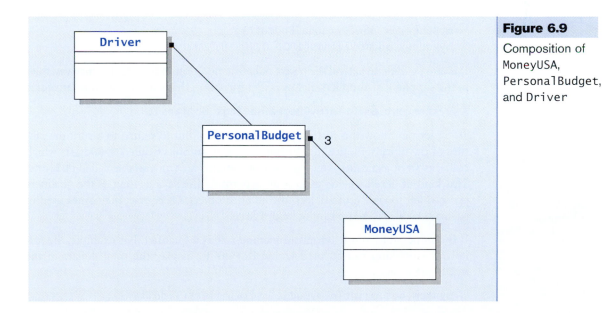

Figure 6.9

Composition of MoneyUSA, PersonalBudget, and Driver

Figure 6.10

Object diagram for MoneyUSA, PersonalBudget, and Driver

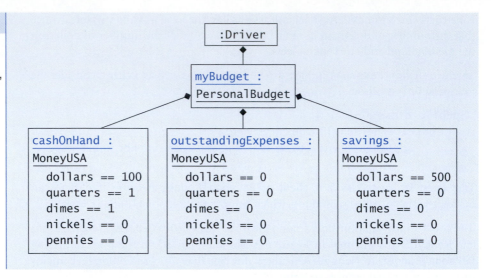

to connect an object with variables that are contained within the object. Primitive instance variables are included in object rectangles, along with their values.

Each object diagram captures the state of objects at one instant in time. It is a kind of snapshot of a particular point during program execution. Figure 6.10 pictures an instant when the three MoneyUSA objects have been constructed and cashOnHand totals $100.35, outstandingExpenses is $0, and savings is $500.

At the execution time pictured by Figure 6.10, a myBudget variable has been constructed within Driver. Therefore, Driver can use the public features of PersonalBudget with instructions such as the following:

```
myBudget = new PersonalBudget();
myBudget.addToSavings(100, 0, 0, 0, 0);
```

It is also possible to extend the object reference notation to refer to instance variables in the suppliers of suppliers. Below is an instruction that can be placed in Driver:

```
System.out.println(myBudget.savings.dollars);
```

To understand how this instruction works, it is helpful to return to a runtime picture of the objects. Notice that Driver contains an object called myBudget, which contains an object called savings, which contains an int variable called dollars. This kind of dereferencing expression is permitted in Java as long as the qualifiers proceed left to right from object to contained object. Of course, the names used in such a variable reference cannot be private.

It is also possible to use a nonvoid method call as a qualifier. For example, the following expression can be used within Driver to display the total dollars in the myBudget assets:

```
System.out.println(myBudget.totalAssets().dollars);
```

software
engineering *Hint*

Reference expressions can become complex. If a qualified expression contains three or more periods reading becomes a challenge. Often it is preferable to use another variable to alias a subexpression object.

6.4 ■ Scope and Lifetime

Three categories of Java variables have been explained thus far in this text.

1. `private` instance variables
2. `public` instance variables
3. local variables

Each of these categories has different **visibility** characteristics. A `private` instance variable is only visible within the class in which it is declared. A `public` instance variable is visible anywhere that an object of the supplier type can be referenced. The visibility of a local variable is the most restrictive of all, being limited to the body of the enclosing method.

Scope is the word that programmers use to refer to such visibility. The scope of a `private` instance variable is its class, and the scope of a local variable is its method. Formal parameters have scope as well. The scope of a formal parameter is the method in which it is declared, just like any of that method's local variables.

Just like variables, methods also have scope. The *scope of a method* refers to the region from which the method can be called. A `private` method has scope restricted to the class in which it is declared. The scope of a `public` method extends to anywhere where an object of the supplying class is available.

In addition to scope, variables have a second property, known as **lifetime**. (Lifetime is a property of variables, *not* a property of methods.) The lifetime of a variable is the portion of runtime during which the variable exists. Local variables have a lifetime that corresponds to their scope. In other words, the lifetime of a local variable begins when the enclosing scope (method body) starts to execute, and its lifetime ends when the enclosing scope completes execution.

The lifetime of an instance variable is dependent upon the object that contains it. When an object is constructed, the lifetime of all of its instance variables (both `private` and `public`) begins. An instance variable's lifetime ends only when the object is orphaned. Figure 6.11 summarizes the scope and lifetime of various program entities.

Good software engineers practice **defensive programming**, just as good drivers practice defensive driving. One important tenant of defensive programming is to protect supplier code from undesirable use by client code. This is analogous to a defensive driver guarding against the conduct of other drivers.

One way to program defensively is to restrict scope as much as possible. The reasoning behind this philosophy is that if clients do not have access to a variable or method, then they cannot utilize them in unwanted ways.

This preference for more restrictive declaration suggests that it is better to declare a method to be `private` than `public`. Of course, some methods need to be `public`, but the programmer has an obligation to use caution before choosing to make a method `public`.

software *Hint*
engineering

Whenever possible, variables should be declared to be local. This limits access to these variables in a form of defensive programming.

Figure 6.11

Scope and lifetime of various program entities

	Scope	Lifetime
local variable	The body of the enclosing method	The period of time during which the enclosing method is running
formal parameter	The body of the enclosing method	The period of time during which the enclosing method is running
private instance variable	The class in which the variable is declared	The period of time during which the object containing the instance variable is accessible
public instance variable	Anywhere that a reference to the object containing the instance variable is available	The period of time during which the object containing the instance variable is accessible
private method	The class in which the method is declared	
public method	Anywhere that a reference to the object belonging to the method's class is available	

software engineering *Hint*

The public parts of a class are those that form the class interface. It is best to declare other class parts as private.

From a defensive programming perspective, the most preferred scope for a variable is local. However, variables sometimes need to be retained from one method call until a subsequent call of the same (or some other) method. In such cases, the variable cannot be local, so it should be declared as a `private` instance variable.

To illustrate the need for various kinds of scope and lifetime, consider the problem of implementing the class described by the diagram and interface definition in Figures 6.12 and 6.13.

Figure 6.12

NestedCircles class diagram

```
┌─────────────────────────────────────┐
│           NestedCircles             │
├─────────────────────────────────────┤
│  - int lastCircleRadius             │
├─────────────────────────────────────┤
│ «constructor»                       │
│    + NestedCircles(int, int, int )  │
│                                     │
│ «update»                            │
│    + void addToContainer(Container )│
│    + void setBackground(Color )     │
│    + void insertCircle()            │
└─────────────────────────────────────┘
```

Figure 6.13

NestedCircles
class
specification

Invariant

A `NestedCircles` object

■ is a filled circular region, possibly with black, concentric circles upon it.

Constructor Methods

`public NestedCircles(int x, int y, int r)`

> **pre:** $r > 0$
>
> **post:**   A new black filled `NestedCircle` object is created with upper left
> corner at (x, y)
> **and** *lastCircleRadius* == r.

Update Methods

`public void setBackground(Color c)`

> **pre:**   c is a valid `Color`
>
> **post:**   This filled `NestedCircles` is recolored using color c.

`public void insertCircle()`

> **post:**   *lastCircleRadius* == 0.8 * *lastCircleRadius***@pre**
> **and** a black circle with radius of *lastCircleRadius* is added
> concentrically to this object.

Query Method

`public Oval addableContent(Container c)`

> **post:**   *result* is this image suitable for passing as an argument to add.

A `NestedCircles` object behaves somewhat like an `Oval`. The most unique feature of `NestedCircles` is the `insertCircle` method. Each call to `insertCircle` draws a new concentric black circle upon the `NestedCircles` object, and each circle has a radius that is 80 percent of the radius of the prior circle. Figure 6.14 contains suitable code for the `NestedCircles` class.

The variables of the `NestedCircles` class illustrate why programmers choose one category of variable over another. The `initialOval` variable is bound to an `Oval` to which all concentric circles are added. `initialOval` is constructed by the `NestedCircles` method, colored by the `setBackground` method, returned by the `addableContent` method, as well as being used by `insertCircle`. Since all of these methods share `initialOval`, it is impossible to declare it as a local variable.

The choice between declaring `initialOval` to be `public` or `private` does not involve correctness because the program would be correct for either public or private scope. However, if `initialOval` is public, then the client code is free to

Figure 6.14

NestedCircles
class

```java
import java.awt.Color;
/** Class Invariant
 *      A NestedCircles object...
 *          is a filled circular region, possibly with black,
 *          concentric circles upon it
 */
public class NestedCircles {
    private Oval initialOval;
    private int lastCircleRadius;

    /** pre:   r > 0
     * post:  A new black filled NestedCircle object is created
     *              with upper-left corner at (x, y)
     *              and lastCircleRadius == r   */
    public NestedCircles(int x, int y, int r) {
        initialOval = new Oval(x, y, 2*r, 2*r);
        lastCircleRadius = r;
    }

    /** post:  result is this image suitable for passing as
     *              an argument to add.   */
    public Oval addableContent() {
        return initialOval;
    }

    /** pre:   c is a valid Color
     * post:  initialOval is recolored using color c   */
    public void setBackground(Color c) {
        initialOval.setBackground(c);
        initialOval.repaint();
    }

    /** post:  lastCircleRadius == 0.8* lastCircleRadius@pre
     *              and a black circle with radius of lastCircleRadius
     *              is added concentrically to this object   */
    public void insertCircle() {
        Oval newOval, circleCenter;
        int newX;
        lastCircleRadius = (int)(lastCircleRadius *.8);
        newX = (initialOval.getWidth() - 2*lastCircleRadius) / 2;
        newOval = new Oval(newX, newX,
            2*lastCircleRadius, 2*lastCircleRadius);
        initialOval.add(newOval, 0);
        circleCenter = new Oval(1, 1, newOval.getWidth()-2,
            newOval.getHeight()-2);
        circleCenter.setBackground(initialOval.getBackground());
        newOval.add(circleCenter, 0);
        newOval.repaint();
    }
}
```

change `initialOval`'s dimensions, relocate it, or modify it in many other potentially undesirable ways. These are the kinds of unwanted variable corruption that motivate defensive programming. In this case, the defensive thing to do is declare `initialOval` as a `private` instance variable.

The `lastCircleRadius` variable is somewhat similar to `initialOval`. `lastCircleRadius` needs to be maintained between consecutive calls to `insertCircle` so that each call can draw a circle outline that is 80 percent of the previous circle outline. Since the lifetime of local variables does not span consecutive calls, `lastCircleRadius` must be an instance variable. Once again, it is better defensive programming to declare `lastCircleRadius` to be `private` rather than `public`.

The `newOval` and `circleCenter` variables are used to construct a new circle outline. These variables are not needed outside the `insertCircle` method, nor are their values needed by subsequent calls to `insertCircle`. Therefore, `newOval` and `circleCenter` are properly declared local to `insertCircle`. The program would still work properly if `newOval` and `circleCenter` were declared as instance variables, but there is no reason to do so. Worst of all, if `newOval` and `circleCenter` were `public` instance variables, they would most likely be a distraction for anyone reading the client code, because they are essentially implementation details of a single method.

The variable `newX` is even more of an implementation detail of `insertCircle`. As a matter of fact, `newX` can be eliminated altogether by passing more complicated arguments to the call to the `Oval`constructor. As with the `newOval` and `circleCenter` variables, sound defensive programming practice favors local declarations whenever possible.

One additional design decision of interest in `NestedCircles` has to do with how to add such an object to a container. `Oval` objects are normally added to a `JFrame` by calling `add` as shown below.

```
theJFrame.add(myOval, 0);
```

However, the `add` method is part of the `java.awt.JFrame` class and a `NestedCircles` argument is not permitted. The solution that is used in this case is to include a nonvoid method called `addableContent` that returns an `Oval` object, i.e., the background object for this class. Using this method, it is possible to add to a content pane with the following statement.

```
theJFrame.add(myNestedCircles.addableContent(), 0);
```

software engineering *Hint*

The need-to-know concept is useful in determining whether to use public or private. The supplier class needs to make things public only when clients "need to know." Otherwise, private is a better choice than public for variables and methods.

6.5 ■ Class Interface Design Principles

In a large programming project, it is typical to assign software development work by classes, so that each programmer has responsibility for his/her own classes. These classes must work cooperatively with others. It can be expected that one class will access instance variables belonging to other classes and call methods written by other programmers.

This environment of separate classes, often written by different developers, places extreme importance on the quality of the **software interfaces**. A software interface is the connection between a supplier and its client classes/objects. In other words, software interfaces consist of things such as `public` instance variables and `public` methods, and the specifications of how they behave.

One of the critical steps in a software development project is designing the software interfaces. During this step of design, the following decisions must be made:

- What different classes are needed to implement the program?
- Which class is responsible for storing various required information?
- Which class is responsible for various required operations?
- What is the class invariant for each class?
- What are the `public` instance members of each class?
- What are the parameter lists of each method?
- What are the preconditions and postconditions for each method?

Obviously, designing software interfaces for large projects is a complex activity that requires considerable insight and skill.

The tools and techniques used in software interface design for larger projects are also quite useful for smaller programs. Class diagrams and class specifications are good examples of such tools. Even the smallest object-oriented programs use other supplier classes, and class diagrams and specifications are the best known tools for defining these suppliers. A good approach to designing software interfaces is to begin with the class diagram, then proceed to the class specification.

There are two important design principles that are key to designing a good class interface.

> **Class Interface Design Principles**
>
> **1.** Locate members in the classes with strongest association.
> **2.** Keep the interface thin.

The first principle is particularly important when first beginning to write suppliers. Designers must regularly choose the class that is the best location for a particular instance variable or method. When a program consists of a single `Driver` class, there is no decision—everything is a member of `Driver`. As soon as you begin to write your own supplier classes, you must begin to choose where to place members.

The first design principle suggests that members should be located within the class that is most strongly associated. For example, the `valueInCents` method is more closely associated with `MoneyUSA` than with `Driver`. Similarly, the `addToSavings` method is logically associated with `PersonalBudget` and not `MoneyUSA`.

One technique for measuring the association of a potential instance variable and a class is to answer the question, "Is it natural for this class to *contain* this variable?" The answer is positive for all of the following:

- Yes, it is natural for `MoneyUSA` to contain a `pennies` variable.
- Yes, it is natural for a `PersonalBudget` to contain `outstandingExpenses`.
- Yes, it is natural for a `NestedCircles` object to contain a `lastCircleRadius`.

Sometimes the answer to the question is clearly negative.

- No, it does not make sense for `MoneyUSA` to contain a `background` of type `Oval`.
- No, it does not make sense for `NestedCircles` to contain `cashOnHand`.

At other times, it is a matter of one alternative being preferred over the other.

- It is more logical for `MoneyUSA` to contain `dimes` than for `PersonalBudget` to contain `dimes`.

Selecting the best class for a method involves a slightly different question, "Is it natural for this method to be applied to an object of this type?" Using this question as a measure of previous methods leads to the following conclusions.

- It seems natural for `insertCircle` to be applied to a `NestedCircles` object.
- It does not make sense to apply the `consolidate` method to a `NestedCircles` object.
- It is more sensible to apply `valueInCents` to a `MoneyUSA` object than a `PersonalBudget`.

One of the most difficult decisions is whether or not to locate methods and instance variables within the `Driver` class. Prior to this chapter, all variables and methods were located within `Driver`, so it is natural to want to continue to keep things in `Driver`. Generally, `Driver` needs to contain only a few key features—perhaps a window that is shared by many objects and a few initial objects that are widely shared. Your designs will improve as you find classes other than `Driver` in which to locate members.

Opening the Black Box

When deciding which class will contain a feature, it may be helpful to know why the name `Driver` was chosen for the initial objects used in the programs of this text. A common pattern among object-oriented programs is for one object to play a central role in the program's execution. Like the person behind the wheel of the automobile, the `Driver` starts the action, must keep track of various other objects, and generally controls program execution.

The second design principle, "Keep the interface thin," is related to early comments about defensive programming. Every `public` feature adds to the "thickness" of an interface. A `public` instance variable contributes more thickness than a `public` method, and update methods are thicker than queries. A **thin interface** is one that restricts the number of methods, especially those that provide opportunity for corrupting an object by unintended access.

The best technique for keeping interfaces thin is called **information hiding**. A class uses information hiding whenever it "hides" variables and methods by declaring them to be `private` or local. Information hiding leads to thin interfaces, and thin interfaces are a key aspect of defensive programming.

As an example of the use of these principles, consider a program that uses a `ThreeButtonFrame` for zooming in and out on a shadowed red dot. Figure 6.15 contains a picture of the initial window.

The requirements for this program stipulate that at all times the window must display a centered red circular dot. Furthermore, this dot must have a shadow of the same size. The location of the shadow is a distance that is 10 percent of the dot's diameter above and 10 percent to the right of the dot. Initially, the dot should have a diameter of 200 pixels. The actions to be performed by the three buttons are described below.

LEFT   Each LEFT button click causes the dot (and its shadow) to increase in size by 20 percent, while remaining centered.

MID   Each MID button click causes the dot (and its shadow) to reset to original size and location.

RIGHT Each RIGHT button click causes the dot (and its shadow) to decrease in size by 30 percent, while remaining centered.

Figure 6.15

Shadowed red dot display

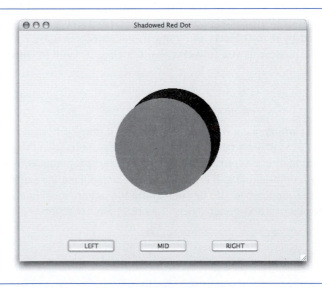

This set of requirements can be satisfied by a program with a single Driver class alone. However, the shadowed red dot seems like an obvious candidate for its own supplier class. This suggests the use of two classes, namely Driver and ShadowedRedDot.

The program appears to involve three main objects: a red dot, the dot's shadow, and a ThreeButtonFrame (together with its content pane and buttons). The designer must locate each of these objects within one of the two classes. Using the design principle of close association, it seems best to locate the dot and shadow objects within ShadowedRedDot. However, the window object is best left in Driver. The decision to locate window in Driver is based on two observations: (1) windows are not really "contained" within a ShadowedRedDot and (2) windows tend to be central to a program and are likely to be shared. (In this case, the buttons and the shadowed dot share the same window.)

Designing methods begins by investigating the actions to be performed. For this set of requirements the dot must be able to *grow*, *shrink*, and be *reset* to its original size. The *grow* and *shrink* behaviors are similar to a camera lens that zooms in and zooms out. By using a parameter to capture the amount of zooming, *grow* and *shrink* can be combined into a single zoom method. Since reset and zoom methods are applied to dots, these methods are best located within ShadowedRedDot. Figure 6.16 shows class diagrams that match the design as it has been presented so far.

The class diagram for ShadowedRedDot illustrates two additional design decisions. It has been decided to keep the interface thin by declaring dot and shadow as private instance variables. Secondly, the ShadowedRedDot constructor method includes a parameter, so that the circles can be added to their JFrame within the same method that creates them.

Good designers typically review the class diagrams before they add more detailed software contracts. Once these diagrams appear to be complete and well organized, it is time to build class specifications. Figure 6.17 shows a set of class specifications for the ShadowedRedDot class.

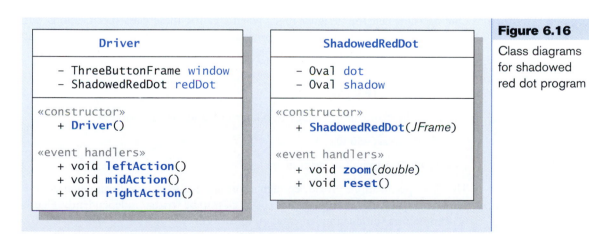

Figure 6.16

Class diagrams for shadowed red dot program

Figure 6.17

ShadowedRedDot class specification

Invariant

A ShadowedRedDot object

- is a filled circular region colored red
- is centered in the Container to which it is added
- has a shadow that is the same size as dot and colored black
- the shadow is delta units left and above dot upon the Container (delta is 10 percent of the diameter of dot)

Constructor Methods

public **ShadowedRedDot**(ThreeButtonFrame *w*)

    post: dot.getWidth() == dot.getHeight() == 200
            and this dot has been added to *w*.

Update Methods

public void **zoom**(double *d*)

    post: dot.getWidth() == dot.getWidth()**@pre** * (100 + *d*)/100
            and dot.getHeight() == dot.getHeight()**@pre** * (100 + *d*)/100.

public void **reset**()

    post: dot.getWidth() == dot.getHeight() == 200

Most of the specifications for a ShadowedRedDot are invariant. Both the dot and its shadow have a fixed color, remain filled, and remain placed throughout the program. The dot is always circular and always stays centered in the window. The diameter of the shadow is the same as the dot's diameter. The placement of the shadow is based on a fixed percentage of the dot's diameter. About the only attribute of ShadowedRedDot that is not invariant is the diameter of the dot.

One decision that the designer made when creating these class specifications was how to utilize the zoom method's parameter. From the specifications, it is clear that the zoom parameter transmits a percentage of diameter change. For example, the following call

    redDot.zoom(65.0);

increases the diameter of redDot by 65 percent, and the call below

    redDot.zoom(-50.0);

reduces redDot to half its prior diameter.

The class specifications provide enough information about the software interface for the Driver class and the ShadowedRedDot class to be written independently. Figure 6.18 contains a suitable implementation for Driver.

Figure 6.18

Driver class for
shadowed red
dot program

```java
/** Driver for Shadowed Dot Program */
public class Driver extends ThreeButtons {
    private ThreeButtonFrame window;
    private ShadowedRedDot redDot;

    /** post:  A window is displayed
     *            and a shadowed red dot is centered in the window
     *            and the shadowed dot has a diameter of 200 pixels.
     */
    public Driver() {
        window = new ThreeButtonFrame("Shadowed Red Dot");
        window.setLayout(null);
        redDot = new ShadowedRedDot(window);
        window.repaint();
    }

    /** post:  the shadowed dot's diameter is enlarged by
     *            20 percent */
    public void leftAction() {
        redDot.zoom(20.0);
    }

    /** post:  the shadowed dot's diameter is reset to
     *            200 pixels */
    public void midAction() {
        redDot.reset();
    }

    /** post:  the shadowed dot's diameter is reduced by
     *            30 percent */
    public void rightAction() {
        redDot.zoom(-30.0);
    }
}
```

The implementation of Driver is quite straightforward because most of the responsibility was shifted, by the various design decisions, to ShadowedRedDot. The resulting Driver is short and easy to read, which is indicative of a good design.

One interesting new idea from the Driver class is how it shares its JFrame with the redDot object. Notice that when the redDot variable is instantiated, window is passed as an argument. Passing in this way permits the ShadowedRedDot code to access the same JFrame as the Driver.

Figure 6.19 contains an implementation for ShadowedRedDot. The assertions (class invariant, preconditions, and postconditions) from the class specifications are included in this class as documentation of code behavior.

Figure 6.19   ShadowedRedDot class (*continues*)

```java
import java.awt.Color;
import javax.swing.JFrame;

/** Class Invariant
 *      A ShadowedRedDot object...
 *          is a filled circular region colored red
 *          and is centered its JFrame
 *          and has a shadow that is the same size as dot and
 *              colored black
 *          and the shadow is delta units left & above dot upon
 *              the window (delta is 10 percent of the diameter
 *              of dot)
 */
public class ShadowedRedDot {
    private Oval dot, shadow;

    /** post:  dot.getWidth() == dot.getHeight() == 200 */
    public ShadowedRedDot(JFrame w) {
        dot = new Oval(w.getWidth()/2-100, w.getHeight()/2-100, 200, 200);
        dot.setBackground(Color.red);
        shadow = new Oval(dot.getX()+20, dot.getY()-20, 200, 200);
        shadow.setBackground(Color.black);
        w.add(shadow, 0);
        w.add(dot, 0);
        w.repaint();
    }

    /** post:  dot.getWidth() == dot.getWidth()@pre * (100 + d)/100
     *         and dot.getHeight() == dot.getHeight()@pre * (100 + d)/100
     */
    public void zoom(double d) {
        dot.setLocation((int)(-d/200*dot.getWidth()) + dot.getX(),
            (int)(-d/200*dot.getHeight()) + dot.getY());
        dot.setSize((int)(dot.getWidth() * (1.0+d/100)),
            (int)(dot.getHeight() * (1.0+d/100)));
        shadow.setSize(dot.getWidth(), dot.getHeight());
        shadow.setLocation(dot.getX()+(int)(dot.getWidth()*0.1),
            dot.getY()-(int)(dot.getHeight()*0.1));
        dot.repaint();
        shadow.repaint();
    }
}
```

Figure 6.19   ShadowedRedDot class (*continued*)

```
    /** post:  dot.getWidth() == dot.getHeight == 200 */
    public void reset() {
        int dotCenterX, dotCenterY;
        dotCenterX = dot.getX() + dot.getWidth()/2;
        dotCenterY = dot.getY() + dot.getHeight()/2;
        dot.setSize(200, 200);
        dot.setLocation(dotCenterX-100, dotCenterY-100);
        shadow.setSize(200, 200);
        shadow.setLocation(dot.getX()+20, dot.getY()-20);
        dot.repaint();
        shadow.repaint();
    }
}
```

Notice how the ShadowedRedDot constructor method makes use of its JFrame parameter (called w). The following statements near the end of ShadowedRed accomplish the essential task of adding the dot and its shadow.

```
w.add(shadow, 0);
w.add(dot, 0);
w.repaint();
```

Since the Driver passed window as an argument to its Jframe parameter w, the above statements cause the shadowed dot to become visible within window.

Most of the work within ShadowedRedDot involves placing and recentering the dot and shadow variables. For example, the first two statements in zoom are as follows.

```
dot.setLocation((int)(-d/200*dot.getWidth()) + dot.getX(),
    (int)(-d/200*dot.getHeight()) + dot.getY());
dot.setSize((int)(dot.getWidth() * (1.0+d/100)),
    (int)(dot.getHeight() * (1.0+d/100)));
```

Executing the first of these two statements recenters dot using the parameter d. This is accomplished by moving dot up and to the left by an amount that is equal to half its growth. Assume that the ShadowedRedDot is supposed to grow by 100 percent (i.e., d == 100). For this value of d the setLocation statement becomes

```
dot.setLocation((int)(-100.0/200*dot.getWidth()) + dot.getX(),
    (int)(-100.0/200*dot.getHeight()) + dot.getY());
```

which simplifies to

```
dot.setLocation((int)(-1.0/2*dot.getWidth()) + dot.getX(),
    (int)(-1.0/2*dot.getHeight()) + dot.getY());
```

or, in other words, the dot moves by one half of its diameter.

The second instruction calls `setSize` to resize `dot`. For example, suppose again that `d == 100`. Substituting the value 100 for `d` results in the following `setSize` method call.

```
dot.setSize((int)(dot.getWidth() * (1.0+100/100)),
    (int)(dot.getHeight() * (1.0+100/100)));
```

which simplifies to

```
dot.setSize(dot.getWidth() * 2,
dot.getHeight() * 2);
```

6.6 ■ Separating Read and Write Access

The concept of information hiding can be carried one step further. To understand this technique it is necessary to investigate variable usage.

Program variables are used in two different ways by code:

1. A variable may be *assigned* a value. (`myVar = someExpression;`)

2. A variable's *value* may be utilized in some other calculation. (`System.out.println(myVar);`)

These two forms of variable usage are often referred to as **write access** and **read access**, respectively. Assigning a new value to a variable is like *writing* to that variable, and utilizing the variable's value in some expression or as a method argument is akin to *reading* the variable's content.

Instructions are permitted read access *and* write access to all instance variables declared within the class. However, instructions have read access only (no write access) to constants (`final` variables). Client classes have *neither* read access nor write access to `private` variables from supplier classes. On the other hand, the supplier's `public` instance variables are available to a client for *both* read and write access.

Sometimes it is best for a supplier to grant *either* read access or write access to clients without granting both. Granting read access without write access is called **read-only access**. Similarly, granting write access without read access is known as **write-only access**. The technique for providing read-only (or write-only) access requires two things:

1. declaring the instance variable to be `private`

2. including a method in the supplier class that provides the desired access to the private variable

For example, suppose that the programmer designing ShadowedRedDot wishes to use a read-only variable to count to the number of times zoom is called. A new zoomCounter instance variable can be included in the ShadowedRedDot class with the following private declaration:

```
private int zoomCounter = 0;
```

The zoom method must also be edited to perform the necessary counting.

The simplest way to grant read-only access to a private variable is accomplished by an **accessor method**—a nonvoid method that returns the variable. The following countOfZoomCalls illustrates use of an accessor method. This method is designed to be included within the ShadowedRedDot class.

```
/** post: result == zoomCounter */
public int countOfZoomCalls() {
    return zoomCounter;
}
```

Granting write-only access is done in much the same way, except that a public void method is used to assign a value to the variable. For example, suppose that the nickels variable of MoneyUSA needs to be write-only. This can be done by declaring nickels to be private and including the following method within MoneyUSA.

```
/** pre:   n >= 0
 * post:  nickels == n
 */
public void setNickels(int n) {
    nickels = n;
}
```

Notice that the setNickels method simply assigns the value of its parameter to the nickels variable. This method gives the client a method for assigning a new value to nickels. However, the client must use a call to setNickels rather than use an assignment instruction.

Using read-only or write-only variables is another technique for "Keep the interface thin." Library classes regularly use this concept for granting read-only and write-only attribute access. The write access methods are often named "set..." and accessor methods are frequently named "get...". Examples of such methods from the *java.awt* and *java.swing* libraries are getX, getWidth, setLocation, and setSize.

Color attributes are often accessed using *both* a read-only method and a write-only method. For example, Oval, Rectangle, Line, java.awt.Label, and java.awt.Container all include both getBackground and setBackground methods. This illustrates that sometimes it is possible to provide both read and write access without declaring the variable as public. Not only is it possible, but also it is

Opening
the Black Box

The following changes to the MoneyUSA class (from Figure 6.5) improve this supplier class because they make the interface thinner.

1. Change the declarations of all of the following instance variables from `public` to `private`: `dollars`, `quarters`, `dimes`, `nickels`, `pennies`

2. Include all of the following accessor methods: **getDollars**, **getQuarters**, **getDimes**, **getNickels**, **getPennies**

3. Include all of the following write access methods: **setDollars**, **setQuarters**, **setDimes**, **setNickels**, **setPennies**

generally a better use of information hiding than using `public` variables. The reason for preferring separate methods is that they give the supplier more control. For example, the `setBackground` method can check its argument before assigning an invalid color, potentially avoiding a runtime error.

6.7 ■ Method Overloading

By now, you may have noticed that Java permits supplier classes to include multiple methods with the same name. Such reuse of method names is known as **overloading**. Overloading method names is allowed within a class as long as any two methods with the same name have different parameter lists (i.e., the number of parameters and/or the type(s) of parameters must differ).

The Math class, described in the previous chapter, provides two versions of the round method. One version rounds from `float` to `int` and the other from `double` to `long`. The specifications of these methods are shown below.

```
/** post:  result == f rounded to the nearest integer */
int Math.round(float f)
```

```
/** post:  result == d rounded to the nearest integer */
long Math.round(double d)
```

Because of the requirement for different parameter lists, overloading does not lead to ambiguity. If the Math.round method is called with a `float` type argument, then it rounds to an `int`. Similarly, if Math.round is called with a `double` argument, it rounds to a `long`. The compiler determines which method to call based on the type of the actual argument.

Another common usage of overloading occurs for constructor methods. Sometimes it is useful to have multiple constructor methods; and since every constructor has the same name as its class, multiple constructors would be impossible without overloading. To illustrate, consider the Color class from the *AWT* library. Figure 6.20 contains a class diagram and Figure 6.21 a class specification for the Color class.

Figure 6.20   Color class diagram

```
                          java.awt.Color

     – int red
     – int green
     – int blue

«constants»
     + Color Color.white     //red, green, blue values of 255,255,255
     + Color Color.black     //red, green, blue values of 0,0,0
     + Color Color.lightGray //red, green, blue values of 192,192,192
     + Color Color.gray      //red, green, blue values of 128,128,128
     + Color Color.darkGray  //red, green, blue values of 64,64,64
     + Color Color.red       //red, green, blue values of 255,0,0
     + Color Color.pink      //red, green, blue values of 255,175,175
     + Color Color.orange    //red, green, blue values of 255,200,0
     + Color Color.yellow    //red, green, blue values of 255,255,0
     + Color Color.green     //red, green, blue values of 0,255,0
     + Color Color.magenta   //red, green, blue values of 255,0,255
     + Color Color.cyan      //red, green, blue values of 0,255,255
     + Color Color.blue      //red, green, blue values of 0,0,255

«constructor»
     public Color(float, float, float)
     public Color(int, int, int)

«other»
     . . .
```

The `Color` class diagram and specification show that this class includes at least two constructor methods—one with three `int` arguments, and one with three `float` arguments. These arguments determine the color intensity for red, green, and blue components, respectively, of a `Color` object. The values of the `int` arguments range from 0 (for least color intensity) to 255 (for most color intensity). The `float` arguments must be in the range from `0.0f` (least color intensity) to `1.0f` (most color intensity).

The term "overloading" is generally used to refer to using the same name for multiple methods. A closely related concept occurs when a single class uses the same name in multiple variable declarations. This is not permitted when all variables have the same scope. However, a variable name *can* be reused when the scopes differ.

The rule for such variable name reuse is: *The identifier declared in the innermost enclosing scope is applicable.* Suppose, as shown below, that the variable `myVar` is declared as both an instance variable of class `MyClass` and also as a local variable within the `myMethod` method of `MyClass`.

Figure 6.21

Color class
specifications

Invariant

A Color object ...

- is a color that can be used in drawing
- 0 <= red <= 255 **and** 0 <= green <= 255 **and** 0 <= blue <= 255

Constructor Methods

public **Color**(float *r*, float *g*, float *b*)

pre: 0.0 <= *r* <= 1.0 *and* 0.0 <= *g* <= 1.0 *and* 0.0 <= *b* <= 1.0

post: A new Color object is created with attributes as follows:
red == r * 255 **and** green == g * 255 **and** blue == b * 255

public **Color**(int *r*, int *g*, int *b*)

pre: 0 <= *r* <= 255 **and** 0 <= *g* <= 255 **and** 0 <= *b* <= 255

post: A new Color object is created with attributes as follows:
red == *r* **and** green == *g* **and** blue == *b*

Other Methods

. . .

software *Hint*
engineering
Figure 6.22
makes it evident
that the rules for
reusing identi-
fiers are messy.
Generally, it is
safer to avoid
reusing names.
One notable
exception is over-
loading, especial-
ly for constructor
methods.

```
public class MyClass {
    public int myVar;

    public void myMethod {
        int myVar;
        . . .
    }
    . . .
}
```

An unqualified reference to myVar within the body of myMethod refers to the local
variable, because this is the innermost scope. An unqualified reference to myVar
within the remainder of MyClass refers to the instance variable, assuming no other
myVar declarations. Figure 6.22 summarizes the rules for reusing identifiers within
a class.

6.8 ■ this

The distinction between class and object is subtle. Classes contain methods and their
associated code. However, at runtime it is *objects* that exist, not classes. So whenever
a method is called, the code for that method is applied to an object, even though the

Within Any Class

1. Reusing (overloading) a name for multiple methods of the same class is allowed as long as the methods have different parameter lists.

2. Reusing a name for declaring two entities (variables, constants, or formal parameters) in the same scope is a syntax error. (For this rule, `private` and `public` entities of the same class are treated as though they have the same scope.)

3. Reusing a name within two different scopes is permitted. (`private` and `public` entities of the same class are treated as though they have the same scope.)

4. Reserved word identifiers cannot be used for any purpose other than their predefined intent.

Figure 6.22

Rules for reusing identifiers

instructions are written within the object's class. For example, consider that a `Driver` class includes the following instruction.

```
theJFrame.setVisible(true);
```

Figure 6.23 contains an object diagram to illustrate this runtime action.

`theJFrame` object can be thought of as a runtime *proxy* for the `JFrame` class. A programmer wrote the instructions for the `setVisible` method within the `JFrame` class. These instructions are applied to the class's proxy, namely `theJFrame`, when the program executes. But how does an instruction refer to the proxy (object) of its own class?

Java includes a special notation to name this otherwise anonymous object. The reserved identifier

   this

always denotes the runtime proxy for the object from the class in which it occurs. So within the code of the `JFrame` class, the `theJFrame` object can be referred to as `this` for the duration of the `theJFrame.setVisible(true)` instruction call. Within the `Driver` class, the name `this` will always refer to the `Driver` object (pictured as an anonymous object in Figure 6.23).

The `this` notation is sometimes necessary when you write supplier classes. For example, consider a program that uses the same identifier to name both an instance variable and a local variable, like `dupVar` in the class skeleton of Figure 6.24.

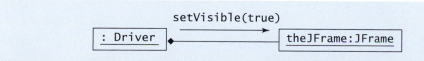

setVisible(true)

`: Driver` → `theJFrame:JFrame`

Figure 6.23

Driver object calling show a JFrame object

Figure 6.24

Class with a
duplicated
variable name

```java
public class SomeClass {
    private int dupVar;

    public void someMethod {
        int dupVar;
        dupVar = 3; // assigns to the local variable
        this.dupVar = 4; // assigns to the instance variable
        . . .
    }
    . . .
}
```

Within the body of someMethod, any reference to dupVar refers to the local variable. However, it is still possible to refer to the instance variable by recalling that an instance variable is contained within an object (i.e., the this object). Therefore, the notation for referencing an instance variable from anywhere within its class is first to reference the object (this), followed by the name of the variable. The following statement from Figure 6.24 demonstrates:

```java
this.dupVar = 4;
```

The this prefix can also be used in a method call. Consider the Driver class sketched in Figure 6.25.

If a Driver class contains a private method such as doIt (from Figure 6.25), then it can call this method with the following instruction:

```java
this.doIt();
```

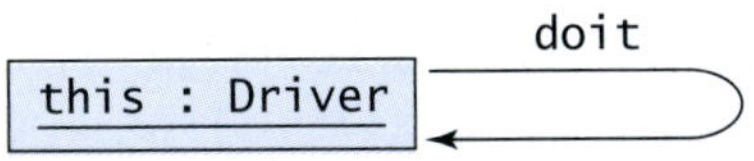

Figure 6.25

Driver
overusing this

```java
// The version of this class shown in Figure 6.26 is preferred.
public class Driver {
    private int aVar;

    public Driver() {
        this.aVar = 3;
        this.doIt();
    }

    private void doIt() {
        . . .
    }
}
```

Figure 6.26

Driver without `this`

```
// This is a better version of the code from Figure 6.25
public class Driver {
    private int aVar;

    public Driver() {
        aVar = 3;
        doIt();
    }

    private void doIt() {
        . . .

    }
}
```

The object diagram to the right of `this.doIt();` illustrates that calling a method within the same class is like sending a message to one's self or applying a method to one's self, because the code for the method is within the same class as the calling object.

Much of the time the `this` prefix is unnecessary because Java provides an abbreviated notation. The abbreviated notation always works for calling private methods and often for references to instance variables. Figure 6.26 shows another version of the `Driver` class that is identical to the one in Figure 6.25 except that it uses the abbreviated notation.

software engineering *Hint*

Private methods can always be called within their class by prefixing the method name with `this`. However, programmers generally omit this notation as superfluous.

6.9 ■ Enumerated Data Types

Not all primitive data types need to be numeric, nor do they need to be predefined. Java includes a mechanism that allows programmers to define their own type. The so-called **enumerated type**[1] is intended for use when data is simple, but no pre-existing data type seems appropriate. Figure 6.27 shows the syntax diagram for enumerated types.

Enumerated type declarations are similar to class definitions with the word `class` replaced by `enum`. The primary difference is that an enumerated type must declare its own constants—a list of identifiers. Consider the following simple example of an enumerated type.

```
public enum Gender {male, female}
```

This declaration creates a new data type, called `Gender`, which can be used in ways similar to a client class. The same declaration also specifies constants (`male` and

---

1. Use of the enumerated data type feature requires Java Version 5.0 or later.

Figure 6.27   ***EnumeratedTypeDeclaration*** description

Syntax

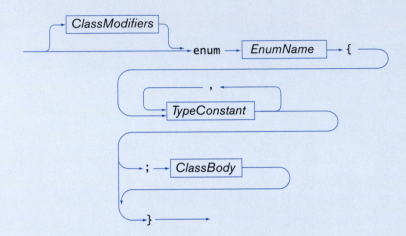

Semantics

EnumName is defined to be a reference data type, which has constants from the list of *TypeConsant* identifiers.

Notes

- *EnumeratedTypeDeclaration* may occur any place that a variable declaration may occur or it can occur in its own file like a class. (The declaration can be preceded by the word `public` or `private` for an instance declaration.)
- *ClassModifiers* can be scope modifiers such as `public` or `private`.
- The *TypeConstant* identifiers are ordered left to right, with the leftmost having an ordinal (integer) value of zero, the next having a value of one, and so forth.
- Like any other statement, *EnumeratedTypeDeclaration* must be followed by a semicolon if it is used inside another class.

female) for the data type. These are the *only* two values that are possible for variables of type `Gender`.

Once an enumerated type is declared, it can be used to specify the type of a variable or parameter, such as the following:

```
private Gender myBabysGender;
private int lifeExpectancy(Gender g) { ... }
```

Such declarations permit an assignment statement such as

```
myBabysGender = Gender.female;
```

or a method call such as this:

```
System.out.println(lifeExpectancy(Gender.male));
```

This code illustrates that proper syntax for specifying enumerated constants consists of the type name, followed by a period, then followed by the name of the constant.

Java allows an enumerated type declaration to be located in places where variables (either instance or local) can be declared. Such an inner declaration can be particularly useful for enumerated types that require only limited scope. For example, the following local declaration of an enumerated type (IceCreamFlavors) is followed by the declaration of two associated local variables.

```
enum IceCreamFlavors { vanilla, chocolate, strawberry,
    neapolitan, cherryNut, butterPecan, rockyRoad };
IceCreamFlavors dereksFavorite, kasandrasFavorite;
```

Each of these variables (dereksFavorite and kasandrasFavorite) may store one of the seven possible values listed in the declaration of the type, but no other value. Within the same local scope as the above declarations, a statement like the following is permitted.

```
dereksFavorite = strawberry;
```

Enumerated types are *not* like the numeric types. You cannot add them, auto-increment them, or compare them using < or >. However, the Java implementation of every enumerated type provides two methods of particular interest: name and ordinal.

software engineering *Hint*

Calls to the name method can often be omitted when using enumerated types. When an enumerated expression is located where a String is required, it is automatically converted, just as though a name were included. This uses a method called toString explained in Chapter 9.

Both of these methods are applicable to every enumerated type and both perform conversions of an enumerated type to a corresponding value in another type. The name method converts an enumerated into a String[2] (i.e., a String identical to the constant identifier). Assuming that dereksFavorite is assigned by the statement above, executing the following instruction outputs "strawberry."

```
System.out.println(dereksFavorite.name());
```

The ordinal method converts enumerated values into an integer equivalent. Each enumerated type declaration must list its enumerated constants, and it is the order of this list that determines the ordinal value of each constant. The first constant in

---

2. Section 6.10 describes the Java String data type.

the list has an ordinal value of zero, the second is one, and so forth. Therefore, the following method outputs the value two, because `strawberry` is the third constant in the list of `IceCreamFlavors`.

```
System.out.println(dereksFavorite.ordinal());
```

The primary benefit of enumerated types is an additional measure of safety from unwanted value assignment. For example, a programmer could store a day of the week in a `weekday` variable using the following declarations.

```
private int weekday;
private final int sunday=0, monday=1, tuesday=2, wednesday=3,
    thursday=4, friday=5, saturday=6;
```

software engineering *Hint*

Enumerated types have two main advantages: readability and safety. Consider the `DayOfWeek` type to the right. It is easier to comprehend the meaning of a constant like wednesday, than its ordinal equivalent of 3. It is also safer to know weekday cannot be assigned a meaningless value, such as −34.

This results in nicely readable code, such as assigning weekday the sixth day of the week:

```
weekday = friday;
```

However, there is nothing to prohibit the weekday variable from being assigned a meaningless value (i.e., a value less than zero or greater than six).

A better solution might be to use code like that below, which relies upon an enumerated type. This code still permits expressions like `weekday.ordinal()` in cases where it is necessary to use an integer representation of the enumerated.

```
private enum DayOfWeek { sunday, monday, tuesday, wednesday,
    thursday, friday, saturday };
private DayOfWeek weekday;
```

This declaration prohibits anything but one of the seven specified constants (or `null`) from being assigned to the weekday variable. The programmer has fewer worries about invalid value assignments.

6.10 ■ String

The `char` data type, presented in Chapter 5, restricts variables and expressions to representing just one character at a time. However, programs must often manipulate sequences of characters, also known as a **strings**. Java provides an appropriate library (supplier) class, called **String**. Figure 6.28 contains a class diagram that describes the most important `String` methods. Figure 6.29 gives the `String` class specifications.

A `String` is the only Java reference data type that recognizes a built-in syntax for constants. This notation consists of any sequence of characters enclosed within double quotations. Each line below contains a separate `String` constant.

```
"This is a string."
"1725 State Street"
"line 1\nline 2\n"
```

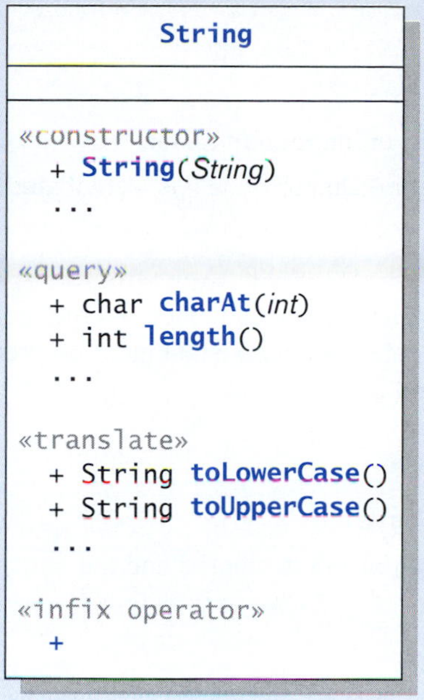

Figure 6.28

String class
diagram

```
                    String
    _____

    «constructor»
      + String(String)
      . . .


    «query»
      + char charAt(int)
      + int length()
      . . .


    «translate»
      + String toLowerCase()
      + String toUpperCase()
      . . .


    «infix operator»
      +
```

The last of the preceding three lines contains two linefeed (\n) characters, specified by escape sequences. (A linefeed character in Java separates a String into separate lines.)

As with primitive types, the String constant yields an object without the use of the new operator. The following example instructions illustrate.

```
stateString = "Wisconsin";
System.out.println("Your message goes here.");
```

A second unique characteristic of the String type is that it supports the infix "+" operator to **concatenate** two String expressions. As an example, the following instruction assigns "David D. Riley" to the nameString variable.

```
nameString = "David D" + "." + " Riley";
```

The "+" operator can also be used to combine a String expression with any other expression of primitive type. When this occurs, the primitive expression is converted to a String representation and concatenated with the string. For example, consider the following instruction sequence.

```
velocity = 12.5;
System.out.println("The value of Velocity is " + velocity);
```

When the above two instructions execute, the second instruction sends the following line of text to the standard output stream.

```
The value of Velocity is 12.5
```

Figure 6.29

String class
specifications

Invariant

A String object

- is a sequence of zero or more char values
- is immutable (cannot be altered once it is instantiated)

String Constant

A String constant consists of any sequence of char constants without enclosing single quotes. The entire string constant must be preceded and followed by double quotation marks (").

Constructor Methods

public String(String s)

> **post:** A new String object is created and the sequence of characters is the same as s.

Other Methods

public char charAt(int p)

> **pre:**   p < length()
>
> **post:** result == the char at position p from this string (note that zero is the position of the leftmost character)

public int length()

> **post:** result == the number of characters in this string

public String toUpperCase()

> **post:** result == this string with every lowercase letter replaced by the corresponding uppercase letter

public String toLowerCase()

> **post:** result == this string with every uppercase letter replaced by the corresponding lowercase letter

Infix Operator

+ evaluates to a string consisting of its two operand strings concatenated (joined).

Objects of type String are **immutable** because they cannot be altered (mutated). The String class includes methods to query selected parts or properties of a String object. However, there are no «update» methods to alter an existing String object. Some of the methods from the String class include

- **length**: to return the number of characters in the String object
- **charAt**: to return any selected char of the String object
- **toLowerCase**: to return a new String object that is the same as the original with uppercase letters replaced by lowercase
- **toUpperCase**: to return a new String object that is the same as the original with lowercase letters replaced by uppercase

---

Any Java object can be output using System.out.println. For primitives and String expressions, System.out.println outputs the value of the expression. The default behavior of System.out.println for other objects is sometimes difficult to read. (The key to open this black box is found in Chapter 9.)

Closed
Black Box

String shares some characteristics with the primitive types. However, String is a reference type, not a primitive, type. As a result, assigning one String to another copies the binding to the same String object. Similarly, each String method returns a new String object.

Unfortunately, as a reference type, String is completely incompatible with char. This incompatibility is mentioned because it is natural to think of a char as a String of length 1. Unfortunately, in Java, the char and String types are as different as int and Oval. Some of the limitations of this incompatibility are listed below.

- You *cannot* pass a char argument to a String parameter (nor the opposite).
- You *cannot* use a char constant in place of a String constant (nor the opposite).
- You *cannot* assign a char expression to a String variable (nor the opposite).

This last restriction is particularly troublesome, because there are many times in programs when char data and String data must be used cooperatively. Fortunately, Java provides tools to work around the incompatibility between char and String.

The **charAt** method is a tool for extracting a char from within a String. The charAt parameter specifies the position of the desired char (0 for leftmost character, 1 for second from the left, etc.). For example, executing the following two instructions, prints the char value 'X.'

```
String stringVar = "VWXYZ";
System.out.println(stringVar.charAt(2));
```

Conversion from char to String requires a different approach. One such approach is to use the + (concatenate) operator described previously. Concatenating any char with a String of length zero (sometimes called an **empty string**), results in a String that consists of that char. The Java notation for an empty string is two consecutive double quotation marks. Therefore, the following expression

```
"" + 'B'
```

evaluates to a `String` of length 1, consisting of the letter B, or `"B"` in `String` constant notation. A more common use of such a conversion might be to convert the content of a `char` variable, as shown below:

```
// Assume that charVar is a variable of type char
// and stringVar a variable of type String
stringVar = "" + charVar;
```

The execution of this instruction assigns to `stringVar` a `String` object that consists of the single character from `charVar`.

This technique of constructing a `String` object from a `char` expression is easily extended to an expression pattern for converting any primitive expression into its `String` representation. As shown in Figure 6.30, any expression of primitive type (denoted *primitiveExpresssion*) can be converted to a `String` object by concatenating the primitive expression with an empty string. The result of applying this pattern is a `String` with the same appearance as that output by `String.out.println(primitiveExpression);`

The expression pattern from Figure 6.30 shows how to convert data of any primitive type into its `String` representation, but this leads to the question, "How can a pro-

---

Figure 6.30

Expression pattern for converting primitive to `String`

$$\text{"" } + \; primitiveExpression$$

Figure 6.31

Scanner class diagram

```
┌─────────────────────────────────┐
│        java.util.Scanner        │
├─────────────────────────────────┤
│                                 │
├─────────────────────────────────┤
│ «constructor»                   │
│     + Scanner(String)           │
│     ...                         │
│                                 │
│ «query»                         │
│     + byte   nextByte()         │
│     + double nextDouble()       │
│     + float  nextFloat()        │
│     + int    nextInt()          │
│     + long   nextLong()         │
│     + short  nextShort()        │
│     ...                         │
└─────────────────────────────────┘
```

gram convert data in the opposite direction?" Suppose for example, that the `String` variable, `str`, is assigned as follows.

```
String str = "75.2";
```

Following the execution of this instruction `str` is assigned text that happens to be consistent with a real number constant. However, since `str` is a `String`, it cannot be treated like a `double` for performing operations such as subtraction, multiplication, and so forth.

In Version 1.5.0 a new standard class was added to the Java libraries (within the *java.util* library). This new class, called **Scanner**, provides several methods for processing `String` data, including converting from `String` to primitive data. Figure 6.31 contains a class diagram for some of the Scanner methods.

software
engineering *Hint*

Care needs to be taken to ensure that the `Scanner` conversion methods are called validly. If the `String` to be converted does not match a constant of the associated primitive type, then a runtime error occurs. For example, calling nextInt for the "75.2" string is an error. Chapter 7 presents a technique for guarding against such errors.

Using `Scanner` to perform conversions is a two-step process: (1) a `Scanner` object must be instantiated passing it the `String` to be translated, and (2) the appropriate query method is called to complete the conversion. Using the `str` variable that was assigned the value `"75.2"` the following instructions will assign the equivalent numeric value of 75.2 to `doub`.

```
Scanner scan = new Scanner(str);
double doub = scan.nextDouble();
```

These two statements can be composed, merging them into the following equivalent instruction.

```
double doub = (new Scanner(str)).nextDouble();
```

Note the following restriction on `Scanner` objects: when the Scanner string consists of a single constant, you cannot call next... method a second time upon the `Scanner` object. In other words, `nextDouble` should not be called multiple times upon the same `Scanner` object, assuming that the `Scanner` object was created with a string representing a single `double` constant.

6.11 ■ JTextField (Optional)

It is common for programs to display `String` data. Prior chapters have provided two ways to do this in Java:

1. Output a `String` to a command line by calling `System.out.println`.

2. Instantiate a `java.awt.Label` object to display the `String`.

Figure 6.32 shows a more complete class diagram of the standard `Label` class. The methods that are newly included are a parameterless `Label` constructor, a `setText` method, and several query methods.

Figure 6.32

Label class
diagram

```
┌─────────────────────────────────────────────┐
│              java.awt.Label                  │
├─────────────────────────────────────────────┤
│                                              │
├─────────────────────────────────────────────┤
│  «constructor»                               │
│      + Label ()                              │
│      + Label (String )                       │
│      . . .                                   │
│                                              │
│  «update»                                    │
│      + void setBackground (java.awt.Color)   │
│      + void setBounds (int, int, int, int )  │
│      + void setForeground (java.awt.Color)   │
│      + void setLocation (int, int)           │
│      + void setSize (int, int)               │
│      + void setText (String)                 │
│      + void repaint ()                       │
│      . . .                                   │
│                                              │
│  «query»                                     │
│      + int getX ()                           │
│      + int getY ()                           │
│      + int getWidth ()                       │
│      + int getHeight ()                      │
│      + String getText ()                     │
│      . . .                                   │
│                                              │
└─────────────────────────────────────────────┘
```

Figure 6.33 demonstrates the use of some of these new methods. This `Driver` class exercises the `MoneyUSA` class from Section 6.3. The program uses a `ThreeButtonFrame`. Upon this window, the program displays the count of dollars, quarters, dimes, and nickels from a monetary amount. Clicking the left button causes the number of dollars to be increased by 1. Clicking the middle button causes the number of quarters to increase by 1 and the number of nickels to increase by 3. The right button is used to consolidate money into the largest possible denominations.

The money program `Driver` makes use of a parameterless Label constructor and assigns text to a `Label` using a `setText` method

The `Driver` class from Figure 6.33 includes a private method, called `updateDisplay`, to update the four labels. Each `setText` call assigns a string that consists of a label followed by the count of the corresponding monetary denomination. Each time that the value of the money changes, `updateDisplay` is called to cause the window to be properly redrawn.

The *Swing* library includes another class, called `JTextField`, that is very similar to `Label`. In fact, `JTextField` is so similar that everything shown in the `Label` class

Figure 6.33   CountingMoney program (*continues*)

```java
import java.awt.*;
public class Driver extends ThreeButtons {
    privateLabel dollarLabel, quarterLabel;
    privateLabel dimeLabel, nickelLabel;
    private MoneyUSA money;
    private ThreeButtonFrame theWin;

    /** post:  A window displays monetary denominations. */
    public Driver() {
        theWin = new ThreeButtonFrame("Money Counter");
        theWin.setLayout(null);
        dollarLabel = newlyAddedLabel(10);
        quarterLabel = newlyAddedLabel(50);
        dimeLabel = newlyAddedLabel(90);
        nickelLabel = newlyAddedLabel(130);
        money = new MoneyUSA(0, 0, 0, 0, 0);
        updateDisplay();
    }

    /** post:  result is displayed upon theWin
     *         and result.getX()==100 and result.getY()==y
     *         and result.getWidth()==100 and result.getHeight()==30
     */
    public Label newlyAddedLabel(int y) {
        Label result;
        result = new Label();
        result.setBounds(100, y, 100, 30);
        theWin.add(result, 0);
        return result;
    }

    /** pre:   money is instantiated
     * post:  money.dollars == money.dollars@pre + 1
     */
    public void leftAction() {
        money.dollars++;
        updateDisplay();
    }

    /** pre:   money is instantiated
     * post:  money.quarters == money.quarters@pre + 1
     *        and money.nickels == money.nickels@pre + 3
     */
```

Figure 6.33   CountingMoney program (*continued*)

```
public void midAction() {
    money.quarters++;
    money.nickels = money.nickels + 3;
    updateDisplay();
}

/** pre:   money is instantiated
 *  post:  money.valueInCents == money.valueInCents@pre
 *         and money consolidated into largest possible denominations
 */
public void rightAction() {
    money.consolidate();
    updateDisplay();
}

/** pre:   money is instantiated
 *  post:  the output labels are updated to reflect the
 *         value of dollars, quarters, dimes, and nickels of the money
 *         variable
 */
private void updateDisplay() {
    dollarLabel.setText("Dollars: " + money.dollars);
    dollarLabel.repaint();
    quarterLabel.setText("Quarters: " + money.quarters);
    quarterLabel.repaint();
    dimeLabel.setText("Dimes: " + money.dimes);
    dimeLabel.repaint();
    nickelLabel.setText("Nickels: " + money.nickels);
    nickelLabel.repaint();
}
}
```

diagram from Figure 6.32 is the same for JTextField. The important difference between the two is that a JTextField is editable by the user, while Label is not. In other words, as your program executes, the user is permitted to type a string value into any JTextField. (You have typed into text fields if you have ever entered a Web page URL in your Web browser or words into a Google search window.)

When using JTextFields, you need to be careful to allow the user time to enter the desired text. For example, the program in Figure 6.34 allows the user to type into three JTextField objects, and then use the buttons to shuffle the content of the three fields. The user is allowed time to type by virtue of button click events. (i.e., nothing is retrieved from a JTextField until a button is clicked.)

Figure 6.34   Shuffling TextFields program (*continues*)

```java
import javax.swing.*;
import java.awt.*;
public class ShuffleFields {
    private TextField topField, midField, bottomField;

    /** post:  topField, midField and bottomField are instantiated
     *         and added to f
     */
    public ShuffleFields(JFrame f) {
        Label directions;
        directions = new Label("Please type in the text fields.");
        directions.setBounds(50, 100, 500, 30);
        directions.setForeground(Color.blue);
        f.add(directions);
        topField = new TextField();
        topField.setBounds(250, 150, 100, 30);
        topField.repaint();
        f.add(topField, 0);
        midField = new TextField();
        midField.setBounds(250, 200, 100, 30);
        midField.repaint();
        f.add(midField, 0);
        bottomField = new TextField();
        bottomField.setBounds(250, 250, 100, 30);
        bottomField.repaint();
        f.add(bottomField, 0);
    }

    /** post:  topField.getText() == midField.getText()@pre
     *         and midField.getText() == bottomField.getText()@pre
     *         and bottomField.getText() == topField.getText()@pre
     */
    public void rotateUp() {
        String topFieldAtPre = topField.getText();
        topField.setText(midField.getText());
        midField.setText(bottomField.getText());
        bottomField.setText(topFieldAtPre);
    }

    /** post:  topField.getText() == midField.getText()@pre
     *         and bottomField.getText() == midField.getText()@pre
     */
    public void copyMiddle() {
        topField.setText(midField.getText());
        bottomField.setText(midField.getText());
    }
```

Figure 6.34   Shuffling TextFields program (*continued*)

```
    /** post:  bottomField.getText() == midField.getText()@pre
     *          and midField.getText() == topField.getText()@pre
     *          and topField.getText() == bottomField.getText()@pre
     */
    public void rotateDown() {
        String bottomFieldAtPre;
        bottomFieldAtPre = bottomField.getText();
        bottomField.setText(midField.getText());
        midField.setText(topField.getText());
        topField.setText(bottomFieldAtPre);
    }
}

public class Driver extends ThreeButtons {
    private ShuffleFields fields;

    /** post:  A window displays three TextFields and directions. */
    public Driver() {
        ThreeButtonFrame theWin;
        theWin = new ThreeButtonFrame("Text Shuffler");
        theWin.setLayout(null);
        fields = new ShuffleFields(theWin);
        theWin.repaint();
    }

    /** post:  the field content has been rotated upward */
    public void leftAction() {
        fields.rotateUp();
    }

    /** post:  The top and bottom fields have a copy of the content of the
     *          middle field @pre
     */
    public void midAction() {
        fields.copyMiddle();
    }

    /** post:  the field content has been rotated downward */
    public void rightAction() {
        fields.rotateDown();
    }
}
```

When this program executes, it displays a `ThreeButtonFrame` like the one shown in Figure 6.35. A `ShuffleField` object places three `JTextField` objects on the window; the names of the associated variables are `topField`, `midField`, and `bottomField` variables.

The `rotateUp` algorithm is a three-way swap in which each field takes on the `String` value from the field below it. (The bottom field gets the prior value of the top field.) This three-way swap uses the following statements:

```
String topFieldAtPre = topField.getText();
topField.setText(midField.getText());
midField.setText(bottomField.getText());
bottomField.setText(topFieldAtPre);
```

The first statement assigns a copy of the `String` value from `topField` to the `topFieldAtPre` variable. The middle two statements use `getText` to retrieve a copy of the `String` from one `TextField` and `setText` to assign this value to another `TextField`.

This program manipulates the values of text fields as `String` data. Another typical use for text fields is to use them for numeric input from the user. Suppose that an online retail company is using a Java program to supply its Web pages, and further assume that the Web pages contain text fields in which customers are expected to type numbers. For example, the following declaration could be used to create a text field for supplying the quantity of items to be purchased.

```
TextField quantityField = new TextField();
```

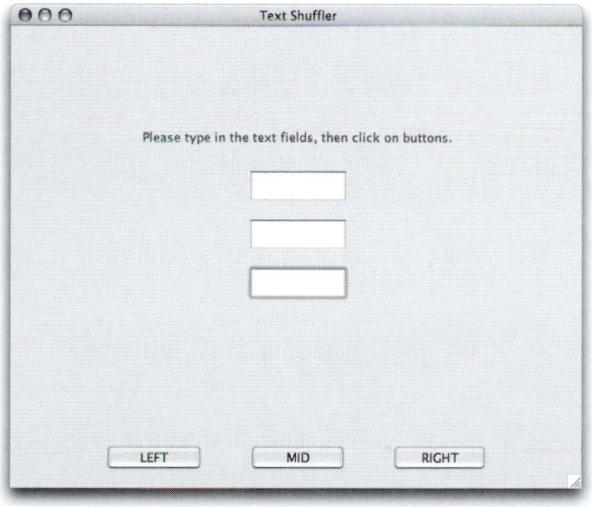

Figure 6.35

Shuffling
`TextFields`
window

Later in the program it will be necessary to inspect the content of quantityField, but the program will most likely use the integer (int) value of the text field, not the String value. One solution is to use a Scanner (discussed in Section 6.9) object to translate from String to int. The following instructions accomplish this.

```
String s = quantityField.getText();
Scanner scanner = new Scanner(s);
int value = scanner.nextInt();
```

These three statements can be merged into the following single, though more complicated, instruction.

```
int value = (new Scanner(quantityField.getText())).nextInt();
```

Inspector *Java*

Below is a collection of hints on what to check when examining code that involves the concepts of this chapter.

- Every feature (method or variable) should be checked for proper scope declaration. It is best to declare variables to be local. However, when the lifetime of a variable must extend beyond one method execution, it must be declared as an instance variable. It is better to declare class members to be `private` than `public`. But when a method is needed by client classes, then it is generally best for it to be declared `public`.

- Qualified expressions should be examined to be certain that they reference the correct object or method. The connections from one object to its `public` members read from left to right.

- Be careful with names that are reused. Check to ensure that the innermost enclosing declaration is the one that is desired.

- Method overloading requires that within one class, two methods with the same name must have different parameter lists. When overloading is used, check the parameter lists for the necessary differences.

- The constant notations for `char` and `String` are easily confused. Remember that char constants are enclosed between single quote characters, while `String` constants are enclosed between double quote characters.

Terminology

accessor method

aggregation (of classes)

ASCII character set

centered

client

client-supplier relation

composition (of classes)

concatenate

defensive programming

empty string

encapsulate

enumerated data type

immutable

information hiding

`JTextField` (from *javax.swing*)

lifetime (a property of objects)

`name` (enumerated method)

`ordinal` (enumerated method)

overloading (methods)

printable character

`private`

`public`

qualified expressions

read access

read-only access

thin interface

Scanner (from *java.util*)

this

scope (a property of class features)

visibility (property of identifiers)

software interface

write access

String

write-only access

supplier

Exercises

1. Consider the following class:

```
public class Auto {
    public int miles;
    public int gas;

    public Auto() {
        miles = 0;
        gas = 0;
    }

    public void addGas(int g) {
        gas = gas + g ;
    }

    // additional methods belong here
}
```

a. Show the exact output that results from executing the following code (in some class other than Auto).

```
Auto car = new Auto();
Auto compact = car;
car.miles = 2;
car.addGas(5);
System.out.println(car.miles);
System.out.println(car.gas);
compact.miles = car.miles + 1;
compact.addGas(7);
System.out.println(compact.miles);
System.out.println(compact.gas);
car = new Auto();
System.out.println(car.miles);
System.out.println(compact.miles);
```

b. Explain the lifetime of every `miles` attribute that occurs during the execution of part (a).

c. How does your answer to part (a) change, if the following declaration is inserted into the addGas method?

```
int gas;
```

d. Rewrite the Auto class so that all instance variables are private, but so that read access is provided by get... methods and write access by set... methods. Next, rewrite part (a) to perform the same algorithm using these new means for reading from and writing to variables.

2. The following class makes use of the Auto class from Exercise 1.

```java
public class FamilyFleet {
    private Auto parentsCar;
    private Auto childrensCar;

    public FamilyFleet() {
        parentsCar = new Auto();
        childrensCar = new Auto();
    }

    public Auto getParentsCar() {
        return parentsCar;
    }

    public void setParentsCar(Auto a) {
        parentsCar = a;
    }

    public Auto getChildrensCar() {
        return childrensCar;
    }

    public void setChildrensCar(Auto a) {
        childrensCar = a;
    }

    // additional methods belong here

}
```

Using the `FamilyFleet` and `Auto` classes, assume that you are writing the code for a `Driver` class that contains the following instance variable declaration.

```java
public class Driver {
   private FamilyFleet ourCars, neighborCars;

   // additional methods belong here

}
```

For each part below, write a single Java instruction that can be placed within the `Driver` class to perform the indicated task. (You may assume that all objects have been assigned some value by the execution of prior code.)

a. an instruction to construct a new object and assign it to `ourCars`

b. an instruction to output (using `System.out.println`) the number of miles traveled by our children's car

c. an instruction to increase the amount of gasoline in the neighbor's parent car by 15 gallons

d. an instruction to copy the amount of gasoline from our children's car into the car of the neighbor's children

3. Draw a class diagram that includes the `Auto`, `FamilyFleet`, and `Driver` classes. Be certain to include all known instance variables and methods, as well as lines to show class composition.

4. Using the environment from Exercise 2, explain what happens when the following instruction executes by drawing *before* and *after* object diagrams:

```java
neighborsCars.setChildrensCar(ourCars.getParentsCar());
```

5. Consider the following two classes.

```java
public class Pizza {
    public int pepperoni;
    private int sausage;
    public int mozzarella;

    public Pizza(int p, int s, int m) {
        pepperoni = p;
        sausage = s;
        mozzarella = m;
    }
}
```

```
    public void enlarge() {
        pepperoni = sausage + 1;
        sausage++;
        mozzarella = sausage * 2;
    }
}


public class MyClass {
    public Pizza dinahsPie;
    private Pizza mamasPie;

    public MyClass() {
        Pizza bigJoesPie;
        dinahsPie = new Pizza(1, 2, 3);
        /* the code goes here */
    }
}
```

For each of the following parts, assume that the single instruction is substituted in place of

```
/* the code goes here */
```

What is the result? Your options are (1) an error in the parameter/argument lists, (2) a null pointer exception, (3) a compile time violation of scope rules, or (4) no compile time or runtime errors will be detected.

a. `dinahsPie = new Pizza(pepperoni, sausage, mozzarella);`

b. `mamasPie = new Pizza(0, 0, dinahsPie.mozzarella);`

c. `dinahsPie = new Pizza(8, 9, 10);`

d. `bigJoesPie = new Pizza(p, s, m);`

e. `dinahsPie.sausage = 1000;`

f. `dinahsPie.mozzarella = 100;`

g. `dinahsPie.enlarge();`

h. `bigJoesPie.enlarge();`

6. Using the classes from Exercise 5, suppose that the following instructions replace `/* the code goes here */`.

```
bigJoesPie = new Pizza(10, 20, 30);
bigJoesPie.enlarge();
bigJoesPie.enlarge();
dinahsPie.enlarge();
```

What is the value of the following objects immediately following the execution of these instructions?

a. `bigJoesPie.pepperoni`

b. `bigJoesPie.mozzarella`

c. `dinahsPie.pepperoni`

d. `dinahsPie.mozzarella`

7. Precisely what is output by executing each of the following code segments?

a. `String s = "ABCdef";`
   `System.out.println(s);`

b. `String s = "ABCdef";`
   `System.out.println(s.toLowerCase());`

c. `String s = "ABCdef";`
   `System.out.println(s + 25 + s);`

d. `String s = "ABCdef";`
   `System.out.println(s.length);`

e. `String s = "ABCdef";`
   `System.out.println(s.charAt(3));`

Programming Exercises

1. Write a separate class to maintain a counter along with `Label` to display the counter, and use your class to perform the following.

   Write a program using a `ThreeButtonFrame` together with two counters. The left counter is for counting the number of times that LEFT is clicked, and the right counter counts the number of times that RIGHT is clicked. Your counters should appear in the positions and sized as shown below. Initially, both counters are zero. Thereafter, the buttons behave as explained below.

   LEFT   This causes the left counter to be incremented by 1.

   MID   This causes both counters to reset to 0.

   RIGHT This causes the right counter to be incremented by 1.

   The following picture shows a state when the LEFT button has been clicked twice and the RIGHT button has been clicked five times since the last reset.

2. Write a program using a `ThreeButtonFrame` that displays a blue triangle with filled blue `ovals` (of diameter 10) centered on each vertex. Initially, the window should appear as illustrated in the picture. Thereafter, the buttons behave as explained below.

  LEFT   This causes the left vertex to move to its left by five pixels. The triangle and `Oval` are adjusted for this change.

  MID   This causes the top vertex to move up by five pixels. The triangle and `Oval` are adjusted for this change.

  RIGHT This causes the right vertex to move to its right by five pixels. The triangle and `Oval` are adjusted for this change.

Your program should include a separate class to encapsulate the triangle and its associated parts. (Note that you should look up the `Line` specifications if you are not familiar with this class.)

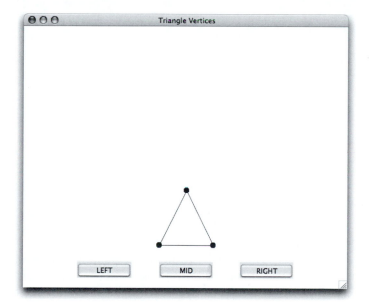

3. This program allows the user to play a game that is like a mixture of anagrams and a slot machine. When the program begins, the five four-letter words pictured below must be displayed with the same approximate size and spacing. The object of the game is to rearrange the letters to form five words that name various animals, using the three buttons, as follows.

  LEFT   The second letter of each word shifts down to the same position in word below it. The second letter of the bottom word becomes the second letter of the top. (Note that this is like a slot machine wheel spinning down one notch.)

MID The third letter of each word shifts down to the same position in word below it. The third letter of the bottom word becomes the third letter of the top.

RIGHT The last letter of each word shifts down to the same position in word below it. The last letter of the bottom word becomes the last letter of the top.

The leftmost letter of each word never moves throughout the program execution. Your program must use a separate class to hold the words and associated features.

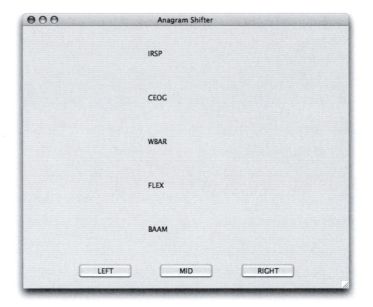

4. This program implements a clock face, using screen buttons to advance an hour hand and a minute hand. You must use a class called ClockHand that maintains a single one of the clock hands and associated features. Initially the clock is displayed as a 300 by 300 filled yellow circle upon a ThreeButtonFrame. Button clicks produce the following results.

LEFT The minute hand (the longer hand) is advanced by the equivalent of one minute.

MID The value of the current hour and current minutes as displayed by the clock are output to the standard output stream. (It is okay if 12 o'clock displays as zero.)

RIGHT The hour hand (the shorter hand) is advanced by the equivalent of one hour.

[*Hints:* A `ClockHand` centered in a `Container` works well. Using cosine and sine is useful in determining the outside endpoints of the clock hands. The `Line` class can be used for drawing line segments.]

The picture below shows this clock at 12:10.

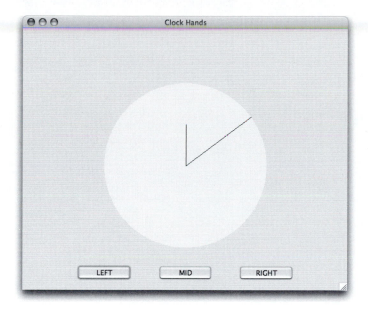

Logic and Selection

*Two roads diverged
in a yellow wood,
And sorry I could
not travel both
And being one traveler,
long I stood . . .*

—Robert Frost,
"The Road not Taken"

Objectives

- To explore the concept of selection and the need for selection control structures
- To examine the *if* instruction in its two basic forms: *if-then* and *if-then-else*
- To emphasize the need for proper indentation styles and use of braces in control structures
- To examine Java facilities for constructing relational expressions, including == and != for all data types and <, <=, >, and >= for primitive types
- To explore the forms of Boolean expressions that are supported by Java, especially the *AND* (&&), *OR* (||) and *NOT* (!) operations
- To introduce the concept of conditional (short-circuit) evaluation and how it is used to avoid certain runtime errors
- To examine the boolean data type and illustrate how it is used in methods (predicates), variables, and parameter passage
- To introduce the discipline of logic and explore how logical reasoning and logical rules can be used to improve Boolean expressions

- To revisit the notion of assertions, examine the form of assertions that involve selections, and suggest a method for assertion testing

- To examine how *if* instructions can be nested and used as multiway selection instructions, including cascading conditions

- To introduce the *switch* instruction

- To introduce testing concepts and how logic plays a significant role in both functional testing and structural testing

*M*athematics provides a foundation for science and engineering. Physics, for example, owes much of its foundation to the mathematical field of calculus. Similarly, computer science is largely founded upon the mathematical field known as *logic*. Software requirements documents are expressed as logical statements; computer hardware is constructed from circuitry described as "digital logic"; and computer programming is a logic-based activity.

The ancient Greeks thought of logic as the basis for human reasoning. Computer scientists also use logic for reasoning—reasoning about program behavior. In addition to *reasoning* about programs with logic, it is possible to *control* program execution with a form of logic. In this chapter, logic is examined *both* as a means to control program execution and as a way to understand and explain software semantics.

7.1 ■ The *if* instruction

Humans are constantly making choices. What time shall I get out of bed? Should I write with a pencil or a pen? Which is the best route to work—the freeway or the back roads? How many hours do I need to set aside for meal preparation?

Programs must also make choices. A chess-playing program must choose its next move. A program calculating income tax must choose which tax table is appropriate. A program controlling the antilock brakes on your car must choose when to apply to them and with what force.

Programming language instructions that are designed for the sole purpose of expressing choices are known as **selection instructions**. Java includes the following two selection instructions:

```
if
switch
```

The ***if*** **instruction** is the more widely used. Figure 7.1 describes the most common version of this instruction, known as an ***if-then-else*** **instruction**. An *if-then-else* has three parts

1. a ***then*** clause

2. an ***else*** clause

3. a *condition*

When an *if-then-else* executes, either the *then* clause will execute or the *else* clause will execute, but not both. The choice of which of the two clauses to select (execute) is based upon the value of the condition. (The syntax and semantics of Java conditions are explored in Sections 7.2 through 7.4.)

As an initial example, suppose a program is being developed to assist an all-you-can-eat restaurant with customer billing. This restaurant has a fixed fee of $12 per meal and policy that children under the age of three can eat free. The following *if-then-else* might be used to calculate the appropriate meal charge for a customer.

```
if (customerAge < 3) {
    mealCost = 0;
} else {
    mealCost = 12;
}
```

When this instruction executes, the `int` variable called `mealCost` will either be assigned 0 or 12, depending upon the value of the `customerAge` variable. Like every *if-then-else* instruction, there are two alternative ways for executing this instruction.

Selection instructions are called **control structures** because they control the order in which statements execute. Figure 7.2 contains an **activity diagram** to illustrate the flow of control for an *if-then-else* instruction.

software ***Hint***
engineering

Technically, the braces {...} can be omitted around any clause that consists of a single statement. However, it is often best to include these braces, even when they are optional, for two reasons: (1) notational consistency improves code readability and (2) code maintenance frequently turns single-statement clauses into multistatement clauses.

This activity diagram shows the possible ways in which this Java code may execute. Diamond-shaped polygons in an activity diagram denote locations where the path splits and/or merges. The top diamond in Figure 7.2 represents a choice of two alternative outgoing arrows. A bracketed logical expression accompanies each outgoing arrow. If *Condition* is `true`, then the path labeled "`Condition`" is followed; and `//Then Clause` executes. Otherwise, if *Condition* is `false`, then the path labeled "`NOT Condition`" is followed; and `//Else Clause` executes. Regardless of which clause is selected, the *if-then-else* completes by executing `//Statement after if`. The bottom diamond in Figure 7.2 shows that both paths merge.

Figure 7.1 ***ifThenElseInstruction*** description (a possible *OneStatement*)

Syntax

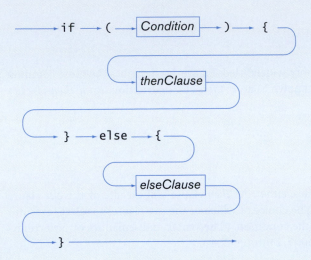

Syntax Notes

- *Condition* can be any valid *BooleanExpression*.
- *thenClause* and *elseClause* can be any valid *StatementSequence*.
- If *thenClause* consists of a single Java statement, then the (curly) braces immediately surrounding *thenClause* are optional.
- If *elseClause* consists of a single Java statement, then the braces immediately surrounding *elseClause* are optional.

Style Note

The reserved word `if` should be aligned with the "}" symbols, and all statements within *thenClause* and *elseClause* should be indented by one tab from the `if`. If *Condition* cannot be completed on one line, then "{" should be placed on a separate line and aligned with its matching "}".

Semantics

Executing *ifThenElseInstruction* causes *Condition* to be evaluated. If *Condition* is found to be `true`, then *thenClause* is executed. If *Condition* is found to be false, then *elseClause* is executed.

The program in Figure 7.3 contains another *if-then-else*. This program is designed to repeatedly move a `Label` displaying "HERE" from right to left across a window. When the HERE text gets within 20 pixels of the window's left edge, the message changes to STOP and is colored red.

Figure 7.2 Control flow of an *if-then-else* instruction

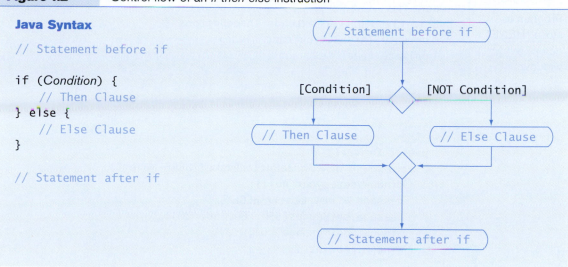

Java Syntax

```
// Statement before if

if (Condition) {
    // Then Clause
} else {
    // Else Clause
}

// Statement after if
```

The *if-then-else* instruction, located in `leftAction`, plays a key role in program behavior. Each call to this `leftAction` (i.e., each left button click event) results in one of two options. If `message` is less than 20 pixels from the left edge of its `Container`, then its text is changed to "STOP" and is colored red. The alternative `leftAction` behavior occurs when `message` is 20 pixels or more from the left edge. In this case, the *else* clause is executed which causes `message` to be repositioned 20 pixels farther left. Therefore, the effect of repeatedly clicking the left button is to move a black "HERE" message left until it nearly reaches the window's edge, and then turn it into a frozen red "STOP" message.

There are actually two forms of the Java *if* instruction. The *if-then-else* is one form and the second form is known as an ***if-then***. Figure 7.4 describes this form.

The *if-then* instruction provides a way to execute *optional* tasks. The *then* clause of an *if-then* instruction is executed when the instruction's condition is `true`, but the condition executes from an *if-then* with a condition that is found to be `false`. It is as though the execution of the *then* clause is optional. This behavior of an *if-then* is pictured in the activity diagram from Figure 7.5.

> **software**
> **engineering** *Hint*
>
> Indentation patterns play an important role in code readability. The clauses of every *if* instruction must be indented by 3 to 4 spaces (one tab setting) from the shell of the instruction. Examples in this section illustrate proper indentation.

The following code segment demonstrates the use of an *if-then* instruction.

```
// Assume outsideTemp is a double variable in Fahrenheit.
if (outsideTemp > 100) {
    System.out.println("Heat advisory!");;
}
```

Figure 7.3

Program to
move "HERE"
across a
window

```java
import java.awt.*;
public class Driver extends ThreeButtons {
    private ThreeButtonFrame window;
    private Label message;

    /** post:  window is created
     *         and message.getText() == "HERE"
     *         and message.getX()==60 and message.getY()==60
     */
    public Driver() {
        window = new ThreeButtonFrame("HERE Mover");
        window.setLayout(null);
        message = new Label("HERE");
        message.setBounds(550, 60, 50, 30);
        window.add(message, 0);
        window.repaint();
    }

    /** pre:    message != null
     * post:    (message.getX()@pre<20
     *              implies (message.getText()=="STOP"
     *              and message.getForeground()==red))
     *           and (message.getX()@pre>19 implies
     *              message.getX() == message.getX()@pre-20)
     */
    public void leftAction() {
        if (message.getX() < 20) {
            message.setText("STOP");
            message.setForeground(Color.red);
        } else {
            message.setLocation(message.getX()-20,
                message.getY());
        }
        message.repaint();
    }

    public void midAction() {
    }

    public void rightAction() {
    }
}
```

Syntax

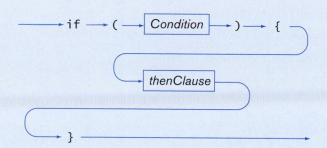

Figure 7.4

ifThenInstruction
description
(a possible
OneStatement)

Syntax Notes

- *Condition* can be any valid *BooleanExpression*.
- *thenClause* can be any valid *StatementSequence*.
- If *thenClause* consists of a single Java statement, then the braces immediately surrounding *thenClause* are optional.

Style Note

The reserved word `if` should be aligned with the "}" symbols and all statements within *thenClause* should be indented by one tab from the `if`. If *Condition* cannot be completed on one line, then "{" should be placed on a separate line and aligned with its matching "}".

Semantics

Executing *ifThenInstruction* causes *Condition* to be evaluated. If *Condition* is found to be `true`, then *thenClause* is executed. If *Condition* is found to be `false`, then execution proceeds to the statement following the *if-then*.

Java Syntax

```
// Statement before if

if (Condition) {
    //Then Clause
}

// Statement after if
```

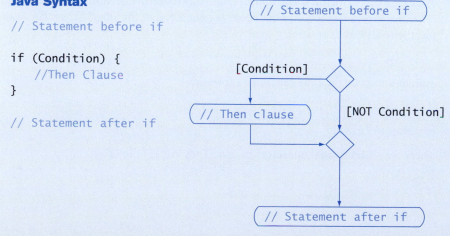

Figure 7.5

Control flow of
an *if-then*
instruction

There are two possible scenarios for executing this code:

- **Scenario 1** (`outsideTemp > 100`)

  In this scenario the heat advisory message is displayed.

- **Scenario 2** (`outsideTemp < 100`)

  In this scenario no message is displayed.

software *Hint*
engineering

Sometimes programmers write an *if-then*, when an *if-then-else* should be used. This tends to occur when the programmer is concentrating on handling one particular situation (the *then* clause) and overlooks the case where the situation does not exist. To be safe, it is wise to begin with an *if-then-else* instruction and be certain that the *else* clause is empty, prior to choosing an *if-then*.

7.2 ■ Relational Expressions

A 19th century English mathematician, **George Boole** studied a form of a **logical expression**, which became known as a **Boolean expression**. Java makes use of Boolean expressions in many places, including as the syntax for *if* instruction conditions.

When a numeric expression is evaluated, the result is a number. When a character expression is evaluated, the result is a character. When a Boolean expression evaluates, the result is a Boolean (logical) value. The only two options for a Boolean value are **true** or **false**. Not surprisingly, these two possible values for a Boolean expression coincide with the two paths for executing an *if* instruction.

In Java, the basic, and most commonly used form of a Boolean expression, is called a **relational expression**. Figure 7.6 describes the syntax and semantics of Java relational expressions.

Each relational expression is a comparison of two other expressions of compatible type, labeled *Operand1* and *Operand2*. At execution time, the relational expression is evaluated by performing the appropriate comparison. The result of evaluating a relational expression is either the Boolean value `true` or the value `false`. For example, the relational expression

    3 < 4

evaluates to `true`, and the relational expression

    'A' >= 'X'

evaluates to `false`.

There are six **relational operators** in Java. They are as follows:

Operator	Meaning
==	equal
!=	not equal
<	less than
<=	less than or equal
>	greater than
>=	greater than or equal

Like any other operator, the relational operators require that their operands have compatible types. In other words, int expressions cannot be compared to JFrame expressions. For primitive types, automatic widening occurs as needed to create compatible expressions in the same way that widening occurs in the evaluation of

Figure 7.6   *RelationalExpression* description

Syntax

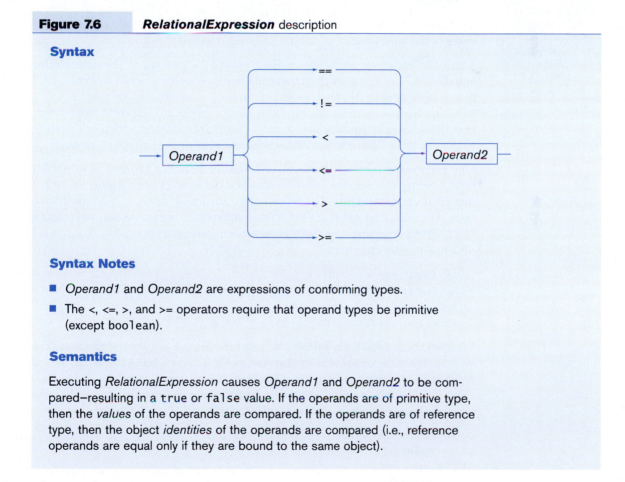

Syntax Notes

- *Operand1* and *Operand2* are expressions of conforming types.
- The <, <=, >, and >= operators require that operand types be primitive (except boolean).

Semantics

Executing *RelationalExpression* causes *Operand1* and *Operand2* to be compared—resulting in a true or false value. If the operands are of primitive type, then the *values* of the operands are compared. If the operands are of reference type, then the object *identities* of the operands are compared (i.e., reference operands are equal only if they are bound to the same object).

other numeric operators. A second restriction is that four of the relational operators (<, <=, >, and >=) are supported only for non-`boolean` primitive expressions.

The == and != operators can be used on either primitive or reference type expressions. However, the meaning of these two operators is somewhat different for primitive data than it is for reference data. When two expressions of primitive type are compared for equality, it is their *value* that is compared. For example, the relational expression

```
myInt == yourInt
```

is `true` exactly when the value of the `myInt` integer variable is identical to the value of `yourInt`.

When a comparison for == or != involves two reference types, then object bindings are compared. For example, the relational expression

```
myOval == yourOval
```

is `true` exactly when `myOval` and `yourOval` (variables of type `Oval`) are both references to the same object.

These two variations on the meaning of == and != give rise to the names **value equality** (the two values are the same) and **identity equality** (the two references bind to the same object). Applying == to primitive operands checks for value equality, while applying == to reference operands checks for identity equality. (The differences between value equality and identity equality are consistent with the differences in the way the assignment instruction behaves for primitive and reference data.)

One particularly common Boolean condition for reference variables is to test for `null` bindings. (Recall that a variable that is equal to `null` often means that it has not yet been instantiated.) The following *if* instruction shows how to use the == operator to check for `someLabel` that is instantiated. This *if* instruction will print its "ERROR" message any time that the subsequent `setLocation` call is about to fail on a null pointer exception.

```
if (someLabel == null) {
    System.out.println("ERROR - someLabel not assigned!");
}
someLabel.setLocation(0, 0);
```

Each relational operator is paired with another operator of opposite meaning. The == operator is the opposite of !=, because A==B is `true` when A!=B is `false` and A==B is `false` when A!=B is `true`. Similarly, < is the opposite of >=, and > is the opposite of <=. These opposite notations lead to alternative ways to express the same algorithm. For example, the following *if* instruction

```
if (someExpression < otherExpression) {
    doThis();
} else {
    doThat();
}
```

has exactly the same runtime behavior as the following.

```
if (someExpression >= otherExpression) {
    doThat();
} else {
    doThis();
}
```

Neither of these alternatives is better than the other, but they do point out yet another example of how the same algorithm may take various forms.

7.3 ■ Boolean Expressions

Relational expressions are just a subset of the more complete Java notation for Boolean expressions, the more complete notation for expressing an *if* condition. Figure 7.7 describes the more general syntax of Boolean expressions.

Figure 7.7	*BooleanExpression* syntax

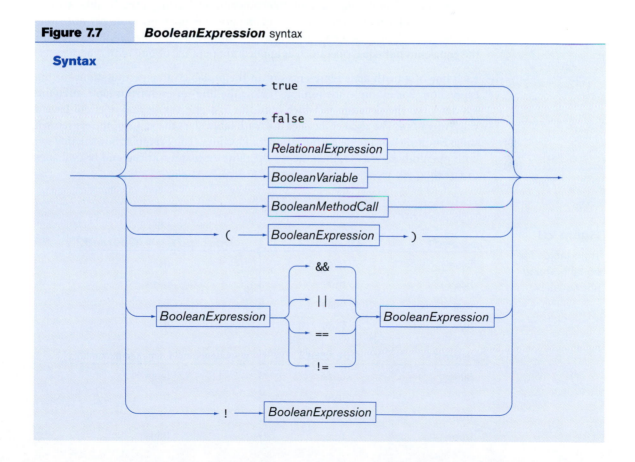

Boolean expressions are so important in Java that the language includes a separate **boolean type**. The `boolean` type is a primitive data type. Like many of the other primitive data types, `boolean` has a notation for constants. The two valid `boolean` constants are identifiers:

```
true
false
```

Java Boolean expressions support five operators.

- equal operator (==)
- not equal operator (!=)
- NOT operator (!)
- AND operator (&&)
- OR operator (||)

The first two of these operators (equal and not equal) are the same relational operators discussed in the prior section. These operators check for equality (or inequality) of values (either both `true` or both `false`).

It is often helpful to explain a Boolean expression by drawing a **truth table**. A truth table is a tabular representation of all of the possible operand value permutations and the resulting expression values. Figure 7.8 shows a truth table definition for both the equal and not equal operators, as applied to operands of `boolean` type.

Each line of a truth table represents one of the possible value permutations for the expression. For example, the top line (below the line) of each truth table in Figure 7.8 describes the situation in which both the first and the second operand have a value of `false`. The right column of the truth table gives the value of the expression value resulting from these particular operand values. The example shows that when both operands are `false`, then the == operator evaluates to `true` and != evaluates to `false`.

Figure 7.8

Truth tables for equal (==) and not equal(!=)

Operand1	Operand2	Operand1 == Operand2
false	false	true
false	true	false
true	false	false
true	true	true

Operand1	Operand2	Operand1 != Operand2
false	false	false
false	true	true
true	false	true
true	true	false

Operand	! Operand
false	true
true	false

Figure 7.9

Truth tables for *NOT* (!)

A truth table is also a good way to define the other `boolean` operators. Figure 7.9 defines the *NOT* operator by way of its truth table. There are only two rows in the truth table from this figure, because *NOT* only applies to one operand. Sometimes the *NOT* operation is called a **logical negation** operation, because it evaluates to the opposite Boolean value of its operand.

The `boolean` *AND* operation has a meaning consistent with the use of "and" in English sentences. The only time that an *AND* operator evaluates to `true` is when both its operands are `true`. Figure 7.10 contains the truth table definition for *AND*.

The `boolean` *OR* operation is sometimes called an **inclusive OR** because it evaluates to `true` whenever one or the other, *or both* of its operands are `true`. Figure 7.11 contains the truth table definition for *OR*.

The *NOT*, *AND*, and *OR* operators can be composed to form more complicated `boolean` expressions. For example, the following *if* instruction prints a "first shift" message when the value of the integer variable `hour` is within the range from 7 through 16. (Note that a mathematician might abbreviate the above condition as 7<=hour<=16, but Java compilers treat this mathematical abbreviation as a syntax error.)

Operand1	Operand2	Operand1 && Operand2
false	false	false
false	true	false
true	false	false
true	true	true

Figure 7.10

Truth tables for *AND* (&&)

Operand1	Operand2	Operand1 || Operand2
false	false	false
false	true	true
true	false	true
true	true	true

Figure 7.11

Truth tables for *OR* (\|\|)

```
if (7 <= hour && hour <= 16) {
    System.out.println("First shift");
}
```

A second example of Boolean operators is shown below. This *if* instruction prints a message based on the value of a char variable, called grade. The *then* clause executes for a grade value of 'A,' 'B,' or 'C,' otherwise the *else* clause executes.

```
if (grade=='A' || grade=='B' || grade=='C') {
    System.out.println("Course grade is 'C' or better");
} else {
    System.out.println("Course grade is below 'C'.");
}
```

These most recent two *if* instructions are a reminder of the importance of operator precedence. The conditions in these instructions are correct, because relational operators have a higher precedence than the boolean && and || operators. Figure 7.12 adds the precedence of the Boolean operators to a table of selected int operators. The two most important relationships to remember for writing Boolean expressions are as follows.

1. The common numeric operations have higher precedence than the relational operators.

2. The precedence of the relational operators is higher than other Boolean operators.

Boolean expressions are similar to other primitive expressions in many ways. It is possible to parenthesize Boolean expressions to force any desired order on operator evaluation. It is also possible to declare variables, constants, and methods to store Boolean values, using the word "boolean" with all lowercase letters.

If an attribute of state information must either be true or false, then it is a good candidate for storing as a boolean variable. Figure 7.13 illustrates with a program that uses buttons to toggle a window label.

The message toggling program from Figure 7.13 uses a boolean instance variable named isAdded. The Driver constructor method assigns isAdded the value true to reflect the fact that the message label has been added to window. Each time that the left button is clicked the *if* instruction uses the value of isAdded as a condition to select between removing the message and adding the message. This causes the message to appear for one left button click and disappear on the subsequent click.

Each call to leftAction must also assign isAdded a value that is consistent with the state of the message variable. This is accomplished by toggling the value of isAdded to its opposite value (true becomes false and false becomes true) via the following instruction.

```
isAdded = !isAdded;
```

---

software *engineering Hint*

Variables of type boolean should be named with action phrases such as

isAdded,
isAlive,
hasChildren

Such names improve readability.

---

software *engineering Hint*

There is a temptation to express the *if* instruction from Figure 7.13 as follows.

```
if (isAdded == true) {...
```

The semantics of this new version are the same as the original version.

```
if (isAdded) {...
```

However, the original version is more succinct and potentially more efficient. Ultimately, code that avoids the use of "==true" or "==false" is better code.

Precedence	Operator	Operation	Order within
highest	-- ++	postfix autodecrement postfix autoincrement	left to right
	-- ++ - !	prefix autodecrement prefix autoincrement unary minus Boolean *NOT*	right to left
	/ * %	division multiplication remainder	left to right
	+ -	addition subtraction	left to right
	< <= > >=	less than less than or equal greater than greater than or equal	left to right
	== !=	equal not equal	left to right
	&&	Boolean *AND*	left to right
lowest	||	Boolean *OR*	left to right

Figure 7.12

Precedence of selected int and Boolean operators

7.4 ■ Conditional Evaluation

The Boolean *AND* (&&) and *OR* (||) operators are evaluated in a way that is unique to these two operations. This evaluation technique is called **conditional evaluation**, because the only portion of the expression that is essential in determining its value is evaluated. To explore the reasoning behind conditional evaluation, consider the evaluation of the following expression.

operand1 && *operand2*

If the value of *operand1* is false, then the entire expression is also false, regardless of *operand2*'s value. The Java VM takes advantage of this fact. Whenever the left operand of an *AND* operation is found to be false, the right operand is ignored. It is said that the evaluation of the right operand is "short-circuited" in such cases. This gives rise to the name **short-circuit evaluation**—a synonym for "conditional evaluation." Of course, if the left operand of an *AND* operation is true, then the operation cannot be short-circuited, and both operands must be evaluated.

Conditional evaluation is also applied to *OR* operations. If two operands are ORed together, then the right operand is short-circuited whenever the left operand evalu-

Figure 7.13

Program to
toggle
"COLLEGE"

```java
import java.awt.*;
public class Driver extends ThreeButtons {
    private ThreeButtonFrame window;
    private Label sweatshirtMsg;
    private boolean isAdded;

    /** post:  window is constructed
     *         and sweatshirtMsg.getText()=="COLLEGE"
     *         and sweatshirtMsg has been added to window's
     *            content pane
     *         and isAdded
     */
    public Driver() {
        window = new ThreeButtonFrame("Flashing Message Window");
        window.setLayout(null);
        sweatshirtMsg = new Label("COLLEGE");
        sweatshirtMsg.setBounds(250, 200, 100, 30);
        window.add(sweatshirtMsg, 0);
        isAdded = true;
        window.repaint();
    }

    /** pre:   sweatshirtMsg!=null and window!=null
     *  post:  (isAdded@pre implies
     *             sweatshirtMsg is removed and not isAdded)
     *         and (not isAdded@pre implies
     *             sweatshirtMsg is added and isAdded)
     */
    public void leftAction() {
        if (isAdded) {
            window.remove(sweatshirtMsg);
        } else {
            window.add(sweatshirtMsg, 0);
        }
        window.repaint();
        isAdded = !isAdded;
    }

    public void midAction() {
    }

    public void rightAction() {
    }
}
```

ates to `true`, because in this case the entire expression is `true` regardless of the right operand's value.

One advantage of conditional evaluation is to avoid wasting time evaluating unnecessary expressions. An even greater advantage of conditional evaluation is to permit a left operand to *guard* a right operand from producing unwanted behavior (usually a runtime error). For example, suppose that `totalWaterConsumed` is an `int` variable representing the water consumption for a period of time given by `daysPassed` (another `int` variable). The following *if* instruction calculates the average water consumption per day.

```
if (daysPassed != 0 && totalWaterConsumed/daysPassed > 100) {
    System.out.println("WARNING: water consumption is high.");
    System.out.prinltn("This house is consuming more than 100
        units/day.");
} else {
    System.out.println("Water consumption is acceptable.");
}
```

The *if* condition above guards against a division by zero that might occur when calculating the average by dividing by `daysPassed`. (Division by zero is a runtime error in Java, because it is an undefined arithmetic calculation.) The solution (shown in the code above) is to include a guard condition prior to potential division by zero. The guard expression in this case is `daysPassed!=0`. Since this guard is the left operand of an *AND* operation, the guard is evaluated first. If the guard is `true`, then `daysPassed` is nonzero and the remainder of the *if* condition is evaluated. However, if the guard expression is `false`, then the right operand is short circuited, avoiding a runtime (division by zero) error.

7.5 ■ Predicates

Methods that return a `boolean` value are given a special name; they are called **predicates**. One such predicate is built into the `java.awt.Container,` as well as `Oval`, `Rectangle`, `Label`, and the content panes of `JFrame` and `ThreeButtonFrame`. It is a parameterless predicate named `isShowing`. A call to `isShowing` returns the value `true` if the associated object is displayed (although possibly obscured by a different object). This method plays a similar role to the `isAdded` variable from the Figure 7.13 example. The following instruction illustrates how to use `isShowing` in place of `isAdded` to add a removed or remove an added message from window.

```
if (sweatshirtMsg.isShowing()) {
    window.remove(sweatshirtMsg);
} else {
    window.add(sweatshirtMsg, 0);
}
```

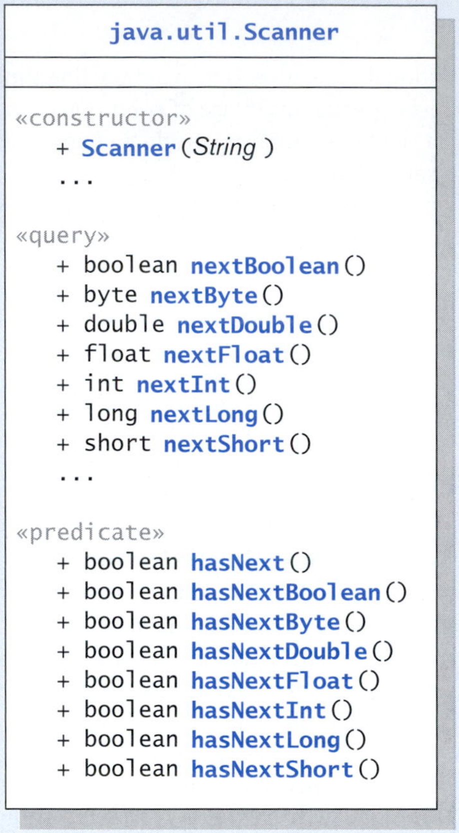

Figure 7.14

Class diagram
for Scanner

java.util.Scanner

«constructor»
+ **Scanner** (*String*)
. . .

«query»
+ boolean **nextBoolean** ()
+ byte **nextByte** ()
+ double **nextDouble** ()
+ float **nextFloat** ()
+ int **nextInt** ()
+ long **nextLong** ()
+ short **nextShort** ()
. . .

«predicate»
+ boolean **hasNext** ()
+ boolean **hasNextBoolean** ()
+ boolean **hasNextByte** ()
+ boolean **hasNextDouble** ()
+ boolean **hasNextFloat** ()
+ boolean **hasNextInt** ()
+ boolean **hasNextLong** ()
+ boolean **hasNextShort** ()

Predicates are often useful in guarding against potential runtime errors. The standard Scanner class, introduced in the previous chapter, contains several predicates for this reason. Figure 7.14 lists these methods within a class diagram.

Assuming that the String assigned to a Scanner object represents a single value,[1] the hasNext method will return true; if the Scanner object String is empty or contains only white space, then hasNext returns false. The other predicates check the kind of value represented in the Scanner string. In other words, hasNextBoolean is true if and only if the text true or false is found in the Scanner string. Similarly, hasNextInt tests for text representing a valid int literal.

Suppose that your program contains two text fields (operand1Field and operand2Field) in which the user is expected to type two numbers (either real or integer). The following code averages these two numbers.

---

1. It is possible for Scanner to convert more than a single value from a string. See Chapter 13 for a description of how to use Scanner for more complex purposes.

```
/* assert: operand1Field and operand2Field are non-null
           javax.swing.JTextField objects and average is a
           double */
String operand1Str = operand1Field.getText();
String operand2Str = operand2Field.getText();
Scanner scan1 = new Scanner(operand1Str);
Scanner scan2 = new Scanner(operand2Str);
if (scan1.hasNextDouble() && scan2.hasNextDouble()) {
    average = (scan1.nextDouble() + scan2.nextDouble()) / 2;
} else {
    System.out.println("ERROR - one text field is non-numeric");
}
```

This code segment begins by retrieving the text from the two operand fields and assigning each to a different `String` variable (`operand1Str` and `operand2Str`). Each of these `String` values is passed to a separate `Scanner` object (`scan1` and `scan2`). Good defensive programming methodology is employed by calling `hasNextDouble` before calling `nextDouble` on `scan1` and `scan2`. If either `Scanner` object contains an invalid string (i.e., something that is fails to represent a numeric value), then the *if* instruction will detect the problem and print the error message.

User-written predicates are also particularly useful for localizing code that is tedious or messy. A condition to test a character variable to see if it stores a symbol representing an English language vowel is certainly a bit messy.

```
if (character == 'A' || character == 'E' || character == 'I'
   || character == 'O' || character == 'U' || character == 'Y'
   || character == 'a' || character == 'e' || character == 'i'
   || character == 'o' || character == 'u' || character == 'y')
{
    System.out.println("character is a vowel.");
}
```

The clutter of the above instruction is reduced, and its readability improved, by using an `isVowel` predicate as shown below.

```
if (isVowel(character)) {
    System.out.println("character is a vowel.");
}
```

The code for the `isVowel` predicate is given in Figure 7.15. Like many predicates, `isVowel` has a body that consists of a single return instruction.

As a second example predicate, consider the task of checking whether or not two `Container` objects are added to the same background in such a way that they overlap on the display. (`java.awt.Container` objects include virtually everything that can be added to a `Container`.) Figure 7.16 contains such a predicate called `areOverlapping`.

The *if* instruction from the `areOverlapping` method separates the check into two cases. The first case (captured by the *then* clause) occurs when the two parameter

---

software engineering *Hint*

Many predicates are included in classes to permit programmers to guard against runtime errors. The `hasNext...` methods from `Scanner` are a good example. It is sound software engineering to use an *if* instruction to guard a call to nextInt, by checking hasNextInt in the if condition.

software engineering *Hint*

Predicate should be named with action phrases, like Boolean variables. The `isVowel` and `areOverlapping` predicates illustrate.

Figure 7.15

isVowel
predicate

```
/* post:   result == c is an uppercase or lowercase vowel
           (a, e, i, o , u, or y) */
private boolean isVowel(char c) {
    return c=='A' || c=='E' || c=='I' || c=='O' || c=='U'
       || c=='Y' || c=='a' || c=='e' || c=='i'
       || c=='o' || c=='u' || c=='y';
}
```

Figure 7.16

areOverlapping
predicate

```
/** pre:   c1 is non-null and c2 is non-null
 * post:   result == c1 and c2 are overlapping regions added
 *         to the same background Container
 */
private boolean areOverlapping(Container c1, Container c2) {
    boolean overlapHorizontally, overlapVertically;
    if (c1.getParent()==null || c2.getParent()==null
        || c1.getParent() != c2.getParent())
    {
        return false;
    } else {
        overlapHorizontally
            = c1.getX() < c2.getX()+c2.getWidth()
            && c1.getX()+c1.getWidth() > c2.getX();
        overlapVertically
            = c1.getY() < c2.getY()+c2.getHeight()
            && c1.getY()+c1.getHeight() > c2.getY();
        return overlapHorizontally && overlapVertically;
    }
}
```

objects are *not* added to the same background `Container`. A `Container` method, named `getParent`, is called on each `c1` and `c2`. The `getParent` method is defined to return the `Container` to which a `c1` (or `c2`) is added. (Notice that `c1==null` and `c2==null` are used to short-circuit potential null pointer exception errors that could result from the calls to `getParent` when either `c1` or `c2` has not yet been constructed.)

The *else* clause from `areOverlapping` handles the case where `c1` and `c2` are both added to the same `Container`. In this situation, the code checks separately for overlapping in the horizontal and in the vertical directions. Overlapping of the two `Container` parameters occurs only when *both* horizontal and vertical directions, so the final expression *AND*s the two `boolean` variables.

In order for the two containers to overlap it must be that c1's left edge lies to the left of c2's right edge (c1 < c2.getX()+c2.getWidth()) at the same time that c1's right edge lies to the right of c2's left edge (c1.getX()_c1.getWidth() > c2.getX()). Checking for vertical overlap is analogous to checking for horizontal overlap.

7.6 ■ The Use of *implies*

You may have noticed that postconditions for code involving *if* instructions often include the word **implies**. Figure 7.17 contains an example method.

In English it is common to think of the statement "A implies B." as synonymous with "If A, then B." Therefore, the postcondition of the minimum method is saying that if d1 is less or equal to d2, then the minimum method returns d1; and if d1 is greater than d2, then minimum returns d2.

> **software engineering Hint**
>
> Software specifications often contain implications to describe what occurs under various conditions. Implications in specifications generally result in selection instructions in the associated code.

The word *implies* also has a (closely related) meaning in the field of mathematical logic. implies is short for the logical operation known as **implication**. An implication is written in the form

> *premise* **implies** *conclusion*

where *premise* is a logical statement that uniquely defines the computational state that produces this case and *conclusion* describes the outcome of the case. The implication

> (d1 <= d2) *implies* result == d1

describes that for the case in which d1 is smaller than or equal to d2, the outcome is that the method returns the value of d1.

```
/** post:   (d1 <= d2) implies result == d1
 *          and (d1 > d2) implies result == d2
 */
private double minimum(double d1, double d2) {
    double result;
    if (d1 <= d2) {
        result = d1;
    } else {
        result = d2;
    }
    return result;
}
```

Figure 7.17

minimum method

implies is *not* a valid Java `boolean` operator. However, implication is a commonly-used logical operation. Figure 7.18 shows the truth table for implication.

As the truth table indicates, the implication

$$(d1 \text{ <= } d2) \text{ } \textit{implies} \text{ } result == d1$$

is true any time that `d1 > d2`. Such situations in which the premise of an implication is false should be thought of as vacuously true. When the premise of an implication is false, that implication may be true but this says nothing about the truth or falsity of the conclusion. The truth table also shows that when the premise is true, the conclusion must also be true, lest the entire implication be false.

The truth table's rightmost column is for a different expression, namely *not Operand1 or Operand2*. Since this last column's values are row by row identical to the ***implies*** column, the two logical expressions are equivalent. This is the key to implementing ***implies*** in Java. Figure 7.19 includes an `implies` predicate that illustrates.

The `implies` method is passed two `boolean` parameters, corresponding to the premise (p) and conclusion (q) of the implication. The method returns the value of *not* p *or* q in the form of the following Java `boolean` expression: `!p || q`

The `implies` method illustrates how to create your own logical methods. This method is also quite useful for testing assertions at runtime, as discussed in Section 7.12.

Figure 7.18   Truth tables for the logical ***implies*** operation

Operand1	Operand2	Operand1 *implies* Operand2	*not* Operand1 *or* Operand2
false	false	true	true
false	true	true	true
true	false	false	false
true	true	true	true

Figure 7.19

implies
predicate

```
/** post:  result == p implies q */
private boolean implies(boolean p, boolean q) {
    return !p || q;
}
```

7.7 ■ **Nesting *if* Instructions**

Some algorithms involve more complicated selections than possible with a single *if* instruction. Often the solution is **nesting**. An *if* instruction is said to be *nested* within another *if* instruction when it is contained within either the *then* clause or the *else* clause. An example of nested is shown in the gradePassFail method of Figure 7.20. This method returns a grade from a corresponding exam score. The particular

Figure 7.20   gradePassFail method and its activity diagram

```
/** post: (s < 0 || s > 100) implies result == 'X
 *        and (60<=s<=100) implies result=='P'
 *        and (0<=s<=59) implies result=='F'
 */
private char gradePassFail(int s) {
    char result;
    if (s < 0 || s > 100) {
        System.out.println("ERROR - invalid test score.");
        result = 'X';
    } else {
        if (s >= 60) {
            result = 'P';
        } else {
            result = 'F';
        }
    }
    return result
}
```

exam has a potential range of 0 to 100 points and is scored Pass/Fail with a grade of 60 or more constituting a pass. The gradePassFail method receives the exam score as a parameter and returns a 'P' for passing or an 'F' for failing. This method also returns an 'X' and prints an error message when the parameter is out of range for a valid test score. Figure 7.20 also includes an activity diagram that pictures the control flow for gradePassFail.

The gradePassFail method contains an *if* instruction that is nested inside the *else* clause of another *if* instruction. The outer *if* checks for a valid score, while the inner *if* checks to see whether the score is passing or not. The *then* clause of the outer *if* prints an error message when the number of points is invalid (less than 0 or more than 100). The *else* clause of the outer *if* executes for any valid exam score. This outer *else* clause executes another *if* instruction to select between passing and failing.

Java's use of (curly) braces becomes a more significant issue as the number of braces increases due to nesting. To understand the reasoning behind braces, it is helpful to understand that the *if* instruction is designed to have a single-statement *then* clause and a single-statement *else* clause. For single-statement clauses, there is no need for braces.

The braces are included in the language as a mechanism to group several statements into what is sometimes referred to as a **compound statement**. A *then* clause or *else* clause that is enclosed in braces is treated just like a single (compound) statement. Figure 7.21 describes the syntax and semantics of a compound statement.

Sometimes braces (compound statements) are unnecessary. The code below is a segment of the gradePassFail method (from Figure 7.20) with nonessential braces removed.

Figure 7.21	*CompoundStatement* description

Syntax

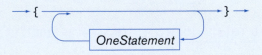

Semantics

Executing *CompoundStatement* causes the *OneStatement* statements to execute in order.

Style notes

- Statements in a sequence are best placed one per line and each line justified to the same left position (i.e., tabbed the same distance from the left margin).
- The precise location of the braces depends upon usage. The statements within a compound statement are indented to show this containment.

```java
if (s < 0 || s > 100) {
    System.out.println("ERROR - invalid test score.");
    result = 'X';
} else
if (s >= 60)
    result = 'P';
else
    result = 'F';
```

This second version of the `gradePassFail` algorithm is valid Java, and it executes the same as the original nested *if*. However, omitting the braces from control structures is discouraged because properly indented braces make the code more readable by clearly marking the beginning and ending of control structures.

Including braces also helps to avoid a problem known as the **dangling else problem**. A dangling else code pattern consists of an *if-then-else* instruction with an *if-then* nested as the *then* clause. Figure 7.22 contains this code pattern along with its associated activity diagram.

As shown in Figure 7.22 with braces, the dangling else pattern is never problematic. Executing this statement produces one of three outcomes:

1. If both *condition1* and *condition2* are `true`, *thenStatement* executes.

2. If *condition1* is `false`, *elseStatement* executes.

3. If *condition1* is `true` and *condition2* is `false`, then no further code executes within this code segment.

The problem with the dangling else pattern only surfaces when nonessential braces are removed. The resulting code is shown in Figure 7.23.

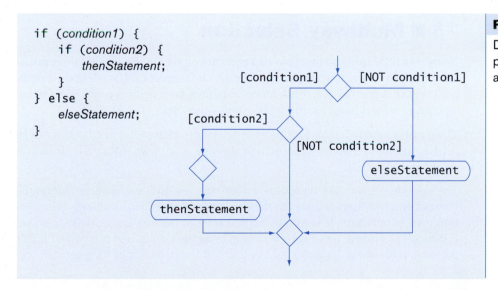

Figure 7.22

Dangling else pattern code and activity diagram

Figure 7.23   Problematic dangling else code and activity diagram

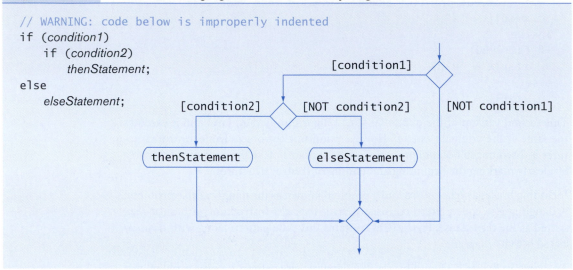

```
// WARNING: code below is improperly indented
if (condition1)
    if (condition2)
        thenStatement;
else
    elseStatement;
```

software *Hint*
engineering

The dangling
else problem is
just one more
reason for includ-
ing braces even
when they are
optional.

The absence of braces in this code fails to clearly indicate the end of the *then* clause from the outer *if* instruction. In the absence of braces, the Java compiler matches *else* clauses with the most recent possibility. Therefore, the *else* clause in the code from Figure 7.23 is paired with the *inner if*, instead of the outer *if*, and the outer *if* has no *else* clause. The activity diagram in the figure illustrates the control flow of this code, and this activity diagram is inconsistent with the indentation of the code.

7.8 ■ Multiway Selection

Many selections involve more than two alternatives. An automobile has three possible directions of travel when passing through an intersection (turn left, turn right, go straight). A baseball player has nine alternatives for a fielding position. Selecting a playing card yields one of fifty-two possible outcomes.

The *if* instruction is designed for two-way selections. However, *if* instructions can be used as **multiway selection** instructions through nesting *if*s within *else* clauses, as shown in Figure 7.24.

The code in Figure 7.24 represents a four-way selection using three *if-then-else* instructions, two that are nested as the *else* clause of outer *if* instructions. The notation used in this example is correct, but it is inferior because the four-way selection is difficult to discern; matching the closing braces is tedious and messy; and if this pattern continues too long, the code will run off the right side of the page.

Figure 7.24   Multiway selection instructions through nested *if*s

```
// a better notation for
// this multiway branch
// pattern is found in
// Figure 7.25.
if (cond1) {
    alternative1;
} else {
    if (cond2) {
        alternative2;
    } else {
        if (cond3) {
            alternative3;
        } else {
            alternative4;
        }
    }
}
```

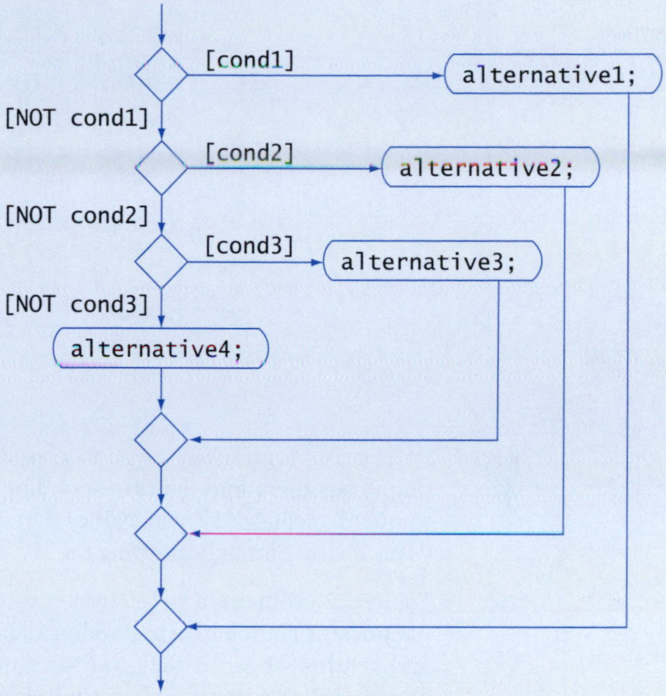

A better notation pattern for multiway selection via nested *if* instructions is shown in Figure 7.25. This formatting indents all of the alternatives by the same distance and omits the unnecessary braces for every *else* clause.

```
if (condition1) {
    alternative1;
} else if (condition2) {
    alternative2;
} else if (condition3) {
    alternative3;
...
} else if (conditionN) {
    alternativeN;
} else {
    alternativeNplus1;
}
```

Figure 7.25

Preferred notation for multiway selection using *if* instructions

Figure 7.26

Telephone
keypad

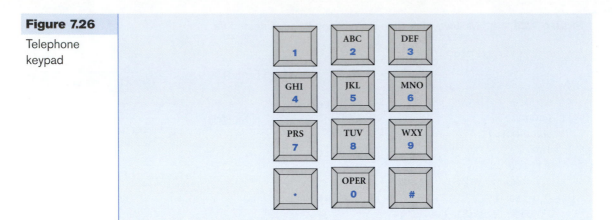

As an example multiway selection, consider a method to translate a letter from a telephone key press into the corresponding digit that is dialed. Figure 7.26 shows the standard telephone keypad. Notice that if the phone user presses the "H" key, then a "4" is dialed. Similarly, pressing the "W" key dials "9."

Figure 7.27 contains a `teleDigit` method to translate an alphabetic key press (the parameter `c`) into the corresponding digit. The `teleDigit` method displays an error and returns −1 when the `char` parameter represents something other than the uppercase letters contained on a telephone keypad.

One common pattern of multiway selection uses a concept known as **cascading conditions** to simplify the Boolean expressions used within the nested *if* instructions. To illustrate cascading conditions, consider a code segment to randomly color `Label` foreground in the following manner.

New Label Color	Probability
green	0.1
yellow	0.3
orange	0.2
cyan	0.4

In other words 10 percent of the time the `Label` should be recolored green, 30 percent of the time it should be recolored yellow, 20 percent of the time it should be recolored orange, and the remaining 40 percent of the time it should be recolored cyan. The following is a code segment to perform recoloring in this way. This code code uses a `double` variable, named `rand`.

```
rand = Math.random();
if (rand <= 0.1) {
    myLabel.setForeground(Color.green);
} else if (rand <= 0.4) {
    myLabel.setForeground(Color.yellow);
```

Figure 7.27   `teleDigit` method

```java
/** post:  (c is NOT a valid uppercase letter from the telephone keypad
 *             implies an error message is output and result == -1)
 *         and (c is a valid uppercase letter from the telephone keypad
 *             implies result == the keypad digit corresponding to c)
 */
private int teleDigit(char c) {
    if ('A' <= c && c <= 'C') {
        return 2;
    } else if ('D' <= c && c <= 'F') {
        return 3;
    } else if ('G' <= c && c <= 'I') {
        return 4;
    } else if ('J' <= c && c <= 'L') {
        return 5;
    } else if ('M' <= c && c <= 'O') {
        return 6;
    } else if (c == 'P' || c == 'R' || c == 'S') {
        return 7;
    } else if ('T' <= c && c <= 'V') {
        return 8;
    } else if ('W' <= c && c <= 'Y') {
        return 9;
    } else {
        System.out.println("ERROR - non digit key character.");
        return -1;
    }
}
```

```java
    } else if (rand <= 0.6) {
        myLabel.setForeground(Color.orange);
    } else {
        myLabel.setForeground(Color.cyan);
    }
```

The code above begins execution by generating a random number through a call to the `random` method from `Math`. Since random returns a value randomly chosen between 0.0 to 1.0, the remainder of the code can use this value to determine recoloring probabilities. This is done as follows:

■ There is a probability of 0.1 that `rand` is less than 0.1.

■ There is a probability of 0.3 that `rand` is between 0.1 and 0.4.

■ There is a probability of 0.2 that `rand` is between 0.4 and 0.6.

■ There is a probability of 0.4 that `rand` is between 0.6 and 1.0.

The cascading effect comes from the fact that the first *if* instruction checks for a rand value less than 0.1. Therefore, the second *if* instruction does not need to check for rand greater than 0.1, since it is impossible to reach the second *if* unless rand is greater than 0.1. Therefore, the second condition builds (or cascades) from the first condition by avoiding the check for rand greater than 0.1. Similarly, the third *if* instruction is written (rand <= 0.6) instead of 0.4 < rand && rand <= 0.6) because the conditions build upon one another in a cascade.

7.9 ■ The *switch* Instruction

Java includes a second selection instruction (the ***switch* instruction**) that is applicable for certain algorithms. Figure 7.28 describes the syntax and semantics of the *switch* instruction.

Figure 7.28   ***SwitchInstruction*** description (a possible *OneStatement*)

SwitchInstruction Syntax

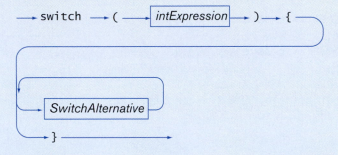

SwitchAtlernative Syntax

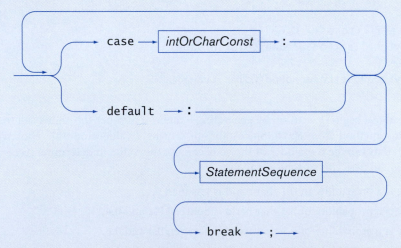

The *switch* instruction differs from the *if* instruction in two important ways:

1. A *switch* instruction is not restricted to two-way selection, but supports multiway selection without any nesting.

2. The clause selection is based upon the value of an `int` (or `char`) expression, rather than a `boolean` condition.

The syntax of a *switch* instruction consists of the reserved word **switch**, followed by the **switch expression** in parentheses, followed by zero or more **case clauses**. *Case* clauses begin with the reserved word **case**, followed by a **case constant**, followed by a colon and the code for the clause. (One of the case clauses for a *switch* instruction may use the reserved word **default** in place of `case`.) Each *case* clause should end with a `break` instruction. Figure 7.29 shows an example *switch* instruction in which the `switch` expression is a `char` variable, called `letterGrade`. The corresponding activity diagram is shown in Figure 7.29 on the right.

software *Hint*
engineering

A common error when writing *switch* instructions is to omit a break instruction at the end of a clause. Such an omission does not produce a compile time error, but it is a poor programming practice. The run-time effect of executing a case clause without a break is that the subsequent case clause is executed.

Syntax Notes

- *intExpression* is an expression of type `int` or `char`.
- *intOrCharConst* is a constant of type `int` or `char`.
- Every *intOrCharConst* must be different from all others within the same *switch* instruction.
- Only one `default` option is permitted within a single `switch` instruction.
- Technically, the `break` instruction is optional, but it is dangerous to omit it.

Style Notes

The reserved word `switch` should be aligned with the "}" symbol. Each case and `default` should be on a separate line. Each *StatementSequence* should be indented from its preceding `case` or `default`. Each `break` should be indented to match the *StatementSequence* that precedes it.

Semantics

Executing *SwitchStatement* causes *intExpression* to be evaluated. If the value of *intExpression* is equal to one of the *intOrCharConst* values, then the *StatementSequence* beneath the constant is executed. If none of the *intOrCharConst* is equal to *intExpression*, then the *StatementSequence* beneath `default` is executed. If none of the *intOrCharConst* is equal to *intExpression* and no `default` option is included, then no other statements from the `switch` instruction executes.

The execution of a *switch* instruction begins by evaluating the `switch` expression (`letterGrade`). When the value of `switch` expression is equal to any of the case constants, then the clause prefixed by that constant is executed. For example, the *switch* instruction from Figure 7.29 will output two lines indicating that the grade is a C, which is an average grade whenever `letterGrade == 'C'`.

software
engineering *Hint*

Default clauses should be included in *switch* statements unless it is certain that they are not needed. It is best to place the default clause as the last of the clauses within a *switch*.

The *switch* instruction clause prefixed by `default` is known as the **default clause**. The *default* clause executes when none of the case constants match the *switch* expression. The example executes its *default* clause, displaying the `"Invalid grade"` message, any time that `letterGrade` has a value other than `'A'`, `'B'`, `'C'`, `'D'`, or `'F'`. Like an *else* clause, *default* clauses are optional. If a *default* clause is omitted, no clause executes when the *switch* expression has a value different from every case constant.

There are several restrictions imposed upon case constants.

■ *Switch* expressions must be of type `int` or `char`.

■ Case constants must be *constants* (not expressions involving variables, operations, or methods).

Figure 7.29   Activity diagram for the `letterGrade` switch example

```
switch (letterGrade) {
    case 'A' :
        System.out.println("Your grade is an A.");
        System.out.println("Excellent work!");
        break;
    case 'B' :
        System.out.println("Your grade is a B.");
        System.out.println("Above average.");
        break;
    case 'C' :
        System.out.println("Your grade is a C.");
        System.out.println("Average grade.");
        break;
    case 'D' :
        System.out.println("Your grade is a D.");
        System.out.println("Below average.");
        break;
    case 'F' :
        System.out.println("Your grade is an F.");
        System.out.println("Failing.");
        break;
    default :
        System.out.println("Invalid grade");
        break;
}
```

- No case constant may appear more than once within a single switch instruction.

- No more than one default clause may be included in a single switch.

There are no restrictions on the number or the ordering of case constants within a switch instruction. Furthermore, multiple case constants can be used for the same case clause. The following code segment illustrates.

```
// assert 0 <= someDecimalDigit <= 9
switch (someDecimalDigit) {
    case 2 :
        System.out.println("An even prime number");
        break;
    case 3 :
    case 5 :
    case 7 :
        System.out.println("An odd prime number");
        break;
    case 0 :
```

```
        case 4 :
        case 6 :
        case 8 :
            System.out.println("An even number that is not prime");
            break;
        case 9 :
            System.out.println("An odd number that is not prime");
            break;
        case 1 :
            System.out.println("The number 1");
            break;
        default :
            System.out.println("someDecimalDigit is not a decimal
                digit.");
            break;
    }
```

Executing the preceding *switch* instruction causes one of six alternatives to occur. If the value of someDecimalDigit is 3, 5, or 7, then the "An odd prime number" message is output. Similarly, if someDecimalDigit is 0, 4, 6, or 8, then the message output is "An even number that is not prime".

Software developers must often choose between using an *if* instruction and using a *switch* instruction. In making this choice it is best to view *switch* as a special purpose instruction and *if* as the more widely used option. A *switch* instruction is a possible choice when there is a natural integer expression to determine the selection and when the number of clauses is greater than two. The disadvantages of a *switch* instruction are the restrictions imposed upon the switch expression and case constants and the potential for neglecting to include break instructions.

7.10 ■ Software Testing

Software testing is the process of exercising a program in order to uncover faults (bugs). A software tester constructs a **test suite**, consisting of different **test cases** designed to check the program under varying situations.

Testing that is done without using specific code details is called **black box testing**, because the program is treated like a black box. Another name for black box testing is **functional testing**, since the idea is to exercise the various functionalities of the code without knowledge of their implementation. One of the advantages of functional testing is that writing test cases can begin as soon as the program requirements are known. On large programming projects it is typical to have software testers writing test suites at the same time that other software engineers are working on program design and implementation.

Logic plays an integral role in functional testing because functional testing relies upon software requirements and software requirements are logical statements of code behavior. For example, suppose that a software tester is assigned the task of testing a single method. The best way to proceed is to examine the precondition and postcondition for the method. Since postconditions are frequently expressed as implications, one technique for selecting different test cases is to be certain to test different permutations of premises of these implications. A postcondition such as

```
/** post: (premise1 implies conclusion1)
           and (premise2 implies conclusion2) */
```

can be tested once when both *premises* are `true`, once when both premises are `false`, once when just *premise1* is `true`, and once when just *premise2* is `true`. These four test cases represent four different functional situations.

Another type of functional testing examines the code for **robustness**. A robust program is one that continues to work reasonably even under unexpected conditions. Executing a method when the precondition is `false` is an extreme example of checking the robustness of code. A more useful form of robustness would be to consider unexpected sequences of user input events.

Unlike black box testing, **white box testing** is done with full knowledge of code details. White box testing is more likely to be performed by the programmer who wrote the code, because he/she is already familiar with it. Test cases for white box testing cannot be written until almost the end of the software implementation, because they depend upon the final implementation.

Another name for white box testing is **structural testing**. As the name implies, structural testing is focused on testing the code structure. This means that the tester seeks to exercise all the different parts of the code. Test cases are often chosen to be certain to exercise certain parts of the code. The term **statement coverage** is used to measure testing. When a tester has 100 percent statement coverage, this means that every statement in the program has been executed by at least one test case(s). (Note that just because every statement works once, does not mean the code is free of bugs. Untested permutations of statements may still produce faults.)

Another form of coverage, called **path coverage**, refers to a test suite that ensures that every possible control flow path through the program has been followed by at least one test case. Selection instructions lead to alternative control flow paths. Figure 7.30 shows a segment of code consisting of two consecutive *if* instructions with a second *if* nested. The flow diagram on the right of this figure pictures the associated control flow.

There are six alternative paths that can occur when this code executes:

1. When all three *Conds* are `true`, *then-clause1*; *then-clause2* executes.
2. When (*Cond1* & *Cond2* & NOT *Cond3*), *then-clause1*; *else-clause2* executes.
3. When (*Cond1* & NOT *Cond2* & *Cond3*), *else-clause1A*; *then-clause2* executes.
4. When (*Cond1* & NOT *Cond2* & NOT *Cond3*), *else-clause1A*; *else-clause2* executes.
5. When (*NOT Cond1* & *Cond3*), *else-clause1B*; *then-clause2* executes.
6. When (*NOT Cond1* & NOT *Cond3*), *else-clause1B*; *else-clause2* executes.

Figure 7.30   Multiple control flow paths from three *if* instructions

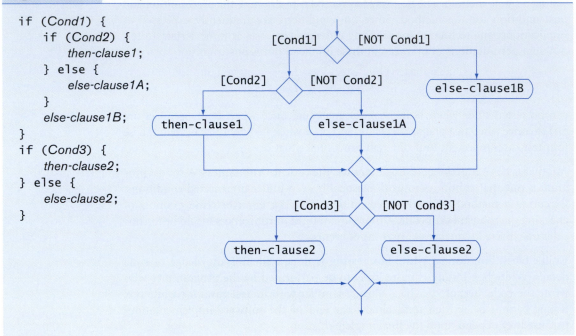

```
if (Cond1) {
    if (Cond2) {
        then-clause1;
    } else {
        else-clause1A;
    }
    else-clause1B;
}
if (Cond3) {
    then-clause2;
} else {
    else-clause2;
}
```

This example illustrates that path coverage can be complicated even for small segments of code. While path coverage may be practical for small segments of code, it is neither practical nor possible for many programs. However, path coverage is a useful concept because it serves as the ultimate goal for structure testing.

7.11 ■ Logic and Programming (Optional)

Programming is based upon the mathematical discipline of **logic**. However, logic did not begin with computers. The ancient Greek philosopher, **Aristotle**, is generally referred to as the "Father of Logic." Aristotle examined how to use logic to reason and as a form of expression. Programmers must also reason about the correctness of their code and use logical statements to express their code.

Two obvious applications of logic in Java programmers come in the form of

■ assertions

■ Boolean expressions

An understanding of the rules of logic is of great benefit to a programmer. These rules are typically expressed in the form of **logical axioms** and **logical theorems**. For example, the following theorem expresses the meaning of double negation.

> ### Double Negation Theorem
>
> $$! \; (!P) \equiv P$$

This theorem states a **logical equivalence.** Two logical expressions are logically equivalent (symbolized by $\equiv$) if they both mean exactly the same thing (i.e., they are both true under the same situations and both false under the same conditions). The Double Negation Theorem states that *NOT* (*NOT* P) is the same as P. The symbol P in this theorem represents an arbitrary logical expression, so this theorem really means that any instance of double negation can be removed without changing meaning.

The Double Negation Theorem can be used by a programmer to rewrite the following *if* instruction

```
if (!(myVar != 3)) { ...
```

with the following.

```
if (myVar == 3) { ...
```

While both of these two *if* instructions have identical behavior, the second is easier to read.

Two other sets of rules that are useful to a programmer are shown in Figure 7.31. In these rules P, Q, R, P1, P2, . . ., Pn all represent arbitrary logical expressions.

These axioms and theorems are useful for simplifying Boolean expressions within Java code. For example, the logical expression

```
(homeTeam==2 && visitor>3) || (homeTeam==2 && visitor==0)
```

can be simplified as follows by applying the second Distributive Axiom.

```
homeTeam==2 && (visitor>3 || visitor==0)
```

Logic axioms and theorems can also be useful in designing code. Consider the problem of overlapping `Containers` presented in the previous section. It may be simpler

software *Hint*
engineering

Using Logical axioms and theorems to simplify Boolean expressions is helpful for readability and debugging. One particularly useful simplification is to eliminate unnecessary *NOT* (!) operators.

Distributive Axioms (numbered 1 and 2)

1. $(P \;||\; Q) \;\&\&\; (P \;||\; R) \equiv \quad P \;||\; (Q \;\&\&\; R)$
2. $(P \;\&\&\; Q) \;||\; (P \;\&\&\; R) \equiv \quad P \;\&\&\; (Q \;||\; R)$

DeMorgan's Laws (numbered 1 and 2)

1. $!(P1 \;\&\&\; P2 \;\&\&\; \ldots \;\&\&\; Pn) \equiv \quad !P1 \;||\; !P2 \;||\; \ldots \;||\; !Pn$
2. $!(P1 \;||\; P2 \;||\; \ldots \;||\; Pn) \equiv \quad !P1 \;\&\&\; !P2 \;\&\&\; \ldots \;\&\&\; !Pn$

Figure 7.31

Distributive Axioms and DeMorgan's Laws

to identify the times that two `Container`s *do not* overlap than it is to identify when they *do* overlap. For example, `Container` c1 does not overlap `Container` c2 in the horizontal direction whenever c1 is completely to the right or completely to the left of c2.

- c1 is right of c2 when: `c1.getX() > c2.getX()+c2.getWidth()`
- c1 is left of c2 when: `c1.getX()+c1.getWidth() < c2.getX()`

Either of the above two conditions is sufficient to ensure that c1 and c2 *do not* overlap. Therefore, the following assignment expresses the condition for horizontal overlapping.

```
isHorizontalOverlapping == ∫
    !(c1.getX() > c2.getX()+c2.getWidth()
    || c1.getX()+c1.getWidth() < c2.getX());
```

The use of the second of DeMorgan's Laws allows this assignment instruction to be simplified as follows.

```
isHorizontalOverlapping ==∫
    c1.getX() <= c2.getX()+c2.getWidth()
    && c1.getX()+c1.getWidth() >= c2.getX();
```

7.12 ■ Assertions Revisited

Another obvious application of logic in programming is the use of program **assertions**. An assertion is a logical statement that defines the state of computation at some location within the code. Below is an assertion in the form of a Java comment.

```
makeTriangle();
/* assert:    side1 > 0 and side2 > 0 and side3 > 0
              and side1 + side2 > side3
              and side1 + side3 > side2
              and side2 + side3 > side1 */
```

The assertion above asserts a common property for triangles, namely that immediately after `makeTriangle` executes `side1`, `side2`, and `side3` all have a positive value and that the sum of any two triangle sides is greater than the third side.

Assertions are not intended to alter a program's execution. They merely document what the programmer believes (asserts) to be true regarding the state. Even though assertions perform no function at runtime, they are still important tools for a programmer. An assertion provides needed insight into the how the program is intended to behave.

Because assertions are logical statements, they define *what* is true about the state of computation and not *how* this state was accomplished. This is just the opposite of program code that instructs the computer *how* to execute, but is less helpful with explaining *what* has happened at any particular code location.

The preceding example assertion, like earlier assertions in this book, is written in the form of a comment. Comments are useful documentation for the programmer reading the program, but sometimes it might be useful to actually check the assertions at runtime. Fortunately, Java includes an `assert` statement for this purpose; Figure 7.32 describes its syntax and semantics.

The `assert` statement includes both a `boolean` expression and an associated message (a `String`). When the `assert` executes, the `boolean` expression is evaluated. If the expression is `false`, then the associated message (an error message) is displayed and execution halts; if the `boolean` expression is `true`, then execution proceeds as though the `assert` were not present. In other words, the `assert` statement turns a comment into a **testable assertion**. The earlier example assertion is properly translated into code including a testable assertion as shown below.

```
makeTriangle();
assert side1 > 0 && side2 > 0 && side3 > 0
    && side1 + side2 > side3
    && side1 + side3 > side2
    && side2 + side3 > side1
    :  "side1, side2 and side3 improper for triangle sides.";
```

Notice that an `assert` statement requires a syntactically correct `boolean` expression. As a result, many notations that are used within comment assertions, such as *and* and *implies*, are not permitted within an `assert`. The example above uses the Java `&&` operator in place of *and*.

When a program checks an `assert` statement and that is `true`-valued, then the `assert` instruction outputs nothing. However, when `assert` condition is found to be `false`, then program execution is terminated and the `assert`'s `String` is output. Below is a sample of the output that results from violating the above assertion.

```
Exception in thread "main" java.lang.AssertionError: side1,
side2 and side3 improper for triangle sides.
```

The `assert` statement is a useful debugging tool that provides runtime testing of conditions. However, executing `assert` statements slows program execution for the usually small amount of time required to test the `boolean` expressions. Due to the additional execution time, most Java implementations require that assertions be

> software
> **engineering** *Hint*
>
> Performing run-time checks of assertions, such as via the assert statement, is a helpful debugging technique. Such checks can uncover hidden bugs and are helpful in locating the source of known bugs.

Syntax

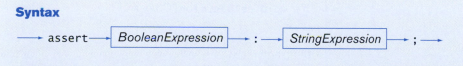

Semantics

When assertions are enabled, executing *assertStatement* causes *BooleanExpression* to be evaluated. If *BooleanExpression* is found to be `false`, then the program execution halts and *StringExpression* is output.

Figure 7.32

assertStatement Description

explicitly enabled in order to activate their testing. For example, from a command line interface runtime assertion checking is activated by including the "`-ea`" flag in the `java` command, as shown below:

```
java -ea run
```

It is also possible to enable assertions by individual classes. For example, the following command enables runtime assertions for all `assert` statements within the `Driver` and `Oval` classes but not other classes.

```
java -ea:Driver -ea:Oval run
```

Two of the most important assertions are preconditions and postconditions. Preconditions and postconditions are a pair of *before* and *after* snapshots that form a precise specification of a method's behavior.

The use of `assert` statement is further illustrated in a more complete example. Figure 7.33 contains a class diagram for a `Die` class that is designed to display one six-sided die.

Figure 7.33

`Die` class diagram

Die
- int **numberOfSpots**
- Rectangle **dieRect**
- Oval **topLeftSpot**
- Oval **midLeftSpot**
- Oval **botLeftSpot**
- Oval **middleSpot**
- Oval **topRightSpot**
- Oval **midRightSpot**
- Oval **botRightSpot**
...
«constructor»
+ **Die**()
«update»
+ void **setSpotCount**(*int*)
+ void **setDieColor**(*Color*)
...
«query»
+ int **spotCount**()
+ Rectangle **getDieRect**()
- boolean **implies**(*boolean, boolean*)
- Rectangle **spotCountSameAsDotsAdded**()

A `Die` object consists of a `Rectangle` (`dieRect`) with from one to six spots displayed. These spots can be in one of seven different locations which leads to seven different variables (`topLeftSpot`, `midLeftSpot`, ..., `botRightSpot`). The `Die` constructor creates an object that is drawn in black with one white spot displayed. A client can change the number of spots by calling `setSpotCount` and change the background (`dieRect`) color by calling `setDieColor`. To see that role that logic plays in the `Die` class, the class's code is shown in Figure 7.34.

Figure 7.34   `Die` class (*continues*)

```
/** class invariant:
 *      This class maintains a single die.
 *      and dieRect.getWidth() == dieRect.getHeight() == 70
 *      and 1 <= numberOfSpots <= 6
 *      and spotCountSameAsDotsAdded()
 */
import java.awt.Color;
public class Die {
    private int numberOfSpots;
    private Rectangle dieRect;
    private Oval topLeftSpot, midLeftSpot, botLeftSpot,
        middleSpot, topRightSpot, midRightSpot, botRightSpot;

    /** post:  spotCount() == 1
     *         and dieRect.getBackground() == Color.black
     */
    public Die() {
        dieRect = new Rectangle(0, 0, 70, 70);
        topLeftSpot = newSpot(10, 10);
        midLeftSpot = newSpot(10, 30);
        botLeftSpot = newSpot(10, 50);
        middleSpot = newSpot(30, 30);
        topRightSpot = newSpot(50, 10);
        midRightSpot = newSpot(50, 30);
        botRightSpot = newSpot(50, 50);
        setSpotCount(1);
        setDieColor(Color.black);
    }

    /** pre:   1 <= j <= 6
     * post:  dieRect has j spots added to it
     */
    public void setSpotCount(int j) {
        assert 1 <= j && j <= 6 : "Invalid number of die spots";
        numberOfSpots = j;
```

Figure 7.34   Die class (*continues*)

```
        dieRect.removeAll();
        if (numberOfSpots == 1) {
            dieRect.add(middleSpot, 0);
        } else if (numberOfSpots == 2) {
            dieRect.add(topLeftSpot, 0);
            dieRect.add(botRightSpot, 0);
        } else if (numberOfSpots == 3) {
            dieRect.add(topLeftSpot, 0);
            dieRect.add(middleSpot, 0);
            dieRect.add(botRightSpot, 0);
        } else if (numberOfSpots == 4) {
            dieRect.add(topLeftSpot, 0);
            dieRect.add(botLeftSpot, 0);
            dieRect.add(topRightSpot, 0);
            dieRect.add(botRightSpot, 0);
        } else if (numberOfSpots == 5) {
            dieRect.add(topLeftSpot, 0);
            dieRect.add(botLeftSpot, 0);
            dieRect.add(middleSpot, 0);
            dieRect.add(topRightSpot, 0);
            dieRect.add(botRightSpot, 0);
        } else {
            dieRect.add(topLeftSpot, 0);
            dieRect.add(midLeftSpot, 0);
            dieRect.add(botLeftSpot, 0);
            dieRect.add(topRightSpot, 0);
            dieRect.add(midRightSpot, 0);
            dieRect.add(botRightSpot, 0);
        }
        dieRect.repaint();
        assert spotCountSameAsDotsAdded()
            : "Number of spots does not match spotCount()";
    }

    /** post: result == numberOfSpots */
    public int spotCount() {
        return numberOfSpots;
    }

    /** post: dieRect.getBackground() == c
     *         and (dieRect.getBackground() == Color.white
     *             implies all spots are colored black)
     *         and (dieRect.getBackground() != Color.white
     *             implies all spots are colored white) */
```

```java
public void setDieColor(Color c) {
    dieRect.setBackground(c);
    if (c == Color.white) {
        setAllSpotColors(Color.black);
    } else {
        setAllSpotColors(Color.white);
    }
    dieRect.repaint();
    assert implies(c == Color.white,
            middleSpot.getBackground() == Color.black)
        && implies(c != Color.white,
            middleSpot.getBackground() == Color.white)
        : "Color of die background inconsistent with spot color";
}


/** post: result == dieRect */
public Rectangle getDieRect() {
    return dieRect;
}


/** post: result is a newly instantiated Oval
 *         and result.getX() == x and result.getY() == y
 *         and result.getWidth == result.getHeight == 10
 *         and result.getBackground() == Color.white
 */
private Oval newSpot(int x, int y) {
    Oval result;
    result = new Oval(x, y, 10, 10);
    result.setBackground(Color.white);
    return result;
}


/** post: result == p implies q */
private boolean implies(boolean p, boolean q) {
    return !p || q;
}


/** post:  topLeftSpot.getBackground() == c
 *         and midLeftSpot.getBackground() == c
 *         and botLeftSpot.getBackground() == c
 *         and middleSpot.getBackground() == c
 *         and topRightSpot.getBackground() == c
 *         and midRightSpot.getBackground() == c
 *         and botRightSpot.getBackground() == c */
```

Figure 7.34   Die class *(continued)*

```java
    private void setAllSpotColors(Color c) {
        topLeftSpot.setBackground(c);
        midLeftSpot.setBackground(c);
        botLeftSpot.setBackground(c);
        middleSpot.setBackground(c);
        topRightSpot.setBackground(c);
        midRightSpot.setBackground(c);
        botRightSpot.setBackground(c);
    }
    /** post: numberOfSpots == count of spots added to dieRect */
    private boolean spotCountSameAsDotsAdded() {
        int dotsAddedCount = 0;
        if (topLeftSpot.getParent() != null)
            dotsAddedCount++;
        if (midLeftSpot.getParent() != null)
            dotsAddedCount++;
        if (botLeftSpot.getParent() != null)
            dotsAddedCount++;
        if (middleSpot.getParent() != null)
            dotsAddedCount++;
        if (topRightSpot.getParent() != null)
            dotsAddedCount++;
        if (midRightSpot.getParent() != null)
            dotsAddedCount++;
        if (botRightSpot.getParent() != null)
            dotsAddedCount++;
        return (dotsAddedCount == numberOfSpots);
    }
}
```

Using the `assert` statement to test preconditions and postconditions is a useful form of defensive programming. The `Die` class demonstrates a limited form of post-condition checking. Consider the `setSpotCount` method. This method is designed to assign the number of `Die` spots from the method's parameter (`j`). The method's precondition is that `j` must be within the range from one through six. The following `assert` statement is included at the beginning of the method body in order to check this precondition:

```java
    assert 1 <= j && j <= 6 : "Invalid number of die spots";
```

It is interesting to notice that without assertion checking an attempt to assign a spot count outside the valid range is likely to go undetected. In such a situation, the `Die` class will cause the die to display six spots due to the final *else* clause and the value of `numberOfSpots` will be incorrect.

The postcondition of `setSpotCount` is also checked by an assertion. In this case, the programmer chose to approximate the postcondition. Instead of checking to see that all of the proper spots have been added to match the value of `j`, this assertion checks to see that the value of `spotCount` matches the total number of spots that have been added to `dieRect`. The postcondition `assert` is repeated below.

```
assert spotCountSameAsDotsAdded()
    : "Number of spots does not match spotCount()";
```

This statement relies upon a separate predicate called `spotCountSameAsDotsAdded` to count the number of spots that are added and compare this to the value of the `numberOfSpots` variable.

The `setDieColor` method also includes an `assert` for checking part of a postcondition. This method controls the color of both the `dieRect` and the spots that are added to it. The normal color for spots is white. However, if `dieRect` is to be colored white, then white spots would be invisible. Therefore, `setDieColor` is responsible for coloring spots black whenever the die is white. The following `assert` statement tests for this correspondence between the color of the die and the color of the spots.

```
assert implies(c == Color.white,
        middleSpot.getBackground() == Color.black)
    && implies(c != Color.white,
        middleSpot.getBackground() == Color.white)
    : "Color of die background inconsistent with spot color";
```

This `assert` statement checks color correspondence only for one spot (`middleSpot`). This code also demonstrates a use of the implies method for expressing `boolean` expressions.

software engineering *Hint*

If you can make only one kind of assertion testable, preconditions are probably the best choice, because this is one of the most frequent causes for run-time errors.

Inspector

Below is a collection of hints on what to check when examining code that involves the concepts of this chapter.

- Indentation patterns are crucial to the readability (and often the correctness) of control structures. If you only have time to check one thing, make it an examination that the indentation is consistent and correctly reflects the intended execution.

- Sometimes programs fail to handle all possible cases properly. One place to find such errors is missing *else* clauses and missing default clauses.

- Each assertion must be consistent with the code it describes. Sometimes as code is modified, the assertions are not properly updated. Do not overlook assertions in a desk check.

- Two-character operators (==, !=, <=, >=, &&, and ||) must be typed as two consecutive symbols with no intervening blanks.

- A common error is to use the assignment operator (=) when an equal operator (==) is needed. The compiler will detect errors unless both operands are `boolean`.

- Each equal and not equal for real numbers should be investigated. Real expressions store approximate values, and testing for equality of two approximations can produce subtle errors.

- Braces should be checked for proper pairing. (A good way to avoid brace pairing problems is to get in the habit of always typing a right brace immediately after its left partner, then back up and insert the code between.)

- Suspicion is indicated whenever an *if* instruction is written without braces. Situations, like the dangling else, should be investigated.

- Sometimes a collection of nested selection instructions is crafted in such a way that certain clauses are unreachable. The conditions inside nested instruction should be checked to make certain that they represent reasonable alternatives.

- Every clause of a `switch` instruction should end with a `break`. This is easily overlooked.

- Humans tend to have difficulty reading *NOT*s. It is wise to replace Boolean expressions that are stated in terms of *NOT* with equivalent expressions that are stated positively. (The rules of double negation and DeMorgan's Laws can help in removing *NOT*s.)

- Using the `assert` statement is an effective tool for debugging. Just turning preconditions into testable assertions can provide valuable information regarding the location and nature of runtime errors.

Terminology

activity diagram

AND operation (`&&`)

Aristotle

`assert` statement

assertion

black box testing

George Boole

Boolean expression

`boolean` type

cascading conditions

case clause

case constant

compound statement

condition

conditional evaluation

control structure

dangling else problem

default clause

DeMorgan's Laws

Distribute Axioms

Double Negation Theorem

else clause

equal operation (`==`)

`false`

functional testing

greater than (`>`)

greater than or equal (`>=`)

identity equality

if instruction

if-then instruction

if-then-else instruction

implication

implies

inclusive *OR*

less than (`<`)

less than or equal (`<=`)

logical axiom

logical equivalence (`≡`)

logical expression

logical negation (*NOT*)

logical theorem

multi-way selection

nesting (of control structures)

NOT operation (`!`)

not equal operation (`!=`)

OR operation (`||`)

path coverage

predicate

relational expression

robustness

`Scanner` (`java.util.Scanner`)

selection instruction

short-circuit evaluation

software testing

statement coverage

structure testing

switch instruction

switch expression

test case

test suite

then clause

`true`

truth table

value equality

white box testing

Exercises

1. What is the value of emuCounter following the execution of each of the following instructions, assuming it has a value of 3 just prior to this execution?

a.
```
if (emuCounter <= 3) {
    emuCounter = 5;
} else {
    emuCounter = 17;
}
```

b.
```
if (emuCounter > 3) {
    emuCounter = 83;
} else {
    emuCounter = 94;
}
```

c.
```
if (emuCounter != 3) {
    emuCounter++;
}
```

2. How do your answers to Exercise 1 change if emuCounter has a value of 4 just before the *if* executes?

3. Assume that each of the following is used as a boolean expression within a Java program. Which of these expressions will evaluate to true, which will evaluate to false, and which will result in syntax errors.

a. 7 == 7

b. 'b' >= 'A'

c. 6 < 8 && 'a' < 'b'

d. true != false || 7 > 7.5

e. Color.red < 3

f. 0 < 3 < 7

g. "CAT" != null

h. "Z" == 'Z'

i. "A" == ""+'A'

4. Complete the following truth tables

a.

P	*Q*	!(*P* || *Q*)
false	false	
false	true	
true	false	
true	true	

b.

P	Q	R	!(P || R) && !Q
false	false	false	
false	false	true	
false	true	false	
false	true	true	
true	false	false	
true	false	true	
true	true	false	
true	true	true	

c.

P	Q	R	!((Q && R) || (P && !R))
false	false	false	
false	false	true	
false	true	false	
false	true	true	
true	false	false	
true	false	true	
true	true	false	
true	true	true	

5. Which two of the following identifiers would make the best names for `boolean` variables or methods?

```
moveThatRascal
rascalHasBeenMoved
heightOfRascal
isARascal
```

6. a. Executing the following *if* instruction can result in a runtime error due to a null-valued variable. Rewrite the instruction guarding the *if* condition (via conditional evaluation) so when `myRect` is `null`, the instruction behaves as though the height of `myRect` were zero.

```
if (myRect.getHeight() >= 200) {
    System.out.println("Height of myRect is 200 or more");
} else {
    System.out.println("Height of myRect is less than 200");
}
```

   b. Executing the following *if* instruction can result in a runtime error due to division by zero. Rewrite the instruction guarding the *if* condition (via conditional evaluation) so that the behavior when `divisor==0` is treated the same as `numerator==0`.

```
if (numerator/divisor > 100) {
    System.out.println("Fraction greater than 100");
} else {
    System.out.println("Fraction less than or equal to 100");
}
```

7. Consider the following predicate.

```java
private boolean exclusiveOR(boolean p, boolean q) {
    return (p || q) && !(p && q);
}
```

What value is returned by each of the following calls to this method?

a. `exclusiveOR(false, false);`

b. `exclusiveOR(false, true);`

c. `exclusiveOR(true, false);`

d. `exclusiveOR(true, true);`

8. Write a Java predicate (`boolean` method) for each of the following.

a. This predicate is called `xor` and has two `boolean` parameters, call them p and q. The `xor` predicate returns `true` exactly when its two `boolean` parameters have different values.

b. This predicate is called `inOrder` and has three `int` parameters, call them a, b, and c. The `inOrder` predicate returns `true` exactly when $a < b < c$.

c. This predicate is called `isWider` and has two `Container` parameters. The `isWider` predicate returns `true` exactly when its first parameter has a *width* attribute greater than its second parameter.

d. This predicate is called `fartherFromOrigin` and has four `int` parameters, called $x1$, $y1$, $x2$, and $y2$. These four parameters must be thought of as the coordinates for two points: the point $(x1, y1)$ and the point $(x2, y2)$. The `fartherFromOrigin` predicate returns `true` exactly when point $(x1, y1)$ is a greater distance from point $(0,0)$ than is $(x2, y2)$.

e. This predicate is called `isUponAndWithin` and has two `Rectangle` parameters, called $r1$ and $r2$. The `isUponAndWithin` predicate returns `true` exactly when $r1$ is added to $r2$ and the boundaries of $r1$ lie completely within the boundaries of $r2$.

f. This predicate is called `isWithin` and has two `Rectangle` parameters, called $r1$ and $r2$. The `isWithin` predicate returns `true` exactly when $r1$ and $r2$ are both added to the same `Container` and the boundaries of $r1$ lie completely within the boundaries of $r2$.

g. This predicate is called `areSidesOfRightTriangle` and has three `int` parameters, called $s1$, $s2$, and $s3$. These three parameters must be thought of as lengths of three sides of a triangle. The `areSidesOfRightTriangle` predicate returns `true` exactly when these three sides represent lengths for a right triangle. (*Hint:* Remember that triangles must have side lengths that are positive and that any of these sides could be the hypotenuse. The Pythagorean theorem can be used to check for proper lengths.)

9. Use the Double Negation Theorem, the Distributive Axioms and DeMorgan's laws, together with your knowledge of opposite relational operators, to simplify each of the following `boolean` expressions. (Assume that all identifiers are `int` variables.)

a. `!(myInt != yourInt)`

b. `!(someBool) && !(anotherBool)`

c. `(distance > 0 || time > 0) && (distance > 0 || time < 100)`

d. `(distance > 0 && time > 0) || (distance > 0 && time < 100)`

10. Write a Java method for each of the following.

a. A method with two `Rectangle` parameters that returns the parameter with the larger area. (If one of the arguments is `null`, then the other is returned; and if both arguments are `null`, then null is returned.)

b. A method with three `double` parameters that returns the value of the largest of its parameters.

c. A method to return the int value of a char parameter, if the char argument is a hexadecimal digit. Below is a table of all hexadecimal digits and their corresponding integer values. Your method should return −1 when its argument is not a valid hexadecimal digit character. (The valid hexadecimals are from '0' through '9' and from 'A' through 'F'.)

Hex	Value
'0'	0
'1'	1
'2'	2
'3'	3
'4'	4
'5'	5
'6'	6
'7'	7
'8'	8
'9'	9
'A'	10
'B'	11
'C'	12
'D'	13
'E'	14
'F'	15

11. Write preconditions and postconditions for each part of Exercise 10.

12. Write a segment of Java code that takes the value from three double variables, d1, d2, and d3 and assigns them to the variables `min`, `mid`, and `max` so that `min <= mid <= max`.

13. Rewrite the `teleDigit` method from Figure 7.26 using a *switch* instruction instead of *if* instructions.

14. Rewrite the two *switch* instruction examples from Section 7.9 to use *if* instructions instead of a *switch*.

15. Write an `assert` statement that could be used to test the entire postcondition of the `setSpotCount` method shown in Figure 7.33.

Programming Exercises

1. Write to cause the LEFT button click to move a `Rectangle` object around a window, "bouncing" off the edges. Your program must begin with single green 300 by 300 `Rectangle`, positioned at location (100, 100) within the window. Initially, the rectangle has a vertical velocity of 25 and a horizontal velocity of 25. The button clicks behave as follows.

    LEFT   Assuming that the rectangle can do so without passing a window boundary, it moves according to its vertical and horizontal velocity. If the horizontal and vertical velocities are both 25, then the rectangle moves right 25 pixels and down 25 pixels. Positive horizontal velocities cause right movement, and negative velocities cause left movement. Similarly, a positive vertical velocity causes movement down, and a negative causes movement up.

                  If the horizontal movement would cause the rectangle to move past the left or right edge of its window, then its horizontal velocity reverses and it moves in this new direction. The vertical movement behaves likewise with respect to the top and bottom of the window. (Note that every LEFT click causes the rectangle to move 25 pixels left or right and 25 pixels up or down.)

    MID   If the rectangle has a vertical velocity moving it up, then its vertical velocity reverses to the downward value. (Note that no movement takes place and nothing happens if the rectangle already has a positive velocity.)

    RIGHT   This button causes the rectangle to change color in the following manner. A color of green becomes cyan. A color of cyan becomes yellow. A color of yellow becomes green.

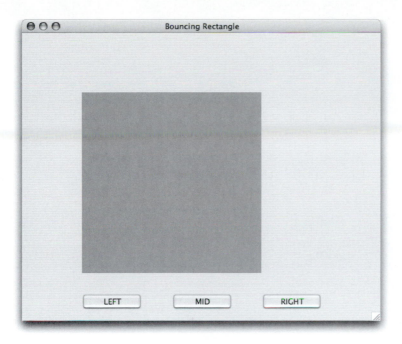

2. Wristwatch manufacturers have devised several clever techniques for setting the clock time using only two buttons on the edge of the clock. For this assignment, you will use a simple one of these techniques to set the value of three-digit number. When the program begins, it displays three large 0 digits in black. The placement and size of these digits is pictured below.

LEFT   This button is used to highlight the particular digit being incremented. A highlighted digit is signified by the color red. At most, one digit at a time is highlighted (colored red). Each time this button is clicked the highlighting moves to the next digit to the left. When the leftmost digit is highlighted, clicking this button turns off all highlighting. When highlighting is turned off, clicking this button highlights the rightmost digit.

MID   The highlighted digit is advanced to the next higher digit. The digit "9" advances to "0". If no digit is highlighted, then clicking this button has no effect.

RIGHT   This button changes the highlighting in the reverse order (i.e., left to right) of the LEFT button.

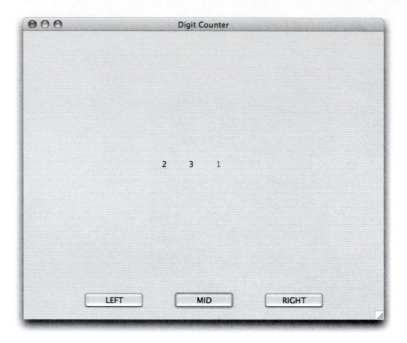

3. For this program it is best to construct a separate class to store/display a single decimal digit in the form of a 7-segment display. (A 7-segment display draws a single digit by lighting some combination of seven filled rectangles positioned as shown in the digit "8" below.) Your program should begin by displaying the digit "0" on your 7-segment display roughly centered in a `ThreeButtonFrame`. The required button click behavior is explained below.

LEFT   Clicking this button causes the digit on the 7-segment display to advance by one. (If nine is displayed, then the digit "advances" to 0.)

MID   Clicking this button causes the digit on the 7-segment display to reduce by one. (If zero is displayed, then the digit "reduces" to 9.)

RIGHT Clicking this button causes the digit to be recolored with the following probabilities: 25 percent of the time this click causes the new color to be orange; 25 percent of the time this click causes the new color to be gray; 50 percent of the time this click causes the new color to be magenta.

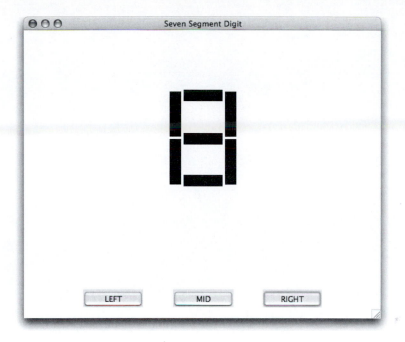

Inheritance

*The meek shall inherit
the earth, but not the
mineral rights.*

—J. Paul Getty

Objectives

- To examine inheritance in Java
- To explore the *is_a* relation as opposed to the *contains_a* relation, and to recognize that *is_a* relations lead naturally to inheritance
- To examine the semantics and limitations of overriding methods in subclasses
- To consider the concept of specialization and the particular version of specialization, known as extension
- To introduce the protected declaration and its role in information hiding
- To demonstrate the utility of the shared variable and callback patterns for event handling
- To examine the way that inheritance is used in event handling via the EventButton, EventTimer, EventSlider, and EventTextField classes

Animals inherit characteristics from their parents. The number of legs on an insect, the shape of a bird's wings, the pattern on a snake's skin—all these exhibit inherited attributes. Similarly, human children have height and hair color determined by genes inherited from their parents.

8.1 ■ Extends

Inheritance plays an important role in object-oriented software development, just as it plays an important role in biological traits. In fact, inheritance is so important that it is often identified as the primary concept separating object-oriented programming from other programming techniques.

There are two things that distinguish software inheritance from biological inheritance.

1. In software, one *class* inherits from another class.

2. In software, inheritance is an "ideal" relationship.

Class inheritance is "ideal" in the sense that it is totally predictable, unlike biological inheritance in which inheritance is typically probabilistic. Software inheritance is also more complete than biological because all traits (i.e., class members) are inherited, not just a subset of traits as is typical in genetic inheritance.

As an initial example of inheritance, consider a software development project for a paper manufacturing company. The program uses a `Parcel` to keep track of the shipping information related to each outgoing paper product. Figure 8.1 is a class diagram for `Parcel`.

`Parcel` objects store the weight and volume of packages, and their class includes a method to calculate shipping cost. The company can ship goods either by airmail or ground. The cost to ship is given below.

Air Freight: \$15 + \$2.75 per kilogram + \$6 per cubic meter (m^3) for a parcel over 1.0 m^3

Ground Freight: \$5 + \$0.04 per kilogram

Figure 8.2 contains the code for `Parcel`.

The two instructions below illustrate how client code might use the `Parcel` class.

```
someParcel = new Parcel(0.56, 0.3, true);
System.out.println("Cost to ship:" +
someParcel.shippingCost());
```

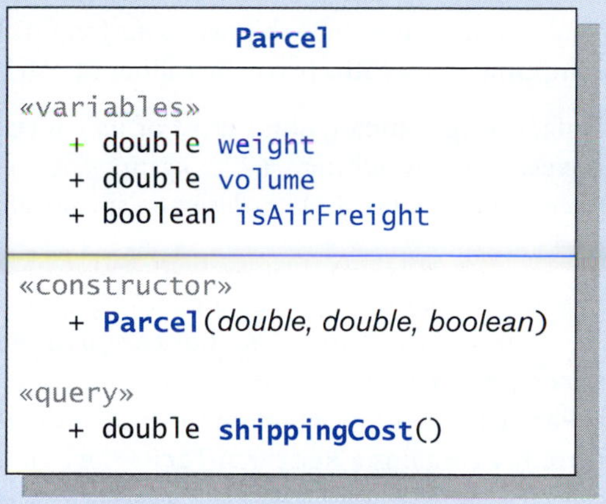

Figure 8.1

Parcel class diagram

```
                    Parcel

«variables»
    + double weight
    + double volume
    + boolean isAirFreight

«constructor»
    + Parcel(double, double, boolean)

«query»
    + double shippingCost()
```

Figure 8.2   Parcel class

```java
public class Parcel {
    public double weight;
    public double volume;
    public boolean isAirFreight;
```

> **Warning:** Declaring instance variables of a superclass as **public** is generally considered to be inferior design. In Section 8.4 a better alternative to these public declarations (the **protected** modifier) is introduced.

```java
    /** post:  weight==w and volume==v and isAirFreight==b */
    public Parcel( double w, double v, boolean b) {
        weight = w;
        volume = v;
        isAirFreight = b;
    }

    /** post:  isAirFreight implies
     *             result == cost to ship as air freight.
     *         and !isAirFreight implies
     *             result == cost to ship by truck. */
    public double shippingCost() {
        double cost;
        if (isAirFreight)
            if (weight > 1.0)
                cost = 15 + 2.75 * weight + 6 * (volume-1);
            else
                cost = 15 + weight * 2.75;
        else // !isAirFreight
            cost = 5 + 0.04 * weight;
        return cost;
    }
}
```

The execution of the first instruction constructs a parcel with a weight of 0.56 kilograms, a volume of 0.3 m³ that is to be shipped as air freight. The second instruction will output the shipping cost of this parcel by calling the shippingCost method.

This paper manufacturing company ships most of its paper goods in various-sized rectangular boxes, all weighing 677 kg/m³. A second class, called RectangularParcel (see Figure 8.3), is designed specifically for these rectangular boxes.

The commonality in the features of RectangularParcel and Parcel are a clue that inheritance can be used to write RectangularParcel. In particular, RectangularParcel uses weight, volume, isAirFreight, and shippingCost in the same way as Parcel. Inheritance is often the proper design for eliminating such duplication. Figure 8.4 contains a RectangularParcel class that uses inheritance in this manner.

The first thing to notice about the RectangularParcel class is the use of the reserved word extends on the class line. The word "extends" is Java notation for "inherits." RectangularParcel inherits the Parcel class. A class that inherits is called a **subclass** (or **child class**), and the class that is being inherited is known as a **superclass** (or **parent class**). In this example, RectangularParcel is a child of the parent class known as Parcel.

Figure 8.3   RectangularParcel class diagram

RectangularParcel
+ double weight
+ double volume
+ double isAirFreight
− int parcelLength
− int parcelWidth
− int parcelHeight
− int weightPerCubicMeter

«constructor»
    + **RectangularParcel** (*double, double, double, boolean*)

«query»
    + double **shippingCost** ()
    + double **length** ()
    + double **width** ()
    + double **height** ()

Figure 8.4   RectangularParcel class

```java
public class RectangularParcel extends Parcel {
    private double parcelLength, parcelWidth, parcelHeight;
    private final int weightPerCubicMeter = 677;


    /** post: parcelLength == len and parcelWidth == w
     *         and parcelHeight == h and volume==len*w*h
     *         and weight == volume * weightPerCubicMeter
     *         and isAirFreight == b */
    public RectangularParcel(double len, double w, double h, boolean b) {
        super(0, 0, b);
        parcelLength = len;
        parcelWidth = w;
        parcelHeight = h;
        volume = parcelLength * parcelWidth * parcelHeight;
        weight = volume * weightPerCubicMeter;
    }
    public double length() {
        return parcelLength;
    }
    public double width() {
        return parcelWidth;
    }
    public double height() {
        return parcelHeight;
    }
}
```

A child class, such as RectangularParcel, automatically inherits *all* of the instance variables and *all* of the methods of its parent class.[1] By inheriting Parcel, RectangularParcel includes all of the following class members.

```
weight
volume
isAirFreight
shippingCost
```

The notation for referencing such inherited features is (with a few exceptions discussed later) the same as the notation used within the parent class. For example, the RectangularParcel constructor refers directly to volume and weight, using the same notation that is permitted inside the Parcel class.

---

1. Technically, all members, not just those that are nonprivate, are inherited. However, any inherited private members are inaccessible in a child class, so effectively, they are not inherited.

Child classes are not restricted solely to those features that they inherit. Just like children often develop characteristics that are not inherited, so too a child class often includes new members. Each child class can declare instance variables and methods, like any other class. These new instance variables and methods are combined with the inherited members to define the subclass. RectangularParcel declares three new private instance variables to store the length, width, and height of a parcel, and corresponding methods to allow client code to inspect, but not alter, these values.

Constructors are handled a bit differently from other methods in Java. Since each class must have a unique name, it must also have its own constructor method(s). The RectangularParcel constructor has a different parameter list from the superclass constructor, reflecting that rectangular parcels have length, width, and height. The RectangularParcel constructor also omits parameters for volume or weight since these can be calculated from its other parameters.

Java prohibits a child class from accessing its superclass constructors by their original names. Fortunately, the language supports a notation to permit the child class to call any constructor from its superclass. However, there are two restrictions: (1) The superclass constructor call uses the reserved word **super**, and (2) such a call to a superclass constructor can only be made within constructor methods and only as their first statement. Subclass constructors should always include such calls to a superclass constructor (Failure to include an explicit call to a superclass constructor causes the compiler to insert an automatic call to super().) RectangularParcel includes the following explicit call to a superclass constructor.

```
super(0, 0, b);
```

When executed, this instruction causes isAirFreight to be initialized to the value of parameter b. The assignment of 0 to instance variables, weight, and volume is unimportant, since these variables are updated to the correct values by other assignments in the constructor.

To continue this example suppose the paper company also ships large rolls of paper in varying sizes. Because of their shape, paper rolls cannot be transported as air freight. The weight of roll paper is slightly less than rectangular boxes at 600 kg/m^3. Figure 8.5 contains a CylindricalParcel class that is appropriate for such a paper roll.

CylindricalParcel is a different subclass of Parcel, so it has different methods and instance variables. It also calls the constructor in a slightly different way, namely super(0, 0, false); because cylindrical parcels never use air freight.

Both RectangularParcel and CylindricalParcel inherit Parcel. This relationship is diagrammed in the class diagram of Figure 8.6. The proper UML class diagram notation for inheritance is a closed-ended arrow drawn from the subclass to its superclass.

Parcel contains four members in addition to its constructor; these members are the weight, volume, and isAirFreight instance variables, as well as the

Figure 8.5   CylindricalParcel class

```java
public class CylindricalParcel extends Parcel {
    private double parcelRadius, parcelLength;

    /** post: parcelLength == len and parcelRadius == r
      *        and volume == len*r*r*PI
      *        and weight == volume*600
      *        and isAirFreight==false */
    public CylindricalParcel(double len, double r) {
        super(0, 0, false);
        parcelLength = len;
        parcelRadius = r;
        volume = parcelLength * Math.PI * Math.pow(parcelRadius,2);
        weight = volume * 600;
    }

    public double length() {
        return parcelLength;
    }

    public double radius() {
        return parcelRadius;
    }
}
```

Figure 8.6   Class diagram showing inheritance relationships

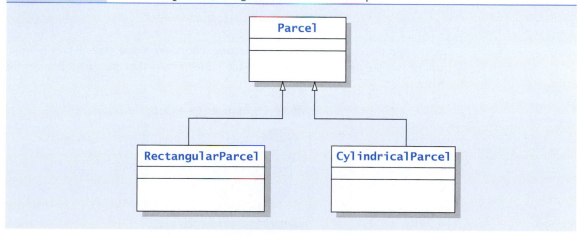

shippingCost method. RectangularParcel and CylindricalParcel both inherit all four of these members. RectangularParcel also includes three of its own methods, namely length, width, and height. CylindricalParcel includes just two more methods than its parent class; these methods are length and radius.

As demonstrated by the Parcel example, it is possible for one class (the parent class) to have more than one child class. On the other hand, Java does not permit any child class to have multiple parents. This restriction is known as **single inheritance**.

8.2 ■ Class Relations: *contains_a* and *is_a*

At first glance, inheritance appears to be a convenient technique for borrowing instance variables and methods from another class (the superclass). However, proper use of inheritance deserves more consideration.

A good place to begin investigating inheritance is with the real-world concept of a *specialization*.

- *Automobile* is a special case of *transportation vehicle*.
- *Shirt* is a particular kind of *clothing*.
- *Bald eagle* is a species of *bird*.
- *Triangle* is a type of *polygon*.

This sort of relation between classes is known as an *is_a* **relation**, because one class *is a* specialized version of the other. An *is_a* relation is an obvious situation for the use of inheritance.

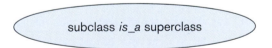

subclass *is_a* superclass

As an example, consider the task of creating a BorderedOval class. Below is a picture of two BorderedOval objects in the same JFrame—one partially obscures the other.

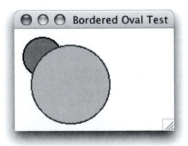

A `BorderedOval` is a solid circular region with a border two pixels wide around its perimeter. `BorderOval` objects differ from `Oval` objects in two ways:

1. `BorderOval` objects are circular (`getwidth() == getHeight()`).

2. `BorderOval` objects have an inner `Oval` object.

Since `BorderedOval` exhibits an *is_a* relationship with `Oval`, inheritance seems like the obvious choice for creating a `BorderedOval` class. Figure 8.7 shows such a class.

The `BorderedOval` constructor method has only three parameters (for *x*, *y*, and diameter) because a `BorderedOval` must be circular. This constructor method begins by calling the inherited `Oval` object constructor; this will be the border of the final image. On top of this inherited object a second `Oval`, called `innerOval` is added.

The `BorderedOval` class also includes methods to permit clients to modify and inspect the color of the border, as well as the oval's center. Calling `setBorderColor` assigns a new color to the border. The `getBorderColor` method returns the border color, while the methods for assigning and retrieving the color of the inner `Oval` are `getInnerColor` and `setInnerColor`, respectively. The following code demonstrates how to create a green `BorderedOval` with a yellow border.

```
someDot = new BorderedOval(10, 10, 100);
someDot.setInnerColor(Color.green);
someDot.setBorderColor(Color.yellow);
```

The fact that a `BorderedOval` is circular suggests a `setSize` method with a single parameter for diameter. Figure 8.7 includes such a `setSize` method, thereby overloading the method because the inherited version of `setSize` has two parameters.

In addition to overloading methods, a subclass is permitted to **override** one or more superclass methods. Overriding occurs whenever a child class includes a definition for a method that has the same name and parameter list as a method inherited from the parent. (The overriding method is required to have the same scope—`public` or `private`, as the inherited method.) The last method of the `BorderedOval`, namely the 2-parameter version of `setSize`, overrides an inherited method. Overriding causes the parent's method to be replaced by a new version for the child class. A call to `setSize` upon a `BorderedOval` object will execute the subclass version of `setSize`, while applying `setSize` upon an `Oval` uses the `Oval` version of the method. The `setSize` method of `BorderedOval` alters the dimensions of *both* this `Oval` and `innerOval`.

Within a child class, it is often necessary to call the parent class's version of a method. Overriding methods can complicate this situation. For example, the code of the `setSize` method must resize both the object and its inner oval. It is not possible to call `setSize` in the usual way to resize the `this` oval because a call to `setSize` would call the method's new (overriding) version, which calls the subclass version of `setSize`, which calls the subclass version of `setSize`, and so forth until the Java VM crashes on a runtime error regarding stack overflow.

Figure 8.7   BorderedOval class (*continues*)

```java
import java.awt.*;
/** Class Invariant
 *      getwidth() == getHeight()
 *      and innerOval.getWidth() == getWidth() - 4
 *      and innerOval.getHeight() == getHeight() - 4
 *      and innerOval.getX() == innerOval.getY() == 2
 *      and innerOval is added to this
 */
public class BorderedOval extends Oval {
    private Oval innerOval;

    /** pre:   d > 4
     * post:   getX() == x and getY() == y
     *         and getWidth() == d and getHeight() == d
     *         and getBackground() == borderColor() == Color.black
     */
    public BorderedOval(int x, int y, int d) {
        super(x, y, d, d);
        innerOval = new Oval(2, 2, d-4, d-4);
        add(innerOval);
    }

    /** post:  getBackground() == c */
    public void setBorderColor(Color c) {
        setBackground(c);
    }

    /** post:  innerOval.getBackground() == c */
    public void setInnerColor(Color c) {
        innerOval.setBackground(c);
    }

    /** post:  result == innerOval.getBackground() */
    public Color getInnerColor() {
        return innerOval.getBackground();
    }

    /** post:  result == getBackground() */
    public Color getBorderColor() {
        return getBackground();
    }

    /** post:  getWidth() == d and getHeight() == d */
    public void setSize(int d) {
        setSize(d, d);
    }
```

Figure 8.7   BorderedOval class (*continued*)

```
    /** pre:   w > 4 and h > 4
     * post:  getWidth() == w and getHeight() == h
     */
    public void setSize(int w, int h) {
        super.setSize(w, h);
        innerOval.setSize(w-4, h-4);
    }
}
```

Java includes a notation that can be used within the child class to refer to the parent class version of any method. Figure 8.8 shows the syntax for this second use for the reserved word **super**. For example, the code within BorderedOval calls the superclass (Oval) version of setSize with the following instruction.

```
    super.setSize(w, h);
```

Not all relationships between two classes are *is_a* relations. Another common relationship is called a ***contains_a* relation**. (This is alternatively known as a ***has_a* relation**.) As the name implies, a *contains_a* relation occurs when an instance of one class is contained within another class.

- An *automobile* contains a *steering wheel*.
- A *shirt* contains a *pocket*.
- A *bald eagle* has a *wing*.
- A *triangle* contains a *vertex*.

Figure 8.8   ***SuperMethodCall*** description (abridged version of *MethodCall*)

Syntax

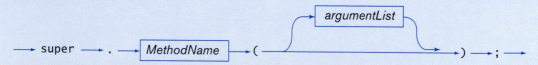

Notes

- *MethodName* is the name of a nonconstructor method from the superclass.
- *argumentList* is a list of argument expressions (separated by commas) that matches in type to the corresponding parameters.
- This super notation is only permitted within a subclass.

Semantics

Executing *SuperMethodCall* causes the superclass version of the method to be executed.

A *contains_a* relation leads to composition—also called aggregation (see Chapter 6). Figure 8.9 demonstrates the class diagram notation for each of these two relations.

The arrow in Figure 8.9 signifies that the class called `subclass` inherits `superclass`. Such a situation is the result of an *is_a* relation (`subclass` *is_a* `superclass`). The diamond-ended line in Figure 8.9 diagrams aggregation (`aggregate` *contains_a* `someclass` object). Such arrows and diamond-ended lines can also be used to illustrate these relations in object diagrams.

The `BorderedOval` class makes use of *both* inheritance and aggregation. `BorderedOval` inherits `Oval`, and it also is a client of `Oval` by way of the `innerOval` instance variable. It is proper to diagram these relations as shown in Figure 8.10. This diagram ornaments the aggregate relation with the name of the associated instance variable.

Figure 8.9

Inheritance and aggregation in class diagrams

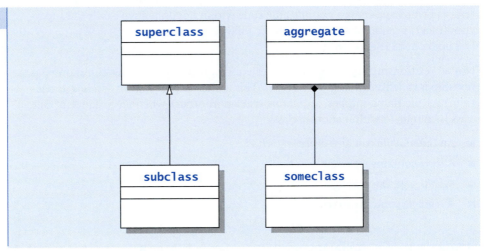

Figure 8.10

Relationship between `Oval` and `BorderedOval`

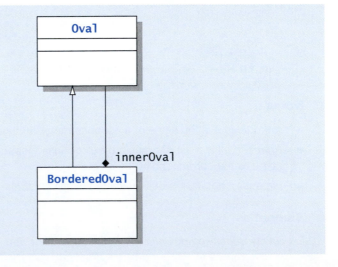

The choice between inheritance and aggregation is not always easy. For example, consider the task of implementing a class to keep track of time in military form. Military time maintains hours in the range 0 through 23 without distinction for A.M. and P.M. Figure 8.11 contains such a `MilitaryTime` class. (The `protected` qualifier in line six is explained in Section 8.4. For now, it is sufficient to know that protected variables are accessible to subclasses.)

Figure 8.11   `MilitaryTime` class (*continues*)

```
/** Class Invariant:
 *      0 <= hour <= 23
 *      and 0 <= minute <= 59
 *      and 0 <= second <= 59 */
public class MilitaryTime {
    protected int hour, minute, second;

    /** post: hour == 1 and minute == 0 and second == 0 */
    public MilitaryTime() {
        hour = 1;
        minute = 0;
        second = 0;
    }

    /** post: hour == 12 and minute == 0 and second == 0 */
    public void setToNoon() {
        hour = 12;
        minute = 0;
        second = 0;
    }

    /** post: (hour@pre < 23 implies hour == hour@pre + 1)
     *        and (hour@pre == 23 implies hour == 0)
     */
    public void advance1Hour() {
        if (hour < 23)
            hour++;
        else
            hour = 0;
    }

    /** post: (minute@pre < 59 implies minute == minute@pre + 1)
     *        and (minute@pre == 59 implies
     *            (minute == 0 and hour advanced by 1))
     */
```

Figure 8.11   MilitaryTime class (*continued*)

```
public void advance1Minute() {
    if (minute < 59)
        minute++;
    else {
        minute = 0;
        advance1Hour();
    }
}


/** post: (second@pre < 59 implies second == second@pre + 1)
 *        and (second@pre == 59 implies
 *            (second == 0 and minute advanced by 1))
 */
public void advance1Second() {
        if (second < 59)
        second++;
    else {
        second = 0;
        advance1Minute();
    }
}


/** post: result == hour */
public int hours() {
    return hour;
}

/** post: result == minute */
public int minutes() {
    return minute;
}

/** post: result == second */
public int seconds() {
    return second;
}
}
```

A MilitaryTime object maintains time in the form of three variables: hour, minute, and second. Consider a second class; call it TimeWithMillisec, which is just like MilitaryTime with the addition of a millisec attribute and an advance1Millisec method for additional precision in the timekeeping. A convincing argument can be made that a TimeWithMillisec timer is really a special case of `MilitaryTime`. Such an *is_a* relation suggests that `TimeWithMillisec` should inherit `MilitaryTime`. The resulting `TimeWithMillisec` class is shown in Figure 8.12.

These implementations of `MilitaryTime` and `TimeWithMillisec` are a good choice, but they are not the only choice. Notice that every `TimeWithMillisec` *contains_a* `MilitaryTime` in the sense that it must include hours, minutes, and seconds. This observation suggests writing a class; call it `TimeWithMillisec2`, which does not inherit, but rather uses aggregation, as sketched in Figure 8.13

Figure 8.12   `TimeWithMillisec` class

```java
public class TimeWithMillisec extends MilitaryTime {
    protected int millisec;
    /** post: hour == 1 and minute == 0
     *         and second == 0 and millisec == 0
     */
    public TimeWithMillisec() {
        super();
        millisec = 0;
    }
    /** post: (millisec@pre < 999 implies millisec == millisec@pre + 1)
     *      and (millisec@pre == 59 implies
     *           (millisec == 0 and second advanced by 1))
     */
    public void advance1Millisec() {
        if (millisec < 59)
            millisec ++;
        else {
            millisec = 0;
            advance1Second();
        }
    }
}
```

Figure 8.13   Partial class to build `TimeWithMillisec2` by aggregation

```java
public class TimeWithMillisec2 {
    private MilitaryTime hourMinuteSecond;
    private int millisec;

    . . .
}
```

software
engineering *Hint*

The decision of
whether to use
aggregation or
inheritance
should generally
be based upon
whether the rela-
tionship between
two classes is
more of an *is_a*
(inheritance) or a
contains_a
(aggregation).

In this case, the better choice seems to be inheritance because `TimeWithMillisec2` will need to repeat all of the query and update methods from `MilitaryTime`, while `TimeWithMillisec` is able to reuse these superclass methods without change. When the choice between *is_a* and *contains_a* is not clear, software developers learn to sketch out partial solutions and draw on past experiences.

8.3 ■ Specialization and Extension— javax.swing.JComponent

The *is_a* relationship that generally links a child class to its parent means that the child is a kind of special case (**specialization**) of the parent. For example, a `RectangularParcel` is a specialization of `Parcel` and `BorderedOval` is a special case of `Oval`. Inheritance is the preferred mechanism for implementing such specialization relationships.

One particular kind of specialization is known as **extension**. Extension occurs whenever a child class adds some functionality that was not present in its parent. The `RectangularParcel` class extends `Parcel` by including new instance variables to store the container's length, width, and height. The `BorderedOval` class exhibits extension by including a border and a method, such as `setBorderColor`, that were not present in its `Oval` superclass. Similarly, the `TimeWithMillisec` class extends `MilitaryTime` to include greater time accuracy through an additional instance variable and method to increment its value.

Inheritance often involves specialization in the form of redefining some methods and extension in the form of the addition of new instance variables and the addition of new methods.

One *javax.swing* class that is designed to be extended is the `JComponent` class. When you wish to create a new graphical image, the best place to begin is the `javax.swing.JComponent` class;[2] `JComponent` is the base class for *Swing* objects that can be added to a `Container`. Figure 8.14 contains a class diagram for key `JComponent` members.

Most `JComponent` methods have been presented and used several times previously. This includes `setBackground`, `setForeground`, `setBounds`, `setLocation`, `setSize`, `repaint`, `getX`, `getY`, `getBackground`, `getForeground`, `getHeight`, and `getWidth`, An additional method, included in Figure 8.14 that plays the central role for graphical display is called `paint`.

In order to understand the role of the `paint` method in creating images, it is important to understand how the Java Virtual Machine (JVM) updates the computer screen (see Figure 8.15). As your program executes, the JVM periodically updates portions of the screen. The executing code can assist by calling `repaint` upon

---

2. `JComponent` is an abstract class with no abstract methods. Abstract classes are explained in Section 9.4.

Figure 8.14   Class diagram for `javax.swing.JComponent`

Figure 8.15

Method interaction between `JComponent` and the JVM

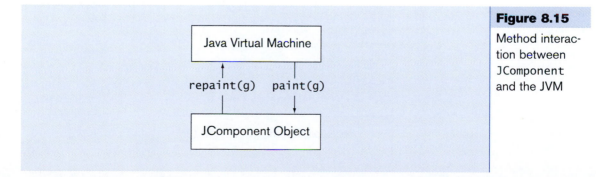

objects that require update, but a call to `repaint` does not ensure immediate change. This is because the JVM has many tasks to perform, not the least of which is executing the statements of the program.

When the JVM is able to update a `JComponent` portion of the display, it does so by calling the `paint` method upon that `JComponent`. As a part of this call to `paint`, an argument of type `java.awt.Graphics` is passed. This parameter provides `paint` with two key resources:

1. The `Graphics` parameter passes the correct drawing context for this particular `JComponent`.

2. The `Graphics` class includes several useful methods for drawing.

The version of `paint` that is inherited from `javax.swing.JComponent` is empty. It is up to the programmer to inherit `JComponent` class and override `paint`, using its `Graphics` parameter to produce an image.

Consider creating a new class for drawing triangle objects. For this class, the images are to be drawn with the triangle's base extending across the bottom of the object's bounding rectangle and the third vertex at the top center of the bounding rectangle. Figure 8.16 diagrams the triangle, enclosed by a dashed bounding rectangle. (Recall that the bounding rectangle is established by calling the `setBounds` method upon the `Container` or `JComponent`.) Figure 8.17 contains the code for a `Triangle` class that draws such a triangle.

The `paint` method of the `Triangle` class consists of four statements; each calls a method upon the `Graphics` parameter g. The first statement, repeated below, establishes the color for subsequent drawing:

```
g.setColor(getBackground());
```

A call to `getBackground()` retrieves the color assigned as the `JComponent`'s background color, and the `setColor` method is the `Graphics` method for establishing a drawing color for the `Graphics` methods that follow.

Figure 8.16

Triangle drawn within its bounding rectangle

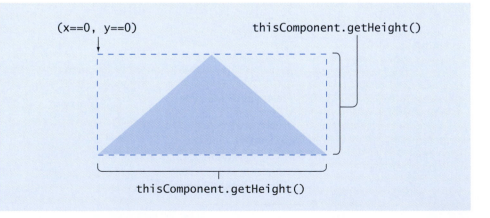

Figure 8.17 Triangle class

```java
import java.awt.Graphics;
import javax.swing.JComponent;
public class Triangle extends JComponent {

    /** post:   getbackGround() is an invisible color
     *          and getWidth() == getHeight() == 0
     */
    public Triangle() {
        super();
    }

    /** post:   a Triangle is drawn with vertices at (getWidth()/2, 0),
     *          (0, getHeight()-1) and (getWidth()-1, getHeight()-1)
     *          and the color of the triangle is getBackground()
     */
    public void paint(Graphics g) {
        g.setColor(getBackground());
        g.drawLine(getWidth()/2, 0, 0, getHeight()-1);
        g.drawLine(0, getHeight()-1, getWidth()-1, getHeight()-1);
        g.drawLine(getWidth()/2, 0, getWidth()-1, getHeight()-1);
    }
}
```

Each call to drawLine draws a line segment. Each line is drawn in the color established by the most recent setColor call, and each line's endpoints are $(x1, y1)$ and $(x2, y2)$ relative to the JComponent's bounding rectangle:

```java
g.drawLine(x1, y1, x2, y2);
```

Figure 8.18 shows a Driver class that makes use of the Triangle class to draw two triangles of different colors, sizes, and locations. The image resulting from executing this program is shown in Figure 8.19.

In order to build your own subclasses of JComponent, you need to be familiar with the possible drawing methods provided by the Graphics class. Figure 8.20 is an abridged set of class specifications for Graphics.

The JComponent class is well designed for being subclassed. Not only does the paint method support a rich collection of drawing facilities by way of the Graphics method, but also the other JComponent methods play a significant role. By virtue of inheritance, the Triangle class inherits methods like setLocation that allow client classes to move the triangle. Similarly, the Triangle class draws its

Figure 8.18

Driver to build
two Triangle
objects

```java
import java.awt.Color;
import javax.swing.JFrame;
public class Driver {
    public Driver() {
        JFrame theWin = new JFrame("Example use of Triangle");
        Triangle leftTriangle, rightTriangle;

        theWin.setBounds(100, 100, 250, 200);
        theWin.setVisible(true);
        theWin.setLayout(null);
        theWin.setBackground(Color.white);

        leftTriangle = new Triangle();
        leftTriangle.setBounds(10, 10, 100, 50);
        leftTriangle.setBackground(Color.lightGray);
        theWin.add(leftTriangle, 0);

        rightTriangle = new Triangle();
        rightTriangle.setBackground(Color.black);
        rightTriangle.setBounds(150, 20, 50, 150);
        theWin.add(rightTriangle, 0);
        theWin.repaint();
    }
}
```

Figure 8.19

Image produced
by executing the
program in
Figure 8.18

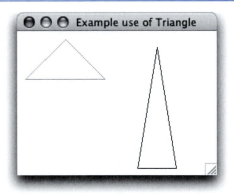

Figure 8.20   `java.awt.Graphics` class specifications

Invariant

All drawing performed upon a `java.awt.Graphics` object

- is done relative to the location of the appropriate `Container` or `JComponent`. (The upper left corner of the `JComponent` is (0, 0).)
- is clipped to the bounding rectangle of the current `Container` or `JComponent`.

Drawing Methods

`public void setColor(java.awt.Color c)`

> **post:** the current drawing color is set to *c*

`public void drawLine(int x1, int y1, int x2, int y2)`

> **post:** a line segment is drawn from point (*x*1, *y*1) to (*x*2, *y*2) using the current drawing color

`public void drawOval(int x, int y, int w, int h)`

> **post:** the outline of an oval is drawn with upper left corner at (*x*, *y*), width of *w*, **and** height of *h* using the current drawing color

`public void drawRect(int x, int y, int w, int h)`

> **post:** the outline of a rectangle is drawn with upper left corner at (*x*, *y*), width of *w*, **and** height of *h* using the current drawing color

`public void drawString(String s, int x, int y)`

> **post:** the text from *s* is drawn with upper left corner at (*x*, *y*) using the current drawing color

`public void fillOval(int x, int y, int w, int h)`

> **post:** a filled oval is drawn with upper left corner at (*x*, *y*), width of *w*, **and** height of *h* using the current drawing color

`public void fillRect(int x, int y, int w, int h)`

> **post:** a filled rectangle is drawn with upper left corner at (*x*, *y*), width of *w*, **and** height of *h* using the current drawing color

`public void clearRect(int x, int y, int w, int h)`

> **post:** a filled rectangle is drawn with upper left corner at (*x*, *y*), width of *w*, **and** height of *h* using the background color of the `JComponent`

. . .

The Oval, Rectangle, and Line classes are all built in the same way—by inheriting JComponent and overriding paint to draw the appropriate image. The Oval class below illustrates.

```
public class Oval extends JComponent {
    public Oval(int x, int y, int w, int h) {
        super();
        setBounds(x, y, w, h);
        setBackground(Color.black);
    }
    public void paint(Graphics g) {
        g.setColor(getBackground());
        g.fillOval(0, 0, getWidth()-1, getHeight()-1);
        paintChildren(g);
    }
}
```

Note that paintChildren causes paint to be called on all objects that are added to this Oval. A call to paintChildren is only needed if add is permitted on objects belonging to the subclass.

shape according to the width and height of its bounding rectangle. Therefore, altering the size of the bounding rectangle by calling setSize also alters the size of the Triangle. Similarly, client code can call setForeground and setBackground while the paint method can access these colors via getForeground and getBackground; this provides two client-controlled colors that are available for use in drawing.

As a second example of the use of JComponent consider the Cube class shown in Figure 8.21. Cube uses several different Graphics methods: getColor, drawRect, drawLine, and fillOval. Cube also makes effective use of inherited methods by using the background color for drawing the edges of the cube and the foreground color for the dot in the center of the cube. The image produced by this class is shown in Figure 8.22.

8.4 ■ Protected Scope

Java permits a subclass to override an inherited method, but the language imposes certain restrictions upon overriding.

■   A child class cannot override private methods because it does not have access to parent features that are private.

■   An overriding method must have the same scope (private, public, or protected) as the inherited method.

Figure 8.21   Cube class

```java
import java.awt.Graphics;
import javax.swing.JComponent;
public class Cube extends JComponent {

    /** post:  getbackGround() is an invisible color
     *         and getX() == x and getY() == y
     *         and getWidth() == getHeight() == s
     */
    public Cube(int x, int y, int s) {
        super();
        setBounds(x, y, s, s);
    }


    /** pre:   getWidth() == getHeight()
     * post:  a cube is drawn with vertices filling the bounding rectangle
     *        and the edge color of the cube is getBackground()
     *        and a dot with color of getForeground() is displayed
     *           on the front face of the cube
     */
    public void paint(Graphics g) {
        int s = getWidth()-1;
        g.setColor(getBackground());
        g.drawRect(0, s/4, s*3/4, s*3/4);
        g.drawLine(0, s/4, s/4, 0);        //left diagonal line
        g.drawLine(s*3/4, s/4, s, 0);    //right top diagonal line
        g.drawLine(s/4, 0, s, 0);              //top horizontal line
        g.drawLine(s*3/4, s, s, s*3/4); //right bottom diagonal line
        g.drawLine(s, 0, s, s*3/4);      //back vertical line
        g.setColor(getForeground());
        g.fillOval(s/4, s/2, s/4, s/4);
    }
}
```

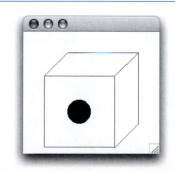

Figure 8.22

Image produced by executing the program in Figure 8.21

■ The parameter list in a child's method must contain the same number of parameters and the same types of parameters as the method from the parent's method. (If the parameter lists differ, then overloading, not overriding, occurs.)

■ Overriding applies only to methods, not to instance variables.

The first two of these restrictions point to a need for more than just `public` and `private` scope. If a method is `public`, then *every* class has access to the method— every client class and every subclass. If a method is `private`, then *no* outside class has access—no client class and no subclass.

In order to provide a scope that differentiates subclasses from client classes, Java includes a third scope option—methods and instance variables can be declared **protected**. The scope of a `protected` feature includes the declaring class itself and all descendant classes. In other words, if `myVar` is a `protected` instance variable of `MyClass`, then `MyClass` can access this variable as can any descendant of `MyClass`. However, client classes (i.e., those that declare variables of type `MyClass`) do *not* have access to `myVar`. Figure 8.23 summarizes the scope differences of `private`, `public`, and `protected` class members.

In class diagrams, `protected` variables and methods are denoted with a prefix symbol of "#," as opposed to "+" for `public` and "-" for `private`. The class diagram in Figure 8.24 illustrates. The three variables in the `MilitaryTime` class are declared to have `protected` scope, while all methods are `public`.

software engineering *Hint*

It is best to avoid declaring instance variables as public. If an instance variable is widely shared by sub-classes, then protected is acceptable. The Parcel class (Figure 8.2) exhibits better information hiding if the declaration of its three instance variables is changed to protected.

To illustrate the utility of the protected scope, consider the task of extending the `MilitaryTime` class to include an additional `setToMidnight` method. Figure 8.25 contains such a class.

`MilitaryTime` declares `hour`, `minute`, and `second` to be protected instance variables. The protected scope of these variables grants subclasses full access to them, as illustrated by `MilitaryTimeWithSet`. Such access permits the assignment instructions that are used in the body of `setToMidnight`.

It would be a poor choice to declare the `MilitaryTime` instance variables with a scope other than `protected`. If these instance variables are declared `private`, then

Figure 8.23   Scope of `private`, `protected`, and `public` members

Member (excepting constructors)	Available within A?	Available in subclass of A?	Available elsewhere?
private member of class A	yes	no	no
protected member of class A	yes	yes	no
public member of class A	yes	yes	yes

Figure 8.24

Class diagram
for
`MilitaryTime`

```
                  MilitaryTime

          # int hour
          # int minute
          # int second

          «constructor»
             + MilitaryTime()

          «query»
             + int hours()
             + int minutes()
             + int seconds()

          «update»
             + void setToNoon()
             + void advance1Hour()
             + void advance1Minute()
             + void advance1Second()
```

child classes, such as `MilitaryTimeWithSet`, are more difficult to implement. On the other hand, if the instance variables of `MilitaryTime` have a `public` scope, then information hiding for client classes is damaged.

Java instance variables are treated differently from methods when it comes to inheritance. While methods can be overridden to replace a parent class's method, instance variables cannot be overridden. Unfortunately, the Java compiler does not generate errors when a child class declares instance variables with the same name as its parent. Instead, when a child declares an instance variable with the same name as a parent's instance variable, then two copies of the variable will be created. The new code of the child has access to the child's variable, and the inherited code from the parent has access to the parent's variable.

Figure 8.26 illustrates with a class called `ParallelDeclarations` that inherits `MilitaryTime`. The `ParallelDeclarations` class is the same as `MilitaryTimeWithSet` except for the inclusion of a declaration for `hour`, `minute`, and `second` in the fourth line.

By including a second set of variable declarations, the `ParallelDeclarations` class has created two parallel sets of variables (`hour`, `minute`, and `second`); the inherited version and the newly declared version. When `super()` is called, the constructor method from `MilitaryTime` will assign values to the parent's variables and the `ParallelDeclarations` variable are unaltered. Similarly, the `advance1Hour`,

software *Hint*
engineering

Declaring methods and instances variables to be protected is often a good choice. As a general rule, it is better to use *protected* rather than *private* any time that there is a chance the class might become a superclass.

Figure 8.25   `MilitaryTimeWithSet` class and class diagram

```
/** Class Invariant
 *      0 <= hour <= 23
 *      and 0 <= minute <= 59
 *      and 0 <= second <= 59
 */
public class MilitaryTimeWithSet extends MilitaryTime {

    /** post: hour == 1
     *         and minute == 0
     *         and second == 0
     */
    public MilitaryTimeWithSet() {
        super();
    }

    /** post: hour == 0
     *         and minute == 0
     *         and second == 0
     */
    public void setToMidnight() {
        hour = 0;
        minute = 0;
        second = 0;
    }
}
```

```
┌─────────────────────────────────┐
│       MilitaryTimeWithSet       │
├─────────────────────────────────┤
│  # int hour                     │
│  # int minute                   │
│  # int second                   │
├─────────────────────────────────┤
│ «constructor»                   │
│    + MilitaryTimeWithSet()      │
│                                 │
│ «query»                         │
│    + int hours()                │
│    + int minutes()              │
│    + int seconds()              │
│                                 │
│ «update»                        │
│    + void setToNoon()           │
│    + void advance1Hour()        │
│    + void advance1Minute()      │
│    + void advance1Second()      │
│    + void setToMidnight()       │
└─────────────────────────────────┘
```

software **engineering** *Hint*

When creating a subclass, avoid declaring instance variables that have the same names as instance variables of the superclass.

advance1Minute, and advance1Second methods increment the parent's variables, not the newly declared variables. When setToMidnight is called, values are assigned to the newly declared variables and the parent's variables are unaltered. If this seems confusing, that is because it is! The moral of this example is that Java programmers should take care *not* to re-declare instance variables from a superclass.

8.5 ■ Inheriting for Event Handling

Method overriding is the key to most event handling in Java. In this chapter, event handling is explored using a few classes written by the author and included on the CD of programs that accompanies this book. These classes are nearly identical to their *Swing* library counterparts, but allow more convenient access to events.

Figure 8.26   ParallelDeclarations class attempt

```
public class ParallelDeclarations extends MilitaryTime {

    /* NOTE: This class doesn't work properly. */
    protected int hour, minute, second;

    /** post: hour == 1 and minute == 0 and second == 0 */
    public ParallelDeclarations() {
        super();
    }

    /** post: hour == 0 and minute == 0 and second == 0 */
    public void setToMidnight() {
        hour = 0;
        minute = 0;
        second = 0;
    }
}
```

> The EventButton, EventSlider, EventTextField, and EventTimer classes introduced in this chapter are built by inheriting similar classes from the standard *Swing* library. The techniques used to build these classes are exposed in Chapter 9 and the code for these classes is revealed there.

Closed
Black Box

A typical library class that supports event handling includes one or more event handler methods. The event handlers of the library class contain only empty bodies. Therefore, an object belonging to such a class responds to events by doing nothing. The key to using such classes is to inherit the provided class and override the event handler method(s).

An example of such a library class supporting event handling is EventButton. (As will be revealed in Chapter 9, EventButton is a child of a *Swing* class called JButton and most of the methods are directly inherited from JButton.) Figure 8.27 contains a class diagram for EventButton.

An EventButton object is essentially a rectangular region that can be clicked by the program user. The two characteristics of EventButton that distinguish it from previously presented *Swing/AWT* classes are

- An EventButton object cannot be colored, but it does have a string label on its surface.
- When the user clicks within the region of an EventButton object, that object's actionPerformed method is called.

Figure 8.27

EventButton
class diagram

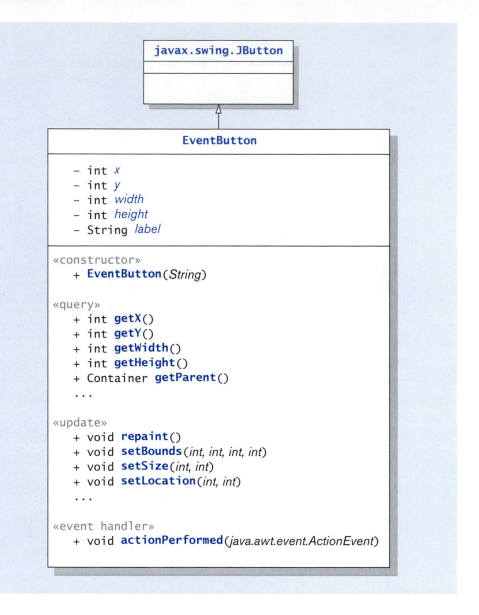

The second of these characteristics, namely the ability to respond to user clicks, is the key reason for the EventButton class. When the user clicks an EventButton object, its actionPerformed method is automatically called by the Java Virtual Machine. In other words, actionPerformed serves as the event handler for button click actions.

The standard Java convention for event handlers is to include a single parameter. In the case of actionPerformed, the parameter is of type ActionEvent (java.awt.event.ActionEvent). The Java VM passes an ActionEvent parameter to the event handler, although this is of little importance for the current discussion.

As explained earlier, the version of the actionPerformed method that is included within EventButton has an empty body, so nothing will happen when a user clicks an EventButton object. In order to use the EventButton class properly, the programmer must replace the default (empty) event handling method. This is accomplished by creating a new child class of EventButton that overrides actionPerformed.

Figure 8.28 shows code for a class called DemoButton and an associated Driver class. A DemoButton is an EventButton with two differences: (1) Each DemoButton is labeled "DEMO" by virtue of the call to super (the EventButton constructor) and (2) A DemoButton stores a count of the number of times it has been clicked, using the clickCount variable.

When the program from Figure 8.28 executes, the Driver constructor creates window and button. The call to the DemoButton constructor initializes the button variable to have a text label of "DEMO" and a clickCount of zero. The Driver method also adds button to window. Figure 8.29 contains a picture that shows window as it appears with the added button.

Following the execution of the Driver constructor, the program awaits button clicks on the demo button. Each such click causes the overridden version of actionPerformed to be called, and each call to actionPerformed causes another line to be appended to the standard output device, creating the following output.

```
Demo click count is 1
Demo click count is 2
Demo click count is 3
    . . .
```

Usually, an EventButton object needs to send messages to other objects, not merely call System.out.println. For example, consider using button clicks to change the location of a Cube object. (This is the same Cube class from Figure 8.21.) The MoveCubeButton from Figure 8.30 demonstrates an EventButton subclass that is used for such a purpose. In particular, each time the user clicks a MoveCubeButton, the appropriate Cube object moves right five pixels and down five pixels.

The behavior of a MoveCubeButton relies upon a new instance variable, called theCube. When MoveCubeButton is instantiated, the third parameter passes a Cube object. The last instruction within the MoveCubeButton constructor causes theCube to be bound to this object. This binding permits theCube to be accessed by future calls to actionPerformed. For example, consider the following client code.

```
Cube smallCube = new Cube(10, 10, 40);
MoveCubeButton exampleButton
    = new MoveCubeButton(20, 30, smallCube);
```

Following the execution of the two statements above, the theCube variable of exampleButton will be an alias for smallCube. Therefore, each time exampleButton is clicked, its actionPerformed method causes theCube (which is really smallCube) to be repositioned.

Figure 8.28   DemoButton class and associated Driver

```java
import java.awt.event.*;
public class DemoButton extends EventButton {
    private int clickCount;

    /** post: getX() == x and getY() == y
     *         and getWidth() == 150 and getHeight() == 30
     *         and getText() is "DEMO" and clickCount == 0
     */
    public DemoButton(int x, int y) {
        super("DEMO");
        setBounds(x, y, 150, 30);
        clickCount = 0;
    }

    /** post: a message indicating clickCount has been sent to standard output
     *         and clickCount == clickCount@pre + 1
     */
    public void actionPerformed(ActionEvent e) {
        clickCount++;
        System.out.println("Demo click count is " + clickCount);
    }
}

/** A client of DemoButton */
import javax.swing.JFrame;
public class Driver {
    private JFrame window;
    private DemoButton button;

    public Driver() {
        window = new JFrame("");
        window.setBounds(10, 10, 200, 100);
        window.setVisible(true);
        window.setLayout(null);
        button = new DemoButton(25, 20);
        window.add(button, 0);
        button.repaint();
    }
}
```

It is quite common for different classes to share the same object in the way that the client code above shares smallCube with exampleButton. Figure 8.31 generalizes this into a pattern for object sharing.

Figure 8.29

The window resulting from the DemoButton program

Figure 8.30

MoveCubeButton class

```java
import java.awt.event.ActionEvent;
public class MoveCubeButton extends EventButton {
    private Cube theCube;

    /** pre:    d != null
     *    post:   theCube == d
     *            and getX() == x and getY() == y
     *            and getWidth() == 100 and getHeight() == 30
     */
    public MoveCubeButton(int x, int y, Cube d) {
        super("MOVE");
        setBounds(x, y, 100, 30);
        theCube = d;
    }

    /** pre:    theCube != null
     *    post:   theCube.getX() == theCube.getX()@pre + 5
     *            and theCube.getY() = theCube.getY()@pre + 5
     */
    public void actionPerformed(ActionEvent e) {
        theCube.setLocation(theCube.getX()+5, theCube.getY()+5);
    }
}
```

Another technique often used for event handling is known as a **callback**. In a callback approach each event is "forwarded" by virtue of a method call to another object. To accomplish a callback, the `actionPerformed` method of an `EventButton` subclass needs to execute one instruction only—a method call on some other object. The reason for the name "callback" is that the object to receive this method call is generally the object that created the button. It is as though every button event results in a "call back" to the object that created the button.

Figure 8.32 illustrates a callback with a class called `recolorCallbackButton`. The `RecolorCallbackButton` class is designed to be used in conjunction with an object

Figure 8.31

Shared object
pattern

A Shared Object Pattern

Suppose that Object A contains an object called *sharedObject* and that Object B must also manipulate *sharedObject*. The following strategy permits such sharing.

- Object A calls one of Object B's methods (often a constructor) and passes *sharedObject* as an argument.
- Object B assigns *sharedObject* to one of its own instance variables. (Now both A and B have variables bound to *sharedObject*.)
- Object A and Object B can access the shared object using their individual bindings.

(See Figure 8.30 for an example.)

Figure 8.32   RecolorCallbackButton class

```java
import java.awt.event.ActionEvent;
public class RecolorCallbackButton extends EventButton{
    private Driver callbackDestination;

    /** pre:   d != null
     * post:  callbackDestination == d
     *        and getX() == x and getY() == y
     *        and getWidth() == 100 and getHeight() == 30
     */
    public RecolorCallbackButton(int x, int y, Driver d) {
        super("RECOLOR");
        setBounds(x, y, 100, 30);
        callbackDestination = d;
    }

    /** pre:   callbackDestination != null
     * post:  the postcondition from callbackDestination.recolor()
     */
    public void actionPerformed(ActionEvent e) {
        callbackDestination.recolor();
    }
}
```

of type `Driver`. The constructor method of `RecolorCallbackButton` begins in much the same way as `MoveCubeButton`. Following the execution of the first two `RecolorCallbackButton` instructions, a button is created and labeled with the name "RECOLOR". The third instruction in the constructor method is different because it assigns d to `callbackDestination`. This constructor method is expecting the `Driver` object to pass its own identity. Subsequently, every `actionPerformed` event causes a call to the `recolor` method to be performed upon the `callbackDestination` object.

The general requirements of the callback pattern are explained in Figure 8.33.

Figure 8.34 completes the code for this example by showing an appropriate `Driver` class. This class creates two cubes and two buttons: one button of type `MoveCubeButton` and one of type `RecolorCallbackButton`.

The `Driver` class from Figure 8.34 begins execution by constructing `smallCube`, coloring it with a red background and black foreground, adding it to the window's content pane, and passing it as the third argument in the construction of `moveButton`. Next, a second and larger cube, called `bigCube`, is constructed. As the `recolorButton` is constructed, it is passed the identity of the `Driver` object (namely *this*). The computer screen should contain a window that appears something like the one shown in Figure 8.35 after the `Driver` constructor finishes execution.

The Figure 8.35 window becomes fully event driven once the `Driver` constructor completes. At such time, the state of the program's execution includes five key

---

A Callback Pattern

Figure 8.33

Callback pattern for event handling

A callback pattern consists of an event-producing object (from class *EventProducer*) forwarding each event by calling a method on another object (from class *Target*). For a true callback, the *Target* object is the one that created the *EventProducer* object.

The following four steps are needed to accomplish this kind of callback scheme for handling events.

1. Class *EventProducer* includes an instance variable of type *Target* (call it `t`), and a method (usually the constructor) to assign this variable.

2. Class *Target* constructs an object of type *EventProducer* and passes its own identity so that `t` is bound to the *Target* object.

3. The body of the event handler method from method *EventProducer* consists of a single instruction of the following form.

   `t.someMethod();`

4. Class *Target* includes a method with the same name and parameter list as `someMethod`.

(See Figures 8.32 and 8.34 for an example in which class *EventProducer* is `RecolorCallback`, class *Target* is `Driver`, and the `t` variable is named `callbackDestination`.)

Figure 8.34   Driver class for the Cube buttons

```
import java.awt.Color;
import javax.swing.JFrame;
public class Driver {
    private JFrame window;
    privateCube smallCube, bigCube;
    private MoveCubeButton moveButton;
    private RecolorCallbackButton recolorButton;

    public Driver() {
        window = new JFrame("Example buttons");
        window.setBounds(10, 10, 500, 450);
        window.setVisible(true);
        window.setLayout(null);

        smallCube = new Cube(10, 10, 40);
        window.add(smallCube, 0);
        smallCube.setBackground(Color.red);
        smallCube.setForeground(Color.black);
        moveButton = new MoveCubeButton(100, 370, smallCube);
        window.add(moveButton);
        bigCube = new Cube(150, 150, 200);
        bigCube.setBackground(Color.green);
        bigCube.setForeground(Color.blue);
        window.add(bigCube, 0);

        recolorButton = new RecolorCallbackButton(300, 370, this);
        window.add(recolorButton, 0);
        window.repaint();
    }

    public void recolor() {
        float redness, greeness, blueness;
        redness = (float) Math.random();
        greeness = (float) Math.random();
        blueness = (float) Math.random();
        Color c = new Color(redness, greenness, blueness);
        bigCube.setForeground(c);
        bigCube.setBackground(new Color(1-redness, 1-greenness, 1-blueness));
        bigCube.repaint();
    }
}
```

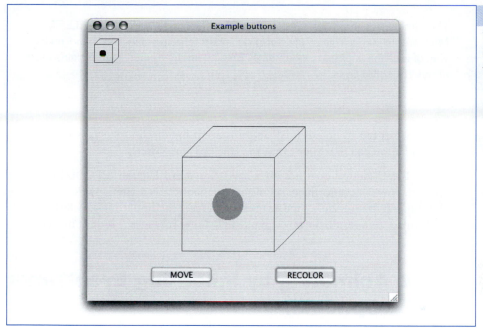

Figure 8.35

Window pro-
duced by code
from Figure 8.34

objects: the `Driver` object, `smallCube`, `bigCube`, and the two buttons. Figure 8.36
shows the key relationships among these five objects, labeling each line with the
appropriate instance variable name.

Figure 8.36 shows a two-way aggregation between the `Driver` object and
`recolorButton`. Such two-way aggregation is typical of a callback pattern. A user
click on the "RECOLOR" button causes the `actionPerformed` method from

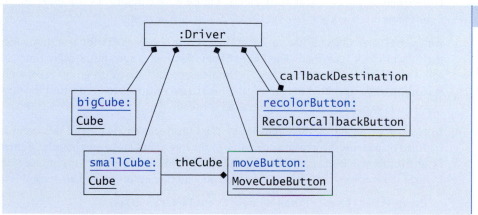

Figure 8.36

Key object bind-
ings from the
Cube button
example

The ThreeButtons class is just a class that declares three buttons (LEFT, MID, and RIGHT). This class is also designed to deliver all event handling by way of a callback pattern. Chapter 9 contains another insert that explains more about ThreeButtons.

recolorButton to be executed, and this event handler in turn calls the recolor method upon callbackDestination (the Driver object).

The "MOVE" button does not use a callback pattern like the "RECOLOR" button. Instead, moveButton contains an instance variable, called theCube. A user click on the "MOVE" button causes the actionPerformed method from moveButton to be performed. As a result, the object named theCube (alias smallCube) moves.

8.6 ■ Animating by Inheriting EventTimer (Optional)

The Callback Object Pattern can also be used to implement animations. This section demonstrates with the assistance of another author-supplied class called EventTimer. (EventTimer is a subclass of the swing Timer class.)

A motion picture results from a sequence of individual photographs stored on film. When these photos are projected in rapid succession, they give the appearance of real motion. A computer animation is produced in much the same way. The primary difference is computer animation results from program execution rather then projecting light through many cells of film.

One effective way to produce animations is the use of events. The EventTimer class is designed to produce just such events. Figure 8.37 contains a class diagram for EventTimer.

An EventTimer object is like an alarm clock. Once the EventTimer is instantiated, the "alarm clock" is armed. The EventTimer parameter specifies a delay time (in milliseconds).[3] A call to the start method causes the "alarm" to go off repeatedly according to the specified time interval. This alarm continues to occur until the program quits executing or the stop method is called.

Instead of a true alarm, the EventTimer class produces an event, and this event is handled by a method with the same name as the EventButton event handler, namely actionPerformed. For example, following code declares and instantiates an EventTimer object, then causes the object to generate events every half second.

```
EventTimer sampleTimer = new EventTimer(500);
sampleTimer.start();
```

---

3. One thousand milliseconds equals a second.

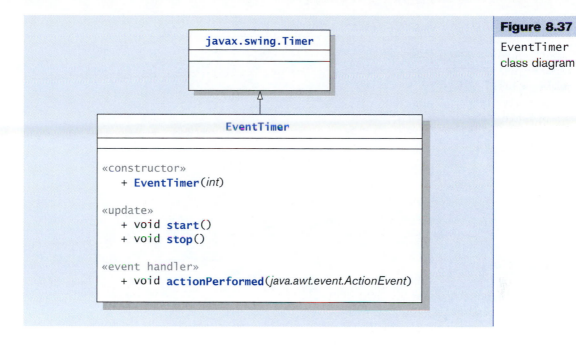

Figure 8.37

EventTimer
class diagram

Consider the problem of animating a Label so that it appears to move side to side within a window. Figure 8.38 contains a Driver class for one solution to this animation problem.

The Driver class in Figure 8.38 relies upon five instance variables. The fishyMsg variable represents a Label displaying the message "FISH" that will be moved back and forth within the JFrame called window. The velocity variable is used to maintain the travel direction of dot. When velocity is 1, fishyMsg is moving to the right; when velocity is –1, fishyMsg is moving to the left.

This program makes use of a callback pattern to animate fishyMsg. The Driver object instantiates an object called clock to initialize the callback, and clock belongs to a class called MsgCallbackTimer that is designed for such a callback. MsgCallbackTimer is shown in Figure 8.39.

A MsgCallbackTimer object contains a single instance variable called theDriver. This theDriver variable is bound to the Driver object that will serve as the true event handler. When MsgCallbackTimer is instantiated, it calls the superclass constructor to establish the event timing interval at the value of the first MsgCallbackTimer parameter. Thereafter, theDriver is assigned the value of the second parameter. Note that every timed event for the MsgCallbackTimer object calls actionPerformed, which in turn calls theDriver.moveMsg.

Returning to the Figure 8.38 Driver class code, it activates a DotTimer object, called clock, with the following instructions.

```
clock = new MsgCallbackTimer(20, this);
clock.start();
```

Figure 8.38   Driver class for message animation

```java
import javax.swing.JFrame;
import java.awt.*;
public class Driver {
    private JFrame window;
    private Label fishyMsg;
    private MsgCallbackTimer clock;
    private int velocity;

    /** post:  window != null
     *         and fishyMsg is placed at the left edge of window
     *         and velocity = 1
     *         and clock is scheduled for 1/50 sec. repeated events
     */
    public Driver() {
        window = new JFrame("Animated Message");
        window.setBounds(10, 10, 400, 200);
        window.setVisible(true);
        window.setLayout(null);
        fishyMsg = new Label("FISH");
        fishyMsg.setBounds(0, 70, 50, 30);
        fishyMsg.setForeground(Color.black);
        fishyMsg.setBackground(Color.blue);
        window.add(fishyMsg, 0);
        window.repaint();
        velocity = 1;
        clock = new MsgCallbackTimer(20, this);
        clock.start();
    }

    /** pre:   fishyMsg != null
     *  post:  (either the left or right edge of fishyMsg@pre lies
     *          outside the boundaries of pane)
     *             implies velocity == - velocity@pre
     *          and fishyMsg.getX() == fishyMsg.getX()@pre + velocity
     */
    public void moveMsg() {
        if (fishyMsg.getX() < 0
            || fishyMsg.getX()+fishyMsg.getWidth() > window.getWidth())
        {
            velocity = -velocity;
        }
        fishyMsg.setLocation(fishyMsg.getX()+velocity, fishyMsg.getY());
    }
}
```

Figure 8.39   MsgCallbackTimer class

```java
import java.awt.event.ActionEvent;
public class MsgCallbackTimer extends EventTimer {
    private Driver theDriver;

    /** pre:    d != null
     *  post:   theDriver == d
     */
    public MsgCallbackTimer(int m, Driver d) {
        super(m);
        theDriver = d;
    }

    /** pre:    theDriver != null
     *  post:   the moveMsg method from theDriver is performed
     */
    public void actionPerformed(ActionEvent e) {
        theDriver.moveMsg();
    }
}
```

Executing the first of the two statements, instantiates clock sets the time interval to 20 milliseconds (fifty events per second), and establishes the Driver object (passed as this) as the callback target. The second statement causes clock to begin generating events.

The key associations among these classes is diagrammed in Figure 8.40. This diagram shows two classes (Driver and MsgCallbackTimer) that are each an aggregate including the other. This two-way aggregation picture is a characteristic of the callback pattern.

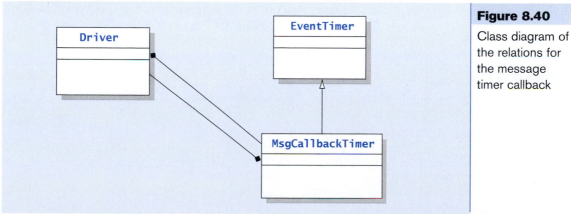

Figure 8.40

Class diagram of the relations for the message timer callback

8.7 ■ Design Example with Sliders and Text Fields (Optional)

In computer programming, the terms **input** and **output** are used to refer to data transfer to and from an executing program. System.out.println is considered to be an output method because programs use this method to provide information from the executing program to the user. Drawing *Swing/AWT* images on a computer screen is another form of computer output.

When an EventButton object is clicked, this is a form of input. The name "input" indicates that the program is receiving something *from* the user. An EventButton object's input is quite limited, since it cannot pass any information to the program except an actionEvent. The author of this book has included two other classes that permit the user to input information. These two classes are **EventSlider** and **EventTextField**.

The EventSlider class supplies a graphical event-driven technique to input integer values. EventSlider objects appear somewhat like the image shown in Figure 8.41. (The actual image may look slightly different on different computer systems.)

On the face of every EventSlider object is a knob. With a pointing device, such as a mouse, the user can drag the knob back and forth. The EventSlider object generates events periodically as the knob is being dragged.

Each EventSlider maintains an int value that increases as the knob is dragged to the right and decreases as the knob moves left. This int value represents the position of the knob, proportional to its minimum and maximum possible values. When the slider knob is dragged all the way to the left, the int value of the slider is at its minimum, and its maximum value occurs when the knob is dragged to its rightmost position.

EventSlider objects can be either horizontal or vertical in orientation. A horizontal scrollbar has a knob that moves left and right, while a vertical scrollbar's knob moves up and down (with maximum at the top and minimum at the bottom).

Figure 8.42 contains a class diagram for EventSlider. The getX, getY, getWidth, getHeight, getParent, repaint, setBounds, setLocation, and setSize methods behave like they do for other *Swing/AWT* classes.

Figure 8.41

An EventSlider image

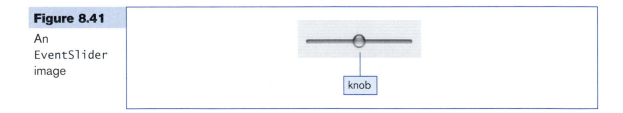

knob

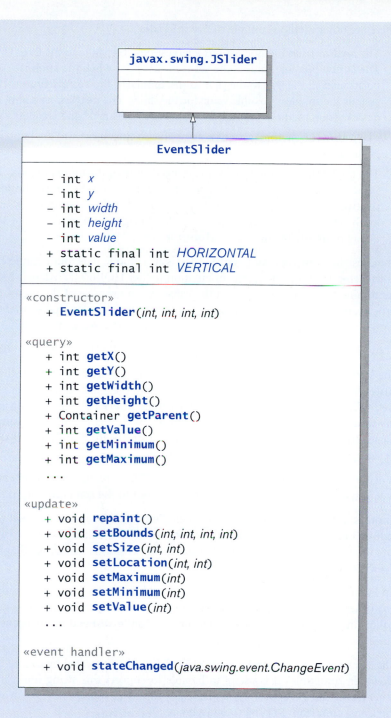

Figure 8.42

EventSlider
class diagram

There are other methods unique to EventSlider.

- The setMaximum method assigns a largest possible value to the EventSlider. The largest possible value is the value of the slider when the knob is positioned all the way to the right (top). Similarly, the setMinimum method assigns the smallest possible value for the slider. The getMaximum and getMinimum methods are called to retrieve these largest and smallest values.

- The setValue method assigns a new value to the object and the knob is positioned appropriately.

- The getValue method returns the integer value of the knob position. This value is proportional to the distance of the knob from the left (or bottom) relative to the minimum and maximum possible values. For example, if the knob is three quarters of the way from left to right for a minimum of 100 and a maximum of 200, then getValue() is 175.

The constructor method for EventSlider is also unique. The four parameters of this constructor are, respectively: the orientation (either HORIZONTAL or VERTICAL), the minimum, the maximum, and the value. As an example of the use of this constructor, the following statement instantiates an EventSlider that is oriented horizontally with a minimum value of 0, a maximum of 10, and an actual value of 5.

```
mySlider = new EventSlider(EventSlider.HORIZONTAL, 0, 10, 5);
```

The slider event handler method has a different name (stateChanged) than previously discussed event handlers. (Note also that the ChangeEvent class for this method's parameter is from the *javax.swing.event* library.) stateChanged is invoked any time that the user drags the slider's knob. Overriding this method permits subclasses to capture user events. Figure 8.43 illustrates the use of scrollbars with a Driver class and an associated PrintingSlider class.

When the Driver in Figure 8.43 executes, two sliders are displayed in a JFrame. Any event on either slider causes its value to be output to the standard output stream.

Another author-created class, called EventTextField, supports textual (String) input. EventTextField is a subclass of the *Swing* class called JTextField that was introduced in Section 6.11. Figure 8.44 contains a class diagram for EventTextField.

An EventTextField object is a rectangular region in which a user can type a single line of text. If the user strikes the *return* key (sometimes called an *enter* key) while typing in an EventTextField, then an actionPerformed event occurs on the object.

The String content of an EventTextField can be inspected by calling getText. However, sometimes it is useful to be able to convert this string input into some other form. The java.util.Scanner class (discussed in Section 7.5) can assist with the translation from String to other types.

As an example of EventTextField and converting the String content to an integer, consider a program to convert temperatures from Fahrenheit to Celsius. Figure 8.45 shows a suitable user interface consisting of two text fields and a slider.

```java
import javax.swing.JFrame;
public class Driver {
    private JFrame window;
    private PrintingSlider upperSlider, lowerSlider;

    public Driver() {
        window = new JFrame("Slider Example");
        window.setBounds(10, 10, 200, 120);
        window.setVisible(true);
        window.setLayout(null);
        upperSlider = new PrintingSlider(100, 200, 100);
        upperSlider.setBounds(10, 10, 100, 30);
        window.add(upperSlider, 0);
        lowerSlider = new PrintingSlider(-100, 100, 0);
        lowerSlider.setBounds(30, 60, 150, 30);
        window.add(lowerSlider, 0);
        window.repaint();
    }
}


import javax.swing.event.ChangeEvent;
public class PrintingSlider extends EventSlider {

    /** post:  this slider object is constructed
     *         and the orientation is horizontal
     *         and getMaximum() == max
     *         and getMinimum() == min
     *         and getValue() == val
     */
    public PrintingSlider(int min, int max, int val) {
        super(HORIZONTAL, min, max, val);
    }

    /** post:  getValue() is output */
    public void stateChanged(ChangeEvent e) {
        System.out.println(getValue());
    }
}
```

Figure 8.43

PrintingSlider
example program

This program accepts events either from the EventTextField object labeled "Fahrenheit" or from the slider. Events on either of these objects should update the other object to the matching value. In response to these events, the program must also translate the associated Fahrenheit temperature into its Celsius equivalent and display this temperature in the JTextField labeled "Celsius."

Figure 8.44

EventTextField
class diagram

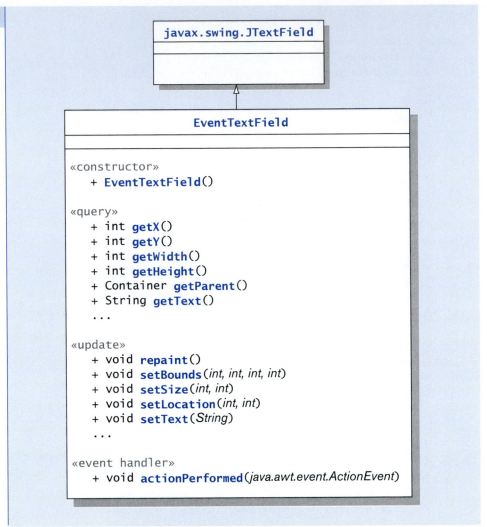

Figure 8.45

User interface
from tempera-
ture conversion
program

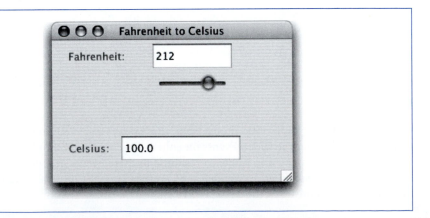

The Fahrenheit to Celsius temperature conversion program is designed around four key objects, as pictured in Figure 8.46. The `Driver` object contains three instance variables: a slider and two text fields (one for Fahrenheit and one for Celsius). If the user updates the value of the Fahrenheit text field, then the resulting event is handled by two callbacks to the `Driver` object—one to update the slider value and one to update the Celsius temperature field. If the user drags the slider, then the resulting `fahrenSlider` event uses the `theField` alias to update the Fahrenheit temperature. (Any slider update will indirectly alter `celsiusFld` by creating a `fahrenFld` event.)

Figure 8.47 contains the code for `FahrenheitField`, the class of the Fahrenheit text field object. `FahrenheitField` inherits `EventTextField`. Note the callback code

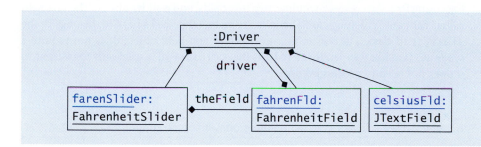

Figure 8.46

Object diagram for temperature conversion

```java
import java.awt.*;
import java.awt.event.ActionEvent;
public class FahrenheitField extends EventTextField {
    private Driver driver;
    /** pre:    d != null
     *  post:   driver == d
     *          and getX() == x and getY() == y
     *          and getWidth() = 100 and getHeight() ==30
     */
    public FahrenheitField(int x, int y, Driver d) {
        super();
        setBounds(x, y, 100, 30);
        driver = d;
    }


    /** pre:    driver != null
     *  post:   the postconditon of driver.updateCelsius()
     */
    public void actionPerformed(ActionEvent e) {
        driver.updateCelsius();
        driver.updateFahrenSlider();
    }
}
```

Figure 8.47

FahrenheitField class from temperature conversion program

that `FahrenheitField` uses to handle events. Whenever the `actionPerformed` method is called, `FahrenheitField` responds by calling `updateCelsius` and `updateFahrenSlider` upon driver. (The identity of driver is passed to `FahrenheitField` when it was instantiated.)

Figure 8.48 contains the slider class that uses the shared object pattern for accessing `Driver` objects. When `FahrenheitSlider` is constructed it must be passed a `FahrenheitField` object. The `theField` variable is bound to this passed object. Whenever the user generates a `FahrenheitSlider` event, the `actionPerformed` method is performed upon `theField`, which updates the Celsius text field. This also illustrates that event-handling methods can be called directly, just like other methods.

A `Driver` class to create the appropriate user interface is given in Figure 8.49. Executing `Driver` creates a window, two text fields, and a slider object. The text field called `fahrenFld` belongs to `FahrenheitField`, while `celsiusFld`, belongs to the `JTextField` class. The reason that this second text field object does not require a separate class, like `FahrenheitField`, is that `celsiusFld` is used only for output so it does not need to process events.

Figure 8.48   `FahrenheitSlider` class from temperature conversion program

```java
import javax.swing.event.ChangeEvent;
public class FahrenheitSlider extends EventSlider {
    private FahrenheitField theField;

    /** pre:    f != null
     *  post:   theField == f
     *          and getMinimum() == min and getMaximum() == max
     *          and getValue() = val and orientation is HORIZONTAL
     *          and theField == f
     */
    public FahrenheitSlider(int min, int max, int val, FahrenheitField f) {
        super(HORIZONTAL, min, max, val);
        theField = f;
    }

    /** pre:    theField != null
     *  post:   theField.intValue == intValue
     *          and the postcondition of theField.actionPerformed(null)
     */
    public void stateChanged(ChangeEvent e) {
        theField.setText("" + getValue());
        theField.repaint();
        theField.actionPerformed(null); //null is a dummy argument
    }
}
```

Figure 8.49   Driver class from temperature conversion (*continues*)

```java
/** Temperature Program Driver */
import javax.swing.*;
import java.awt.*;
import java.util.Scanner;
public class Driver {
    private JFrame window;
    private FahrenheitField fahrenFld;
    private FahrenheitSlider fahrenSlider;
    private JTextField celsiusFld;

    public Driver() {
        window = new JFrame("Fahrenheit to Celsius");
        window.setBounds(10, 10, 300, 200);
        window.setVisible(true);
        window.setLayout(null);
        fahrenFld = new FahrenheitField(125, 5, this);
        window.add(fahrenFld);
        celsiusFld = new JTextField();
        celsiusFld.setBounds(85, 120, 150, 30);
        window.add(celsiusFld, 0);
        fahrenSlider = new FahrenheitSlider(-100, 300, 0, fahrenFld);
        fahrenSlider.setBounds(125, 40, 100, 30);
        window.add(fahrenSlider, 0);
        makeAndAddLabels(window);
        window.repaint();
    }

    /** pre:    c != null
     *  post:   Fahrenheit and Celsius labels have been added to the
     *          left of the respective fields.
     */
    private void makeAndAddLabels(JFrame f) {
        Label celsiusLabel, fahrenLabel;
        fahrenLabel = new Label("Fahrenheit:");
        fahrenLabel.setBounds(20, 5, 100, 30);
        fahrenLabel.setForeground(Color.red);
        f.add(fahrenLabel, 0);
        celsiusLabel = new Label("Celsius:");
        celsiusLabel.setBounds(20, 120, 60, 30);
        celsiusLabel.setForeground(Color.red);
        f.add(celsiusLabel, 0);
    }
```

Figure 8.49   Driver class from temperature conversion (*continued*)

```
/** pre:   celsiusFld != null and fahrenFld != null
 * post:  celsiusFld displays the Celsius equivalent of the temperature
 *        from fahrenFld
 */
public void updateCelsius() {
    double fahrenTemp;
    fahrenTemp = (new Scanner(fahrenFld.getText())).nextDouble();
    celsiusFld.setText("" + (fahrenTemp- 32.0) * 5.0/9.0);
    celsiusFld.repaint();
}

/** pre:   fahrenFld != null and fahrenSlider != null
 * post:  fahrenSlider is set to the value from fahrenFld
 */
public void updateFahrenSlider() {
    double fahrenTemp;
    fahrenTemp = (new Scanner(fahrenFld.getText())).nextDouble();
    fahrenSlider.setValue((int)fahrenTemp);
}
}
```

Figure 8.49 shows the code that is called in response to all user events. The updateCelsius method retrieves the value from the input text field by way of the following method call.

```
fahrenFld.getText()
```

This value must be translated from String to its double equivalent. This is accomplished as follows.

```
fahrenTemp = (new Scanner(fahrenFld.getText())).nextDouble();
```

A Fahrenheit temperature is translated into Celsius by subtracting 32 degrees and then multiplying by 5/9. The resulting value is assigned to celsiusFld by way of a setText method. Recall that the "" + *expr* notation converts the expression value into a String.

8.8 ■ Summary

One important characteristic of successful manufacturing is **reuse**. Automotive designers frequently design the next generation of vehicles by borrowing from preexisting components, such as tires, door handles, and light bulbs. Computer manufacturers design new laptop computers around available processors, LCD panels, and keyboard technologies.

These forms of reuse do not reuse the objects themselves; no one expects to remove spark plugs from an older car in order to insert them into a new vehicle. Instead, this is reuse of design and architecture. The automotive designer can avoid the cost of designing spark plugs by using existing designs. The computer manufacturer can avoid considerable expense by using existing computer processor architectures.

Object-oriented software development provides two major opportunities for software reuse:

1. reuse of a supplier class
2. reuse of a superclass.

Chapter 6 focused on the concept of supplier classes. By using aggregation, a client class is able to reuse the facilities (instance variables and methods) that are part of a supplier class. This same supplier class may play a similar role in many different programs and/or for many client classes within a single program. Client code developers have the benefits of reusing the design, implementation, prior testing, and documentation associated with any shared supplier class.

This chapter introduces another way that reuse is supported in object-oriented languages, namely *inheritance*. When one class inherits another, it borrows members of the superclass.

Inheritance is a mechanism for one class (the superclass) to be reused to create another *class* (the subclass). This is unlike aggregation, in which a supplier class is used to give form to the objects of the client. Most software libraries make extensive use of inheritance, not only to save development costs, but also to provide software consistency.

Ideally, inheritance represents an *is_a* relationship in which the subclass *is_a* superclass. A subclass is best viewed as a specialization of its superclass. The subclass may provide additional functionality (new methods and instance variables). The subclass may refine the behavior of inherited methods by overriding them. However, the well-conceived subclass should be more than just a way to borrow functionality from another class; it should be a specialized/extended version of its superclass.

One effective application of inheritance is to provide a mechanism for event handling. Each subclass can define its own event-handling behavior by overriding the event handler method of its superclass. This chapter included a discussion of four such author-supplied classes. The `EventButton` class is used to create clickable buttons; the `EventTextField` class provides for GUI window panes where the user can type text; and the `EventSlider` class is for graphical slider objects that maintain an integer value in the form of a sliding knob. The fourth class supporting events is `EventTimer`. The `EventTimer` class is unlike the other three classes in the sense that its events result from the passage of time, instead of some user action.

Inspector

Below is a collection of hints on what to check when examining code that involves the concepts of this chapter.

- Whenever a class is designed, care should be taken to check the scope of each instance variable and method. Those methods that are genuinely needed by clients must be `public`. Most of the remaining members should be `protected`. The `private` declaration should be reserved for those situations when a class will never be inherited or when subclasses will never require the use of the `private` feature.

- The first instruction of any subclass constructor method should call one of the superclass constructors.

- It's a good idea to check the instance variables declared in a child class to be certain they do not duplicate the name of some parent's instance variable. Such parallel variables can be the source of extremely subtle errors.

- When creating a new subclass, each method from the superclass should be checked to be certain that its behavior is proper for the subclass. Those superclass methods that do not behave properly should be overridden.

- If one method is intended to override another, it is always best to check for identical parameter lists. If the parameter lists are different, overloading will occur, potentially leading to unexpected behavior.

- The postcondition for an overriding method should always satisfy the postcondition of the method it overrides. In other words, the child class's version of the method should perform a task upon the object that is analogous to the task performed by the parent version.

- Check each overriding method to be certain that it does not try to call itself accidentally. Calls to the parent's version of an overridden method must be prefixed with `super`.

- Every use of the shared object pattern must include a variable to alias the shared variable and the proper code to assign this variable the correct binding.

- Every use of the callback pattern must include a variable to alias the object that is the destination of the callback and the proper code to assign this variable the correct binding.

- Event-handling objects need to be completely initialized *before* it is possible for the user to generate events. Watch out for any event handling code that modifies other objects that handle events. This can be tricky.

Terminology

callback	`java.awt.Graphics`
child class	`javax.swing.JComponent`
contains_a relation	output
`EventButton`	override
`EventSlider`	`paint` (from the `JComponent` class)
`EventTextField`	parent class
`EventTimer`	`protected`
extends	redefine (a method)
extension	single inheritance
has_a relation	specialization
inheritance	subclass
input	`super`
is_a relation	superclass

Exercises

1. For each part below two classes of real-world objects are given. For each pair of objects select the best of the following five possibilities.

   (1) left class *is_a* right class

   (2) right class *is_a* left class

   (3) left class *contains_a* right class

   (4) right class *contains_a* left class

   (5) none of the above relations seem appropriate

   a. furniture and desk
   b. desk and drawer
   c. hammer and handle
   d. hammer and nail
   e. boat and canoe
   f. bass and fresh water fish
   g. stringed instrument and bass
   h. tuba and brass instrument
   i. tuba and trombone
   j. cockpit and airplane
   k. footwear and shoelace
   l. footwear and boot
   m. footwear and shoe store

   n. retail establishment and shoe store
   o. plant and leaf
   p. rose bush and plant
   q. rose bush and thorn
   r. tea cup and saucer
   s. tea cup and dishes
   t. book and table of contents
   u. book and library
   v. beverage and coffee
   w. liquid and beverage
   x. liquid and coffee
   y. animal and elephant
   z. tail and elephant

2. For each part of Exercise 1 answer the following question: If these were software classes, should inheritance be used, and if so, which should be the child class and which should be the parent?

Use the classes below to complete Exercises 3 through 8.

```java
public class Bird {
    private int wingLength;
    protected double brain;
    public boolean canFly;
    public Bird() {
        wingLength = 11;
        brain = 100;
        canFly = false;
    }

    public void setWingLength(int w) {
        wingLength = w;
    }

    public void setBirdBrain(double d) {
        brain = d;
    }
}

public class Pelican extends Bird {
    public int beakVolume;
    private int age;
    public Pelican() {
        // Pelican instruction here
    }
    public void setBirdBrain(double d) {
        brain = d*2;
    }
}

public class TwoBirds {
    public Bird bigBird;
    public Pelican zeke;

    public TwoBirds() {
        bigBird = new Bird();
        zeke = new Pelican();
        // TwoBirds instruction here
    }
}
```

3. For each part below suppose that this instruction were inserted in place of `// TwoBirds instruction here` in the TwoBirds class. Which of the following best explains the result of this code insertion?

    (1) The instruction references an instance variable or method that is outside its scope.

    (2) The instruction compiles and executes without error.

    a. `zeke.brain = 3.2;`

    b. `zeke.wingLength = 7;`

    c. `zeke.canFly = true;`

    d. `zeke.age = 3;`

    e. `zeke.beakVolume = 4;`

    f. `zeke.setWingLength(7);`

4. For each part below suppose that this instruction were inserted in place of `// Pelican instruction here` in the Pelican class. Which of the following best explains the result of this code insertion?

    (1) The instruction references an instance variable or method that is outside its scope.

    (2) The instruction compiles and executes without error.

    a. `brain = 3.2;`   f. `setBirdBrain(1.2);`

    b. `wingLength = 7;`   g. `setWingLength(4);`

    c. `canFly = true;`   h. `Bird();`

    d. `age = 3;`   i. `super();`

    e. `beakVolume = 4;`

5. Draw a class diagram that shows all of the aggregation and inheritance relationships from the Bird, Pelican, and TwoBirds classes.

6. Suppose that the following instruction is inserted in place of `// Pelican instruction here` in the Pelican class. Precisely what value is assigned to the object's brain attribute as a result executing this code?

    `setBirdBrain( 2.4 );`

7. Suppose that the following instruction is inserted in place of `// Pelican instruction here` in the Pelican class. Precisely what value is assigned to the object's brain attribute as a result executing this code?

    `super.setBirdBrain( 2.4 );`

8. There is one instruction that should be first in the `Pelican` constructor method. What is it?

9. Below is a class designed to construct a button for toggling the color of a `Rectangle` object from black to white, repeatedly.

```java
import java.awt.event.ActionEvent;
public class ToggleButton extends EventButton {
    protected Rectangle theRectangle;

    public ToggleButton(Rectangle r) {
        super();
        setBounds(10, 10, 100, 20);
        setText("Toggle");
        // Instruction missing here
    }

    public void actionPerformed(ActionEvent e) {
        if (theRectangle.getForeground() == Color.white) {
            theRectangle.setForeground(Color.black);
        } else {
            theRectangle.setForeground(Color.white);
        }
    }
}
```

   a. Does this code appear to be using the shared object pattern or the callback pattern?

   b. What instruction needs to be substituted for `// Instruction missing here` in order to complete the pattern?

   c. Show all of the code that the client needs to execute in order to construct and initialize a `ToggleButton` to manipulate a `theRectangle` variable.

   d. Show the complete code for a class called `ToggleButtonWithSet` that inherits `ToggleButton` and adds the functionality necessary to change the `Rectangle` that same `ToggleButton` manipulates at runtime.

   e. Draw a picture of the class diagrams, including all inheritance and aggregation connections between your client class, the `ToggleButton` class, and the `EventButton` class.

10. Below is a client class designed to toggle the color of `myRectangle` object from black to white, repeatedly. This program accomplishes the same basic task as examined in Exercise 9. Supply the necessary code for the `ToggleButton2` class that completes the program.

```java
import javax.swing.JFrame
public class Driver {
    private Rectangle myRectangle;
    private JFrame window;
    private ToggleButton2 button;

    public Driver() {
        window = new JFrame("Toggle Button Window");
        window.setBounds(10, 10, 300, 200);
        window.setVisible(true);
        window.setLayout(null);
        myRectangle = new Rectangle(50, 50, 150, 50);
        myRectangle.setForeground(Color.black);
        window.add(myRectangle, 0);
        button = new ToggleButton2(this);
        window.add(button, 0);
    }

    public void toggleMyRect() {
        if (myRectangle.getForeground() == Color.white) {
            myRectangle.setForeground(Color.black);
        } else {
            myRectangle.setForeground(Color.white);
        }
    }
}
```

11. Draw a picture of the class diagrams, including all inheritance and aggregation connections between the Driver class, the ToggleButton2 class, and the EventButton class from Exercise 10.

12. What specific user actions result in generating an event for each of the following objects?

   a. an EventRectangle object

   b. an EventSlider object

   c. an EventTextField object

13. For Parts a through c, assume that the field variable is defined by the following code:

```java
EventTextField field = new EventTextField();
field.setBounds(10, 10, 150, 20);
```

a. Write a statement, using `System.out.println`, that will output one half the numeric value of the String constant within field. (For this problem, you must assume that the String value of `field` is a `double` constant such as 32.6 or −198.22.)

b. Write a statement, using `System.out.println`, that will output twice the numeric value of the String constant within `field`. (For this problem, you must assume that the String value of field is an `int` constant such as 3 or −625.)

c. Write a segment of code, using `System.out.println`, that will output "abc" if the String constant within `field` is "true" and "xyz" if it is "false."

Programming Exercises

1. Modify the temperature program from Section 8.6 as follows:

   a. it includes a second slider for specifying Celsius temperature

   b. events on either the Celsius field or the Celsius slider result in a translation from Celsius to Fahrenheit

   c. any event on one of the four interactive objects (the Fahrenheit slider and text field, as well as the Celsius slider and text field) update the other three to have the corresponding values

2. Using inheritance, write a class called `SpottedRect`. A `SpottedRect` object displays a `Rectangle` with a filled `Oval` centered within. The `Oval` must be half as wide and half as high as its `Rectangle`. Your constructor must include parameters to allow the `SpottedRect` objects to be added anywhere and be any size. However, once constructed, `SpottedRect` objects should not change in size. Your `SpottedRect` class must include a `setForeground` method with three int parameters for redness, greenness, and blueness. These parameters accept int arguments in the range from 0 through 255 with the same meaning as the `Color` constructor method. Calling this new `setForeground` method must cause the `Rectangle` object to be colored as specified and the inner `Oval` to be colored in the "opposite" color. For example, for `spottedRect.setColor(0, 255, 100)` the `Rectangle` should have redness of 0, greenness of 255, and blueness of 100, while the `Oval` has redness of 255, greenness of 0, and blueness of 155.

   Write a `Driver` class that constructs two `JFrames`. One `JFrame` is filled with four `SpottedRect` objects. The second `JFrame` contains three `EventSliders`, labeled Red, Green, and Blue. All of the `SpottedRect` objects should respond to any change to the scrollbars by taking on the new color specified by the three scrollbars.

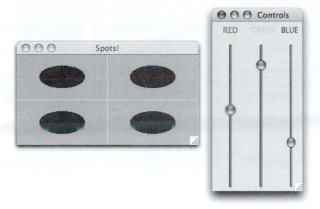

3. This program is an early prototype of an employee payroll system. For this program, three windows appear on the screen. The left window is a place for the user to type information about a single fixed-salary employee. The middle window is a place to enter information about a piece rate employee. The right window is for an hourly employee. All three windows have labeled JTextFields for first name, last name, and job title.[4] All three windows include a Display Employees button across the bottom. Since the three types of employees are all different, the remainder of each window is different. A fixed salary is paid a certain fixed amount each week, so the left window includes a labeled JTextField named Weekly Salary. A piece rate employee is a production worker paid according to the number of items produced. The center window has two labeled JTextFields—one titled Piece Count and the other, Rate per Piece. (If the piece count is 10,000 and the rate per piece is 0.03, then the payment for this work is $300.) The hourly employee is paid an hourly wage, plus time-and-a-half for any work over 40 hours. The right window has two labeled JTextFields named Wage per Hour and Hours Worked.

Your program should display all three windows throughout its execution. The user is expected to type information into the various JTextFields, but no JTextField events need be processed. Clicking the Display Button in the associated window is the user's way to complete the input. This button should cause six lines of output (two for each window) to be appended to the standard output stream. The first line for a window is the name and job title of the employee and the second line is the total wage for the week, given the values specified by the user.

Hint: Use a superclass, called Employee to keep the things that are common to all employees and inherit from this class to make the three different kinds of employee. A separate LabeledField class is also helpful.

---

4. javax.swing.JTextField objects are similar to EventTextField objects, excluding the event handling method.

4. Using inheritance, construct a new class, called `SliderField`. Every `SliderField` object is a filled, rectangular region that is 50 pixels tall and 200 pixels wide. A `SliderField` contains the following three things.

1. a `Label` in the upper left corner with the same background color as the EventSlider, a width of 100 pixels and a height of 20 pixels

2. an `EventTextField` in the upper right corner with a width of 80 pixels and a height of 20 pixels

3. an `EventSlider` centered across the bottom with a width of 150 pixels and a height of 20 pixels

The behavior of a `SliderField` should link the slider and the text field, so that any user action on the slider causes the text field to be updated with the new value of the slider. Similarly, any event upon the text field should cause the scrollbar to take on the value from the text field. In addition, to updating the opposite object, any slider or text field event should call a `SliderField` event, called `SliderFieldUpdated`. This is a parameterless method that can be over-ridden like an event handler. Below is a complete list of the methods that must be included in your `SliderField` class. (Some can be inherited, and others will need to be overridden.)

■ `SliderField()` constructs all the `SliderField` parts described above

■ `getX()` the same as the `getX` for the `JComponent` background

■ `getY()` the same as the `getY` for the `JComponent` background

■ `getWidth()` the same as the `getWidth` for the `JComponent` background

■ `getHeight()` the same as the `getHeight` for the `JComponent` background

■ `setLocation(int, int)` the same as the `setLocation` for the `JComponent` background

■ `repaint()` the same as the repaint for the `JComponent` background

■ `setForeground(Color)` assigns the `JComponent` color and the background color for the `JLabel`

- ■ `setText(String)` same as the `setText` for `JLabel`

- ■ `setMinMaxVal(int, int, int)` sets the values of both the `EventTextField` and the `EventSlider`

- ■ `setValue(int)` sets the values of both the `EventTextField` and the `EventSlider`

- ■ `getValue()` same as the getValue method from `EventSlider`

You should also disable the `setSize` method so that clients cannot alter the size of a `SliderField` object. (Note that your implementation of `SliderField` will require other classes.)

Use two `SliderField` objects to rewrite the temperature conversion program from Section 8.6, so that any change to Fahrenheit updates Celsius and any change to Celsius updates Fahrenheit.

Polymorphism

Yea, all which inherit, shall dissolve, And, like this insubstantial pageant faded, Leave not a rack behind.

—William Shakespeare, *The Tempest*

Objectives

- To explore the concept of hierarchies among classes
- To define type conformance of one object/class to another and to examine the type conformance rules that Java enforces within its expressions, assignments, and parameter passage
- To introduce the `instanceof` notation as a way to test for type conformance
- To examine how methods are associated with objects, rather than the types of variables
- To examine ways in which polymorphism enhances software flexibility and extensibility
- To explore the impact of dynamic binding and polymorphism on runtime execution
- To introduce abstract classes as a mechanism for implementing hierarchical classes that neither require nor permit instantiation
- To introduce the concept of a root class, called `Object`
- To examine the `toString` method as an example of a root class member that is utilized polymorphically

- To compare and contrast identity equality and content equality and to explore how content equality is implemented via the `equals` method
- To introduce the concept of an interface and show how it is used in `java.lang.Comparable`, as well as listener classes
- To introduce the use of interfaces for event delegation

*T*he working world of the modern software engineer consists of a rich collection of interrelated software libraries. There are libraries to provide graphical user interaction, such as *AWT* and *Swing*. There are libraries to provide common system utilities and methods, such as those provided by the `System`, `Scanner`, and `Math` classes. There are also libraries more specifically tailored to the needs of the software development company and project. Remembering, organizing, and utilizing all of these software classes is part of the challenge of modern software development.

The key to using and creating libraries wisely lies in understanding inheritance and the many opportunities it provides. Indeed, most substantive libraries make extensive use of inheritance.

9.1 ■ Inheritance Hierarchies

Like many object-oriented concepts, inheritance is best understood by examining its parallels in the real world. The *is_a* relation and associated concept of specialization provide strong clues to the nature of inheritance.

In the real world are numerous examples of whole *systems* of *is_a* relationships. For example, a chair is a piece of furniture, but so is a bed. Furthermore, there are different specializations of both chairs and beds. Figure 9.1 illustrates one way to look at this system of *is_a* relations.

It is evident from the inheritance relationships of various types of furniture that this system forms a hierarchy. A group of sibling subclasses (i.e., those that share a common parent class) inherit behavior (methods) from their parent. Part of the behavior of a chair is that it is designed for people to sit upon, so child classes of chair should share this behavior. Despite the similar behavior of various chairs, there are also differences. Desk chairs are designed to work ergonomically for office usage; rockers incorporate a rocking mechanism; recliners are capable of tilting backward; and lawn chairs must withstand the weather conditions of the outdoors.

Figure 9.1   A partial hierarchy of *is_a* relations among furniture types

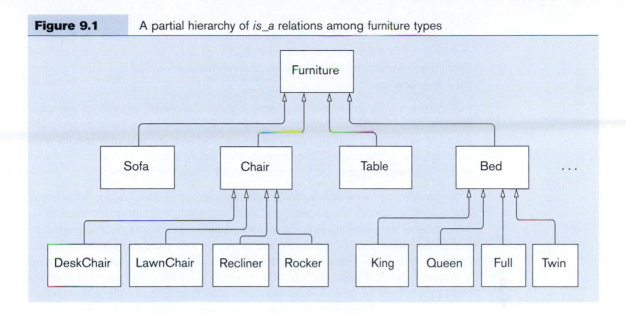

Beds are also furniture, but beds are categorized differently than chairs. A bed is typically classified by its size. A twin bed accommodates a single person, while a king-sized bed is designed for two people. The common property that beds seem to share is that they are designed as places for people to rest.

The furniture hierarchy is one example of a system of *is_a* relations, but there are many others. Perhaps the most complete example of a system of *is_a* relations is the biological classification system. Scientists classify every known animal and plant using an eight-level hierarchy. Each organism belongs to a kingdom, a phylum, a class, an order, a family, a genus, a species, and a variety.

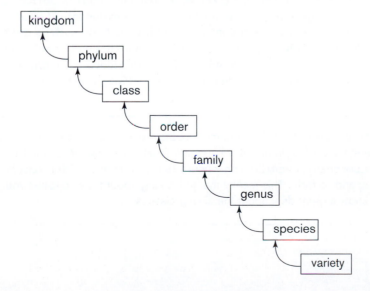

Every *genus* defines certain properties for the organisms that belong to that genus. Some of the properties of a *genus* are inherited from its *family* and are therefore shared by every other *genus* of the same *family*. Similarly, some of the properties of the *family* are inherited from the more general characteristics of the *order* to which the *family* belongs.

Inheritance is really a cumulative process. A particular *species* inherits certain traits from the *genus* to which it belongs; the *genus* inherits some traits from its *family*; the *genus' family* inherits traits from its *order*; and so forth. A particular species is an accumulation of the traits of the *kingdom*, *phylum*, *class*, *order*, *family*, and *genus* to which it belongs; together with the traits that are unique to its *species*.

This cumulative process of inherited characteristics works the same for Java classes. Each subclass inherits the instance variables and methods that are declared in its superclass, as well as all instance variables and methods that may have been inherited by the superclass. For this reason it is helpful to think of the superclass as a **parent** class. This leads to the notion of **ancestor** classes. It is said that class A is an ancestor of class D if and only if A is the parent of D, or the grandparent of D or the great-grandparent of D, and so on. Similarly, class D is defined to be a **descendant** of class A, if A is an ancestor of D. Any Java class can be thought of as the accumulation of its own instance variables and methods together with those inherited from all of its ancestor classes.

The concept of a **system of classes**, or an **inheritance hierarchy**, is extremely useful in software design. Figure 9.2 illustrates such a hierarchy for the JComponent class of the *Swing* library. Each class diagram in the figure includes selected methods that are defined or redefined by the associated class. Informally, JComponent can be thought of as supplying those facilities necessary for implementing a drawable object. Among the many methods of JComponent are add, getParent, getX, getY, getWidth, getHeight, paint, paintChildren, repaint, setBounds, setLocation, and setSize. Some of these methods are inherited from ancestor classes and not overridden. For example, JComponent inherits getBackground, getForeground, getParent, and setBounds from Component. JComponent also inherits add and remove from Container. Other methods, such as getX, getY, getWidth, getHeight, paint, repaint, setBackground, setForeground, setLocation, and setSize; are inherited but overridden by JComponent. Still other methods, like paintChildren, are unique to JComponent objects.

Opening
the Black Box

The author-supplied classes inherit most of their functionality from similar classes in the standard *Swing* and *AWT* libraries. Oval, Line, and Rectangle inherit JComponent; EventButton inherits JButton; EventSlider inherits JSlider; and so forth. This means that in learning about these classes you already know a great deal about the *Swing* classes.

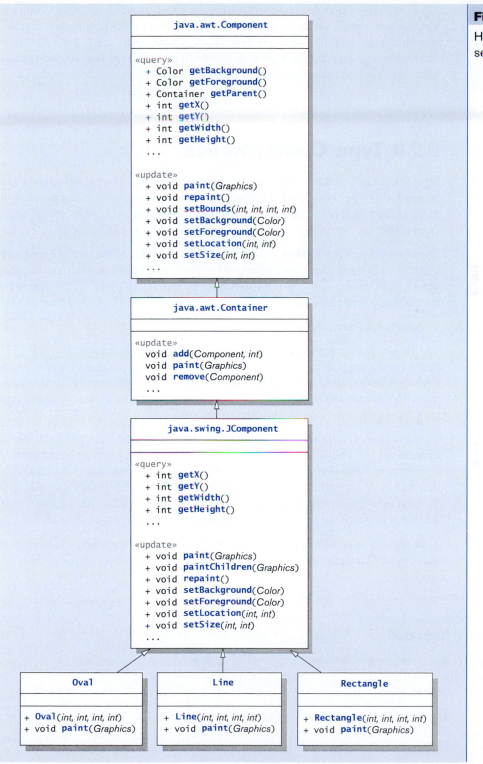

Figure 9.2

Hierarchy of
selected classes

Figure 9.2 shows that `Rectangle` is treated as a specialization of `JComponent`. In fact, the only significant difference between `JComponent` and `Rectangle` is that one is transparent and the other is opaque. Similarly, `Oval` and `Line` are both `JComponent` objects that look a bit different when added. All four of these classes have differing constructor and `paint` methods, but all share the other methods.

9.2 ■ Type Conformance

Figure 9.2 also illustrates that the `add` method, from the `Container` class, has a parameter of type `Component`. This decision may seem unusual, since you are more likely to `add` an `Oval` or a `Rectangle` to a `JComponent` than you are to `add` a `Component`.

The obvious question is: How can user-defined objects be added to a `JComponent`, when the `add` method requires a `Component` parameter? For example, suppose that `donut`, and `donutHole` are both variables of type `Oval`. Why is the following instruction permitted, since `donutHole` belongs to class `Oval` and not `Component`?

```
donut.add(donutHole, 0);
```

The answer to this question lies in Java rules for **type conformance**. You may recall that for primitive data an expression conforms to its own type or any type for which automatic widening is supported. Figure 9.3 contains a definition for type conformance for reference data, along with the associated usage rule. Failure to follow type conformance rules results in compiler errors.

The definition of conformance for reference data states that the type of any object *conforms to* any and all ancestor classes. By this definition, the type of `donutHole` conforms to `Component`, because the type of `donutHole` is `Oval` and `Oval` is a descendant of `Component`. The usage rule from Figure 9.3 points out that it is acceptable to use an expression as long as its type conforms to the required type. Therefore, `donutHole` is an acceptable argument in the previous call to `add`.

Type conformance adds pliability to methods. The same `add` method can be used to place `Oval` (like `donuteHole`) or a `Line` or a `JComponent`, because all of these are

---

Figure 9.3

Type conformance rules for reference types

Definition

A reference expression type *conforms to* its own class or any ancestor class.

Usage Rule

An expression can be used anywhere that its type conforms to the required class type.

descendant classes of (and thereby conform to) `Component`. Type conformance also allows objects of any programmer-created class to be added to `JComponents` or `JFrames`, as long as the developer's new class inherits from `Component` or one of its descendant classes.

As long as inheritance taxonomies represent *is_a* relations, type conformance tends to behave as expected. It is reasonable to expect that if a `Component` can be added to a `JFrame`, then anything else that *is_a* `Component`, such as donut or donutHole, can be added to a `JFrame`.

As a second example of type conformance, consider the task of writing a `boolean` method to identify whether or not two `Rectangle` objects overlap when they are drawn upon the same background. Section 7.5 contains a predicate to check for such situations among `Container` objects. A similar predicate is repeated in Figure 9.4.

This `areOverlapping` predicate accepts two `Component` arguments and checks to see if they overlap. Because of type conformance, the arguments to `areOverlapping` can be of any type conforming to `Component`. Therefore, `areOverlapping` can be used to check whether two `Rectangles` overlap or even to check whether a `Rectangle` overlaps the bounding box of an `Oval`. It would be a waste of time to write a separate predicate to test for overlapping `Rectangles`, since `areOverlapping` already performs such a check for a more general type of parameters (`Component` parameters).

Type conformance is directional. In other words, for any two different types, if the *type1* conforms to *type2*, then *type2* does not necessarily conform to *type1*. To illus-

> software engineering *Hint*
>
> Type conformance of parameters adds pliability to methods.
>
> When the same method is rewritten for different parameter types, this is an indication to consider placing the method in a superclass. The `areOverlapping` method illustrates this.

| Figure 9.4 | `areOverlapping` predicate |

```
/** post:   result == c1 and c2 are overlapping regions placed
 *          upon the same background
 */
private boolean areOverlapping(Component c1, Component c2) {
    boolean overlapHorizontally, overlapVertically;
    if (c1 == null || c2 == null || c1.getParent() == null
        || c1.getParent() != c2.getParent())
    {
        return false;
    } else {
        overlapHorizontally = c1.getX() <= c2.getX()+c2.getWidth()
            && c1.getX()+c1.getWidth() >= c2.getX();
        overlapVertically = c1.getY() <= c2.getY()+c2.getHeight()
            && c1.getY()+c1.getHeight() >= c2.getY();
        return overlapHorizontally && overlapVertically;
    }
}
```

trate the directionality of type conformance, consider the proper classification of the following set of figures as understood from the study of geometry.

- circle
- closed figure (any two-dimensional region with a well-defined perimeter)
- hexagon
- polygon
- quadrilateral
- square
- triangle

The following statements summarize the usual definitions of these figures.

- A circle is a closed figure.
- A polygon is a closed figure.
- A triangle is a three-sided polygon.
- A quadrilateral is a four-sided polygon.
- A hexagon is a six-sided polygon.
- A square is a quadrilateral with four sides of equal length and corners forming right angles.

Figure 9.5 diagrams the appropriate inheritance hierarchy for the *is_a* relations from the above definitions. Assume that these seven classes are implemented with the indicated inheritance taxonomy.

Figure 9.5

Inheritance hierarchy for selected closed figures

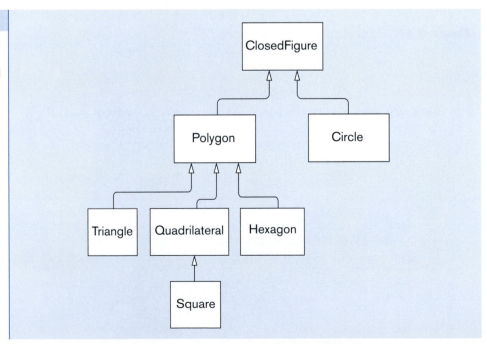

The directional nature of conformance means that it is acceptable to pass an actual argument of type `Square` when the corresponding formal parameter is of type `Polygon`. Similarly, it is acceptable to pass a variable belonging to `Hexagon` for a parameter of `ClosedFigure` type. However, a `Polygon` expression cannot be passed when a `Triangle` parameter is required. Neither can a variable of type `ClosedFigure` be passed when the formal parameter type is `Quadrilateral`.

Previous examples have considered type conformance for parameter passage. A second important use for type conformance applies to assignment instructions. For example, suppose that `myPolygon`, `myTriangle`, `myQuadrilateral`, `myHexagon`, and `mySquare` are all variables of the indicated type. The rules of type conformance permit assignments such as the following.

```
myPolygon = myTriangle;
myQuadrilateral = mySquare;
myPolygon = mySquare;
```

However, the following instructions are all illegal.

```
// The instructions below all violate type conformance rules.
myTriangle = myPolygon;
mySquare = myTriangle;
myTriangle = myHexagon;
```

Once again, the *is_a* relation is the key in understanding how type conformance works in assignment instructions. Since `Triangle`, `Quadrilateral`, `Hexagon`, and `Square` all have an *is_a* relation with `Polygon`, it is sensible to allow a `Polygon` variable to name any of these kinds of objects. (The type of the object is an instance of the type of the variable.) On the other hand, it does not make sense to assign a polygon to a square because the polygon is not guaranteed to be a square. (It might be a hexagon or a triangle.) Similarly, an expression of type `Polygon` cannot be assigned to a variable of type `Hexagon`, such as the following:

```
// The instruction below violates type conformance rules.
myHexagon = myPolygon;
```

On the other hand, every hexagon is certain to be a polygon, so the instruction below is allowed.

```
myPolygon = myHexagon;
```

The ability to assign variables, and therefore objects, of conforming type means that a variable can often bind to different types of objects. Sometimes it is useful for a program to test the type of the variable's binding. Java provides for such a test in the form of a relational operator called **instanceof**. Figure 9.6 describes the syntax and semantics of `instanceof`.

As an example usage of `instanceof`, consider checking the type of object that is assigned to the `myPolygon` variable. The *if* instruction on the following page performs such a test and prints out a message that is appropriate for each possible type. Notice that this code works properly *only* if the condition testing for conformance to one class precedes tests for conformance to ancestor classes.

Figure 9.6   *Instanceof* description (a *BooleanExpression*)

Syntax

Notes

■ *ObjectExpression* is any expression that evaluates to some object, such as a variable name, parameter, method, etc.

■ *TypeName* is the name of some known class or primitive type.

Semantics

Executing an *Instanceof* expression returns the value `true` exactly when the value of *ObjectExpression* conforms to *TypeName*.

```
if (myPolygon instanceof Square) {
    System.out.println("myPolygon references a Square.");
} else if (myPolygon instanceof Quadrilateral) {
    System.out.println("myPolygon references a
        Quadrilateral.");
} else if (myPolygon instanceof Triangle) {
    System.out.println("myPolygon references a Triangle.");
} else if (myPolygon instanceof Hexagon) {
    System.out.println("myPolygon references a Hexagon.");
} else if (myPolygon instanceof Polygon) {
    System.out.println("myPolygon references a Polygon.");
}
```

9.3 ■ Subtype Polymorphism

As explained in the previous section, the rules of type conformance allow a variable of one type to bind to an object of another type (as long as the object type conforms to the variable's class). This permits, for example, a variable belonging to the `ClosedFigure` class to bind to an object of type `Circle` at one time and a `Square` object at a later time. This ability of a variable to bind to varying objects (including objects of varying type) is referred to as **dynamic binding**.

When a variable changes its binding, there is always the potential that the class of the new object differs from the variable's own type (as long as the new type conforms). For example, executing the following instruction binds `myPolygon` to some object of type `Square`.

```
myPolygon = squareExpression;
```

If at some future time, the following instruction executes

```
myPolygon = hexagonExpression;
```

myPolygon becomes dynamically bound to a different object, and this new object belongs to the Hexagon class.

The ability of a single variable (or parameter) to refer to objects of differing type is known as **subtype polymorphism** or just **polymorphism**. The roots of this word come from Greek words "poly," meaning *many* and "morph" meaning *structure* or *shape*.

The key to understanding polymorphism can be expressed in two statements.

1. Objects do not change the class to which they belong, but a variable may be bound dynamically to different types of objects.

2. The behavior of each object (i.e., the method versions that are called) is determined by the *object's* class, rather than the variable's type.

The second statement above is a direct result of encapsulation. An object is very much like the class to which it belongs. The object contains all instance variables that are declared or inherited by its class. Similarly, the object utilizes the methods whose code comes from its class. This connection between object and method is particularly important when methods are overridden, making different versions of the same method available within the class hierarchy.

For example, suppose that the ClosedFigure class includes a method, called perimeter, that returns the perimeter of ClosedFigure objects. Figure 9.7 contains partial classes for Circle and Square. The Circle and Square classes each

```
public class Circle extends ClosedFigure {
    private double radius;
    // Additional code omitted from here.

    /** post: result == radius * 2 * Math.PI */
    public double perimeter() {
        return radius * 2 * Math.PI;
    }
}


public class Square extends Quadrilateral {
    private double sideLength;
    // Additional code omitted from here.

    /** post: result == sideLength * 4 */
    public double perimeter() {
        return sideLength * 4;
    }
}
```

Figure 9.7

Overridden perimeter method for Circle and Square class

contain their own version of the `perimeter` method. Each version uses a calculation for `perimeter` that is appropriate for that particular kind of closed figure. The `Circle` class includes a `radius` variable, so the `perimeter` method returns `(radius * 2 * Math.PI)`. The `Square` class includes a variable called `sideLength`, so the `perimeter` method returns `(sideLength * 4)`.

Now suppose the following instruction is executed.

```
System.out.println(closedFigureVar.perimeter());
```

This instruction calls the version of `perimeter` that is consistent with the object bound to `closedFigureVar`. If `closedFigureVar` has been assigned a `Circle` object, then `Circle`'s method is called, calculating perimeter based upon `radius`. If `closedFigureVar` has been assigned a `Square` type object, then `Square`'s method is called and perimeter is calculated based upon `sideLength`.

As a more complete program demonstrating polymorphism, consider a program to demonstrate cake cutting geometry. Cake cutting is done in different ways for different cake shapes. To slice a rectangular cake into eight slices, most people would cut the pieces as shown below.

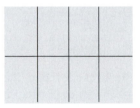

However, when asked to slice a round cake into eight equal pieces, the more typical solution results in the wedge-shaped cake slices shown below.

These options lead to a programming solution that uses a superclass called `Cake` and two subclasses: `CircularCake` and `SquareCake`. Figure 9.8 shows the class diagram for this collection of classes.

There are two polymorphic methods of interest in this example: `paintCake` and `paintEighthCuts`. As its name implies, the `paintCake` method draws the image of the cake (either rectangular or circular) on the `JComponent`. The `paintEighthCuts` method is included to draw black lines to indicate how to cut the cake into eight equal pieces. Both of these methods are passed a `java.awt.Graphics` parameter to give them the context upon which to draw their images. Figure 9.9 shows code for the `RectangularCake` class.

Figure 9.8   Class diagram for cake classes

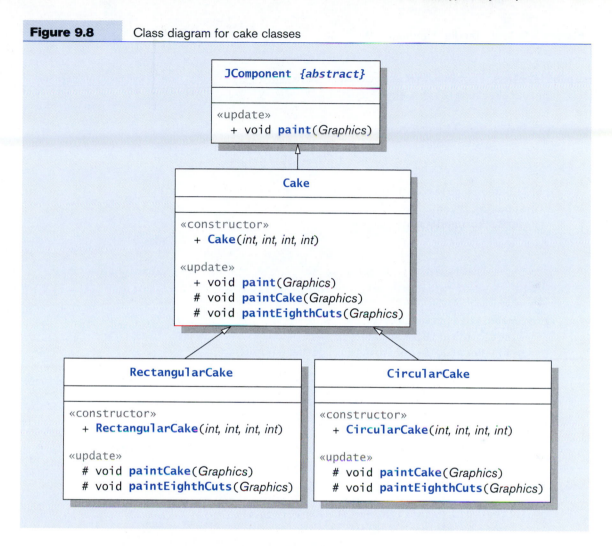

The constructor method for `RectangularCake` calls its superclass constructor, passing values to establish the bounding rectangle for the cake. The constructor also assigns the background color to yellow. Executing `paintCake` causes the cake to be drawn filling the bounding rectangle and using the background color. A call to the `paintEighthCuts` method draws four lines. The first two lines split the cake into quarters by drawing horizontally and vertically through its center. The *if* statement is used to draw two more lines to split the quarters in half perpendicular to their longest side.

Figure 9.10 shows the code for the `CircularCake` class. The `CircularCake` constructor is quite similar to the constructor method from `RectangularCake`, except that only three parameters are needed (for *x*, *y*, and diameter). The `CircularCake` constructor uses for the color (pink) and cake's shape (Oval).

Figure 9.9   The RectangularCake class

```java
import java.awt.*;
public class RectangularCake extends Cake {
    privateRectangle theCake;

    /** post:  getX() == x and getY() == y
     *         and getWidth() == w and getHeight() == h
     *         and getBackground == Color.yellow
     */
    public RectangularCake(int x, int y, int w, int h) {
        super(x, y, w, h);
        setBackground(Color.yellow);
    }

    /** post:  the cake is drawn as a rectangle filling the bounding rectangle
     *         and the color of the cake is getBackground()
     */
    protected void paintCake(Graphics g) {
        g.setColor(getBackground());
        g.fillRect(0, 0, getWidth(), getHeight());
    }

    /** post:  two black lines (one vertical and one horizontal) divide
     *            the cake into fourths
     *         and getWidth() > getHeight() implies the cake is separated by
     *            two more vertical lines making 8 equal-sized pieces.
     *         and getWidth() <= getHeight() implies the cake is separated by
     *            two more horizontal lines making 8 equal-sized pieces.
     */
    protected void paintEighthCuts(Graphics g) {
        g.setColor(Color.black);
        g.drawLine(0, getHeight()/2, getWidth(), getHeight()/2);
        g.drawLine(getWidth()/2, 0, getWidth()/2, getHeight());
        if (getWidth() > getHeight()) {
            g.drawLine(getWidth()/4, 0, getWidth()/4, getHeight());
            g.drawLine(getWidth()*3/4, 0, getWidth()*3/4, getHeight());
        } else {
            g.drawLine(0, getHeight()/4, getWidth(), getHeight()/4);
            g.drawLine(0, getHeight()*3/4, getWidth(), getHeight()*3/4);
        }
    }
}
```

Figure 9.10   The `CircularCake` class

```java
import java.awt.*;
public class CircularCake extends Cake {

    /** post:  getX() == x and getY() == y
     *         and getWidth() == getHeight() == d
     *         and getBackground() == Color.pink
     */
    public CircularCake(int x, int y, int d) {
        super(x, y, d, d);
        setBackground(Color.pink);
    }


    /** post:  the cake is drawn as an oval filling the bounding rectangle
     *         and the color of the cake is getBackground()
     */
    protected void paintCake(Graphics g) {
        g.setColor(getBackground());
        g.fillOval(0, 0, getWidth(), getHeight());
    }


    /** post:  four black lines are drawn through the cake center to form
     *         eight wedge-shaped pieces of equal size.
     */
    protected void paintEighthCuts(Graphics g) {
        int ds, dl;
        g.setColor(Color.black);
        // draw horizontal and vertical lines, respectively
        g.drawLine(0, getHeight()/2, getWidth(), getHeight()/2);
        g.drawLine(getWidth()/2, 0, getWidth()/2, getHeight());

        // draw diagonal lines
        ds = (int)((getWidth() - getWidth()/Math.sqrt(2.0)) / 2.0);
        dl = (int)(getWidth() / Math.sqrt(2.0)) + ds;
        g.drawLine(ds, ds, dl, dl);
        g.drawLine(ds, dl, dl, ds);
    }
}
```

Similar to `RectangularCake`, the `paintEighthCuts` method of `CircularCake` sections the cake by drawing horizontal and vertical lines to quarter the cake. Calculating the coordinates of the endpoints for the two diagonal lines is slightly more involved. Figure 9.11 shows how program variables are used to accomplish the diagonal line positioning.

The dashed-line square in Figure 9.11 represents the border of the `JComponent` background for the cake. The gray oval upon this square has a width that is identical to its height. The local variables `ds` and `dl` are used to calculate the coordinates of the endpoints for the diagonals. One diagonal is drawn from coordinate (`ds`, `ds`) to (`dl`, `dl`), and the second is drawn from coordinate (`ds`, `dl`) to (`dl`, `ds`). Formulas for the values of `ds` and `dl` can be discovered by examining the following circle with a chord (the dotted line) connecting the endpoints of the two diagonals.

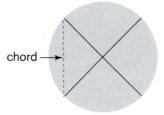

This chord is the hypotenuse of a right triangle that has halves of the diagonal lines for legs. Since the length of each leg is `getWidth()/2`, the Pythagorean theorem can be applied to conclude that

$$\texttt{chord}^2 \;==\; (\texttt{getWidth()}/2)^2 \;+\; (\texttt{getWidth()}/2)^2$$

which simplifies to

$$\texttt{chord} \;==\; \texttt{getWidth()}/\sqrt{2}$$

Figure 9.11

The `CircularCake` diagonal lines

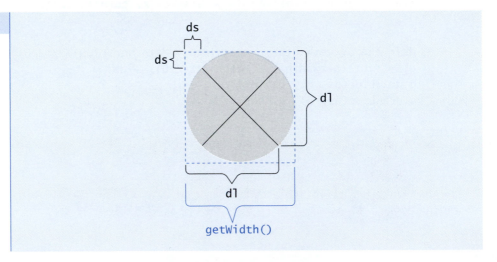

Next notice that the length of one side of the JComponent (getWidth()) is equal to the chord plus twice ds. This leads to the conclusion that

ds == (getWidth() - getWidth()/√2̄)/2

The value of d1 can be calculated by adding the length of the chord to the ds, as shown below.

d1 == (getWidth() / √2̄) + ds

These last two equations for ds and d1 are the two that are used within the CircularCake class.

To observe how nicely polymorphism encapsulates differences *inside* the classes it is useful to examine a client of these two cakes. Figure 9.12 illustrates such client in the form of a Driver class.

Every call to the cutTheCake method in the class from Figure 9.12 constructs a new object and assigns it to theCake. This new object is randomly selected to either be of type CircularCake or RectangularCake. This Driver class is designed for use in conjunction with a button, whose event handler calls back to cutTheCake for every button click action. Figure 9.13 contains the code for such a CakeButton class.

Clicking CakeButton, causes a callback to the Driver's cutTheCake which in turn creates a new cake. So where are the calls to paintCake and paintEighthCuts and how is the polymorphism employed? The answer to this question lies with the Cake class. One version of Cake is shown in Figure 9.14.

Like other JComponent subclasses, Cake overrides the paint method to draw its image. This Cake version of paint provides the key to how polymorphism is used in this program. Every time paint is called, it calls paintCake and paintEighthCuts. Cake includes both methods, but they have only empty bodies.[1] However, it is *not* the Cake version of paintCake and paintEighthCuts that are called when the program executes. Instead, paint calls the subclass versions (polymorphically) thereby drawing the proper cake and cutting lines associated with the particular kind of cake.

Polymorphism frequently improves code **extensibility**. Extensibility refers to the ease with which software can be modified (extended) to solve problems other than the initial intent. To see how the cake program is extensible, consider the problem of adding additional types of cakes (perhaps a heart-shaped cake, a triangular cake, a diamond-shaped cake, or some other geometry). Each new cake is implemented in the form of a class that inherits Cake and overrides paintCake and paintEighthCuts. Clients can use these new cake classes with minimal modification.

Subtype polymorphism relies upon method overriding in the context of inheritance. Dynamic binding means that theCake variable simultaneously assumes both the identity and the associated behavior of each object assigned to it. When theCake is bound to a CircularCake object, then paintCake and paintEighthCuts use cir-

---

1. Figure 9.18 provides a better alternative than using methods with empty bodies.

Figure 9.12   The Driver class for the cake program

```java
import javax.swing.JFrame;
public class Driver {
    private JFrame window;
    private Cake theCake;
    private CakeButton sliceButton;

    /** post:  window is created at (10, 10) with width and height of 400
     *         and sliceButton is added to window
     *         and theCake is constructed as a CircularCake object
     */
    public Driver() {
        window = new JFrame("Cake Cutter");
        window.setBounds(10, 10, 400, 400);
        window.setVisible(true);
        window.setLayout(null);
        theCake = new CircularCake(100, 100, 200);
        window.add(theCake, 0);
        sliceButton = new CakeButton(75, 5, this);
        window.add(sliceButton, 0);
        window.repaint();
    }

    /** pre:   theCake != null
     * post:   theCake@pre is removed from window
     *         and a new theCake is constructed & placed on window
     *             (The new cake has a 50-50 chance of being circular
     *             or rectangular.)
     */
    public void cutTheCake() {
        window.remove(theCake);
        if (Math.random() > 0.5) {
            theCake = new CircularCake(100, 100, (int)(Math.random()*200+1));
        } else {
            theCake = new RectangularCake(100, 150, 200,
                (int)(Math.random()*300+1));
        }
        window.add(theCake, 0);
        window.repaint();
    }
}
```

Figure 9.13   The CakeButton class

```java
import java.awt.event.ActionEvent;
public class CakeButton extends EventButton {
    private Driver driver;

    /** pre:    d != null
     *  post:   getX() == x and getY() == y
     *          and getWidth() == 250 and getHeight() == 30
     *          and getText() == "make and slice a new cake"
     *          and driver == d
     */
    public CakeButton(int x, int y, Driver d) {
        super("make and slice a new cake");
        setBounds(x, y, 250, 30);
        driver = d;
    }

    /** pre:    driver != null
     *  note:   the cutTheCake method from driver is performed.
     */
    public void actionPerformed(ActionEvent e) {
        driver.cutTheCake();
    }
}
```

cular cake behavior. When `theCake` is bound to a `RectangularCake`, then `paintCake` and `paintEighthCuts` use rectangular cake behavior.

The superclass (`Cake` in the example) plays a critical role in this polymorphism for two reasons:

1. Different kinds of objects conform to `theCake`, because they inherit from `Cake`.

2. `Cake` provides superclass methods, such as `paintCake` and `paintEighthCuts`, that can be overridden.

The Java compiler permits a method to be called upon a variable only if that method is appropriate for the declared type of the variable. In other words, since `theCake` is declared as type `Cake`, the compiler will allow only methods that are included in `Cake` to be called upon `theCake`, although it may be descendant class versions of these methods that actually execute. Therefore, `paintCake` and `paintEighthCuts` *must* be included within the `Cake` class.

Figure 9.14   The Cake class

```java
// This class is better implemented as shown in Figure 9.18
import javax.swing.JComponent;
import java.awt.Graphics;
public class Cake extends JComponent {

    /** post:  getX() == x and getY() == y
     *         and getWidth() == w and getHeight() == h
     */
    public Cake(int x, int y, int w, int h) {
        super();
        setBounds(x, y, w, h);
    }

    /** post:  a cake is drawn with lines for cutting into eighths
     */
    public void paint(Graphics g) {
        paintCake(g);
        paintEighthCuts(g);
        paintChildren(g);
    }

    /** post:  the cake is drawn
     * note:  this method must be overridden to be useful
     */
    protected void paintCake(Graphics g) { }

    /** post:  the lines are drawn for cutting the cake into eighths
     * note:  this method must be overridden to be useful
     */
    protected void paintEighthCuts(Graphics g) { }
}
```

This general solution of having a superclass with methods that are ultimately implemented in different forms by subclasses is used so often that it is given a special name, namely the **Template Design Pattern.** The word "template" is appropriate, since the superclass is never really intended to be used for creating objects, but to be inherited only by subclasses that supply object types. Figure 9.15 explains the Template Design Pattern further.

The Template Design Pattern is the usual mechanism through which polymorphism provides extendibility. The template class includes methods, like `paintCake` and `paintEighthCuts`, that allow for extension. A class for a different shaped cake is obligated to provide its own version of these methods.

Figure 9.15

The Template
Design Pattern

Template Design Pattern

When a variable, call it *v*, must take on the value of differing types of objects and perform different tasks for the same method, then one approach is as follows.

- Declare *v* to belong to class *S*.
- Class *S* must include all methods whose behavior will be overridden by subtypes. (Some or all of these methods may have empty bodies or be abstract in *S*.)
- Subclasses of *S* should override the methods and supply the behavior that is specific to their class.
- Assigning *v* objects from the subclasses of *S* permits the overridden methods to use the behavior from the subclass.

(See Section 9.3 for an example.)

The Template Design Pattern also demonstrates another form of encapsulation and information hiding. The differences between each cake are largely encapsulated within different versions of the paintCake and paintEighthCuts methods. This provides effective information hiding, because the client code does not need to know that different types of cakes require different cake-cutting code.

9.4 ■ **Abstract Classes**

There are times when a class exists solely to serve as a template superclass, supplying methods that can be overridden. The Cake class from Section 9.3 illustrates because Cake *never* needs to be instantiated. Client code may declare variables of type Cake, but it is the child classes of Cake that are instantiated and the resulting objects that are bound to Cake variables. If a Cake object is instantiated, it can serve no useful purpose. An object of type Cake has no visible form. Worse yet, an object of type Cake has paintCake and paintEighthCuts methods that do nothing when executed.

Java provides an alternative mechanism for declaring a class that never needs to be instantiated, such as Cake. This mechanism is called an **abstract class**. Abstract classes are virtual entities because it is impossible to construct an object belonging to an abstract class. Abstract classes, however, are still quite useful since they can supply the type for variables and parameters. Abstract classes can also be inherited, and their protected and public instance variables and methods are available for use by a subclass. Classes that are not abstract are often referred to as **concrete classes**.

Figure 9.16 contains the syntax and semantics necessary to specify an abstract class. Syntactically, the only required change for the class shell is the reserved word "abstract" that must appear immediately before the "class" identifier.

software *Hint*
engineering

When a class is needed solely to serve as a template class (i.e., it will never be instantiated), then such a class should be written as an **abstract class**. Abstract classes are still able to supply code and can be inherited, making them useful within a class hierarchy.

Figure 9.16

AbstractClass description (abridged version of *Class*)

Syntax

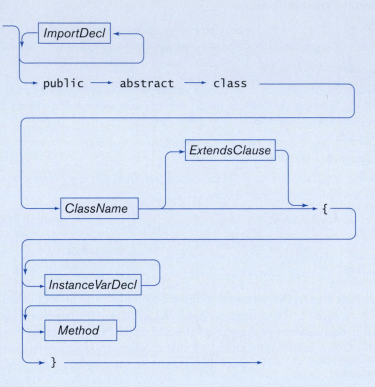

Semantics

An abstract class can be used as the type of a variable or parameter. It can be inherited. Its protected and public instance variables and methods are available to subclasses. An abstract class cannot be instantiated via new.

An abstract class can contain abstract methods (see Figure 9.17). If a class contains an abstract method, then the class must be an abstract class.

Notes

- *ImportDecl* is any single import declaration.
- *ClassName* is an identifier that names the abstract class.
- *ExtendsClause* is an optional inheritance clause.
- *InstanceVarDecl* is any valid instance variable declaration.
- Method is any valid method declaration, including an abstract method.

One of the benefits of an abstract class over a concrete class is the possibility of including **abstract methods**. Figure 9.17 shows the syntax and semantics for an abstract method. An abstract method is one in which the body of the method is left

Figure 9.17   ***AbstractMethod*** description (abridged version of *Method*)

Syntax

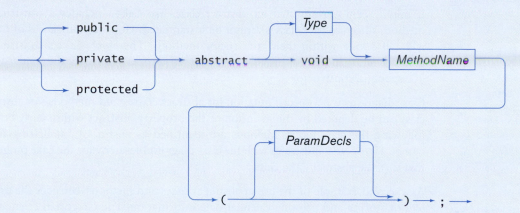

Semantics

An *AbstractMethod* has no body. Therefore, the class that contains an abstract method must be declared as an abstract class. Furthermore, any class that inherits an abstract method must either override it to be nonabstract or be declared as an abstract class.

Notes

- *MethodName* is an identifier. Each method within the same class must either have a unique name or a different number and/or type of parameters.
- *ParamDecls* is a list of formal parameters and their types.
- *Type* can be any accessible class name.

unspecified. Syntactically, Java requires that a semicolon (;) be placed in an abstract method where the curly braces and body are located from nonabstract methods.

There are two key rules regarding the inclusion of abstract methods:

1. Any class that includes an abstract method is required to be an abstract class and must be so declared.

2. Any class inheriting a class with abstract methods must either override the methods or else it, too, is an abstract class.

The Cake class from the program discussed in Section 9.3 is an ideal candidate to be coded as an abstract class. Like many of the template design pattern situations, the Cake class is included only to provide a common superclass for the more specific kinds of cakes. Furthermore, paintCake and paintEighthCuts should be abstract

software *Hint*
engineering
Declaring a method to be abstract forces a subclass to provide an implementation. Abstract methods are a good idea when descendant classes should be forced to tailor the method to their particular needs.

software **Hint**
engineering
Often there is a
choice between
using an abstract
method or a
method that pro-
vides a default
behavior. An
abstract method
is the better
choice if sub-
classes should
be forced to sup-
ply behavior.

methods because there is no sensible implementation without knowing more about the kind of cake being cut. Figure 9.18 contains an appropriate abstract class for Cake.

It might seem curious that an abstract class, like Cake, includes a constructor method, since abstract classes cannot be instantiated. However, subclasses of Cake will call super within their constructor methods. Therefore, Cake's constructor method is included to provide a means to properly invoke the underlying JComponent constructor.

Class diagrams use a special notation for abstract classes and methods. An abstract class can be denoted by the inclusion of the property **abstract** within curly braces following the class name. Methods are identified as abstract by italicizing their names. Figure 9.19 illustrates with the class diagram hierarchy for the cake program that uses the abstract Cake class.

As a second example of the use of abstract classes and methods, consider the problem of storing and printing calendar date information. The Gregorian calendar is

Figure 9.18   The Cake abstract class

```java
import javax.swing.JComponent;
import java.awt.Graphics;
public abstract class Cake extends JComponent {

    /** post:  getX() == x and getY() == y
     *          and getWidth() == w and getHeight() == h
     */
    public Cake(int x, int y, int w, int h) {
        super();
        setBounds(x, y, w, h);
    }

    /** post:  a cake is drawn with lines for cutting into eighths */
    public void paint(Graphics g) {
        paintCake(g);
        paintEighthCuts(g);
        paintChildren(g);
    }

    /** post:  the cake is drawn */
    protected abstract void paintCake(Graphics g);

    /** post:  the lines are drawn for cutting the cake into eighths */
    protected abstract void paintEighthCuts(Graphics g);
}
```

Figure 9.19   Class diagram for cake classes with an abstract Cake class

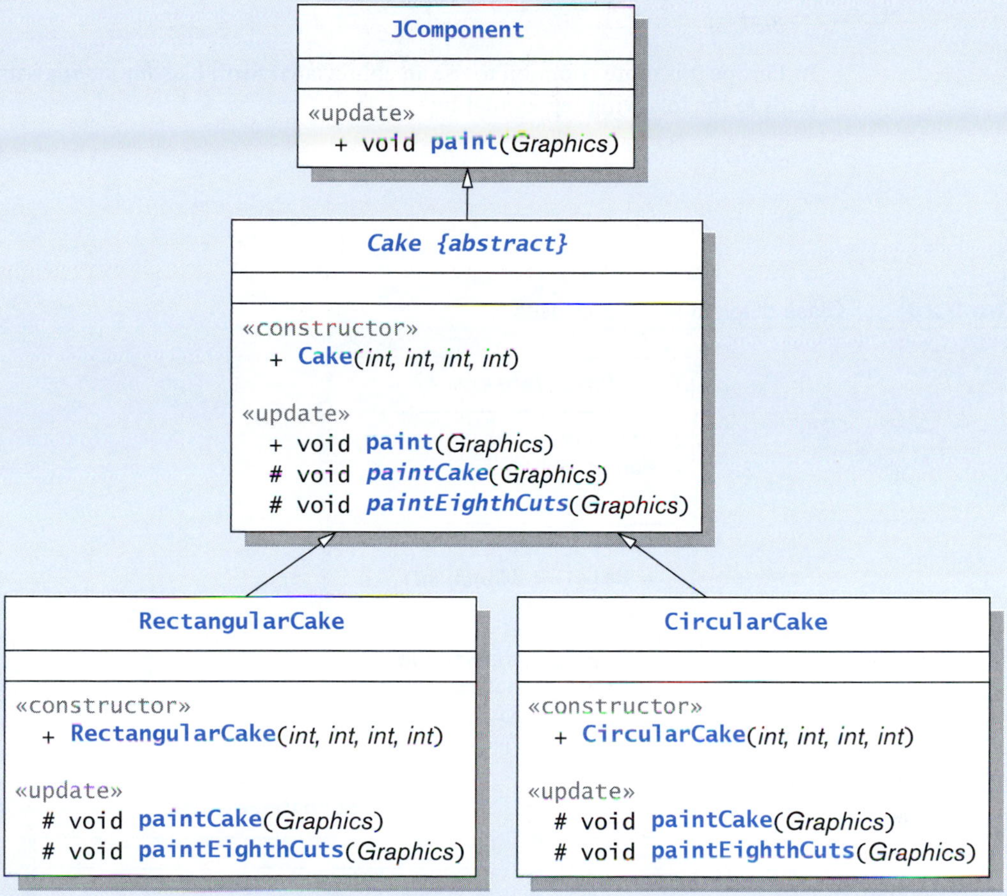

widely recognized around the world, as a way to keep track of a date in terms of a year number (A.D.), a month within the year, and a day within the month.

There is far less agreement about precisely how to represent a date. In written letters, many people represent a date in a form such as the one below.

Mar. 27, 1951

Around the time of the American Revolution, the English language was written in more formal notations. In those days the date above may well have been written as follows.

Day 27 during the month of March in the year of our Lord, 1951

Today, Americans tend to abbreviate dates in the form *month/day/year*, often representing the month as a number and the year with only the last two digits. Using this notation, the above date is denoted as follows.

3/27/51

In Europe it is more common to use an abbreviated form like *day.month.year* which leads to the following representation.

27.3.51

Figure 9.20   Class diagram for date classes

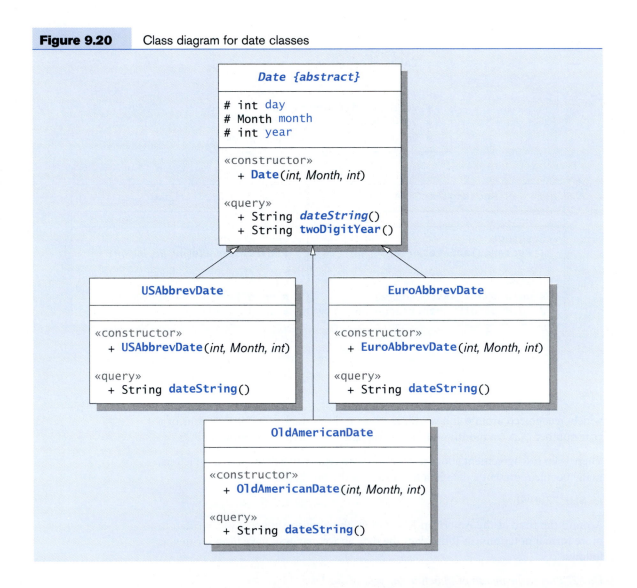

This variation in the way that dates are represented suggests that the template design pattern might be a good way to implement an abstract class called Date. Figure 9.20 contains a class diagram for Date, together with three concrete subclasses. The key abstract method within Date is called dateString. This method is expected to return the desired form of the date representation.

The code for the Date class and the associated Month enumerated type is shown in Figure 9.21. Notice that abstract classes may contain nonabstract members. The Date class contains three instance variables, as well as a constructor and twoDigitYear methods.

Figure 9.21   The Date class

```
/** an enumerated type for months */
public enum Month {
    January, February, March, April, May, June, July,
    August, September, October, November, December;
}

public abstract class Date {
    protected int day;         // day within a month
    protected Month month;
    protected int year;        // full calendar year (A.D.)

    /** pre:   1 <= m <= 12
     *         and d is a sensible day for month m
     *         (Note that this method doesn't check date validity)
     * post:   day == d and month == m and year == y
     */
    public Date(int d, Month m, int y) {
        day = d;
        month = m;
        year = y;
    }

    /** post:  result is the last two digits of year */
    public String twoDigitYear() {
        return "" + year % 100;
    }

    /** post:  result is some appropriate string form of the date */
    public abstract String dateString();
}
```

Abstract classes frequently include nonabstract methods that are expected to be useful to subclasses. The twoDigitYear method is an example. The Date class stores each month as an enumerated (Month) type. Many date abbreviations depict just the last two digits of the year, so the twoDigitYear method is included to translate the full (four-digit) form of the year to the last two digits.

Figure 9.22 shows the code for three possible concrete subclasses, USAbbrevDate, EuroAbbrevDate, and OldAmericanDate. Each of these classes is designed for a different form of date representation.

Figure 9.23 contains a Driver class that can be used to test the four date classes. This Driver illustrates the use of type conformance and polymorphism by declaring its three local variables to belong to the abstract Date class, then assigning them objects from the concrete subclasses.

Figure 9.22	USAbbrevDate, EuroAbbrevDate, and OldAmericanDate

```java
public class USAbbrevDate extends Date {
    /** pre:    1 <= m <= 12
     *          and d is a sensible day for month m
     *          (Note that this method doesn't check date validity)
     * post:    day == d and month == m and year == y
     */
    public USAbbrevDate(int d, Month m, int y) {
        super(d, m, y);
    }

    /** post:   result is a string in the form "m/d/y2"
     *          where m is the month number, d is the day number
     *          and y2 is the last two digits of the year.
     */
    public String dateString() {
        return "" + (month.ordinal()+1) + "/" + day + "/" + twoDigitYear();
    }
}


public class EuroAbbrevDate extends Date {
    /** pre:    1 <= m <= 12
     *          and d is a sensible day for month m
     *          (Note that this method doesn't check date validity)
     * post:    day == d and month == m and year == y
     */
    public EuroAbbrevDate(int d, Month m, int y) {
        super(d, m, y);
    }
```

```java
public class Driver {
    public Driver() {
        Date sandiBirthday;
        Date derekBirthday;
        Date kasBirthday;
        sandiBirthday = new OldAmericanDate(27, Month.March, 1951);
        System.out.println(sandiBirthday.dateString());
        derekBirthday = new USAbbrevDate(17, Month.November, 1981);
        System.out.println(derekBirthday.dateString());
        kasBirthday = new EuroAbbrevDate(9, Month.October, 1979);
        System.out.println(kasBirthday.dateString());
    }
}
```

Figure 9.23

Driver for the date program

```java
    /** post:  result is a string in the form "d.m.y2"
     *         where d is the day number, m is the month number
     *         and y2 is the last two digits of the year.
     */
    public String dateString() {
        return "" + day + "." + (month.ordinal()+1) + "." + twoDigitYear();
    }
}

public class OldAmericanDate extends Date {
    /** pre:   1 <= m <= 12
     *         and d is a sensible day for month m
     *         (Note that this method doesn't check date validity)
     * post:   day == d and month == m and year == y
     */
    public OldAmericanDate(int d, Month m, int y) {
        super(d, m, y);
    }

    /** post:  result is a string in the form
     *         "day d during the month of m in the year of our Lord, y"
     *         where d, m and y are, respectively, day, month & year.
     */
    public String dateString() {
        return "day " + day + " during the month of " + month.name()
                + " in the year of our Lord, " + year;
    }
}
```

The Template Design Pattern is used in the author-supplied class called ThreeButtons. This class has the following general form:

```java
public abstract class ThreeButtons {
    public abstract void leftAction();
    public abstract void midAction();
    public abstract void rightAction();
    ...
}
```

9.5 ■ The Object Class

Class hierarchies are so central to the concept of object-oriented programming that true object-oriented languages incorporate a **root class**. The root class is a class that is automatically inherited by every other class. In Java the name of the root class is Object.

Object is an implicit ancestor class for every other Java class. There is no need for import or the extends syntax in order to inherit Object, nor can a class choose not to inherit from Object. Figure 9.24 contains a class diagram and class specification for two of the most important members of the Object class.

The two Object methods that are shown in Figure 9.24 are toString and equals. Because these are Object methods, they are accessible to every Java object. (The equals method is examined in Section 9.6.) The toString method is intended to be a standard way to translate any object into a useful string representation. The default implementation for toString returns a string that typically includes the object's class and memory location.

For example, the following code can be executed without altering any of the Date classes shown previously.

```java
Date bevBirthday;
bevBirthday = new OldAmericanDate(29, 3, 1948);
System.out.println(bevBirthday.toString());
```

software
engineering *Hint*

The implementation of toString that is inherited from Object is not particularly useful. Overriding toString is an idea always worthy of consideration.

When the last instruction executes, the default implementation of toString that was inherited from Object outputs a line such as the following.

```
OldAmericanDate@1289161
```

This output gives the type of the object OldAmericanDate and an identification number (1289161) that is unique to this object.

Since the default implementation of toString is not particularly useful, many classes will choose to override the method. The Date class (previously shown in Figure 9.21) can be modified to include a better toString method as shown in Figure 9.25.

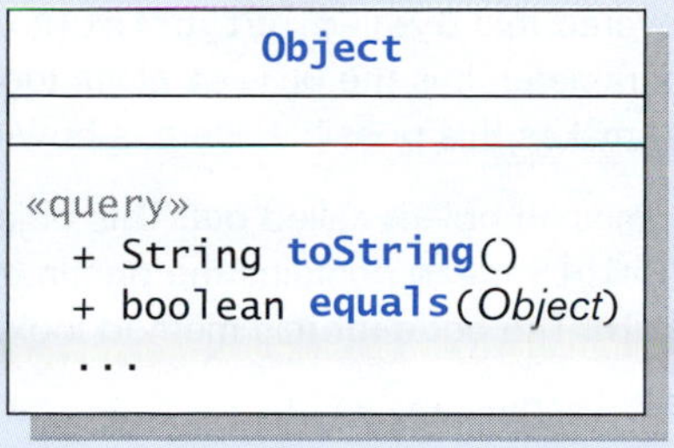

Figure 9.24

A class diagram and specification for `Object`

```
           Object

«query»
  + String toString()
  + boolean equals(Object)
  ...
```

public String **toString** ( )

    post: *result* is some string representation of this object. Subclasses are encouraged to override this method.

public boolean **equals** (Object other)

    post: other is the same as this *implies* *result* == true
        and other is different from this *implies* *result* == false

    note: The default behavior is the same as ==.
        Overriding equals is encouraged to permit testing for content equality

With a `Date` class as modified in Figure 9.25, the following code works differently than before.

```
Date bevBirthday;
bevBirthday = new OldAmericanDate(29, 3, 1948);
System.out.println(bevBirthday.toString());
```

Now when `toString` executes, the `Date` version of `toString` is used. (This version of the method is inherited by `OldAmercianDate`.) Therefore, the following line is output.

```
March 29, 1948
```

Figure 9.25

A `Date` class that includes `toString`

```
public abstract class Date {
    // The innards of the Date class from Figure 9.21 have been
    // omitted for clarity reasons. They should be placed here.
    public String toString() {
        return "" + month.name() + " " + day + ", " + year;
    }
}
```

Opening
the Black Box

In Chapter 5 we discovered that System.out.println could be called with any Java object as a parameter. It is the Object class together with its toString method that makes this possible. Here is how it works:

The System class contains an object called out. This object belongs to a class called PrintStream. PrintStream contains the println method that is called by System.out.println. The code for this method looks like the following.

```
public void println(Object z) {
    println(z.toString());
}
```

When the above version of println is called, it outputs the string returned by z.toString(). In other words, println outputs whatever is returned from calling toString. If the programmer does not override toString, then println outputs the default string from the Object class implementation of toString. However, if toString is overridden for the object to be printed, then println will use the overriding version.

9.6 ■ Equality by Content and by Identity

In Java the "==" operator tests for equality. When two object references are compared as follows

```
object1 == object2
```

the resulting relational expression is true whenever object1 and object2 are bound to the same object, and false otherwise. The kind of equality checked by the "==" operation is called **identity equality** because it tests whether or not the two objects have the same identity.

The default implementation of the equals method that is inherited from Object also checks for identity equality. As long as equals is not overridden, the expression

```
object1.equals(object2)
```

will have the same value as the following expression.

```
object1 == object2
```

The equals method, like toString, is really included in Object with the intention that it will be overridden. The convention that is generally adopted by Java programmers is to define a new version of equals that tests for **content equality**. Two objects are said to have content equality when they have equal state. Generally, two objects are checked for content equality by comparing the values of all instance variables.

Figure 9.26 shows how to include equals to test for content equality in the Date class. Two Date objects are considered to be equal only when day, month, and year all have the same values in both objects.

```
public abstract class Date {
    // The innards of the Date class from Figure 9.21 have been
    // omitted for clarity reasons. They should be placed here.
    public boolean equals(Object z) {
        return
            z instanceof Date
            && day == ((Date)z).day
            && month == ((Date)z).month
            && year == ((Date)z).year;
    }
}
```

Figure 9.26

A Date class that implements equals

The implementation of `equals` from Figure 9.26 relies upon several Java features. Obviously, another object cannot have content equal to a `Date` object, unless that other object is also of type `Date`. However, the `z` parameter of the `equals` method that is being overridden has a type of `Object`. The solution is to include the following in the return instruction.

```
z instanceof Date
```

This test causes `equals` to short circuit and return `false` whenever it is applied to a `Date` object with an argument whose type does not conform to `Date`.

Once the method has verified that the `z` parameter is of type `Date`, it is still impossible to use an expression such as `z.day`. The problem is that `instanceof` is not tested until runtime, so the compiler must still rely upon the declared type of `z`, namely `Object`. Therefore, a cast is needed. In other words, the intended expression

```
z.day
```

must be expressed, using a cast, as follows.

```
((Date)z).day
```

The following code illustrates a potential use for the `equals` method.

```
Date jasonBirthday, jeremyBirthday;
jasonBirthday = new USAbbrevDate(20, 4, 1976);
jeremyBirthday = new USAbbrevDate(20, 4, 1976);
if (jasonBirthday.equals(jeremyBirthday)) {
    System.out.println("Content Equality");
} else {
    System.out.println("Content Inequality");
}
```

In the event that the `Date` class used for the above code was redefined to include an `equals` method as shown in Figure 9.26, then executing the code above outputs the following message.

software engineering *Hint*

There are many times when content equality tests are useful. The proper technique for providing tests for content equality is to overload the `equals` method.

```
Content Equality
```

If `equals` is not overloaded, then the `Object` version of `equals` is used and the resulting output is shown below.

```
Content Inequality
```

9.7 ■ Using Interfaces

The `Object` class cannot provide every possible method that might be of use to a particular subclass, nor is it possible to anticipate the needed code for various polymorphic situations. For this reason, Java includes a class-like mechanism called an **interface**. Numerous standard interfaces are included in the standard Java libraries.

An interface can be thought of as a class with no instance variables and no code for any method. It is a bit like the ultimate abstract class—where nothing can be concrete. The purpose of an interface, like that of an abstract class, is to be inherited and used polymorphically by overriding all methods. In other words, interfaces provide a foundation for the use of the Template Design Pattern. One of the most commonly used standard Java interfaces is called `Comparable`.[2] Figure 9.27 contains a class diagram for `Comparable`.

The purpose of `Comparable` is to provide a standard way for a programmer to declare a class to be **ordered**. An ordered class means that any two of its objects can be compared for greater than, less than, and equal to. Numeric types are ordered; Java supports this kind of ordering through the primitive types and operators such as $<$, $>$, and ==. It is also common to think of text values as ordered alphabetically. Java also supports alphabetical order comparisons (more-or-less[3]) by virtue of the `char` data type and its use of Unicode. For all reference data Java includes the `Comparable` interface.

The `Comparable` interface relies on one method—`compareTo`. A call to `compareTo` compares two objects, the object to which the method is applied and the object sent as a parameter. Each call to `compareTo` is expected to return a negative value if the

Figure 9.27

Diagram for the standard Comparable interface

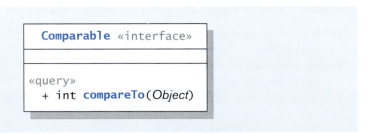

---

2. `Comparable` is part of the *java.lang* library, which does *not* require import.

3. Alphabetical ordering is preserved within case, but all uppercase letters have lesser value than any lowercase letter.

object to which it is applied is *less* than the argument object. The method returns a positive value if the object is *greater* than the argument. The method returns zero if the object is *equal* to the argument, as described in Figure 9.28.

Many of the standard library classes inherit (implement) interfaces. The String class, for example, implements the Comparable interface. For String the compareTo operation compares two objects by comparing their characters from left to right. The following expressions illustrate this.

> Assuming that s is a String variable that stores "www" ...
>
> ■ s.compareTo("xyz") evaluates to a number less than 0
>
> ■ s.compareTo("waz") evaluates to a number greater than 0
>
> ■ s.compareTo("www") evaluates to 0

The notation for inheriting interfaces is different from inheriting classes in two ways: (1) Interfaces are inherited using the syntax of "implements *interfaceName*" instead of "extends *className*"; (2) You can inherit more than one interface in which case all interfaces are included in the same implements clause separated by commas. (An implements clause must follow the extends clause if both are present in the same class.)

Figure 9.29 shows how to use the Comparable interface to provide ordering to a class called SimpleName. A SimpleName stores a person's first name and last name. The ordering of names is alphabetical by last name, followed by first name. For example, the name "Sam Jones" is less than "Mary Smith," because a last name of "Jones" alphabetically precedes the last name of "Smith." The name "Mary Jones" is less than "Sam Jones" because the last names are equal, but the first name of "Mary" alphabetically precedes the first name of "Sam."

Interfaces play a key role in Java event handling. Both the *java.awt.event* and *javax.swing.event* libraries include **listeners** for supporting event handling. A listener is nothing more than a java interface that includes an event handling method. Figure 9.30 shows a class diagram for the standard ActionListener interface. This interface is used for event handling associated with buttons, text fields, and other GUI objects.

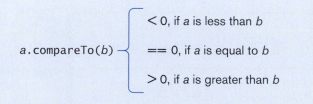

Figure 9.28

Ordering test of the compareTo method

Figure 9.29   A SimpleName class implementing Comparable

```java
public class SimpleName implements Comparable {
    private String firstName;
    private String lastName;

    /** post:  firstName == first and lastName == last */
    public SimpleName(String first, String last) {
        firstName = first;
        lastName = last;
    }

    /** post:  comparison done alphabetically last name before first */
    public int compareTo(Object s) {
        if (!(s instanceof SimpleName))
            System.out.println("Cannot compareTo SimpleName to other type");
        if (lastName.compareTo(((SimpleName)s).getLast()) < 0)
            return -1;
        else if (lastName.compareTo(((SimpleName)s).getLast()) > 0)
            return 1;
        else
            return firstName.compareTo(((SimpleName)s).getFirst());
    }

    public String getFirst() {
        return firstName;
    }

    public String getLast() {
        return lastName;
    }
}
```

Figure 9.30   Diagram for the standard java.awt.event.ActionListener interface

```
┌─────────────────────────────────────────────────┐
│         java.awt.event.ActionListener            │
│                  «interface»                     │
├─────────────────────────────────────────────────┤
│                                                  │
├─────────────────────────────────────────────────┤
│ «event handler»                                  │
│   + void actionPerformed(java.awt.event.ActionEvent) │
└─────────────────────────────────────────────────┘
```

Any class can handle events for the associated GUI object by doing two things:

1. The event handling class must `implement` the appropriate listener class. (This includes overriding the event handler method.)

2. The proper add listener method must be applied to the object that generates the events. These methods are names like the events (`addActionListener` for `ActionEvents`, `addChangeListener` for `ChangeEvents`, and so forth).

Figure 9.31 contains a sample of how to implement a listener interface for event handling. In this case, the `Driver` class creates a `JButton` and handles its events without the need for other programmer written classes.

The `Driver` class implements `ActionListener`, which is the event listener interface associated with `JButton`. The `Driver` class also includes the following statements:

```
simpleButton = new JButton("Click Me");
simpleButton.setBounds(50, 80, 100, 40);
simpleButton.addActionListener(this);
```

Figure 9.31   A `Driver` class that serves as a delegate for `JButton`

```
import java.awt.event.*;
import javax.swing.*;
public class Driver implements ActionListener {
    private JFrame window;
    private JButton simpleButton;

    /** post:  window is created at (10, 10) with width and height of 200
     *         and simpleButton is added to window
     */
    public Driver() {
        window = new JFrame("JButton Delegate");
        window.setBounds(10, 10, 200, 200);
        window.setVisible(true);
        window.setLayout(null);
        simpleButton = new JButton("Click Me");
        simpleButton.setBounds(50, 80, 100, 40);
        simpleButton.addActionListener(this);
        window.add(simpleButton, 0);
        window.repaint();
    }

    /** post:  a CLICKED message has been output. */
    public void actionPerformed(ActionEvent e) {
        System.out.println("CLICKED");
    }
}
```

The first of these statements instantiates a `JButton` and assigns it a label, and the second statement establishes the boundaries of the button. The third statement fulfills the second requirement for event handling by adding `this` (i.e., the `Driver` object) as action listener. Following this third statement, every click on `simpleButton` will generate a call to the `actionPerformed` method within this `Driver`.

Event handling that relies upon such calls to add listeners is known as **event delegation**. Event handling for the `JButton` object has been delegated to another object. For the example in Figure 9.32, the `Driver` object serves as the delegate handling the events generated by `simpleButton`.

It is often convenient to have the same object serve as delegate for multiple GUI objects, but if the GUI objects require the same listener, then distinguishing between the objects requires extra work. For example, suppose the example `Driver` class from Figure 9.31 is extended to include not one but two buttons. If this new `Driver` is to serve as delegate for both buttons, then the same `actionPerformed` method will be called regardless of which button is clicked. So how can the code distinguish and perform different tasks for different buttons? The answer lies in the parameter that is included with every standard event handling method. Such parameters belong to a standard event class like `ActionEvent`. These standard event classes support a parameterless method, called `getSource`, that returns the identity of the object that generated the event. Figure 9.32 illustrates how to implement such two-button code.

This `Driver` serves as a delegate for both the `simpleButton` object and the `anotherButton` object. When the `actionPerformed` method is called, an `if` instruction, repeated below, is used to select different tasks for different buttons.

```
if (e.getSource() == simpleButton)
    System.out.println("CLICKED");
else
    System.out.println("CLACKED");
```

When `actionPerformed` is called, the `e` parameter is passed to it. Calling `getSource` on this parameter returns the identity of either `simpleButton` or `anotherButton`, because these are the only two objects for which `Driver` is a delegate. The then clause executes if it was `simpleButton` that is clicked and the else clause executes if `anotherButton` is clicked.

Figure 9.32   A Driver as delegate for two JButtons

```java
import java.awt.event.*;
import javax.swing.*;
public class Driver implements ActionListener {
    private JFrame window;
    private JButton simpleButton, anotherButton;

    /** post:  window is created at (10, 10) with width and height of 200
     *         and simpleButton is added to window
     *         and anotherButton is added to window
     */
    public Driver() {
        window = new JFrame("Two Buttons");
        window.setBounds(10, 10, 200, 200);
        window.setVisible(true);
        window.setLayout(null);
        simpleButton = new JButton("Click Me");
        simpleButton.setBounds(50, 20, 100, 40);
        simpleButton.addActionListener(this);
        window.add(simpleButton, 0);
        anotherButton = new JButton("Clack Me");
        anotherButton.setBounds(50, 80, 100, 40);
        anotherButton.addActionListener(this);
        window.add(anotherButton, 0);
        window.repaint();
    }

    /** post:  simpleButton clicked implies CLICKED was output
     *         and anotherButton clicked implies CLACKED was output
     */
    public void actionPerformed(ActionEvent e) {
        if (e.getSource() == simpleButton)
            System.out.println("CLICKED");
        else
            System.out.println("CLACKED");
    }
}
```

Opening
the Black Box

Earlier several event-supporting classes were used in examples. These classes were called EventButton, EventSlider, EventTimer, and EventTextField. Each of these classes used the same basic design, as pictured below:

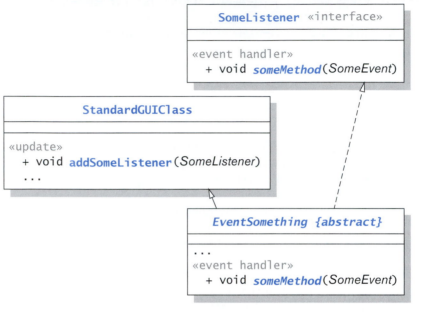

The class named EventSomething represents either EventButton, EventSlider, EventTimer, or EventTextField. The StandardGUIClass represents JButton for EventButton, JSlider for EventSlider, Timer for EventTimer, and JTextField for EventTextField. The SomeListener interface represents the standard interface that is associated with StandardGUIClass (i.e., java.awt.event.ActionListener is associated with JButton, Timer, and JTextField, while javax.swing.event.ChangeListener is associated with JSlider.

Each of the author-supplied classes establishes itself as the event-handling delegate, but leaves the event handling method abstract. The code below demonstrates a complete author-written class.

```java
import java.awt.event.*;
import javax.swing.JButton;
public abstract class EventButton extends JButton
                      implements ActionListener {
    public EventButton(String s) {
        super(s);
        addActionListener(this);
    }
    public abstract void actionPerformed(ActionEvent e);
}
```

The ThreeButton class, used in earlier chapters, combines the use of the concepts of abstract classes, interfaces, and event delegation as shown below. (Note that declaring the ThreeButtonFrame class inside ThreeButtons restricts access to the outer class.)

Opening **the Black Box**

```java
import javax.swing.*;
import java.awt.*;
import java.awt.event.*;
public abstract class ThreeButtons {
    public abstract void leftAction();
    public abstract void midAction();
    public abstract void rightAction();

    protected class ThreeButtonFrame extends JFrame
            implements ActionListener {
        private JButton leftButton, midButton, rightButton;

        public ThreeButtonFrame(String s) {
            super(s);
            setBounds(20, 20, 600, 500);
            setVisible(true);
            ...    // create the buttons & add to this content pane
                   // & delegate the button actions to this
        }

        //Event Handler
        public void actionPerformed(ActionEvent e) {
            if (e.getSource() == leftButton)
                leftAction();
            else if (e.getSource() == midButton)
                midAction();
            else if (e.getSource() == rightButton)
                rightAction();
        }
    }
}
```

Inspector

Below is a collection of hints on what to check when examining code that involves the concepts of this chapter.

- With any collection of several classes, it is generally helpful to sketch out a class diagram that shows the inheritance relationships.

- Every assignment instruction of nonprimitives should be checked for type conformance. The expression on the right of the assignment must have the same type or a descendant type as the variable on the left. (Syntax errors result from nonconformance.) Sometimes the code may need to include an `instanceof` check to ensure type conformance.

- Every nonprimitive argument should be checked for type conformance to its formal parameter. The argument must have the same type or a descendant type of the formal parameter. (Syntax errors result from nonconformance.)

- Overriding methods should be examined to ensure that their parameter lists match that of the method they override. If the parameter lists differ, then overloading occurs without causing a syntax error.

- A method that overrides an inherited method should accomplish at least as much as the postcondition from the superclass version.

- When the template design pattern is being used, then it is wise to check the superclass (i.e., the template) to be certain that it contains all of the methods that require override.

- When polymorphism is involved, each class should be considered to ensure that the version of each polymorphic method is correct for objects of this type.

- Each class from which no objects are created should be considered a candidate to become an abstract class.

- Overriding the `toString` method should be considered for each class.

- Providing a content equality test by overriding `equals` should be considered for each class.

- When using event delegation there are two steps to remember: (1) the delegate's class must inherit the proper listener and override its event handler method, (2) a call to an add listener method must be performed passing the delegate as argument.

Terminology

abstract class

abstract method

ancestor class

`Comparable` (a standard interface)

`compareTo` (method from
  `Comparable`)

`Component` (an *AWT* class)

concrete class

`Container` (an *AWT* class)

content equality

delegate (for event handling)

descendant classes

dynamic binding

`equals` (method from `Object`)

extensibility (of software)

`getSource`

identity equality

inheritance hierarchy

`instanceof`

interface

`JComponent` (a *Swing* class)

listener (for event handling)

`Object` (the root class)

ordered (a property of classes)

parent class

polymorphism

root class

subtype polymorphism

system of classes

Template Design Pattern

`toString` (method from `Object`)

type conformance

Exercises

Use the five classes below to complete Exercises 1 and 2.

```java
public class Great {
    // several methods not shown
}

public class Greater extends Great {
    // several methods not shown
}

public class Greatest extends Greater {
    // several methods not shown
}

public class Wonderful extends Greater {
    // several methods not shown
}

public class Superlative {
    public Wonderful wonder;
    // several methods not shown
}
```

1. Draw a class diagram that shows all of the inheritance and aggregation relationships among these classes.

2. Using the five classes above, assume the following instance variable declarations.

```
public Great g;
public Greater ger;
public Greatest gest;
public Wonderful won;
public Superlative sup;
```

Which of the following parts are valid according to the rules of type conformance?

a. g = ger;

b. gest = ger;

c. gest = won;

d. won = ger;

e. sup = won;

f. won = sup;

g. g = won;

h. ger = sup.wonder;

Use the classes below to complete Exercises 3 and 4.

```
public class Weather {
    // other methods omitted
    public void report {
        System.out.println("No Warnings or watches.");
    }
}

public class HighWind extends Weather {
    // other methods omitted
    public void report {
        System.out.println("Wind Advisory.");
    }
}

public class StormWatch extends Weather {
    // other methods omitted
}
```

```
public class TornadoWarning extends StormWatch {
    // other methods omitted
    public void report {
        System.out.println("TORNADO WARNING!!");
    }
}
```

```
public class MyWarning {
    public TornadoWarning bigWind;
    // other methods omitted
}
```

3. Using the five classes above, assume the following instance variable declarations.

```
public Weather w;
public HighWind hw;
public StormWatch sWatch;
public TornadoWarning tWarn;
public MyWarning warn;
```

Which of the following assignment instructions are valid according to the type conformance rules of Java?

a. w = hw;

b. w = sWatch;

c. sWatch = warn;

d. warn = tWarn;

e. tWarn = hw;

f. warn.bigWind = tWarn;

g. tWarn = warn.bigWind;

h. w = warn.bigWind;

4. Assuming that all variables from Exercise 3 have been attached to objects of the same type, give the output that results from executing the following code segment.

```
w.report();
w = tWarn;
w.report();
w = sWatch;
w.report();
```

5. Figures 9.9, 9.10, and 9.18 contain the RectangularCake, CircularCake, and Cake classes, respectively.

   a. Show all of the modifications needed to include a toString method within RectangularCake to properly override the toString from the Object class.

   b. Show all of the modifications needed to include a toString method within CircularCake to properly override the toString from the Object class.

   c. Show all of the modifications needed to include an equals method within RectangularCake to properly overload the equals from the Object class and implement content equality.

   d. Show all of the modifications needed to include an equals method within CircularCake to properly overload the equals from the Object class and implement content equality.

   e. Show all of the modifications needed to implement the Comparable interface for CircularCake. Use the area of a cake as the ordering property (i.e., assume that one CircularCake is less than another if and only if it has less area).

   f. Which version of equals is used when a RectangularCake object is compared to a CircularCake argument as follows?

      myRectangularCake.equals(myCircularCake)

   g. Why does it seem unnecessary to override toString within Cake?

   h. Why does it seem unnecessary to overload equals within Cake?

6. Consider the following three classes.

```java
public class Bumper {
    public int theNum;

    public Bumper() {
        theNum = 1;
    }

    public void bumpIt() {
        theNum = theNum + 1;
    }

    public void printTheNum() {
        System.out.println(theNum);
    }
}
```

```
public class Bumper20 extends Bumper {
   public Bumper20() {
      theNum = 100;
   }
   public void bumpIt() {
      theNum = theNum + 20;
   }
}
```

```
public class Bumper300 extends Bumper20 {
   public Bumper300() {
      super();
   }

   public void bumpIt() {
      the_num = the_num + 300;
   }
}
```

Assume the following instance variable declarations use the classes declared above.

```
public Bumper bumped;
public Bumper20 lumped;
public Bumper300 gumped;
```

Precisely what is output when the following code segment executes?

```
lumped = new Bumper20();
gumped = new Bumper300();
gumped.printTheNum();
lumped.bumpIt();
lumped.printTheNum();
bumped = lumped;
bumped.bumpIt();
bumped.printTheNum();
bumped = new Bumper300();
bumped.bumpIt();
bumped.printTheNum();
```

7. Write the complete code for a SameBumper class. Your class must inherit the Bumper class from Exercise 6. SameBumper must also implement the equals method in such a way that two SameBumper objects are considered equal exactly when theNum of the first has the same value as theNum of the second.

Programming Exercises

1. Dr. Seuss wrote a story, entitled "The Zax"[4] about two fictional characters that were so stubborn that they refused to walk in any direction but one. The North-Going Zax walks only northward and the South-Going Zax walks only to the south. You are expected to write a program to simulate this Zax problem. The window for this program begins with the following content.

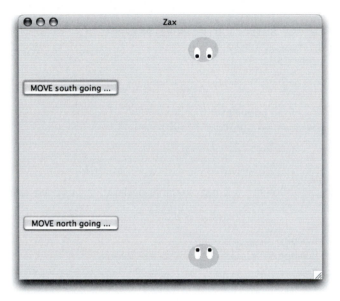

Each Zax is displayed as an oval with blue eyes pointing in the direction of movement. The South-Going Zax is at the top of the window, and the North-Going Zax is at the bottom. Each Zax moves only when its associated button is clicked. A Zax moves forward by two pixels unless it bumps into the other Zax, then no one moves because they are deadlocked.

Your program must include a superclass called `Zax` and two subclasses for each type of `Zax`. A method, called `goForward`, must be used polymorphically in all three classes.

2. Young children are often taught about real-world objects by using manipulatives. This programming assignment is to construct a "busy box" that can be used to teach about three objects: an automobile, a balloon, and a helicopter. Your program should use a `ThreeButtonFrame` to display the three objects above the buttons as shown on the next page.

---

4. Published in *The Sneetches and Other Stories*, Random House, 1953.

Each of the three buttons *selects* the object above (thereby deselecting the previously selected object). Slider events manipulate only the selected object. If the selected object is the automobile then it moves horizontally to match the slider value (i.e., as the slider is dragged left the auto moves left). When the helicopter is selected, it moves up or down to respond to slider changes. When the balloon is selected it grows and shrinks with changes to the slider.

You must have a superclass from which you create classes for the three screen images. Use polymorphism to implement the action of the slider.

(Note that if you wish to use graphic files for this program, you can use the `Image` class included in Appendix D.)

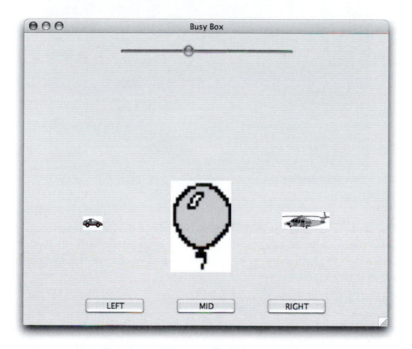

3. The basic idea of this program is to provide a programming tool for performing room layout. This program is capable of manipulating a sofa, two chairs, a desk, a table, and the room itself. The user tools include a horizontal slider, vertical slider, and two buttons. The Select Next Item button is used to select one of the items. It cycles through the possibilities, leaving the selected item highlighted as a red solid rectangle. (The nonselected items are outlines.) The picture on the following page shows the program appearance.

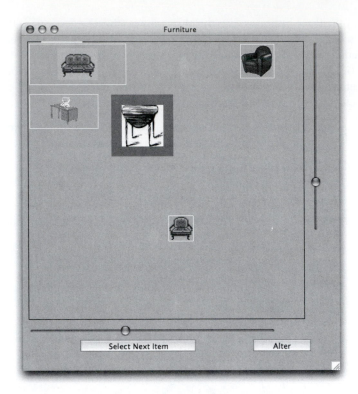

The two sliders and the Alter button operate upon the selected item. When a sofa, chair, desk, or table is selected then the sliders work to reposition the selected item within the room space. The sliders change the size of the room when it is selected.

The Alter button behaves differently for different objects.

■ For the *sofa:*

The Alter button causes the sofa to turn 90 degrees. (The image need not change.)

■ For the *chairs:*

The Alter button causes the chair to toggle between a 30″-by-30″ chair using one chair image to a 22″-by-22″ chair using a different chair image.

■ For the *desk:*

The Alter button causes the desk to cycle between four possible configurations: (1) a 60″ wide by 30″ high desk, (2) a 72″-by-36″ desk, (3) a 36″-by-72″ desk, and (4) a 30″-by-60″ desk. (The image does not change.)

■ For the *table:*

The Alter button does nothing.

- For the *room:*

  The Alter moves the door opening (the white opening) from one wall to another.

(Note that if you wish to use graphic files for this program, you can use the Image class included in Appendix D.)

4. Computer-drawn sketches are useful in many ways. For example, law enforcement officials often use computer drawing to help identify suspects. For this assignment, you will create a prototype drawing program to display and manipulate faces. Your solution should be designed to take advantage of inheritance and polymorphism.

The program uses two windows, one to draw the face and the other to control the drawing. Initially, the windows should appear as shown below.

The face consists of a head, two eyes, a nose, and a mouth. Each of these parts is selected by clicking the mouse within the border of the object. The eyes are selected as a pair, so clicking either eye selects them both. When one face part is selected, all previous selections are forgotten.

The control window (called Inspector) operates upon only the selected object. A click on the Change Image button performs the following task, depending upon the selected face part.

(Note that if you wish to use graphic files for this program, you can use the Image class shown in Appendix D.)

- For a selected *head:*

  The head changes color from green to yellow to purple back to green.

- For a selected *nose:*

  The nose image changes to another of three possible nose images.

- For a selected *mouth:*

  The mouth image changes to another of three possible mouth images.

- For a selected *eyes:*

  The eye images change to another of four possible pairs of images.

The slider behavior also depends upon the selected image.

- For a selected *head:*

  The head gets wider or narrower with slider value changes.

- For a selected *nose:*

  The nose image moves up or down with slider value changes.

- For a selected *mouth:*

  The mouth gets wider or narrower with slider value changes.

- For a selected *eyes:*

  The eyes move closer together or farther apart with slider value changes.

(Note that if you wish to use graphic files for this program, you may wish to use the `Pict` class included in Appendix D.)

`JComponent` objects supports the following mouse events: `mouseClicked`, `mousePressed`, `mouseReleased`, `mouseEntered`, and `mouseExited`, via the `MouseListener` interface and `MouseEvent` class. They also support `mouseDragged`, and `mouseMoved` events via the `MouseMotionListener` interface and `MouseEvent` class. These classes and interfaces are located within *java.awt.event*. See Appendix D.4 for a more complete description.

Repetition

10

Round and round and round she goes, and where she stops nobody knows.

—Ted Mack, "The Original Amateur Hour"

Objectives

- To introduce the concept of repetition in control structures
- To examine the syntax and semantics of Java's three repetition instructions, namely *while*, *do*, and *for*
- To emphasize the importance of loop initialization, primary work, and making progress code in the correctness of a loop
- To introduce the TextArea object as a multiline output object
- To caution against common loop difficulties, including infinite loops and off-by-one loops
- To examine nested loops
- To explore loop invariants and their role in loop design
- To introduce the event loop mechanism used by the Java Virtual Machine
- To examine the impact of loops on software testing

C omputers are often thought of as faithful servants because they perform large numbers of instructions with accuracy and without protest. This characteristic equips computers particularly well for performing repetitive procedures.

Java includes three instructions whose purpose is to control repetitive execution. The three instructions are while, do, and for.

These instructions are referred to as **repetition control structures** because of their ability to control execution by causing statements to execute repeatedly. This chapter explores these instructions.

10.1 ■ The *while* Loop

The **while instruction** or *while* **loop** is the most commonly used of all repetition structures and is included in many programming languages. Figure 10.1 describes the Java syntax and semantics for this statement.

A *while* loop has two main parts:

1. a loop condition

2. a loop body

The loop condition is a Boolean-valued expression, similar to the condition used in an *if* instruction. The condition of a *while* loop determines how long the repetition will continue. As the name of the instruction implies, a *while* loop iterates (repeats) as long as its loop condition remains true-valued.

software *Hint*
engineering

Good programming style dictates that the body of a loop must always be indented from the notation that begins and ends the loop. Such consistent indentation greatly enhances readability.

The group of statements that are repeated for each loop iteration are called the "loop body." The loop body in Java is treated like a single unit in the same way that the *then* clause and the *else* clause of an *if* instruction are treated as units.

Figure 10.1 demonstrates two possible alternatives for while instruction syntax. The first alternative is generally preferred. This syntax can be used in all cases. The Alternative Syntax can only be used when the loop body consists of a single statement.

Figure 10.2 contains a description of the runtime behavior of a while instruction in the form of an activity diagram.

Figure 10.1   ***whileInstruction*** description (a possible *OneStatement*)

Syntax

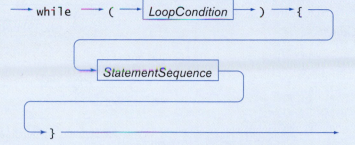

Alternate Syntax (when the loop body is a single statement)

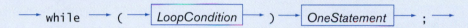

Note

LoopCondition can be any valid Boolean-valued expression.

Style Notes

The reserved word while should be aligned with the "}" symbol that ends the *whileInstruction* and all statements within *StatementSequence* should be indented by at least one tab from the while. If *LoopCondition* requires multiple lines, then the initial loop brace "{" should be placed on a separate line and indented the same as its matching "}".

Semantics

Executing *whileInstruction* causes *LoopCondition* to be evaluated. If *LoopCondition* is found to be true, then *StatementSequence* (or *OneStatement*) executes and the process repeats. If *LoopCondition* is found to be false, then execution proceeds to the next statement following the while instruction.

A while instruction begins execution by evaluating the loop condition. If the value of the loop condition is true, then execution proceeds to execute the loop body. Following each loop body execution the loop condition is reevaluated, and the body executes again as long as the condition is true. Whenever the loop condition is evaluated and found to be false, then execution proceeds to the next statement after the loop.

Figure 10.2   The control flow of a `while` instruction

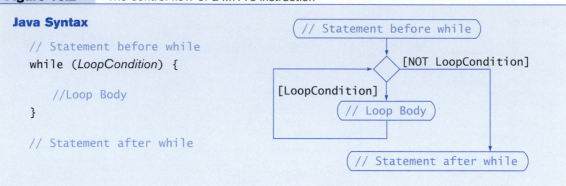

The control flow depicted in Figure 10.2 illustrates this repetition by following the arrow to the loop body when the loop condition is `true` and the arrow to the statement following the loop when the condition is `false`. The control flow path that passes through the loop body returns to the loop condition. This circular control path is common for all repetition control structures, and the circular nature of the path is the reason for the name "loop" for this kind of control.

Below is a sample *while* loop that uses an `int` variable called `powerOfTwo`. (A `//(n)` comment is included to number certain statements.)

```
int powerOfTwo;
powerOfTwo = 2;                                            //(1)
while (powerOfTwo < 10) {                                  //(2)
    System.out.println("Next power: " + powerOfTwo);      //(3)
    powerOfTwo = powerOfTwo * 2;                          //(4)
}
System.out.println("the end.");                           //(5)
```

A trace of the execution of the above code is shown in Figure 10.3. Execution proceeds from the top of this trace to the bottom. The number of each statement executed is indicated in the leftmost column, labeled "Line No." The action taken during the execution of each statement is explained briefly in the Execution Action column. The value assigned to the `powerOfTwo` variable is shown in the third column, and the rightmost column shows the output, if any, generated by the statement.

Another way to display program output is to make use of a `TextArea`[1] object. `TextArea` is an *AWT* class designed for displaying lines of text. Figure 10.4 contains a class diagram for `TextArea`.

`TextArea` is different from `JTextField` because `TextArea` does not support input, nor does it supply any event handling. `TextArea` is different from `Label` because a

---

1. There is a `javax.swing.JTextArea` class, but it is not discussed because the `TextArea` class includes automatic sliders, making it more useful for output with many lines.

Figure 10.3   Trace of the execution of the powerOfTwo loop

Line No.	Execution Action	powerOfTwo	Output
//(1)	powerOfTwo assigned 2	2	
//(2)	(powerOfTwo < 10) evaluates to true		
//(3)	Output		Next power: 2
//(4)	powerOfTwo updated	4	
//(2)	(powerOfTwo < 10) evaluates to true		
//(3)	Output		Next power: 4
//(4)	powerOfTwo updated	8	
//(2)	(powerOfTwo < 10) evaluates to true		
//(3)	Output		Next power: 8
//(4)	powerOfTwo updated	16	
//(2)	(powerOfTwo < 10) evaluates to false		
//(5)	Output		the end.

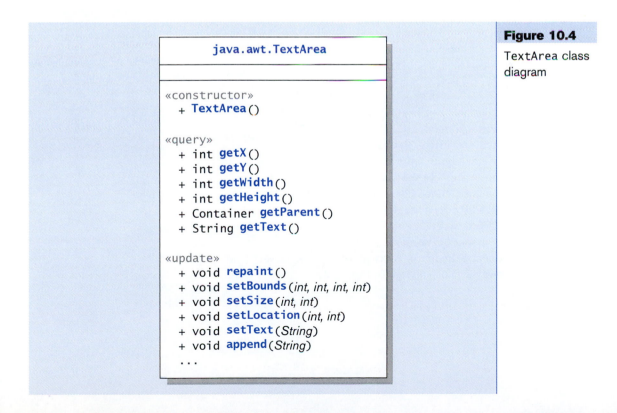

Figure 10.4

TextArea class diagram

TextArea object may contain several lines of text, while `Label` objects can display only one line. The text content of a `TextArea` object (returned by the `getText` method) is a `String` made up of all its lines of text concatenated together with `"\n"` characters between lines.

`TextArea` includes mostly methods examined previously in this book. The two new methods that distinguish this class are as follows.

- `setText(s)` .... replaces the entire content (all lines) of the text area with *s*
- `append(s)` .... appends *s* onto the end of the text area's string

Figure 10.5 illustrates how to use the `TextArea` class to create an output region. This `Driver` class contains a loop similar to the one presented earlier for calculating powers of two. However, this new version of the loop sends output to the `outPane` object rather than using `System.out.println`.

Figure 10.5   A `Driver` for the `powerOfTwo` loop

```java
import javax.swing.JFrame;
import java.awt.TextArea;
public class Driver {
    private JFrame window;
    private TextArea outPane;

    /** post:  A window is created containing a text area
     *         and the text area contains the powers of 2 less than 100
     */
    public Driver() {
        int powerOfTwo;
        window = new JFrame("Powers of 2");
        window.setBounds(10, 10, 200, 140);
        window.setVisible(true);
        window.setLayout(null);
        outPane = new TextArea();
        outPane.setBounds(20, 20, 150, 80);
        window.add(outPane, 0);
        powerOfTwo = 2;
        while (powerOfTwo < 100) {
            outPane.append("Next power: " + powerOfTwo + "\n");
            powerOfTwo = powerOfTwo * 2;
        }
        window.repaint();
    }
}
```

Executing the `Driver` code from Figure 10.5 displays the following window. Notice how the `TextArea` automatically provides a scrollbar to allow the user to scroll to any text that lies outside the region that displays. In the case below, the first three lines have scrolled off the top of the text area but can be viewed by pulling up on the right scrollbar knob.

An algorithm to display the Fibonacci number sequence is also a good use for a *while* loop. Fibonacci numbers were discovered by a thirteenth-century mathematician, Leonardo Fibonacci. Originally, this sequence of numbers was used to model the population growth of rabbits, but has since been observed in numerous other natural situations.

The complete collection of Fibonacci numbers form an infinite sequence of positive integers. The first two integers in the sequence are both 1. Thereafter, each number in the sequence is calculated by adding the two numbers that immediately precede it. The first ten numbers of the sequence are 1, 1, 2, 3, 5, 8, 13, 21, 34, and 55. Figure 10.6 contains a `Driver` class to output the first 30 Fibonacci numbers to a `TextArea` object.

Every loop contains at least three critical parts:

1. the **initialization** code
2. code to accomplish the **primary work** to be performed
3. code for **making progress** to loop termination

The initialization code is responsible for initializing the state properly to begin the loop. This code must execute prior to the `while` and is best placed immediately before `while`. The initialization code for the powers of two loop is the following single statement.

```
powerOfTwo = 2;
```

This instruction assigns `powerOfTwo` the proper value to begin the loop. If this instruction is removed, the resulting program prints nothing but zeros.

The second part of a loop performs the primary work of the loop body. This portion of the loop is generally the reason that the loop was written. The primary work of the powers of two loop is performed by the following instruction.

```
outPane.append("Next power: " + powerOfTwo + "\n");
```

Figure 10.6

A Driver to display Fibonacci numbers

```java
import javax.swing.JFrame;
import java.awt.TextArea;
public class Driver {
    private JFrame window;
    private TextArea outPane;

    /** post:  the first 30 Fibonacci numbers are displayed,
     *          one per line, on a TextArea object
     */
    public Driver() {
        int aFibo, nextFibo, newFibo, linesOutput;
        window = new JFrame("Fibonacci Numbers");
        window.setBounds(10, 10, 300, 400);
        window.setVisible(true);
        window.setLayout(null);
        outPane = new TextArea();
        outPane.setBounds(20, 20, 120, 300);
        window.add(outPane, 0);
        aFibo = 1;
        nextFibo = 1;
        linesOutput = 0;
        while (linesOutput != 30) {
            outPane.append(aFibo + "\n");
            newFibo = aFibo + nextFibo;
            aFibo = nextFibo;
            nextFibo = newFibo;
            linesOutput++;
        }
        window.repaint();
    }
}
```

Loop termination (completion) for a *while* loop is defined as the time when the loop condition is false. The loop body generally includes instructions to *make progress* toward this eventual termination. The powers of two program makes progress with the following instruction.

```java
powerOfTwo = powerOfTwo * 2;
```

To further illustrate the three loop parts, Figure 10.7 labels the Fibonacci program loop appropriately.

The linesOutput variable from the Fibonacci program is used in the loop condition, so it seems an obvious candidate to be initialized. By assigning linesOutput

```
aFibo = 1;                                  ┐
nextFibo = 1;                               ├─────  initialization
linesOutput = 0;                            ┘
while (linesOutput != 30) {
    outPane.append(aFibo + "\n");           ┐
    newFibo = aFibo + nextFibo;             │
    aFibo = nextFibo;                       ├─────  primary work
    nextFibo = newFibo;                     ┘
    linesOutput++;                          ──────  make progress
}
```

Figure 10.7

Fibonacci
program loop
parts identified

the value zero, it is properly established to count the number of lines that have been appended to the outPane object.

The need for the assignments to aFibo and nextFibo within initialization may be less obvious. aFibo maintains the Fibonacci number about to be output and nextFibo maintains the successor to aFibo. Both of these variables must store consecutive Fibonacci numbers for the loop body to be able to calculate subsequent Fibonacci numbers.

10.2 ■ Counting Loops

There is one looping pattern that occurs so frequently that it is given a special name. The **counting loop pattern** is, as its name implies, characterized by counting. This counting is accomplished by a variable, called a counter variable. The typical counting loop uses its counter variable to determine when to stop repeating. The types of tasks that are well suited to counting loop solutions include the following.

- Display the first fifteen prime numbers.
- Print the first fifty Unicode characters.
- Display twelve 10-by-10 blue rectangles across a JFrame.
- Show the value of PI approximated to thirty digits.

All of these tasks involve a count of times (fifteen, fifty, twelve, and thirty) that a task must be performed. The counting pattern, and associated *while* loop template, are shown in Figure 10.8.

The Fibonacci number loop from Figure 10.6 is an example of a counting loop. The counter variable is linesOutput for the Fibonacci program.

Not all counting loops match the pattern perfectly. Sometimes it makes sense to start the counting with a value other than zero, so the initialization might become

```
someCounter = n;
```

Figure 10.8

Counting loop
pattern

Counting Loop Pattern

A counting loop is a good choice for any algorithm (a task) that needs to be repeated some fixed number of times. Below is a skeleton of this code.

```
someCounter = 0;
while (someCounter != numberOfRepetitions) {
    // perform primary work
    someCounter++;
}
```

An application of this pattern requires the following:

- *numberOfRepetitions* is replaced by the count repetitions required.
- *//perform primary work* is replaced by the code for a single task.
- someCounter is some variable declared as one of the integer data types.

where n is 1 or some other integer. Sometimes it is more convenient to decrease the counter, rather than increase it, so the loop body instruction for making progress might be

```
someCounter--;
```

Sometimes it is better to count by some other integer than one. There are many variations in this counting loop pattern, but they all follow the basic theme of using a counter variable and the following:

- initializing the counter before the loop
- incrementing (or decrementing) the counter in the body of the loop
- using the counter in the condition to determine when to terminate repetition

A second example of a counting pattern is the displayPrimes method shown in Figure 10.9. This method has a single int parameter called n. When displayPrimes is called, it displays the first n prime numbers. displayPrimes uses primeCount as its counter variable.

The displayPrimes method represents a variation on the basic counting loop pattern, because it does not increment primeCount each time the loop body is executed. Instead, the loop body tests the value of potentialPrime using a Boolean method called isPrime, which returns true if and only if its parameter is a prime number. (The code for isPrime will be given shortly.) As a result, primeCount is incremented only when potentialPrime is found to be a prime number.

Figure 10.10 contains the code for the isPrime method referred to by displayPrimes. This method is designed to identify whether or not parameter p is a prime number. This is accomplished by yet another variation on a counting loop pattern. The isPrime algorithm tests each potential divisor from 2 through the

Figure 10.9

displayPrimes
method

```
/** pre:    n >= 0
 * post:   the first n prime numbers are output in outPane
 */
public void displayPrimes(int n) {
    int potentialPrime, primeCount;
    outPane.setText(" "); // clear the pane
    outPane.append("Primes\n");
    potentialPrime = 2;
    primeCount = 0;
    while (primeCount != n) {
        if (isPrime(potentialPrime)) {
            outPane.append(" " + potentialPrime + "\n");
            primeCount++;
        }
        potentialPrime++;
    }
}
```

Figure 10.10

isPrime method

```
/** pre:    p >= 2
 * post:   result == (p is a prime number)
 */
public boolean isPrime(int p) {
    int divisor;
    boolean looksPrime;
    looksPrime = true;
    divisor = 2;
    while (divisor <= Math.sqrt(p)) {
        if (p/divisor == (double)p/divisor) {
            looksPrime = false;
        }
        divisor++;
    }
    return looksPrime;
}
```

square root of p. A boolean variable, looksPrime, is initially assigned true and is changed to false only if a factor of p is found.

The loop counter for the isPrime method is divisor. This variable is initialized to 2 before the loop begins. Each time through the loop body the next divisor value is tested and if `divisor` turns out to be a factor of p, then `looksPrime` is assigned `false`. If the loop completes and `looksPrime` is still `true`, then there can be no factors of p from 2 through $\sqrt{p}$ so p must be prime. The following condition is used to test whether or not `divisor` is a factor of p.

```
(p/divisor == (double)p/divisor)
```

This condition compares the integer value of p divided by `divisor` to the same division done on `double` numbers. If these two divisions are equal, then a factor has been found.

10.3 ■ Sentinel Loops

Not all loops follow the counting loop pattern. Many loops simply repeat the body until some threshold condition exists. Such noncounting loops are often called **sentinel loops**. The tasks below suggest the use of sentinel loops.

- Display all prime numbers up to and including 37.
- Print all of the Unicode characters that precede the letter "Z."
- Display as many 10-by-10 blue rectangles across a `JFrame` as possible.

Another example of repeating to a noncounting threshold is the action of dropping an object from height H until it reaches earth's surface. Earth's gravity causes falling objects to accelerate at a rate of 9.81 meters per second. This means that the velocity (meters per second) of the frictionless object falling from a resting position can be calculated as V in the following equation.

$V = 9.81 * T$

T in this equation denotes the number of seconds of free fall from rest. The distance, D (meters), that the object falls is explained by the following equation.

$D = 4.9 * T^2$

If the object begins falling from a height, H, then its height after falling for T seconds can be described as shown below.

ActualHeight $= H - D = H - 4.9*T^2$

For example, suppose that a bowling ball is dropped from a helicopter hovering over the ocean at a height of 177 meters. Figure 10.11 demonstrates the results. This picture displays three values for each second of bowling ball travel:

1. The number of seconds that have passed since the ball was dropped.
2. The bowling ball's height (in meters) above earth's surface.
3. The downward velocity of the ball at that particular instant in time.

Figure 10.11
Bowling ball
dropping into
ocean

	Seconds	Height	Velocity
	0	177 m	0 m/sec
	1	172 m	9.81 m/sec
	2	157 m	19.62 m/sec
	3	132 m	29.43 m/sec
	4	98 m	39.24 m/sec
	5	54 m	49.05 m/sec
	6	0 m	58.86 m/sec

A typical `JFrame` image for a program to demonstrate this drop is shown in Figure 10.12. This program uses a `TextArea` to display the heights and velocities for a drop.

Figure 10.13 contains the code for the bowling ball program.

Figure 10.12

Output from the bowling ball program

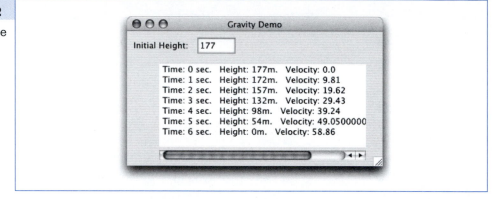

Figure 10.13   Falling object program (*continues*)

```
import javax.swing.*;
import java.awt.TextArea;
public class Driver {
    private JFrame window;
    private TextArea outPane;
    private HeightField inField;
    private Label label;

    /** post:  window != null and outPane != null and inField!=null
     *         and outPane, inField are both displayed in window
     */
    public Driver() {
        window = new JFrame("Gravity Demo");
        window.setBounds(10, 10, 400, 230);
        window.setVisible(true);
        window.setLayout(null);
        outPane = new TextArea();
        outPane.setBounds(50, 50, 340, 150);
        window.add(outPane, 0);
        label = new Label("Initial Height:");
        label.setBounds(10, 10, 100, 25);
        window.add(label, 0);
        inField = new HeightField(110, 10, this);
        window.add(inField, 0);
        window.repaint();
    }
```

Figure 10.13   Falling object program (*continued*)

```
    /** pre:   h > 0 and outPane != null
     * post:   outPane is reset to contain one line for each second of
     *         drop from a height of h until through last height before
     *         zero. Each line gives the height of the dropped object
     *         and its velocity at that second.
     */
    public void displayFall(int h) {
        int seconds;
        outPane.setText(""); // clear the text area of prior content
        seconds = 0;
        while (h-seconds*seconds*4.9 > 0) {
            outPane.append("Time: " + seconds +" sec. ");
            outPane.append("Height: "+(int)(h-seconds*seconds*4.9)+"m.");
            outPane.append(" Velocity: " + seconds*9.81 + "\n");
            seconds++;
        }
        outPane.repaint();
    }
}


import javax.swing.JTextField;
import java.awt.event.*;
public class HeightField extends JTextField
        implements ActionListener {
    private Driver driver;

    /** pre:   d != null
     * post:   driver == d
     *         and getX() == x and getY() == y
     *         and getWidth() == 60 and getHeight() == 25
     */
    public HeightField(int x, int y, Driver d) {
        super();
        setBounds(x, y, 60, 25);
        addActionListener(this);
        driver = d;
    }

    /** pre:   driver != null
     * post:   the displayFall method from driver is performed
     *         upon the integer value of this.
     */
    public void actionPerformed(ActionEvent e) {
        driver.displayFall((new Integer(getText())).intValue());
    }
}
```

The key loop of the falling object program occurs in the `displayFall` method. This method simulates the fall by advancing one second for each loop repetition. This loop has many similarities to counting loops because the `seconds` variable is assigned an initial value of zero and is incremented by one for each loop repetition. The difference between this loop and most counting loops is that the loop condition is the following.

```
(h-seconds*seconds*4.9 > 0)
```

This condition tests to see if the height of the falling object is greater than zero, which is a sentinel condition.

10.4 ■ Loop Design Cautions

The process of designing loops can be tricky. Consider the following program loop that is designed to print the integers from 1 through `num`.

```
counter = 1;
while (counter != num+1) {
    System.out.println(counter);
    counter++;
}
```

This loop works properly if `num` has an initial value greater than or equal to one. However, if `num` has a negative value initially, then this loop will continue to increment `counter` "forever." A loop like this that never stops repeating is known as an **infinite loop** or a **dead loop**. A common way to create an infinite loop accidentally is by forgetting to include a portion of the loop body to make progress toward loop completion. For example, the loop above is guaranteed to be an infinite loop if the following line is omitted from the loop body.

```
counter++;
```

The first time you encounter an infinite loop, you may believe that the program has stopped running. Actually, just the opposite has occurred; the program cannot stop running!

A second potential difficulty in loop design is the subtle relationships between the three portions of the loop code:

■ the initialization part

■ the primary work part

■ making progress part

For the loop counting from 1 to *n* these three parts are identified as follows:

```
initialization ─────────── counter = 1;
                  while (counter != num+1) {
primary work ──────────  System.out.println(counter);
making progress ──────────  counter++;
                  }
```

The examples shown so far are largely organized so that the primary work part precedes the making progress part. This is one typical way to write many algorithms. However, it is almost always possible to write equivalent loops with the primary work and making progress parts reversed. For example, the following loop performs the same task of printing the integers from 1 through num, but increments counter *before* the println call.

```
counter = 1;
while (counter != num+1) {
    counter++;
    System.out.println(counter-1);
}
```

In order to make this code produce the proper output, the argument to println is changed to counter-1. Yet a third equivalent loop is shown below.

```
counter = 0;
while (counter != num) {
    counter++;
    System.out.println(counter);
}
```

This last example uses a println argument of counter, but alters the initialization and loop condition code to compensate. These equivalent loops point out the close relationships among loop initialization, loop conditions, the primary work part, and the making progress part. Any change to one of these parts may induce needed changes to the others.

One additional common programming error is the **off-by-one loop**. An off-by-one loop results when a loop body is repeated one time too many or one time too few. The following code results in such an error because it will print only the values from 1 through num-1 (not 1 through num).

```
counter = 1;
while (counter != num) {
    System.out.println(counter);
    counter++;
}
```

software **engineering** *Hint*

A loop has four interrelated parts:

■ the loop initialization

■ the loop condition

■ the primary work part

■ the making progress part

Most programmers find it easiest to write their code according to a pattern. The most common pattern is to place the loop initialization code before the loop (as close as possible), and place the primary work part before the making progress part.

software **engineering** *Hint*

Programmers must always be on the lookout for off-by-one loops. These can usually be avoided by tracing loop execution for typical data.

10.5 ■ **Nested Loops**

Nested loops occur when one loop is placed within the body of another. The inner loop is said to be "nested" within the outer loop. As an illustration of how to use nested loops, Figure 10.14 contains the code for a polka dot program.

To observe the runtime behavior of the polka dot program, consider the shell of its two loops, along with the corresponding activity diagram on the next page.

Figure 10.14   Polka dot program

```java
import javax.swing.JFrame;
import java.awt.Color;
public class Driver {
    private JFrame window;

    public Driver() {
        int yCount, xCount;
        Oval dot;
        Color rowColor;
        window = new JFrame("Polkadots");
        window.setBounds(10, 10, 200, 200);
        window.setVisible(true);
        window.setLayout(null);

        yCount = 0;
        while (yCount != 12) {
            rowColor = new Color(yCount/13.0f, yCount/13.0f, yCount/13.0f);
                // rowColor is gray an intensity of yCount/13.
                // (0.0f is black and 1.0f is white)
            xCount = 0;
            while (xCount != 8) {
                dot = new Oval(xCount*25, yCount*15, 10, 10);
                dot.setBackground(rowColor);
                window.add(dot, 0);
                xCount++;
            }
            yCount++;
        }
        window.repaint();
    }
}
```

```
yCount = 0;
while (yCount != 12) {
    ...
    xCount = 0;
    while (xCount != 8) {
        ...
        xCount++;
    }
    yCount++;
}
```

This shell reveals that the outer loop is a counting loop that counts from 0 through 12, and the inner loop is also a counting loop, counting from 0 through 8. Tracing this skeleton code shows that for yCount==0 the inner loop body executes eight times. When yCount==1, the inner loop executes another eight times, and so forth. Below is a trace table of the order in which yCount and xCount are assigned values.

yCount	xCount	yCount	xCount
0	0	1	2
0	1	...	...
0	2	1	8
0	3	2	0
0	4	2	1
0	5	...	...
0	6	2	8
0	7	.	.
0	8	.	.
1	0	.	.
1	1	12	8

Every time that the outer loop body executes, the inner loop body executes eight times. Therefore, the total number of Oval dots constructed in the body of the inner loop is 12 * 8 or 96.

Examining the execution of the outer loop reveals more about how the dots are arranged. Each time that the body of the outer loop executes, the value of yCount increases by one. This yCount value is used to determine the intensity of the rowColor object. The twelve executions of the outer loop body result in twelve different rowColor values that range from black for the first outer loop body repetition to a very light gray for the last repetition.

The inner loop body constructs a new Oval for each repetition. Since xCount is initialized to zero before the inner loop, the first Oval constructed will be located at x==0*25==0 and y==0*15==0. The second Oval will be located at x==25 and y==0, the third at x==50 and y==0, and so forth. In other words, the xCount variable is changing value more frequently than yCount, resulting in Ovals that are drawn across rows. Figure 10.15 shows the complete JFrame displayed by executing the polka dot program.

The pattern of nesting one loop within a single outer loop, such as the polka dot loops, is sometimes called **doubly nested loops**. The two dimensional nature of the polka dots is typical for a doubly nested pattern. The outer loop proceeds from row to row, and the inner loop proceeds across columns within a row. The result is the construction of Ovals that proceeds from the top of the window to the bottom, and left to right within each row.

There is no reason that the creation of Ovals must always be done row by row. Suppose that a programmer wishes to construct Ovals, column by column, with the left column as black dots and proceeding to lighter gray dots on the right. Figure 10.16 shows such a window.

The shell of the looping structure that proceeds across the columns is shown below.

```
xCount = 0;
while (xCount != 8) {
    rowColor = new Color(xCount/9.0f, xCount/9.0f, xCount/9.0f);
    yCount = 0;
    while (yCount != 12) {
        . . .
        yCount++;
    }
    xCount++;
}
```

software *Hint*
engineering

The bodies of the inner nested loops have the greatest potential for repetition. Programmers looking to improve the execution speed of their programs often look first at speeding up the innermost loops.

The primary difference between this code and that of the original polka dot program is that the role of the two loops is interchanged. The outer loop of the new algorithm changes xCount, thereby proceeding from left to right across the columns. For each outer loop repetition, the inner loop varies yCount so as to advance from top to bottom row.

A **triply nested** loop pattern consists of a doubly nested loop that is nested within a third loop. Triply nested loops are well suited to processing three-dimensional structures in the same way that doubly nested loops work well for two-dimensional structures.

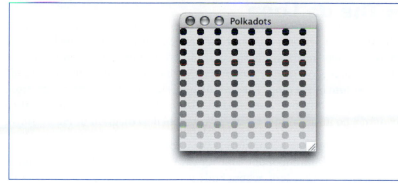

Figure 10.15

Window displayed by the polka dot program

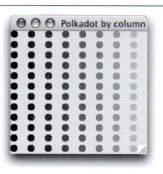

Figure 10.16

Window displayed by looping across columns

Nested loop repetition can be deceptively repetitious. For example, consider triply nested loops in which each loop is repeated one hundred times. The skeleton of such a structure is given below.

```
x = 0;
while (x != 100) {
    y = 0;
    while (y != 100) {
        z = 0;
        while (z != 100) {
            // work of innermost loop goes here
            z++;
        }
        y++;
    }
    x++;
}
```

When the above code executes, the `// work of innermost loop goes here` line is executed 100*100*100 or one hundred thousand (100,000) times!

10.6 ■ **The *do* Loop**

While loops are said to perform their test for loop exit at the **top of the loop**. The phrase "top of the loop" refers to the fact that the *while* loop's condition is checked *before* the loop body is executed. Java supports a second kind of loop that checks for loop exit at the **bottom of the loop**. This instruction is referred to as a **do instruction**. Figure 10.17 describes the syntax and semantics of the Java do instruction. The runtime behavior of a do instruction is shown as a control flow diagram of Figure 10.18.

The fact that *do* loops test their condition at the bottom of the loop means that the loop body executes a minimum of one time for each execution of the entire *do* loop. This is different from a *while* loop whose body is not executed when the loop condition is initially `false`. Except for this difference, however, a *do* loop behaves like a *while* loop.

Figure 10.17	*doInstruction* description (a possible *OneStatement*)

Syntax

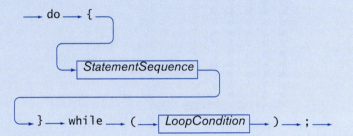

Alternate Syntax (when the loop body is a single statement)

Note

LoopCondition can be any valid Boolean-valued expression.

Style Notes

The reserved word do should be aligned with the "}" symbol that ends the *doInstruction* body and all statements within *StatementSequence* should be indented by at least one tab from the `while`.

Semantics

Executing *doInstruction* causes *StatementSequence* to execute once. Following each execution of *StatementSequence*, *LoopCondition* is evaluated. If *LoopCondition* is found to be `true`, then the process repeats. If *LoopCondition* is found to be `false`, then execution proceeds to the next statement following the do instruction.

Figure 10.18

The control flow of a *do* instruction

Java Syntax

```
// Statement before do
do {
     //Loop Body
} while (LoopCondition);

// Statement after do
```

Figure 10.19 contains an example program, using a *do* loop. This program displays a table of sine and cosine values for degree measurements from 0 degrees through 90 degrees (in 10-degree increments). The table is placed in three `TextArea` objects: `degreePane` displays the degrees, `sinePane` displays the corresponding sine values, and `cosinePane` displays the cosine values.

Each time the body of the `do` instruction from `displayTable` repeats, another line is appended to each of the three `TextArea` objects. When the program completes execution, the window that is displayed appears as shown in Figure 10.20.

The choice to use a *do* loop in the program to display a table of sine and cosine values is reasonable because this program must display more than one row of the table. The same algorithm could also have been written with a *while* loop instead of a *do* loop.

software *Hint*
engineering

How does a software developer choose between a *while* loop and a *do* loop? Most of the time, either loop will work well. In such cases *while* loops are generally used. The preference for *while* is simply that a *do* instruction always executes its loop body at least once, and the *while* works even if the loop body should not execute.

10.7 ■ **The** *for* **Loop**

Java includes a third looping instruction that generally is considered to be more specialized in nature than a `while` or `do`. The common form of the **for instruction** is described in Figure 10.21.

Below is a sample of the use of a *for* loop.

```
for (int k=1; k!=100; k++) {
    System.out.println(k);
}
```

software *Hint*
engineering

The alternative syntax for loop instructions omits braces. This should generally be avoided because code modifications tend to be easier if multiinstruction loop bodies are assumed.

Figure 10.19   A program to display a table of sine and cosine values

```java
import javax.swing.JFrame;
import java.awt.TextArea;
public class Driver  {
    private JFrame window;
    private TextArea degreePane, sinePane, cosinePane;

    public Driver()    {
        window = new JFrame("Table of sine and cosine");
        window.setBounds(10, 10, 300, 300);
        window.setVisible(true);
        window.setLayout(null);
        degreePane = new TextArea();
        degreePane.setBounds(10, 20, 50, 240);
        window.add(degreePane, 0);
        sinePane = new TextArea();
        sinePane.setBounds(70, 20, 100, 240);
        window.add(sinePane, 0);
        cosinePane = new TextArea();
        cosinePane.setBounds(180, 20, 100, 240);
        window.add(cosinePane, 0);
        displayTable();
        window.repaint();
    }

    /** post:  degreePane, sinePane and cosinePane contain s table of
     *           sine and cosine values beginning with 0 degrees through
     *           90 degrees in 10-degree increments.
     */
    private void displayTable( )    {
        int degrees = 0;
        degreePane.append("Deg. \n");
        degreePane.append("---- \n");
        sinePane.append("Sine \n");
        sinePane.append("------- \n");
        cosinePane.append("Cosine \n");
        cosinePane.append("------- \n");
        do {
            degreePane.append(degrees + "\n");
            sinePane.append(Math.sin(degrees/180.*Math.PI) + "\n");
                // Math trig functions use radian measures for angles
            cosinePane.append(Math.cos(degrees/180.*Math.PI) + "\n");
            degrees = degrees + 10;
        } while (degrees != 100);
    }
}
```

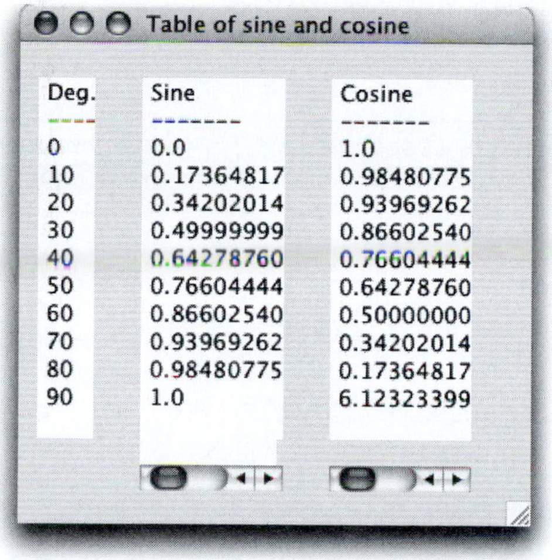

Table of sine and cosine

Deg.	Sine	Cosine
0	0.0	1.0
10	0.17364817	0.98480775
20	0.34202014	0.93969262
30	0.49999999	0.86602540
40	0.64278760	0.76604444
50	0.76604444	0.64278760
60	0.86602540	0.50000000
70	0.93969262	0.34202014
80	0.98480775	0.17364817
90	1.0	6.12323399

Figure 10.20 Output from the sine/cosine table program

The Semantics section of Figure 10.21 describes the behavior of a *for* loop in terms of an equivalent *while* loop. According to this description, the following code defines the behavior of the sample *for* loop.

```
int k=1;
while (k!=100) {
    System.out.println(k);
    k++;
}
```

Therefore, this example *for* loop is a counting loop with `k` as its counter variable. When the loop executes, the values from 1 through 99 are output.

Another way to explain the execution of *for* loops is in terms of the key parts of the loops (using names borrowed from Figure 10.21).

- *initInstr* is a single initialization instruction that is executed before the rest of the loop begins.
- *LoopCond* is tested at the top of the loop. If *LoopCond* is `true` then the body of the loop is executed, and the process repeats. When *LoopCond* is tested and found to be `false`, then the loop terminates.
- *StatementSequence* is the loop body.
- *progressInstr* is a single instruction that is executed immediately after every loop body repetition.

The *for* loop is a good choice for counting loops because *initInstr* can be used both to declare and initialize a counter variable. Declaring the counter within *initInstr* is a good idea, because it localizes the scope and the lifetime of the variable to the execution of the `for`. The *progressInstr* is also useful for counting loops as a way to assist the programmer to remember to include the "make progress" part of the loop body.

Figure 10.21   *forInstruction* description (a possible *OneStatement*)[2]

Syntax

Alternate Syntax (when the loop body is a single instruction)

Notes

- *initInstr* is some valid instruction. If this includes a variable declaration, then the variable is local with scope and lifetime restricted to this execution of the for instruction.
- *LoopCond* can be any valid Boolean-valued expression.
- *progressInstr* is some valid instruction.

Style Notes

The reserved word for should be aligned with the "}" symbol that ends the *forInstruction* and all instructions within *InstructionSequence* (i.e., the loop body) should be indented by at least one tab from the *for*. If the parenthesized code cannot be completed on one line, then "{" should be placed on a separate line and aligned with "}".

Semantics

Executing *forInstruction* behaves like the following code.

```
initInstr;
while (LoopCond) {
    StatementSequence;
    progressInstr;
}
```

---

[2] More specialized versions of the *for* loop are shown in Chapters 11 and 12.

Often *progressInstr* is used to increment (or decrement) the counter variable.

Figure 10.22 revisits the polka dot program previously given in Figure 10.14. This version of the program performs exactly the same function as the earlier one, but does so using *for* loops instead of *while* loops.

Using *for* loops tends to reduce the number of lines in a program because the initialization and make progress parts of the loop can all be combined. For example, the inner loop of the polka dot program when using a *while* loop is as follows:

```
xCount = 0;
while (xCount != 8) {
    . . .
    xCount++;
}
```

Using a *for* loop reduces the code as shown below:

```
for (int xCount=0; xCount != 8; xCount++) {
    . . .
}
```

Figure 10.22   Polka dot program using for loops

```java
import javax.swing.JFrame;
import java.awt.Color;
public class Driver {
    private JFrame window;

    public Driver() {
        Oval dot;
        Color rowColor;
        window = new JFrame("Polkadots");
        window.setBounds(10, 10, 200, 200);
        window.setVisible(true);
        window.setLayout(null);

        for (int yCount=0; yCount != 12; yCount++) {
            rowColor = new Color(yCount/13.0f, yCount/13.0f, yCount/13.0f);
            // rowColor is gray an intensity of yCount/13.
            // (0.0f is black and 1.0f is white)
            for (int xCount=0; xCount != 8; xCount++) {
                dot = new Oval(xCount*25, yCount*15, 10, 10);
                dot.setBackground(rowColor);
                window.add(dot, 0);
            }
        }
        window.repaint();
    }
}
```

software *Hint*
engineering

The default choice for a loop should be the *while* loop, since it works reasonably well for all situations. However, the *for* loop works well for simple counting loops or when the number of loop repetitions is known in advance. When using a **for** instruction, it is typical to use *initInstr* to declare and initialize a counting variable, *progressInstr* to increment the counter, and *LoopCond* to test the counter.

In addition, incorporating a declaration into the for eliminates the need for declaring xCount. All of these characteristics of the for make the code slightly more readable for simple counting loops.

When writing a loop, the programmer can always choose any of the three—while, do, or for. The choice depends upon the task at hand. Most programmers use while as the default because it works best in the widest variety of cases and is never really a bad choice. However, in situations where it is clear that the loop body will always execute at least once, the *do* loop is a viable choice. The *for* loop tends to be more specialized in purpose; a *for* loop should generally be avoided except for counting loops or certain sequential styles of data processing. Furthermore, when the parenthesized (...) clauses of the *for* loop exceed one line in length, there is a significant loss in readability.

10.8 ■ Loop Invariants

Assertions have been shown to be useful as class invariants, as well as method preconditions and postconditions. Assertions can also be useful in loop design. The particular kind of assertion that is used within loops is known as a **loop invariant**. (Not to be confused with a *class* invariant.)

A loop invariant captures the state of computation within a loop. This assertion should be placed just prior to the loop condition. Figure 10.23 shows how a loop invariant is located within a *while* loop.

Informally, a loop invariant captures the work of the loop by showing relationships that hold each time this location is encountered during code execution. For example, the following counting loop sums the numbers from 1 through num.

Figure 10.23   Placement of a loop invariant within a *while* loop

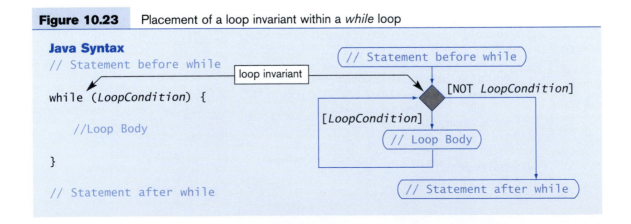

```
sum = 0;
counter = 1;
while /*invariant location*/ (counter != num+1) {
    sum = sum + counter;
    counter++;
}
```

The loop invariant for this code can be discovered by tracing the code, while writing down the values of both variables. Such a trace results in the following table.

sum	counter	
0	1	before the loop body executes the first time
1	2	before the loop body executes the second time
3	3	before the loop body executes the third time
6	4	before the loop body executes the fourth time
10	5	before the loop body executes the fifth time
15	6	before the loop body executes the sixth time
etc.	etc.	

A careful examination of this table shows that the following relation between sum and counter exists for each line of the table.

$$sum == 0 + 1 + 2 + \ldots + (counter-1)$$

This is a loop invariant for this loop.

As another example loop invariant, reconsider the Fibonacci loop.

```
aFibo = 1;
nextFibo = 1;
linesOutput = 0;
while (linesOutput != 30) {
    outPane.append(aFibo + "\n");
    newFibo = aFibo + nextFibo;
    aFibo = nextFibo;
    nextFibo = newFibo;
    linesOutput++;
}
```

An appropriate loop invariant for this code is given below.

The first linesOutput Fibonacci numbers have been output
and aFibo == the (linesOutput+1)*th* Fibonacci number
and nextFibo == the (linesOutput+2)*th* Fibonacci number

> software **engineering** *Hint*
>
> Writing loop invariants can be challenging at first. However, the unique perspective provided by a loop invariant is valuable.

Once the loop invariant is known, it can be used in many ways. A loop invariant can be used to test to see if initialization is done properly. This is accomplished by substituting the result of loop initialization into the loop invariant and checking to see if the resulting expression accurately describes the state immediately before loop execution. For example, the initialization code for the Fibonacci loop assigns `linesOutput==0`, `aFibo==1`, and `nextFibo==1`. Substituting these three values for their variables in the loop invariant results in the following:

> The first 0 Fibonacci numbers have been output
> *and* 1 == the (0+1)*th* Fibonacci number
> *and* 1 == the (0+2)*th* Fibonacci number

The above statement is clearly true since nothing is output before the loop begins and since 1 is both the first and second Fibonacci number. The fact that this statement is true reveals that the initialization code is correct.

The loop invariant can also be used to verify that the loop condition is correct. For example, consider the summing loop. An appropriate loop invariant follows.

> `sum == 0 + 1 + 2 + ... + (counter-1)`

Since this loop's condition is (`counter != num+1`) it must be that `counter == num+1` when the loop terminates. Substituting `num+1` for `counter` into the loop invariant results in the following assertion, which verifies that the loop has assigned the correct value to `sum` when it completes.

    sum == 0 + 1 + 2 + ... + (num+1-1) == 1 + 2 + ... + num

Similarly, the loop invariant for the Fibonacci loop states, among other things, that "The first `linesOutput` Fibonacci numbers have been output." Therefore, a loop that is supposed to output the first thirty Fibonacci numbers should properly begin with the following.

    while (linesOutput != 30)

The position of a loop invariant for a *do* loop should also be just prior to the loop condition. Below is an example, using a loop borrowed from the sine/cosine table program.

```
degrees = 0;
do {
    degreePane.appendln(" " + degrees);
    sinePane.appendln(" " + Math.sin(degrees/180.*Math.PI));
    cosinePane.appendln(" " + Math.cos(degrees/180.*Math.PI));
    degrees = degrees + 10;
    // Loop Invariant:
    //     the sine/cosine table is completed from 0 through
    //     degrees-10
} while (degrees != 100);
```

Some programmers also use loop invariants to design their code. The general procedure for designing a loop from a loop invariant consists of the following steps.

Step   Action

1. Select a loop invariant.
2. Choose loop initialization statements to make the loop invariant `true` initially.
3. Select a loop condition that when `false` ensures that the loop invariant implies the intended loop postassertion (i.e., the state that is required just following the loop).
4. Complete a loop body that preserves the invariant, while making progress.

As an example of using this four-step procedure to create a loop, consider the task of writing a loop to calculate the factorial of *n*, an integer variable. The factorial of *n* is defined to be 1*2*...*n. The notation "n!" is used to denote *n* factorial.

Figure 10.24 contains the shell of a loop to calculate n!. The italicized portions of this figure show code that remains to be designed. The *assert* comments (assertions) express desired runtime for their respective code locations. The assertion following the loop captures the intended purpose of the loop.

The first step in designing the *n* factorial loop is to select a loop invariant. An appropriate choice for this loop is

```
// Loop invariant: factorial == j!
```

This choice is based on the knowledge that a loop invariant generally has the same form as the assertion following the loop, but needs to represent an intermediate condition. Figure 10.25 shows the shell of the loop following Step 1.

Step 2 of the loop design is to use the loop invariant to derive the initialization code. Initialization code must guarantee that the loop invariant is `true` the first time it is encountered. The simplest initialization code in this situation sets both `factorial` to 1 and j to 0. (Note that 0! = 1 by the definition of factorial.) Figure 10.26 shows the loop shell with this initialization code included.

```
// Assume the declaration of three int variables: n, j, factorial
// assert: 0 <= n <= 12
// initialization code
while // Loop invariant
(SomeCondition) {
    // Loop Body
}
// assert: factorial = n!
```

Figure 10.24

Shell of a loop to calculate n! (n factorial)

Figure 10.25

Shell of *n*! loop with loop invariant (after Loop Design Step 1)

```
// Assume the declaration of three int variables: n, j, factorial
// assert: 0 <= n <= 12
// initialization code
while // Loop Inv: factorial == j!
(SomeCondition) {
    // Loop Body
}
// assert: factorial = n!
```

Figure 10.26

Shell of *n*! loop with initialization (after Loop Design Step 2)

```
// Assume the declaration of three int variables: n, j, factorial
// assert: 0 <= n <= 12
factorial = 1;
j = 0;
while // Loop Inv: factorial == j!
(SomeCondition) {
    // Loop Body
}
// assert: factorial = n!
```

Step 3 of loop design is to use the loop invariant to determine the proper loop condition. This step is achieved by noting that the assertion following the loop must be true when the loop terminates. If factorial==n! (from the assertion after the loop) and factorial==j! (from the loop invariant), then it must be that n==j. A loop condition of

    (j != n)

ensures that n==j when the loop terminates, which in turn assures the desired assertion following the loop. Figure 10.27 shows the loop shell with this loop condition inserted.

Figure 10.27

Shell of n! loop with condition (after Loop Design Step 3)

```
// Assume the declaration of three int variables: n, j, factorial
// assert: 0 <= n <= 12
factorial = 1;
j = 0;
while // Loop Inv: factorial == j!
(j != n) {
    // Loop Body
}
// assert: factorial = n!
```

The final step of loop design, Step 4, is to complete the code for the body of the loop. This step involves recognizing two things:

1. A loop must make progress toward completion.

2. A loop must preserve its loop invariant.

The initialization code causes the variable, j, to have an initial value of 1. The loop condition makes it clear that j will have a value of n when the loop terminates. Therefore, the value of j must increase if the loop body is to make progress. The following loop body makes progress and ensures that the loop invariant is still `true`.

```
j++;
factorial = factorial * j;
```

Inserting this loop body completes the factorial program as shown in Figure 10.28.

Most programmers do not perform the loop design in this detailed, step-by-step manner. However, they do borrow from the reasoning that is used in these four steps. Furthermore, several remarkably efficient algorithms have been discovered using this procedure to design loops from their invariants.

software *Hint*
engineering
The four-step procedure for using a loop invariant to design a loop should be remembered even when it is not used explicitly. The four-step procedure assists in writing loops that are correct *the first time.*

10.9 ■ Looping and Event Handling

Loops appear to provide a tempting approach to perform animation. For example, the following code may seem like a way to cause a Label to move across a window.

```
// Warning: The following code may be deceptive.
JFrame window;
Label label;
window = new JFrame("Poor attempt to animate");
window.setBounds(10, 10, 300, 100);
window.setVisible(true);
window.setLayout(null);
label = new Label("Help Me");
```

```
// Assume the declaration of three int variables: n, j, factorial
// assert: 0 <= n <= 12
factorial = 1;
j = 0;
while // Loop Inv: factorial == j!
(j != n) {
    j++;
    factorial = factorial * j;
}
// assert: factorial = n!
```

Figure 10.28

Shell of *n*! loop with body (after Loop Design Step 4)

```
label.setBounds(0, 30, 100, 30);
window.add(label, 0);
while (label.getX() + label.getWidth() < 300) {
    label.setLocation(label.getX() + 20, label.getY());
}
```

Clearly, the initialization code places `label` on the left edge of `window`. Just as clearly, the loop body causes `label` to move to the right for each repetition. However, when this code executes, `label` does *not* move. Instead, all that is seen when the program executes is the label positioned at the right side of the window. The behavior of this code relies upon an understanding of the workings of the Java Virtual Machine. The opened black box below is another reminder of how the JVM works at runtime.

Opening
the Black Box

> Java programs can be thought of as largely *reactive*. A program may begin by executing the Driver constructor, but then it becomes idle. Whenever an event occurs, the program reacts by executing an event handler, then once again the program is idle. The next event results in another event handler "reaction." This pattern of reacting to events then becoming idle is precisely what the Java VM expects from a program.

In order to support this react-then-become-idle pattern, the Java VM essentially leaves the graphical display unaltered until an idle time. In other words, a call to `repaint()` does not result in an immediate change to a display. Instead, the display is updated only when the program becomes idle. Therefore, using a loop to animate is futile.

The correct way to animate a `Label` so that it moves across a window is accomplished with events, using a class such as `EventTimer` shown in Chapter 8 or to use `javax.swing.Timer` as described in Chapter 9.

10.10 ■ Testing and Loops

In Chapter 7, we examined the idea of structure testing. Loops pose unique problems for software testers who are concerned with testing paths through the control flow. It is essentially impossible to achieve path coverage when testing most code that contains one or more loops. The problem is that the control path for executing a loop body just once is different from the path for executing it twice and from the path for executing it three times, and so forth. This leads to the conclusion that there are an enormous number (often infinite) of possible execution paths for even a single loop.

A reasonable alternative to path coverage, called **loop coverage**, is to ensure that each loop body is executed multiple times. It is a good practice to include at least three possibilities in the loop coverage:

- Ensure that at least one test case checks the loop for the fewest possible executions of its loop body—zero for `while` and `for` and one for `do` (i.e., the loop condition causes loop exit the first time it is tested).
- Ensure that at least one test case checks for a loop body that executes exactly once.
- Ensure that at least one test case checks for multiple consecutive loop body executions.

For example, consider a loop that is designed to calculate the total of all consecutive odd integers from 1 through n, assuming that n is odd. In other words, this loop should assign the `oddTotal` variable the value of 1+3+5+ ... +n. Such a loop is shown in Figure 10.29.

Testing this loop might proceed as follows:

- One test case could be for `n == 1`. This checks the case where the loop executes just once. (The final value of `oddTotal` will correctly be 1.)
- A different test case could check when `n == 7`. This checks the loop in a situation when it executes a few times. (The final value of `oddTotal` will correctly be 1+3+5+7 or 16.)
- Yet another different test case could check when `n == -3`. This checks the loop in a situation when it executes zero times. (The final value of `oddTotal` will correctly be 0.)
- You might even test the code to see how robust it is by violating the initial assertion. In this case, a test value of n that is even (say `n == 4`). (The final value of `oddTotal` will be 1+3+5 or 9; it is not clear whether this is correct or incorrect.)

```
// assert: n is an odd integer
int oddtotal = 0;
int oddNum = -1;
while (oddNum < n) {
    oddNum = oddNum + 2;
    oddTotal = oddTotal + oddNum;
}
// assert: oddTotal == 1+3+...+n
```

Figure 10.29

Loop to total consecutive odd integers

Inspector

Below is a collection of hints on what to check when examining code that involves the concepts of this chapter.

■ It is always a good idea to simulate the execution of a loop on your desktop by tracing a few repetitions. Ideally, the loop should be traced for its first two or three repetitions and its last two or three.

■ Most programmers concentrate on the portion of the loop body that performs the primary work of the loop. It is always wise to check that the portion of the loop body that makes progress is correct.

■ Every loop needs some initialization. A loop should be examined to ensure proper initialization before its first repetition.

■ One extremely effective means of verifying a loop is to express a loop invariant, and then use it to check the loop in the following ways:

1. Is the initialization code sufficient to assure that the loop invariant is true the first time it is encountered?

2. Do the loop invariant and the negation of the loop condition imply the desired result of the loop?

3. Does the loop body preserve the invariant after each repetition?

■ When loops are nested, it is the inner loop that does most of the work. The inner loop should always be examined for statements that can be moved outside of its body without changing the final result of the code. Such statements should be moved outside of the inner loop for more efficient code.

■ If a *do* loop is used, it is best to check that its loop body must always execute at least once. If the loop might need to skip the body under certain circumstances, then a *while* loop is better.

■ If a *for* loop is used, it is best to check that its first line is not too long or complex. In such cases it may be that the loop would be easier to read if written as a *while* loop.

■ When expressing a counting loop using a for statement, you should check to see if it is possible to include the declaration of the counting variable into the initialization portion of the for statement because this is better defensive programming.

■ The Java VM event loop can get swamped by inefficient event handlers. Each event handler should be examined for unnecessary code or inefficiencies. Can some of the event handler code be performed when the object is initialized? Are there any repaint calls that are unnecessary?

Terminology

bottom of a loop

counting loop pattern

dead loop

do instruction

do loop

doubly nested loops

event loop

for loop

infinite loop

initialization (of a loop)

loop body

loop condition

loop coverage

loop invariant

making progress (in a loop body)

nested loops

repetition control structures

top of a loop

triply nested loops

while instruction

while loop

Exercises

1. Show the exact output that is produced by executing each of the following loops.

a.
```java
int k;
k = 0;
while (k < 9) {
    System.out.println(k*5);
    k++;
}
```

b.
```java
int k;
k = 11;
while (k != 19) {
    System.out.println(k);
    k = k + 2;
}
```

c.
```java
int k;
k = 10;
while (k != 13) {
    System.out.println(k);
    k = k + 2;
}
```

```
d. int k;
   k = 0;
   while (k != -9) {
       k = k - 1;
       System.out.println(k);
       k = k - 2;
   }

e. int k;
   k = 1;
   while (k != 9) {
       System.out.println(k);
   }

f. int k;
   k = 1;
   while (k != 9) {
       k = k + 2;
       System.out.println(k);
       k = k - 1;
   }

g. int k, j;
   k = 33;
   j = 1;
   while (k < j) {
       k = k + 10;
       System.out.println(k);
       j = j * 2;
   }

h. int k;
   k = 1;
   do {
       k++;
       System.out.println(k);
   } while (k != 9);

i. int k;
   k = 1;
   while (k != 33) {
       k++;
       System.out.println(k);
       k++;
   }

j. for (int k=1; k != 33; k++) {
       System.out.println(k);
   }
```

k. ```
   for (int k=1; k != 33; k++) {
       k++;
       System.out.println(k);
       k++;
   }
   ```

l. ```
   for (int k=1; k != 33; k = k + 2) {
       System.out.println(k);
   }
   ```

m. ```
   for (int k=0; k != 33; k = k + 2) {
       System.out.println(k);
   }
   ```

**2.** Which of the Exercise 1 loops are infinite loops?

**3.** Show the content of outPane following the execution of each of the following code segments.

a. ```
   JFrame window = new JFrame("");
   window.setBounds(10, 10, 200, 200);
   window.setVisible(true);
   window.setLayout(null);
   TextArea outPane = new ATextArea();
   outPane.setBounds(50, 50, 100, 100);
   window.add(outPane, 0);
   outPane.append("This is a test\n");
   outPane.append("of an ATextArea object.");
   outPane.append("This is only a test.\n");
   ```

b. ```
   JFrame window = new JFrame("");
   window.setBounds(10, 10, 200, 200);
   window.setVisible(true);
   window.setLayout(null);
   TextArea outPane = new ATextArea();
   outPane.setBounds(50, 50, 100, 100);
   char oneChar;
   window.add(outPane, 0);
   oneChar = 'a';
   while (oneChar < 'y') {
       outPane.append(oneChar);
       oneChar++;
   }
   outPane.append("/" + "\n");
   ```
   ```

4. Show the exact output that is produced by executing each of the following loops.

a.
```java
int j, k;
k = 0;
while (k < 3) {
    j = 5;
    while (j > 0) {
        System.out.println("j == " + j);
        j = j - 2;
    }
    System.out.println("k == " + k);
    k++;
}
```

b.
```java
int j, k;
k = 1;
while (k < 7) {
    j = 5;
    while (j > 0) {
        System.out.println("j == " + j);
        System.out.println("k == " + k);
        j--;
    }
    k = k * 2;
}
```

c.
```java
int j, k;
k = 1;
j = 10;
while (k < 8) {
    while (j > 0) {
        System.out.println("j == " + j);
        System.out.println("k == " + k);
        j--;
    }
    k = k * 2;
}
```

d.
```java
int j, k;
k = 1;
while (k < 8) {
    j = 5;
    while (j > k) {
        System.out.println("j == " + j);
        System.out.println("k == " + k);
        j--;
    }
    k = k * 2;
}
```

5. What is the value of the `sum` variable following the execution of the following code segment?

```
int j, k, m, n, sum;
sum = 0;
j = 0;
while (j != 20) {
    k = 0;
    while (k != 100) {
        m = 0;
        while (m != 50) {
            n = 0;
            while (n != 10) {
                sum++;
                n++;
            }
            m++;
        }
        k++;
    }
    j++;
}
```

6. Consider the code below.

```
int k, prod;
// initialization code here
while (k != lastInt) {
    prod = prod + 7;
    k = k + 1;
}
/* Assert: prod == 7 * lastInt */
```

Below is a proper loop invariant for this loop.

```
prod = 7 * k
```

a. What initialization code needs to be inserted to make this loop work properly?

b. Which part of this code is the primary work and which is the make progress part of the loop?

c. For what values of `lastInt` does this code result in an infinite loop?

d. How does the assertion following the loop change if the two instructions of the loop body are reversed to become

```
k = k + 1;
prod = prod + 7;
```

e. What is the proper loop invariant resulting from the changes described in Part c?

f. Rewrite this code to perform the original task (i.e., the assertion after the loop is the same) but the value of k *decreases* by one for each loop body execution.

g. Rewrite this code to perform the original task, using a *do* loop, instead of a *while* loop.

7. Each part below shows a final assertion and a loop invariant for a *while* loop. Your task is to write a loop that, when executed, makes the final assertion true and also has the given loop invariant. Be certain to include the declaration of all needed variables and proper initialization code. You may assume that all variables are of type int.

a. final assertion
```
sum = 1 + 2 + ... + 100
```

loop invariant
```
sum = 1 + 2 + ... + intVar
```

b. final assertion
```
sum = 1 + 3 + 5 + ... + 999
```

loop invariant
```
sum = 1 + 3 + ... + intVar and intVar % 2 = 1
```

c. final assertion
```
sum = 3 + 4 + 5 + ... + 999
```

loop invariant
```
sum = intVar + (intVar+1) + (intVar+2) + ... + 999
```

Programming Exercises

1. Write a program to factor any positive integer. Below is an example of such a program that accepts the value to be factored in a JTextField and displays all of the prime factors in a TextArea.

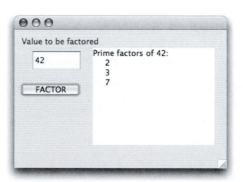

2. Write a program that calculates both the greatest common divisor (GCD) and least common multiple (LCM) of two positive integers. If either input value is nonpositive or not an integer, a proper error message should be displayed. Below is an example of such a program, using `JTextField` objects and a button for user input.

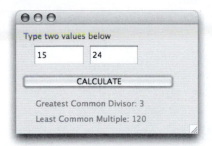

The greatest common divisor is the largest integer that divides evenly (with a remainder of zero) both input numbers. The least common multiple is the smallest integer that can be evenly divided by both input numbers.

3. This program is designed to draw a ruler of up to 10 inches in length. The interface to this program is a Control Window with two text fields and a button. The top text field is for the user to specify the length of the ruler (in whole inches). The bottom text field allows the user to specify graduations (1 for inches only; 2 for inches and halves; 4 for inches, halves, and quarters; 8 for inches, halves, quarters, and eighths; 10 for inches and tenths; and everything else for inches, halves, quarters, eighths, and sixteenths).

The ruler is drawn in a separate window in response to a button click. Be certain that every button click draws a new ruler using the text field values at that time. Below is a picture of the way a ruler should be drawn. Note that each button click causes the ruler to redraw to the user's specifications.

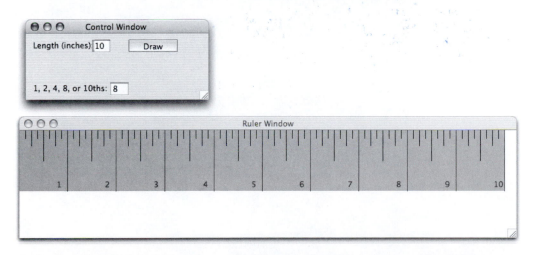

4. Pythagorean triples are any three positive integers for which the square of the largest equals the sum of the squares of the other two. For example, 3, 4, and 5 are a Pythagorean triple because $3^2 + 4^2 == 5^2$. Write a program to display all Pythagorean triples whose individual values are less than a user-specified value. Below is an example in which the maximum value is 17.

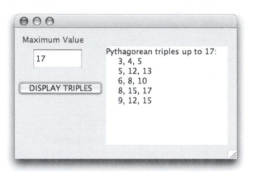

5. For this assignment you must design and implement the code necessary to display a calendar for any specified month and year. When the program begins, it must display a single window that appears like the one below. The user is expected to type a year and a month (as integers) into two text fields and then to click the Show Calendar button. In response to the Show Calendar click, your program must display a calendar for that particular month (i.e., dates must be arranged in columns for the correct week days). Every month must be displayed with the leftmost column of numbers corresponding to Sunday.

Where did our calendar come from?

It takes the earth approximately 365.24219878 days to orbit the sun. The ancient Egyptians invented a calendar with a 365-day year. While this may have kept the seasons consistent with the calendar during the length of the Egyptian empire, this calendar clearly drifts after time. In fact, the calendar loses an entire year after 1508 years. The Romans detected the error in the Egyptian calendar and created the so-called Julian calendar, which added a day to every fourth year. It takes the Julian calendar about 47 centuries to gain a year of time, but it still has considerable drift. In 1582, Pope Gregory XIII approved the calendar, which was named the Gregorian calendar for him. We continue to use the Gregorian calendar today.

Using the Gregorian calendar there are still 365 days in most years, and every year that has 366 days (i.e., leap year) does so by virtue of February 29. The rule for determining leap year is as follows. Leap year occurs for any year that is evenly divisible by four (i.e., year % 4 == 0) that is not evenly divisible by 100, unless it is evenly divisible by 400.

Why the long description of leap year? Because you need to calculate the number of days that have passed in order to decide which day of the week is day 1 for a particular month. In other words, if you calculate the total number of days that occurred since the first day A.D. modulo (%) seven through October 1999, then you will find the weekday for November 1, 1999. (By the way, January 1 in year 1 was a Monday.)

Containers

11

Objectives

- To examine the utility of containers as both a receptacle for items and a way to organize items
- To explore `Bag<ItemType>` as a simple generic container
- To introduce the importance of type safety
- To present wrapper classes and show how to manually and automatically box and unbox
- To examine a class, called `SimpleList` that implements a list container with an internal iterator
- To explore how an iterator is used in conjunction with other list operations
- To introduce the concept of a list traversal algorithm pattern and examine several such algorithms
- To examine a specialized version of the *for* loop that is useful for simple iterator processing
- To explore linear searching algorithms as a method of looking for list data satisfying certain properties
- To introduce the concept of a sorted container and show how to maintain a sorted list by means of the insertion method
- To examine generic parameters, including those constrained by an *extends* clause

Vending machines, video rental stores, and banks all have something in common. They all store items that are dispensed to their clients. A vending machine stores snack foods, video rental stores offer DVDs, and banks are repositories for money.

In programming terminology, an entity that exhibits this ability to store and dispense items as needed is referred to as a **container**. Vending machines, video rental stores, and banks are all real world examples of containers.

11.1 ■ Containers

People often think of computers as machines for implementing containers. An employee payroll program utilizes a *container of employees*. An airline reservation system relies upon *containers of airplane seat assignments*. A university transcript is a *container of collegiate courses*.

In an object-oriented environment, containers are themselves objects, but a container is unique in the sense that its primary purpose is to serve as a storehouse for other objects. Typical container methods include the following:

- methods for initializing the container
- methods to insert objects into the container
- methods to remove objects from the container
- methods to inspect the content of the container
- methods to return the size and other container properties

In addition, container classes sometimes include other methods to organize their content or to assist client software in locating content with special properties.

The standard Java *AWT* library includes a class called `Container` that is a particular kind of container. Objects belonging to `Container` are used to keep track of items that are being displayed. The graphical classes used as examples throughout this text are descendants of `Container`. Figure 11.1 shows the inheritance structure of several such classes.

The method that is called by classes in order to insert a new object into a `Container` is named **add**. When an object is `add`ed to a `Container` it can be displayed. Java also provides a `remove` method to take an object out of its `Container`, thereby erasing its image. An `Oval`, a `JComponent`, and the content pane of every `JFrame` all inherit this behavior from `Container`.

Figure 11.1   Inheritance structure of the `Container` and related classes

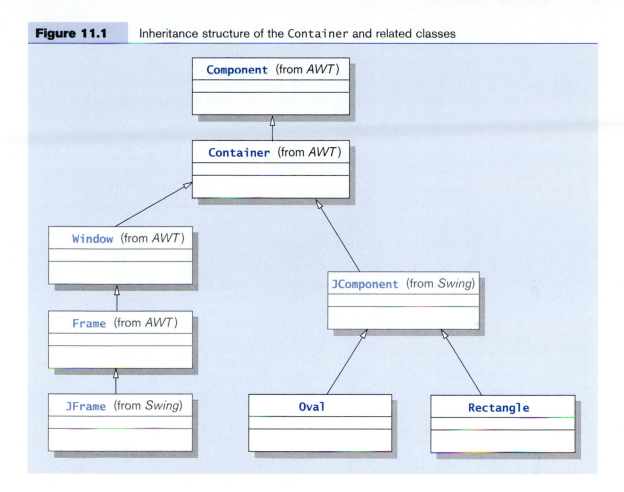

One characteristic of `Container` that is not true of all containers is the restriction that no two `Container` objects may contain the same object simultaneously. This restriction is enforced by the `add` method; if `add` is called upon an object that is already in another `Container`, then that object is automatically removed from its prior containment.

In addition to their ability to be added and removed, objects belonging to descendants of `Component` share another method related to `Container`. A `getParent()` method is included in all of these classes to return the `Container` to which the object is added. (The value of `getParent() == null` for an object that isn't added.)

11.2 ■ **Generic Containers**

The `Container` class from the *AWT* library is a useful technique for storing graphical objects, but as a container it is highly specialized. There are many other kinds of containers that cannot be implemented using `Container`. Perhaps you need a container to store the addresses of friends, or perhaps you need a container of favorite URLs, or perhaps you would like a container of quiz scores—a container that stores only `Component` objects is not sufficient.

One way to meet these other needs is to use a general purpose container. Among the most general purpose containers are those known as **generic containers**. A generic container class is one designed to support the creation of containers for storing different kinds of objects.

Figure 11.2 contains a class diagram for a simple generic container, called `Bag`. `Bag` is not a standard library; it is included to better illustrate the characteristics of a simple container. (An implementation of `Bag` is included on the CD that accompanies this book.) The methods of the `Bag` class are typical for a container class. These methods include the following:

- `add`—to put an item into a `Bag`
- `remove`—to remove an item from a `Bag`
- `item`—a method to return (inspect) one value entity from within a `Bag` without removing it
- `size`—a method to return the integer count of the number of items in a `Bag`

A generic class supports containers for different types of content, but the individual containers need not be generic. The class diagram reflects this with the notation `<ItemType>` as a suffix to the class name. When an actual container is declared and instantiated Java requires that an actual type (an expression referring to some known class or interface) be supplied inside angle brackets < ... > immediately following the container class name. The following statements illustrate:

```
Bag<String> nameCollection;
nameCollection = new Bag<String>();
```

Figure 11.2

Bag class diagram

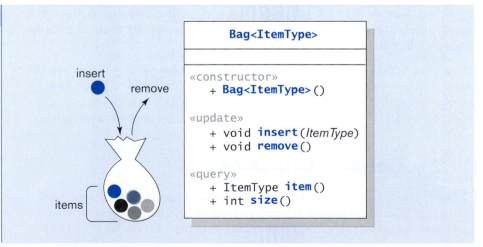

The first statement declares a `Bag` container, known as `nameCollection`. The `<String>` suffix signifies that `nameCollection` stores items that must conform to `String`. When a container object is instantiated, as in the second statement, it is also necessary to specify the item type.

Genericity provides flexibility in the sense that the same class can be used to create different kinds of containers. A `Bag<Color>` object is a container for `Color` items. A `Bag<JFrame>` is a container for `JFrame` items. A `Bag<Money>` is a container for `Money` items.

Figure 11.3 explains more details about the `Bag` class and its methods in the form of a class specification. Notice that the lack of a precondition on `add` means that there is no limit on the number of items that can be inserted.

Invariant

A `Bag<ItemType>` object

- is a container of zero or more other objects
- is capable of storing anything that conforms to the instantiated argument for `ItemType` (This instantiated argument can be any class name.)

Constructor Method

`public Bag<ItemType>()`

post: `this` is an empty bag (i.e., `size() == 0`)

Query Methods

`public int size()`

post: *result* == the number of items in `this` Bag

`public ItemType item()`

pre: `size() > 0`

post: *result* == one of the items from `this` Bag

Update Methods

`public void add (ItemeType z)`

post: `this == this@pre` with z inserted

    and `size() = size()@pre + 1`

`public void remove()`

pre: `size() > 0`

post: `this == this@pre` with one item removed

    and `size() = size()@pre - 1`

Figure 11.3

Bag<ItemType> class specifications

Below is a segment of code that creates a `Bag` object and inserts `String` objects into it.

```
Bag<String> nameCollection;
nameCollection = new Bag<String>();
nameCollection.add("Richard");
nameCollection.add("Eddie");
nameCollection.add("Marion");
nameCollection.add("Richard");
nameCollection.remove();
System.out.println("Number of names stored: "
    + nameCollection.size());
```

When the above code executes, it constructs an empty bag of strings, called `nameCollection`. The code continues by adding four `String` objects, `"Richard"`, `"Eddie"`, `"Marion"`, and `"Richard"` again. Next, one of the names is removed from the bag. The final instruction outputs the message.

```
Number of names stored: 3
```

Sometimes generic classes are called **parameterized classes** because the generic part(s) behave like parameters. The generic parameter in the `Bag` class is called `ItemType`, and when the class is declared and instantiated a class name, such as `<String>`, it must be supplied like an argument for the `ItemType` parameter. Generic parameters are always specified by an identifier placed immediately after the class name and enclosed within < ... > symbols. (Multiple generic parameters are possible as long as they are placed within the same < ... > brackets and separated by commas.)

Within the class a generic parameter can be used as though it named an actual class. Figure 11.3 demonstrates by specifying the type of the parameter for the `add` method to be `ItemType`. The return type for the `item` method is also declared to be `ItemType`.

Arguments for generic parameters must be supplied in two places—once in the declaration of the generic class and again whenever the class is instantiated. A class name must be used for both arguments. The class used as an argument during instantiation must conform to that of the declaration. (Although in practice they are generally the same.) The generic parameter takes on the type from instantiation. For the `nameCollection` container the actual class supplied for `ItemType` is `String`. Therefore, the following code satisfies all type conformance rules because both the argument of the `add` method and the value returned by `item` method are assumed to be of type `String`.

```
Bag<String> nameCollection;
String nameString;
nameCollection = new Bag<String>();
nameCollection.add("Lea");
nameString = nameCollection.item();
```

This code creates a Bag<String> called nameCollection and adds the String object, "Lea", to nameCollection. The fifth instruction assigns "Lea" to nameString. (The item method is guaranteed to return "Lea" because "Lea" is the only object within the container.)

The program in Figure 11.4 demonstrates another use of Bag. This program creates a JFrame displaying two JButtons. Each click on one button (addBtn) causes a new randomly located black line to appear on the JFrame and each click of the other button (redBtn) causes one of the previously added lines to be recolored in red. (Note that a redBtn click will appear to do nothing in the event that the selected line is already red.)

The Driver class for the random line program declares and instantiates a Bag<RandomLine> variable called bagOfLines. (The RandomLine class is also included in Figure 11.4.) Each click of addBtn causes a new RandomLine object to be created and added into bagOfLines. Each click of redBtn executes the following code.

```
if (bagOfLines.size() != 0) {
    someLine = bagOfLines.item();
    someLine.setBackground(Color.red);
}
```

The *if* instruction guards against calling item when the bag is empty bag. For a nonempty bag this code causes the someLine variable (of type RandomLine) to be assigned one item from bagOfLines and then someLine is colored red. As the program executes some of the lines to be colored red may have already been colored red and some may not.

The Java mechanism for generic classes provides support for **type safety** in the sense that the Java compiler generates errors for attempts to add items of nonconforming type. For example, bagOfLines is declared and instantiated to be Bag<RandomLine>. Therefore, only objects conforming to RandomLine can be added to bagOfLines. Similarly, a call to bagOfLines.item() is guaranteed to return an object conforming to RandomLine.

Programmers can weaken type safety by declaring types too broadly. For example, suppose that Bag is declared and instantiated to be a container of Object as follows:

```
Bag<Object> bagOfLines = new Bag<Object>();
RandomLine insertObject = new RandomLine();
bagOfLines.add(insertObject);
RandomLine inspectedObject;
inspectedObject = (RandomLine)(bagOfLines.item());
```

software *Hint*
engineering

Every type cast is potentially dangerous. The need for type casts should be viewed as a sign that the code may not be type safe.

For the code above ItemType is Object. Since the type of insertObject is RandomLine and since RandomLine conforms to Object, the third statement (the call to add) is acceptable. In fact, any kind of object can be added to a Bag<Object>. However, the cast to (RandomLine) in the fifth statement is essential to avoid a com-

Figure 11.4   The `Driver` and associated `RandomLine` classes

```
import javax.swing.*;
import java.awt.event.*;
import java.awt.Color;
public class Driver implements ActionListener {
    private JFrame window;
    private JButton addBtn, redBtn;
    private Bag<RandomLine> bagOfLines;

    /** post:  window is created at (10, 10) with width and
     *              height of 400
     *          and addBtn & redBtn are added to window
     */
    public Driver() {
        window = new JFrame("Random Lines");
        window.setBounds(10, 10, 400, 400);
        window.setVisible(true);
        window.setLayout(null);
        addBtn = new JButton("Add a Line");
        addBtn.setBounds(10, 330, 180, 30);
        addBtn.addActionListener(this);
        window.add(addBtn, 0);
        redBtn = new JButton("Color Line Red");
        redBtn.setBounds(210, 330, 180, 30);
        redBtn.addActionListener(this);
        window.add(redBtn, 0);
        window.repaint();
        bagOfLines = new Bag<RandomLine>();
    }

    /** post:  e.getSource() == addBtn
     *              implies a new randomly drawn line segment appears.
     *          and e.getSource() == redBtn
     *              implies one line from pane@pre has been removed
     */
    public void actionPerformed(ActionEvent e) {
        RandomLine someLine;
        if (e.getSource() == addBtn) {
            someLine = new RandomLine();
```

piler error. Unfortunately, type casts weaken type safety because the compiler does not check that the cast is valid until runtime.

A `Bag<Object>` may contain any kind of object, because all classes conform to `Object`, but this flexibility comes at a cost. Without knowing precisely what is in the

```
            window.add(someLine, 0);
            bagOfLines.add(someLine);
        } else {
            if (bagOfLines.size() != 0) {
                someLine = bagOfLines.item();
                someLine.setBackground(Color.red);
            }
        }
    }
    window.repaint();
    }
}

import javax.swing.JComponent;
import java.awt.*;
public class RandomLine extends JComponent {
    private int x1, y1, x2, y2;

    /** post:  0 <= x1 <= 399 and 0 <= y1 <= 399
     *         and 0 <= x2 <= 399 and 0 <= y2 <= 399
     *         and getBackground() == Color.black
     */
    public RandomLine() {
        setBounds(0, 0, 400, 400);
        x1 = (int)(Math.random()*400);
        x2 = (int)(Math.random()*400);
        y1 = (int)(Math.random()*400);
        y2 = (int)(Math.random()*400);
        setBackground(Color.black);
    }

    /** post:  a black line is drawn from (x1,y1) to (x2,y2)
     *         and the line is colored getBackground()
     */
    public void paint(Graphics g) {
        g.setColor(getBackground());
        g.drawLine(x1, y1, x2, y2);
    }
}
```

container, it is impossible to inspect container content because the value returned by the item method requires a cast for treatment of any type except Object. Of course, instanceof can be used, but this only allows a program to test for some fixed set of possible types.

11.3 ■ Wrapper Classes and Autoboxing/Unboxing

The distinction between primitive types and reference types has implications for generic classes. The primitive types (`int`, `boolean`, `byte`, `char`, `double`, `float`, `long`, and `short`) are not classes in Java. This means that the primitive types do *not* conform to `Object`. This also means that a primitive type name cannot be used to specify a generic parameter. For example, the following declaration is not permitted.

```
Bag<int> attemptedBag; //invalid declaration
```

Fortunately, the *java.lang* library includes a set of classes to compensate for this inconsistency between the primitive and reference types. These classes are known as the **wrapper classes** because their purpose is to provide a way to wrap a primitive value within a reference object. As shown in Figure 11.5, there is a separate wrapper class for every primitive type. Wrapper classes usually take the name of their corresponding primitive type, except for capitalizing the first letter of the name. For example, the wrapper class for `boolean` types is `Boolean` and the wrapper class for `double` types is `Double`. The two exceptions to this rule are for primitive types `int` and `char`. The wrapper class for `int` is `Integer`, and the wrapper class for `char` is `Character`.

Each wrapper class includes two key methods:

1. A constructor method that accepts a single parameter of its corresponding primitive type. This constructor creates an object that stores the value of its argument.

2. A method to return the primitive value stored within the wrapper. These methods are always named with the primitive type followed by the suffix "`Value`", and they are parameterless.

Figure 11.6 illustrates these two methods by supplying the class specifications for the `Integer` wrapper class.

Figure 11.5

Wrapper classes corresponding to primitive types

Primitive Class	Corresponding Wrapper Class
boolean	Boolean
byte	Byte
char	Character
double	Double
float	Float
int	Integer
long	Long
short	Short

Figure 11.6

Integer class specifications

Invariant

An Integer object

- is a wrapper around an embedded value of type int.
- implicitly inherits Object like other classes.
- does not support int operators such as +, -, <, etc.

Constructor Method

public Integer (int j)

    post: the embedded value of this == *j*

Query Method

public int intValue ()

    post: *result* == the embedded value of this

    . . .

Converting from a primitive value to its corresponding wrapper class object is called **boxing**. The wrapper class constructors are methods that perform boxing. For example, the second statement below boxes the value of myInt, wrapping this value (396) into an Integer object bound to the yourInteger variable.

```
int myInt = 396;
Integer yourInteger = new Integer(myInt);
```

The process of converting from a wrapper class object to its primitive equivalent is called **unboxing**. Each wrapper class provides a nonvoid (*type*Value) method that unboxes the object by returning its unwrapped equivalent. For example, the second statement below unboxes herInteger, storing its unwrapped int value (784) in hisInt.

```
Integer herInteger = new Integer(784);
int hisInt = herInteger.intValue();
```

The advantage of a wrapper class object is that its type conforms to Object. This means that wrapper class objects can be placed within a Bag just like other objects whose type conforms to Object. This also means that you can declare and instantiate generic classes with wrapper class generic arguments such as Bag<Integer>.

Beginning with Version 1.5.0, Java incorporates mechanisms known as **autoboxing** and **autounboxing** for using primitive types with generic classes. As the names imply, values are automatically boxed and unboxed as necessary when used in conjunction with generic types. This saves the programmer from worrying about when

software *Hint*
engineering
Autoboxing and autoun-
boxing can be confusing.
The assignments to the left
are unnecessary and
potentially difficult for other
programmers to read. It is
best to avoid autoboxing
and autounboxing unless
you have a good reason,
such as using primitives in
generic classes.

to box and when to unbox. For example, the Java compiler allows the following instructions:

```
Integer itsInteger = 17;
int itsInt = itsInteger;
```

These two instructions would seem to be erroneous because primitive types and reference types are generally incompatible. However, the Java compiler compensates for this apparent error by autoboxing the 17 in the first instruction and autounboxing itsInteger in the second. It is even possible to write instructions such as the following:

```
Integer herInteger = yourInteger * hisInteger;
```

When this instruction executes the value of yourInteger and hisInteger must be autounboxed, because the multiplication operation (*) applies only to primitive, not wrapper class, values. Once the two primitive values are multiplied the result must be autoboxed in order to store it in herInteger.

This autoboxing and autounboxing is particularly useful when you need to use a primitive argument for a generic parameter. For example, the compiler will not permit the declaration of Bag<int> because int is a primitive, not a class. Fortunately, Bag<Integer> achieves the same intent given autoboxing and autounboxing. The following code segment demonstrates.

```
Bag<Double> doubleBag = new Bag<Double>();
doubleBag.add(85.1);
double primitiveVar = doubleBag.item();
```

In order to declare and instantiate doubleBag it is necessary to use the Double wrapper class. In the second statement the value 85.1 is autoboxed in order to conform to the type of Double. In the third statement the value returned by item() is of type Double so it is autounboxed to be assigned to primitiveVar.

11.4 ■ Lists

The Bag class provides for useful illustrations of the basics of generic Java container classes, but programmers rarely use a class like Bag. Bag's primary shortcoming is that it provides no mechanisms for controlling the order of items within the container. The remove method from Bag removes an item, but the program cannot control *which* item will be removed. Similarly, a call to item inspects (returns) one of the items from a Bag, but which one? Most algorithms require containers that provide better control over the order in which items are removed and inspected.

One of the best known ordered containers is called **list**. Lists treat their content as a single file line of items. Every item in the list, except the front item, has another item preceding it, and every item, except the back item, has an item behind it. Like links on a chain, list items are located in specific positions within the list. Also like a chain, inserting or removing links does not alter the relative position of the other links in the chain.

front ←——————————————————————————————→ back

Actually, a list is not a single kind of container because there are many different kinds of lists. For the purposes of this text, a particular kind of list known as `SimpleList`, is examined and a class implementing `SimpleList` is supplied. Figure 11.7 contains the class diagram for `SimpleList`. This diagram shows that `SimpleList` is designed to implement two standard Java interfaces: `java.util.Iterator` and `java.util.Collection`.

Figure 11.7   `SimpleList` class diagram

```
           java.util.Iterator<ItemType>                    java.util.Collection<ItemType>
                   «interface»                                     «interface»

    «update»
      + void remove()
                                                            java.util.AbstractCollection<ItemType>
    «query»                                                            {abstract}
      + boolean hasNext()
      + ItemType next()


                                    SimpleList<ItemType>


                             «constructor»
                               + SimpleList<ItemType>()

                             «update»
                               + boolean add(ItemType)
                               + void remove()
                               + void reset()

                             «query»
                               + boolean hasNext()
                               + ItemType next()
                               + int size()
```

In addition to its constructor, `SimpleList` includes three methods that are different from `Bag`, namely `reset`, `next`, and `hasNext`. Figure 11.8 shows the class specifications for these three methods, as well as the other methods.

Nearly every `SimpleList` method involves the notion of an **iterator**. The iterator is a device to keep track of a list position. Like a timer on a CD player, an iterator measures how much of the list precedes its current position. For example, below is a picture of a list containing three string items. The front item in the list is the string "Moe", the middle item is "Larry", and the back item is "Curly".

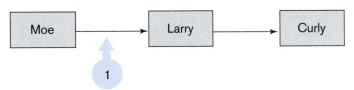

Figure 11.8   `SimpleList` class specifications

Invariant

A `SimpleList` object

- is a container of zero or more objects arranged in a linear order.

- maintains an *iterator* that is positioned either in front of the first item, beyond the last item, or between two consecutive list items. (The iterator can be thought of as an integer that counts the number of items preceding its position.)

- maintains an `isRemovable` Boolean value to tell when a call to remove is allowed.

Constructor Method

public `SimpleList<ItemType>` ( )

> **post:** `this` is empty (i.e., `size()` == 0)
>   ***and*** *iterator* == 0 (i.e., the iterator has zero items before it)
>   ***and*** `isRemovable` == `false`

Update Methods

public boolean **add** (ItemType *z*)

> **post:** `this` == `this`***@pre*** with *z* inserted at the *iterator****@pre*** position
>   ***and*** `size()` = `size()`***@pre*** + 1
>   ***and*** *iterator* == *iterator****@pre*** + 1
>   ***and*** `isRemovable` == `false`

> **note:** The add method returns a `boolean` value to be consistent with inheritance constraints. However, in practice we shall treat this as a void method.

Each `SimpleList` container has a single iterator built into the container. It is best to think of this iterator as always positioned *between* items, unless it precedes or follows the entire list. The arrow attached to the oval in the previous diagram denotes the iterator for the list. At this time, the iterator is positioned between the "Moe" item and the "Larry" item. The value shown within the iterator is "1" reflects the fact that the number of items preceding the iterator is one. (The `SimpleList` class specifications explain the iterator in terms of this integer value.)

The `SimpleList` class includes methods specifically to manipulate the position of the iterator. Whenever the `reset` method is called upon a list, the iterator is positioned at the very front of the list, as shown below.

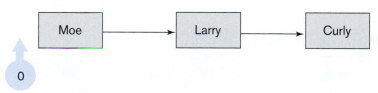

```
public void remove ()
```
    pre: isRemovable

    post: `this` == `this@pre` with the item preceding *iterator@pre* removed
         and size() == size()@pre - 1
         and *iterator* == *iterator@pre* - 1
         and isRemovable == false

```
public void reset ()
```
    post: *iterator* == 0 (i.e., the *iterator* has zero items before it)
         and isRemovable == false

Query Methods

```
public boolean hasNext ( )
```
    post: *result* == (*iterator* == size()) (i.e., *result* is false exactly when *iterator* is positioned at the rear of this list)

```
public ItemType next ()
```
    pre: hasNext()

    post: *iterator* == *iterator@pre* + 1
         and *result* == the item immediately preceding *iterator*
         and isRemovable == true

```
public int size ()
```
    post: *result* == the number of items in this list

Advancing the iterator past its reset position is generally accomplished by calling the next method. Each proper call to next accomplishes two tasks: (1) it advances the iterator by one item and (2) it returns the value of the item immediately preceding the iterator's new position. For example, the two pictures below show "before" and "after" states when forth is called between.

BEFORE executing `String s = next();`

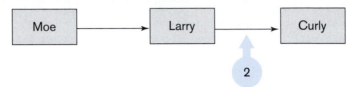

AFTER executing `String s = next();`

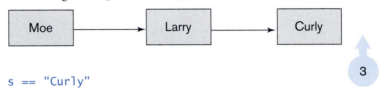

`s == "Curly"`

When the iterator is positioned at the back of the list (as shown immediately above), it is said that the iterator is **off the list**. Calling next when the iterator is off the list is an error that causes a runtime exception.

SimpleList includes a method to check whether or not the iterator is off the list. The hasNext method returns false when the iterator is positioned off the list and true otherwise. In other words, hasNext is true precisely when it is okay to call next.

A call to add[1] inserts the new item at precisely the location of the iterator. To illustrate, the following two pictures show the list *before* and *after* adding the string "Bozo".

BEFORE calling `add("Bozo");`

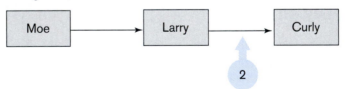

AFTER calling `add("Bozo");`

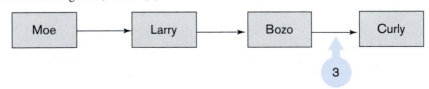

---

1. For SimpleList it is best to treat **add** as a void method, although technically it returns a boolean.

Notice that a call to add leaves the previous list items intact. In addition, the iterator is always positioned just after the item that was inserted. If the iterator is positioned at the front of the list (has a value of zero) prior to an add, then the inserted item becomes the new front of the list. If the iterator is off the list at the time of an add, then the new item is appended to the back of the list.

The remove method is unique. The intent of this method is to provide the client the ability to remove an item only immediately after inspecting it (i.e., the item removed is the one last returned by next). In order to accomplish this, remove differs from other SimpleList methods in three ways: (1) remove deletes the item immediately *preceding* the iterator, (2) the iterator moves one position *backward* (i.e., toward the list's front) following a remove, and (3) remove can only be called following a call to next. This third restriction means that if the most recent method called on a SimpleList is reset, add, or remove, then it is necessary to call next again before a remove. This may seem like an odd restriction, but disallowing calls to reset, add, and remove ensures that the iterator is not positioned at the start of the list, thereby guaranteeing that the item to be removed actually exists. The pictures below illustrate the use of remove.

BEFORE executing String s = next();

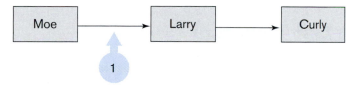

BEFORE calling remove();

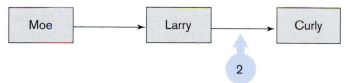

AFTER calling remove();

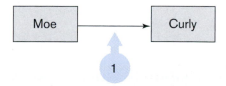

The following code combines several SimpleList method calls into a larger segment of code, shown on the next page.

```
String str;
SimpleList egList<String>;
egList = new SimpleList<String>();
egList.add("Maria");
egList.reset();
egList.add("Michael");
egList.reset();
str = egList.next();
egList.add("Susan");
str = egList.next();
egList.add("Patty");
egList.add("Diane");
egList.add("Gillian");
```

A careful trace of this code reveals that the resulting list can be pictured as follows.

11.5 ■ List Traversal

The SimpleList class provides three methods (reset, next, and hasNext) that assist client code in manipulating iterators. The previous section illustrates how these methods can be used to control the order in which items are inserted, removed, and/or inspected.

These three methods also provide the tools needed to perform **list traversal algorithms**. A list traversal algorithm consists of processing each list item, one at a time. Figure 11.9 contains an example method, called printList, to output all of the String items of its list parameter.

When printList executes, it begins by positioning the list's iterator at the front of the list using the following instruction.

```
list.reset();
```

Figure 11.9

printList
method

```
private void printList(SimpleList<String> list) {
    String str;
    list.reset();
    while(list.hasNext()) {
        str = list.next();
        System.out.println(str);
    }
}
```

Each time through the loop, the next item is inspected and assigned to a local variable as shown below.

```
str = list.next();
```

The final instruction in the loop body outputs this item.

```
System.out.println(str);
```

The printList method is but one illustration of a list traversal algorithm. In particular, this is a traversal that outputs each item. However, there are many other algorithms such as the following:

- a list traversal of a list of JComponent objects recolor of each JComponent
- a list traversal of a list of double values to calculate the square root of each item
- a list traversal of a list of JTextField objects to input the value from each item

These, and countless other list traversal algorithms, can all be accomplished using the same algorithmic pattern shown in Figure 11.10.

As a further illustration of list traversal algorithms, consider the program in Figure 11.11. The Driver constructor method constructs a horizontal row of Oval objects, placing them upon a JFrame. Each Oval is also inserted into a list called ovalList.

The actionPerformed method from Figure 11.11 contains two list traversal algorithms. When coordinateBtn is clicked the algorithm uses a traversal to output the horizontal coordinate for every item of ovalList. This traversal algorithm is repeated below.

```
// NOTE: See Figure 11.13 for a better version of the
// loop below.
ovalList.reset();
while(ovalList.hasNext()) {
    tempOval = ovalList.next();
    System.out.println("X coordinate of oval:
        " + tempOval.getX());
}
```

software **engineering** *Hint*

The two loop body instructions in printList can be combined into one:

System.out.println(list.next());

However, many traversal algorithms involve more complicated use of list items, which require that each item be saved temporarily in a variable such as str. It is a good idea to get in the habit of using such a temporary variable.

The following pattern assumes list is of type SimpleList<ActualType>

```
ActualType   temp;
list.reset();
while (list.hasNext())   {
    temp = list.next();
    // Process temp
}
```

Figure 11.10

List traversal algorithm pattern for SimpleList

Figure 11.11   List traversal algorithm for a list of Ovals

```java
import java.awt.*;
import java.awt.event.*;
import javax.swing.*;
public class Driver implements ActionListener {
    private JFrame window;
    private JButton greenBtn, blueBtn, coordinateBtn;
    private SimpleList<Oval> ovalList;

    /** post: window is created
     *          and a row of black ovals spans window horizontally
     *          and the row of ovals is stored in ovalList
     */
    public Driver() {
        Oval tempOval;
        int horizontalPos;
        window = new JFrame("Manipulate the Ovals");
        window.setBounds(10, 10, 600, 500);
        window.setVisible(true);
        window.setLayout(null);
        greenBtn = newButton(20, 430, "Color Green");
        blueBtn = newButton(210, 430, "Color Blue");
        coordinateBtn = newButton(400, 430, "Print Coordinates");
        ovalList = new SimpleList<Oval>();

        horizontalPos = 5;
        ovalList.reset();
        while (horizontalPos < window.getWidth()) {
            tempOval = new Oval(horizontalPos, 100, 10, 10);
            window.add(tempOval, 0);
            ovalList.add(tempOval);
            horizontalPos = horizontalPos + 15;
        }
        window.repaint();
    }

    /** pre:   window != null
     *  post:  result is a newly created button
     *          and result.getX()==x and result.getY()==y
     *          and result.getWidth()==180 and result.getHeight()==30
     *          and result.getParent() == window's pane
     *          and this is the action listener for result
     */
```

```java
public JButton newButton(int x, int y, String s) {
    JButton button;
    button = new JButton(s);
    button.setBounds(x, y, 180, 30);
    button.addActionListener(this);
    window.add(button, 0);
    return button;
}

/** post:   greenBtn was clicked
 *              implies all ovals are recolored green
 *          and blueBtn was clicked
 *              implies all ovals are recolored blue
 *          and coordinateBtn was clicked
 *              implies the X coordinate of all ovals are output
 */
public void actionPerformed(ActionEvent e) {
    Oval tempOval;
    if (e.getSource() == coordinateBtn) {
        // NOTE: See Figure 11.13 for a better version of the
        // loop below.
        ovalList.reset();
        while(ovalList.hasNext()) {
            tempOval = ovalList.next();
            System.out.println("X coordinate of oval: "
                + tempOval.getX());
        }
    } else { // either greenBtn or blueBtn was clicked
        // NOTE: See Figure 11.13 for a better version of the
        // loop below.
        ovalList.reset();
        while(ovalList.hasNext()) {
            tempOval = ovalList.next();
            if (e.getSource()==greenBtn)
                tempOval.setBackground(Color.green);
            else
                tempOval.setBackground(Color.blue);
            tempOval.repaint();
        }
    }
}
```

When either `greenBtn` or `blueBtn` is clicked a list traversal algorithm is used to assign the proper color to every `ovalList` item. The loop to perform this traversal is as follows.

```
// NOTE: See Figure 11.13 for a better version of the loop below.
ovalList.reset();
while(ovalList.hasNext()) {
    tempOval = ovalList.next();
    if (e.getSource()==greenBtn)
        tempOval.setBackground(Color.green);
    else
        tempOval.setBackground(Color.blue);
    tempOval.repaint();
}
```

For simple loop traversals (i.e., traversals that do not require calls to `add`, `remove`, or process other lists in parallel) Java provides a special version of the *for* loop that is

Figure 11.12   *forCollectionInstruction* description (a possible *OneStatement*)[2]

Syntax

Notes

- *Collection* represents an object that conforms to `java.util.Collection<Type>` or an array[3].
- *ItemType* conforms to the *Type* of the items in *Collection*.
- *itemID* is an identifier.
- *ItemType* and *itemID* must be separated by white space.
- *StatementSequence* cannot include statements that alter or access *Collection* except via *ItemID*.
- The braces { ... } are not optional if *StatementSequence* is a single statement.

Style Notes

- The reserved word for should be aligned with the "}" symbol that ends the *forInstruction* and all instructions within *InstructionSequence* (i.e., the loop body)

---

2. More specialized versions of the *for* loop are shown in Chapters 12 and 13.

3. Arrays are presented in Chapter 12.

easier to read. Such a loop is possible for any class that implements `java.util.Collection`. Figure 11.12 shows the syntax of such a *for* statement.

This special version of *for* loop is particularly useful for writing traversals of a `SimpleList<ItemType>` named `list`. More specifically, a traversal of the form

```
ItemType temp;
list.reset();
while (list.hasNext()) {
    temp = list.next();
    // Process temp
}
```

is better expressed by the following *for* statement:

```
for (ItemType temp : list) {
    // Process temp
}
```

- should be indented by at least one tab from the *for*. If the parenthesized code cannot be completed on one line, then "{" should be placed on a separate line and aligned with "}".

Semantics

- Executing *forCollectionInstruction* causes *ItemID*, to bind to each item in *Collection*—the first item is bound for the first loop body iteration, the second item is bound for the second body iteration, and so forth.
- The *ItemID* variable has lifetime and scope that extend only to the loop's execution.
- For a *Collection* of type `SimpleList<ItemType>` the semantics of the loop are as follows:

```
ItemType ItemID;
Collection.reset();
while (Collection.hasNext()) {
    ItemID = Collection.next();
    StatementSequence
}
```

- There is a major restriction to this style of *for* statement—you cannot add, remove, or `replace` items; nor can you `reset` the list's iterator within the loop's body.

software *Hint*
engineering
The version of
the *for* loop
defined in Figure
11.12 is only
applicable to sim-
ple traversal
algorithms.
However, its syn-
tactic elegance is
the reason that
should be used
whenever
possible.

Figure 11.13 demonstrates the use of such a `for` instruction by showing a better version of the traversal loops for the `Driver` class from Figure 11.11.

Appropriately used, the *for* loop is generally considered to be more readable than a *while* loop. This is particularly true for the version of the *for* loop that processes `Collections`. However, this Collection *for* loop can only be used for certain algorithms—primarily just a simple traversal that processes the entire list and does not add, remove, or replace any list items. An algorithm that needs to alter the list, traverse only a part of the list, access the iterated item outside of the loop body, or traverse two lists in parallel is not a candidate for this kind of *for* statement.

11.6 ■ Linear Searching

`SimpleList` containers are useful for countless purposes. A program to store the customer database of a Web-based retailer might store all customers within a `SimpleList`. A university's student information program might store each student as an item in a `SimpleList`. A dairy farmer's program for maintaining milk production information might utilize a `SimpleList` to store relevant data for each cow.

One algorithm that is commonly employed by nearly all list programs is called a **search algorithm**. The Web-based retailer may need to *search* for a customer who has just requested the status of a purchase. The registrar's office responds to student requests for college transcripts by *searching* for the student's record. In response to a recent illness for some cow, the dairy farmer might wish to *search* for that cow's milk production records.

Figure 11.13

actionPerformed
method from
Figure 11.11–
improved
version

```java
public void actionPerformed(ActionEvent e) {
    if (e.getSource() == coordinateBtn) {
        for(Oval tempOval : ovalList) {
            System.out.println("X coordinate of oval: "
                + tempOval.getX());
        }
    } else { // either greenBtn or blueBtn was clicked
        for(Oval tempOval : ovalList) {
            if (e.getSource()==greenBtn)
                tempOval.setBackground(Color.green);
            else
                tempOval.setBackground(Color.blue);
            tempOval.repaint();
        }
    }
}
```

All search algorithms share the need to locate some object (or some set of objects) within a container. The most common kind of search is to locate a particular object, given an identifying characteristic, such as a customer name or a student ID number.

An algorithm to search a `SimpleList` is really just a special kind of list traversal algorithm. Like other traversals, a search algorithm processes the list from front to back in a linear order. For this reason, searches within `SimpleList` are classified as **linear searches**.

Figure 11.14 contains a subclass of `SimpleList` that adds a new method called `isIn` that has a single parameter of type `ItemType`. It performs a linear search of the `SimpleList` and returns true exactly when the parameter's value is found to be one of the items in the container.

A call to `isIn` initiates a linear search of the list until one of two things occurs.

1. The item identified by the iterator is the same item as the search object (z). (The `found` variable is true when this occurs.)

2. The iterator has been advanced off the list

```java
public class SearchList<ItemType> extends SimpleList<ItemType> {

    /** post:   size() == 0
     *          and iterator == 0
     */
    public SearchList() {
        super();
    }


    /** post:   result == (this contains z as one or more of
     *                  its items)
     *          and iterator == 0
     */
    public boolean isIn(ItemType z) {
        boolean found;
        ItemType temp;
        reset();
        found = false;
        while (!found && hasNext()) {
            temp = next();
            found = (temp == z);
        }
        reset();
        return found;
    }

}
```

Figure 11.14

SearchList class

The loop terminates the first time that either of these conditions is true. Following the loop, found is returned. This particular isIn method alters the location of the iterator. Both the method's postcondition and the call to reset immediately after the search loop highlight this fact.

SearchList provides a sample of how to write your own generic class. The generic parameter(s) (e.g., <ItemType>) must be listed inside angle brackets following the class name and the constructor name. Throughout the class, the generic name (ItemType) can be used as though it were an actual class name. The following code segment shows an example of how to create a SearchList and call the isIn method.

```
SearchList<Character> goFish = new SearchList<Character>();
goFish.add('a');
goFish.add('x');
goFish.add('b');
goFish.add('f');
System.out.println("The value x is in the list:
    " + goFish.isIn('x'));
System.out.println("The value z is in the list:
    " + goFish.isIn('z'));
```

The isIn method of SearchList searches for an item that is identical to its argument. A different kind of search might look for other properties. For example, suppose you have a container of Component objects and wish to be able to test whether any of them has the same dimensions as some specific JButton object. Figure 11.15 contains a class with such a search.

The only thing that needs to change for a search with different properties is the assignment to the found variable. In Figure 11.14, searching for an identical object used the following instruction to compare temp and the search object z.

```
found = (temp == z);
```

The search for matching dimensions in Figure 11.15 uses the following instruction to compare temp to the search object b.

```
found = (temp.getWidth()==b.getWidth()
    && temp.getHeight()==b.getHeight());
```

Such boolean methods as isIn and containsSameSize provide only information regarding the existence of an item with the necessary characteristics. Sometimes it is helpful not only to know about existence but also to have access to the object found by the search. For example, the nextWithSameSize method in Figure 11.16 would be appropriate for inclusion in the SearchForSizeList class.

When the nextWithSameSize locates a container item with appropriate characteristics, the method is similar to the standard next method in that it performs two tasks: (1) the method returns this item and (2) the iterator is positioned immediately after the item. Returning the item supports algorithms that wish to remove, add, or replace relative to the item.

Figure 11.15   SearchForSizeList class

```java
import javax.swing.JButton;
public class SearchForSizeList extends SimpleList<JButton> {

    /** post:  size() == 0
     *         and iterator == 0
     */
    public SearchForSizeList() {
        super();
    }

    /** post:  result == (this contains an item with identical
     *             getWidth() and getHeight() values as c)
     *         and iterator == 0
     */
    public boolean containsSameSize(JButton b) {
        boolean found;
        JButton temp;
        reset();
        found = false;
        while (!found && hasNext()) {
            temp = next();
            found = (temp.getWidth()==b.getWidth()
                    && temp.getHeight()==b.getHeight());
        }
        reset();
        return found;
    }
}
```

11.7 ■ Sorting by Insertion

Sometimes it is helpful to maintain lists in a **sorted** fashion. Residential portions of telephone books are sorted by peoples' last names. The index for this textbook is sorted in alphabetic order. Teachers often sort exam scores from highest to lowest.

There are two important ways in which to sort items. An **ascending sort** arranges items from least to greatest, and a **descending sort** arranges items from greatest to least. Correspondingly, a list that is sorted by an ascending sort is said to be in **ascending order**, while a descending sort produces a list in **descending order**, as illustrated on the next page.

Figure 11.16   nextWithSameSize method

```
/** note:   This method is intended for inclusion in
 *           the SearchForSizeList class, see Figure 11.15
 * post:    containsSameSize(b) implies
 *           (result has the same dimensions as b and the iterator is
 *           positioned after result)
 *         and (not containsSameSizeList(b)) implies
 *           result == null
 */
public JButton nextWithSameSize(JButton b) {
    boolean found;
    JButton temp = new JButton();
    found = false;
    while (!found && hasNext()) {
        temp = next();
        found = (temp.getWidth()==b.getWidth()
            && temp.getHeight()==b.getHeight());
    }
    if (found)
        return temp;
    else
        return null;
}
```

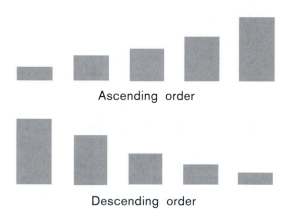

Ascending order

Descending order

One convenient technique for producing a sorted list is accomplished by a different insertion method that ensures every new item is located so as to preserve the desired sort property (either ascending or descending). As an initial example of a sorted list, consider the AscendingListOfInt class shown in Figure 11.17. This class is not

Figure 11.17   AscendingListOfInt class

```
/** CLass Invariant
 *      An AscendingListOfInt contains Integers sorted in ascending order.
 */
public class AscendingListOfInt extends SimpleList<Integer> {

    /** post:  this is empty
     *         and iterator == 0
     */
    public AscendingListOfInt() {
        super();
    }

    /** post:  this list == this@pre with k inserted (note that the
     *              sort property from the class invariant is maintained)
     *         and iterator is positioned immediately after
     *              the newly inserted k
     */
    public boolean add(Integer k) {
        boolean found;
        int tempInt = 0;
        reset();
        found = false;
        while (!found && hasNext()) {
            tempInt = next();
            found = (k <= tempInt);
        }
        if (!found) {
            super.add(k);
        } else {
            remove();
            super.add(k);
            super.add(tempInt);
        }
        return true;  // because add is a boolean method
    }
}
```

generic even though it inherits SimpleList. (Notice that the first line of the class specifies that the item type be Integer, the wrapper class for int data.)

The key code that keeps the AscendingListOfInt sorted is the loop within the add method, shown again on the next page.

```
reset();
found = false;
while (!found && hasNext()) {
    tempInt = next();
    found = (k <= tempInt);
}
```

This loop searches for the first list item that is greater than or equal to the value to be inserted (k). When such a bigger value is found, the loop terminates. In the case that the loop terminates only when the iterator is off the list, then k can simply be inserted at the back of the list as shown below:

```
super.add(k);
```

When the search for the place to insert k does not reach the end of the list, the situation is more complicated. This occurs whenever the loop has located a list item that is greater than or equal to k. This item has just been returned by next and assigned to tempInt. It would be wrong to merely insert k into the list in this situation. To preserve the ascending order k needs to be inserted *before*, not after, tempInt. One solution is to remove the last (tempInt) item, then insert k, then reinsert the removed (tempInt) item after k. The following code does this.

```
// assert: The item about to be removed is tempInt
remove();
super.add(k);
super.add(tempInt);
```

To investigate the behavior of sorting a sequence of numbers consider the following code.

```
AscendingListOfInt sortList = new AscendingListOfInt();
sortList.add(3);
sortList.add(1);
sortList.add(5);
sortList.add(2);
sortList.add(1);
```

When this code executes, the first call to the add method passes the argument 3, which is autoboxed as an Integer. The sortList is empty at this time, so hasNext is immediately false and the insertion value (3) is inserted as the only item in the list.

k == 3

3

The second call to add, namely sortList.add(1), passes the value 1 as an argument corresponding to parameter k. This call to add causes the list iterator to be reset to the start of the list and the value of the first call to next (3) is assigned to tempInt. Since the value of k is 1 and the value of tempInt is 3, the loop terminates with found == true. This causes the tempInt value to be replaced by k (1) followed by tempInt (3).

The third call to insert is `sortList.add(5)`. This call to add passes the value 5 for parameter k and causes the list iterator to be reset to the start of the list, as shown below.

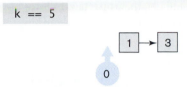

Since `next()` has a value of 1 at this time, the add method's while loop condition is true. This results in the first execution of the loop body, as pictured below.

Now `next()` has a value of 3, and the add method's while loop condition is true again. The resulting second loop body execution produces the following state.

At this time, `hasNext` is `false`, so the loop terminates execution and the value of k (5) is inserted at the iterator position (i.e., at the end of the list).

The fourth call to insert is `sortList.add(2)`. This call to add passes the value 2 for parameter k and causes the list iterator to be reset to the start of the list, as shown below.

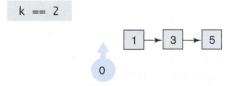

The first loop condition test for this call of insert finds that the value of k (2) is greater than the value of `next()`, which is 1. Therefore, the loop body is executed once to advance the iterator, as shown on the next page.

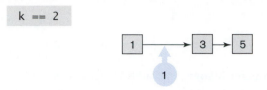

Now the value of k (2) is less than the value of next(), so the loop terminates, removes the tempInt value (3), then inserts k followed by tempInt. The fifth and final call to add resets the iterator to the loop beginning, as shown below.

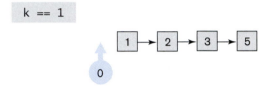

Since the value of k (1) is equal to the value of next(), the loop terminates immediately, removes the tempInt (1) value, then inserts k followed by tempInt, as shown below.

This example illustrates how each call to add searches the list to find the proper location for the new value and then inserts the value in its place. The property of sortedness is thereby maintained.

11.8 ■ Generic Sorting (Optional)

With all of the earlier discussion of generic classes, it is less than satisfying that AscendingListOfInt can sort integer data, but is not useful for sorting double or String or any other kind of orderable values. It would be nice to be able to construct a class that could sort any orderable data. In other words, we would like to design a container class that is *partially generic* in the sense that content must be orderable. Fortunately, Java provides the tools to do this by way of two facilities:

1. the Comparable interface (discussed in Section 9.6)

2. a way to restrict generic parameters by including an extends clause

The second of these two language features deserves additional comment. When you declare a class that includes generic parameters, each parameter can be made partially generic by appending the suffix *extends C*, where *C* denotes a known class or interface. The *extends C* suffix must be located after the classname, but still within the <> brackets. This suffix constrains any corresponding generic argument to be a class that conforms to *C*. Figure 11.18 illustrates how this can be used to produce a more generic sorted list class.

Figure 11.18   AscendingList class

```
/** Class Invariant
 *     An AscendingListOfInt contains objects sorted in ascending order.
 */
public class AscendingList<ItemType extends Comparable>
    extends SimpleList<ItemType> {

    /** post:  this is empty
     *         and iterator == 0
     */
    public AscendingList() {
        super();
    }

    /** post:  this list == this@pre with z inserted (note that the
     *             sort property from the class invariant is maintained)
     *         and iterator is positioned immediately after the newly inserted z
     */
    public boolean add(ItemType z) {
        boolean found;
        ItemType temp = null;
        reset();
        found = false;
        while (!found && hasNext()) {
            temp = next();
            found = (z.compareTo(temp) <= 0);
        }
        if (!found) {
            super.add(z);
        } else {
            remove();
            super.add(z);
            super.add(temp);
        }
        return true; // because add is a boolean method
    }
}
```

There are two key differences between the AscendingList class and the less generic AscendingListOfInt class from the prior section. The first difference occurs in the first noncomment line repeated below.

```
public class AscendingList <ItemType extends Comparable>
    extends SimpleList<ItemType> {
```

This declares `AscendingList` to have a generic parameter, called `ItemType`, but it also includes an *extends* clause on `ItemType`. This *extends* clause stipulates that the actual class supplied for `ItemType` must conform to the standard `Comparable` interface.

The second key difference between `AscendingList` and `AscendingListOfInt` is the way that each compares the list items to the item to be inserted. For `AscendingListOfInt` the insertion value, called k, is compared to a list item, stored in `tempInt`, by the following instruction.

```
found = (k <= tempInt);
```

The corresponding instruction from `AscendingList` for comparing object z to the list item in `temp` is repeated below.

```
found = (z.compareTo(temp) <= 0);
```

The call to `compareTo` is permitted because the *extends* clause ensures that the actual class be a descendant of `Comparable`, which means it must implement the `compareTo` method.

To illustrate the use of this new class, both of the following declarations would be valid instantiations.

```
AscendingList<Double> doubleList = new AscendingList<Double>();
AscendingList<String> stringList = new AscendingList<String>();
```

These are allowed because `Double` and `String` are both descendants of `Comparable`.

Inspector Java

Below is a collection of hints on what to check when examining code that involves the concepts of this chapter.

- Generic classes provide parameters for specifying actual types. When declaring a variable/parameter or class inheriting a generic class, you need to include the specification for the actual type in angle brackets following the generic class's name. You also need to include the actual type in angle brackets within any instruction that instantiates a generic type.

- Wrapper classes are best avoided within client code, except for supplying the argument for a generic parameter.

- The `next` method for lists should always be examined for the possibility of a call when the iterator is off the list. The `hasNext` method can be used to guard against such illegal calls.

- Take care that when you call the `remove` method for lists that the `next` method has just been called on the same list.

- Every list traversal algorithm should be checked to ensure that the `next` method has been called within the loop body. Forgotten `next`s are a common cause for infinite loops.

- Do not forget to test code that manipulates a container to be certain that it works when the container is empty.

- Be careful about assuming too much regarding an iterator. Many methods, such as search methods, can disturb the position of an iterator.

- Type safety is a significant concern for generic containers. For the most part generic classes provide type safety. Including an *extends* clause on a generic parameter provides additional restrictions without damaging type safety. If you still find it necessary to perform type casts, it is best to guard them with if instructions that use `instanceof` to ensure proper type conformance and safety.

Terminology

add (a container method)

ascending order

ascending sort

autoboxing

autounboxing

bag

`Boolean` (the wrapper class)

boxing (to a wrapper class value)

`Byte` (the wrapper class)

`Character` (the wrapper class)

container	list container
`Container` (the *AWT* class)	list traversal algorithm
descending order	`Long` (the wrapper class)
descending sort	`next` (a container method)
`Double` (the wrapper class)	parameterized class
extends clause (for generic parameters)	`remove` (a container method)
`Float` (the wrapper class)	`reset` (a list method)
`forth` (a list method)	search algorithm
generic container	`Short` (the wrapper class)
`hasNext` (a list method)	`size` (a container method)
`Integer` (the wrapper class)	sort
`item` (a Bag method)	type safety
iterator	unboxing (to a primitive value)
linear search	wrapper classes

Exercises

1. Following the execution of each code segment below, indicate how many `String` items are stored in `myBag` and the strings these items represent.

a.
```
Bag<String> myBag;
myBag = new Bag<String>();
myBag.add("abc");
myBag.add("xyz");
myBag.add("abc");
```

b.
```
Bag<String> myBag;
myBag = new Bag<String>();
myBag.add("abc");
System.out.println(myBag.next());
myBag.add("xyz");
myBag.add("abc");
```

c.
```
Bag<String> myBag;
myBag = new Bag<String>();
myBag.add("abc");
myBag.reset();
System.out.println(myBag.next());
myBag.remove();
myBag.add("xyz");
myBag.add("abc");
```

d. ```
Bag<String> myBag;
myBag = new Bag<String>();
myBag.add("abc");
myBag.add("xyz");
myBag.add("abc");
myBag.reset();
System.out.println(myBag.next());
System.out.println(myBag.next());
myBag.remove();
```

e. ```
Bag<String> myBag;
myBag = new Bag<String>();
myBag.add("abc");
myBag.add("xyz");
myBag.add("abc");
myBag.reset();
myBag.remove();
```

2. Suppose you are writing a section of code that includes a variable called bagOfJComponent, belonging to the Bag class.

a. Show how to declare bagOfJComponent as a local variable.

b. Give an assignment instruction that will assign the value of one of the items from bagOfJComponent to myComponent. (You should assume that myComponent has already been declared as a JComponent variable.)

3. Suppose you are writing a section of code that includes a variable called letterBag, belonging to the Bag class. Show how to declare letterBag so that it can be used to store char values.

4. Each of the following examples gives a "BEFORE" picture of the state of a SimpleList<String>, named myList, just prior to executing the code. You should assume that all list items contain String values. Draw the new picture that results after the code executes.

a. **BEFORE**

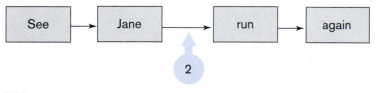

CODE
```
myList.add("and Jim");
myList.reset();
```

b. **BEFORE**

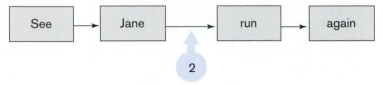

CODE

```
String s;
s = myList.next();
myList.remove();
s = myList.next();
myList.add("?");
myList.reset();
myList.add("May I");
```

c. **BEFORE**

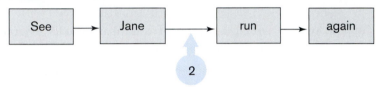

CODE

```
String s;
myList.reset();
while(myList.hasNext()) {
    s = myList.next();
}
myList.insert("and again");
```

d. **BEFORE**

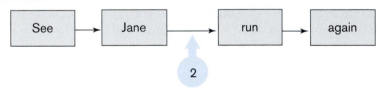

CODE

```
for(String s : myList) {
    System.out.println(s);
}
```

5. Figure 11.9 contains the code for a `printList` method. Write an equivalent method that uses the special version of `for` statement detailed in Figure 11.12.

6. Complete the code for the body of the following methods that use a parameter(s) of type `SimpleList`.

a.
```
/** pre:    list.size() > = 2
 *  post:   list == list@pre with the first and last items
 *          removed */
private void trimEnds(SimpleList<String> list) {
    // your code goes here.
}
```

b.
```
/** post:   destList is a copy of the content of sourceList
 */
private void copyList(SimpleList<String> sourceList,
    SimpleList<String> destList) {
    // your code goes here.
}
```

c.
```
/** post:   destList is destList@pre with every item that is
 *          somewhere in sourceList removed */
private void removeDups(SimpleList<String> sourceList,
    SimpleList<String> destList)
{
    // your code goes here.
}
```

7. Complete the code for the body of the following methods that use a parameter(s) of type `SimpleList<Oval>`.

a.
```
/** pre:    oList.size() > = 3
 *  post:   result == the width of the third item of oList
 */
private Color thirdWidth(SimpleList<Oval> oList) {
    // your code goes here.
}
```

b.
```
/** post:   all items in oList are the same as oList@pre
 *          except all are colored white. */
private void whiteWash(SimpleList<Oval> oList) {
    // your code goes here.
}
```

c.
```
/** pre:    oList.size() > = 1
 *          post:   result == getX() value of oList item that
 *                  is farthest left in its location */
private int leftmostX(SimpleList<Oval> oList) {
    // your code goes here.
}
```

d. ```
   /** post: oList contains the same items as oList@pre, but
    *   these items are reordered so that the getY
    *   values are arranged in descending order */
   private void sortDescendingOnY(ListOfOval oList) {
       // your code goes here.
   }
   ```

# Programming Exercises

1. This program permits the user to create and manipulate a night sky as a container. Initially, the program displays a black ThreeButtonFrame. Each click on the black window creates a new gray "star" at the position of the user's mouse click. (Note that Rectangles can handle mouseClick events, and getX(), getY() methods applied to a MouseEvent parameter retrieve its position.) Stars are Ovals with a diameter of 2. The three buttons of the window behave as follows.

   **LEFT**     A click on this button causes the first, third, fifth, seventh, etc., stars to be recolored in white.

   **MID**      A click on this button causes the second, fourth, sixth, eighth, etc., stars created to be recolored in yellow.

   **RIGHT**    A click on this button causes the most recently created star to be recolored in red.

2. This program is designed to use a ThreeButtonWindow to control the behavior of space ships. (*Hint:* The gif images can be displayed using the Image class described in Appendix D.) When the program begins the window appears as follows.

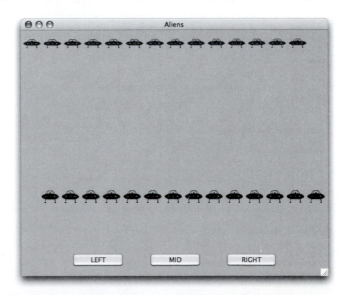
   ```

Thereafter the buttons behave as explained below.

LEFT   A click on this button causes the top row of spaceships to all move downward by 2 pixels. In addition, these ships should all be recolored—blue ships become red, red ships become green, green ships become black, and black ships become blue.

MID   A click on this button affects the ships in the bottom row. It causes the rightmost ship, the ship third from the right, the ship fifth from the right, . . . to all move up by 2 pixels.

RIGHT   A click on this button removes the rightmost space ship from the bottom row.

3. Write a program to maintain a list of names with associated telephone numbers. Your user interface should appear like the one below.

The two ATextFields below "Name" and "Phone Number" display one name and the corresponding phone number from the list. Initially, they are blank because the list is empty. The four buttons behave as described below.

PREVIOUS
           A click on this button causes the "Name" and "Phone Number" fields to be updated to display the previous phone number in the list. If the first number is displayed, then clicking this button has no effect.

NEXT   A click on this button causes the "Name" and "Phone Number" fields to be updated to display the subsequent phone number in the list. If the last number is displayed, then clicking this button causes the fields to turn blank. If the fields are already blank, then clicking this button has no effect.

INSERT A click on this button inserts the value in the "Name" and "Phone Number" field to be inserted into the list immediately *before* the fields that were displayed. Furthermore, fields should again display the item that follows immediately after the newly inserted item. (The expectation is that the user will use PREVIOUS and NEXT to position the display, then type new values into the fields, then click INSERT.)

REMOVE A click on this button removes the displayed item and updates the "Name" and "Previous Number" fields to the subsequent item. The fields are updated to blank when the last list item is removed.

4. This program gives the user certain controls over a festive light display. Initially, the program consists of a large dark gray window with small Ovals just inside the window's perimeter. (There should be 40 to 50 Ovals on each side of the window. The Ovals are to be treated as a continuous, circular string of light bulbs so that all the way around the window there are consecutive pairs of yellow Ovals with a blue Oval separating them from adjacent pairs. These lights should be operating as a marquee light moving in the counterclockwise direction. At a rate of five times per second, the color of each Oval should be assigned to its counterclockwise neighbor. In addition a large "LIGHT SHOW!" message should blink on and off in the center of the window at a rate of once per second.

In a separate small window are three buttons that behave as described below.

MARQUEE

Causes the behavior to revert to the initial program behavior.

REVERSE Causes the Ovals to become pairs of blue Ovals separated by yellow, and the marquee action should be clockwise.

FLASH Causes the entire string to take on a single color and flash from one color to another at a rate of five times per second. All Ovals first become green, then all become red, then all become white, then all become green and the sequence repeats.

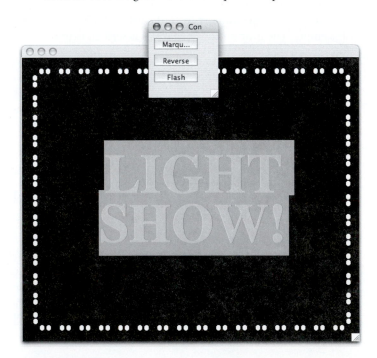

Introduction to Arrays

The tiled floor was thick with dust, and a remarkable array of miscellaneous objects was shrouded in the same grey covering.

—H.G. Wells,
The Time Machine

Objectives

- To explore the concept of arrays as direct access containers
- To examine the syntax and semantics of array declaration and instantiation
- To explore the use of index expressions for referencing array items
- To introduce the possibility of index boundary violations
- To examine uses for the length feature for arrays
- To explore the container version of *for* loop for array processing
- To examine aggregate treatment of arrays in parameter passage, method value return, and assignment instructions, as well as to introduce the Java syntax for an aggregate array expression
- To examine the use of arrays to store tabular information
- To illustrate inherent limitations of arrays
- To examine the selection sort algorithm
- To introduce two-dimensional arrays

*T*ape recorders are **sequential access** storage devices. As the tape rolls forward, the music (or video) that is stored on the tape is played in the same order it was recorded. The only way to play a song from the middle of a tape is to advance (fast forward) past the front portion. List containers, like those presented in Chapter 11, also exhibit sequential access. The only way to reach the middle of a list is to call next multiple times.

Compact disks and DVDs are **direct access devices**. The term "direct access" stems from their ability to skip directly to a particular track without scanning all preceding information. This chapter is all about direct access containers.

12.1 ■ One-Dimensional Arrays

Containers, as described in Chapter 11, are receptacles used to store other objects. The most commonly used direct access container is the **array**. Like a compact disk (CD) of music, an array stores a collection of data that is conceptually linear. The music CD is considered linear because musical songs (cuts) are ordered one after another from the first cut to the last. Arrays store objects in a similar linear sequence. Figure 12.1 pictures an example array in which all items are String objects.

Another similarity between musical CDs and arrays is that they both number their items. The songs of a CD are numbered 1, 2, 3, . . . and the items of an array are numbered 0, 1, 2, ... An array identification number is called an **index** (**indices** when plural) or **subscript**. An index is needed to reference a particular array item in the

Figure 12.1	
An example array of Strings	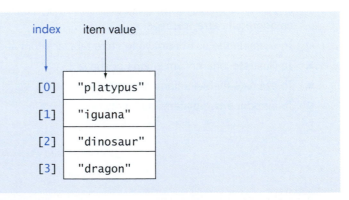

Figure 12.2   *ArrayDecl* description (a possible *OneVarDecl*)

Syntax

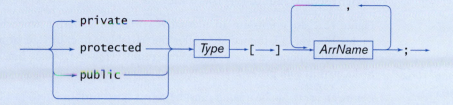

Alternative Syntax

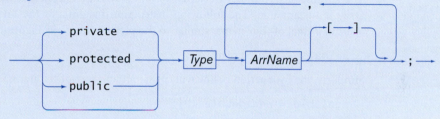

Note

Type and *ArrName* must be *Identifiers*. *Type* must either be a primitive type or it must name a class name that is known within this scope.

Usage

Each *ArrName* from Syntax, as well as each *ArrName* that is followed by [ ] from Alternative Syntax, refers to an array in which each item must conform to *Type*.

same way that a song number is needed to advance directly to a cut on a CD. The example in Figure 12.1 depicts an array in which the item with an index of zero (0) is "platypus," and the item with index of two (2) is "dinosaur."

In Java, arrays must be declared just like other variables. Such a declaration of an array may occur as an instance variable or as a local variable. Figure 12.2 shows the syntax needed to specify an array declaration.

An array declaration defines both the name of the array and the type of items that it is permitted to contain. For example, the declaration below specifies a private instance variable, called `animals`, that names an array in which every item is a `String`.

```
private String[] animals;
```

The following line declares a local variable, called `ageTable`, which is an array of `double` items.

```
double[] ageTable;
```

Below is a declaration that declares a protected instance variable, rowOfButtons, that will serve as an array of JButton items.

```
protected JButton[] rowOfButtons;
```

Figure 12.2 also points out an alternative syntax for declaring arrays by placing the square brackets [] immediately after the variable name, instead of after the type name. Either notation produces the same result. (However, square brackets must not be located in *both* places.)

software *Hint*
engineering

Arrays have a size that is fixed at the time they are instantiated. Unlike lists that grow and shrink with insert and remove methods, array sizes do not change

Before an array can be used, it must be constructed (instantiated) just like any other object. Figure 12.3 describes the Java notation for instantiating an array.

The specific size (number of items) of an array is determined at the time that the array is instantiated. The following instruction instantiates the animals array to contain a total of four items, similar to the picture shown in Figure 12.1.

```
animals = new String[4];
```

Similarly, the instruction below will construct an array of ten items.

```
ageTable = new double[10];
```

Java always numbers array indices beginning at zero. Therefore, the index range for the ageTable array is 0 through 9. The following instruction constructs an array of one hundred JButton items with indices ranging from 0 through 99.

```
rowOfButtons = JButton[100];
```

Once an array has been declared and instantiated, array items can be treated as though they were variables. The notation that is used to refer to such items is described in Figure 12.4. This array item syntax consists of the name of the array, followed by an integer expression for an index enclosed in square brackets. Therefore,

Figure 12.3 *ArrayConstruction* description (a possible *Expression*)

Syntax

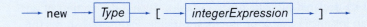

Note

integerExpression is an expression of type int.

Semantics

integerExpression is first evaluated. Assuming that the *integerExpression* has a non-negative value, an array is instantiated to contain this number of items. The items will be indexed from 0 through *integerExpression*–1. If *integerExpression* is negative, then a runtime exception occurs when this construction executes.

Figure 12.4   **ArrayItemReference** description (a possible *Variable*)

Syntax

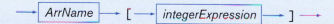

Note

integerExpression is an expression of type `int`.

Semantics

integerExpression is first evaluated. Assuming that the *integerExpression* is a valid index, then *ArrayItemReference* refers to the item within the array named *ArrName* that has an index of *integerExpression*. If *integerExpression* is not valid, then a run-time exception (*ArrayIndexOutOfBoundsException*) occurs.

`animals[2]` references the item from the `animals` array that has an index of 2. Likewise, `ageTable[0]` refers to the item of the `ageTable` array with an index of 0.

To illustrate the complete process of declaring, constructing, and using an array, consider the execution of the following segment of Java code.

```java
char[] initials;
int someInt;
initials = new char[6];
initials[2] = 'B';
initials[0] = 'E';
initials[3] = 'S';
initials[1] = 'M';
initials[4] = 'R';
System.out.println(initials[3]);
someInt = 2;
System.out.println(initials[someInt*2]);
initials[someInt+1] = initials[0];
```

The first statement in the code segment above declares an array object. This statement specifies that the name of the array is `initials` and that each of its individual items will store a `char` value. Therefore, after the following two statements are executed

```java
char[] initials;
int someInt;
```

the state of execution includes the two variables pictured on the next page. (Notice that `initials` array is `null` at this point in the execution.)

> software
> **engineering** *Hint*
>
> The use of an array always involves three tasks.
>
> - *declare* the array (to provide the array name and the type of its items)
> - *instantiate* the array (to provide the size—number of items)
> - *use* the array items as though they were variables (using array item reference notation)

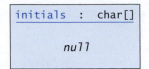 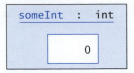

Executing the instruction below causes the `initials` array to be instantiated with six items (indexed from 0 through 5).

```
initials = new char[6];
```

Following the execution of this instruction, the state of execution changes as shown below.

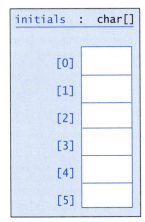 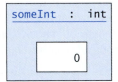

Execution proceeds to a number of assignment instructions that use indices to refer to specific items of the `initials` array. For example, the first assignment instruction is

```
initials[2] = 'B';
```

Following the execution of this instruction, the item with index of 2 is assigned the character 'B'. The resulting state is shown below.

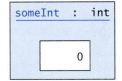

The remainder of the consecutive assignment instructions from this example are as follows.

```
initials[0] = 'E';
initials[3] = 'S';
initials[1] = 'M';
initials[4] = 'R';
```

Following the execution of these instructions, the state of execution is updated, as shown in the following picture.

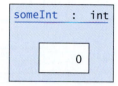

The next instruction executed

```
System.out.println(initials[3]);
```

causes the value of the array item with an index of 3 to be output. In this case, the character 'S' is output.

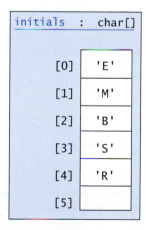
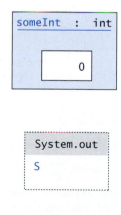

The instruction that follows is

```
someInt = 2;
```

Executing the previous instruction assigns someInt the value 2, as shown below.

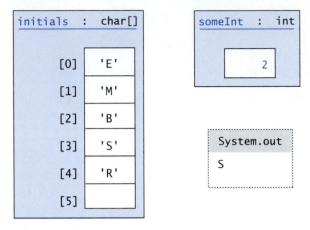

The next instruction to execute is repeated below.

```
System.out.println(initials[someInt*2]);
```

This instruction has a more complicated integer expression for an index. Every array index expression must be evaluated before the item can be identified. In this case, the expression someInt*2 must first be evaluated in order to discover that the necessary index is 4. Therefore, executing this instruction causes 'R' to be output.

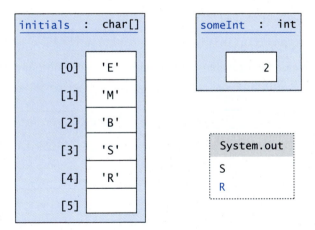

The final instruction in this code segment is as follows.

```
initials[SomeInt+1] = initials[0];
```

When this instruction executes, the index expression SomeInt+1 is evaluated to the value 3. Therefore, this instruction results in the state pictured on the next page.

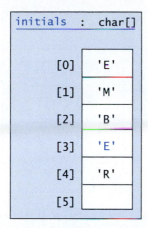

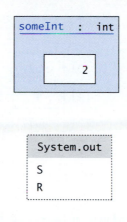

Array items behave like variables of the same type. Since the `initials` array contains items of primitive (`char`) type, these items can be used just like any other `char` variable.

Items that belong to classes also behave like variables of the same type. For example, the following code declares and instantiates an array of three `java.awt.Label` items.

```
Label[] labels;
labels = new Label[3];
```

Following the execution of these two instructions, the array contains three items, but none of the items are bound.

labels : Label[]	
[0]	*null*
[1]	*null*
[2]	*null*

Instructions such as the following are needed in order to construct the content of the individual array items.

```
labels[1] = new Label("milk");
```

Executing this last instruction alters the state as follows.

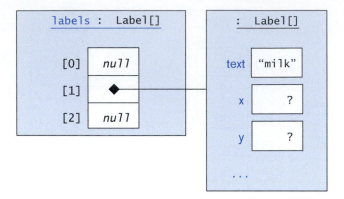

Once the second item of `labels` has been assigned a `Label` in this manner it can be used just like any other `Label` variable. Therefore, the following instructions produce the usual `Label` behavior.

```
labels[1].setLocation(100, 200);
labels[1].repaint();
```

12.2 ■ Keeping Indices in Bounds

The most common programming error associated with arrays is an index that is **out of bounds**. An out of bounds index is any index expression that evaluates to an integer that is one of the following:

- less than zero
- greater than the array's maximum possible index

For an array of 25 items, all index expressions must be within the range from 0 through 24. Any other value for an index is invalid (out of bounds) for the array.

When an index is found to be out of bounds, a **boundary violation** has occurred. Boundary violations are detected as runtime exceptions by the Java VM. The resulting error messages from such errors contain information like the following.

```
ArrayIndexOutOfBoundsException
```

Since all arrays begin with a smallest index of zero, a Java program can easily test to ensure that an index isn't too small using code similar to that shown below.

```
if (indexExpression >= 0) {
    CodeUsingIndexExpression
}
```

Java also includes an additional feature to assist in testing array indices from becoming too large. This feature is called **length**. An array reference (array name) can be followed by

```
.length
```

to form an int expression returning the number of items in the array. The following instruction uses length to ensure that the integer variable index is valid for the initials array.

```
if (0 <= index && index < initials.length) {
    System.out.println(initials[index]);
}
```

Notationally, length behaves like a public read-only (final) variable of every array. length cannot be directly assigned a value, and it does not require a variable declaration.

12.3 ■ **Sequential Processing with** *for* **Loops**

Index expressions permit a program to directly access any array item. Nonetheless, in practice, arrays are often processed sequentially from the array cell with index 0 through the cell with index length-1 or in reverse. Such sequential algorithms are reminiscent of list traversal algorithms.

Just as the for statement was a good choice for expressing list traversal and counting algorithms, the for statement is also a good choice for many array processing loops. Figure 12.5 shows the two typical patterns using *for* loops that are most useful for array processing.

Index *for* **Pattern**

The following for instruction can be used to sequentially process the array called arr from the first item to the last.

```
for (int ndx = 0; ndx!=arr.length; ndx++) {
    // process cell indexed by ndx
}
```

Collection *for* **Pattern**

The following for instruction can be used to sequentially process the array called arr from the first item to the last. The cells of arr must be of type CellType.

```
for (CellType item : arr) {
    // process item
}
```

Figure 12.5

Algorithm patterns for sequential array processing

The following loop is an example of the Index *for* Pattern. This loop visits every cell of the `labels` array, outputting the `String` displayed in each `Label`.

```
for (int k=0; k!=labels.length; k++) {
    if (labels[k] != null)
        System.out.println(labels[k].getText());
}
```

This same behavior can be expressed more succinctly using the Collection *for* Pattern as follows:

```
for (Label lab : labels) {
    if (lab != null)
        System.out.println(lab.getText());
}
```

This Collection *for* Pattern uses the same kind of special purpose *for* loop that is used for `SimpleList` traversal algorithms (see Chapter 11). When the pattern is possible, it is usually the preferable (most readable) choice. However, the following restrictions limit the applicability of the Collection *for* Pattern:

1. There is no available index variable within the loop body of the Collection *for* Pattern.

2. Within the loop body any assignment to the item variable *cannot* alter the array.

3. The loop body cannot refer to two or more different array cells.

4. The Collection *for* Pattern visits *every* array cell.

5. The Collection for Pattern processes an array in only one direction—from the cell with index of zero to the last cell in the array.

The first restriction makes it impossible to write any loop that requires access to an index. For example, consider an algorithm to resize every `Oval` in an array to have a radius equal to its own index plus 10 (i.e., `ovals[0]` will be set to a radius of 10, `ovals[1]` will be set to a radius of 11, `ovals[2]` will be set to a radius of 12, and so forth). This algorithm cannot be expressed using only a Collection *for* Pattern without introducing additional variables. However, the algorithm can be expressed with the following Index *for* Pattern:

```
/* assert: ovals[0] through ovals[99] are all
 *         instantiated Oval objects
 */
for (int n=0; n!=100; n++) {
    ovals[n].setSize(n+10, n+10);
}
```

The second restriction means that the Collection *for* Pattern is useless for assigning values to an array. For example, the following loop assigns the value 53.67 to every cell of the `doubles` array.

```
/* assert: doubles is instantiated with cells of type double.
 */
for (int d=0; d!=doubles.length; d++) {
    doubles[d] = 53.67;
}
```

It is tempting to try the following erroneous use of the Collection *for* Pattern. This attempt fails because the cell reference (called **doub** in this example) is a variable that is local to the **for** statement that is *assigned* to each array cell. In other words, doub stores a copy of each cell's value (for cells of primitive type) or stores an alias of each cell's binding (for cells of reference type).

```
// WARNING: The following code accomplishes nothing.
for (double doub : doubles) {
    doub = 53.67;
}
```

> software
> **engineering** *Hint*
>
> Never attempt to assign to the cell reference a variable in a Collection *for* Pattern. The Java compiler fails to report any error, but such an assignment accomplishes nothing and is confusing code.

Perhaps the most limiting restriction of the Collection *for* loop is that its body can only access one cell of the array at a time. This restriction means that many algorithms cannot be expressed using the Collection *for* Pattern; among them are **shift** algorithms. A shift algorithm shifts array cell contents to neighboring cells according to some particular rule(s). For example, one kind of shift would move each cell's content to the cell with next lower index. In other words `doubles[0]` is assigned `doubles[1]`**@pre**, `doubles[1]` is assigned `doubles[2]`**@pre**, and so forth. Below is a picture depicting this shift followed by the code to perform it.

doubles array:

```
/* assert: doubles is instantiated with cells of type double.
 */
for (int d=0; d!=doubles.length-1; d++) {
    doubles[d] = doubles[d+1];
}
```

This loop is a slightly modified form of the Index *for* Pattern because the loop index variable, d, ranges up to `doubles.length-1` rather than up to `doubles.length`. This change is necessary so that the expression `[d+1]` does not produce an array index out of bounds exception.

This shift algorithm is impractical to express using a Collection *for* Pattern for several reasons, among them is the restriction against the loop body referring to more than one array cell. The shift algorithm needs to refer to two different cells in order to assign one to the other. This shift also violates the fourth restriction because it executes length-1 times, while every Collection *for* Pattern loop must execute length times.

The fifth restriction for the Collection *for* Pattern is that cells must be processed in increasing index order (i.e., the cell with index 0 is processed for the first loop iteration, the cell with index 1 for the second iteration, and so forth). A simple modification of the Index *for* Pattern allows array cells to be processed in the opposite order. The following shift algorithm demonstrates by shifting doubles cells in the opposite order from the prior shift. In other words, the cell with index doubles.length-1 is assigned the cell with index doubles.length-2, then the cell with index doubles.length-2 is assigned doubles.length-3, and so on.

doubles array:

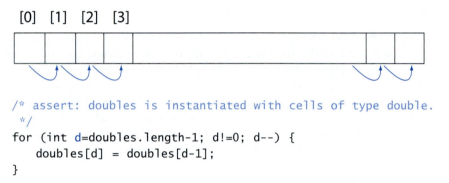

```
/* assert: doubles is instantiated with cells of type double.
   */
for (int d=doubles.length-1; d!=0; d--) {
    doubles[d] = doubles[d-1];
}
```

This *for* loop initializes its counting variable, d, to the value of doubles.length-1. After each loop iteration, the value of d is decremented by one. The last time the loop body executes is when d == 1, because loop termination occurs when d == 0.

To illustrate proper use of both *for* loop patterns in a full program, Figure 12.6 contains a Driver that randomly permutes Strings. This program allows the user to type a String into a JTextField called inField.

When the user clicks the GUI button, the program responds by calling the Driver's actionPerformed method, which randomly rearranges the letters from the text field and displays the message via outLabel. This permutation makes use of a char array called message. The first *for* loop makes use of the Index *for* Pattern to copy all of the characters from inStr into the corresponding cells of message:

```
for (int j=0; j!=message.length; j++) {
    message[j] = inStr.charAt(j);
}
```

The second loop is responsible for permuting characters of the message array. This loop is *not* a sequential array processing loop. Instead, the variable is used as a loop counter to count from 1 through twice the number of characters in the message.

Figure 12.6   Program to randomly permute strings (*continues*)

```java
import java.awt.Label;
import java.awt.event.*;
import javax.swing.*;
public class Driver implements ActionListener {
    JFrame window;
    JTextField inField;
    Label inLabel, outLabel;
    JButton button;

    /** post: window is instantiated to contain inField, inLabel
     *            outLabel and button
     *         and outLabel.getText() == ""
     *         and button's events are delegated to this
     */
    public Driver() {
        window = new JFrame("Word Scramble");
        window.setBounds(20, 20, 300, 200);
        window.setLayout(null);
        window.setVisible(true);

        inLabel = new Label("Type your message below.");
        inLabel.setBounds(10, 10, 200, 20);
        window.add(inLabel, 0);
        inField = new JTextField();
        inField.setBounds(30, 40, 250, 25);
        window.add(inField, 0);

        button = new JButton("Click here to scramble");
        button.setBounds(20, 90, 260, 25);
        button.addActionListener(this);
        window.add(button, 0);
        outLabel = new Label("");
        outLabel.setBounds(30, 130, 200, 20);

        window.add(outLabel, 0);
        window.repaint();
    }

    /** post:  outLabel is updated to be a randomly chosen
     *            permutation of inField.getText()
     */
```

Figure 12.6 Program to randomly permute strings (*continued*)

```
public void actionPerformed(ActionEvent e) {
    String inStr = inField.getText();
    String outStr;
    char[] message = new char[inStr.length()];
    int rnd1, rnd2;
    char temp;
    for (int j=0; j!=message.length; j++) {
        message[j] = inStr.charAt(j);
    }

    for (int r=1; r != inStr.length()*2+1; r++) {
        rnd1 = (int)(Math.random()*message.length);
        rnd2 = (int)(Math.random()*message.length);
        temp = message[rnd1];
        message[rnd1] = message[rnd2];
        message[rnd2] = temp;
    }

    outStr = "";
    for (char c : message) {
        outStr = outStr + c;
    }
    outLabel.setText(outStr);
    window.repaint();
}
}
```

Each time through this loop, two random array indices are selected and the corresponding cells of message are swapped.

The final loop, repeated below, constructs a `String` named `outStr` from the message array. This loop makes use of the Collection *for* Pattern. The `outStr` variable is initialized to the empty `String`. Each successive loop iteration appends the next cell of the `message` array.

```
outStr = "";
for (char c : message) {
    outStr = outStr + c;
}
```

Figure 12.7 shows a second example program that also makes use of the Index *for* pattern. This program simulates the action of marquee lights.

Figure 12.7   Marquee dots program (*continues*)

```java
import java.awt.Color;
import java.awt.event.*;
import javax.swing.*;
public class Driver implements ActionListener{
    privateOval[] dots;
    privateJFrame window;

    /** post: window is created
     *        and a row of filled ovals is assigned to dots
     *            (These ovals span the window horizontally.)
     *        and any dot with a multiple of 3 for an index
     *            is dark gray, while all other dots are white.
     */
    public Driver() {
        window = new JFrame("Marquee Lights");
        window.setBounds(10, 10, 600, 500);
        window.setVisible(true);
        window.setLayout(null);
        window.setBackground(Color.black);
            JButton button = new JButton("Click to change light colors.");
            button.setBounds(100, 420, 400, 30);
            button.addActionListener(this);
            window.add(button, 0);

        int xPos = 5;
        dots = new Oval[32];
        for (int j=0; j!=32; j++) {
            dots[j] = new Oval(xPos, 100, 10, 10);
            if (j % 3 == 0) {
                dots[j].setBackground(Color.darkGray);
            } else {
                dots[j].setBackground(Color.white);
            }
            window.add(dots[j], 0);
            xPos = xPos + 15;
        }
        window.repaint();
    }

    /** post: all dots' old colors are moved to the left by one dot
     *        and the rightmost dot gets the previous color of
     *            the leftmost dot
     */
```

Figure 12.7   Marquee dots program (*continued*)

```
public void actionPerformed(ActionEvent e) {
    Color leftmostDotColor;
    leftmostDotColor = dots[0].getBackground();
    for (int j=0; j!=31; j++) {
        dots[j].setBackground(dots[j+1].getBackground());
    }
    dots[31].setBackground(leftmostDotColor);
    window.repaint();
  }
}
```

An array of Oval objects called **dots** plays the role of the light string. The Driver constructor method instantiates this array. Next, Driver includes a *for* loop to instantiate 32 Oval circles. Each Oval is constructed and assigned to a unique array item by the following instruction.

```
dots[j] = new Oval(xPos, 100, 10, 10);
```

One third of the dots items (i.e., those with an index that is a multiple of 3) are colored dark gray and the others are colored white.

The actionPerformed method from Figure 12.7 contains an algorithm for simulating marquee lighting that is somewhat similar to a shift algorithm. Executing this method causes each of the dots items (except the last) to take on the background color of its neighbor with next greater index. The following *for* loop accomplishes such recoloring.

```
for (int j=0; j!=31; j++) {
    dots[j].setBackground(dots[j+1].getBackground());
}
```

The repetitions of this loop perform the following work.

```
dots[0]  is assigned the color of dots[1]
dots[1]  is assigned the color of dots[2]
dots[2]  is assigned the color of dots[3]
...
dots[30] is assigned the color of dots[31]
```

This process of reassigning colors causes the previous color of the first item in the dots array to be replaced in the very first loop repetition. Since the last item needs to be assigned the previous color of the first, it must be saved prior to the loop. A variable, called leftmostDotColor stores this color until it can be assigned to the last dots item.

12.4 ■ **Treating Arrays in Aggregate**

Previous sections have demonstrated that array items behave like variables. The dots array, declared in Figure 12.7, consists of items of type Oval. Therefore, any item of dots can be assigned a new Oval with an instruction such as

```
dots[3] = new Oval(10, 10, 50, 50);
```

This instruction instantiates an Oval object and assigns it to dots[3] array item.

Methods can also be applied to array items, such as the following two method calls, which apply the setBackground and repaint methods to the object assigned to the dots[3] array item.

```
dots[3].setBackground(Color.orange);
dots[3].repaint();
```

Furthermore, any array item can be passed as an argument, as long as its type conforms to the corresponding formal parameter type. The following call to the add method illustrates by passing the object assigned to the dots[3] item as an argument.

```
window.add(dots[3], 0);
```

For some algorithms, this ability to process an array by way of its individual items isn't enough. There needs to be a way to treat an array as a whole. A so-called **aggregate array operation** is one in which the *entire* array behaves as a single entity. One variety of aggregate array manipulation in Java is **aggregate array parameter passage**. When an array is passed in aggregate, the whole array is passed via a single parameter. In order to pass an aggregate array, the formal parameter must be declared using the syntax shown in Figure 12.8.

Figure 12.8	*aggregateArrayParmeter* description (a possible *Type* for declaring formal parameters)

Syntax

$$\longrightarrow \boxed{\textit{Type}} \longrightarrow [\ \longrightarrow\ ] \longrightarrow$$

Notes

Type is a primitive type or a class name known within this scope.

Semantics

Any aggregate array of items in which the item type conforms to *Type* is permitted for a parameter of this type.

As an example of aggregate array parameter passage, consider a method called `countOfZeros` that returns the number of zero-valued items from an array of `int`. Figure 12.9 contains such a method. This method utilizes an aggregate array parameter, named `arr`, to pass the particular array to be examined.

Within the `countOfZeros` method, `arr` is treated like any other array of `int`. The `countOfZeros` algorithm is expressed using the Collection *for* Pattern, checking each item (`cell`) of the array.

A program could use the `countOfZeros` method to count the number of students who received an exam score of zero. Such a program could declare the exam scores in an array as follows.

```
int[] examScores;
examScores = new int[15];
```

The `countOfZeros` method has a single parameter, called `arr`. This parameter will accept an aggregate array of `int` items. For example, it is appropriate to call `countOfZeros` as shown below.

```
int studentsAbsent = countOfZeros(examScores);
```

This call passes `examScores` in aggregate, and within the code of the `countOfZeros` method this array is given the `arr` alias. This permits `countOfZeros` access to every part of the `examScores` array.

As a second example of passing an aggregate array as a parameter, consider the `initializeTo` method from Figure 12.10. This method illustrates that the content of an array can be altered when it is passed in aggregate.

When `initializeTo` is called, it is passed an array of `double` values. The second parameter for `initializeTo` is named `d` and is of type `double`. Executing `intializeTo` causes every cell of its array parameter to be assigned the value of `d`. This method demonstrates the usefulness of `length` to determine the size of the array argument. To illustrate calling `initializeTo`, suppose the following three statements are executed.

Figure 12.9

countOfZeros method

```
/** post:  result == the count of arr items that == 0 */
public int countOfZeros(int[] arr) {
    int result;
    result = 0;
    for (int cell : arr) {
        if (cell == 0) {
            result++;
        }
    }
    return result;
}
```

```
/** post:  for all j from 0 through arr.length, arr[j] == d */
public void initializeTo(double[] arr, double d) {
    for (int k=0; k!=arr.length; k++) {
        arr[k] = d;
    }
}
```

Figure 12.10

initializeTo
method

```
double[] measureTable;
measureTable = new double[1000];
initializeTo(measureTable, Math.PI);
```

The result of these three instructions is to instantiate an array of one thousand cells, called measureTable, and to assign the value of the mathematical constant PI to every cell of this array.

A second kind of aggregate array operation supported by Java is an aggregate assignment. This allows one array to be assigned to another in a single assignment instruction. For example, if someDoubles is declared as shown below

```
double[] someDoubles;
```

then the following assignment instruction is permissible.

```
someDoubles = measureTable;
```

This is called an **aggregate assignment** because it assigns an entire array, as opposed to a single item of the array. Aggregate assignments behave like any other assignment of one reference object to another. The variable name on the left of the assignment is bound to the same array as the expression on the right. For the example above, someDoubles becomes an alias for the measureTable array. The array expression that is bound must have item type that conforms to the item type of the array name being assigned.

A third way that arrays can behave in aggregate is when returned as the value of a nonvoid method. Figure 12.11 illustrates with a method called arrayCopy.

When called, the arrayCopy method returns a complete copy of its source parameter. For example, the following statement causes someIntArray to be assigned an array that has the same length and item content as examScores, but is a separate array.

```
int[] someIntArray = arrayCopy(examScores);
```

Executing the body of arrayCopy begins by declaring a local array called result. The result array is instantiated to have the same length of the source parameter. A *for* loop copies the value of every item from source into result. The return instruction at the end of arrayCopy returns the aggregate result array.

Java supports an **aggregate array expression** notation as another way to treat arrays in aggregate. This notation is particularly useful for initializing arrays. Figure 12.12 describes the syntax and semantics of aggregate array expressions.

Figure 12.11

arrayCopy method for double arrays

```
/** post:   result.length == source.length
 *          and for 0 <= j < source.length [result[j]==source[j]]
 */
private int[] arrayCopy(int[] source) {
    int[] result;
    result = new int[source.length];
    for (int ndx = 0; ndx != source.length; ndx++) {
        result[ndx] = source[ndx];
    }
    return result;
}
```

Figure 12.12   ***aggregateArrayExpression*** description (a possible *Expression*)

Syntax

Notes

itemExpression is a valid expression of the same type as the array item.

Semantics

An aggregate array is instantiated with length equal to the number of *itemExpressions*.
Each item of this array has the value of the corresponding *itemExpression*.

Each aggregate array expression instantiates a new array. For example, the following array picture is repeated from the beginning of the chapter.

[0]	"platypus"
[1]	"iguana"
[2]	"dinosaur"
[3]	"dragon"

This array can be declared as follows.

```
private String[] animals;
```

The assignment instruction below makes use of an aggregate array expression to construct the content of the array as pictured above.

```
animals = {"platypus", "iguana", dinosaur", "dragon"};
```

An aggregate array expression determines both the length of the array and the value of every array item. The assignment above instantiates an array of length four with particular `String` constants for item values.

Below is a second use of an aggregate array expression that creates an array of two items, each bound to separate `Oval` objects.

```
Oval[] bubbles = {new Oval(0,0,5,5), new Oval(10,10,8,8)};
```

12.5 ■ Tables

A **table**, sometimes called a **look-up table**, is a convenient way to store and retrieve information. Chemists use the periodic table to record facts regarding the elements, such as their atomic weight. Tax tables are often used to determine personal income tax. An international banker performs monetary conversions using tables of exchange rates.

Arrays provide an efficient tool for implementing many tables. Figure 12.13 contains a table of the number of days in a month during a non-leap year.

Month	Num	Length
January	1	31
February	2	28
March	3	31
April	4	30
May	5	31
June	6	30
July	7	31
August	8	31
September	9	30
October	10	31
November	11	30
December	12	31

Figure 12.13

Table of the length of each month in a non-leap year

Figure 12.14 shows a Java method that returns the number of days in a month, without the use of an array. This daysPerMonth method assumes that its parameter is the month number and uses a collection of *if* instructions to select the correct number of days.

A more efficient implementation of daysPerMonth is possible by using an array. Figure 12.15 contains a monthLength array constant and the associated daysPerMonth method. A call to this new method returns the appropriate monthLength item. Note that the array index is m-1, because humans number months from 1, while arrays have a lowest index of zero.

Using an array look-up to replace a system of *if* instructions is referred to as **table-driven** code. Figure 12.16 contains a second example of table-driven code. This table shows the gravitational force of the planets relative to earth.

Figure 12.14   daysPerMonth method using if instructions

```
/**     pre:    1 <= m and m <= 12
 *      post:   result == number of days in month m (non-leap year)
 *      note:   see Figure 12.15 for an alternative.
 */
private int daysPerMonth(int m) {
    if (m==1 || m==3 || m==5 || m==7 || m==8 || m==10 || m==12) {
        return 31;
    } else if (m==4 || m==6 || m==9 || m==11) {
        return 30;
    } else {
        return 28;
    }
}
```

Figure 12.15   daysPerMonth method using an array

Array (table) Declaration

```
private final int[] monthLength
    = {31, 28, 31, 30, 31, 30, 31, 31, 30, 31, 30, 31};
```

Method Using the Table

```
/**     pre:    1 <= m <= 12
 *      post:   result == number of days in month m (non-leap year)
 */
private int daysPerMonth(int m) {
    return monthLength[m-1];
}
```

The information from this gravity table can be stored in the `relativeGravity` array declared and initialized below.

```
private final double[] relativeGravity
    = {0.37, 0.78, 1.00, 0.38, 2.64, 1.16, 1.07, 1.21, 0.05};
```

To make this array easier to use and the program easier to read, the following enumerated type declaration might be included.

```
public enum Planet {
    Mercury, Venus, Earth, Mars, Jupiter, Saturn, Uranus,
        Neptune, Pluto
}
```

Given these constants, looking up the relative gravity of Saturn is expressed as

```
relativeGravity[Planet.Saturn.ordinal()];
```

software engineering *Hint*

Sometimes table keys do not map naturally onto integer indices. At such times, an enumerated type can enhance readability.

12.6 ■ **Arrays with Reference Items**

Arrays are containers of items. Sometimes the array items have a primitive type in which case the array is really a container of primitive values. At other times the array items belong to a class, and in these cases, the array consists of an array of objects. Like any variable that belongs to a class, the items from an array of objects really store bindings. For example, suppose a class called `Name` is used to declare arrays. The `Name` class is shown in Figure 12.17.

Below is a declaration of two arrays with items that belong to the Name class.

```
private Name[] politicians, presidents;
```

Planet	Gravity
Mercury	0.37
Venus	0.78
Earth	1.00
Mars	0.38
Jupiter	2.64
Saturn	1.16
Uranus	1.07
Neptune	1.21
Pluto	0.05

Figure 12.16

Table of relative gravity for planets

Figure 12.17

Name class

```java
public class Name {
    public String first;
    public String last;

    public Name(String fs, String ls) {
        first = fs;
        last = ls;
    }

    public Name deepClone() {
        Name result;
        result = new Name(String(first), String(last));
        return result;
    }
}
```

These arrays can be instantiated as follows.

```java
politicians = new Name[3];
presidents = new Name[3];
```

Following the execution of the two instructions above, all array items are null. The pictures below illustrate.

politicians

[0]	null
[1]	null
[2]	null

presidents

null	[0]
null	[1]
null	[2]

Next, assume that these instructions assign values to items of the `politicians` array.

```java
politicians[0] = new Name("George", "Washington");
politicians[1] = new Name("Abraham", "Lincoln");
```

Following the execution of these assignments, the first two items from politicians are updated as shown below.

Executing the following three instructions assigns the first two items from politicians to the corresponding items of presidents.

```
presidents[0] = politicians[0];
presidents[1] = politicians[1];
```

Since the items of these arrays are objects, these assignments copy the bindings, resulting in the following.

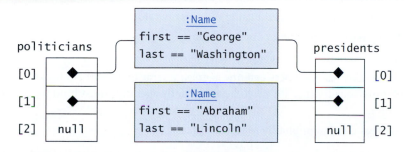

The result of these last assignments leaves both arrays bound to the same two objects. For many applications, such multiple bindings are acceptable. However, there are other times when the program needs to ensure that each array contains separate objects.

To make such a complete copy it is necessary to construct a second set of item objects. The deepClone method from the Name class provides a facility for returning a complete copy of any Name object. This method can be used as follows to create and assign item copies.

```
presidents[0] = politicians[0].deepClone();
presidents[1] = politicians[1].deepClone();
```

The picture below shows the structure following the execution of these last two instructions.

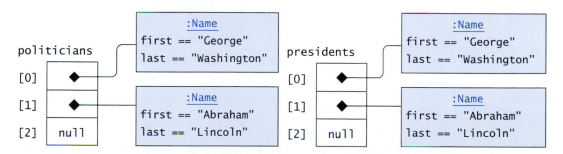

The result of executing the two assignment instructions is that both the items of the presidents array are bound to their own copies of objects with the same content as those objects bound to the politicians array.

12.7 ■ Arrays and Objects

In many ways, arrays act as though they are regular objects. These similarities between arrays and other objects include the following.

1. Every array name must be declared before it is used.

2. Array variables have a value of `null` until they are bound to an array of conforming type.

3. Arrays must be instantiated using the `new` operator.

4. An aggregate assignment copies a binding.

5. A method may return an aggregate array.

6. An equality test (`==`) between one aggregate array and another checks for identity equality (i.e., for `==` to be `true`, both operands must bind to the same array).

7. Aggregate arrays implicitly inherit `Object`.

This last similarity deserves special comment. Since an array inherits `Object`, every aggregate array conforms to `Object` and can be assigned to a variable of type `Object`. For example, `SimpleList<Object>` (presented in the previous chapter) is a container in which each item must be of type `Object`. This container permits the objects belonging to any class, as well as aggregate array objects to be added.

All the similarities between arrays and objects tend to suggest that arrays are really objects with a special notation for indexing. However, there are two ways in which Java treats arrays unlike full-fledged objects:

1. It is impossible to inherit from an array.

2. The methods inherited from `Object` cannot be overridden by any array.

There are many places where the Java syntax requires a *type* be specified:

Variable declarations require a type.

```
private type varName;
```

Formal parameters must specify their type.

```
public void methodName(type parameterName) {...}
```

The type must precede the name of each method.

```
public type methodName() {...}
```

In all of these example cases, an aggregate array may be used as a valid type. However, it is *not* possible to use an aggregate array in an inheritance specification.

aggregate array **invalid**

```
public class className extends type {...}
```

The second way in which arrays are unlike other objects has to do with overriding methods. All Java classes implicitly inherit `Object`. Among other things, inheriting `Object` gives each class the ability to override `Object` methods such as `toString` and `equals`. Aggregate arrays share this property of inheriting `Object`. However, an array is incapable of overriding inherited methods such as `toString` and `equals`.

12.8 ■ Sorting—the Selection Sort

In Chapter 11, a **sorting algorithm**, namely insertion sort, was introduced. Sorting algorithms rearrange the items within a container to place them in some particular order. The most common kinds of sorting algorithms perform either an ascending sort (ordering items from smallest to largest) or a descending sort (ordering items from largest to smallest).

There are many different algorithms for sorting arrays. One of the most common is the **straight selection sort**, informally called a **selection sort**. The name "selection" comes from the fact that this algorithm repeatedly *selects* items in sorted order.

People commonly utilize selection sorts in their everyday activities. For example, a selection sort to order the batting averages of nine professional baseball players in descending order would proceed as follows.

1. Select the largest batting average and place it first in the new order, removing it from further consideration in the sorting process.

2. Select the next largest batting average and place it second, removing it from further consideration in the sorting process.

3. Select the next largest batting average and place it third, removing it from further consideration in the sorting process.

    . . .

8. Select the next largest batting average and place it eighth, removing it from further consideration in the sorting process.

9. Place the remaining batting average ninth.

The shell of this algorithm can be expressed shown in Figure 12.18. (Note that all comments in this algorithm are informal statements requiring further implementation.)

Suppose that the name of the array to be sorted in descending order is `arr`. Then the first time the body of this loop executes, it selects a value for `arr[0]`. The second loop body execution selects the value for `arr[1]`. Each subsequent loop body repetition selects another item and assigns it to the `arr` item with next greater index.

```
/* Loop initialization code goes here */
while (/* the array is not yet sorted */) {
    /* Select the largest value from those remaining */
    /* Move the largest value into "next" position */
}
```

Figure 12.18

Step 1 of the design of the selection sort algorithm

As the sorting algorithm proceeds, the array remains partitioned into two parts: the front part of the array (with lower indices) contains the sorted values that have already been selected and the rear part of the array contains the unsorted values that have not yet been selected. Figure 12.19 pictures this situation.

Figure 12.20 shows how an `int` variable, called `lastSorted`, can be used to maintain the index of the last item that was selected and assigned.

One effective way to identify a selected array item is to store the index of the selected item in an `int` variable. Using a variable called `selectedIndex`, the selection sort algorithm can be refined as shown in Figure 12.21.

Figure 12.19

The state of the `arr` array in the midst of selection sort

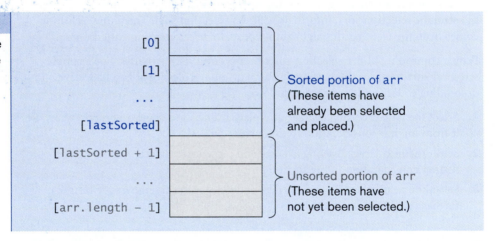

Figure 12.20

Step 2 of the design of the selection sort algorithm

```
int lastSorted = -1;
while (lastSorted != arr.length-1) {
    /* Select the largest value from those remaining */
    lastSorted++;
    /* Move the largest value into the lastSorted position */
}
```

Figure 12.21

Step 3 of the design of the selection sort algorithm

```
int selectedIndex;
int lastSorted = -1;
    while (lastSorted != arr.length-1) {
        /* Assign the index of the largest value from those
            unsorted to selectedIndex */
        lastSorted++;
        /* Swap arr[selectedIndex] and arr[lastSorted] */
}
```

The portion of the selection sort algorithm that selects the largest valued item begins by assuming that `arr[lastSorted+1]` is largest then checks all subsequent `arr` items to find the largest. This search for the largest value is accomplished by the following code.

```
selectedIndex = lastSorted+1;
for (int k = lastSorted+2; k<arr.length; k++) {
    if (arr[k] > arr[selectedIndex]) {
        selectedIndex = k;
    }
}
```

Plugging this code and the swap code into the algorithm shell results in the completed selection sort code shown in Figure 12.22. This method assumes that the array items are of type `double`.

The behavior of the selection sort algorithm can be observed by tracing the execution of `selectionSort` for specific array content. Figure 12.23 contains such a trace. This picture progresses left to right. The leftmost column depicts the array and `lastSorted` value just before executing the body of the `selectionSort` *while* loop for the first time. The state of execution just prior to each subsequent repetition of the *while* loop body is shown in the next column. Arrows indicate swapped array items.

```
/** post:   arr is the same as arr@pre with item values permuted
 *          and for all j [0<=j<arr.length-1)
 *             [arr[j] >= arr[j+1]]
 */
public void selectionSort(double[] arr) {
    int selectedIndex;
    double selectedValue;
    int lastSorted = -1;
    while (lastSorted != arr.length-1) {
        selectedIndex = lastSorted+1;
        for (int k = lastSorted+2; k<arr.length; k++) {
            if (arr[k] > arr[selectedIndex]) {
                selectedIndex = k;
            }
        }
        lastSorted++;
        // swap arr[selectedIndex] with arr[lastSorted]
        selectedValue = arr[selectedIndex];
        arr[selectedIndex] = arr[lastSorted];
        arr[lastSorted] = selectedValue;
    }
}
```

Figure 12.22

The complete selection sort method

Figure 12.23   Execution trace of `selectionSort`

	arr	arr	arr	arr	arr
[0]	290	**325**	325	325	325
[1]	250	250	**306**	306	306
[2]	325	**290**	290	**290**	290
[3]	306	306	**250**	250	**290**
[4]	290	290	290	290	**290**

lastSorted ==	-1	0	1	2	3
selectedIndex ==	?	2	3	2	4

12.9 ■ Two-Dimensional Arrays

The arrays examined thus far are called **one-dimensional arrays**. As demonstrated, a one-dimensional array is a linear sequence of items. Java also supports arrays of greater dimension, because each array item can be any object, including another array. For example, a **two-dimensional array** is an array in which each array item is a separate one-dimensional array. Figure 12.24 shows a picture of the one-dimensional arrays by comparison to two-dimensional arrays.

Two-dimensional arrays can be thought of as having rows and columns. Each item is in one row and one column of the array. Therefore, two indices are required.

Figure 12.24   One-dimensional and two-dimensional arrays

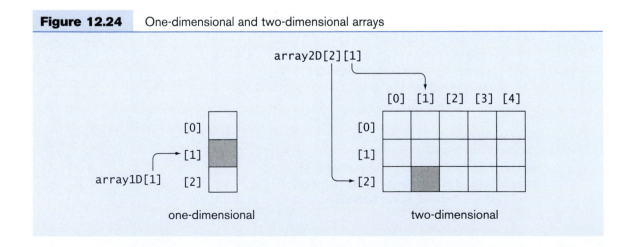

Figure 12.25 shows that the syntax for declaring a two-dimensional array uses two sets of square brackets, signifying the two indices for each item.

As an example, consider a two-dimensional array for storing a table of mileage for highway travel between cities. Figure 12.26 diagrams such a table.

Figure 12.25 **_ArrayDec2D_** description (a possible `OneVarDecl`)

Syntax

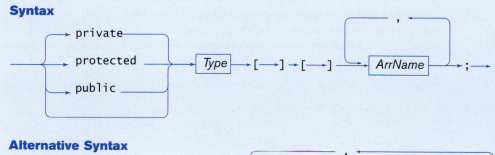

Alternative Syntax

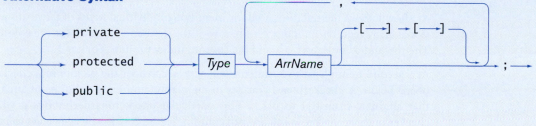

Note

Type and _ArrName_ must be _Identifiers_. _Type_ must either be a primitive type or it must name a class name that is known within this scope.

Usage

Each _ArrName_ from Syntax, as well as each _VarName_ that is followed by [ ] from Alternative Syntax, refers to a two-dimensional array in which each item must conform to _Type_.

	Chicago	Los Angeles	Miami	New York
Chicago	0	2095	1360	840
Los Angeles	2095	0	2713	2915
Miami	1360	2713	0	1330
New York	840	2915	1330	0

Figure 12.26

Table of mileage between four cities

The information from this mileage table can be stored in a two-dimensional `mileage` array using the following code.

```
private enum City{Chicago, Los_Angeles, Miami, New_York}
private int mileage[][] = {{0, 2095, 1360, 840},
                          {2095, 0, 2713, 2915},
                          {1360, 2713, 0, 1330},
                          {840, 2915, 1330, 0}};
```

The declaration of `mileage` demonstrates that Java extends the aggregate array notation to allow an aggregate to contain aggregates. Each row of the two-dimensional array corresponds to one of the inner aggregate array expressions (shown on separate lines). The inner array expressions are separated by commas and enclosed in braces to form the two-dimensional array expression.

The instructions below can be used to print the mileage from Miami to New York:

```
int miamiToNY = mileage[City.Miami.ordinal()]
                      [City.New_York.ordinal()];
System.out.println(miamiToNY);
```

As shown above the notation used for identifying individual items of a two-dimensional array requires an index for the row of the item and an index for the column. The row index for `Miami` is 2 and the column index for `New_York` is 3.

As a second example of two-dimensional arrays, consider the picture of a checkerboard below. A checkerboard consists of eight rows and eight columns of squares that alternate from red to black. This particular checkerboard contains a white checker in the second row and seventh column. Figure 2.27 is a `Driver` class to construct this image.

The checkerboard program from Figure 12.27 illustrates several characteristics that are common to programs that utilize two-dimensional arrays. The two-dimensional array to store the checkerboard is declared with the following line.

```
private Rectangle[][] checkerboard;
```

To instantiate a two-dimensional array as a full grid requires specifying both the number of rows and the number of columns. The following instruction instantiates `checkerboard` to have eight rows and eight columns (each indexed from 0 through 7).

```
checkerboard = new Rectangle[8][8];
```

Figure 12.27   Program to draw a checkerboard

```java
import java.awt.Color;
import javax.swing.JFrame;
public class Driver {
    private Rectangle[][] checkerboard;
    private JFrame window;
    private Oval whitePiece;

    public Driver() {
        JFrame window = new JFrame("Checkerboard");
        window.setBounds(100, 100, 160, 160);
        window.setVisible(true);
        window.setLayout(null);
        checkerboard = new Rectangle[8][8];
        for (int row=0; row!=checkerboard.length; row++) {
            for (int col=0; col!=checkerboard[0].length; col++){
                checkerboard[row][col] = new Rectangle(col*20, row*20, 20, 20);
                if ((row+col) % 2 == 0) {
                    checkerboard[row][col].setBackground(Color.black);
                } else {
                    checkerboard[row][col].setBackground(Color.red);
                }
                window.add(checkerboard[row][col], 0);
            }
        }
        whitePiece = new Oval(2, 2, 16, 16);
        whitePiece.setBackground(Color.white);
        checkerboard[1][6].add(whitePiece, 0);
        window.repaint();
    }
}
```

The items of two-dimensional arrays require two consecutive index expressions—a row index and a column index. Two-dimensional array items, like one-dimensional array items, can be used like variables of the same type. The following instruction assigns a `Rectangle` object to an array item.

```java
checkerboard[row][col] = new Rectangle(col*20, row*20, 20, 20);
```

Similarly, the instruction below places an item from `checkerboard` on the window.

```java
window.add(checkerboard[row][col], 0);
```

Placing the white checker piece onto the square in the second row and seventh column is performed by the following instruction.

```java
checkerboard[1][6].add(whitePiece, 0);
```

The checkerboard program also includes an instance of a common pattern for processing all of the items of an array. This pattern is explained in Figure 12.28.

In Java, two-dimensional arrays are actually a one-dimensional array of items that are one-dimensional arrays. Therefore, the notation `checkerboard.length` refers to the number of rows in the checkerboard. The number of columns can be found by accessing the `length` attribute of any of the rows, such as `checkerboard[0].length`.

While two-dimensional arrays often have rows of equal length, this is not required in Java. Each row can be instantiated separately and assigned to the row item, thereby creating different lengths for different rows.

Java also permits more than two dimensions in an array. A **multidimensional array** is any array of dimension two or greater. The same notations that are used in two-dimensional arrays are extended to dimensions of three and more.

Figure 12.28

Two-dimensional array processing pattern

Two-Dimensional Array Processing Pattern

Processing every item in a two-dimensional array (`arr`), proceeding row by row and column by column within each row is accomplished by the following pattern.

```
for (int r=0; r!=arr.length; r++) {
    for (int c=0; c!=arr.length[0].length; c++) {
        // process item arr[r][c]
    }
}
```

An application of this pattern requires that the `arr` array must be instantiated with all rows of equal length.

Inspector *Java*

Below is a collection of hints on what to check when examining code that involves the concepts of this chapter.

- Array index out of bounds exceptions are arguably the most common difficulty in array processing. Each index expression should be considered as a potential runtime error.

- Java arrays always begin with an index of zero. When an array is instantiated with a length of n, the largest valid index is $n-1$. Index expressions need special attention to ensure that the 0th item is not forgotten.

- When the type of array items belong to classes, the items are bound to objects. These bindings are like variables. Instantiating such arrays does not instantiate the individual items. You should check to ensure that the items are instantiated separately.

- Arrays have many of the properties of classes. However, arrays lack some polymorphic properties because they cannot be inherited, nor can they override `Object` methods. In a few cases, a different type of container may be required to circumvent these restrictions.

- If an array is accessed only via sequential algorithms, then perhaps a list would be a better container choice.

Terminology

aggregate array parameters	multidimensional array
aggregate assignment	one-dimensional arrays
array	out of bounds
boundary violation	selection sort (straight selection)
Collection *for* Pattern	sequential access
direct access device	sorting algorithm
for instruction	subscript
Index *for* Pattern	table
index (indices)	table-driven code
length (of an array)	two-dimensional arrays
look-up table	

Exercises

1. Draw a picture of the array that results from executing each of the following code segments. Be certain that your picture clearly shows the number of items and content of each item.

   a. ```
   String[] message;
   message = new String[6]
   message[1] = "Write home.";
   message[3] = "Send money.";
   message[5] = "I cannot tell a lie.";
   message[3] = "Please retransmit";
   ```

   b. ```
   double[] number;
   number = new double[4];
   number[0] = 1.2;
   number[1] = 3.4;
   number[2] = 5.6;
   number[3] = 7.8;
   number[0] = number[3];
   number[2] = number[1] + number[3];
   ```

   c. ```
   int[] distance;
   distance = new int[6];
   distance[0] = 4;
   distance[1] = 3;
   distance[2] = 2;
   distance[3] = 1;
   distance[4] = distance[distance[1]};
   distance[5] = 2 + distance[distance[3]-1] + distance[1+1]
   ```

   d. ```
   Oval[] elipse;
   elipse = new Oval[4];
   elipse[0] = new Oval(0, 0, 10, 10);
   elipse[1] = new Oval(1, 1, 21, 21);
   elipse[2] = new Oval(2, 2, 32, 32);
   elipse[3] = elipse[2];
   elipse[1].setBackground(Color,green);
   elipse[3].setSize(43, 43);
   elipse[1].setLocation(elipse[0].getX(), elipse[3].getX());
   ```

2. Draw a picture of the array that results from executing each of the following code segments. Be certain that your picture clearly shows the number of items and content of each item.

   a. ```
   double[] number;
   number = new double[5];
   ```
   ```

```
    for (int j = 0; j != 5; j++) {
        number[j] = (j+1) * 3;
    }
```

b.
```
int[] money;
money = new int[8];
for (int k = 1; k != 7; k++) {
    money[k-1] = k * k;
}
```

c.
```
int[] pizza;
pizza = new int[8];
for (int k = 0; k != 8; k++) {
    pizza[k] = k;
}
for (int j = 1; j != 8; j++) {
    pizza[j-1] = pizza[j];
}
```

d.
```
int[] inventory;
inventory = new int[8];
for (int k = 0; k != 8; k++) {
    inventory[k] = k;
}
for (int j = 6; j != 0; j--) {
    inventory[j-1] = inventory[j];
}
```

e.
```
int[] box;
box = new int[8];
for (int k = 0; k != box.length; k++) {
    box[k] = k;
}
for (int j = box.length-2; j != 0; j--) {
    box[j] = box[j]*box[j];
}
```

f.
```
int[] canoe, kayak;
canoe = new int[5];
kayak = new int[5];
for (int k = 0; k != canoe.length; k++) {
    canoe[k] = k*2;
    kayak[k] = canoe[k] + 1;
}
for (int j = 0; j != 3; j++) {
    canoe[j] = kayak[j]+ canoe[j+1];
}
```

3. Show the output that results from executing each of the following segments of code.

a.
```java
double[] dog, cat;
dog = new double[8];
cat = new double[8];
for (int j = 0; j != 8; j++) {
    dog[j] = j;
}
for (int j = 0; j != 8; j++) {
    cat[j] = dog[j];
}
for (int j = 0; j != 8; j++) {
    cat[j] = j*10;
}
for (int j = 0; j != 8; j++) {
    System.out.println(dog[j]);
    System.out.println(cat[j]);
}
```

b.
```java
double[] tree, shrub;
tree = new double[5];
for (int j = 0; j != 5; j++) {
    tree[j] = j;
}
shrub = tree;
for (int j = 0; j != 5; j++) {
    shrub[j] = j*10;
}
for (double t : tree) {
    System.out.println(t);
}
for (double s : shrub) {
    System.out.println(s);
}
```

c.
```java
Rectangle[] frontFace, backFace;
frontFace = new Rectangle[3];
for (int k = 0; k != 3; k++) {
    frontFace[k] = new Rectangle(0, 0, k*20, k*10);
}
backFace = new Rectangle[3];
for (int k = 0; k != 3; k++) {
    backFace[k] = frontFace[k];
}
for (Rectangle r : backFace) {
    r.setSize(1, 2);
}
```

```
for (Rectangle r : frontFace) {
    System.out.println(r.getHeight());
    System.out.println(backFace[k].getHeight());
}
```

4. Draw a picture of the array that results from executing each of the following code segments. Be certain that your picture clearly shows the number of items and content of each item.

a. `double[] number = {1.05, 2.05, 3.05, 4.05, 5.05};`

b. `char[] initial = {'w', 'x', 'y', 'z'};`

c. `String[] color = {"red", "green", "blue"};`

d. `Oval[] pane = {new Oval(0, 0, 50, 50),`
   `      new Oval(100, 100, 60, 60),`
   `      new Oval(200, 200, 70, 70)};`

5. Show all of the code needed for a table lookup to perform the same task as the following *if* instructions.

a.
```
/** pre:   0 <= c and c <= 4 */
private int monetaryValue(int c) {
    if (c==0) {
        return 1;
    } else if (c==1) {
        return 5;
    } else if (c==2) {
        return 10;
    } else if (c==3) {
        return 25;
    } else {
        return 100;
    }
}
```

b.
```
/** pre:   2 <= m and m <= 10 */
private int mysteryValue(int m) {
    if (m==2 || m==3 || m==5 || m==7) {
        return 100;
    } else if (m==4 || m==6 || m==8) {
        return 200;
    } else {
        result = 500;
    }
}
```

6. Complete each of the following method bodies so that each method follows the specifications from the precondition, postcondition, and modifies clauses.

a.
```
/** post:  all items in names are assigned the letter 'R'
 */
private void makeAllRs(char[] names) {
    // your code goes here.
}
```

b.
```
/** pre:    arr.length > = 2
 * post:  the values in arr[0] and arr[1] are swapped from
 *        their previous values */
private Color swapFirstTwo(double[] arr) {
    // your code goes here.
}
```

c.
```
/** pre:    dArray.length > = 1
 * post:  result is the largest value of any item in
 *        dArray */
private double biggestValue(double[] dArray) {
    // your code goes here.
}
```

d.
```
/** pre:    dArray.length > = 1
 * post:  result is the index of the largest-valued item
 *        in dArray */
private int biggestIndex(double[] dArray) {
    // your code goes here.
}
```

e.
```
/** pre:    target.length == dest.length
 * post:  the item values in target are assigned items
 *        from dest in reversed in order */
private void copyReversed(char[] dest, char[] target) {
    // your code goes here.
}
```

Programming Exercises

1. Write a program to analyze user messages. Your program should display a JTextField in which the user types a message. When the user strikes the *return* key on the JTextField, a set of 26 histogram bars are displayed across the bottom of the window. Each bar represents the number of times the corresponding alphabetic letter occurs in the user's message. The most frequently occurring letter should be 150 pixels high and all others proportional to their occurrence count relative to the maximum. A picture of a typical analysis follows.

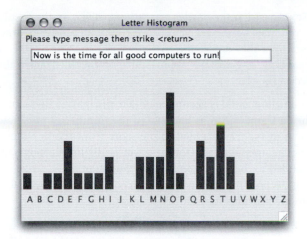

2. Write a program to score a bowling game. The initial GUI of the program should appear as shown below. The user enters the appropriate scores in the JTextField cells and then clicks the Score the game button. The program responds by completing the scores and filling in a frame-by-frame running total.

AFTER SCORING:

Here is a brief summary of bowling scoring. Ten frames make up a single bowling game. (Each frame in this program is represented by the larger square. The first nine frames are alike. At the beginning of each frame, ten bowling pins are reset on the alley and the bowler throws a first ball. The number of pins downed on this first ball is always placed in the leftmost JTextField for the frame. If all ten pins are downed, this is called a strike and the bowler is finished for the frame. If less than ten pins are downed on the first ball, then a second ball is thrown at the remaining pins and the number of pins downed by the second ball is recorded in the right JTextField for the frame. If all the pins are downed after the second ball, this is called a spare. The tenth frame begins the same with all ten pins reset and the number of pins downed by the first ball recorded in the left JTextField. If the bowler gets a strike on the first ball of the tenth frame, then the pins are reset and a second ball is thrown. If there was no strike, then the user throws a normal second ball at the remaining pins. The number of pins downed by the second ball in the tenth frame is placed in the center JTextField. If the bowler gets either a strike on the first ball or a spare on the second ball, he/she is given a third roll. If all pins were downed after the second ball, then they are again reset, otherwise the third ball is thrown at the pins left standing. The number of pins rolled on the third ball of the tenth frame is recorded in the rightmost JTextField.

Scoring a bowling game is accumulated left to right. If there are no strikes or spares, then a frame's score is the total of the number of pins downed by both balls thrown in the frame added to the score from the previous frame. If the frame is a spare, then the score for the frame is 10 plus the next ball thrown after the spare added to the score from the previous frame. If a strike is thrown, then the score is 10 plus the total pins downed on the next *two* balls added to the score from the previous frame.

For some extra effort you might want to substitute a "/" in place of any score that constitutes a spare and "X" in the roll for a strike. (In all but the tenth frame, the strike "X" should be placed in the right ATextField of the frame.) See the example above.

3. Below is a picture of the GUI for this program. It consists of a red dot upon a two-dimensional (3-by-4) grid of squares, along with four buttons. Clicking any of the buttons causes the dot to move to the next grid cell in the direction indicated. The dot cannot move off the grid, so some button clicks must be ignored. Be certain to use a two-dimensional array of Rectangle in your solution.

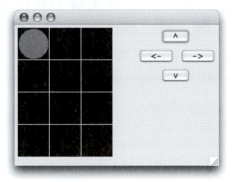

4. Write a program that draws a grid of JTextField objects in five rows and three columns, like the picture below. This grid is to be treated like a ledger in which each JTextField stores a single real number. When the Total Rows button is clicked, the program responds by subtotaling across every row, leaving the sum subtotals in Labels to the right of the gird. Similarly, a button click to Total Columns causes the five columns to be subtotaled. You must use a two-dimensional array of JTextField for the grid and loops to perform the algorithms.

Summing Ledger					
0	1	2	3.0		Total Rows
10	11	12	33.0		Total Columns
20	21	22	63.0		
30	31	32	93.0		
40	41	42	123.0		
100.0	105.0	110.0			

5. The program should construct an array of ten bars. (Each bar is 40 units wide and 1 unit tall. Ten units separate consecutive bars.) Store the bars in an array and display them on a window

   Clicking the Update one button causes one bar to change height. The particular bar to resize is supplied by the user in the Bar Number field. (The bars are numbered from the left, beginning with one (1).) The new height for the selected bar comes from the New Height field.

   A click of the New bars button causes all of the previous bars to be destroyed and replaced by an evenly spaced row of bars. The height of these new bars is 1 pixel, and the Bar count field gives the number of new bars. The width of each bar should be 400 divided by the number of bars, and the space between bars is 25 percent of a bar's width. You will want to create a new array, using the same array name, after first removing all of the items from the old array.

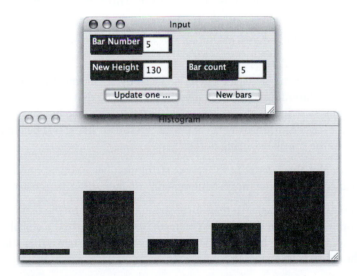

6. Cryptography (i.e., the science of how to send secret messages) has long been an important area of study within computer science. For this program, you will use a simple translation table to encode a message. The user interface for this program is shown below.

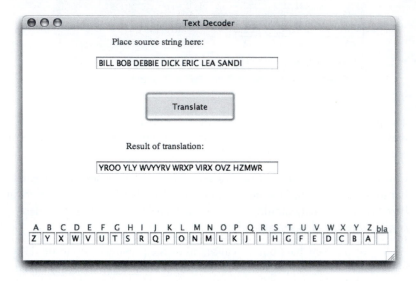

The user is expected to type a message string into the top text field and to define the translation mappings via the bottom row of text fields. When the Translate button is clicked, your program must display the correct decoded form of the message in the text field just below the button. This translation must proceed as follows:

■ The decoded message will contain the same number of characters as the source.

■ Every alphabetic character will be replaced by the leftmost character from the corresponding translation field box, assuming that that the field is not the empty string. (i.e., if the user has placed a "+" in the box below "H", then every occurrence of "H" or "h" in the source string will be replaced by "+" in the translated string.)

■ Every alphabetic letter in the source string that has a corresponding text field containing an empty string remains unaltered in the translated string.

■ Every blank character in the source string is replaced by the first character from the string in the text field beneath blank. (Just like the alphabetic translation, if the blank text field contains an empty string, then blanks should remain unaltered.)

■ All other characters (i.e., nonalphabetic and nonblank) remain unchanged in the decoding process.

File Input and Output

13

If you have an anecdote from one source, you file it away. If you hear it again, it may be true. Then the more times you hear it, the less likely it is to be true."

—Anthony Holden, *International Herald Tribune*, June 9, 1979.

Objectives

- To introduce the concept of a file system and the associated use of files and directories

- To examine the way that files are named with both relative and absolute file names

- To examine the `File` class as a way to manage files and file systems programmatically

- To introduce the exception handling mechanisms needed to perform I/O in Java

- To explore the Java concepts of streams, readers, and writers, and the way such objects are used to read from and write to files

- To suggest a general purpose algorithm for file input and another for file output

- To explore binary file I/O using `DataInputStream` and `DataOutputStream`

- To examine the concept of an end of file condition and the many different ways in which it is detected

- To explore text file I/O using `PrintWriter` and `BufferedStream`

- To introduce terminal-style file I/O using `System.in` and `System.out`

- To explore persistent object implementation using
  `ObjectInputStream` and `ObjectOutputStream`
- To introduce the use of `JFileChooser` as a means to allow
  the user to specify file names

*P*rograms store and manipulate data. Sometimes the program's data is of primitive type and sometimes it consists of objects belonging to one or more classes. Sometimes data is referenced by a variable and sometimes it is part of a container of data. Sometimes the data is publicly accessible and sometimes its scope is more restricted.

There is one important property of the entire program data examined thus far—such data is *transient* in the sense that when the program completes execution all of this program data is lost. The lifetime of some data, such as local variables and formal parameters, can even end long before the program terminates.

This transient nature of program data leads to questions regarding the potential need for more permanent forms of data storage. For example, an insurance company is likely to have many programs to manipulate its client data. There might be one program to enter a new client, another to generate notices for premium invoices, and a third to process an insurance claim. Certainly, client data must be retained from the time that any of these programs is run until the next is run.

13.1 ■ Files

The need to retain data between program executions is supported by something called a **file**. Files are categorized as **persistent**, rather than transient, because the data of the file *persists* even when programs are not executing.

If you've ever written and executed a Java program, then you have used at least two files. A Java program typically consists of many source code files. A `Driver` class is generally stored as a file called *Driver.java*. When the *Driver.java* program is compiled, a second file, a bytecode file called *Driver.class*, is produced. This *Driver.class* file is used by the Java VM during program execution. In other words, the *Driver.java* file is shared by the text editor and the Java compiler, while the *Driver.class* file is shared by the Java compiler and the Java VM.

A second difference between program variables and files is the physical devices where they are stored. The data referenced by program variables and parameters are stored within computer memory (sometimes called the "main memory" or "RAM") of the computer.[1] The transient nature of this kind of data is underscored by the fact that turning off the power to most computers causes main memory to be erased.

Files are retained by different devices than main memory. Hard disks, floppy disks, compact disks, flash memory devices, various forms of computer tapes, and DVDs are all capable of storing files. The name **secondary storage** is commonly used to identify the type of storage used for files, and the devices that manipulate secondary storage are called **secondary storage devices**. Since data stored in secondary storage must be persistent, secondary storage devices *do not* automatically erase their content when power to the computer is lost.

Computer systems use **file systems** to organize all of secondary storage. Modern file systems organize their storage using files and directories. The **file** is the basic unit of secondary storage. Data must first be collected into a file before it can be stored within secondary storage.

A **directory** is a mechanism for cataloging. A group of files can be grouped together into a single directory. Sometimes directories, and possibly other files, are grouped together into other directories. Many computer systems refer to directories as **folders** because of the similarity between a computer directory and a file folder. Just as printed documents can be grouped together in file folders, computer files can be grouped together in computer folders.

Figure 13.1 pictures a small segment of a typical file system. Each rectangle in this picture depicts a separate file or directory. The rectangles with folder icons are directories and those without the icon are files.

The root of the file system shown in Figure 13.1 is a directory named *Users*. The *Users* directory contains two other directories: *jones* and *smith*. The *jones* directory consists of two files: *addresses* and *email*. The *smith* directory contains one file called *addresses* and one directory called *Java*.

Figure 13.1 also illustrates that each file and each directory has its own name. These **file names** and **directory names** follow a syntax that is defined by the particular file system. In general, these names can include alphabetic letters and periods. It is also possible for two files and/or directories to share the same name as long as they are not within the same immediate directory.

The file system provides two different ways to identify a particular file. The first technique uses a **path name**. The complete path name for a file is formed by joining all the containing directories (from most distant to immediate) followed by the file name. Each directory/file name is separated from adjacent names using a separator symbol ("/" for Unix and Apple file systems and "\" for Windows.) The path name for the *read.me* file would be as follows for a Unix or Apple file system.

```
/Users/smith/Java/read.me
```

---

1. In computer systems with virtual memory, it is possible for program data to be stored outside of the main computer memory. However, such situations do not alter the transient nature of this data.

Figure 13.1

Example file system

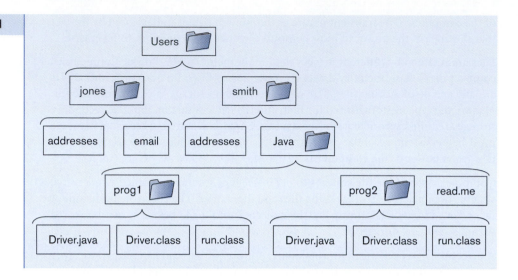

The path name for this same file in a Windows file system is shown below.

    \Users\smith\Java\read.me

The first symbol in each of these names is a file separator to signify that the path name begins with the master directory for the entire device.

The second way to identify a file uses a **current directory** (also called a **working directory**). Many programs keep track of such a working directory, and it is generally possible to change the working directory from one folder to another. For example, Unix shells and Windows (command line application) use the **cd command** to allow the user to type a new current directory.

The purpose of a current directory is to simplify the identification of files. When a current directory is established, a file can often be identified by a **relative path name** that consists of the substring of the complete path name that omits the names up to and including the current directory. For example, the complete path name for the *run.class* file that is within prog2 is given below.

    /Users/smith/Java/prog2/run.class   (in Unix/Apple notation)

                or

    \Users\smith\Java\prog2\run.class   (in Windows notation)

However, if the current directory is set to the *prog2* folder, then the following relative path name will uniquely identify the same file.

    run.class

Notice that complete path names begin with a file separator symbol and relative path names omit this leading character.

It is common for a Java Virtual Machine and the Java compiler to treat the directory of the class that initiates program execution (such as directory containing *run.class*) as its current directory. This explains why import declarations are unnecessary in situations where all class files are grouped in a common directory and the CLASSPATH variable is properly set. (See Chapter 15 for a discussion of the CLASSPATH system variable.)

13.2 ■ The Java File Class

Java includes many file-related classes within a library package called *java.io*. Some of these classes are used to build objects to extract data from files and some are used to place data within files.

Still another of the classes from the *java.io* package is designed to provide Java programs with a mechanism for interacting with the file system. This class is called **File**. Figure 13.2 contains a class diagram and Figure 13.3 contains a class specification for some of the most common used methods of the File class.

Using the standard File class, it is possible to check for the existence of a file and print an appropriate message with the segment of code on the following page.

Figure 13.2

File Class Diagram

```
                java.io.File

    - String FileName

«constructor»
    + File(String)
    ...

«query»
    + boolean canRead()
    + boolean canWrite()
    + boolean exists()
    + String getAbsolutePath()
    + boolean isFile()
    + boolean isDirectory()
    + long length()
    ...

«update»
    + boolean createNewFile()
    + boolean delete()
    + void deleteOnExit()
    + boolean mkdir()
    ...
```

```
// Note that the code below requires exception handling
// (see Section 13.3)
    File file = new File("EXAMPLE");
    if (!file.exists()) {
        System.out.println("No file or directory with a
            relative path name " + "of EXAMPLE exists.");
    } else if (file.isFile()) {
        System.out.println("A file with name EXAMPLE
            exists.");
    } else if (file.isDirectory()) {
        System.out.println("A directory with name EXAMPLE
            exists.");

    }
```

The code above demonstrates that an object of type `File` can be used to examine a file system by checking for the existence of a file (`exists`) and by checking to see whether the relative path name represents a file (`isFile`) or a directory (`isDirectory`). It is also possible, but not shown, to use `File` to ascertain the complete path name (by calling `getAbsolutePath`) or to check a file's size (by calling `length`).

To illustrate how a `File` object can be utilized to create a new file, consider the following code.

```
// Note that the code below requires exception handling
// (see Section 13.3)
    File file = new File("myFile.fil");
    boolean operationOK;
    if (!file.exists()) {
        operationOK = file.createNewFile();
    } else {
        System.out.println("A file/directory with name
            myFile.fil exists.");
    }
```

When the file variable is instantiated, it is associated with the relative name of *myFile.fil*. If a file with this name already exists, then the *else* clause executes, displaying a suitable message. If no file named *myFile.fil* already exists, then the *then* clause will execute. The resulting call to `createNewFile` in the above example performs two functions. This method attempts to create a new file with the given name. Secondly, the `createNewFile` method returns a `true` or `false`, indicating whether or not such a creation was properly performed.

Figure 13.3 summarizes a class specification for the most widely used of the `File` class members.

Figure 13.3

File Class
Specifications
(*continues*)

Invariant

A `File` object

■ represents the file with the name given by *FileName*. (This name can either be a complete path name or a name relative to the current directory used by the Java VM.)

Constructor Method

public `File` (*String s*)

post: A new `File` object is created and if possible, associated with a file named *s*
and *FileName* == *s* (either a complete path name or a relative name)

Query Methods

public boolean `canRead`( )

post: *result* == true if and only if the file exists and it is permissible for the program to read from this file

public boolean `canWrite`( )

post: *result* == true if and only if the file exists and it is permissible for the program to write to this file

public boolean `exists`( )

post: *result* == true if and only if the *FileName* file or directory already exists

public String `getAbsolutePath`( )

post: *result* == the complete path name associated with *FileName* (even if the file doesn't exist)

public boolean `isFile`( )

post: *result* == true if and only if a file identified by *FileName* already exists

public boolean `isDirectory`( )

post: *result* == true if and only if a directory identified by *FileName* already exists

public int `length`( )

post: (exists() **implies** *result* == the number of bytes occupied by the file/directory)
and (not exists()) **implies** *result* == 0)

Figure 13.3

File Class
Specifications
(*continued*)

Update Methods

`public boolean` **`createNewFile`**`( )`

> **post:** A new, empty file called *FileName* was created (Note that any existing
> file with the same name was replaced.)
> **and** *result* == the file creation was properly performed

`public boolean` **`delete`**`( )`

> **pre:** `exists()`
>
> **post:** The file identified by *FileName* has been deleted from the
> file system
> **and** *result* == the deletion was properly performed

`public void` **`deleteOnExit`**`( )`

> **pre:** `isFile()`
>
> **post:** At the time that the currently executing program terminates, the file
> identified by *FileName* will be deleted from the file system

`public boolean` **`mkdir`**`( )`

> **pre:** *note* `exists()`
>
> **post:** An empty directory identified by *FileName* has been constructed
> **and** *result* == the directory creation was properly performed

`public void` **`setToReadOnly`**`( )`

> **pre:** `isFile()`
>
> **post:** The file identified by *FileName* has permissions that prohibit writing
> new values into the file.

13.3 ■ I/O Exceptions

Many things can go wrong when a program accesses files or the file system. For
example, file systems generally enforce security restrictions that protect files and
directories from unwanted access. These security systems may prohibit file access to
certain programs.

Java incorporates a mechanism known as **exception handling**, to manage runtime
errors that are detected by the Java VM, including those that result from illegal file
usage. The term **exception** refers to a runtime failure. The program **throws** an
exception when it encounters a runtime error that is too severe to continue normally. For example, a runtime file security violation throws an exception. Similarly,
when a program attempts to create a new file on a hard disk with no available space
an exception is thrown.

The creators of Java felt that most of the exceptions associated with files are so severe
that they are categorized as **checked exceptions**. Any checked exception forces programs to include special code to account for such possibilities.

The preferred way to deal with checked exceptions is to include **exception handling code** and in Java this requires the use of a **try instruction**. Figure 13.4 contains a description of the *try* instruction.

A *try* instruction is a Java statement that has a body, much like a method has a body. When the *try* statement executes, its body executes. If no exceptions are thrown

Figure 13.4   ***tryStatement*** description (a possible *OneStatement*)

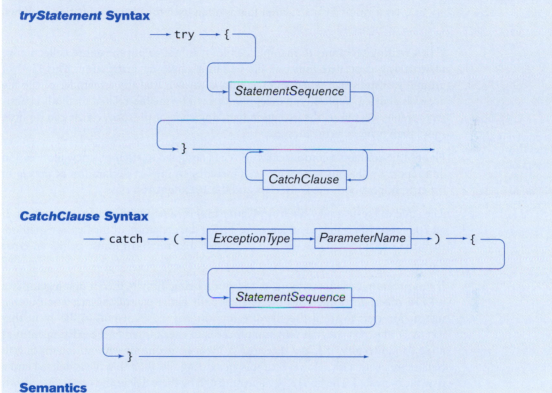

tryStatement Syntax

CatchClause Syntax

Semantics

When a *try* is executed, its *StatementSequence* is executed. If an exception matching the *ExceptionType* of one of the catch clauses is thrown while executing the *try*, then the matching *StatementSequence* is executed and the remainder of the *try* instruction is aborted.

Note

■ *ExceptionType* is an identifier that names a valid Java exception.

Style Notes

■ The body of the *try* instruction should be indented.

■ The catch clauses should be left aligned with their corresponding *try* and their bodies should be indented.

software *Hint*
engineering

The entire collection of related code that would be impacted by an exception should be collected together within a *try* instruction body. For file-related code, this usually means all of the code for a single algorithm performed upon the same file should be kept together.

within the *try's* body, then the *catch* clauses are ignored, and execution proceeds as though there were no *try* instruction.

Every Java exception has some type, and if an exception is thrown within a *try* body and if that exception has a type matching one of the *catch* clauses, then the remainder of the *try* body is skipped and the matching *catch* clause is executed.

The type of exceptions that can occur while using methods from the file-related classes all belong to the `IOException` type. Therefore, the particular form of *try* instruction that is often used for file manipulation is shown in Figure 13.5.

When writing programs to manipulate files it is best to put the entire collection of instructions associated with one file within a single *try* instruction. This kind of grouping ensures that when an exception is thrown that the remainder of the file access is aborted. Typically, an exception thrown by the file-related methods is non-recoverable. Therefore, the exception handling code of the *catch* clause can do little more than print an error message.

software *Hint*
engineering

Catch clauses typically display an error message to notify the user that something has gone wrong.

Figure 13.6 contains a complete `Driver` class designed to attempt a new file creation and report on the outcome. This class includes an import declaration of *java.io* in order to import both the `File` class and the `IOException` class.

The code to create a new file from Figure 13.6 is nested within a *try* instruction. If an `IOException` is thrown at any time during the execution of the `Driver` method, then the remainder of the method is aborted and the *catch* clause prints an error message.

If this program executes without an exception being thrown, then it first instantiates a `File` object for a file with the relative path name of *example.txt*. The outer *if* instruction tests to see if this file/directory already exists or not. In the event that `exits()` returns `true`, the program proceeds to check whether the existing entity is a file or a directory. If it is a directory, a message is output without attempting to replace this with a file. However, if it is an existing file, then that file is deleted and a new file is created. The `boolean` value returned by these delete and create operations are assigned, respectively, to the `deleteOK` and `createOK` variables. These variables are used to print an appropriate message. If the file does not exist in the first place, then a new file is created and an appropriate message is displayed.

Figure 13.5	
Form of the *try* instruction needed for file-related methods	```try { // Code with potential to throw exceptions goes here. } catch (IOException e) { // Code to handle the exception goes here. }```

Figure 13.6   Driver class to attempt to create a new file

```java
import java.io.*;
public class Driver {
    public Driver() {
        try{
            File file;
            boolean createOK;
            file = new File("example.txt");
            if (file.exists()) {
                if (file.isDirectory()) {
                    System.out.println(file.getAbsolutePath()
                        + " is a directory. No file created.");
                } else {
                    boolean deleteOK = file.delete();
                    if (deleteOK) {
                        System.out.println("Existing file deleted.");
                        createOK = file.createNewFile();
                        if (createOK) {
                            System.out.println("File created. ");
                        } else {
                            System.out.println("Unable to create file "
                                + file.getAbsolutePath());
                        }
                    } else {
                        System.out.println("Unable to delete file "
                            + file.getAbsolutePath());
                    }
                }
            } else { // file doesn't exist
                createOK = file.createNewFile();
                if (createOK) {
                    System.out.println("File created. ");
                } else {
                    System.out.println("Unable to create file "
                        + file.getAbsolutePath());
                }
            }
        }
        catch (IOException e) {
            System.out.println("I/O error occurred");
        }
    }
}
```

13.4 ■ **Input and Output**

Computer scientists use the term **I/O** (short for **Input/Output**) to refer to the transfer of data between a program and some external device, such as a secondary storage device. The operation of sending data *to* a device is called **writing**, and the data are the program **output**. The operation of retrieving data *from* a device is called **reading**, and the data are the program **input**.

The File class includes methods for creating new files and deleting existing files. However, a File object alone is incapable of reading from or writing to a file. Fortunately, the *java.io* package includes a rich collection of different classes to support I/O. Different classes provide different ways for programs to organize and retrieve data. Various classes accommodate the differences between the various I/O devices.

The notion of a **stream** is fundamental to Java I/O. Java programs do not communicate directly with external devices. Instead, a program creates a stream object to connect a program to some device. Each stream functions like a conduit that establishes a path for the data to flow between the program and the I/O device. Figure 13.7 illustrates this connection by showing an executing program with an input stream to serve as a conduit for reading data from a file and an output stream to serve as a conduit for writing data to a file.

In this book, **sequential files** are examined. An essential characteristic of every sequential file is that data is processed from the beginning. An input stream will supply the data from the file in precisely the order in which that data is stored, starting with the first data item. An output stream causes data to be written from the file's beginning and in the order that write methods are executed.

Java supports several different kinds of streams for different purposes. Figure 13.8 diagrams some of the most commonly used Java stream classes, all from the *java.io* package. This figure also includes arrows to depict the inheritance relations among these classes.

Figure 13.7

Using streams with readers and writers

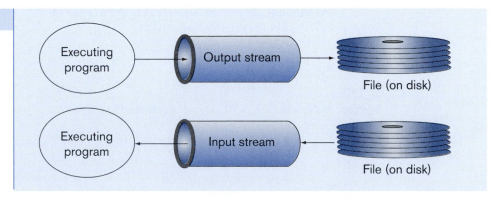

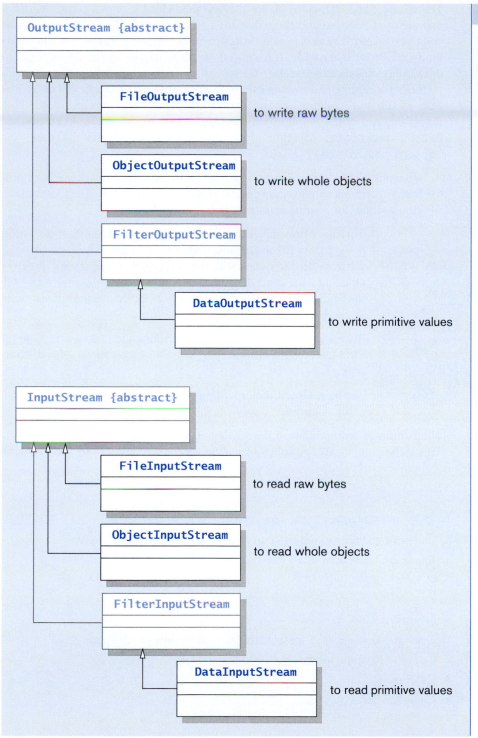

Figure 13.8

Inheritance relations for selected stream classes

The stream classes shown in Figure 13.8 are subdivided into two categories: those that are used for input and those that are used for output. The `FileInputStream` and `FileOutputStream` classes are not particularly useful by themselves, since these kinds of streams provide for data flow only in the form of bytes. The `DataInputStream` and `DataOutputStream` are more useful since they provide methods for reading and writing data of any primitive data type, as well as `String` data. The `ObjectInputStream` and `ObjectOutputStream` classes include methods for reading and writing whole objects. Section 13.5 discusses `DataInputStream` and `DataOutputStream`; Section 13.7 examines `ObjectInputStream` and `ObjectOutputStream`.

Before exploring the particulars of each of these streams, it is instructive to explore the basic algorithms employed by programs that perform I/O. Figure 13.9 contains a basic algorithm for reading from a file.

software *Hint*
engineering

Streams are closed automatically when the program completes with or without a call to a close method. However, it is still best to explicitly call close for two reasons.

1. An explicit close makes it clear when the programmer expects to be finished performing I/O.

2. Once a file is closed it is possible to reopen the file.

This algorithm shows that files must be **opened** before it is possible to read from them. Opening a file for input consists of associating a file from the file system with the appropriate input stream object(s). Opening a file generally positions the file data so that it is read from the beginning of the file. The Java stream objects include constructor methods that are used to open files.

After a program is finished reading from a file it is wise to close the file. Most streams include a parameterless `close` method for this purpose.

The basic algorithm for writing to a file is similar to the reading algorithm. Figure 13.10 contains the writing algorithm.

The additional requirement of the writing algorithm is called "*Flush the stream.*" This step is usually accomplished by calling a parameterless `flush` method upon

Figure 13.9

General algorithm for reading from a file

1. Open the file for input, instantiating associated stream objects.
2. Call read methods to retrieve part of or the entire stream's content.
3. Close the file/stream.

Figure 13.10

General algorithm for writing to a file

1. Open the file for output, instantiating associated stream objects.
2. Call read methods to write data into the stream.
3. Flush the stream.
4. Close the file/stream.

the appropriate output stream. Flushing ensures that no data is left in the stream conduit.

Another difference between input and output algorithms is the behavior of their open operations. When a file is opened for input, it is expected that the file already exists. The stream for the newly opened input file begins to supply the first data that is stored within the file. When a file is opened for output, it is because the program intends to place data into a file. For all but a few specialized streams, the program will place *all* of the data into the file. Therefore, the process of opening a file for output typically creates a new file. Even if the file already exists, opening an output stream on a file should be expected to create a new file.

The stream class constructors in Java are designed in a curious way. Only two of the *java.io* streams, namely `FileInputStream` and `FileOutputStream`, can be connected directly to a file. No other *java.io* stream class includes the proper constructor methods to allow the program to specify a file name or to use a `File` object. This unique property of `FileInputStream` and `FileOutputStream` gives these two classes special importance. Figure 13.11 contains a class diagram and class specifications for the `FileInputStream` class.

software engineering *Hint*

Before opening a file for output, it is best to check if a file with the same name already exists. For most Java streams, opening a new output stream deletes any earlier file with the same name.

Figure 13.11 `FileInputStream` class diagram and specifications (*continues*)

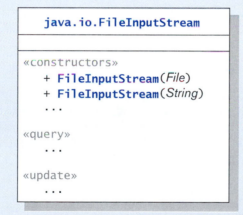

```
java.io.FileInputStream

«constructors»
    + FileInputStream(File)
    + FileInputStream(String)
    ...

«query»
    ...

«update»
    ...
```

Invariant

A `FileInputStream` object

■ serves as a conduit for input from a file specified at the time this object is instantiated.

Figure 13.11 FileInputStream class diagram and specifications (*continued*)

Constructor Methods

public **FileInputStream** (*File f*)

    pre: *f*.isFile()

    post: A new FileInputStream object is created and if possible, associated with a file named *f* **and** the file is positioned to begin reading from the beginning.

    throws: If file *f* does not exist, is a directory, or cannot be opened, then a FileNotFoundException (subclass of IOException) is thrown.

public **FileInputStream** (*String s*)

    pre: *s* is a pathname for an existing file.

    post: A new FileInputStream object is created and if possible, associated with a file named *s*. (*s* may be a complete path name or a relative name) **and** the file is positioned to begin reading from the beginning.

    throws: If file *s* does not exist, is a directory, or cannot be opened, then a FileNotFoundException (subclass of IOException) is thrown.

There are only two FileInputStream methods of interest to this discussion—the two constructor methods. These methods make FileInputStream unique from other streams. The first constructor instantiates a stream object and connects it to the file from a File object. The code segment below illustrates how to open a file using this constructor.

```
try{
    File file;
    FileInputStream inStream;
    file = new File("sampleFile");
    inStream = new FileInputStream(file);
    // The code to read the file and close it belongs here.
}
catch (IOException e) {
    System.out.println("I/O error occurred");
}
```

When this code executes, a file object is instantiated and connected to a file with the relative path name *sampleFile*. Next, a FileInputStream object named inStream is instantiated and connected to the same file by passing file as an argument to the constructor method. The *try* instruction captures any I/O exceptions that might occur.

This first example of opening a stream via a File object is useful whenever the program needs to check other file properties, through File queries like isDirectory(), exists(), or length(). However, if the program does not require such tests, then using the second constructor method leads to abbreviated code for opening the same file. This code is shown below.

```
try{
    FileInputStream inStream;
    inStream = new FileInputStream("sampleFile");
    // The code to read the file and close it belongs here.
}
catch (IOException e) {
    System.out.println("I/O error occurred");
}
```

The FileOutputStream class includes two constructor methods that parallel those from FileInputClass. Figure 13.12 contains their specifications.

Figure 13.12   FileOutputStream constructor specifications

public **FileOutputStream** (*File f*)

pre: *not f.*isDirectory()

post: A new FileOutputStream object is created and if possible, associated with an empty file named *f*
and the file is positioned to begin writing from the beginning.

throws: If file *f* is a directory, cannot be created, or cannot be opened for any reason, then a FileNotFoundException (subclass of IOException) is thrown.

public **FileOutputStream** (*String s*)

pre: *s* is not the path name for an existing directory.

post: A new FileOutputStream object is created and if possible, associated with an empty file named *s*. (*s* may be a complete path name or a relative name)
and the file is positioned to begin writing from the beginning.

throws: If the file named s is a directory, cannot be created, or cannot be opened, then a FileNotFoundException (subclass of IOException) is thrown.

13.5 ■ DataInputStream and DataOutputStream

As mentioned previously, the DataInputStream and DataOutputStream classes are well suited for reading and writing data of primitive type. Figure 13.13 illustrates this by showing that DataOutputStream includes a separate method to output each primitive type.

Opening a DataOutputStream is complicated by the fact that the constructor method has a parameter of type OutputStream rather than File or String (for the file's name). However, FileOutputStream inherits from OutputStream. This permits a DataOutputStream to be opened by first instantiating a FileOutputStream object, then passing this object as an argument to instantiate a DataOutputStream. The resulting situation is illustrated in Figure 13.14.

Figure 13.15 shows the code needed to open a file in this way. The Figure 13.15 also illustrates how to write, flush, and close such a file.

The first four statements in the body of the *try* instruction constitute the code needed to open the stream for a file named *example.bin*. The third statement instantiates a FileOutputStream object called outStream, and the fourth statement uses outStream as an argument to instantiate dataStream. All subsequent method calls are appropriately directed to dataStream, not outStream.

Figure 13.13   DataOutputStream Class Diagram

```
            java.io.DataOutputStream


«constructor»
    + DataOutputStream (OutputStream)
    . . .

«update»
    + void close ()
    + void flush ()
    + void writeBoolean (boolean)
    + void writeByte (byte)
    + void writeChar (char)
    + void writeDouble (double)
    + void writeFloat (float)
    + void writeInt (int)
    + void writeLong (long)
    + void writeShort (short)
    + void writeUTF (String)
    . . .
```

Figure 13.14   Connecting a DataOutputStream to a file

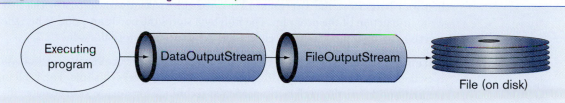

Figure 13.15

Driver to write
to a binary file

```java
import java.io.*;
public class Driver {
    public Driver() {
        try{
            FileOutputStream outStream;
            DataOutputStream dataStream;
            outStream = new FileOutputStream("example.bin");
            dataStream = new DataOutputStream(outStream);
            dataStream.writeInt(12);
            dataStream.writeBoolean(true);
            dataStream.writeDouble(98.7);
            dataStream.writeUTF("hello world");
            dataStream.writeChar('Z');
            dataStream.flush();
            dataStream.close();
        }
        catch (IOException e) {
            System.out.println("ERROR writing.");
        }
    }
}
```

The DataOutputStream and DataInputStream classes are designed to perform
I/O using a storage format that essentially matches the format used to store data in
memory. So, the content of the *example.bin* file following the execution of the code
from Figure 13.15 can be illustrated as follows.

Content of the *example.bin* file:

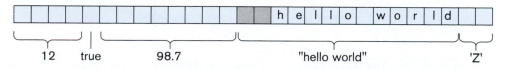

Each of the small squares in the preceding picture represents one byte of the file. The first four bytes store the `int` value 12 because this is what was output by the first write instruction of the program. The fifth byte stores the `boolean` value. When the `writeDouble` method is called, eight bytes are written to store the value 98.7.

You might be wondering why `DataOutputStream` has no `writeString` method. As is evident in the above example, the `writeUTF` method[2] plays this role. The UTF in the name of this method refers to a particular technique for storing `String` data efficiently. A single Unicode character occupies two bytes of storage. However, a UTF encoding reduces this to one byte for most commonly used symbols. The above example shows each character in the "hello world" string stored within a single byte. The two bytes preceding this string are also part of the overhead required for UTF encoding.

The methods of `DataInputStream` parallel those of `DataOutputStream`. Figure 13.16 shows a class diagram for `DataInputStream`.

The most significant differences between `DataOutputStream` and `DataInputStream` are (1) `DataInputStream` has no `flush` method and (2) the void write methods from `DataOutputStream` are replaced by nonvoid parameterless read methods in `DataInputStream`. Figure 13.17 illustrates how to use `DataInputStream` to read the file that was created by the code from Figure 13.15.

Figure 13.16   `DataInputStream` Class Diagram

```
            java.io.DataInputStream

«constructor»
    + DataInputStream(InputStream )
    . . .

«query»
    + boolean readBoolean()
    + byte readByte()
    + char readChar()
    + double readDouble()
    + float readFloat()
    + int readInt()
    + long readLong()
    + short readShort()
    + String readUTF()
    . . .

«update»
    + void close()
```

2. The acronym UTF stands for "Unicode Transformation Format."

```java
import java.io.*;
public class Driver {

    public Driver() {
        try {
            int inInt;
            boolean inBool;
            double inDouble;
            String inStr;
            char inCh;
            FileInputStream inStream;
            DataInputStream dataStream;
            inStream = new FileInputStream("example.bin");
            dataStream = new DataInputStream(inStream);

            inInt = dataStream.readInt();
            inBool = dataStream.readBoolean();
            inDouble = dataStream.readDouble();
            inStr = dataStream.readUTF();
            inCh = dataStream.readChar();
            dataStream.close();

            System.out.println(inInt);
            System.out.println(inBool);
            System.out.println(inDouble);
            System.out.println(inStr);
            System.out.println(inCh);
        }
        catch (IOException e) {
            System.out.println("ERROR reading.");
        }
    }
}
```

Figure 13.17

Driver to read and print the binary file created by Figure 13.15

The Driver method from Figure 13.17 opens the file for input using a FileInputStream object in the same way that FileOutputStream was used for opening an output stream. Each of the values is read from the input file and assigned to a separate variable. The method uses System.out.println to display each of these variables.

The most important thing to remember when using DataInputStream is that *data must be read (by type) in the same order it was written*. The order used to write the *example.bin* file is as follows.

an int → a boolean → a double → a String → a char

Therefore, it must be read with the following order of calls:

readInt, readBoolean, readDouble, readUTF, readChar.

Reading data in the wrong order from a `DataInputStream` can produce extremely unusual behavior. Consider the following code segment (a variation from the Figure 13.17 code).

```
inStream = new FileInputStream("example.bin");
dataStream = new DataInputStream(inStream);
inBool = dataStream.readBoolean();
inInt = dataStream.readInt();
```

When `readBoolean` is called, it will consume the first byte from the file. Unfortunately, the file's first byte was one fourth of an `int` value. When the `readInt` method is called, it consumes the next four bytes from the file. The result is that `inInt` is assigned a value formed from three fourths of an `int` value appended to a `boolean` value. The values assigned to `inBool` and `inInt` resulting from the execution of this code are simply not sensible, but no error will be reported.

Sometimes the author of the input program does not know the exact amount of data in a file. In such cases, the program must test for a condition known as **end of file**. An end of file condition becomes `true` when all data from an input file has been read.

`DataInputStream` handles an end of file condition by throwing an `EOFException` when any read method is called that would retrieve more bytes of data than remain unread in the stream. This condition can be caught by a separate *catch* clause. For example, suppose that *fileOfInts* is a file that is known to contain exclusively `int` values. The following code will read every value from this file and print it with `System.out.println`.

```
try {
    FileInputStream inStream;
    DataInputStream dataStream;
    inStream = new FileInputStream("fileOfInts");
    dataStream = new DataInputStream(inStream);
    while (true) {
        System.out.println(dataStream.readInt());
    }
}
catch (EOFException e) {
    // This occurs normally when reading past the last int.
}
catch (IOException e) {
    System.out.println("ERROR reading.");
}
```

The loop in the above program may appear to be infinite, but remember that each time through the loop another `int` value is read from the stream. When `readInt` is called after all values from the stream have been read, then an `EOFException` is thrown. The exception is handled by its own *catch* clause, which does nothing.

13.6 ■ Text Files

A file that contains exclusively char data is called a **text file**. Memos, letters, and manuals are often stored in the computer in the form of text files. Your source code (*.java*) files are also stored as text files. Text editors are programs that create and modify text files.

Not all files are in text file format. For example, any file created using DataOutputStream is unlikely to be a text file, unless only writeChar methods are used. Nontext files are referred to collectively as **binary files**. When a binary file is opened by a text editor, it tends to appear as a random collection of symbols.

Since humans prefer to read text separated into separate lines, text files make use of a special character (written '\n' in Java) to separate consecutive lines. Figure 13.18 shows three lines of text the way they would be read by humans, and the corresponding characters as they would be stored in a text file.

The *java.io* package includes several classes to manipulate text files. Many of these classes use the concepts of **reader** and **writer** objects to massage stream data.

In a sense, the data that comes from a stream is like crude oil. It is possible to use crude oil in its natural form. However, crude oil is useful in a wider variety of applications after it has been refined and repackaged. Readers and writers provide tools to refine and repackage data.

Figure 13.19 illustrates a typical way to utilize readers and writers for performing I/O. In order to write to a file, a program creates two objects—a writer object and an output stream. The actual output methods will be performed upon the writer. Similarly, a program can input from a file by way of a reader object that is connected to an input stream object.

Figure 13.20 contains a class diagram for one writer class, called PrintWriter. The PrintWriter class is an output class that produces text files only.

On the surface, the PrintWriter class looks somewhat similar to DataOutputStream. Both classes use the same close and flush methods. Both

Three lines of text:

This

is a

test

Content of a text file storing the three lines:

T	h	i	s	\n	i	s		a	\n	t	e	s	t

Figure 13.18

Text file storage format for lines

Figure 13.19   Using streams with readers and writers

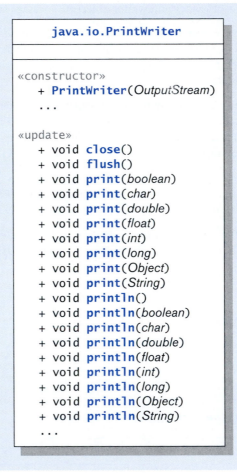

Figure 13.20

PrintWriter
Class Diagram

java.io.PrintWriter

«constructor»
    + **PrintWriter**(*OutputStream*)
    . . .

«update»
    + void **close**()
    + void **flush**()
    + void **print**(*boolean*)
    + void **print**(*char*)
    + void **print**(*double*)
    + void **print**(*float*)
    + void **print**(*int*)
    + void **print**(*long*)
    + void **print**(*Object*)
    + void **print**(*String*)
    + void **println**()
    + void **println**(*boolean*)
    + void **println**(*char*)
    + void **println**(*double*)
    + void **println**(*float*)
    + void **println**(*int*)
    + void **println**(*long*)
    + void **println**(*Object*)
    + void **println**(*String*)
    . . .

classes include separate methods for most of the primitive data types, although `PrintWriter` does so by overloading its `print` and `println` methods. Even the constructor method of the two classes uses the same type of stream parameter.

The primary difference between `DataOutputStream` and `PrinterWriter` is that `DataOutputStream` writes data in binary form, while `PrintWriter` must transform all data into a textual form before writing. For example, the following `DataOutputStream` method call writes its data in the form of an eight-byte double.

```
dataStream.writeDouble(1234567890.1);
```

However, the corresponding `PrintWriter` method call below writes a sequence of 12 characters, including the decimal point, to represent the same output data in textual form.

```
printWriterObject.print(1234567890.1);
```

The `PrintWriter` class includes `println` methods to make the insertion of end of line separations more convenient. Each call to the parameterless version of `println` writes a single end of line character into the output stream. In other words, a call to the following method

```
println();
```

performs the same function as the following instruction.

```
print('\n');
```

When an argument is passed to `println`, then an end of line character is appended to the stream *following* the textual representation of the argument.

Figure 3.20 contains a complete `Driver` method that uses `PrintWriter` to create a text file. The file created by executing the `Driver` method writes the same data as the class from Figure 13.15. Figure 13.21 also shows the content of the text file that is produced by executing the `Driver` method.

Opening
the Black Box

The notation `System.out` refers to a variable of type `PrinterWriter`. Therefore, method calls like

```
System.out.println()
```

are calling the methods described in this section.

Reading from a text file can be accomplished in many ways. One way to read from a text file is one character at a time. Another way to read from a text file is to read an entire line in a single method call. The `BufferedReader` class provides for both of these options. Figure 13.22 contains a class diagram for `BufferedReader`.

The constructor method of `BufferedReader` differs from previously presented input classes because it cannot accept an argument of type `FileInputStream`.

Figure 13.21

Driver using
PrintWriter

```java
import java.io.*;
public class Driver {

public Driver() {
    try {
        FileOutputStream outStream;
        PrintWriter printWriter;
        outStream = new FileOutputStream("example.txt");
        printWriter = new PrintWriter(outStream);
        printWriter.print(12);
        printWriter.print(true);
        printWriter.println(98.7);
        printWriter.print("hello world");
        printWriter.print('Z');
        printWriter.flush();
        printWriter.close();
    }
    catch (IOException e) {
        System.out.println("ERROR writing.");
    }
}
}
```

Content of the resulting *example.txt* file:

1	2	t	r	u	e	9	8	.	7	\n	h	e	l	l	o		w	o	r	l	d	Z

Figure 13.22   BufferedReader Class Diagram

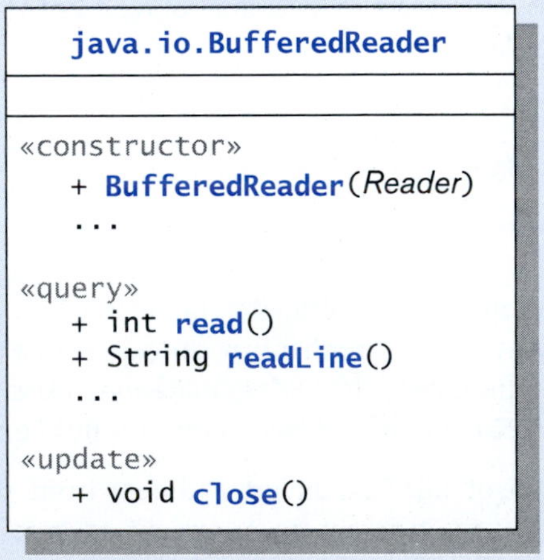

```
┌─────────────────────────────────────┐
│       java.io.BufferedReader        │
├─────────────────────────────────────┤
│                                     │
├─────────────────────────────────────┤
│ «constructor»                       │
│    + BufferedReader(Reader)         │
│    ...                              │
│                                     │
│ «query»                             │
│    + int read()                     │
│    + String readLine()              │
│    ...                              │
│                                     │
│ «update»                            │
│    + void close()                   │
│                                     │
└─────────────────────────────────────┘
```

However, there is another *java.io* class, called FileReader, that is a subclass of Reader and can be used in the same way as FileInputStream.

Each call to the BufferedReader readLine method returns the next unread line as a String value. There are two important things to remember when calling readLine.

1. The String returned by readLine does *not* include the end of line character ('/n'), but the end of line is consumed by the method call.

2. When readLine is called after reaching the end of file, then null is returned.

Below is a segment of code to open the *example.txt* file and read its contents line by line.

```
try {
    String inStr;
    FileReader inReader;
    BufferedReader bReader;
    inReader = new FileReader("example.txt"));
    bReader = new BufferedReader(inReader);
    inStr = bReader.readLine();
    while (inStr != null) {
        System.out.print(inStr + "//");
        inStr = bReader.readLine();
    }
    bReader.close();
}
catch (IOException e) {
    System.out.println("ERROR reading.");
}
```

In order to read a file character by character, BufferedReader provides a method called read. The read method is a bit unusual because it returns an int value, rather than a char. A cast is required before the read method's value can be used as a char. Another characteristic of the read method is that it returns the value −1 to indicate any attempt to read past the end of file. The following code is an example of reading an entire text file character by character, while checking for end of file.

```
try {
    int inInt;
    char inChar;
    FileReader inReader;
    BufferedReader bReader;
    inReader = new FileReader("example.txt");
    bReader = new BufferedReader(inReader);
    inInt = bReader.read();
    while (inInt != -1) {
        inChar = (char) inInt;
        System.out.println(inChar);
        inInt = bReader.read();
```

```
            }
            bReader.close();
        }
        catch (IOException e) {
            System.out.println("ERROR reading.");
        }
```

The BufferedReader class is somewhat limited in the sense that it can only input text in the form of individual characters or sequences of characters, but it cannot translate the characters into any other form than char or String. The Scanner class, previously discussed in Chapters 6 and 7 provides more flexibility for the input of text values. Figure 13.23 contains a more complete class diagram than shown previously for this class.

Two methods not previously presented appear in Figure 13.23—a second Scanner constructor with a parameter of type InputStream and a close method. These methods allow Scanner to function as a stream reader for text files. (Actually, Scanner either processes text from a file or a String, depending upon which constructor method is chosen.)

When a Scanner processes text, it does so left to right, treating the text as a sequence of **tokens**. A token is defined to be a consecutive group of characters with no intervening delimiters. (The default delimiters are white space characters like blanks, tabs, ends of lines, and so forth.) In other words, a Scanner views a block of text as though it were a sequence of tokens, using white space as separators between the tokens. For example, consider the following block of text.

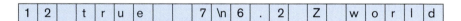

A Scanner would identify six tokens in this text: the integer 12, the word *true*, the integer 7, the real 6.2, the letter *Z*, and the word *world*. Calls to the next . . . methods of Scanner proceed left to right, each call locating the next token from the text. The code below illustrates one way to read from a file (*example.txt*), while translating each token into its corresponding primitive data type.

```
    try {
        FileInputStream inStream;
        Scanner inScan;
        inStream = new FileInputStream("example.txt");
        inScan = new Scanner(inStream);

        while (inScan.hasNext()) {
            if (inScan.hasNextBoolean())
                System.out.println("Boolean value: " +
                    inScan.nextBoolean());
            else if (inScan.hasNextLong())
                System.out.println("Integer value: " +
                    inScan.nextLong());
```

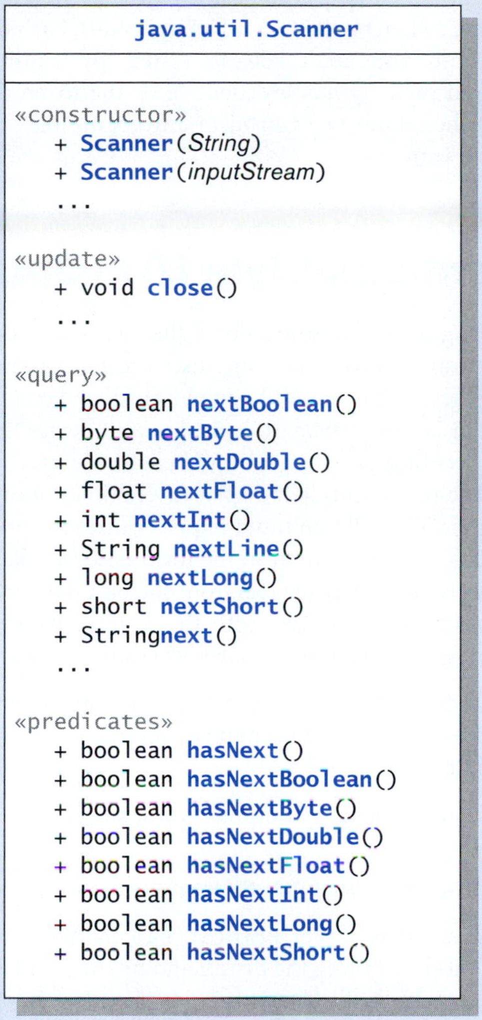

Figure 13.23

Class diagram for Scanner

```
else if (inScan.hasNextDouble())
    System.out.println("Double value: " +
        inScan.nextDouble());
else // it must be a String
    System.out.println("String value: " +
        inScan.next());
}
inScan.close();
}
catch (IOException e) {
    System.out.println("ERROR reading.");
}
```

This code segment uses a loop to repeatedly process `inScan` until all tokens have been processed (i.e., when `hasNext` is no longer `true`). Each time the loop body executes, the current `inScan` token is tested by calling `hasNextBoolean`, `hasNextLong`, and possibly `hasNextDouble`. If the token does not satisfy any of these conditions, then it must be a string of unrecognizable characters, in which case it is input as a `String`.

13.7 ■ **Terminal-Style I/O (Optional)**

Prior to the use of graphical user interfaces, the most common form of I/O between an executing program and the program's user was **terminal-style I/O**. This type of I/O is so named because it behaves like an old-fashioned computer terminal. A computer terminal consists of a keyboard and an output device (either a video screen or a printer). An executing program typically communicates with the terminal in a kind of dialog. The program might display several lines of output and then request input from the user. Typically, an input request causes the program to suspend execution until the user supplies input in the form of keystrokes. Even though textual computer terminals are largely devices from the past, terminal-style I/O is still utilized in many places. For example, both the command line application from the Windows operating system and Unix shell programs operate on terminal-style I/O.

The creators of Java felt that terminal-style I/O was sufficiently important that they included two objects to provide programs convenient access to a standard way of emulating computer terminal-like I/O.

1. The `System.out` object is an output stream, analogous to a computer terminal display.

2. The `System.in` object is an input stream for the computer keyboard.

The `System.out` object is of type `PrintStream`. `System.out` can be used directly without initialization by calling the `print` and `println` methods. Executing either of these methods causes the argument to be displayed in the standard output stream (usually a window of textual display).

The `System.in` object is of type `InputStream`, so using `System.in` requires a bit of initialization in order to accomplish terminal-style I/O. In particular, since computer terminals typically read data one line at a time, it is best to use a `Scanner` to process the input from `System.in`. Figure 13.24 illustrates.

The `Driver` method from Figure 13.24 connects to `System.in` using a `Scanner` object named `inScan`. Thereafter `inScan` will process all terminal input.

Terminal-style I/O usually begins when the program displays a prompt for the user. The following instruction is an example of how to produce such a user prompt.

```
System.out.print("Type a token: ");
```

Next, the program executes the following instruction.

```
userInput = inScan.next();
```

```
import java.util.Scanner;
public class Driver {
    public Driver () {
        String userInput;
        Scanner inScan = new Scanner(System.in);
        System.out.print("Type a token: ");
        userInput = inScan.next();
        System.out.println("Your token: " + userInput);
    }
}
```

Figure 13.24

Example of terminal-style I/O

Since this particular `Scanner` is reading from `System.in`, the execution of this instruction will cause the program to delay until the user has typed a complete input token. That token will then be assigned to `userInput`.

13.8 ■ Persistent Objects (Optional)

Sometimes whole objects must be retained from one program execution to the next. Such persistent objects require that a program store the complete state of the object in some file. This object and its state can be restored later by reading the data back from the file.

One situation that calls for persistent objects is a program that keeps track of its final state to use as the initial state the next time the program is executed. For example, consider a computer program that plays the game of chess against the human who executes the program. It might be desirable to write the chess-playing program so that the user could suspend a game and turn off the computer to resume the game at a later date. Such a program is written by making the game board persistent, along with its associated chess piece objects.

It is possible to use *java.io* streams, like `DataOutputStream` and `DataInputStream`, as a crude mechanism for implementing persistent objects. Using `DataOutputStream` and `DataIntputStream` to implement persistence requires that all of its key individual attributes of the persistent object be written and read. This is a tedious approach for complicated objects. A better technique for implementing persistent objects is provided by way of the `ObjectOutputStream` and `ObjectInputStream` classes. These classes include methods to read or write an entire object at once.

Figure 13.25 contains an example use of `ObjectOutputStream`. Executing this `Driver` method writes two objects (from `window` and `dot`) to a binary file.

The method used to write persistent objects to an `ObjectOutputStream` is `writeObject`. Executing `writeObject` method outputs the complete state of its

Figure 13.25   Writing objects with `ObjectOutputStream`

```java
import java.io.*;
import javax.swing.JFrame;
public class Driver {

    public Driver() {
        JFrame window;
        Oval dot;
        window = new JFrame("Persistent Objects");
        window.setBounds(10, 10, 300, 200);
        window.setVisible(true);
        window.setLayout(null);
        dot = new Oval(125, 75, 50, 50);
        window.add(dot, 0);
        window.repaint();

        try{
            FileOutputStream outStream;
            ObjectOutputStream objStream;
            outStream = new FileOutputStream("example.obj");
            objStream = new ObjectOutputStream(outStream);
            objStream.writeObject(window);
            objStream.writeObject(dot);
            objStream.flush();
            objStream.close();
        }
        catch (IOException e) {
            System.out.println("ERROR writing.");
        }
    }
}
```

software
engineering *Hint*

Care must be
taken when
using serializable
classes. The files
created as
`ObjectOutput-`
`Streams` could
be reloaded by
other programs
so access to
these files should
be carefully
restricted and
confidential data
not included in
the files.

argument object. If the object is an aggregate, then the state of its instance variables is also written. This inclusion of referenced objects is applied transitively so that the complete state of the object can be retained.

One requirement of the use of `ObjectOutputStream` is that any argument to the `writeObject` method must be **serializable**. A class is made serializable by implementing the standard Java `Serializable` interface. Both `JFrame` and `Oval` do so.

If a persistent object is stored using `ObjectOutputStream`, then it should be restored using `ObjectInputStream` and its `readObject` method. Figure 13.26

Figure 13.26   Reading objects with `ObjectInputStream`

```java
import java.io.*;
import javax.swing.JFrame;
public class DriverReload {

    public DriverReload() {
        JFrame window;
        Oval dot;
        try{
            FileInputStream inStream;
            ObjectInputStream objStream;
            inStream = new FileInputStream("example.obj");
            objStream = new ObjectInputStream(inStream);
            window = (JFrame) objStream.readObject();
            dot = (Oval) objStream.readObject();
            objStream.close();
            window.setVisible(true);
        }
        catch (Exception e) {
            System.out.println("ERROR reloading object.");
        }
    }
}
```

demonstrates with a `DriverReload` class to restore the objects written by the Figure 13.25 code.

There are three requirements that must be observed to input objects using `ObjectInputStream`.

1. Objects must be read in the same order they were written.

2. The value returned by `readObject` is of type `Object` and must be cast to the proper type.

3. A call to `readObject` may throw various exceptions, requiring a different *catch* clause.

The code in Figure 13.26 observes all of these requirements. The first object read is assumed to be a `JFrame`, and the second is an `Oval`. Both of the calls to `readObject` are immediately cast to the proper type. The *catch* clause uses a parameter of type `Exception`, which is a superclass of `IOException` and includes all of the required types of exceptions that must be handled by this code. The only additional instruction included in `DriverReload` is a call to `setVisible` to ensure that the `JFrame` becomes active and visible.

13.9 ■ JFileChooser (Optional)

Most modern operating systems include graphical file browser windows to make it easier for the user to select a file from within the file directory. It is also common for computer applications to permit the user to select an input file input or an output file using a similar file browser.

The *Swing* package includes a graphical file browser class for just this purpose. Figure 13.27 contains a class diagram for this JFileChooser class. A picture of a typical JFileChooser window, as it would appear to a user, is shown in Figure 13.28.

Figure 13.27

JFileChooser Class Diagram

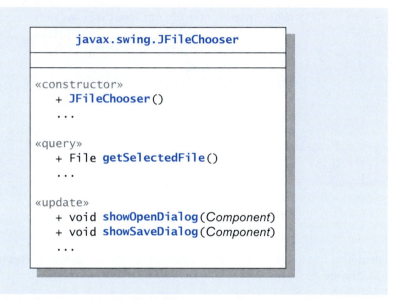

Figure 13.28

JFileChooser sample image

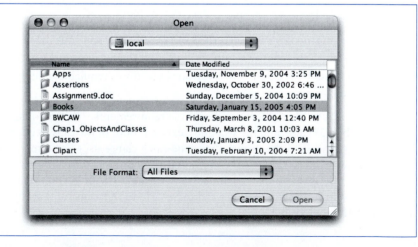

A JFileChooser object can be instantiated from a parameterless constructor. Such an object becomes visible by executing either of two methods.

1. **showOpenDialog** is called to display a JFileChooser that is appropriate for selecting an input file.

2. **showSaveDialog** is called to display a JFileChooser that is appropriate for selecting a new output file.

Note that null can be used as an argument for both showOpenDialog and showSaveDialog.

After having called showOpenDialog or showSaveDialog to display the file finder, the program should call getSelectedFile. This method performs three tasks:

1. Execution is suspended until the user selects a file or cancels the action in the JFileChooser window.

2. A File object is returned for the user-selected file (null is returned if the user canceled this action or selected an invalid file).

3. If a valid file is selected, then that file is opened for input or output from the beginning of the file.

Figure 13.29 illustrates how to use a JFileChooser object to open a file for input. The code in this example reads all characters from a user-specified text file, writing them to System.out.

```java
import java.io.*;
import javax.swing.JFileChooser;
public class Driver {

    public Driver() {
        try {
            JFileChooser chooser = new JFileChooser();
            int tmp = chooser.showOpenDialog(null);
            File file = chooser.getSelectedFile();
            if (file != null) {
                FileInputStream inStream;
                InputStreamReader reader;
                int inInt;
                inStream = new FileInputStream(file);
                reader = new InputStreamReader(inStream);
                inInt = reader.read();
                while (inInt != -1) {
                    System.out.print((char)inInt);
                    inInt = reader.read();
                }
```

Figure 13.29

Using JFileChooser to read from a file (*continues*)

Figure 13.29

Using
JFileChooser
to read from a
file (*continued*)

```
            reader.close();
        } else {
            System.out.println("No file name selected.");
        }
    }
    catch (FileNotFoundException e) {
        System.out.println("ERROR opening input stream.");
    }
    catch (IOException e) {
        System.out.println("ERROR reading.");
    }
  }
}
```

The three lines from this example that are needed to display a `JFileChooser` and open the specified file are as follows.

```
JFileChooser chooser = new JFileChooser();
int tmp = chooser.showOpenDialog(null);
File file = chooser.getSelectedFile();
```

Executing the first of these three lines instantiates a `JFileChooser` object called `chooser`. The second instruction displays `chooser` in a form that is proper for opening an existing file. The call to `getSelectedFile` causes the program to suspend execution until the user has selected some file or canceled the selection via the `chooser` window. If the user selects a valid file name, then the associated file is opened and assigned to the `file` variable. If the user makes an invalid selection or cancels the selection, then `file` is assigned `null`.

Inspector *Java*

Below is a collection of hints on what to check when examining code that involves the concepts of this chapter.

■ The standard Java I/O packages are located together in the *java.io* folder. It is best to include a declaration like the following when using these libraries: `import java.io.*;`

■ When a program opens a file with its path name, care must be taken to be certain that the file's name and directory match the file system upon which the program executes.

■ Always check to be certain that the file is properly opened before attempting to read from it or write to it.

■ Opening a file for output generally deletes any existing file with the same path name. If this deletion is unwanted, then a `File` object should be used to check for its existence prior to executing the opening code.

■ Always ensure that a file is closed after the I/O is complete on it. Output files usually require the additional step of calling `flush` before closing.

■ Most I/O operations throw checked exceptions. You must remember to handle these exceptions by enclosing your I/O code within a *try* instruction and catching the appropriate type of exceptions. (`IOException` is the superclass for most exceptions that occur during I/O.)

■ Java contains many classes for I/O. The proper selection of classes is needed to perform I/O properly. Below is a list of the classes associated with certain types of I/O.

> To read *bytes* from a binary file
> ...connect a `FileInputStream` object to the file.

> To write *bytes* to a binary file
> ...connect a `FileOutputStream` object to the file.

> To read *primitive values* and/or *Strings* from a binary file
> ...connect a `DataInputStream` object to a `FileInputStream` object connected to the file.

> To write *primitive values* and/or *Strings* to a binary file
> ...connect a `DataOutputStream` object to a `FileOutputStream` object connected to the file.

> To read *chars* and/or *Strings* from a text file
> ...connect a `BufferedReader` object to a `FileReader` object connected to the file.

> To read *primitive values* and/or *Strings* from a text file
> ...connect a `Scanner` object to a `FileInputStream` object connected to the file.

To write *primitive values* and/or *Strings* to a text file
...connect a `PrintWriter` object to a `FileOutputStream` object connected to the file.

To read persistent *Objects* from a binary file
...connect an `ObjectInputStream` object to a `FileInputStream` object connected to the file.

To write persistent *Objects* to a binary file
...connect an `ObjectOutputStream` object to a `FileOutputStream` object connected to the file.

To read *primitive values* and/or *Strings* in terminal-style from the standard input stream
...connect a `Scanner` object to `System.in`.

To write *primitive values* and/or *Strings* to the standard output stream
...use `PrintWriter` methods upon `System.out`. (No additional objects are required).

■ When reading from a file, there must be some familiarity with the type of data stored within the file. If the file is a binary file, then it must be read as a binary file. If there are different types of data in the file, then the data must be read in the order (by type) that they were written. Failure to read in the proper order results in meaningless input and/or thrown exceptions.

■ Always check input code to ensure proper handling of the end of file condition. Java provides different ways to check for end of file. When reading past end of file on a `DataInputStream` object, an `EOFException` is thrown. When reading reference data (such as a `readLine` applied to a `BufferedReader` object) an attempt to read past end of file returns `null`. A call to read that normally returns the next character from a `BufferedReader` object will return −1 when reading beyond the end of file. For input via `Scanner`, the `hasNext` method is used to check for more unprocessed input.

■ Objects that are made persistent via `ObjectInputStream` and `ObjectOutputStream` must belong to classes that implement `Serializable`.

Terminology

binary file	file
current directory	file name
directory	file system
end of file condition	folder
exception	input
exception handler	I/O (Input/Output)

output

path name

persistent object

read (from an input device)

reader (file input object)

relative path name

secondary storage

sequential file

serializable

stream

terminal-style I/O

text file

throw (an exception)

token

try instruction

write (to an output device)

writer (file output object)

Exercises

1. Figure 13.1 contains a sample file directory. Using this particular directory, specify the names for each of the following files.

   a. the complete path name for the `email` file

   b. the complete path name for the *Driver.java* file from `prog1`

   c. the complete path name for the *Driver.class* file from `prog2`

   d. the relative path name for the `email` file if the current directory is `/Users`

   e. the relative path name for the *Driver.class* file from `prog2` file if the current directory is `/Users/smith`

   f. the relative path name for the *Driver.class* file from `prog2` file if the current directory is `/Users/smith/prog2`

2. Figure 13.25 depicts the connections that are used to write to a file called *example.bin*. This figure names the classes involved in this output and shows the proper connection sequence. For each part below draw a picture in this same style, which describes the indicated example.

   a. the objects used to read from *example.bin* within the code in Figure 13.27

   b. the objects used to write to *example.txt* within the code in Figure 13.21

   c. the objects used to write to *example.obj* within the code in Figure 13.25

   d. the objects used to read from *example.obj* within the code in Figure 13.26

3. Label each of the following standard Java I/O-related classes with the best choice from the following

   (1) writes data in binary form

   (2) reads data in binary form

(3) writes data in textual form

(4) reads data in textual form

a. `BufferedReader`

b. `DataInputStream`

c. `DataOutputStream`

d. `PrintWriter`

e. `ObjectInputStream`

f. `ObjectOutputStream`

g. `Scanner`

4. Suppose that following code segment is executed.

```
try{
    FileOutputStream outStream;
    DataOutputStream dataStream;
    outStream = new FileOutputStream("Ex3File");
    dataStream = new DataOutputStream(outStream);
    dataStream.writeInt(34);
    dataStream.writeLong(644);
    dataStream.writeFloat(7.3f);
    dataStream.writeDouble(12.345);
    dataStream.writeFloat(9.87f);
    dataStream.flush();
    dataStream.close();
}
catch (IOException e) {
    System.out.println("ERROR writing.");
}
```

a. Assuming that no file named *Ex3File* exists prior to executing this code, how many bytes in total are written to *Ex3File* after the code finishes execution?

b. How does your answer to part (a) change if a file with the name *Ex3File* already exists before this code executes?

c. Picture the content of the *Ex3File* created by this code, depicting the number of bytes devoted to each output value.

5. Suppose that following code segment is executed.

```
try{
    FileOutputStream outStream;
    PrintWriter printWriter;
    outStream = new FileOutputStream("Ex4File");
```

```
        printWriter = new PrintWriter(outStream);
        printWriter.print(34);
        printWriter.println(644);
        printWriter.print(7.3f);
        printWriter.print(12.345);
        printWriter.print(9.87f);
        printWriter.flush();
        printWriter.close();
    }
    catch (IOException e) {
        System.out.println("ERROR writing.");
    }
```

a. Assuming that no file named *Ex4File* exists prior to executing this code, how many bytes in total are written to *Ex4File* after the code finishes execution?

b. Picture the content of the *Ex4File* created by this code, depicting the actual characters devoted to each output value.

6. Assume that the following code has just executed.

```
try {
        FileOutputStream outStream;
        DataOutputStream dataStream;
        outStream = new FileOutputStream("sample");
        dataStream = new DataOutputStream(outStream);
        dataStream.writeInt(101);
        dataStream.writeDouble(102.0);
        dataStream.writeInt(103);
        dataStream.writeInt(104);
        dataStream.writeInt(105);
        dataStream.flush();
        dataStream.close();
        outStream = new FileOutputStream("sample");
        dataStream = new DataOutputStream(outStream);
        dataStream.writeInt(201);
        dataStream.writeDouble(202.0);
        dataStream.writeInt(203);
        dataStream.writeInt(204);
        dataStream.writeInt(205);
        dataStream.flush();
        dataStream.close();
        outStream = new FileOutputStream("sample2");
        dataStream = new DataOutputStream(outStream);
        dataStream.writeUTF("Cows R not us");
        dataStream.writeUTF("Cows R them");
        dataStream.flush();
        dataStream.close();
```

```
            int j1, j2, j3, j4;
            String str;
            FileInputStream inStream;
            DataInputStream dataInStream;
            inStream = new FileInputStream("sample");
            dataInStream = new DataInputStream(inStream);
            j1 = dataInStream.readInt();
            j2 = dataInStream.readInt();
            j2 = dataInStream.readInt();
            j2 = dataInStream.readInt();
            dataInStream.close();
            inStream = new FileInputStream("sample");
            dataInStream = new DataInputStream(inStream);
            j3 = dataInStream.readInt();
            dataInStream.close();
            inStream = new FileInputStream("sample2");
            dataInStream = new DataInputStream(inStream);
            str = dataInStream.readUTF();
            dataStream.close();
            // variable values from HERE.
        }
        catch (IOException e) {
            System.out.println("ERROR in I/O.");
        }
```

a. Is the first output file created above a *binary* file or a *text* file?

b. What values are assigned to the variables below by the end of this second code segment?

j1 _____

j2 _____

j3 _____

str _____

Programming Exercises

1. For this assignment you must write a program that copies text files in a peculiar manner. When your program executes it accepts input from a file called *source.txt*. The program creates a new text file called *copyOfSource.txt* that contains the same lines as *source.txt* except that the order of the lines has been reversed. Note that keeping both files in the same folder as your code is easiest. Also, note that you can use a text editor program to create text files for *source.txt*.

2. Using your favorite program that utilizes *java.swing.** to construct a graphical display, modify the program so that the objects of the display are made persistent. In particular, the program must remember the state of the display each time that it quits and reload this state each time it starts. (You may use a separate Save button to cause the state to be saved and assume that the user clicks this button prior to terminating the program's execution.)

3. Programming Exercise 1 from Chapter 12 analyzes the characters that are typed into a JTextField object. Write this same program except your version must analyze all of the characters from a text file named *letters.txt*.

4. Programming Exercise 2 from Chapter 12 displays bowling scores that are typed into several JTextField objects. Write this same program except your version must input all scores as consecutive int values from a binary file called *pins.bin*. (Note that you will need to create a separate program to create the initial content of a *pins.bin* file to use for test data.)

5. Modify Programming Exercise 1 above to allow the user to select the name for the output file by using a JFileChooser object.

Recursion

He (Waclaw Sierpinski) was a creative mind and liked creative mathematics.

—Rotkiewicz (a student of Sierpinski)

Objectives

- To introduce recursion as a form of control
- To explore the concept of recursive definition and how it leads naturally to recursive methods
- To examine the runtime behavior of recursion in the form of activation records
- To compare and contrast loops and recursion
- To examine more complicated forms of recursion, including multiple recursive calls from a single method and indirect recursion

*P*rogramming languages often include instructions, called **control structures** that are tools for manipulating control flow. An *if* instruction is a control structure that supports selection. The *while*, *do*, and *for* loops are control structures, providing repetition. The call and return mechanism of a method is still another control structure, often called "control abstraction."

This chapter explores a way to utilize control abstraction to produce a repetition-like form of control. The result is a sufficiently different form of control to deserve its own name—**recursion**.

14.1 ■ Recursive Definition

Long before computer programs made use of recursion as a form of control flow, people were using recursion as a definitional tool. In fact, mathematicians have long accepted recursion as a sound method for defining properties.

Informally, a **recursive definition** can be described as a definition of some property that is self-referential. In other words, a property is defined in terms of itself. For example, consider the task of defining *odd positive integer*.

Mathematicians might offer two relevant observations about the *odd positive integers*.

1. The smallest odd positive integer is 1.

2. Every odd positive integer, except 1, is two greater than some other odd positive integer.

These two observations are transformed into a recursive definition, presented in Figure 14.1. This definition is expressed in two parts: a **basis clause** and a **recursive clause**. All recursive definitions include these two parts.

The basis clause defines the property for one or more specific situations that can be defined nonrecursively. The basis clause can be thought of as defining the property for the simplest case(s). In the definition of an odd positive integer, the basis clause

Figure 14.1 Recursive definition of *odd positive integer*	**Basis Clause** The number 1 is an *odd positive integer*. **Recursive Clause** If $K == N + 2$ and N is an odd positive integer, then K is an *odd positive integer*.

defines that 1 is an odd positive integer. The number 1 is the "simplest case" because it is the smallest of all odd positive integers.

The recursive clause defines the property for all cases not examined in the basis. This makes the recursive clause the more general case. For the definition of *odd positive integer*, the recursive clause defines that any value, K, is an odd positive integer as long as it is $K == N + 2$ where N is also an odd positive integer.

A recursive clause is characterized by the fact that it defines a property by using the same property. The recursive clause from Figure 14.1 defines an *odd positive integer* K by using another *odd positive integer* called N.

To see how this definition is applied, consider the question of whether or not the integer 3 is an *odd positive integer*. Substituting *3* for K in the recursive clause leads to the following statement.

If $3 == N + 2$ and N is an *odd positive integer*, then 3 is an *odd positive integer*.

According to the above statement, it is possible to conclude that 3 is an odd positive integer by satisfying two requirements: (1) to find some value N for which $3 == N + 2$ and (2) to verify that this same value N is itself an odd positive integer. If the value 1 is selected for N, then $3 == N + 2$ is satisfied. Furthermore, 1 is guaranteed to be an odd positive integer according to the basis clause.

It is more complicated to reason why a larger number, such as 9, is an odd positive integer. The five steps below offer an appropriate analysis.

Step 1: According to the recursive clause,

If $9 == N + 2$ and N is an *odd positive integer*, then 9 is an *odd positive integer*.

Since $9 == 7 + 2$, the above statement means

If 7 is an *odd positive integer*, then 9 is an *odd positive integer*.

Step 2: To decide about 7, according to the recursive clause,

If $7 == N + 2$ and N is an *odd positive integer*, then 7 is an *odd positive integer*.

Since $7 == 5 + 2$, the above statement means

If 5 is an *odd positive integer*, then 7 is an *odd positive integer*.

Step 3: To decide about 5, according to the recursive clause,

If $5 == N + 2$ and N is an *odd positive integer*, then 5 is an *odd positive integer*.

Since $5 == 3 + 2$, the above statement means

If 3 is an *odd positive integer*, then 5 is an *odd positive integer*.

Step 4: To decide about 3, according to the recursive clause,

If $3 == N + 2$ and N is an *odd positive integer*, then 3 is an *odd positive integer*.

Since $3 == 1 + 2$, the above statement means

If 1 is an *odd positive integer*, then 3 is an *odd positive integer*.

Step 5: To decide about 1, according to the basis clause,

One (1) is an *odd positive integer*.

software *Hint*
engineering

Using recursion in programming begins with **recursive thinking**. Studying recursive definitions is a good way to learn thinking recursively.

Every recursive definition (and every recursive Java method) has both a basis and a recursive part. The basis must work for specific situation(s). The recursive part is self-referential in such a way that it makes progress toward the basis.

Therefore, by the reasoning in Step 4, 3 is an odd positive integer; by Step 3, 5 is an odd positive integer; by Step 2, 7 is an odd positive integer; and by Step 1, 9 is an odd positive integer.

The previous five steps follow a typical pattern of repeatedly applying the recursive clause until the issue is reduced to something that is satisfied by the basis clause. This repeated application of the recursive clause permits recursive definitions to define properties that extend to an infinite number of elements.

A recursive definition is useful only if the basis and recursive clauses of a recursive definition work in concert with one another. The recursive clause must be written so that repeated applications of this clause will eventually lead to the basis clause and the basis clause must define the property for some small number of elements.

The key characteristic of the basis clause is that it must provide the first occurrence(s) of the definition. Suppose that the basis clause for *odd positive integer* was changed as shown below.

INCORRECT ATTEMPT TO DEFINE: *odd positive integer*

Basis Clause

Seven (7) is an *odd positive integer*.

Recursive Clause

If $K == N + 2$ and N is an *odd positive integer*, then K is an *odd positive integer*.

This basis clause may be a correct statement regarding the number seven. However, this new basis makes it impossible to conclude that 1, 3, and 5 are odd positive integers, which is contrary to the usual notion of odd positives.

The key characteristic of a proper recursive clause is that it provides a way to make progress toward use of the basis clause. Suppose that the recursive clause of the odd positive integer definition were altered as shown below.

ANOTHER INCORRECT ATTEMPT TO DEFINE: *odd positive integer*

Basis Clause

One (1) is an *odd positive integer*.

Recursive Clause

If $K == N - 2$ and N is an *odd positive integer*, then K is an *odd positive integer*.

This new recursive clause may be a correct statement mathematically, but it is not useful in a recursive definition. For example, consider applying this recursive clause to consider if the value 11 is an odd positive integer. The recursive clause can be translated into the following by substituting 11 for K.

If $11 == N - 2$ and N is an *odd positive integer*, then 11 is an *odd positive integer*.

Since $11 == N - 2$, N must have a value of 13. However, this is progressing *away* from the basis clause in the sense that the basis clause defines the property for 1 and 13 is a greater distance from 1 than 11.

Technically, every recursive definition should also include a third clause, known as an **extremal clause**. The extremal clause defines the situations where the property is *not* true. Figure 14.2 adds an extremal clause for the definition of odd positive integer. Frequently, extremal clauses are not included in definitions because they are taken for granted. In the case of odd positive integer, it is reasonable to assume that any number that satisfies neither the basis nor the recursive clause must *not* be an odd positive integer.

Some recursive definitions are more complicated. For example, Figure 14.3 contains a definition of *even integer*. This definition requires a two-part recursive clause

Basis Clause

One (1) is an *odd positive integer*.

Recursive Clause

If $K == N + 2$ and N is an *odd positive integer*, then K is an *odd positive integer*.

Extremal Clause

Anything that cannot satisfy the basis clause and cannot satisfy the recursive clause is *not* an *odd positive integer*.

Figure 14.2

Recursive definition of *odd positive integer* with extremal

Basis Clause

Zero (0) is an *even integer*.

Recursive Clause

(Option 1)
If $K == N - 2$ and N is an *even integer*, then K is an *even integer*.

(Option 2)
If $K == N + 2$ and N is an *even integer*, then K is an *even integer*.

Figure 14.3

Recursive definition of *even integer*

because there are even integers that are greater than the basis value of zero, and there are even integers that are smaller than zero.

This definition contains two possible alternatives, labeled Option 1 and Option 2, within the recursive clause. Both of these options are true, and both can be used when applying the definition. Option 1 must be applied repeatedly in order to reason that a value less than zero is an *even integer*. Option 2 must be applied repeatedly for reasoning about positive numbers.

The basis clause of the definition of *even integer* is also interesting. The value zero really is not the first even integer. The *even integer* property is a somewhat unusual situation in which any particular even number can be substituted for zero and the basis will still lead to an equivalent workable definition.

Recursive definitions can also be applied to nonmathematical properties. For example, consider the task of defining what it means to be an *ancestor of Person X*.

Both of X's parents are ancestors of X.

A parent of a parent of X (i.e., a grandparent of X) is an ancestor of X.

A parent of a parent of a parent of X (i.e., a great-grandparent of X) is an ancestor of X.

. . .

Figure 14.4 supplies a recursive definition for *ancestor of X*.

Arguably, the simplest form of an ancestor is a parent. Therefore, Figure 14.4 supplies a basis clause that defines *ancestor of X* in terms of *parent of X*. To see how the recursive clause can be applied to make progress toward the basis, consider the partial family tree for Tim shown on the next page.

The definition of ancestor from Figure 14.4 can be used to see that Martha is an ancestor of Tim by the following reasoning steps.

Step 1:   According to the recursive clause,
   Every parent of an ancestor of Tim is an ancestor of Tim.

Figure 14.4

Recursive definition of ancestor

Basis Clause

Every parent (mother or father) of X is an ancestor of X.

Recursive Clause

Every parent of an ancestor of X is an ancestor of X.

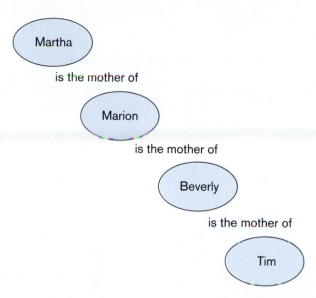

Since Martha is Marion's mother (parent), it is concluded that Martha is Tim's ancestor as long as Marion is an ancestor of Tim.

Step 2: Using the recursive clause a second time, it is concluded that Marion is Tim's ancestor as long as Beverly is Tim's ancestor because Marion is Beverly's parent.

Step 3: According to the basis clause,

Every parent of Tim is an ancestor of Tim.

Since Beverly is Tim's mother (parent), it is concluded that Beverly is an ancestor of Tim.

Therefore, using Step 2, Marion is Tim's ancestor.

Therefore, using Step 1, Martha is Tim's ancestor.

Recursive definitions can also be an effective tool for defining programming language syntax. For example, Figure 14.5 contains the definition of a Boolean expression that partially defines the syntax supported in Java. This definition of Boolean expression syntax includes two options in the basis clause, one for each Boolean constant. The recursive clause options define the syntax of various Boolean operators and parentheses.

Using the definition from Figure 14.5, it is possible to conclude that each of the lines below represent valid syntax for a *Boolean expression.*

```
true
! true
(false)
false && (true)
!(false || (true && !false))
```

Figure 14.5

Recursive definition of *Boolean expression* syntax

Basis Clause

The strings below are each syntactically valid *Boolean expressions*.

```
true
false
```

Recursive Clause

(Option 1)
If *expr* is any syntactically valid *Boolean expression*, then so is each of the following lines

```
! expr
(expr)
```

(Option 2)
If *expr1* and *expr2* are both syntactically valid *Boolean expressions*, then so is each of the following lines

```
expr1 && expr2
expr1 || expr2
```

Some properties, like the Java Boolean expression, are inherently recursive. Syntax diagrams regularly utilize recursion in the form of a box that refers to the expression being defined. For example, the following syntax diagram for `booleanExpression` refers to itself in order to define the proper use of parentheses to surround a Boolean expression.

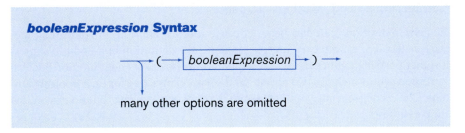

***booleanExpression* Syntax**

many other options are omitted

The concept of ancestor, discussed earlier, is another example of a definition that is inherently recursive. It is impossible to define properties such as ancestor or a parenthesized Boolean expression without resorting to recursion, formally or informally.

14.2 ■ From Recursive Definition to Method

The Fibonacci sequence is another example of something that is an inherently recursive concept. Figure 14.6 supplies a definition for the *j*th value in the Fibonacci number sequence.

The recursive clause of the Fibonacci definition indicates that the fourth Fibonacci number is the sum of the third Fibonacci number plus the second. The recursive clause also indicates that the third Fibonacci number is the sum of the second plus the first Fibonacci numbers. Since the basis clause states that the first and second Fibonacci numbers are both 1, the whole definition indicates that the third Fibonacci number is 2 and the fourth Fibonacci number is 3.

This definition for the *j*th Fibonacci number can be transformed into a recursive Java method. Figure 14.7 contains this code.

Basis Clause

(Option 1)
1 is the 1st *Fibonacci number.*

(Option 2)
1 is the 2nd *Fibonacci number.*

Recursive Clause

If *J1* is the (*j* − 1)st *Fibonacci number* and *J2* is the (*j* − 2)nd *Fibonacci number*, then *J1* + *J2* is the *j*th *Fibonacci number.*

Figure 14.6

Recursive definition of *j*th *Fibonacci number*

```
/** pre:    j >= 1
 *  post:   result == the jth number in the Fibonacci sequence
 */
// CAUTION: There are more efficient ways to write this code.
private int jth_Fibonacci(int j) {
   if (j == 1 || j == 2) {
      return 1;
   } else {
      return jth_Fibonacci(j-1) + jth_Fibonacci(j-2);
   }
}
```

Figure 14.7

jth_Fibonacci method

The jth_Fibonacci method uses its parameter to indicate the position of the value within the Fibonacci sequence (j==1 for the first Fibonacci, j==2 for the second, etc.). Whenever the j parameter is 1 or 2, the method returns 1. This corresponds to the two options of the basis clause in the definition of Fibonacci. Whenever the j parameter value is greater than 2, the jth_Fibonacci returns the sum of the (j − 1)st and (j − 2)nd Fibonacci numbers. This is consistent with the recursive clause of the Fibonacci number definition.

The thought of a method calling itself may seem unusual, but it is perfectly acceptable Java code. A method that calls itself is known as a **recursive method**. Figure 14.8 explains the values returned by this method for arguments 1 through 6. The source of the values of the later calls can be found in the earlier ones.

As a second example of a recursive method, consider the problem of testing whether or not one *Swing/AWT* object is an ancestor container for another. Figure 14.9 gives a recursive definition for the meaning of *ancestor container*. This method is based upon the notion that JComponent objects (such as buttons and Rectangles) can

Figure 14.8   Values returned by jth_Fibonacci method for arguments 1 to 6

jth_Fibonacci(1)

    return 1

jth_Fibonacci(2)

    return 1

jth_Fibonacci(3)

    return jth_Fibonacci(2) + jth_Fibonacci(1) == 1 + 1 = 2

jth_Fibonacci(4)

    return jth_Fibonacci(3) + jth_Fibonacci(2) == 2 + 1 = 3

jth_Fibonacci(5)

    return jth_Fibonacci(4) + jth_Fibonacci(3) == 3 + 2 = 5

jth_Fibonacci(6)

    return jth_Fibonacci(5) + jth_Fibonacci(4) == 5 + 3 = 8

Figure 14.9

Recursive definition of ancestor container

Basis Clause

If c.getParent() == *a*, then *a* is an ancestor container of *c*.

Recursive Clause

If *a* is an ancestor container of c.getParent(),

then *a* is an ancestor container of *c*.

be added to Container objects (such as windows and JFrames). The *Swing/AWT* getParent returns the Container to which its object is added, unless there is no placement in which case getParent returns null.

The definition of the concept of an ancestor container is turned into a boolean in Figure 14.10. The isAncestorContainer is designed to return true exactly when its first argument is an ancestor container of its second argument.

The isAncestorContainer closely resembles the definition from Figure 14.9 except for the first check for c == null. This check corresponds to an extremal clause test; it handles the situation where all possibilities have been exhausted and false must be returned.

14.3 ■ **Recursive Methods**

Void methods, as well as nonvoid methods can be recursive. For example, consider the problem of displaying all ancestor containers of a Component. In particular, a method called displayAncestorWidths is designed to print the width of each ancestor container from the most distant ancestor to the closest ancestor. To illus-

Figure 14.10   isAncestorContainer

```
/** post:  result == a is an ancestor container of c */
private boolean isAncestorContainer(Container a, JComponent c) {
    if (c == null) {
        return false;
    } else if (c.getParent() == a) {
        return true;
    } else {
        return isAncestorContainer(a, c.getParent());
    }
}
```

trate this, Figure 14.11 diagrams a collection of JComponent objects. In this picture, each rectangle is placed upon the next larger rectangle with the largest rectangle placed upon the window.

If the displayAncestorWidths method is called upon the smallest rectangle from Figure 14.11, the widths of each JComponent should be output in the following order.

400
350
250
100

Figure 14.12 shows the code for this method. Like many recursive methods, displayAncestorWidths is deceptively short for the algorithm performed.

When this method is called, it is passed a JComponent, c. If this component is the same as the pane parameter, then the work of the method is complete, and it simply prints the pane's width. If displayAncestorWidths is called with a parameter other than pane, then it first proceeds to call itself recursively with c's parent container as an argument. This recursive call should cause the widths of all ancestor containers to be displayed, and when the recursive call returns, the System.out.println instruction displays the width of c.

Figure 14.11

A group of ancestor containers

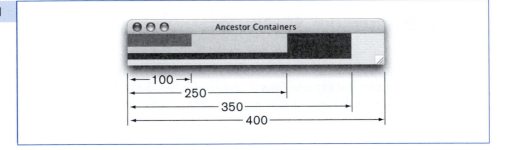

Figure 14.12   displayAncestorWidths method

```
/** post:  all ancestor widths are displayed
 *             - most distant ancestors first
 */
private void displayAncestorWidths(JComponent c, Container pane) {
    if (c != pane && c != null)
        displayAncestorWidths(c.getParent(), pane);
    System.out.println("Width: " + c.getWidth());
}
```

It is wise to remember two points when designing recursive methods.

1. There must be a nonrecursive way to execute the method.

2. Every recursive call must make progress toward the nonrecursive alternative.

The first point is analogous to the basis clause of a recursive definition. There must be a way to exit the recursion in the same way that there must be at least one basis situation. The second point is also just reminiscent of recursive definitions. Each time a method is called recursively, it is important that the call is moving the algorithm closer to the nonrecursive (basis) alternative.

In the case of `displayAncestorWidths` a nonrecursive call occurs when the parameter c is `pane` or when the recursion exhausts all container enclosures (i.e., when `c == null`). The recursive call in `displayAncestorWidths` is guaranteed to make progress because it passes a parent container as the argument for the next call. If recursion to the parent container is repeated enough times, either the window frame at the background of the placement or `null` will be encountered.

software _engineering Hint_

When writing a recursive method, think first about the simplest, or first case(s). These can often be found by answering the question, "Under what circumstances can this method complete its work nonrecursively?"

14.4 ■ Recursive Execution

Tracing the execution of a recursive method reveals the runtime behavior of recursion. In order to trace recursion it is important to keep track of all **activations**. A method activation is defined to be a separate, single call to that method. Each activation has its own copy of all parameters and local variables, collectively called an **activation record**. This activation record also includes the location of the currently executing instruction. Consider a trace of the `displayAncestorWidths` method upon the smallest rectangle from Figure 14.11. When `displayAncestorWidths` is called with the smallest rectangle and the content pane of the background `JFrame` as arguments, its activation record can be pictured as shown in Figure 14.13.

This activation record shows that the c parameter is bound to the smallest rectangle. The activation also records the point of execution within the method's code (pic-

Figure 14.13   Initial activation of `displayAncestorWidths`

```
Initial activation record of displayAncestorWidths
Parameter
    c   smallest rectangle
Method code (arrow indicates point of execution)
→   if (c != pane && c != null)
        displayAncestorWidths(c.getParent());
    System.out.println("Width: " + c.getWidth());
```

tured as a colored arrow). This arrow points just before the *if* instruction to indicate that execution is about to begin to execute the *if* instruction.

As this first activation proceeds to execute, it is discovered that c is neither equal to the content pane nor `null`. Therefore, the `displayAncestorWidths` method is called recursively and the parent container of c (the middle rectangle) is passed as the argument. This second call produces a second activation record, as shown in Figure 14.14.

This second activation is drawn on top of the first activation to illustrate that both activations are in progress at the time of this execution snapshot. The first activation is on hold in the sense that it has performed a recursive call. The location of the instruction that caused this call is illustrated by the faded arrow. The second activation is beginning to execute at the solid arrow.

Notice that both activations have their own c parameter. The c parameter of the first activation continues to bind to the smallest rectangle, while the c parameter of the second activation is bound to the middle rectangle.

As the execution of this second activation proceeds, it will call `displayAncestorWidths` a third time passing the parent container (i.e., the larger rectangle). The recursive third activation, results in yet a fourth activation of the method that passes the background pane. Figure 14.15 illustrates the state of the four activation records as this fourth call begins.

The execution snapshot from Figure 14.15 shows the different values for each c parameter. The first three activations are executing in the midst of their call instruction. The fourth activation is about to begin executing. Executing this fourth activation is different because the value c is equal to pane. Therefore, the *if* condition is `false` and the activation proceeds to output the width of c (pane) which is 400.

Figure 14.14   Two activations of `displayAncestorWidths`

Initial activation record of `displayAncestorWidths`
Parameter
  c [smallest rectangle]
Method code (arrow indicates point of execution)

    if (c !=
    ➡️displa
    System.out

Second activation record of `displayAncestorWidths`
Parameter
  c [middle rectangle]
Method code (arrow indicates point of execution)

    ➡️
        if (c != pane && c != null)   {
            displayAncestorWidths(c.getParent());
        System.out.println("Width: " + c.getWidth());

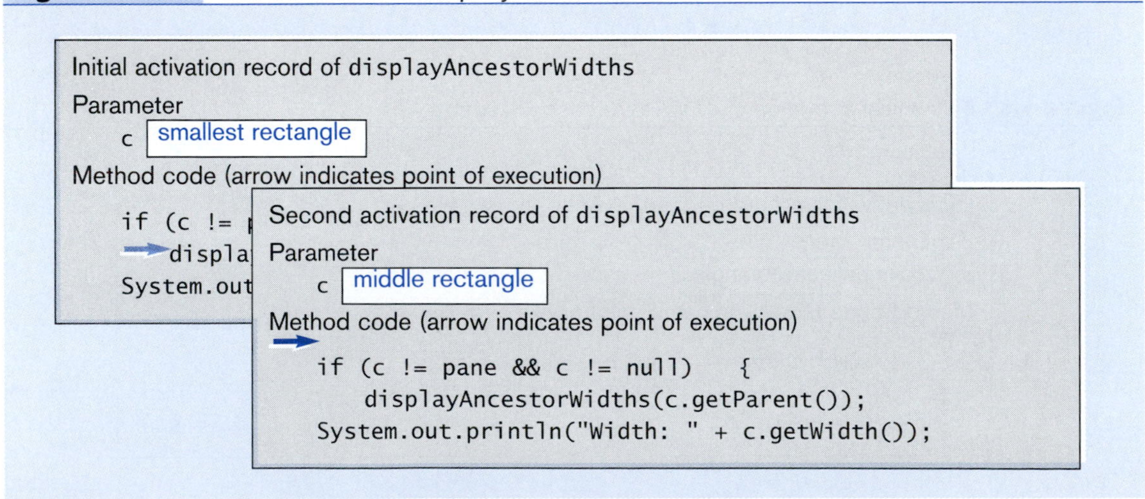

Figure 14.15 Four activations of `displayAncestorWidths`

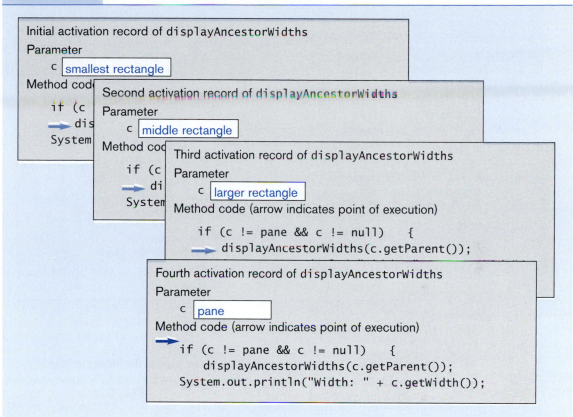

This fourth activation proceeds to return to the third activation at the location shown in Figure 14.16.

The third activation proceeds to display the width of the larger rectangle (350). Then the third activation returns to the second. Similarly, the second activation displays the width of the middle rectangle (250) and returns to the first activation. Finally, the first activation returns the width of its smallest rectangle parameter (100), then returns.

14.5 ■ **Recursion and Repetition**

Recursion resembles looping (repetition) in many ways. Just like looping, recursion is used to perform repetitive tasks. Both forms of control require attention to initialization and making progress. Both have the potential for unending execution.

software *Hint*
engineering

Tracing the activation records of recursion is useful only for understanding the mechanics of runtime recursive execution. Writing recursively requires the developer to learn to think recursively—i.e., in terms of basis and recursive clauses.

Figure 14.16   Upon return from the 4th activation of `displayAncestorWidths`

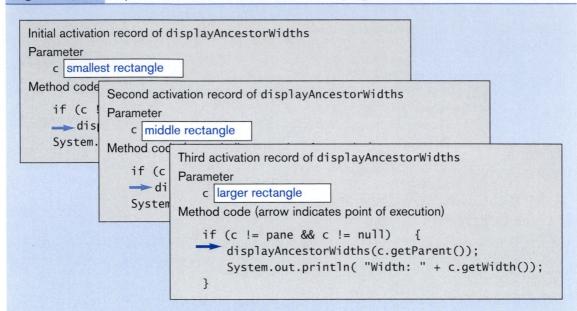

It is always possible to replace repetition with recursion. To illustrate, Figure 14.17 contains a pattern for translating any *while* loop into a recursive method that performs the same algorithm.

Calling the `recWhile` method results in the same operation as the *while* algorithm of Figure 4.17. The execution of `recWhile` begins by checking the value of

Figure 14.17

A *while* loop and the corresponding recursive method

a while algorithm

```
while (theCondition) {
    loopBody;
}
```

the corresponding recursive method

```
private void recWhile() {
    if (theCondition) {
        loopBody;
        recWhile;
    }
}
```

theCondition. If this `boolean` condition is `false`, then *recWhile* returns in the same way that the *while* loop algorithm completes execution whenever *theCondition* is found to be `false`. Whenever the test finds *theCondition* to be `true`, then *recWhile* executes *loopBody* and calls itself recursively. This is the same behavior as the *while* algorithm that executes *loopBody* whenever *theCondition* is `true`.

Translating recursion into loops is not always so simple, nor is it always feasible. Part of the difficulty stems from the fact that recursive methods incorporate parameter passage, which is not easily mimicked by a loop.

Despite the difficulties in translating from recursion to loops, there is one category of recursion, called **tail recursion**, which can be routinely translated into repetition. Tail recursion is a category of recursive methods in which the recursive call is the last instruction to be executed by an activation. For example, the `isAncestorContainer` repeated below, uses tail recursion.

```
private boolean isAncestorContainer(Container a, Component c)
{
    if (c == null) {
        return false;
    } else if (c.getParent() == a) {
        return true;
    } else {
        return isAncestorContainer(a, c.getParent());
    }
}
```

Whenever `isAncestorContainer` makes a recursive call, it does so from within the *else* clause. Such a recursive call is the last task `isAncestorContainer` performs prior to its return.

Tail recursion can be eliminated by using a loop that does the following:

- captures the recursive work within the loop body
- utilizes a loop condition(s) corresponding to the basis step of the recursion

For example, a nonrecursive version of `isAncestorContainer` is shown in Figure 14.18. This new version utilizes a local variable called `newC`, to play the same role as the `c` parameter within the recursive version. The loop causes the value of `newC` to change from `Component` to its parent container, just as occurred in the recursive calls. The loop terminates when either of the two basis conditions, (`newC == null`) or (`c.getParent == a`), is `true`.

software *Hint*
engineering

In contrast to `isAncestorContainer`, the `displayAncestorWidths` method, repeated below, is not tail recursive. This is because the `System.out.println` is called *after* the recursive call. It is typically quite difficult to translate non-tail recursive code into loops. A loop to do the work of `displayAncestorWidths` would need

Recursion is generally less efficient than repetition. This is due to the time required to manage the multiple environments of the recursive activations. Therefore, eliminating tail recursion tends to improve algorithm efficiency. Some optimizing compilers are capable of eliminating tail recursion, freeing the programmer from worrying about the inefficiencies of recursion.

Figure 14.18 Nonrecursive version of `isAncestorContainer`

```
private boolean isAncestorContainer(Container a, JComponent c)
{
    JComponent newC = c;
    while (newC!=null && c.getParent != a) {
        newC = newC.getParent();
    }
    return newC != null;
}
```

to progress through all parent `Container`s, while somehow remembering all of the `JComponent`s along the way.

```
private void displayAncestorWidths(JComponent c,
                                   Container pane) {
    if (c != pane && c != null)
        displayAncestorWidths(c.getParent(), pane);
        System.out.println("Width: " + c.getWidth());
}
```

software *Hint*
engineering

A stack overflow exception usually means that some recursive method has recursed too deeply.

A final similarity between recursion and loops is that both have the potential for infinite execution. A method that calls itself without making progress toward the basis clause is similar to an infinite loop. The only difference is that such infinite recursion halts with a **stack overflow** exception.

The name "stack overflow" comes from the fact that the Java VM stores each activation record within a so-called "runtime stack." When a method is called recursively without end, the Java VM will eventually exhaust all of the available space for method activations and the exception message results.

14.6 ■ More Complicated Forms of Recursion

Nontail recursion is more complicated than tail recursion in the sense that nontail recursion is not easily translated into an equivalent loop. Another way in which one algorithm can be more complicated than another is to perform multiple recursive calls per activation. The `jth_Fibonacci` method from Section 14.2 is such an example of a method that calls itself twice for each recursive activation.

Many **fractal** algorithms also require such multiple recursive calls. Fractals are visualized as drawing patterns that repeat in varying scales. For example, the Sierpinski gasket is a particular kind of fractal created by Waclaw Sierpinski, a famous Polish mathematician (1882–1969). The Sierpinski gasket appears within an equilateral tri-

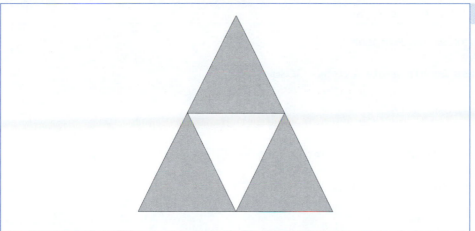

Figure 14.19

The Sierpinski
gasket pattern

angle with apex pointing directly up. (Call this outer gray triangle the *bounding tri-angle.*) The recursive pattern used to draw a Sierpinski gasket is to draw a second equilateral triangle inside and upside down to the bounding triangle, as shown in Figure 14.19. In this picture, the bounding triangle is a solid gray and the second triangle is the white center triangle. The white triangle is half the width and height of the bounding triangle, and perfectly centered. A Sierpinski gasket is formed by applying this drawing pattern recursively using the remaining gray triangles as bounding triangles.

Drawing fractals, like the Sierpinski gasket, is performed recursively by levels. A level $N + 1$ fractal consists of a level N fractal with the next smaller copy of the pattern included. For the Sierpinski gasket, a level $N + 1$ fractal is formed by drawing half-sized triangles in the center of every solid gray (bounding) triangle of a level N gasket. Figure 14.20 illustrates.

Figure 14.21 shows a class, called `DownTriangle`, which creates an appropriate triangle for use in a Sierpinski gasket fractal. The `DownTriangle` constructor is a non-

Figure 14.20   Level 1 through Level 4 Sierpinski gasket fractals

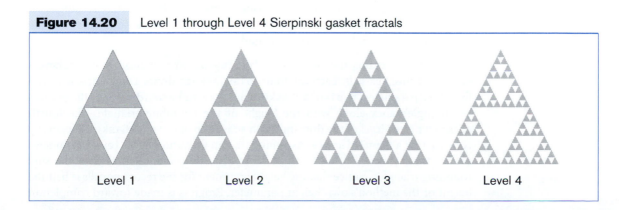

Level 1   Level 2   Level 3   Level 4

Figure 14.21   `DownTriangle` class

```java
import javax.swing.JComponent;
import java.awt.*;
public class DownTriangle extends JComponent {

    /** post:   getX() == x-h/2 and getY() == y+h/2
     *          and getWidth() == h/2 and getHeight() == h/2
     */
    public DownTriangle(int x, int y, int h) {
        super();
        setBounds(x-h/4, y+h/2, h/2, h/2);
    }

    /** post:   a black triangle is drawn with vertices at upper
     *          left, upper right and center bottom of the
     *          bounding rectangle
     */
    public void paint(Graphics g) {
        g.setColor(Color.black);
        g.drawLine(0, 0, getWidth()-1, 0);
        g.drawLine(0, 0, getWidth()/2, getHeight()-1);
        g.drawLine(getHeight()-1, 0, getWidth()/2, getHeight()-1);
    }
}
```

recursive method that is passed the apex (x,y) and height (h) of a bounding triangle. DownTriangle draws a downward pointing triangle within the specified bounding triangle.

Figure 14.22 diagrams how a DownTriangle is drawn with respect to its parameters (x, y, and h). The dashed triangle represents the boundary to be partitioned into four equal smaller triangles. The gray shaded rectangle is the bonding rectangle, set by setBounds, in the DownTriangle constructor. The black solid lines are the actual triangle drawn by the paint method.

Figure 14.23 contains the code for a displayGaskets method that recursively draws Sierpinski gaskets. Each call to displayGaskets draws a single triangle. The first three parameters to displayGaskets are the x and y coordinates of the bounding triangle's apex along with the height of the bounding triangle. The fourth parameter is the level of the drawing. Each activation of displayGaskets begins by constructing a DownTriangle. Assuming that an activation has a level parameter greater than 1, it will result in three more activations—one for each of the surrounding triangles. Notice that the height argument for the recursive calls is half the height of the method's own height parameter. Progress is made toward completion

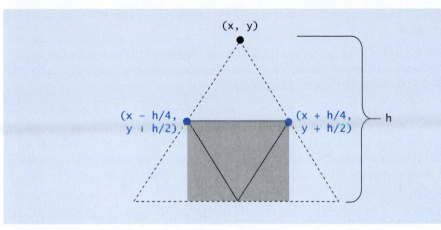

Figure 14.22

DownTriangle drawing

```java
import javax.swing.JFrame;
import java.awt.*;
public class Driver {
    private JFrame win;

    public Driver() {
        win = new JFrame("Sierpinski Gasket");
        win.setBounds(10, 10, 600, 620);
        win.setVisible(true);
        win.setLayout(null);
        displayGaskets(300, 0, 600, 5);
        win.repaint();
    }

    /** pre:   lev > 0
     *  post:  Sierpinski gaskets of level lev are drawn on win
     *         within a triangle with upper apex at (x, y)
     *         and height of h
     */
    private void displayGaskets(int x, int y, int h, int lev) {
        DownTriangle gasket;
        gasket = new DownTriangle(x, y, h);
        win.add(gasket, 0);
        if (lev > 1) {
            displayGaskets(x, y, h/2, lev-1);
            displayGaskets(x-h/4, y+h/2, h/2, lev-1);
            displayGaskets(x+h/4, y+h/2, h/2, lev-1);
        }
    }
}
```

Figure 14.23

Sierpinski gasket program

because each recursive call uses a level argument that is one less than its calling activation.

The `displayGaskets` method requires three recursive calls to accomplish its task. This leads to a more complicated form of recursion that is extremely difficult to implement without the use of recursion.

Another form of recursion is known as **indirect recursion**. Indirect recursion occurs when a method can produce simultaneous activations of itself without calling itself directly. Such a situation occurs only when a method calls some sequence of other methods that eventually result in another call to the original method. Figure 14.24 shows a variation on the Sierpinski gasket program that is accomplished by indirect recursion.

The `displayDownTriangle` method is similar to the method by the same name from the Sierpinski gasket program. This method draws a `DownTriangle` in the same way as before. However, this new method does not call itself, but calls `displayUpTriangle` instead. The `displayUpTriangle` method mirrors the behavior of `displayDownTriangle`. The `displayUpTriangle` method uses a bounding triangle with its apex at the bottom. A call to one of these methods draws a triangle and passes the newly drawn triangle to the other method, where it will be used as a bounding triangle. `displayUpTriangle` calls `displayDownTriangle`, and `displayDownTriangle` calls `displayUpTriangle`. The indirect recursion terminates when the `lev` parameter is no longer greater than 1. The picture drawn by calling these methods is a collection of triangles nested inside each other as shown in Figure 14.25.

Figure 14.24   `displayDownTriangle` and `displayUpTriangle`

```
private void displayDownTriangle(int x, int y, int h, int lev) {
    DownTriangle triangle;
    triangle = new DownTriangle(x, y, h);
    win.add(triangle, 0);
    if (lev > 1) {
        displayUpTriangle(x, y+h, h/2, lev-1);
    }
}

private void displayUpTriangle(int x, int y, int h, int lev) {
    UpTriangle triangle;
    triangle = new UpTriangle(x, y, h);
    win.add(triangle, 0);
    if (lev > 1) {
        displayDownTriangle(x, y-h, h/2, lev-1);
    }
}
```

Figure 14.25   Image from `displayDownTriangle` and `displayUpTriangle`

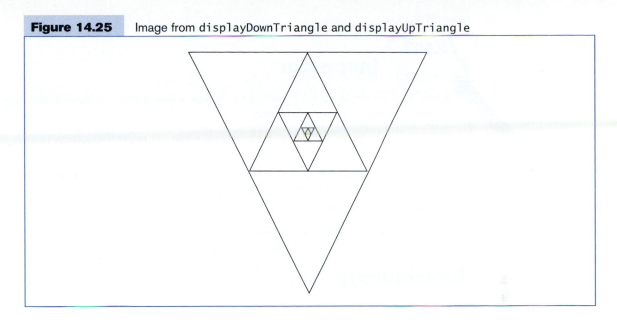

Both multiple recursive calls and indirect recursion contribute to algorithm complexity. Both can be difficult to replace with loops.

Inspector

Below is a collection of hints on what to check when examining code that involves the concepts of this chapter.

- Every recursive method needs a basis clause that causes the recursion to terminate. Checking for the presence of such a clause is always helpful.

- When a recursive method calls itself, it must be making progress toward the basis clause. Checking for such progress can often eliminate the stack overflow errors.

Terminology

activation	indirect recursion
activation record	recursion
basis clause	recursive clause
control structure	recursive definition
direct access device	recursive method
extremal clause	tail recursion
fractals	

Exercises

1. Write a recursive definition for each of the following.

   a. Define what it means for one positive expression to be greater than (>) another positive expression. This should be defined in terms of + and ==.

   b. Define what it means for an airline to have to fly from A to B. Note that flying from A to B may require several individual connecting flights.

2. Consider the following method.

```
private void munge(int x) {
   System.out.println(x);
   if (x != 10) {
      munge(x+3);
   }
   System.out.println(x);
}
```

a. What output results from the following call?
```
munge(10);
```

b. What output results from the following call?
```
munge(1);
```

c. What output results from the following call?
```
munge(11);
```

d. What output results from the following call?
```
munge(0);
```

3. Consider the following method.

```
private int times(int k, int m) {
    if (k != 0) {
        return m + times(k-1, m);
    } else {
        return 0;
    }
}
```

a. What output results from the following instruction?
```
System.out.println(times(3, 2));
```

b. What output results from the following instruction?
```
System.out.println(times(2, 3));
```

c. What output results from the following instruction?
```
System.out.println(times(100, 75));
```

d. What output results from the following instruction?
```
System.out.println(times(-1, 2));
```

e. Write a precondition and a postcondition to describe the behavior of this times method.

4. Show how to replace each of the following methods with a recursive method that produces the same output without a loop.

```
a. private void printProducts(int j, int k) {
       while (j < k) {
           System.out.println(j*k);
           j++;
           k = k - 2;
       }
   }
```

```
b. private void print0toN(int n) {
       for (int k=0; k!=n+1; k++) {
           System.out.println(k);
       }
   }
```

5. Rewrite the code for the jth_Fibonacci function so that it performs the same task as the method from Figure 14.7 without using recursion in your method.

6. Show how to replace the following method with a recursive method that returns the same values when executed.

```
private int sum1ThruN(int n) {
    int sum = 1;
    int k = 1;
    while (sum <= n) {
        sum = sum + k;
        k++;
    }
    return sum;
}
```

7. Figure 14.17 shows a recursive method that mimics the execution of a *while* loop.

   a. Supply a similar recursive method to mimic the behavior of the following *do* loop pattern.

   ```
   do {
       loopBody;
   } while (theCondition);
   ```

   b. Supply a similar recursive method to mimic the behavior of the following *for* loop pattern.

   ```
   for (; theCondition; progressStatement) {
       loopBody;
   }
   ```

Programming Exercises

1. Write a program to draw a Sierpinski carpet fractal pattern. This Sierpinski carpet begins with a black background square. The drawing pattern is a black square with a filled white square centered within the black square. The side length of the white square is one-third the side length of the black square on which it is placed.

The fractal pattern is repeated upon the eight black squares that surround the white center square. Dashed lines below show the location of these eight squares.

Your program must be capable of drawing Sierpinski carpets to different levels. Below is an illustration of the repeated pattern.

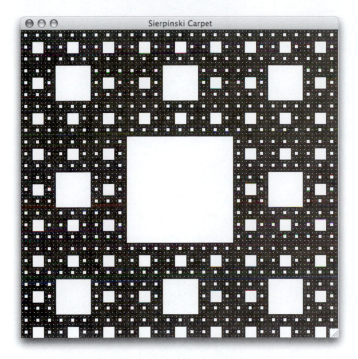

2. Write a program to produce fractal images based upon a regular hexagon. A level 0 image consists of a hexagon with the following form.

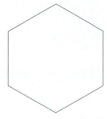

The repeated pattern is to draw six more hexagons at the corners of the larger hexagon. These six new hexagons have side length that is half of their predecessor. The level 1 picture below illustrates.

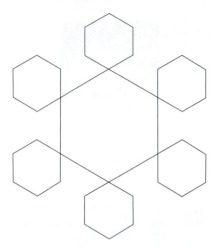

The picture below shows a level 4 version of this fractal pattern.

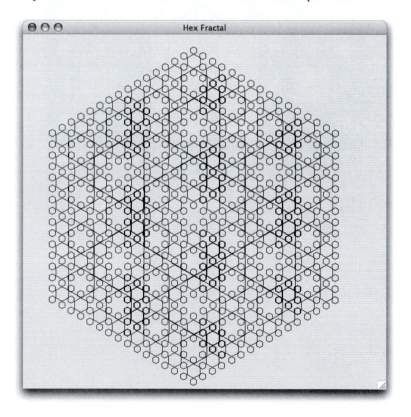

Applications and Applets

Objectives

- To explore the use of `static` variables for sharing constants and for sharing data storage among objects
- To introduce the concept of `static` methods and their utility in designing libraries of pure functions, such as the `Math` package
- To examine applications, the `main` method, and the *run.java* file used to implement the applications in this text
- To explore Java applets and a convenient way to turn applications into applets
- To examine how Java uses `import` declarations and the `CLASSPATH` variable to support package access
- To introduce applets and how they are invoked by browsers via `HTML` files
- To explore how Java packages are grouped into package libraries

J

ava supports two different mechanisms for initiating program execution. A program can be delivered either as an **application** or as an **applet**. The reason for this distinction has to do with the source of the program and the environment in which it executes.

Traditionally, computer programs (the so-called **standalone programs**) have been stored and executed on the same computer. Your text editor is an example of such a standalone program. You have a copy of the program on your computer that you execute when you wish to edit a text file. Such standalone programs are called applications in Java terminology. An application is executed by your computer's operating system or virtual machine in the case of Java.

Modern reliance on the Internet has led to a second kind of program, often known as a **Web application**, which is called an applet in Java terminology. Applets are designed to be delivered not from your local computer, but rather across a network from a Web server. Unlike applications that are executed by your operating system, an applet is usually executed by a Web browser such as Internet Explorer, Firefox, Netscape Navigator, Mozilla, or Safari.

Executing a standalone program (i.e., a Java application) that is object-oriented presents something of a dilemma. If a program is a collection of communicating objects that can create other objects, who creates the first object? The answer to this question is the most interesting issue in describing how to create a Java application. However, before we can answer this question, there is an important Java concept that we need to understand—namely static declarations.

15.1 ■ static Variables

Not everything in a program is object-oriented, and not all libraries are associated with objects. The Math library is a good example of a library that is not object-oriented and does not require any objects, except parameters. If you look closely at the members (both variables and methods) of the Math class, you will discover that every member is static.

Members that are declared to be static are not really associated with any particular object. Instead, a static member belongs to a class. In fact, static variables and `static` methods are often called **class variables** and **class methods**, respectively. This is quite unlike nonstatic members that depend upon an object for their very existence.

The `Math` library class includes two **static variables**. The E and PI constants are declared within the `Math` class as shown below:

```
public final static double E = 2.7182818284590452354;
public final static double PI = 3.14159265358979323846;
```

Notice the syntax for declaring a `static` variable is to insert the `static` reserved word before the variable's type, as shown below:

ScopeQualifier `static` *VariableType VariableName*;

The following declarations illustrate.

```
public static int gamesHighScore;
static String textMessage;
```

Since `static` variables belong to classes, there is no need to instantiate any object in order to use a `static` variable. Furthermore, `static` variables can be referenced using the class name of the containing class in place of an object reference. This means that any external class can refer to the PI constant as

```
Math.PI
```

Understanding the difference between objects and classes is the key to understanding `static` variables. An object must be instantiated via a `new` expression before the object's instance variables actually exist. A class, on the other hand, exists from the time that it is first written—even before the program begins execution. Therefore, a program can refer to a `static` variable at any time. Additionally, there is no Java runtime mechanism for creating classes, like there is for creating objects. This means that there is only one class for a given name—and therefore only one set of `static` variables associated with that class. All of these properties mean that when a variable is declared as `static`, that variable exists throughout the execution of a program, and there cannot be a second variable from the same class with the same name.

Figures 15.1 and 15.2 illustrate the difference between `static` and non-`static` variables. Figure 15.1 contains a supplier class called `NonStat` and a segment of client code using `NonStat`. The object diagram in this figure illustrates the usual behavior of non-`static` instance variables. Each of the three objects (`non1`, `non2`, and `non3`) contain their own copy of the instance variable called `nonStatVar`. Each of these copies can be assigned independently.

Figure 15.2 contains an example that is almost the same as Figure 15.1, except that the supplier's non-`static` instance variable has been replaced by a `static` instance variable. The binding lines in the object diagram demonstrate that none of the objects (`stat1`, `stat2`, and `stat3`) contains its own copy of the `static` variable (`statVar`). Instead, all three objects share the same variable. Therefore, if the value of `statVar` is changed in one of the objects, then it is changed for all.

Figure 15.1

Creating objects containing non-static variables

Supplier class:

```java
public class NonStat {
    private int nonStatVar;
    public NonStat() { //The constructor method.
    }
}
```

Client code:

```java
NonStat non1, non2, non3;
non1 = new NonStat();
non2 = new NonStat();
non3 = new NonStat();
```

Object diagram after executing client code:

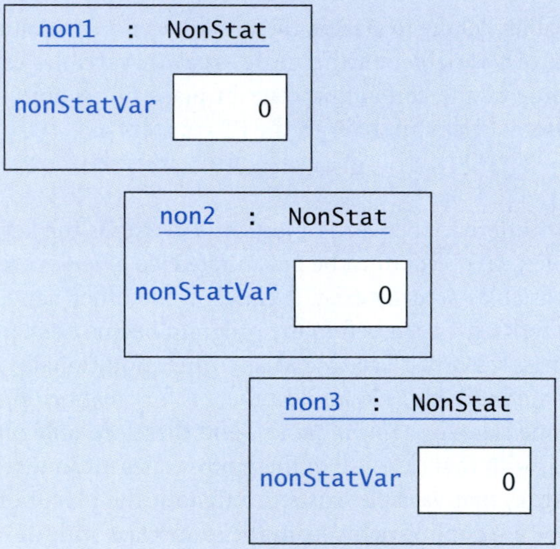

```
        non1  :  NonStat

     nonStatVar        0

             non2  :  NonStat

          nonStatVar        0

                  non3  :  NonStat

               nonStatVar        0
```

This example also shows another way to reference a `static` variable. Actually, there are three ways to reference `static` variables:

1. *ClassName .VarName* when *VarName* is the name of a `static` variable declared within the class called *ClassName*

2. *ObjRef.VarName*   when *ObjRef* is an expression referencing an object that belongs to a class containing a `static` variable called *VarName*

3. *VarName*   when *VarName* is the name of a static variable declared within the current scope

Supplier class:

```java
public class Stat {
    private static int statVar;
    public Stat() { //The constructor method.
    }
}
```

Client code:

```java
Stat stat1, stat2, stat3;
stat1 = new Stat();
stat2 = new Stat();
stat3 = new Stat();
```

Object diagram after executing client code:

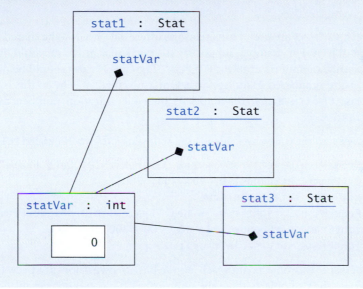

Figure 15.2

Creating objects containing static variables

The Label class from the *AWT* library implements three `static` constants: LEFT, CENTER, and RIGHT. A program causes a Label, called myLabel, to be centered within its bounding rectangle via the following instruction.

```java
myLabel.setAlignment(Label.CENTER);
```

Opening
the Black Box

Figure 15.3   JFrameWithID class

```
import javax.swing.JFrame;
/** This class is a version of JFrame that maintains its own ID number. */
public class JFrameWithID extends JFrame {
    private static int totalJFrameCount = 0;
    private int ID;

    public JFrameWithID(String s) {
        super(s + " -- #" + (totalJFrameCount+1));
        totalJFrameCount++;
        ID = totalJFrameCount;
    }
}
```

static variables are useful for situations where data needs to be shared among different objects. For example, suppose that a particular program would like to assign an identification number to each JFrame. The first JFrame should be numbered 1, the second numbered 2, and so forth. One convenient way to do this is to design a subclass of JFrame that maintains its own identification number, as shown in Figure 15.3.

Suppose that the following code is used to instantiate two JFrameWithID objects.

```
JFrameWithID leftFrame = new JFrameWithID("Left Frame");
leftFrame.setBounds(10, 10, 200, 200);
leftFrame.setVisible(true);
JFrameWithID rightFrame = new JFrameWithID("Right Frame");
rightFrame.setBounds(310, 10, 200, 200);
rightFrame.setVisible(true);
```

This creates two objects and each object has its own (non-static) ID variable. However, the two objects share the same totalJFrameCount variable. This shared variable is assigned the value 0 before either object is instantiated. When leftFrame is instantiated, totalJFrameCount is incremented to 1 and this value (1) is assigned to the ID variable of leftFrame. When rightFrame is instantiated, totalJFrameCount is incremented a second time to 2 and it (2) is assigned to rightFrame's ID.

software engineering *Hint*

The advantage implementing JFrameWithID using a static variable is that the task of maintaining unique ID numbers is encapsulated solely within the class—no other class needs to worry about keeping track of these numbers. This is particularly useful when JFrameWithID objects are created in multiple different classes, since none of these classes needs to worry about the responsibility.

While static variables provide an easy way to share data, they should be used with caution. Programmers *expect* that each object has its own variables, so the fact that a static variable is shared across all objects causes potential confusion. A good designer must weigh the options. For example, consider the possibility of creating self-adding Ovals, as suggested in Figure 15.4.

Figure 15.4   SelfAddingOvalBad class

```
/** Note that this class relies upon a specific kind of Driver class,
 * and is an inferior design than the original Oval class.
 * A better alternative is shown in Figure 15.5
 */
public class SelfAddingOvalBad extends Oval {

    /**pre:    The Driver class must include a public, static
     *         variable, called window, of type JFrame
     *         and window != null
     * post:   this is instantiated
     *         and getX() == x and getY() == y
     *         and getWidth() == w and getHeight() == h
     *         and getParent() == window.getContentPane()
     */
    public SelfAddingOvalBad(int x, int y, int w, int h) {
        super(x, y, w, h);
        Driver.window.add(this, 0);
        repaint();
    }
}
```

A SelfAddingOvalBad is an Oval that performs two additional tasks: it adds itself to the Driver's window and it repaints itself. The add instruction only works if (1) Driver includes a declaration of a variable called window, (2) the Driver's window variable is both static and public, and (3) the Driver's window variable has been previously assigned an instantiated JFrame. These restrictions are listed in the precondition of the SelfAddingOvalBad constructor.

One of the signs of strong software design is minimized dependencies between different classes. The SelfAddingOvalBad class depends more than necessary upon the Driver class. Furthermore, SelfAddingOvalBad lacks the flexibility to be initially adding to any JFrame except window. A better design is shown in Figure 15.5.

The SelfAddingOval class constructor includes an additional fifth parameter—win. This requires the code creating a SelfAddingOval to supply a JFrame argument, but it does not require that this argument be named window or be public and static. Additionally, it is not essential that the Driver class include such a variable. The price for the significant reduction in dependencies is one additional parameter.

software *Hint*
engineering

The SelfAddingOval constructor method shows two telltale signs of bad design: (1) excessive restrictions on constructor preconditions and (2) preconditions that rely too much on characteristics of another class.

software *Hint*
engineering

Even though using an additional parameter is preferable in SelfAddingOval, such is not always the case. Sometimes a program is written so that nearly all objects need access to the same variable. The cost of passing this shared variable as a parameter to numerous objects must be weighed against other dependencies associated with static variables. Sometimes using a static variable is better.

Figure 15.5

SelfAddingOval
class

```java
import javax.swing.JFrame;
public class SelfAddingOval extends Oval {

    /** pre:    win != null
     * post:   this is instantiated
     *         and getX() == x and getY() == y
     *         and getWidth() == w and getHeight() == h
     *         and getParent() == win.getContentPane()
     */
    public SelfAddingOval(int x, int y, int w, int h, JFrame win) {
        super(x, y, w, h);
        win.add(this, 0);
        repaint();
    }
}
```

The characteristics of a `static` variable can be combined with the characteristics of a `final` variable (constant) to form a **static constant**. A `static` variable declaration guarantees that there is just a single instance of the variable, but it fails to ensure that the binding to this variable cannot change. As a program executes, a `static` variable can be bound to different objects at different times. A `final` variable cannot be rebound. A `static final` variable has both properties—it has only one instance and is bound just once.

For example, the standard Java libraries include a class, called `System`. The `System` class has a `static final` variable called `out` that is bound to the standard output stream for your program. This is what makes it possible to execute an instruction such as the one below.

```java
System.out.println("Hello World!");
```

This notation calls a method named `println` upon the `out` variable, thereby writing the message to the standard output device—the same standard output device that is used by every other call to `System.out.println`.

As a second example of static constants, consider `java.awt.Color` class. The `Color` class declares `Color` constants using declarations like the following.

```java
public final static blue = new Color(0,0,255);
```

Such a declaration specifies `blue` as a `static` constant and assigns `blue` to the object returned by the `Color` constructor method. This initialization of `blue` will occur only once during a program's execution, so the `Color.blue` constant is shared throughout the program with the same object binding.

Suppose that a Java program assigns a blue color to an `Oval` with the following code.

```
Oval dot;
dot = new Oval(0, 0, 10, 10);
dot.setBackground(Color.blue);
```

A later test, such as the one below, tests for the same blue color:

```
if (dot.getBackground() == Color.blue) {...
```

Normally, checking for identity equality like this is dangerous for objects. In this case, there is no danger because a static color constant is only instantiated once (any reference to `Color.blue` refers to the same *variable*) and because color constants cannot change their binding (any reference to `Color.blue` refers to the same *object*).

Opening
the Black Box

The `Color` class from the *AWT* library uses `static` constants for 13 predefined colors.

```
public final static Color black = new Color(0,0,0);
public final static Color blue = new Color(0,0,255);
public final static Color cyan = new Color(0,255,255);
public final static Color darkGray = new Color(64,64,64);
public final static Color gray = new Color(128,128,128);
public final static Color green = new Color(0,255,0);
public final static Color lightGray = new
    Color(192,192,192);
public final static Color magenta = new Color(255,0,255);
public final static Color orange = new Color(255,200,0);
public final static Color pink = new Color(255,175,175);
public final static Color red = new Color(255,0,0);
public final static Color white = new Color(255,255,255);
public final static Color yellow = new Color(255,255,0);
```

The `Color` constructor method specifies, respectively, the amount of redness, greenness, and blueness (255 is the maximum intensity of each color).

Because they are `static`, each of these constants can be referenced using the `Color` class name, as illustrated below.

```
Color.black
```

15.2 ■ static Methods

Methods can be declared `static` in the same way as variables. The syntax for declaring a **static method** is the same as any other method with the exception of the inclusion of the `static` reserved word between the scope identifier (either `private`, `protected`, or `public`) and the method's return type.

```
private static TypeName methodName (. . . )
```

A `static` method, just like a `static` variable, is associated with the class in which it is declared and it does not rely upon the creation of objects. This can be particularly useful for nonvoid methods that are not applied to an object. Such methods are sometimes called **pure functions** because, like a mathematical function, they return the result of some calculation that is based solely upon their parameters. The square root function (`Math.sqrt`) is a pure function. A `double` argument is passed to the square root method and it returns the square root of this value without the need for any object except the argument. In fact, every method within the `Math` class is a pure function and so each one is declared as a `static` method.

Opening **the Black Box**

The `Math` class contains many `static` methods. A sample of these methods is listed below:

```
public static double abs(double num)
public static int    abs(int num)
public static double cos(double num)
public static double pow(double b, double exp)
public static double random()
public static int    round(float b)
public static long   round(double b)
public static double sin(double num)
public static double sqrt(double num)
public static double tan(double num)
```

Since these methods are all static methods, there is no need to instantiate an object of type `Math`. To invoke a method you need only to prefix the method name with the class name. This is why the following instruction is valid.

```
double rand = Math.random();
```

software **engineering** *Hint*

static methods are best avoided except for rare cases. One good use for static methods is for methods that return values based solely upon primitive-type.

static methods have one major disadvantage—the body of a `static` method is prohibited from referencing any non-`static` instance method or non-`static` instance variable. This restriction is imposed because, unlike non-`static` methods, `static` members do not involve a `this` object. If the `this` object does not exist, then its instance variables do not exist nor can its instance methods be invoked. Note that the inability of a `static` method to utilize non-`static` instance variables does *not* prohibit a `static` method from constructing and manipulating *local* non-`static` objects, as will be demonstrated in the next section.

15.3 ■ Applications

Java follows the tradition of programming languages like C and C++ that use one particular `static` method as the predefined starting point for program execution. Every Java application begins its execution with a method called `main`. Furthermore, the `main` method *must* be `static` and `void` and it is required to have an array of `String` for a parameter list. Figure 15.6 contains a very simple example.

The Hello World program is designed as a Java application to print a one-line message. When the application executes, it "magically" calls the `main` method, which in turn executes a `println` method on the `System.out` `static` variable.

Once you have compiled the Hello World program how can you test its execution? In order to execute the Hello World program from a command line, you must first set the current directory[1] to the folder that contains *HelloWorld.class*. The command to execute a Java program is the word *java* followed by the class name. The Hello World application is executed by the following command.

```
java HelloWorld
```

Another way to execute a Java application is to build an application bundle. Application bundles have icons that can be double-clicked from the desktop or executed from a menu. Unfortunately, every operating system is unique in the way that it handles the desktop, desktop icons, and executables. Therefore, there is no one single way to construct an application bundle.

If you are building an application bundle for OS X, then you need to execute a software tool called *Jar Bundler*. (The Jar Bundler tool is located within the system's Developer/Applications/JavaTools folder.) Jar Bundler provides a graphical interface to assist the user in building the bundle. The user must include all of the nonstandard *.class* files and select an icon for the bundle. There are tools similar to Jar Bundler that can be purchased for other operating systems. It is not practical to discuss any single such commercial product.

One tool included in the standard Java development kit deserves mention—namely the **jar files**. The word *jar* stands for *Java Archive*. A jar file is a single file that contains a complete Java application or applet and is, at the same time, stored in a com-

```
public class HelloWorld {
    public static void main(String[] args) {
        System.out.println("Hello World!");
    }
}
```

Figure 15.6

Hello World Program

---

1. Files, folders, and establishing the current directory are explained in Section 13.1.

pressed format. If a jar file is stored as an application,[2] then it can be executed by a double-click in most operating systems. The four steps that are necessary to build such an application jar file are shown below:

1. Compile all files into *.class* files within the same folder. (One of these, call it *mainClass.class*, must contain the `static` void `main` method for the application.)

2. Within the same folder used in Step 1 create a text file, call it *manifest.mf*, to serve as the manifest. This file needs only to contain the following single line. (You can use a text editor to create this file.)

   `Main-Class:` *mainClass*

   Note that *mainClass* should be replaced by the actual name of the class (without *.class* suffix) as described in Step 1. Note also that the file's line must be terminated with an end of line (usually inserted by striking the *return* key at the end of the line while editing).

3. Within a command line or shell set the current directory to match the folder used in Step 1.

4. Type the following command, where *manifest.mf* must match the name of the manifest file and *my.jar* is the name you wish to use for the resulting jar file.

   `jar cmf` *manifest.mf my.jar* `*.class`

The Hello World program demonstrates how to build an application, but it uses only static methods and variables. A second application, one that instantiates objects, is shown in Figure 15.7.

This second version of the Hello World program creates three objects: `window`, `dot`, and `helloMsg`. The key point to notice is that all three are declared as local variables.

Opening **the Black Box**

The primary reason for naming the initial class `Driver` is to allow for convenient conversion to a Java application. All that is needed is a separate `run` class, as shown below. To start the application's execution, use the command `java run`. This class contains a `main` method that performs just one task—instantiate a `Driver` object, calling the `Driver` constructor.

run.java:

```java
public class run {
    public static void main(String args[]) {
        Driver driver = new Driver();
    }
}
```

---

2. When a jar file executes, it uses the system console for its standard output device. This means that `System.out.println` output can only be viewed by identifying the operating system tool that displays the console.

Figure 15.7

Hello World
program with
objects

```
/** This program adds a Hello World message to a filled green
 *      oval in the center of a JFrame.
 */
import javax.swing.JFrame;
import java.awt.*;
public class HelloRevisited {
    public static void main(String[] args) {
        JFrame window = new JFrame("Hello World");
        window.setBounds(10, 10, 400, 400);
        window.setVisible(true);
        window.setLayout(null);
        Oval dot = new Oval(100, 100, 200, 200);
        dot.setBackground(Color.green);
        dot.repaint();
        window.add(dot, 0);
        Label helloMsg = new Label("Hello World!");
        helloMsg.setBounds(20, 85, 160, 30);
        helloMsg.setAlignment(Label.CENTER);
        helloMsg.repaint();
        dot.add(helloMsg, 0);
        window.repaint();
    }
}
```

Local objects are acceptable within a `static` method, even though instance variables are not. In other words, the program would no longer be correct if `window`, `dot`, and/or `helloMsg` were declared as instance variables.

To construct a jar file for the Hello World program from Figure 15.7 you would begin by gathering the two compiled classes `HelloRevisited.class` and `Oval.class` in the same folder. Next, use an editor to create a file called *HELLO.MF* as shown below.

HELLO.MF

```
Main-class: HelloRevisited
```

The `HELLO.MF` file must be located within the class file folder. The command used to build the final jar file is as follows. (This command will create a new jar file called *runHello.jar*.)

```
jar cmf HELLO.MF runHello.jar *.class
```

15.4 ■ **Applets**

One of the design principles of Java is to support programs that are delivered by the Internet. The kind of program that Java designers chose to deliver software through a network is called an **applet**. A properly written applet can be executed by any Java-enabled Web browser.

The requirements for building an applet are as follows:

■ A class that conforms to `Applet` or `JApplet`

■ An HTML (Web page) file to invoke the applet's execution

`JApplet` is a class that is part of the standard *Swing* library. The purpose of `JApplet` is to serve as a superclass for building applets. Figure 15.8 shows a class diagram for `JApplet`.

Browsers utilize five predefined parameterless methods to control the execution of an applet: `JApplet` (the constructor), `init`, `start`, `stop`, and `destroy`. The non-constructor methods have no behavior, so they are included for subclasses to over-ride. These methods are called automatically by Web browsers. Sun's documentation describes their use as follows:

■ `init`   "called . . . to inform this applet that it has been loaded into the system."

■ `start`   "called . . . to inform this applet that it should start its execution."

■ `stop`   "called . . . to inform this applet that it should stop its execution."

■ `destroy` "called . . . to inform this applet that it is being reclaimed and should destroy any resources it has allocated."

Figure 15.8

JApplet class diagram

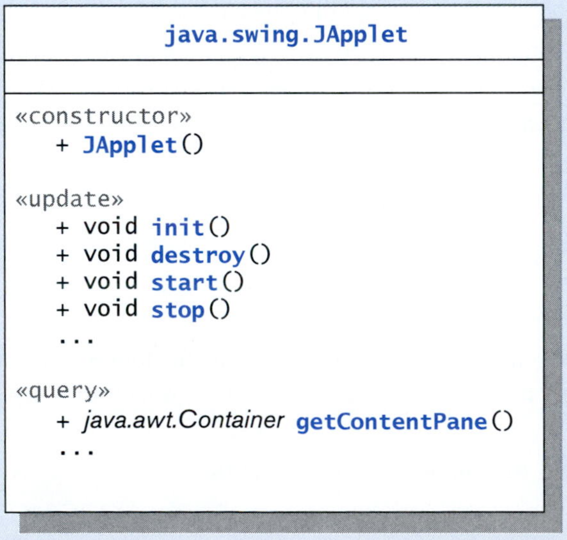

```
               java.swing.JApplet
────────────────────────────────────────────────

«constructor»
    + JApplet()

«update»
    + void init()
    + void destroy()
    + void start()
    + void stop()
    . . .

«query»
    + java.awt.Container getContentPane()
    . . .
```

In practice, most Web browsers call methods in the indicated sequence for each of the Web browser functions, as listed below:

software **engineering** *Hint*

For `JApplet` subclasses it is technically best to locate initialization code, such as the instantiation of instance variables, within the subclass constructor and place other executable code within the `start()` method. However, most browsers execute both methods so this text takes the simpler approach of locating all code within the constructor.

- **Initial Applet load** (by accessing the proper Web page for the first time)

  JApplet() → init() → start()

- **Selecting a different Web page** (by entering a new URL or back button with an active applet)

  stop() → destroy()

- **Clicking the reload button** (with an active applet)

  stop() → destroy() → JApplet() → init() → start()

As you can see, Web browsers do not typically take advantage of all of the possibilities that the Java designers had intended. For this reason, you can write most Java applets by locating your code within a constructor. Since the `JApplet` method is called every time that a subclass constructor is called, creating a Java applet consists of creating a class that inherits `JApplet` and supplies a constructor.

software **engineering** *Hint*

It is better to use local variables than instance variables within a constructor method of a `JApplet` subclass. This avoids potential "leftover" objects.

Figure 15.9 shows a version of the Hello World program written as an applet. Note that the `HelloApplet` class inherits `JApplet`, and all code is located within the `HelloApplet` constructor.

You should also notice that `HelloApplet` does not contain a `JFrame` object, like the earlier `HelloRevisited` application. This is because every `JApplet` has its own built-

```java
import javax.swing.JApplet;
import java.awt.*;
public class HelloApplet extends JApplet {
    public HelloApplet() {
        super();
        setLayout(null);
        Oval dot = new Oval(100, 100, 200, 200);
        dot.setBackground(Color.green);
        dot.repaint();
        add(dot, 0);
        Label helloMsg = new JLabel("Hello World!");
        helloMsg.setBounds(20, 85, 160, 30);
        helloMsg.setAlignment(Label.CENTER);
        helloMsg.repaint();
        dot.add(helloMsg, 0);
        repaint();
    }
}
```

Figure 15.9

HelloApplet class

in JFrame. As a result, subclasses of JApplet can apply methods to this that would normally be applied to a JFrame. Evidence of this is visible in the instructions such as

```
setLayout(null);
```

which causes the HelloApplet's content pane to use a null layout manager. Similarly, the following instruction adds the dot (Oval) object to HelloApplet's JFrame.

```
add(dot, 0);
```

The reason that JApplet incorporates JFrame and applications do not is that applets are designed to be executed by a Web browser and every Web browser incorporates a visible window to display Web pages. The JApplet's JFrame is expected to occupy a region within the Web browser window. This does not mean that a JApplet is prohibited from instantiating additional JFrame objects (commonly known as popup windows) to be displayed outside the browser window, but it does allow an applet to display things within the browser window.

Just like an application, you cannot execute an applet unless it has first been compiled and is grouped in the same folder together with other associated nonstandard classes. The HelloApplet class must be compiled and the resulting *HelloApplet.class* file should be grouped in the same folder as *Oval.class* to prepare for execution. Once a folder has been prepared, there are two ways to initiate the execution of an applet that will be discussed here: (1) executing an applet from a Web browser and (2) executing an applet from a command line.

Internet Web browsers display information in the form of **Web pages**. Web pages are generally stored as text files using a notation called **hypertext markup language** or **HTML**. This notation is the reason that Web pages are also referred to as **HTML files**. HTML files are named with a suffix of *.html* (or sometimes *.htm*). A Web browser that is fully configured to run Java applets will run the example applet by opening the associated page, call it *helloPage.html*. (This is usually accomplished by double-clicking the HTML file.)

A complete discussion of HTML files is outside the range of this book. All that you really need to know for executing Java applets is that a text file like the one in Figure 15.10 will work for any applet by changing the three parts highlighted in blue. You supply the name of your applet class replacing *HelloApplet.class*, and supply values for the initial applet container dimensions replacing the two *400* strings. (The title can also be updated, but even that is not essential.) The resulting HTML file should be stored in the same folder as your applet and related classes.

Executing your applet with a Web browser requires only that you open the HTML file (e.g., *helloPage.html*) with the browser. Often this is accomplished by double-clicking *helloPage.html*.

The Java distribution also includes a tool for executing applets directly from a command line. This tool also requires the use of an HTML file. Assuming that the cur-

```
<HTML>
<HEAD>
    <TITLE>Hello World Applet</TITLE>
</HEAD>
<BODY>
    <APPLET CODE="HelloApplet.class"
        WIDTH=400
        HEIGHT=400
        CODEBASE="." >
    </APPLET>
</BODY>
</HTML>
```

Figure 15.10

helloPage.html file

rent directory is set to the folder containing the applet along with the HTML file, the following command will initiate applet execution.

```
appletviewer helloPage.html
```

As a second example, consider an applet to simulate the sun's rising. This program is designed to show the sun's rising within the JApplet window and use a separate JFrame for a button to start the sunrise. Figure 15.11 shows the code for the applet (GrowingDot) and a separate class to implement the button and its JFrame.

This program demonstrates that applets can use external windows, like any other Java program. In this case, ButtonFrame inherits JFrame to display a window, separate from the JApplet. When the program executes both windows will appear, and both will disappear when the applet terminates. In order to execute this program, you need to compile GrowingDot, ButtonFrame, along with Oval. The resulting files—*GrowingDot.class*, *ButtonFrame.class*, and *Oval.class*—should be gathered into the same folder, along with an HTML file, such as *sunrise.html* from Figure 15.12.

The run class (from the previous section) is a universal way to turn programs from this book into Java applications. Similarly, we can write a different class, call it AppletRun, that is a universal way to turn book programs into Java applets. Figure 15.13 illustrates.

15.5 ■ Creating Packages (Optional)

The collection of related library classes that are available in a programming environment is called an **Application Programming Interface** or **API**. The complete API of a Java system includes all of the library classes that are available.

Figure 15.11   GrowingDot and associated ButtonFrame classes

```java
import java.awt.Color;
import java.awt.event.*;
import javax.swing.*;
/** Class Invariant:
 *      redDot.getWidth() == redDot.getHeight()
 *      and redDot.getX() == 100 - redDot.getWidth()/2
 *      and redDot.getY() == 100 - redDot.getHeight()/2
 */
public class GrowingDot extends JApplet implements ActionListener {
    private Oval redDot;
    private Timer clock;
    private ButtonFrame startBtn;
    private int darkness;

    /** post:  redDot is added on this
     *         and startBtn != null
     *         and this is colored black
     *         and clock is scheduled for 0.1 sec. repeated events
     */
    public GrowingDot() {
        setLayout(null);
        redDot = new Oval(98, 98, 4, 4);
        redDot.setBackground(Color.red);
        add(redDot);
        clock = new Timer(100, this);
        clock.setRepeats(true);
        startBtn = new ButtonFrame(clock);
        darkness = 0;
        setBackground(new Color(darkness, darkness, darkness));
    }

    /** pre:   redDot != null
     * post:   (redDot@pre.getWidth() == 200) implies
     *             redDot is resized to 4 by 4 and this recolored to black
     *         and (redDot@pre.getWidth() != 200) implies
     *             (redDot resize to 2 by 2 larger than redDot@pre
     *             and this is recolored whiter)
     */
    public void actionPerformed(ActionEvent e) {
        if (redDot.getWidth() == 200) {
            redDot.setSize(4, 4);
```

```java
            redDot.setLocation(98, 98);
            darkness = 0;
            setBackground(new Color(darkness, darkness, darkness));
            clock.stop();
        } else {
            redDot.setSize(redDot.getWidth()+2, redDot.getHeight()+2);
            redDot.setLocation(100-redDot.getWidth()/2,
                100-redDot.getHeight()/2);
            darkness = darkness + 5;
            if (darkness > 255)
                darkness = 255;
            setBackground(new Color(darkness, darkness, darkness));
        }
        redDot.repaint();
        repaint();
    }
}

import javax.swing.*;
import java.awt.event.*;
public class ButtonFrame extends JFrame implements ActionListener {
    private Timer theTimer;

    /** post: theTimer == t */
    public ButtonFrame(Timer t) {
        super("");
        setBounds(100, 100, 200, 80);
        setVisible(true);
        setLayout(null);
        JButton btn = new JButton("Start Sunrise");
        btn.setBounds(10, 10, 180, 30);
        btn.addActionListener(this);
        add(btn, 0);
        repaint();
        theTimer = t;
    }

    public void actionPerformed(ActionEvent e) {
        theTimer.start();
    }
}
```

Figure 15.12

sunrise.html file

```
<HTML>
<HEAD>
    <TITLE>Sunrise Applet</TITLE>
</HEAD>
<BODY>
    <APPLET CODE="GrowingDot.class"
        WIDTH=200
        HEIGHT=100
        CODEBASE="." >
    </APPLET>
</BODY>
</HTML>
```

Figure 15.13

appletRun
class and
associated
run.html

```
import javax.swing.JApplet;
public class AppletRun extends JApplet {
    public void AppletRun() {
        Driver Driver = new Driver();
    }
}
```

run.html:

```
<HTML>
<HEAD>
    <TITLE>Universal HTML for Driver applets </TITLE>
</HEAD>
<BODY>
    <APPLET CODE="Driver.class"
        WIDTH=100
        HEIGHT=100
        CODEBASE="." >
    </APPLET>
</BODY>
</HTML>
```

The Java API is further subdivided into **packages**, where each package is a group of related classes. Some packages, like *AWT* and *Swing*, are standard to all current Java systems. Other packages are provided by other vendors. Figure 15.14 shows a few of the packages that are part of the standard Java API. Selected classes from several of these packages have been used in earlier examples of this text.

Java provides the tools to permit programmers to build their own packages. Creating a new package begins by placing the source code for all of the package's classes (i.e.,

Package	Purpose
java.lang	Includes wrapper classes and System, String, Object
java.util	Includes classes for building containers, dates, etc.
java.applet	Includes Applet
java.io	Includes classes for file manipulation
java.net	Includes classes to support Internet communication
java.awt	Includes graphical user interface classes
java.awt.event	Includes various event handling classes
javax.swing	Includes graphical user interface classes

Figure 15.14

A partial list of packages from the standard Java API

the *.java* files) into a single folder. Each of these classes must be edited to insert a **package declaration** containing the name for the package. Figure 15.15 shows the syntax for a package declaration.

Suppose that the Java library of an international bank includes software classes for currency for individual nations: Dollar for United States currency, Euro for European currency, Yen for Japanese currency, etc. These different monetary classes can be grouped into a single package called money by performing the following three steps.

Step 1:

Include the following package declaration in every class to be included in the package.

```
package money;
```

Figure 15.16 sketches the skeleton of the three classes for the different money types.

Step 2:

Place all of the source files within a single folder. For this example, suppose that the folder is called *MoneyPackage*. Figure 15.17 pictures the file directory hierarchy at this stage for the three money files.

Step 3:

Compile all of the files in the *MoneyPackage* folder. The proper shell command to compile this package is as follows. (This must be typed in a windows command prompt or Unix shell with *MoneyPackage* as the current directory.)

```
javac -d . *.java
```

This will create a new folder within *MoneyPackage* that stores the compiled code (i.e., the *.class* files.) Figure 15.18 illustrates.

> **software engineering** *Hint*
>
> The Java compiler allows any combination of classes to be included in a package. It is up to the programmer to group classes that are logically related to one another.

Figure 15.15 *PackageDeclaration* description

Syntax

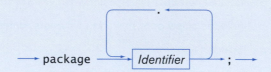

Notes

- If included, a *PackageDeclaration* is the first noncomment, nonblank line in the class file. (This declaration precedes the "class" line.)
- There may be no more than one *PackageDeclaration* per file.

Semantics

- Following their compilation, the class(es) within the file containing a *PackageDeclaration* become part of the package.
- The name of the package is formed by the *Identifiers* used in the declaration. For example, `package A.B;` specifies that the class(es) of the file should be compiled into a package called "A.B".
- The *.class* files of the package that result from compilation will be placed into a folder with the same name as the package. To ensure such placement the following command should be used in the Windows command prompt or Unix shell: `javac -d . *.java`
- Compiling a file with the declaration, `package A.B;` places the resulting *.class* file(s) into a folder called "B" that is within a folder called "A".

Figure 15.16

Three source files of the money package

Dollar.java file:

```
package money;
public class Dollar {
    /* innards omitted
}
```

Euro.java file:

```
package money;
public class Euro {
    /* innards omitted
}
```

Yen.java file:

```
package money;
public class Yen {
    /* innards omitted
}
```

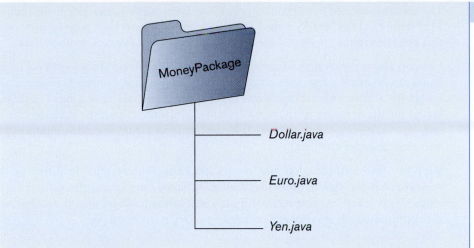

Figure 15.17

The *MoneyPackage* folder prior to compilation

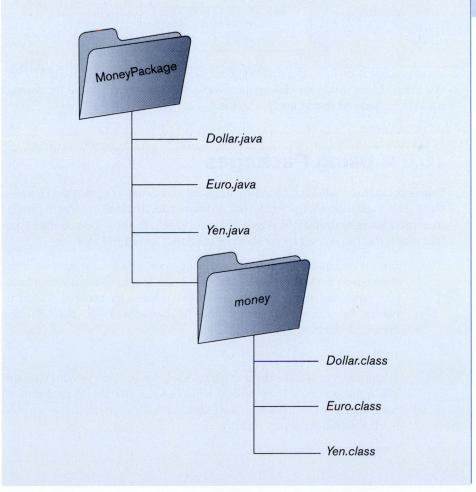

Figure 15.18

The *MoneyPackage* folder following compilation

The classes examined throughout this text have been *public classes*. The word "public" before "class" marks a class as public. Public classes, like public methods and public variables, have a scope that makes them available to any other class.

Java also allows the creation of classes that have **package scope**. A class with package scope can be used by any other class from the same package, but nowhere else. The syntax for a class with package scope is identical to the syntax of a public class, except for the omission of the word "public" from the class line. (Package scope may also be applied to instance variables and methods, using the same notation of omitting the scope qualifier.)

Suppose, for example, that the *money* package requires the facilities of a MoneyExchanger class in order to calculate exchange rates among the various currencies. If it is best to encapsulate this class within the package, then the following file appropriately defines MoneyExchanger to have package scope.

MoneyExchanger.java file:

```
package money;
class MoneyExchanger {
    /* innards omitted
}
```

Package scope is useful in this situation because MoneyExchanger is needed by several other classes within the class and nowhere else. However, the need for package scope is limited and should not be overused.

15.6 ■ Using Packages

Once a package is created and compiled, its public classes become available. However, client classes and subclasses generally include **import declarations** in order to provide reasonable access to the public classes of the packages. An import declaration specifies classes that can be used by the client or subclass. Figure 15.19 explains.

software *Hint*
engineering

Technically, an import declaration is unnecessary if the full path name (using period separators) is included for references to features from some external class. However, import declarations should always be included to send a clear signal of class interdependencies.

Import declarations denote classes using a syntax that is essentially a file system path name. The names of classes being imported begin with a package name and proceed using periods as separators between folder/file names. For example, to import the Dollar.class file, the following import declaration is used.

```
import money.Dollar;
```

Frequently, a class is the client of many other classes from the same package. When this occurs, it is convenient to include an asterisk (*) to denote all matching names. For example, the following declaration imports *every* public class within the *money* package.

```
import money.*;
```

Figure 15.19 *ImportDeclaration* description

Syntax

Notes

- If included, an *ImportDeclaration* must follow any *PackageDeclaration* and precede the "class" line.
- There may be several *ImportDeclarations* per file.
- The *java.lang* package is automatically available without import.

Semantics

- The notation of Identifiers with period separators refers to file folders. For example,

      import A.B;

  specifies that the class called "B.class" is to be imported from a folder called "A".
- The naming of a class to be imported begins with the name of the folder that contains the package.
- An asterisk (*) signifies that all possible identifiers should be included.

The standard Java API package, called *java.lang*, is imported by default. This one package can be used without an import declaration. The *java.lang* package includes, among other classes, the following:

```
System
String
Object
```

This explains why these classes are always accessible, but never imported.

Opening
the Black Box

Import declarations work properly only if the Java system performing the compile and/or executing the program knows where to search for the packages. Most Java systems use a system variable called **CLASSPATH** for this purpose.

Inspector

Below is a collection of hints on what to check when examining code that involves the concepts of this chapter.

■ `static` methods and `static` variables should be eliminated whenever possible. Public, non-`final` `static` variables are especially risky. If an alternative exists to `static`, it should be given serious consideration.

■ When creating packages, all classes of the package must include the package declaration and it must be the first noncomment line of the file.

■ The *.class* files stored within a package are available only when the client class includes a proper import declaration.

Terminology

applet	package
appletviewer	package declaration
application	package scope
class library	pure function
class method	standalone program
class variable	`static` constant
CLASSPATH	`static` method
Hypertext Markup Language (HTML)	`static` variable
import declaration	Web application
main (method)	Web page

Exercises

1. Suppose that the first line of some class is as follows:

```
package MyPackage;
```

Further, suppose that the CLASSPATH variable includes the following reference that is intended to include the package for the class mentioned above:

```
/Java/Library
```

a. In what folder should the *.class* file for this class be placed?

b. Where in the directory system should this folder be located?

2. Suppose that you are creating a new class, call Blob. A Blob object is a three-dimensional object that can be added to the content pane of a JFrame. Each of the methods below is being considered for inclusion within the Blob class. Which of the following are suitable candidates for static methods and which must be non-static?

a. A parameterless method that returns the volume of the this Blob.

```
private static double volume() { ... }
```

b. A method that is passed a Blob parameter and returns its volume.

```
private static double volume(Blob b) { ... }
```

c. A method that is passed two Blob parameters and returns the one with greater volume.

```
private static double biggerBlob(Blob b1, Blob b2) { ... }
```

d. A method to recolor a Blob.

```
private static void recolor(Color c) { ... }
```

e. An equals method to compare the this Blob to another Blob passed as a parameter.

```
private static boolean equals(Blob b) { ... }
```

3. Suppose that a Java application is written without the use of the run class. Instead, the application will begin executing from a class called TestApplication, shown in part below:

```
public class TestApplication {
    private static Oval squirrel;
    private Oval moose;
    public static void main(String args[]) {
        //code goes here
    }
}
```

Which of the following code segments can validly be located in place of //code goes here and which will cause compile-time errors?

a. squirrel = new Oval(10, 10, 50, 50);

b. moose = new Oval(10, 10, 50, 50);

c. Oval localSquirrel = new Oval(10, 10, 50, 50);

d. static Oval localSquirrel = new Oval(10, 10, 50, 50);

4. Consider the following class:

```
public class ThreeSquares {
   public Rectangle square1 = new Rectangle(0, 0, 10, 10);
   public static Rectangle square2 = new
      Rectangle(0,0,10,10);
   public static final Rectangle square3 = new
      Rectangle(0,0,1,1);
   public static void ThreeSquares() {
      square2 = new Rectangle(0, 0, 100, 100);
   }
}
```

For each part that follows, identify whether or not the code is syntactically correct. If it is incorrect, then why? If it is correct, show what values are output when this code executes.

a. `System.out.println(ThreeSquares.square1.getWidth());`

b. `System.out.println(ThreeSquares.square2.getWidth());`
   `System.out.println(ThreeSquares.square3.getWidth());`

c. `ThreeSquares squarePair;`
   `squarePair = new ThreeSquares();`
   `System.out.println(squarePair.square1.getWidth());`
   `System.out.println(squarePair.square2.getWidth());`
   `System.out.println(squarePair.square3.getWidth());`

d. `ThreeSquares squarePair;`
   `squarePair = new ThreeSquares();`
   `squarePair.square3 = new Rectangle(0, 0, 200, 200);`
   `System.out.println(squarePair.square1.getWidth());`

e. `ThreeSquares squarePairA, squarePairB;`
   `squarePairA = new ThreeSquares();`
   `squarePairB = new ThreeSquares();`
   `squarePairB.square1 = new Rectangle(0, 0, 200, 200);`
   `squarePairB.square2 = new Rectangle(0, 0, 2000, 2000);`
   `System.out.println(squarePairA.square1.getWidth());`
   `System.out.println(squarePairA.square2.getWidth());`
   `System.out.println(squarePairB.square1.getWidth());`
   `System.out.println(squarePairB.square3.getWidth());`

5. Which of the following parts output the message "Same color" when executed?

a. `Color lightColor, whiteColor;`
   `lightColor = Color.white;`
   `whiteColor = Color.white;`
   `if (lightColor == whiteColor) {`
   `   System.out.println("Same color");`
   `}`

b.
```
Color lightColor, whiteColor;
lightColor = new Color(0, 0, 0);
whiteColor = new Color(0, 0, 0);
if (lightColor == whiteColor) {
    System.out.println("Same color");
}
```

c.
```
Color lightColor, whiteColor;
lightColor = Color.white;
whiteColor = new Color(0, 0, 0);
if (lightColor == whiteColor) {
    System.out.println("Same color");
}
```

d.
```
Color lightColor, whiteColor;
lightColor = new Color(0, 0, 0);
whiteColor = lightColor;
if (lightColor == whiteColor) {
    System.out.println("Same color");
}
```

Introduction to Computing Systems

Objectives

- To introduce the basic hardware components of a computer
- To examine the difference between digital and analog devices as an explanation for some of the behavior of digital computers
- To explore the fundamentals of bit strings and binary numbers, as used by computers to represent information
- To relate common terminology used to measure computer memory size and computer speed
- To introduce basic networking techniques and terminologies

*T*oday's computers are sophisticated devices. Even an ordinary home computer is capable of executing millions of instructions per second, storing billions of individual pieces of data, and transferring messages throughout the world in a fraction of a second. Appendix A provides a glimpse of some of the fundamental issues of computing systems that make this possible.

A.1 ■ What Is a Computer?

Technically, any device that performs automated calculations can be called a **computer**. Computers are embedded in everything from cameras to automobiles and are frequently hidden from sight. However, when most people use the word "computer," they usually refer to a separate, visible, machine. The most common such computer is called a **personal computer** because it serves a single person.

Computers have four basic hardware components.

- I/O devices
- main memory
- central processing unit
- secondary storage

The first things that most people notice about a computer are the I/O devices. I/O is an abbreviation for input/output, and an I/O device is anything that is intended to get information into or out of a computer. Most I/O devices are designed to interact with humans. The most obvious I/O devices on personal computers are **keyboards, mice, printers,** and **computer monitors** (also called **computer displays**), as shown in Figure A.1.

Less obvious than the I/O devices is the box that contains the innards of the computer, often referred to as the **system unit** (see Figure A.1). Inside the system unit are the main memory and the central processing unit of the computer. Main memory is the part of the computer that stores data while it is being processed. Section A.3 examines the basics of computer storage.

The central processing unit (**CPU** or **processor**) is the computational part of the computer. Some of the common brand names for current processors include the Athalon, Celeron, Itanium, Pentium IV, PowerPC G5, and Xenon. Processors are measured primarily in terms of their **clock speed**. The processor's clock is an inter-

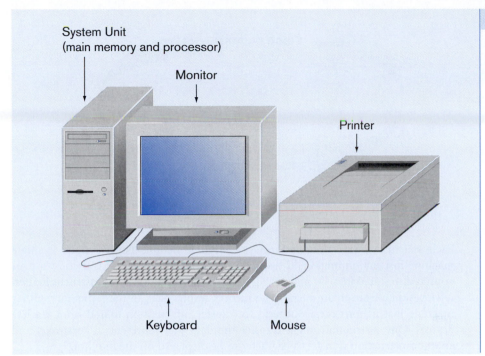

Figure A.1

Parts of a typical personal computer

nal device that regulates the speed at which the processor functions. Generally, a computer with a higher clock speed is faster than one with a lower clock speed. Clock speeds for computers in 2005 are typically in the range from 800 MHz to 5 GHz.

"Mhz" stands for a measure of frequency known as **megahertz**. One megahertz is equal to one million cycles per second, so a 500 MHz clock "ticks" a half billion times per second. Around the year 2000, many personal computer processors passed into the **gigahertz** (GHz) range. One gigahertz is one billion cycles per second. Computer processor speeds continue to double approximately every 18 months.

When the computer is turned on, its processor begins to execute instruction after instruction in what is known as the **fetch-execute cycle** (see Figure A.2). Conceptually, the CPU fetches an instruction from main memory, and then it executes that instruction. Next, the CPU fetches another instruction and the process repeats.

The instructions that are fetched from main memory constitute the **program** that is being executed. These instructions are called **machine language** because they are in a form that is conveniently decoded by the machine (i.e., the CPU). CPUs cannot usually execute one machine instruction per clock. However, the exact number of instructions that are executed per second is difficult to measure because this rate depends upon the speed of main memory, the processor's ability to overlap the execution of multiple instructions, and the task performed by each particular instruction.

Figure A.2

The fetch-execute cycle

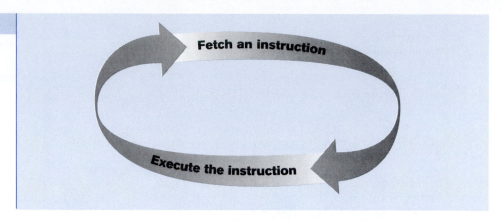

Each machine instruction performs a simple function. For example, a single machine instruction might add two pieces of data. The data that is used by a program is also stored in main memory. Therefore, the execution of an instruction often retrieves data from main memory and stores results back in main memory. Other machine instructions carry out tasks to transfer information to and from the I/O devices. One instruction might transfer the data that represents a keystroke, and another instruction transfers a character to be displayed on the monitor.

The dual usage of main memory to store both program instructions and data is called the **von Neumann architecture**. This is named after John von Neumann who developed the concept in the 1940s.

Data stored in main memory is transient. Before a program begins to execute, both the instructions and the data for the program must be placed (loaded) into memory. Since there is only one main memory, it must be reused. A newly executing program is frequently loaded into memory space made available from an earlier program that has completed. This means that a program should consider everything it stores in main memory to be lost once its execution is finished. A second way in which main memory is transient is that it is usually built using technologies that erase when the current is shut off. This transient nature of data stored in main memory is the reason why computers generally include more permanent storage, called **secondary storage**.

Data stored on secondary storage can be maintained indefinitely. Many secondary storage devices have removable media that can be transported from one computer to another.

A secondary storage device is often named after its media. For example, a floppy disk drive uses floppy disks for a storage media. Other common forms of secondary storage media include the following.

- **hard disks** (the primary storage for large files and programs integral to computer operation)
- **floppy disks** (removable magnetic disks approximately 3.5 inches square)

- **compact disks (CDs)** (plastic disks storing information as reflective/nonreflective dots)
- **DVDs** (CD-like medium with greater capacity)
- **magnetic tapes** (ribbons of magnetically coated plastic)
- **flash memory** (computer memory chip packaged to plug into a USB or PCI computer slot)

Sometimes the same basic technology has variations. A **CD-ROM** device is capable of playing data that has been previously stored on a CD. However, a CD-ROM cannot write new data to CDs. The acronym "ROM" represents "read only memory," which means that the CPU is restricted to reading from the CD. A different form of secondary storage, known as **CD-RW,** can both retrieve data from a CD and store (burn) new data onto the CD. The "RW" symbols stand for "read" (retrieve data) and "write" (store new data).

A.2 ■ Analog or Digital?

Most of today's computers are **digital computers**, although certain special-purpose nondigital (**analog**) computers exist. Many aspects of computer behavior are defined by its digital nature.

Analog devices are based on continuously varying systems, while digital devices support only a fixed (discrete) number of alternatives. An elevator is an analog device because it rises gradually and continuously, from one floor to the next. A stairway is discrete, not analog, because it divides its rise into a certain number of steps. A motion picture exhibits this same discrete property. Every motion picture is made from a film of individual photos (frames) that when played at the rate of 30 frames per second gives the illusion of continuous motion. Figure A.3 lists several real-life systems that have both discrete and continuous (analog) counterparts.

Discrete systems are conveniently represented as digits. A light switch is either off or on. The off position can be represented by the digit 0 and the on position by the digit 1. Similarly, the clicking volume buttons can be used to raise and lower the value of an integer ranging from 0 (no sound) to 100 (maximum volume).

Two of the more common devices that are available in either digital or analog are automobile speedometers and wristwatches. An analog speedometer has a needle that moves continuously from 0 miles per hour and up. Digital speedometers display the auto's speed in the form of numeric digits. A digital speedometer displays "25" or "26," but nothing between. An analog wristwatch has hands that sweep around the dial in an infinite number of positions, while its digital counterpart displays time in the form of a fixed collection of numbers.

The concept of digitization is key to understanding the modern computer. Images displayed on a computer monitor are not drawn as a collection of continuous lines, but rather are displayed in a grid of small rectangular figures called **pixels** (short for

Figure A.3

Discrete systems as opposed to continuous systems

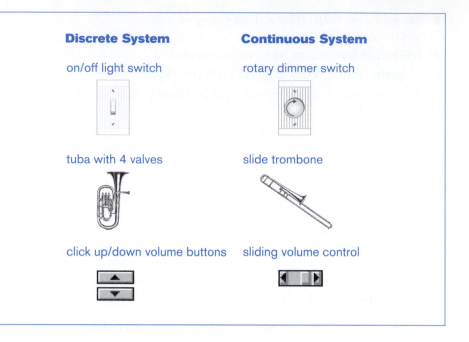

"picture elements"). Figure A.4 illustrates. The letter "A" on the right is displayed in a grid of pixels that is 7 wide and 9 high. Most modern computer displays have sufficiently many pixels that the quality of images is better than the pixelized "A" from Figure A.4. (A common computer monitor today measures 17 inches diagonally and has a visible region of 1280 pixels horizontally by 1024 pixels vertically.) However, even the best computer displays have limitations.

The color and intensity of graphical images are also digitized. Color resolution can differ. One commonly used digitization technique is like mixing three colors of paint. Every color is made from mixing a certain amount of redness, greenness, and blueness. The colors are digitized by storing the intensity of each color as an integer in the range from 0 through 255. This means that 256 different intensities of red can be mixed with 256 different intensities of green and 256 different intensities of blue. The result is $256 \times 256 \times 256 = 16,777,216$ potential colors.

Figure A.4

Displaying a letter in a continuous and pixelized form

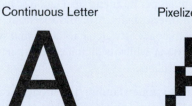

Sound on a computer is also stored digitally. Phonograph records and analog tape recorders store sound in analog form as an infinite number of different frequencies and amplitudes. Compact disks and MP3s encode sound as a sequence of numbers that are sampled thousands of times per second. Playing this digitized sound is like playing a motion picture, stringing the sound associated with the numbers so close together that the human ear hears continuity.

A.3 ■ **How Is Data Stored?**

By now it should be clear that a digital computer stores data in digitized (i.e., numeric) form. Images are stored as numbers, sounds are stored as numbers, and machine instructions are stored as numbers. Everything that is stored within a digital computer is encoded as a number.

The numbers stored in a computer are actually stored in an elementary form, known as a **bit string**. A bit string is a sequence of several **bits**, where "bit" is an abbreviation for **binary digit**. A bit is limited to just two possible values: 0 or 1.

To understand why bits are important, it is necessary to examine a little more about computer technology. Computers store things in one of three forms: electrical, magnetic, or optical. The main memory and CPU use largely electrical storage. CDs and DVDs store data optically. Most secondary storage, including hard disks, floppy disks, and tapes utilize magnetic storage technologies.

Figure A.5 shows that each of these storage techniques has a natural method for encoding a bit. An electrical circuit can be designed to store either a positive voltage (V+) or an electrical ground (gnd). A positive voltage can represent a bit value 1 and

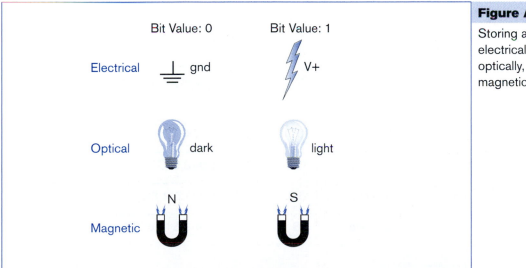

Figure A.5

Storing a bit electrically, optically, or magnetically

a ground can represent 0. An optical circuit is either light or dark, representing 0 or 1. A magnetic field can be polarized in one of two opposing directions, commonly referred to as "north" and "south." One of these two magnetic polarities can be used to represent a 0 and the other a 1.

Since a single bit of data can only store one of two configurations, storing more complex forms of data requires that bits be strung together in sequence. Conceptually, a string of eight bits is like eight parallel wires, each with its own value (V+ or gnd), or eight spots on a CD each capable of reflecting light or dark. A bit string that is exactly eight bits long is called a **byte**.

One byte of storage is sufficient to store a simple character or an integer in the range from 0 through 255. A byte is also the base measurement used to describe the volume of data. Figure A.6 shows several common measurements that are based in quantities of bytes.

One **kilobyte (KB)** of data is roughly one thousand bytes. The transfer of data over telephone lines is still in the range of 20 to 60 kilobytes per second. One **megabyte (MB)** is slightly more than a million bytes. Main memory sizes are generally measured in megabytes. Digital photographs are a few megabytes in size. A personal computer may be advertised with 512 MB of main memory. Secondary storage is typically much larger and much slower than main memory. Therefore, secondary storage devices are generally measured in **gigabytes (GB)**. One gigabyte exceeds a billion bytes. While a typical hard disk size is 60 GB, it is not unusual for a large computer installation to have computing databases measured in **terabytes (TB)**. One terabyte is over a trillion bytes.

Main memory is a sequence of **words** of data, where each word is a bit string. The size of a word of memory depends on the particular computer with one to eight bytes being a common word length. Figure A.7 diagrams this view by showing a portion of main memory.

Figure A.6

Commonly used computer storage measures

Measure	Abbrev	Quantity (in bytes)
byte	B	$2^0 = 1$
kilobyte	KB	$2^{10} = 1{,}024$
megabyte	MB	$2^{20} = 1{,}048{,}576$
gigabyte	GB	$2^{30} = 1{,}073{,}741{,}824$
terabyte	TB	$2^{40} = 1{,}099{,}511{,}627{,}776$

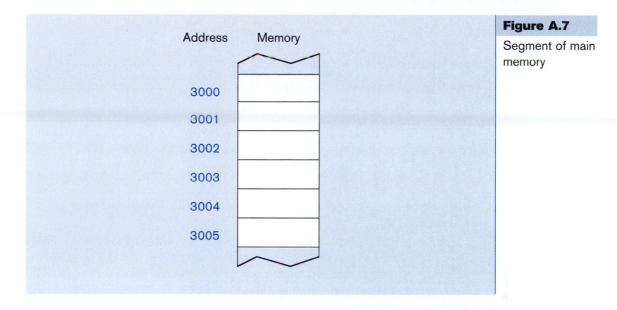

Figure A.7 also illustrates that each separate word of memory has its own numeric address. Like the street address of a townhouse, the memory address uniquely identifies the location of a particular word of data. The CPU fetches an instruction by specifying the address of the memory word(s) where the instruction is stored. Similarly, an address is required any time that the CPU retrieves data from or stores data into memory.

A.4 ■ What Are Binary Numbers?

When bit strings must represent numeric values, the obvious encoding choice is that of **binary numbers**. A binary number, also known as a **base-2 number**, uses 0 and 1 as its only two digits.

To understand binary numbers, it is helpful to review the more familiar **decimal** numbers. A decimal integer is written as a sequence of decimal digits (0 through 9) in which each digit position has a different weight, and this weight indicates how much a position contributes to the integer's value. The rightmost digit position is called the 1's position, because the rightmost digit represents a number of 1's in the integer value. The second position from the right is the 10's position, because the digit in this position contributes ten times its value to the integer. The third position from the right is the 100's position; the fourth position is the 1000's position; and so on.

Figure A.8 illustrates with a particular decimal number, namely "3704." The integer value of this number is calculated as $3 \times 1000 + 7 \times 100 + 0 \times 10 + 4 \times 1$.

Figure A.8

The value of a decimal integer

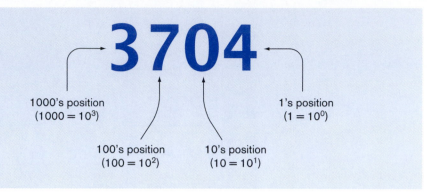

1000's position
$(1000 = 10^3)$

100's position
$(100 = 10^2)$

10's position
$(10 = 10^1)$

1's position
$(1 = 10^0)$

From Figure A.8 it is evident that the weight of each position in a decimal number is a power of ten and that these powers increase from right to left. The weight of the rightmost position in a decimal integer is $1 = 10^0$; the second position from the right has a weight of $10 = 10^1$; the third position has a weight of $100 = 10^2$; and the fourth position has a weight of $1000 = 10^3$.

The binary number system is like the decimal system if you substitute 2 for 10. The decimal system has ten digits (0 through 9); and the binary system has two digits (0 and 1). The weights of the digit positions of a decimal number are powers of 10. The weights of the digit positions in a binary number are powers of 2. Therefore, the rightmost digit in a binary number is still the 1's position (2^0). The second position from the right in a binary number is the 2's position (2^1). The third position is the 4s position (2^2). The fourth position is the 8's position (2^3).

The decimal value of any binary number can be calculated by summing the product of each digit times its weight. The value of the binary number 1101 (shown in Figure A.9) is $1 \times 8 + 1 \times 4 + 0 \times 2 + 1 \times 1 = 13$. Figure A.10 illustrates how to count from 0 through 16 (decimal) with binary numbers.

Just as with decimal numbers, leading zeros (zeros on the left of an integer) contribute nothing to the value of a binary number. This means that $00010 = 10$.

Figure A.9

The value of a binary integer

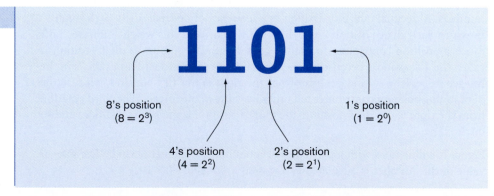

8's position
$(8 = 2^3)$

4's position
$(4 = 2^2)$

2's position
$(2 = 2^1)$

1's position
$(1 = 2^0)$

Binary		Decimal
0	=	0
1	=	1
10	=	2
11	=	3
100	=	4
101	=	5
110	=	6
111	=	7
1000	=	8
1001	=	9
1010	=	10
1011	=	11
1100	=	12
1101	=	13
1110	=	14
1111	=	15
10000	=	16

Figure A.10

Binary numbers from 0 through 16 (decimal)

Since the positional weights of binary digits grow by powers of 2, it is helpful to be familiar with powers of 2 when using this system. Figure A.11 diagrams a table of the powers of 2 from 2^0 through 2^{10}. The powers of 2 table explains why one kilobyte is

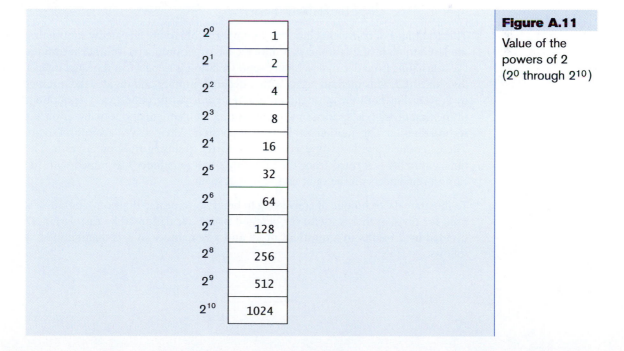

Figure A.11

Value of the powers of 2 (2^0 through 2^{10})

2^0	1
2^1	2
2^2	4
2^3	8
2^4	16
2^5	32
2^6	64
2^7	128
2^8	256
2^9	512
2^{10}	1024

1024 bytes, rather than 1000 bytes. Additionally, it provides insight about why the main memory of a computer is generally 64 KB or 256 KB, rather than more even decimal quantities.

The powers of 2 can also be used to count the number of unique values for a bit string of a given length. For example, there are 32 (2^5) different bit strings that can be formed from a string of five bits. Similarly, there are 256 (2^8) different bit strings that have a length of eight bits.

The powers of 2 table can also be used to assist in the conversion of a decimal number into its binary representation. For example, the value of 625 can be converted to a decimal number as follows.

- The largest power of 2 contained within 625 is 512 (2^9). Subtracting 625–512 leaves 113.

- The largest power of 2 contained within 113 is 64 (2^6). Subtracting 113–64 leaves 49.

- The largest power of 2 contained within 49 is 32 (2^5). Subtracting 49–32 leaves 17.

- The largest power of 2 contained within 17 is 16 (2^4). Subtracting 17–16 leaves 1.

Using the above reasoning, the binary equivalent of 625 can be constructed as follows.

$$
\begin{aligned}
625 \text{ (decimal)} \quad = \quad & 1 \times 2^9 + 1 \times 2^6 + 1 \times 2^5 + 1 \times 2^4 + 1 \times 2^0 \\
= \quad & 1 \times 2^9 + 0 \times 2^8 + 0 \times 2^7 + 1 \times 2^6 + 1 \times 2^5 + 1 \times 2^4 + 0 \times 2^3 \\
& + 0 \times 2^2 + 0 \times 2^1 + 1 \times 2^0 \\
= \quad & 1001110001 \text{ (binary)}
\end{aligned}
$$

This technique of converting a decimal number to binary by repeatedly subtracting the largest power of 2 is somewhat difficult for larger numbers. Another technique for translating from decimal to binary representation is to perform repeated integer divisions by 2. This method starts with a decimal number and divides the number by 2, recording both the quotient and the remainder of this division. The quotient of the first division is divided by 2 again, noting the quotient and remainder of this second division. The quotient of the second division is divided by 2 again, and so on. These repeated divisions by 2 continue until the resulting quotient is zero. The binary number is formed from the bit string of all remainder bits joined with the earliest remainders on the right end of the bit string.

To illustrate the technique of converting to binary by repeated division, a notation is used for division that is useful for pen and paper calculations. The calculation **97 divided by 2 results in a quotient of 48 and a remainder of 1** is diagrammed as follows.

$$
2 \mid \overline{ 97 }
$$

$$
48 \qquad \text{R: } 1
$$

Figure A.12 demonstrates the conversion of 625 (decimal) into its binary equivalent through repeated division by 2. It is important to notice that the remainders form the binary value from *bottom to top*.

Just like decimal numbers, binary numbers can represent fractional values. Decimal numbers use a decimal point to separate the integer part of the number from the fractional part. The weight of the digits to the right of the decimal point continue the sequence of powers of 2 by using negative powers of 10. (Recall that $10^{-X} = 1/10^X$.) Binary numbers also use a period to separate the integer portion from the fractional part and the weight of the positions right of the period are negative powers of 2. Figure A.13 illustrates.

Converting a binary value into decimal is done the same with or without fractional parts. That is, you sum the weights of each binary 1 bit position. Below are two examples.

11.01 (binary) = 2 + 1 + 1/4 = 3.25

0.101 (binary) = 1/2 + 1/8 = 0.625

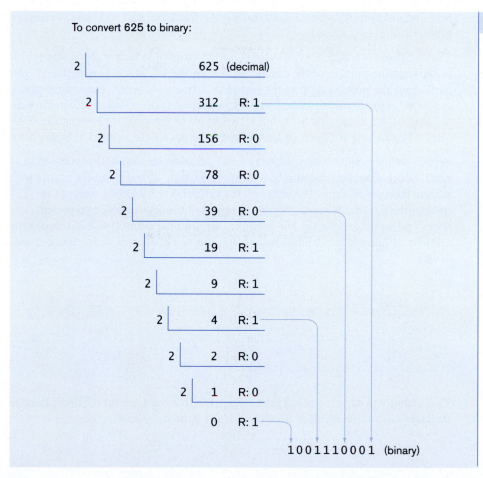

To convert 625 to binary:

1001110001 (binary)

Figure A.12

Convert 625 (decimal) into binary via repeated division by 2

Figure A.13

The value of a
binary integer
with fractional
part

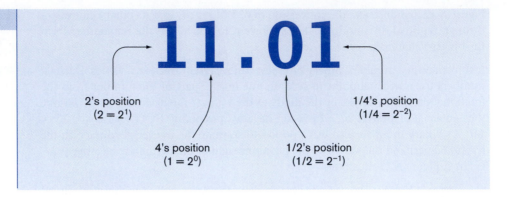

Converting a decimal number into its binary representation is slightly different
when the number contains a fractional part. The technique of repeatedly subtracting powers of two still works as previously described; however, the technique of
repeated division by 2 does not. To convert the fractional part to binary, a repeated
multiplication by 2 is used.

The complete technique for converting decimal values into binary representations is
to separate the portion of the binary number to the left of the period (the integer
part) from the portion right of the period (the fractional part). The integer part is
converted as previously described. The fractional part is converted by repeatedly *multiplying* the fractional part by 2, and retaining all of the resulting integer bits. (The
integer bits are ordered from greatest weight to least.) This is pictured in Figure A.14.

Representing fractional parts in binary form sometimes makes it impossible to store
exact values. Even decimal numbers cannot represent all real numbers exactly with
a finite number of digits. For example, the value $1/3 = 0.33333\ldots$ where the "$\ldots$"
denotes the fact that 3s repeat forever. The binary numbers are able to represent even
fewer real numbers exactly. For example, the decimal number 0.2 is a repeating
number in binary, as demonstrated by the following steps of converting 0.2 into
binary.

$$
\begin{array}{ccc}
.2 & .8 & .2 \\
\underline{\times\,2} & \underline{\times\,2} & \underline{\times\,2} \\
0.4 & 1.6 & 0.4 \\
\\
.4 & .6 & \\
\underline{\times\,2} & \underline{\times\,2} & \\
0.8 & 1.2 & \\
\end{array}
$$

This inability to store fractional values exactly with a fixed number of digits leads to
the fact that computers often store numbers as approximations.

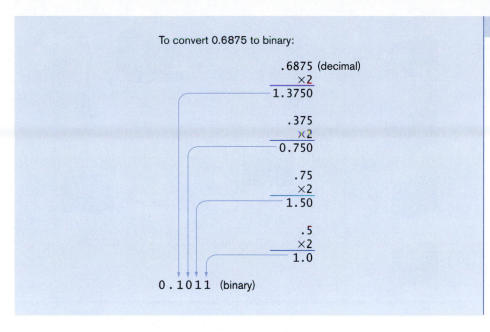

To convert 0.6875 to binary:

.6875 (decimal)
×2
1.3750

.375
×2
0.750

.75
×2
1.50

.5
×2
1.0

0.1011 (binary)

Figure A.14

Convert decimal into binary via repeated multiplication by 2

A.5 ■ How Do Computers Communicate?

One of the most important facilities of the modern computer is its ability to communicate with other computers, and thereby with other people. Such communication is made possible by connecting computers to one another in a computer **network**. The computers within a particular office suite or small building often form a **local area network** (**LAN**). The technologies that are used to manage LAN communications are often restricted by distance to a few hundred meters. Networks that cover larger distances are referred to as **wide area networks** (**WANs**).

Most of today's LANs and WANs are ultimately connected to each other by the **Internet**. The Internet is not really a single entity, but a collection of separate networks that are interconnected with few regulations and largely decentralized management. However, computers on the Internet do share a few **protocols** (communication conventions).

Internet Service Providers (**ISPs**) are companies that sell physical connections to the Internet. Each ISP has its own connection to the Internet that is made available to customers who connect to ISP computers.

A home computer typically makes use of existing telephone lines to communicate with an ISP. Telephone lines, commonly referred to as **voice lines**, are not specifically designed to handle computer communication, so a device called a **modem** is

Figure A.15

Networked
computers

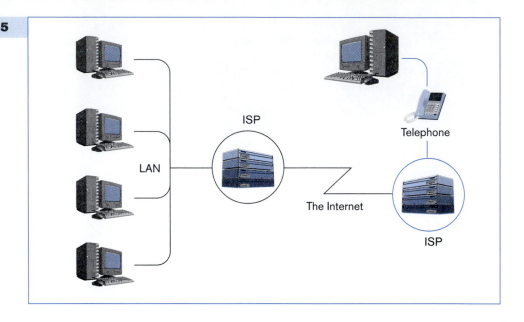

required within any computer communicating this way. Modems are typically capable of a communications **bandwidth** (i.e., capacity) of 56 Kb per second. (Note that communication speeds are given in *kilobits* per second, not kilobytes per second. The small "b" in Kb denotes this difference.) A second technology that is gaining popularity among home computer users borrows the use of cable television wires. **Cable modems** transfer data at a rate of 1.5 Mbps (megabits per second).

A LAN is more likely to use so-called **data lines,** instead of telephone wires, to carry computer transmissions. Data lines are preferred because of their additional bandwidth. LAN bandwidth typically ranges from 10 Mbps for the commonly used **Ethernet** technology to 12.8 Gbps (gigabits per second) for **Asynchronous Transfer Mode (ATM)**. Wireless technologies use radio signals to transfer at rates in the 1 Mbs to 10 Mbs range. Wireless communication is limited by the relatively short range of radio transmission—at maximum, a few hundred meters from computer to network hub.

Data lines used to transmit over longer distances, such as those connecting LANs to an ISP, often use T*x* lines to communicate. The most common such communication uses either T1 lines (1.5 Mbps) or T3 lines (45 Mbps).

There is more to a network than just wires. Networks actually consist of at least three different kinds of devices.

- client computers
- network interconnection devices
- servers

A client computer refers to any computer that makes use of the services provided by a network. Home computers and office computers are generally thought of as client computers. A network interconnection device is any piece of equipment needed to connect the wires of the network and make certain that transmissions are directed along the proper paths. Switches, routers, and hubs are among the devices that provide such network infrastructure.

One of the greatest advantages of a computer network is for sharing resources. Servers are the primary resource providers. A server is just another computer, but unlike client computers, servers are designed to respond to requests from other computers. A database server stores data for access by selected individuals. A computer server provides the ability to perform calculations at high speeds. A Web server provides World Wide Web pages to be displayed on client computers using a Web browser such as Internet Explorer, Firefox, or Safari.

Suppose that you wish to send e-mail to a friend. You compose your e-mail on your personal computer (a client computer) and then request that the message be sent. Your message is directed through the Internet from router to router using the address you specify in the "to field" to guide it to its destination. Eventually, this message will be stored in the e-mail server that is used by your friend. Still later, your friend, using another client computer, requests mail from the e-mail server and your message is delivered. This example illustrates that even a simple e-mail message requires the cooperation of many different devices, including client computers, servers, and the network interconnection devices that lie between.

So if a computer is connected to a LAN operating at 10 Mbps, then why do Web pages sometimes arrive at speeds less than 10 Kbps? The answer to this question is as complicated as the Internet itself. It is possible that the Web server is simply receiving requests for its Web pages faster than it is able to retrieve them from disk, so it selectively puts client computers "on hold." Another possible explanation is that the local computer is busy performing other tasks that restrict the CPU time that is available for network communication. While these end computers may be the source of some bottlenecks, a more likely reason for slow communication is the network itself.

LANs and WANs make use of shared interconnections. For example, a LAN may operate at 10 Mbps, but if there are 100 computers on the LAN, the average bandwidth available to each is less than 0.1 Mbps. Similarly, data transmission lines that connect two ISPs act like trunk lines that can be shared by thousands of individual computers. This explains why the Internet is often called the "data superhighway." A frequent concern is that there are more "on-ramps" onto the Internet than the "number of driving lanes" can handle.

A.6 ■ Why Are Computers Called "Systems"?

We have seen that modern computer hardware can perform some remarkable feats: execute millions of machine instructions per second, store trillions of bytes on a hard disk, and communicate with other computers at a rate of thousands of bytes per second. However, computer hardware can do none of these things without computer **software**. Computer hardware without software is like a DVD player without a DVD disk, a baseball glove without a ball, or a movie projector without film.

The term "software" refers to any collection of computer instructions. These instructions serve as commands for the CPU. Software instructions might command the CPU to add two values, to store something into main memory, to display the character "R" on the computer monitor, or to transmit a byte of information to some other Internet address.

Instructions are grouped to form computer programs. A single program is designed to perform one application. Word processors are programs to help people write and edit textual documents. Database applications are programs to assist computer users with information storage and retrieval. Web browsers are programs designed to make it convenient to "surf" the Internet.

At the center of all computer activity is a very special program known as the **operating system (OS)**. Common operating systems for personal computers include Unix, Linux (a version of Unix), OS X, Solaris (another version of Unix), and Windows XP. The operating system is responsible for coordination of all computer functions, including how various parts of the hardware interact with each other and with the executing software. The following items are some of the key functions performed by operating systems.

- The OS maintains a file system to keep track of all data stored on secondary storage. Such a file system identifies each file by a name and allows files to be organized into folders (also called "directories").

- The OS manages the main memory, loading new programs into memory so they can execute and reserving separate memory space to store the program's data.

- The OS ensures the integrity of several programs that are simultaneously active. If you run a word processor at the same time as a Web browser, it is the operating system that does the "behind the scenes" work needed to guarantee that both of these programs can operate independently and simultaneously.

- The OS provides a **graphical user interface (GUI)**. The elements of a typical GUI include menus for selecting tasks, windows for displaying text and graphics on a computer monitor, buttons for clicking, and scrollbars for dragging. The GUI elements work closely with the computer keyboard and mouse to give the user control over the computer.

- The OS provides for basic host-level security, such as user accounts (with user names and passwords), local firewalls (to restrict which network transmissions are received and sent by the computer), file (and other resource) access privilege enforcement, support for system event logging, tools for system maintenance (to load software corrections), and support for secure network communication.

Computers are called "computer systems" as a reference to the collaborative nature of the computer hardware and its operating system.

Terminology

analog device

asynchronous transfer mode (ATM)

bandwidth

base-2 number

binary digit

binary number

bit

bit string

cable modem

CD-ROM

CD-RW

central processing unit (CPU)

client computer

clock speed

compact disk (CD)

computer

data line

decimal number

digital computer

display

DVD

Ethernet

fetch-execute cycle

floppy disk

gigabits per second (Gbps)

gigabyte (GB)

gigahertz (GHz)

graphical user interface (GUI)

hard disk

Internet

Internet service provider (ISP)

Input/Output (I/O) device

keyboard

kilobits per second (Gbps)

kilobyte (GB)

local area network (LAN)

machine language

magnetic tape

main memory

megabits per second (Mbps)

megabyte (MB)

megahertz (MHz)

modem

monitor

mouse

network

network interconnection device

operating system (OS)

personal computer

pixel

printer

processor

program

protocol

secondary storage

server

software

system unit

terabyte (TB)

voice line

von Neumann architecture

wide area network (WAN)

word (of main memory)

Java Syntax Diagrams

appendix

Appendix B defines the syntax of the Java programming language in syntax diagram format. Each rectangle contains the name of a separate syntax diagram. Semantic qualifiers are denoted using a <...> suffix. For example, **ID <class>** denotes the syntax diagram called "ID" that names a class. Below is an alphabetized list of diagram names and their corresponding page numbers.

Compilation Unit

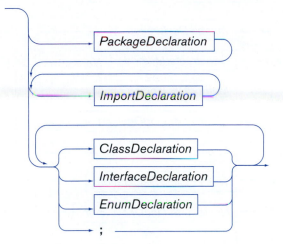

PackageDeclaration

ImportDeclaration

ClassBody

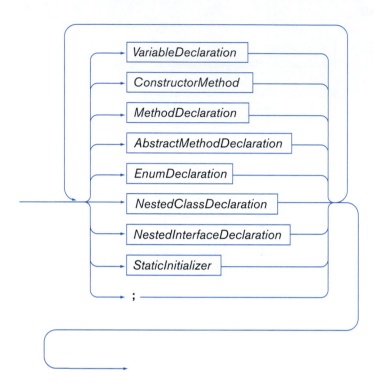

ClassDeclaration

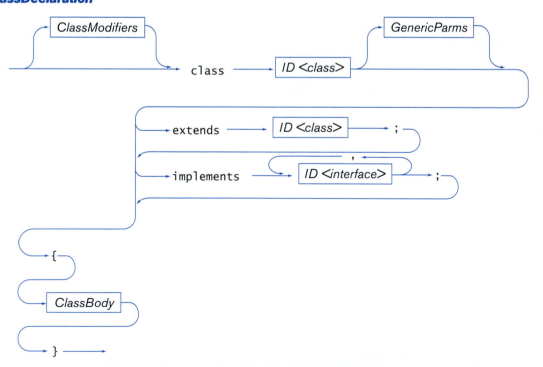

ClassModifiers

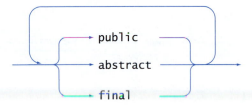

Note: Each modifier can occur once, at most, for the same modified unit.

InterfaceDeclaration

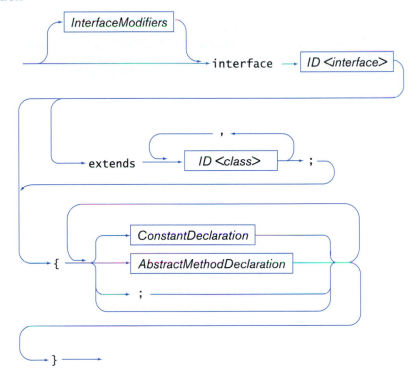

InterfaceModifiers

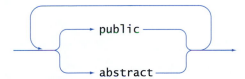

Note: Each modifier can occur once, at most, for the same modified unit.

EnumDeclaration

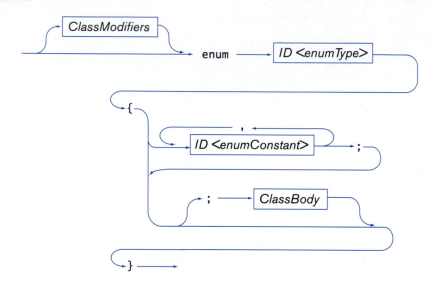

GenericParms

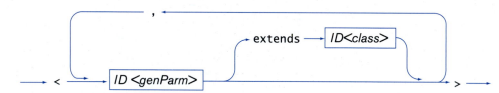

NestedClassDeclaration

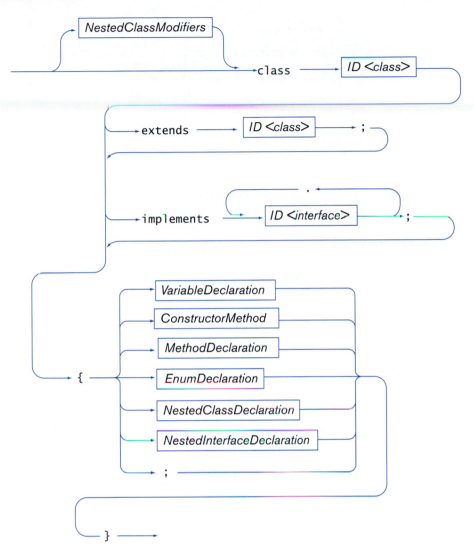

Note: Each modifier can occur once, at most, for the same modified unit. The following modifiers are mutually exclusive `public`, `protected`, `private`.

NestedClassModifiers

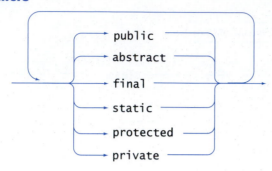

Note: Each modifier can occur once, at most, for the same modified unit. The following modifiers are mutually exclusive `public`, `protected`, `private`.

NestedInterfaceDeclaration

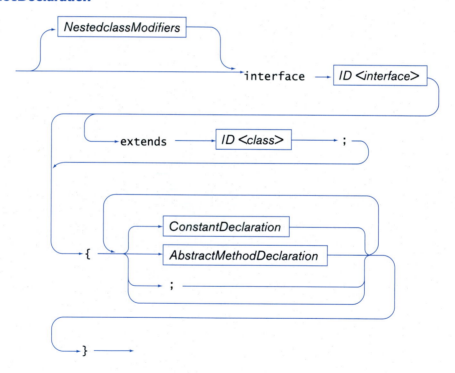

ConstantDeclaration

Note: ConstantDeclaration must include "final" as a modifier.

AbstractMethodDeclaration

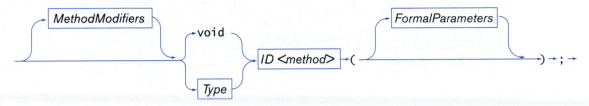

ConstructorMethod

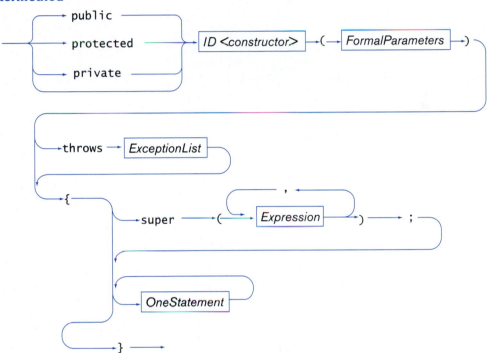

FormalParameters

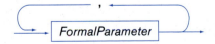

FormalParameter

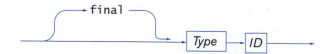

ExceptionList

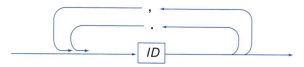

Type

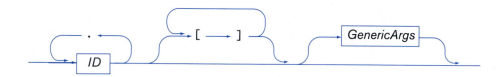

MethodDeclaration

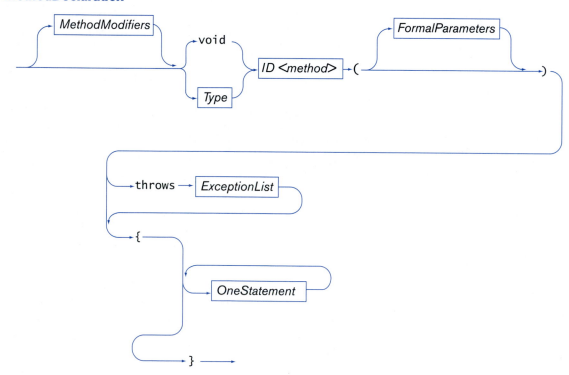

MethodModifiers

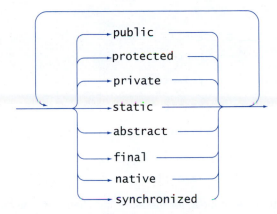

Note: Each modifier can occur once, at most, for the same modified unit. The following modifiers are mutually exclusive: `public`, `protected`, `private`.

GenericArgs

VariableDeclaration

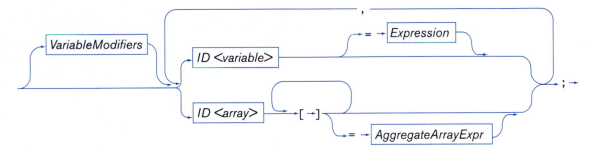

VariableModifiers

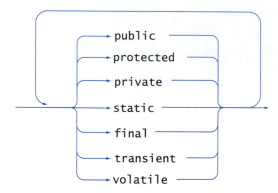

Note: Each modifier can occur once, at most, for the same modified unit. The following modifiers are mutually exclusive: `public`, `protected`, `private`.

StaticInitializer

OneStatement

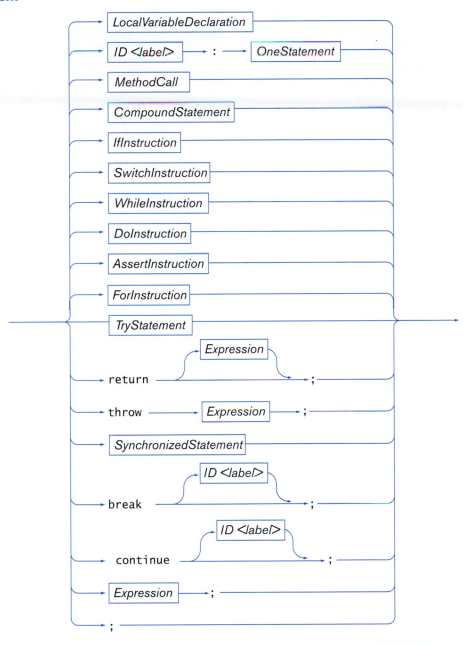

LocalVariableDeclaration

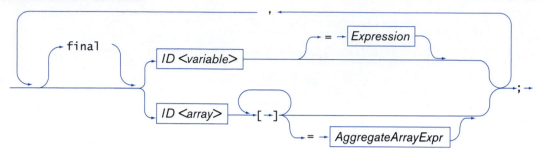

AggregateArrayExpr

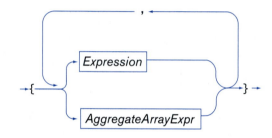

MethodCall

Arguments

CompoundStatement

IfInstruction

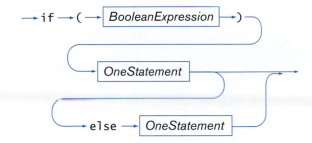

SwitchInstruction

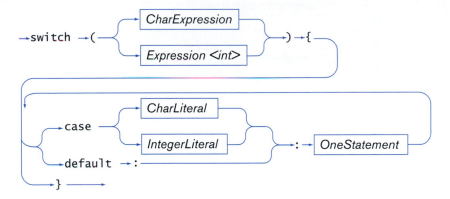

Note: No more than one *default* clause is permitted per switch instruction.

WhileInstruction

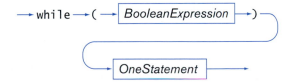

DoInstruction

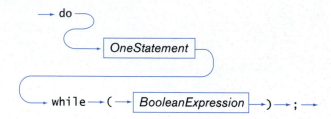

ForInstruction

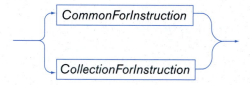

CommonForInstruction

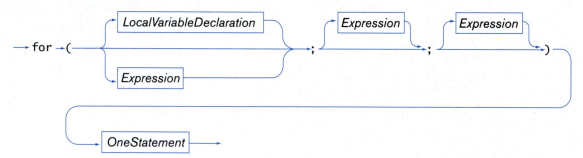

CollectionForInstruction

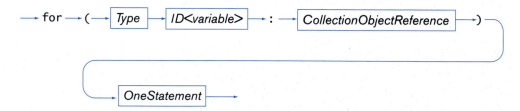

CollectionObjectReference

Note: A *CollectionObjectReference* must have type conforming to either an array or the *java.util.Collection* interface.

AssertInstruction

TryStatement

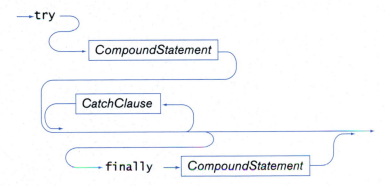

CatchClause

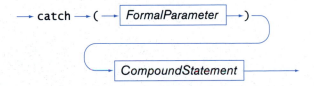

SynchronizedStatement

Expression

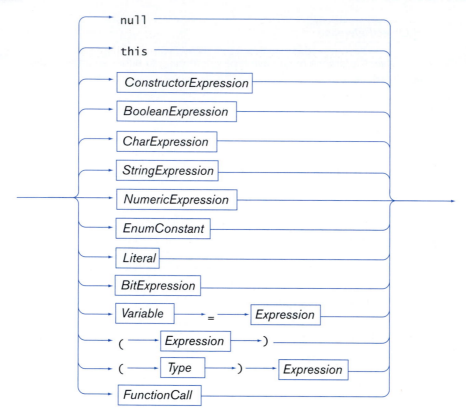

ConstructorExpression

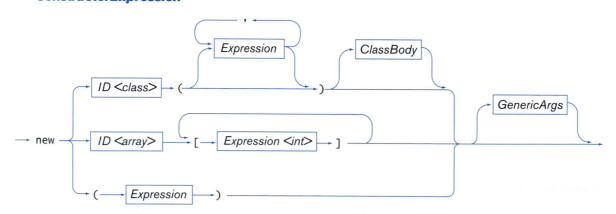

PrimitiveExpression

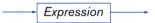

Note: A *PrimitiveExpression* must be of type `boolean`, `byte`, `char`, `double`, `float`, `int`, `long`, or `short`.

BooleanExpression

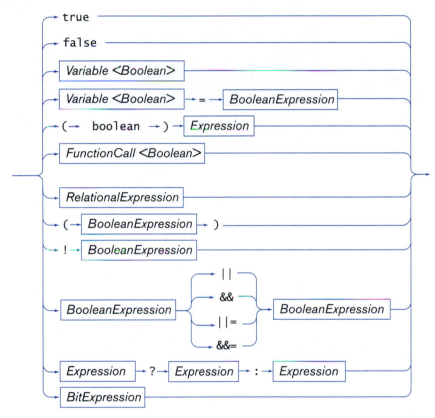

RelationalExpression

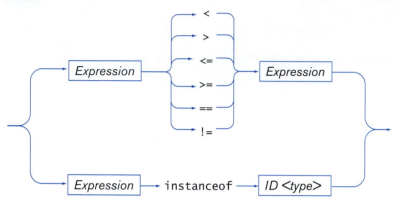

CharExpression

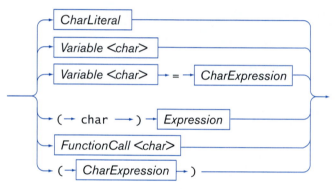

CharLiteral

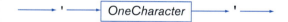

StringExpression

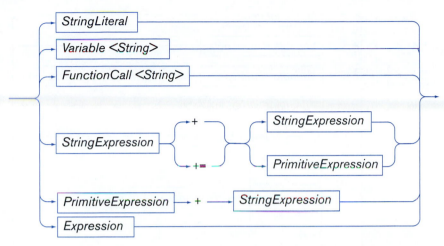

StringLiteral

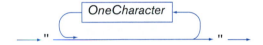

NumericExpression

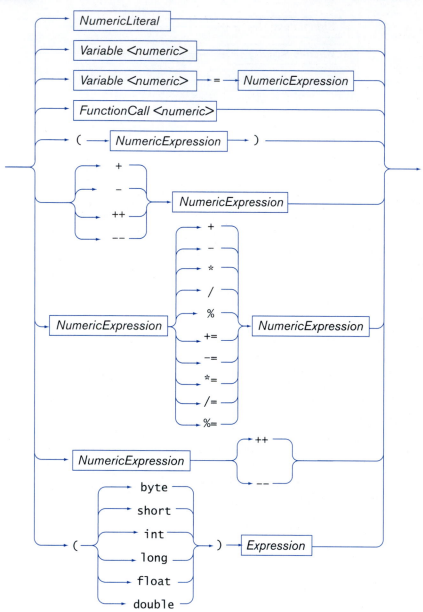

EnumConstant

$ID<enumType>$. $ID<enumConstant>$

NumericLiteral

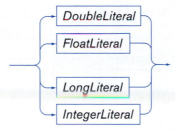

DoubleLiteral

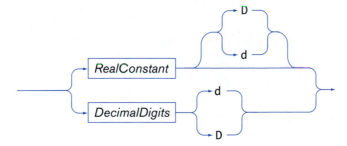

Note: Blanks, tabs, and line breaks are not permitted within *DoubleLiteral*.

FloatLiteral

Note: Blanks, tabs, and line breaks are not permitted within *FloatLiteral*.

LongLiteral

Note: Blanks, tabs, and line breaks are not permitted within *LongLiteral*.

RealConstant

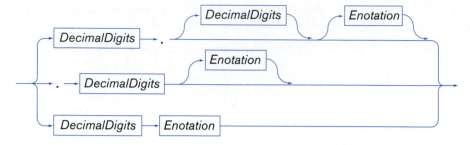

Note: Blanks, tabs, and line breaks are not permitted within *RealConstant*.

Enotation

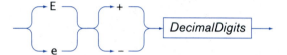

Note: Blanks, tabs, and line breaks are not permitted within *Enotation*.

IntegerLiteral

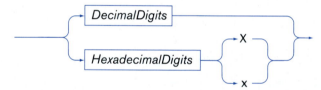

Note: Blanks, tabs, and line breaks are not permitted within *IntegerLiteral*.

Literal

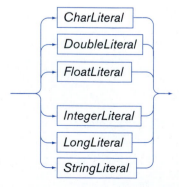

BitExpression

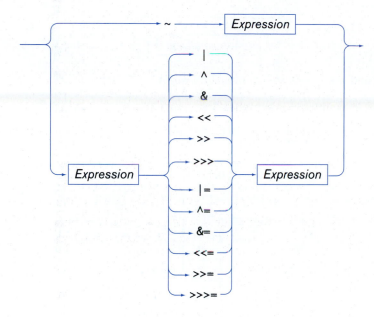

DecimalDigits

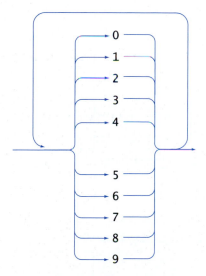

Note: Blanks, tabs, and line breaks are not permitted within *DecimalDigits*.

HexadecimalDigits

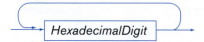

Note: Blanks, tabs, and line breaks are not permitted within *HexadecimalDigits*.

HexadecimalDigit

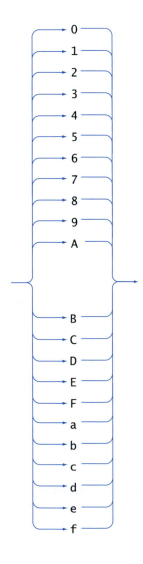

FunctionCall

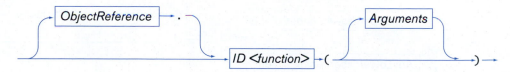

ObjectReference

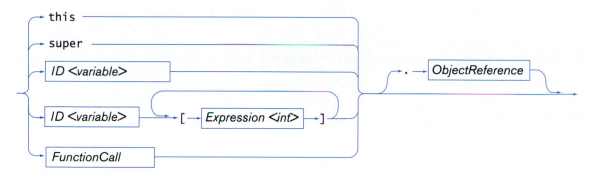

Variable

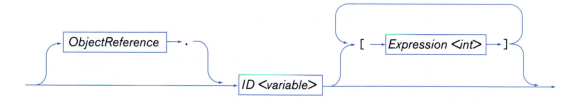

NumericVariable

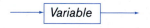

Note: Numeric Variable is a variable of type `byte`, `double`, `float`, `int`, `long`, or `short`.

ID

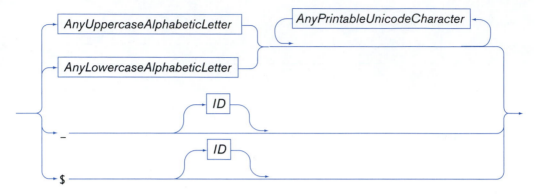

Note: Blanks, tabs, and line breaks are not permitted within *ID*.

OneCharacter

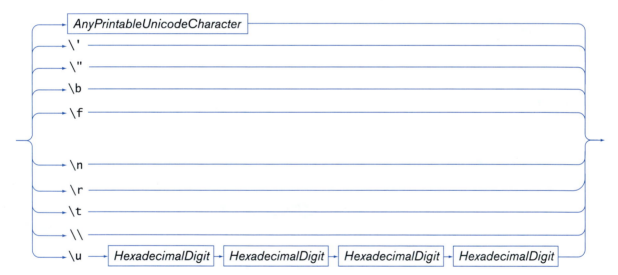

Note: Blanks (except for a single blank character), tabs, and line breaks are not permitted within *OneCharacter*.

Comment

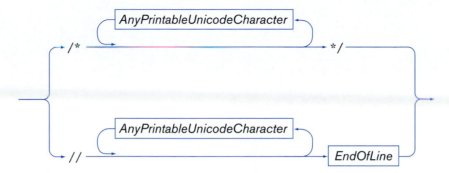

Precedence of Java Operations

The following table indicates the 15 Java precedence levels and associated operators. The book sections that describe the various operations are included. (N.C. means not covered.)

Precedence	Operator	Operation	Text Coverage	Order within
high	`--`	postfix autodecrement	Sect. 5.2	Left to right
(Postfix)	`++`	postfix autoincrement	Sect. 5.2	
	`.`	qualified expression	Sect. 2.2 and 6.2	
	`[ ]`	array indexing	Sect. 12.1	
2nd	`+`	unary plus	N.C.	Right to left
(Unary)	`-`	unary minus	Sect. 5.2	
	`!`	`boolean` NOT	Sect. 7.3	
	`--`	prefix autodecrement	N.C.	
	`++`	prefix autoincrement	N.C.	
	`~`	bitwise NOT	N.C.	
3rd	`new`	object construction	Sect. 2.4	Right to left
(Cast)	`( type )`	cast	Sect. 5.6	
4th	`/`	division	Sect. 5.2	Left to right
(Multiplicative)	`*`	multiplication	Sect. 5.2	
	`%`	remainder (modulo)	Sect. 5.2	
5th	`+`	addition	Sect. 5.2	Left to right
(Additive)	`-`	subtraction	Sect. 5.2	
	`+`	String concatenation	Sect. 6.10	
6th	`<<`	shift left	N.C.	Left to right
(Shift)	`>>`	shift right	N.C.	
	`>>>`	shift right with 0	N.C.	
7th	`<`	less	Sect. 7.2	Left to right
(Relational)	`<=`	less or equal	Sect. 7.2	
	`>`	greater	Sect. 7.2	
	`>=`	greater or equal	Sect. 7.2	
	`instanceof`	type comparison	Sect. 9.2	
8th	`==`	equality (identity)	Sect. 7.2 and 9.6	Left to right
(Equality)	`!=`	inequality	Sect. 7.2	
9th	`&`	bitwise AND	N.C.	Left to right

Precedence	Operator	Operation	Text Coverage	Order within
10th	^	bitwise XOR	N.C.	Left to right
11th	|	bitwise OR	N.C.	Left to right
12th	&&	boolean AND	Sect. 7.3	Left to right
13th	||	boolean OR	Sect. 7.3	Left to right
14th	?:	conditional	N.C.	Right to left
15th	=	assignment	Sect. 2.4	Right to left
(Assignment)	+=	add, then assign	N.C.	
	+=	concatenate, then assign	N.C.	
	/=	divide, then assign	N.C.	
	*=	multiply, then assign	N.C.	
	-=	subtract, then assign	N.C.	
	<<=	shift left, then assign	N.C.	
	>>=	shift right, then assign	N.C.	
	&=	bitwise AND, then assign	N.C.	
	|=	bitwise OR, then assign	N.C.	
	^=	bitwise XOR, then assign	N.C.	

Library Software

Class libraries are central to the object-oriented approach to software development. This text includes a wide array of library classes–some are standard classes included in the Java Application Programming Interface (API). Appendix D discusses how these libraries are used and extended.

D.1 ■ Overview of Standard Libraries

The Java 2 Platform Standard Edition API is partitioned into three major groups: the base (*java*) library, extensions to the basic library (*javax*), and the *org* classes, which are supplied to maintain compatibility with standards organizations.

Early versions of Java included a library, known as *AWT* (short for **Abstract Windowing Toolkit**). The *AWT* library includes numerous classes that are useful for building graphical user interfaces. As the Java language matured, it was felt that *AWT* lacked some of the features needed for certain graphical applications, so the *Swing* library was developed as an extension of *AWT*. By Version 1.2 of Java, both *AWT* and *Swing* were standard parts of the Java API.

It is virtually impossible to separate *AWT* and *Swing* because most of the key *Swing* classes inherit much of their functionality from *AWT* classes. Furthermore, many of the *Swing* classes are clients of other *AWT* classes. Therefore, the notation "*Swing/AWT*" is often used to refer to the collective programming environment formed by these combined libraries.

Figure D.1 diagrams the inheritance relationships for most classes used in this book. The number in parentheses at the bottom of a class icon indicates the section(s) in which the class is most fully described. The highlighted classes are supplied with the book and tend to be very thin shells over underlying *AWT* and *Swing* classes.

Two other groups of classes that are examined in the book, but not included individually in Figure D.1, are the wrapper classes and I/O classes. Figure D.1 has placeholders for each group. Figure D.2 contains the details for the I/O classes.

D.2 ■ Containers and Windows

Creating computer display images with *Swing/AWT* begins with the concept of a window. The *Swing/AWT* libraries include many classes for creating windows. Among the possibilities are `Window`, `Panel`, `Frame`, `JFrame`, `Applet`, and `JApplet`. Chapter 4 includes an author-written window called `ThreeButtonFrame`.

Underlying the concept of a window is an *AWT* class called `Container` while its counterpart in the *Swing* library is called `JComponent`.[1] Using the computer desktop metaphor, a `Container` is something that can have objects placed upon it. Windows are `Containers` because a window is designed for display upon a computer "desktop" while graphical images can be placed upon the window. Figure D.3 supplies the specifications for some key `Container` methods.

As an object, a `Container` is a transparent region, although its descendant classes often are not transparent. This region has a bounding rectangle that defines its region in terms of a *width*, *height*. The location of every `Container` is defined with respect to the `Container`'s background. The upper left corner of the `Container` is

---

1. All of the methods discussed for `Container` also apply to `JComponent`.

Figure D.1 Class hierarchy for classes used in this book

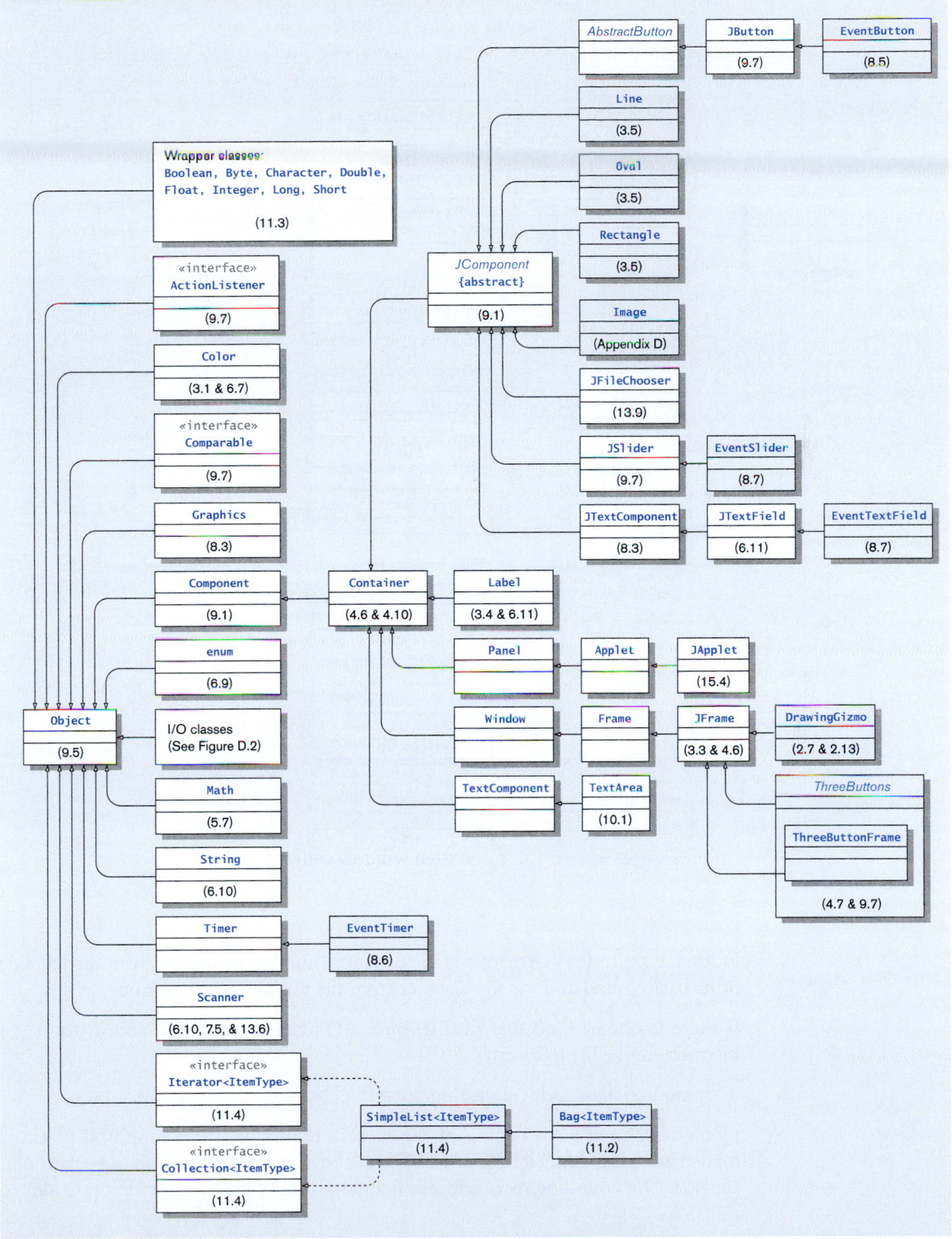

Figure D.2   *java.io* class hierarchy for classes used in this book

located at point (x, y), where x is the distance (number of pixels) from the left side of its background and y is the distance from the top of its background.

If there is one method that distinguishes a `Container`, it is the `add` method. An instruction like the following

   someContainer.`add`(*someComponent*, `0`);

places *someComponent* on top of the *someContainer* object. A graphical object is made visible by adding it to another visible `Container` object (a kind of background canvas). The bounding rectangle also defines visibility in the sense that portions of

Invariant

A `java.awt.Container` object

■ is a transparent rectangular region.

■ has its upper left corner *x* pixels from the left and *y* pixels from the top. (The upper left corner of the container is (0, 0).)

Below is a `Container` added to the content pane of a `JFrame`. The `Container` is shown in black, although it would be transparent on any computer display.

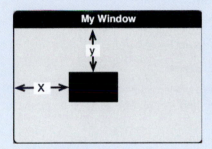

Constructor Methods

public `Container`( )

    post: A new Container object is created
        and *backColor* **and** *foreColor* are transparent.
        (Note that Containers also do not appear until added.)

Update Methods

public void `add`(java.awt.Component c, int *j*)

    pre: *j* == 0 (for this book)

    post: *c* is placed on top of this Container located c.getX() pixels from the left and c.getY() pixels from the top of this Container.

public void `remove`(java.awt.Component c)

    post: The *c* graphical object will be removed from this Container.

    note: Nothing occurs if *c* was not added to this Container at the time of the call.

public void `setBackground`(java.awt.Color c)

    post: *backColor* == c

public void `setBounds`(int *initX*, int *initY*, int *w*, int *h*)

    post: *x* == *initX* **and** *y* == *initY* **and** *width* == *w* **and** *height* == *h*

Figure D.3

Container
class
specifications
(*continued*)

```
public void setForeground(java.awt.Color c)
```
> **post:** *foreColor == c*

```
public void setLayout(java.awt.LayoutManager m)
```
> **post:** *m* is established as the layout manager for this Container.
>
> **note:** For this text an argument of null is suggested. This method need not
> be called except for the content pane of a JFrame.

```
public void setLocation(int initX, int initY)
```
> **post:** *x == initX* **and** *y == initY*

```
public void setSize(int w, int h)
```
> **post:** *width == w* **and** *height == h*

```
public void repaint( )
```
> **post:** Causes the Java virtual machine to update the display of this
> Container and its content, as soon as possible.

Query Methods

```
public java.awt.Color getBackground( )
```
> **post:** *result == backColor*

```
public java.awt.Color getForeground( )
```
> **post:** *result == foreColor*

```
public int getX( )
```
> **post:** *result == x*

```
public int getY( )
```
> **post:** *result == y*

```
public int getHeight( )
```
> **post:** *result == height*

```
public java.awt.Container getParent( )
```
> **post:** *result ==* background Container upon which this is added
> (null if not added)

```
public int getWidth( )
```
> **post:** *result == width*

the added graphics that lie outside the bounding rectangle are clipped. The second argument of the add method specifies the order of placement. A second argument of zero is used throughout this book because it follows the usual desktop metaphor in which each newly added object is placed above any previously added objects. (Note that add can be called without this second parameter, but such an add places an object *underneath* previously added objects.)

A program sometimes instantiates objects of type Container. The primary reasons for such objects are (1) to use as a transparent background for a group of objects or (2) for a background to clip. A spaceship animation that consists of several separately placed objects might use a Container because the separate objects can be moved collectively as a unit by simply moving the underlying Container. A half circle can be implemented by clipping a circle to the edge of a background Container.

The repaint method is a key to understanding how the Java VM updates screen images. The VM does not normally respond immediately to methods that change the display. Instead, it updates the display between event handling and various housekeeping chores. You should not expect your program to be in exact control of the time at which the screen is updated. You can however, assist in ensuring that update is performed as soon as possible on selected objects by calling the repaint method. Calling repaint on an object is a signal to the VM that the image of the object and its content need to be updated as soon as possible. Note that you cannot expect an object's image to be updated without calling repaint. You should not call repaint unnecessarily because it can slow down image update.

The descendant classes of Container are typically not transparent, which explains why Container includes methods like setBackground and setForeground that serve no useful purpose in the base class. Among these descendant classes are the window classes.

Arguably, the most often used window classes are Frame and JFrame. These classes are designed for full-fledged GUI windows in the sense that they incorporate title bars with close buttons and resizer insets. The *Swing* class, JFrame, is specified in Figure D.4.

There are several extensions that distinguish JFrame from Container:

- A JFrame has a title bar; the text for the title is set by the argument to the JFrame constructor.
- A JFrame requires a layout manager (null is used for an argument in this book).
- A JFrame only becomes visible on the desktop by calling setVisible(true).
- The setBackground method establishes the color of the window's content pane.
- A JFrame incorporates a separate Container upon which content is added.

Figure D.4

JFrame class specifications and diagram

Invariant

A JFrame object

- is a rectangular window.
- is placed on a computer screen with its upper left corner *x* pixels from the left and *y* pixels from the top. (The upper left corner of the screen is (0, 0).)
- has an overall dimension of *width* pixels from side to side and *height* pixels from top to bottom; this region has a background color of *backColor*.

Below is a Frame with a gray *backColor* on a white screen.

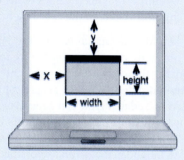

Constructor Methods

public **JFrame**(String *s*)

   post: A new JFrame (window) object is created
   and *s* is displayed in the bar at the top of the Frame.
   (Note that this method needs to be followed by calls to setBounds
   and setVisible in order to make the object appear.)

Update Methods

public void **setLayout**(java.awt.LayoutManager *m*)

   pre: *m* == null (for use in this book).

   post: Objects added to the frame will be arranged via *m*.

public void **setVisible**(boolean *b*)

   post: (*b* == true) ***implies*** this frame is made visible and brought to the
   foreground (in front of other windows).

Creating and displaying a JFrame requires a call to the constructor, to setBounds, to setLayout, and to setVisible. Below is a typical sequence of instructions.

```
JFrame myFrame = new JFrame("Example Frame");
myFrame.setBounds(10, 10, 500, 400);
myFrame.setLayout(null);
```

Query Methods

```
public java.awt.Container getContentPane( )
```
> **post:** *result ==* the content pane (the drawable region of the JFrame)

javax.swing.JFrame
– int *x*
– int *y*
– int *width*
– int *height*
– Color *backColor*
«constructor»
+ **JFrame**(*String*)
«update»
+ void **add**(*java.awt.Component, int*)
+ void **remove**(*java.awt.Component*)
+ void **repaint**()
+ void **setBackground**(*java.awt.Color*)
+ void **setForeground**(*java.awt.Color*)
+ void **setBounds**(*int, int, int, int*)
+ void **setLayout**(*java.awt.layoutManager*)
+ void **setLocation**(*int, int*)
+ void **setSize**(*int, int*)
+ void **setVisible**(*boolean*)
. . .
«query»
+ *java.awt.Container* **getContentPane**()
+ *java.awt.Color* **getBackground**()
+ *java.awt.Color* **getForeground**()
+ *int* **getX**()
+ *int* **getY**()
+ *int* **getHeight**()
+ *int* **getWidth**()
. . .

```
myFrame.setVisible(true);
myFrame.setBackground(Color.white);
// Now objects can be added to myFrame
```

A JFrame consists of a drawing region surrounded by a border. (This border consists of a title bar and often includes resizers and scroll bars.) The drawing region is a Container known as the **content pane**. Normally, graphical objects are added to this content pane. However, the JFrame class also overloads methods such as add, remove, and setLayout, so that an instruction such as

    myFrame.add(*someComponent*, 0);

performs the same function as follows:

    myFrame.getContentPane().add(*someComponent*, 0);

D.3 ■ Graphical Objects–JComponent

The Container and JFrame classes are designed to display the content of other objects. These *other* objects are descendants of the java.awt.Component or javax.swing.JComponent classes. In this section, we examine the JComponent class, which is the alternative used within this book. Figure D.5 contains specifications for JComponent.

Figure D.5

JComponent class specifications and diagram (*continues*)

Invariant

A JComponent object

■ has a bounding rectangle, like any other Container.

■ the bounding rectangle has a width of *width* pixels and a height of *height* pixels.

■ can be added to a Container with its upper left corner *x* pixels from the left and *y* pixels from the top. (The upper left corner of the parent container is (0, 0).)

Below is a JComponent that has been added to a Frame called myWindow. This JComponent (by virtue of its paint method) has the appearance of a black rectangle.

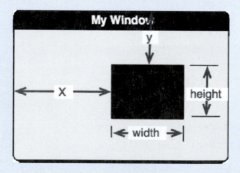

Figure D.5

JComponent
class
specifications
and diagram
(*continued*)

Update Methods

public void **paint**(java.awt.Graphics *g*)

pre: This method is called by the Java VM in order to update the screen display, and when called, the g parameter is passed by the VM to provide a graphical environment for drawing.

post: The default version of this method does nothing.

note: This method is designed to be overridden by child classes.

public void **paintChildren**(boolean *b*)

post: This causes the paint method to be called upon all objects that are added to this.

---

javax.swing.JComponent *{abstract}*

– int *x*
– int *y*
– int *width*
– int *height*
– Color *backColor*
– Color *foreColor*

«constructor»
  + **JComponent**

«update»
  + void **paint**(*java.awt.Graphics*)
  + void **paintChildren**(*java.awt.Graphics*)
  + void **repaint**()
  + void **setBackground**(*java.awt.Color*)
  + void **setForeground**(*java.awt.Color*)
  + void **setBounds**(*int, int, int, int*)
  + void **setLocation**(*int, int*)
  + void **setSize**(*int, int*)
  + void **add**(*java.awt.Component*)
  . . .

«query»
  + *java.awt.Color* **getBackground**()
  + *java.awt.Color* **getForeground**()
  + *java.awt.Container* **getParent**()
  + *int* **getX**()
  + *int* **getY**()
  + *int* **getHeight**()
  + *int* **getWidth**()
  . . .

JComponent is an abstract class. In order to use it properly, it needs to be inherited and its paint method overridden. The paint method defines the appearance of a JComponent. If the paint method draws a red automobile, then its JComponent appears as a red automobile. As discussed earlier, the Java VM controls when images are updated. It does so by calling the paint methods of the objects that it chooses to update. Programs should not normally call paint directly.

When you write your own subclass of JComponent, you must override the paint method to define the image that represents objects of this type. Overriding paint usually involves queries to JComponent methods such as getBackground, getForeground, getX, getY, getWidth, and getHeight together with calls to Graphics methods that perform the actual image drawing. In order to draw the paint code calls methods upon the Graphics parameter, g. Figure D.6 demonstrates with a class that draws the image of a filled circle, colored with the JComponent's background color and a five-pointed star drawn from line segments in the JComponent's foreground color.

The paint method in StarOnDot calls setColor to establish the drawing color. Next, it calls methods like fillOval and drawLine to perform the actual drawing in the most recently set color. The call to paintChildren at the end of the method is optional. If it is included, then the image will draw all objects that are added to it. Without a call to paintChildren, the objects placed upon this JComponent will not appear. In other words, calling paintChildren allows a JComponent to act like a Container. A more extensive collection of potential Graphics methods for drawing and filling images is given in Figure D.7.

There are two methods that must be called in order to create a JComponent or descendant class object—you need to call its constructor method, followed by setBounds to establish its bounding rectangle. To make the object visible, it also needs to be added to some visible Container. Figure D.8 shows a class that creates two StarOnDot objects. Figure D.9 illustrates the associated JFrame.

If you wish to draw an image that comes from a GIF, JPG, or PNG file, then it is best to use the class called Image that is supplied with this book. Figure D.10 shows a class diagram for Image and provides specifications for the methods not previously described.

Figure D.11 contains a Driver class that demonstrates how to use Image. This program adds a brown Rectangle to a JFrame. This Rectangle serves as a picture frame for the Image.

The key instructions in the program are repeated below:

```
castle = new Image(10, 10, 270, 203, "Wartburg.gif");
pictureFrame.add(castle, 0);
```

The first instruction creates the Image object, using the castle variable. The image is retrieved from a file called *Wartburg.gif* that must be located with the same folder as *Driver.class*. An Image uses the height and width of the bounding rectangle to

Figure D.6   StarOnDot class

```java
import javax.swing.*;
import java.awt.*;
public class StarOnDot extends JComponent {

    public StarOnDot() {
        super();
    }

    public void paint(Graphics g) {
        double diameter = getWidth();
        if (getHeight() < diameter)
            diameter = getHeight();

        // draw the filled circle
        g.setColor(getBackground());
        g.fillOval(0, 0, (int)diameter-1, (int)diameter-1);

        /* Draw the 5-pointed star using points at the following degree
         * measurements (270 degrees would be the top apex of the star):
         * 54, 126, 198, 270, and 342 degrees */
        g.setColor(getForeground());
        g.drawLine((int)(diameter/2+Math.cos(Math.toRadians(54))*diameter/2),
                   (int)(diameter/2+Math.sin(Math.toRadians(54))*diameter/2),
                   (int)(diameter/2+Math.cos(Math.toRadians(198))*diameter/2),
                   (int)(diameter/2+Math.sin(Math.toRadians(198))*diameter/2));
        g.drawLine((int)(diameter/2+Math.cos(Math.toRadians(126))*diameter/2),
                   (int)(diameter/2+Math.sin(Math.toRadians(126))*diameter/2),
                   (int)(diameter/2+Math.cos(Math.toRadians(270))*diameter/2),
                   (int)(diameter/2+Math.sin(Math.toRadians(270))*diameter/2));
        g.drawLine((int)(diameter/2+Math.cos(Math.toRadians(198))*diameter/2),
                   (int)(diameter/2+Math.sin(Math.toRadians(198))*diameter/2),
                   (int)(diameter/2+Math.cos(Math.toRadians(342))*diameter/2),
                   (int)(diameter/2+Math.sin(Math.toRadians(342))*diameter/2));
        g.drawLine((int)(diameter/2+Math.cos(Math.toRadians(270))*diameter/2),
                   (int)(diameter/2+Math.sin(Math.toRadians(270))*diameter/2),
                   (int)(diameter/2+Math.cos(Math.toRadians(54))*diameter/2),
                   (int)(diameter/2+Math.sin(Math.toRadians(54))*diameter/2));
        g.drawLine((int)(diameter/2+Math.cos(Math.toRadians(342))*diameter/2),
                   (int)(diameter/2+Math.sin(Math.toRadians(342))*diameter/2),
                   (int)(diameter/2+Math.cos(Math.toRadians(126))*diameter/2),
                   (int)(diameter/2+Math.sin(Math.toRadians(126))*diameter/2));
        paintChildren(g);
    }
}
```

Figure D.7 `java.awt.Graphics` class specifications and diagram

Invariant

All drawing performed upon a `java.awt.Graphics` object

- is done relative to the location of the appropriate JComponent. (The upper left corner of the JComponent is (0, 0).)
- is clipped to the bounding rectangle of the current JComponent.

Drawing Methods

`public void setColor(java.awt.Color c)`

   post: The current drawing color is set to c.

`public void drawImage(java.awt.Image img, int x, int y, int w, int h, ImageObserver z)`

   post: Tthe *img* image is drawn scaled to width *w* and height *h*.

   note: Within a JComponent subclass this can be used for an *ImageObserver*.

`public void drawLine(int x1, int y1, int x2, int y2)`

   post: A line segment is drawn from point ($x1$, $y1$) to ($x2$, $y2$) using the current drawing color.

`public void drawPolygon(int[] xVertices, int[] yVertices, int nPoints)`

   post: A polygon is drawn with vertices at (*xVertices*[0], *yVertices*[0]) through (*xVertices*[*nPoints*−1], *yVertices*[*nPoints*−1]).

`public void drawOval(int x, int y, int w, int h)`

   post: The outline of an oval is drawn with upper left corner at (x, y), width of *w*, and height of *h* using the current drawing color.

`public void drawRect(int x, int y, int w, int h)`

   post: The outline of a rectangle is drawn with upper left corner at (x, y), width of *w*, and height of *h* using the current drawing color.

`public void drawString(String s, int x, int y)`

   post: The text from *s* is drawn with upper left corner at (x, y) using the current drawing color.

public void **fillOval**(int *x*, int *y*, int *w*, int *h*)

> **post:** A filled oval is drawn with upper left corner at (x, y), width of w, and height of h using the current drawing color.

public void **fillPolygon**(int[] *xVertices*, int[] *yVertices*, int *nPoints*)

> **post:** A filled polygon is drawn with vertices at ($xVertices$[0], $yVertices$[0]) through ($xVertices$[$nPoints$−1], $yVertices$[$nPoints$−1]).

public void **fillRect**(int *x*, int *y*, int *w*, int *h*)

> **post:** A filled rectangle is drawn with upper left corner at (x, y), width of w, and height of h using the current drawing color.

public void **clearRect**(int *x*, int *y*, int *w*, int *h*)

> **post:** A filled rectangle is drawn with upper left corner at (x, y), width of w, and height of h using the background color of the JComponent.

---

javax.awt.Graphics

«update»
```
+ void setColor(java.awt.Color)
+ void drawImage(java.awt.Image, int, int, int, int, ImageObserver)
+ void drawLine(int, int, int, int)
+ void drawOval(int, int, int, int)
+ void drawPolygon(int[ ], int[ ], int)
+ void drawRect(int, int, int, int)
+ void drawString(String)
+ void fillOval(int, int, int, int)
+ void fillPolygon(int[ ], int[ ], int)
+ void fillRect(int, int, int, int)
+ void clearRect(int, int, int, int)
. . .
```

Figure D.8

Example driver for StarOnDot class

```java
import javax.swing.JFrame;
import java.awt.Color;
public class Driver {
    private JFrame window ;
    private StarOnDot leftStar, rightStar;

    public Driver() {
        window = new JFrame("Two stars on dots");
        window.setBounds(50, 50, 320, 250);
        window.setVisible(true);
        window.setLayout(null);

        leftStar = new StarOnDot();
        leftStar.setBounds(10, 10, 100, 100);
        leftStar.setBackground(Color.green);
        leftStar.setForeground(Color.red);
        window.add(leftStar, 0);
        leftStar.repaint();

        rightStar = new StarOnDot();
        rightStar.setBounds(90, 10, 200, 250);
        rightStar.setBackground(Color.darkGray);
        rightStar.setForeground(Color.white);
        window.add(rightStar, 0);
        rightStar.repaint();
    }
}
```

Figure D.9

Image produced by executing program in Figure D.8

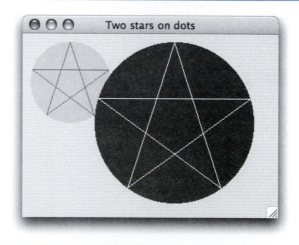

Invariant

An `Image` is a `JComponent` for drawing pictures from GIF, JPG, or PNG files. The image is resized to fit exactly within the bounding rectangle.

Constructor Methods

`public Image(int x, int y, int w, int h)`

post: The bounding rectangle is assigned dimensions from x, y, w, h **and** there is no image file assigned.

`public Image(int x, int y, int w, int h, String f)`

post: The bounding rectangle is assigned dimensions from x, y, w, h **and** the image is assigned from the file named f.

Update Method

`public void setImage(String f)`

post: The image is assigned from the file named f.

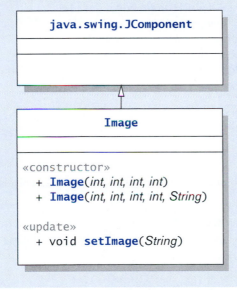

Figure D.11

Specifications for a Driver using the Image class

```java
/** This is a driver to display a picture of a Castle */
import javax.swing.JFrame;
import java.awt.*;
public class Driver {
    private JFrame window ;
    private Rectangle pictureFrame;
    private Label label;
    private Image castle;

    public Driver() {
        window = new JFrame("Wartburg Picture");
        window.setBounds(50, 50, 320, 280);
        window.setVisible(true);
        window.setLayout(null);
        pictureFrame = new Rectangle(15, 13, 290, 223);
        pictureFrame.setBackground(new Color(64, 52, 23));
        window.add(pictureFrame, 0);
        castle = new Image(10, 10, 270, 203, "Wartburg.gif");
        pictureFrame.add(castle, 0);
        label = new Label("Wartburg Castle");
        label.setForeground(Color.white);
        label.setBackground(Color.black);
        label.setBounds(70, 180, 105, 20);
        castle.add(label, 0);
        window.repaint();
    }
}
```

shape the picture. [2]For castle, the image is sized to be 270 pixels wide and 203 pixels high.

It is also possible to add Component objects to Image objects. The castle program does so, placing a label on the castle. The complete JFrame for this program is shown in Figure D.12.

D.4 ■ Event Handling

The *Swing/AWT* libraries include many classes for processing events. There are classes for creating GUI objects, using classes such as JButton, JSlider, and JTextField whose primary program interaction is through event handling. There

---

2. If the bounding rectangle of an image differs from the image file, then the picture will be distorted.

Figure D.12

Image produced by castle program

are ways to incorporate keyboard events and mouse events into JComponent. There is even a javax.swing.Timer class for support of timed interrupts.

All Java event handling shares the following characteristics:

- Each event is associated with an object and standard classes are provided for many such objects.
- Each event generates the equivalent of a method call to a method with a specific name. The name of these so-called *event handler* methods is determined by the class for the event. When a runtime event occurs, the Java VM invokes the event handler—passing an argument with type from the standard event class.
- Listener interfaces are provided for each event type. (Standard listener interfaces are stored in the same library as their corresponding event class.)
- Delegation is used to assign events to objects.

Figure D.13 contains a table of some of the more commonly used standard events. This table gives the *Swing* class that is capable of generating such events, the associated standard event class, the name of the standard event handler, and the listener interface.

By default, events are ignored. In other words, instantiating the JSlider class and adding the resulting object to a JFrame will create a visible slider, but that slider will do nothing when manipulated by the user. To activate event handling, three more steps must occur:

1. Your program must include a class that implements the listener interface associated with the event. The implementing must override the event handler(s) for the event(s) you wish to capture.
2. An object from the class described in Step 1 must be instantiated.

Figure D.13   Summary of various events

General Event Category	*Swing Generator Class*	Standard Event Class	Handler Method(s)	Listener Interface
button click	`JButton`	`java.awt.ActionEvent`	`actionPerformed`	`ActionListener`
slider drag	`JSlider`	`javax.swing.ChangeEvent`	`stateChanged`	`ChangeListener`
text field	`JTextField`	`java.awt.ActionEvent`	`actionPerformed`	`ActionListener`
time passage	`Timer`	`java.awt.ActionEvent`	`actionPerformed`	`ActionListener`
mouse buttons	`JComponent`	`java.awt.MouseEvent`	`mouseClicked` `mouseEntered` `mouseExited` `mousePressed` `mouseReleased`	`MouseListener`
mouse movement	`JComponent`	`java.awt.MouseMotionEvent`	`mouseDragged` `mouseMoved`	`MouseMotionListener`
keystroke	`JFrame`	`java.awt.KeyEvent`	`keyPressed` `keyReleased` `keyTyped`	`KeyListener`

3. The object that will be generating events must receive a method call to delegate events to the listener object from Step 2.

As an example, consider the two classes shown in Figure D.14. The `Driver` object in this program creates a `JButton` object, called `btn`, and a `ButtonHandler` object, called `listener`. Each time `btn` is clicked, an `actionPerformed` event is generated. (This means that `btn` is an event generator.) The `listener` object is delegated responsibility for handling all of `btn`'s events by virtue of the call to `addActionListener`.

There is nothing to prohibit an object from delegating events to itself. Chapter 8 proposes such classes as `EventButton`, `EventSlider`, `EventTextField`, and `EventTimer` for this purpose. These four classes have event handler methods that are empty, so that they can be overridden by subclasses.

The `Timer` class is unique because it generates events independent of user interaction. Figure D.15 contains the specifications for the key members of `Timer`.

Notice that the `Timer` constructor method performs three tasks:

1. It instantiates the object.
2. It establishes the interval separating timer events.
3. It sets up an event delegate (`actionListener`).

```java
import javax.swing.*;
public class Driver {
    private JFrame window;
    private JButton btn;
    private ButtonHandler listener;

    public Driver() {
        window = new JFrame("Button Click Example");
        window.setBounds(10, 10, 200, 150);
        window.setVisible(true);
        window.setLayout(null);
        btn = new JButton("Click Here");
        btn.setBounds(50, 50, 100, 30);
        window.add(btn, 0);
        btn.repaint();
        listener = new ButtonHandler();
        btn.addActionListener(listener);
    }
}

import java.awt.event.*;
public class ButtonHandler implements ActionListener {

    public ButtonHandler() {
        super();
    }

    public void actionPerformed(ActionEvent e) {
        System.out.println("A button click event occurred");
    }
}
```

Unlike other event generator objects, Timer objects are incapable of generating events until one more method is called—namely start. Once start is called, the object begins to generate repeated events until the program completes or until stop is called.

JButton and Timer events are simple in the sense that all the code usually needs to know is that an event has occurred. There are other types of events, however, that are coupled to additional information. For example, changing a JSlider is coupled with the new position of the slider. Typing (striking the *return* key) within a JTextField is coupled to the text typed within the field.

Sometimes access to this coupled information is provided via the generator classes and other times it is available by calling methods upon the parameter that is passed to the event handler method. A list of some of the most useful methods follows.

Figure D.15   `javax.swing.Timer` class specifications and diagram

Invariant

A `javax.swing.Timer` object

- is designed to generate timed events (i.e., events occur according to some time interval).
- *interval* represents the time (in milliseconds) separating consecutive events.

Constructor

public **Timer**(int *delay*, java.awt.event.ActionListener *z*)

  post: *interval* == delay
      and *z* is added as the event handler.

  note: A call to the `Timer` construct arms the timer, but you must call `start()` to begin event generation.

Update Methods

public void **addActionListener**(java.awt.event.ActionListener *z*)

  post: *z* is added as event handler.

public void **setDelay**(int *delay*)

  post: *interval* == *delay*

public void **start**( )

  post: Events will begin to occur repeatedly with *interval* milliseconds separation between events.

public void **stop**( )

  post: Events from this object will terminate unless `start` is called again.

---

javax.swing.Timer
- int **interval**
«constructor»   + **Timer** (*int, java.awt.event.ActionListener*)

«update»
  + void **addActionListener** (*java.awt.event.ActionListener*)
  + void **setDelay** (*int*)
  + void **start** ()
  + void **stop** ()
  ...

From the JSlider class

```
public int getValue( )
```

> **post:** *result* == the position of the slider within the range from
> getMinimum() through getMaximum()

From the JTextField class

```
public String getText( )
```

> **post:** *result* == the text currently displayed within this text field

From the KeyEvent class
(i.e., the parameter passed to key event handlers)

```
public char getKeyChar( )
```

> **post:** *result* == the character associated with the key that caused the
> event

```
public int getKeyCode( )
```

> **post:** *result* == the integer value associated with the key that caused
> the event
>
> **note:** This method is useful for keys, like function keys and arrow keys,
> that are not associated with any character. This method does *not*
> work for keyTyped events, but does for keyPressed and
> keyReleased.

From the MouseEvent class
(i.e., the parameter passed to mouse and mouse motion event handlers)

```
public int getX( )
```

> **post:** *result* == the X position (within the context of the event generator)
> at the time that the event occurs

```
public int getY( )
```

> **post:** *result* == the Y position (within the context of the event generator)
> at the time that the event occurs

One additional method is provided by all of the event classes (i.e., the parameters passed to the event handler methods). This method is called getSource, and is defined as follows.

```
public Object getSource( )
```

> **post:** *result* == the object that generated this event

The getSource method is particularly useful when several objects delegate their events to the same handler object. Calling getSource can be used to determine which object generated the event. Suppose that your program contains two JButton objects: bigButton and tinyButton. The following actionPerformed method allows a single delegate shared by these two buttons to perform different tasks for each button.

```java
public void actionPerformed(ActionEvent e) {
    if (e.getSource() == bigButton) {
        // place bigButton handler code here
    } else if (e.getSource() == tinyButton) {
        // place tinyButton handler code here

        ...
    }
}
```

A KeyEvent occurs as the result of striking one of the keys on the keyboard. Such an event is delivered to the frame that has focus (i.e., the Frame or JFrame that is highlighted in the foreground of the screen). There are three possible kinds of key events, named below by their corresponding event handler methods.

- keyPressed—occurs when the key is pressed down.
- keyReleased—occurs when the key is released from being pressed.
- keyTyped—occurs when the key has been both pressed and released.

Key events can be handled by a subclass of a JComponent using the following steps:

1. The JComponent object must receive a call to addKeyListener (which delegates keyPressed, keyReleased, and keyTyped events).
2. The object delegated to handle key events must include an implements clause for java.awt.event.KeyListener.
3. The delegate's class must include event handler methods for all three events that are delegated to its objects. Each key event handler has a single parameter of type KeyEvent.

Figure D.16 illustrates how to delegate key events in this manner. The Driver class in this example creates a JFrame object. Executing the following instruction

```java
win.addKeyListener(this);
```

establishes the Driver object as the delegate for handling key events. Correspondingly, the Driver class implements KeyListener and overrides the three event handlers.

When the application executes, a window is displayed. When this window is in the screen's foreground, it will add a message to the standard output stream every time a key is struck. The message will indicate the integer value of the key that was struck. This example illustrates how to use getKeyCode() (a method from KeyEvent) in order to determine which key was struck.

A mouse event (from the MouseListener interface) occurs as the result of some user action that involves the computer's pointing device (a mouse, trackball, etc.). There are five possible kinds of events, named on the next page by their corresponding event handler methods.

```java
import javax.swing.JFrame;
import java.awt.event.*;
import java.awt.*;
public class Driver implements KeyListener {
    private JFrame window;

    public Driver(){
        window = new JFrame("Keystroke Example");
        window.setBounds(10, 10, 200, 200);
        window.setLayout(null);
        window.addKeyListener(this);
        window.setVisible(true);
    }

    public void keyTyped(KeyEvent e) {
    }

    public void keyPressed(KeyEvent e) {
        System.out.println("The key which was struck is "
            + e.getKeyCode());
    }

    public void keyReleased(KeyEvent e) {
    }
}
```

mouseClicked—occurs when the mouse button is pressed, then released, while pointing to a JComponent.

mousePressed—occurs when the mouse button is pressed down, while pointing to a JComponent.

mouseReleased—occurs when the mouse button is released from being pressed, while pointing to a JComponent.

mouseEntered—occurs when the mouse button is moved from the outside into the region of a JComponent.

mouseExited—occurs when the mouse button is moved from the inside to outside the region of a JComponent.

In addition, there are two more event handler methods provided by the MouseMotionListener interface.

mouseDragged—occurs when the mouse button is held down at the same time that the mouse is moved within the region of a JComponent.

mouseMoved—occurs when the mouse is moved within the region of a JComponent, but the mouse button is *not* held down.

Mouse events can be handled by a subclass of a `JComponent` using the following steps:

1. The `JComponent` object must receive a call to `addMouseListener` (which delegates `mouseClicked`, `mousePressed`, `mouseReleased`, `mouseEntered`, and `mouseExited` events) and/or a call to `addMouseMotionListener` (to delegate `mouseDragged` and `mouseMoved` events).

2. The object delegated to handle mouse events must include an `implements` clause for either `java.awt.event.MouseListener` (for the first five `MouseListener` events) or `java.awt.event.MouseMotionListener` (for the last two `MouseMotionListener` events) or `javax.swing.MouseInputListener` (for all seven events).

3. The delegate's class must include event handler methods for all events that are delegated to its objects. Each mouse event handler has a single parameter of type `MouseEvent`.

Figure D.17 illustrates how to delegate mouse events in this manner. The `Driver` class in this example creates a `Rectangle` object. Executing the following instruction

```
mouser.addMouseMotionListener(this);
```

establishes the `Driver` object as the delegate for handling mouse motion events. Correspondingly, the `Driver` class implements `MouseMotionListener` and overrides the `mouseDragged` and `mouseMoved` methods.

When the application executes, a black rectangle is displayed within a `JFrame`. Anytime that the user drags the mouse or moves the mouse across this black rectangle, the application will generate events, thereby outputting messages. It is worth noting that events depend upon the bounding rectangle of the `JComponent` and not the image that it draws. If an oval were used instead of a rectangle, events would still be generated outside the oval's image as long as they were within its bounding rectangle.

Figure D.17 also illustrates how to ascertain the exact position of the cursor at the time that a mouse event occurs. The `MouseEvent` parameter that is sent to all mouse event handlers supports `getX()` and `getY()` calls to return the position of the cursor relative to the `JComponent`'s coordinates.

```java
import javax.swing.JFrame;
import java.awt.event.*;
public class Driver implements MouseMotionListener {
    private JFrame window;
    private Rectangle mouser;

    public Driver(){
        window = new JFrame("Mouse Motion");
        window.setBounds(10, 10, 200, 200);
        window.getContentPane().setLayout(null);
        mouser = new Rectangle(10, 10, 100, 100);
        mouser.addMouseMotionListener(this);
        window.getContentPane().add(mouser);
        mouser.repaint();
        window.setVisible(true);
    }

    public void mouseDragged(MouseEvent e) {
        System.out.println("Mouse dragged event");
    }

    public void mouseMoved(MouseEvent e) {
        System.out.println("Mouse moved event");
        System.out.println(" x: " + e.getX());
        System.out.println(" y: " + e.getY());
    }
}
```

Figure D.17

Driver handling mouse events for a rectangle

UML Notation

The Unified Modeling Language (UML) is a collection of many graphical notations used to diagram various aspects of software artifacts. The standards for these notations were published by the Object Management Group (OMG) in September 1997. UML has seen widespread adoption and is commonly used throughout the software engineering community. Appendix E explains the subset of UML that is used within this book. For a more complete explanation of UML, see *The Unified Modeling Language Reference Manual* by Rumbaugh, Jacobson, and Booch (Addison Wesley).

E.1 ■ **Class Diagrams**

Class diagrams capture classes, their key properties, and their relationships with other classes. These pictures represent a view of classes as they appear at compile time (i.e., a *static* view).

Using this notation, each class is diagrammed as a separate rectangle with three compartments, separated by horizontal lines. The top compartment contains the name of the class, the middle compartment contains the class's instance variables, and the bottom compartment contains the class's methods. Some or all of the variables and methods may be omitted, in order to highlight the remaining members and/or class relationships. Three consecutive dots are sometimes included to indicate that variables or methods have been omitted. (It is acceptable to draw class diagrams in such an incomplete way in order to omit details not relevant for the intended audience.)

Each variable is specified on a separate line with its type followed by its name. Note that this is a common notation for C-based languages, such as Java. An alternative UML notation is to specify the variable as its name, followed by a colon, followed by the variable's type.

Each method is specified on a separate line with its return type, followed by its name, followed by a parameter list. Constructor methods have no return type. Parameters are specified by their type, but are not necessarily named. (UML allows an alternative notation for methods that is similar to that for variables. The alternative notation has the return type at the end, preceded by a colon.)

Every variable and method is optionally preceded by a symbol to indicate its scope. The appropriate symbols for Java are public (+), private (-), and protected (#). Methods can be grouped into categories that are preceded by notations like «constructor», «query», and «update».

Figure E.1 contains an example class diagram that shows a typical class, called StreetAddress. The corresponding Java code is shown to the right of the class diagram.

Interfaces and abstract classes are diagrammed similarly to classes. An interface is distinguished from a class by including the stereotype «interface» above the class name in the top compartment of the interface rectangle. An abstract class is distinguished by italicizing the class name (and abstract methods). For clarity, the name abstract should also be included in braces following the class name. Figure E.2 shows an example interface, and Figure E.3 diagrams an abstract class.

There are two kinds of relationships among classes that are diagrammed in this text. **Association** is a relationship that occurs any time that one class is used within another. If the association results from the declaration of a parameter or local variable, then it is diagrammed as a line segment connecting the two classes.

Aggregation is a special kind of association that results when a client class contains one or more instance variables belonging to another type. Aggregation is diagrammed as a line segment connecting the aggregate (client) to any constituent

Figure E.1   Example class diagram with matching Java code

```java
public class StreetAddress {
    private String city;
    private String state;
    private int zipcode;
    public StreetAddress(String h, String st, int z) {
        //code omitted
    }
    public String getStreet() {
        //code omitted
    }
    public String getCity() {
        //code omitted
    }
    public String getState() {
        //code omitted
    }
    public int getZipcode() {
        //code omitted
    }
    public String getAddress() {
        //code omitted
    }
    public void setCityState
        (String c, String s) {
        //code omitted
    }
    protected void setZipcode(int z) {
        //code omitted
    }
}
```

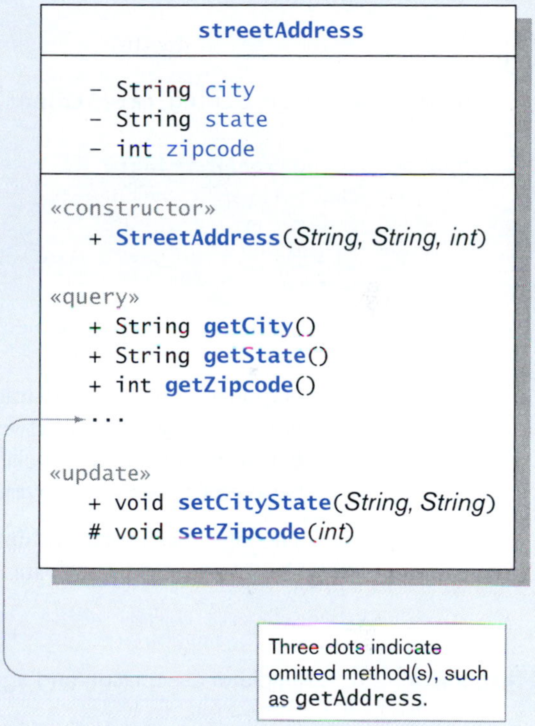

streetAddress

- String city
- String state
- int zipcode

«constructor»
+ **StreetAddress**(*String, String, int*)

«query»
+ String **getCity**()
+ String **getState**()
+ int **getZipcode**()
...

«update»
+ void **setCityState**(*String, String*)
# void **setZipcode**(*int*)

Three dots indicate omitted method(s), such as getAddress.

Figure E.2   Example interface

```java
public interface ActionListener {
    // All variables and methods omitted
}
```

«interface»
ActionListener

Figure E.3   Example abstract class

```java
public abstract class Date {
    protected int day;
    protected int month;
    protected int year;

    public Date(int, int, int) {
        // code omitted
    }

    public abstract String dateString();

    public String monthString() {
        // code omitted
    }
}
```

Date {abstract}
int day
int month
int year
«constructor»
+ **Date**(*int, int, int*)
«query»
+ String *dateString*()
+ String **monthString**()

(supplier) class with a diamond drawn on the aggregate end of the line. Figure E.4 illustrates aggregation between `Person` and `String` and `Person` and `Date`. Figure E.4 also shows two associations that are not aggregation. These associations are between `Person` and `JFrame` and `Person` and `JTextArea`.

The inheritance relationship is diagrammed as an arrow connecting a subclass (child class) to its superclass (parent class). The head of the arrow points toward the super-

Figure E.4   Example of association and aggregation

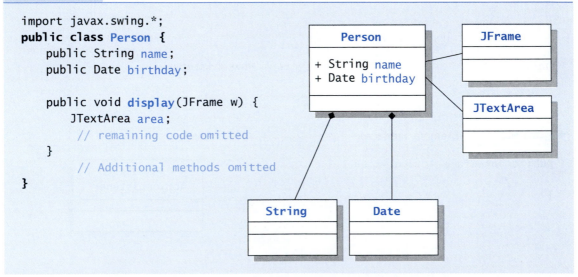

```java
import javax.swing.*;
public class Person {
    public String name;
    public Date birthday;

    public void display(JFrame w) {
        JTextArea area;
        // remaining code omitted
    }

    // Additional methods omitted
}
```

class. Implementing an interface is diagrammed similar to inheritance, except that a dashed arrow points from the implementation to the interface. Figure E.5 illustrates both inheritance and interface implementation.

E.2 ■ Object Diagrams

Object diagrams picture the runtime (dynamic) behavior of a program. Each object diagram is a snapshot of one particular computational state. An object diagram shows a collection of objects and their assigned values from a specific instant in time.

The UML notation for a single object consists of a rectangle with the name of the object at the top of the rectangle, followed by a colon, followed by the object's type. The name and type are underlined to distinguish object rectangles from class rectangles. This text uses the additional notation of shading (☐) to denote object diagrams.

An object diagram typically pictures instance variables within the object in which they are created. The value assigned to a primitive instance variable is shown following the variable name and a "==" separator. Figure E.6 contains an object diagram that depicts a local variable, called watch, after it has been created via the instruction in the gray box. The StopWatch class to which watch belongs is shown on the right side of Figure E.6.

When an object is the aggregate of other objects, the instance variables of the aggregate can be diagrammed by using the same symbol (a line segment with a diamond on the aggregate end) as a class diagram. Figure E.7 illustrates.

Figure E.5	Example of inheritance

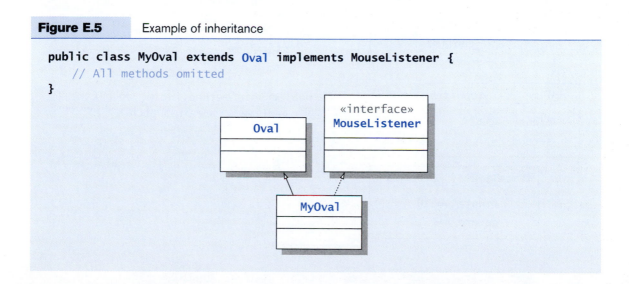

```
public class MyOval extends Oval implements MouseListener {
    // All methods omitted
}
```

Figure E.6   Example object diagram and associated `StopWatch` class

```
Stopwatch watch;
watch = new StopWatch(4, 9.3);
```

The object diagram below shows the state
of watch upon executing the two statements
above.

```
watch : StopWatch

   minute == 4
   second == 9.3
```

```java
public class StopWatch {
    private int minute;
    private double second;

    public StopWatch(int m, double s) {
        minute = m;
        second = s;
    }
}
```

Figure E.7   Example object diagram and associated `SplitTimer` class

```
SplitTimer clock = new SplitTimer();
clock.setStart(10, 5.3);
clock.setEnd(12, 7.1);
```

The object diagram below shows the
state that results from executing the
above statements.

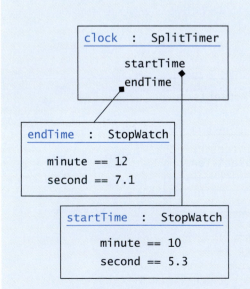

```java
public class SplitTimer {
    public StopWatch startTime;
    public StopWatch endTime;

    public SplitTimer() {}

    public void setStart(int m, double s) {
        startTime = new StopWatch(m, s);
    }

    public void setEnd(int m, double s) {
        endTime = new StopWatch(m, s);
    }
}
```

Figure E.8   Example object diagram

```
SplitTimer clock = new SplitTimer();
clock.setStart(10, 5.3);
clock.endTime = clock.startTime;
```

The object diagram at right shows the state that
results from executing the above statements.

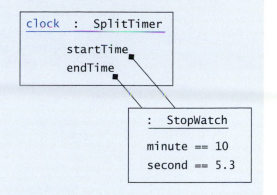

Variable names, like startTime and endTime, are repeated both inside the aggregate object and inside the object. Including instance variable names within the
aggregate object is useful in situations where an object is assigned multiple names
(aliases). Figure E.8 demonstrates with an object diagram for an object that has been
assigned to both startTime and endTime.

Figure E.8 also demonstrates that it is acceptable to omit the name within an object
rectangle, such as the StopWatch object. This omission is commonly used for
anonymous objects and when an object has more than one name.

E.3 ■ Activity Diagrams

An activity diagram pictures actions and their dependencies. Each activity diagram
in this book is used to show the alternative control flows for possible program executions. In this context, an action consists of the execution of one or more Java statements.

The left side of Figure E.9 contains an activity diagram for the Java code segment on
the right. Each action is diagrammed as an oval that contains the Java statement.
Runtime control flow is indicated by arrows directed from each action state to its
subsequent action.

Alternatives in control flow require **branch** and **merge** symbols. A branch symbol is
a small diamond with multiple outgoing arrows. The outgoing arrows symbolize
alternative execution paths, and each is labeled with a guard condition (in square
brackets). An outgoing arrow is followed only when its guard condition is true. If
alternative execution flows eventually merge to perform the same actions, then a diamond may be used with multiple incoming arrows and a single outgoing arrow. It is
also possible to combine branching and merging in a single diamond.

Figure E.9   Activity diagram for sequential actions

```
int length = 12;
int width = 7;
int perimeter = length*2 + width*2;
int area = length * width;
```

int **length** = 12;

int **width** = 7;

int **perimeter** = length*2 + width*2;

int **area** = length * width;

Figure E.10 illustrates a single branch (the top diamond). This branch represents a choice in program execution. If the condition a > b is true, then execution follows the left arrow, otherwise the right arrow is followed. Regardless of the chosen branch, both paths merge prior to executing the System.out.println call.

Figure E.10   Activity diagram including branching

```
public void printMax(int a, int b) {
    int max;
    if (a > b) {
        max = a;
    } else {
        max = b;
    }
    System.out.println(max);
}
```

int **max**;

[a > b]   [a <= b]

max = a;   max = b;

System.out.println(max);

Programming Using Windows

While it is recommended that programmers use an integrated development environment such as BlueJ, Code Warrior, Eclipse, or JBuilder, Appendix F is included if you choose to run Java applications without such tools. The various applications discussed are included in all versions of Windows XP except for the Java Development Kit (JDK), which may be downloaded free from Sun Microsystems Web site (java.sun.com), as well as the CD that accompanies this book.

F.1 ■ Installing the Java JDK

The Java Standard Edition Development Kit includes all of the files for the standard Java libraries along with a Java compiler, a Java Virtual Machine implementation, and many other programming tools. For use with this book it is essential that you use a version of the JDK that is labeled 1.5 or later. The JDK is normally installed by double-clicking the installation file and following the directions of the installation wizard.

Once the JDK has been installed, you should ensure that the **path** environment variable is properly assigned. The path variable is used by the Windows operating system to locate key JDK software, including the compiler and the virtual machine. To set the path environment variable, you must first activate the System Properties, then select the *Advanced* tab. Figure F.1 shows the associated pop-up window.

Next, click the *Environment Variables* button. Figure F.2 shows the pop-up window that results from this button click.

To edit the path variable, select the `Path` line within the pane labeled System variables and click the *Edit* button. If the path address of your JDK tools is not already within the definition of the path variable, then you should append it to the line. (*Note:* Be careful not to disturb the existing path variable definitions.) You should append the following:

```
;C:\folder\jdk1.5.version\bin
```

Figure F.1

System Control
Panel Properties

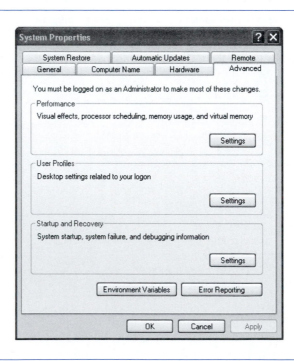

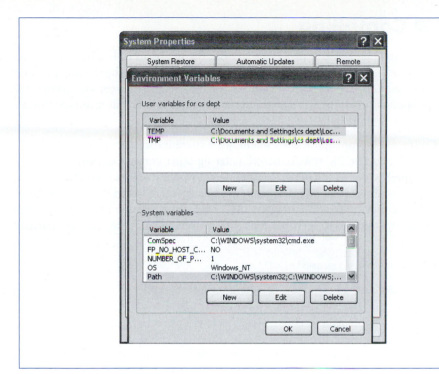

Figure F.2

Environment variables

where *folder* denotes the folder into which you loaded the JDK during installation and *version* denotes the particular version number that was installed. For example, if you loaded version 1.5.0 at the root of the file system, then you would append the following: ;C:\jdk1.5.0\bin. Take care to type the new path definition correctly, including the semicolon and no white space.

F.2 ■ Editing

Java programs can be edited with many text editors. Windows XP includes two editors: WordPad and NotePad. (Both can be found by clicking the *start* menu and selecting *All Programs → Accessories*.) When editing the programs that accompany this book you should avoid using NotePad because it may not properly recognize line separations. You should also avoid using a word processor such as Microsoft Word, unless you are willing to go through the additional steps required to ensure that files are stored in text format. Be aware that when switching between text editors indentation patterns can become scrambled due to different tab settings.

When you create Java class files, it is best to store each class in a separate file. The file should be named *something*.java where *something* is the name of the Java class. All files used by a single program are normally stored within the same folder.

F.3 ■ **Compiling**

In order to compile and run programs without the use of an IDE, you will want to use Microsoft's *Command Prompt* application. This can be found by clicking the *start* menu and selecting *All Programs → Accessories → Command Prompt*. The Command Prompt application is a line-oriented interface that permits the user to type system commands.

The Command Prompt application maintains a **current directory** that can be set to any folder within the file system. Before entering other commands, you should set the current directory to the folder containing your program files. The command to set the current directory is "cd" followed by white space, followed by the path name of the folder containing your program files. For example, if the program folder is c:\javaprogs\example, then the following command properly sets the current directory:

```
cd c:\javaprogs\example
```

Having set the current directory, the command to compile all Java program files within follows:

```
javac *.java
```

Be warned that like most compilers, the Java compiler will not store a compiled version of a program when it contains syntax errors. When an error-free program is compiled, the Java compiler creates a *.class* file for every class file within the folder that has been compiled. Compile-time error messages are reported to the Command Prompt application.

F.4 ■ **Execution**

The programs that accompany this book are written in a consistent way specifically to make them more convenient to execute. They are all written to begin execution as applications with an initial object called `Driver`. So long as you follow this convention, you can initiate a program's execution by including a copy of the *run.class* file that is included with every application program on the CD accompanying this book, then typing the following command:

```
java run
```

If the executing program contains any runtime errors they will be reported to the Command Prompt application window. System.out.println messages are also displayed in this same application window.

A running program can be terminated in various ways. Entering *Ctrl+C* (holding down the *Ctrl* key while pressing the *C* key) will terminate a running program and close all associated windows.

Index